HEALTH, ILLNESS, and OPTIMAL AGING

In the course of working on this book, both of us have lost our last remaining parent, and we would like to dedicate this book to them—Anne F. Aldwin, R.N., and Abe L. Fox, M.A.

HEALTH, ILLNESS, and OPTIMAL AGING

Biological and Psychosocial Perspectives

Carolyn M. Aldwin
University of California at Davis

Diane F. Gilmer
University of California at Davis

Foreword by James Birren

SAGE Publications
International Educational and Professional Publisher
Thousand Oaks ■ London ■ New Delhi

For information:

Sage Publications, Inc.
2455 Teller Road
Thousand Oaks, California 91320
E-mail: order@sagepub.com

Sage Publications Ltd.
6 Bonhill Street
London EC2A 4PU
United Kingdom

Sage Publications India Pvt. Ltd.
B-42, Panchsheel Enclave
Post Box 4109
New Delhi 110 017 India

Printed in the United States of America

Library of Congress Cataloging-in-Publication Data

Aldwin, Carolyn M.
Health, illness, and optimal aging: biological and psychosocial perspectives /
Carolyn M. Aldwin, Diane F. Gilmer ; with a foreword by James Birren.
    p. cm.
Includes bibliographical references and index.
ISBN 978-0-7619-2259-9 (paper : alk. paper)
   1. Aging. I. Gilmer, Diane F. II. Title.
QP86 .A44 2003
612.6´7—dc21

                                                            2002153451

Printed on acid-free paper

11   12   13   14   15   10   9   8   7   6   5   4

Acquiring Editor:	Jim Brace-Thompson
Editorial Assistant:	Karen Ehrmann
Production Editor:	Claudia A. Hoffman
Copy Editor:	Kate Peterson
Typesetter:	C&M Digitals (P) Ltd.
Indexer:	Molly Hall
Cover Designer:	Janet Foulger

ACKNOWLEDGMENTS

A number of individuals have been extremely supportive in this endeavor. Drs. Lois Aldwin, Mary Bisson, and Marylynn Barkeley lent their considerable expertise in immunology, cellular biology, and endocrinology. Drs. Andrew Duxbury's and John S. Werner's impressive command of geriatric medicine greatly improved the clinical sections. Drs. Beth Ober, Crystal Park, and Avron Spiro III provided very useful comments on cognition, personality, and statistical methods, respectively. We are very grateful for these reviewers' careful readings and corrections and also appreciate the comments of four anonymous reviewers. The graduate students who took the first author's class on Adaptation and Aging—including Mattie Gabston, Patricia Jennings, Linda Kelly, Danielle Rife-Larsen, and Ray Shiraishi—also provided very helpful feedback. Laurel deLapp and Amber Mills Despotes gave helpful suggestions from the undergraduate point of view. Donnya Hafich kindly proofread much of the manuscript and spent many hours tracking down articles for us. Loriena Yancura, Yuri Rodriguez, and Barry Burns provided very capable assistance with the figures and illustrations. The first author is grateful to Dr. Ana Paula Cupertino for lending her house in Brazil, which afforded the solitude to finish the first draft of this book. Victoria Davis brilliantly found the positive aging quote in Shakespeare. Our editor, Jim Brace-Thompson, was very patient and supportive. Finally, our spouses, Drs. Michael R. Levenson and David S. Gilmer, provided much-needed support and encouragement. Dr. Levenson (Rick) lent us so much of his own writing for use in Chapter 9 that we ended by sharing authorship with him on that chapter.

CONTENTS

Foreword   xv
   James Birren

1.   Introduction and Basic Concepts in Aging   1
    Basic Definitions   4
    Organization of the Book   9

SECTION I.DEMOGRAPHIC, THEORETICAL,
AND METHODOLOGICAL ISSUES   13

2.   Demography of Aging   15
    Aging in the World   16
       Population Aging in the United States   16
       International Aging   25
    Demographic Factors and Rate of Aging   28
       Gender   28
       Marital Status   30
       Ethnicity   33
       Socioeconomic Status (SES)   37
    Summary   41

3.   Theories of Aging   43
    Biological Theories of Aging   45
       Genetic Theories   46
       Molecular/Cellular Theories of Aging   49
       System-Level Theories   51
       Interrelationships Among Levels of Analysis   53
    Psychosocial Theories of Aging   53
       Classical Theories   54
       Current Theories   58
       Interrelationships Among Theories   61
    Psychosocial Factors and Aging   62
    Summary   64

4. Understanding Change in Aging Research   65

     Basic Definitions   66
         Basic Statistical Terms   66
         Summary of Common Statistical Techniques   68
         Research Designs   68
     Age-Related Designs   73
         Cross-Sectional Versus Longitudinal Designs   73
         Sequential Designs   75
     Statistics for Assessing Change   77
         Mean-Level Change   78
         Relative Change   80
         Structural Change   82
         Ipsative Change   83
     Statistics That Predict Change   86
         Two-Point Designs   86
         Cross-Lagged Panel Designs and Analyses   87
         Analyzing Multiple-Point Longitudinal Data   89
     Summary   92

SECTION II. AGING OF BIOLOGICAL SYSTEMS   95

5. Aging of the Skin and Musculoskeletal System   97

     Skin   98
         Basic Anatomy and Physiology   98
         Age-Related Changes   99
         Disease-Related Processes   100
         Promoting Optimal Aging   103
     Musculoskeletal System   104
         Basic Anatomy and Physiology   104
         Age-Related Changes   106
         Disease-Related Processes   109
         Promoting Optimal Aging   117
     Summary   119

6. Aging of the Internal Organ Systems   120

     Cardiovascular System   120
         Basic Anatomy and Physiology   120
         Age-Related Changes   124
         Disease-Related Processes   125
         Promoting Optimal Aging   131
     Respiratory System   132

Basic Anatomy and Physiology 132
Age-Related Changes 134
Disease-Related Processes 134
Promoting Optimal Aging 140
Gastrointestinal System 141
Basic Anatomy and Physiology 141
Age-Related Changes 145
Disease-Related Processes 146
Promoting Optimal Aging 152
Renal/Urinary System 152
Basic Anatomy and Physiology 152
Age-Related Changes 154
Disease-Related Processes 156
Promoting Optimal Aging 160
Summary 162

7. Aging and the Regulatory Systems 163

Sensory System 163
Age- and Disease-Related Changes 164
Promoting Optimal Aging 171
Nervous System 171
Basic Anatomy and Physiology 171
Age-Related Changes 176
Disease-Related Processes 178
Promoting Optimal Aging 184
Endocrine System 185
Basic Anatomy and Physiology 185
Age-Related Changes 190
Disease-Related Processes 193
Promoting Optimal Aging 197
Immune System 198
Basic Anatomy and Physiology 198
Age-Related Changes 203
Disease-Related Processes 205
Promoting Optimal Aging 205
Summary 207

8. Functional Health, Health Promotion, and Quality of Life 208

Functional Health 209
Assessing Functional Health 209
Functional Losses, Morbidity, and Mortality 215

Promoting Optimal Functional Health   216
Health Promotion in Older Adults   217
     Models of Health Behavior Change   217
     Health Promotion Programs for Older Adults   219
     Environmental Competence   222
Quality of Life   223
Summary   226

SECTION III. PSYCHOSOCIAL FACTORS AFFECTING PHYSICAL HEALTH   227

9.   The Interface Between Physical and Mental Health   229

Carolyn M. Aldwin, Michael R. Levenson, and Diane F. Gilmer

Personality Processes and Disease   230
     Psychological Risk Factors and Health   232
     Psychosocial Protective Factors and Health   239
     Alcohol and Aging   245
Differentiating Between Mental and Physical
     Health Problems   251
Summary   253

10.   Stress, Coping, and Health   254

Stress   255
     Stress as a Physiological State   255
     Stress as a Characteristic of the Environment   267
     Stress as a Transaction Between the Person
        and the Environment   271
Coping With Stress   274
     Theoretical Approaches to Coping   274
Summary   281

11.   Social Support, Health, and Aging   283

Characteristics of the Social Support Network   283
     Functions of Social Support   284
     Social Support Networks   284
     Assessment of Social Support   290
     Change in Network Size With Age   291
     Reciprocity   292
     Negative Effects of Social Support   293
Social Support, Morbidity, and Mortality   294
     Social Support, Mortality, and Physical Health   295

Social Support and Recovery From Illness   296
Organizational Memberships and Health   297
Social Support, Stressful Events, and Mental Health   297
Caregiving   298
Spouse Caregiving   298
Summary   300

SECTION IV. AGING ACCELERATORS AND DECELERATORS   301

12.   What Is Optimal Aging?   303

Models of Optimal Aging   303
Rowe and Kahn's Model of Successful Aging   304
Vaillant's Model of Aging Well   309
Wisdom and Optimal Aging   312
Religiousness, Spirituality, and Optimal Aging   316
Ars Moriendi—The Art of Dying   318
Summary   321

References   323

Author Index   381

Subject Index   405

About the Authors   417

LIST OF TABLES

Table 4.1   Summary of Common Statistics   67
Table 4.2   Sequential Designs Indicating Ages at Different
             Periods for Different Cohorts   75
Table 4.3   Summary of Longitudinal Statistics   78
Table 7.1   Selected Small-Molecule, Rapidly Acting Transmitters
             and Their Functions   173
Table 7.2   Selected Large-Molecule, Slow-Acting Neuropeptides
             and Their Functions   187
Table 7.3   Illustrative Changes in the Neuropeptide
             Transmitters With Age   194
Table 7.4   Leukocyte Types, Locations, and Functions   199

LIST OF FIGURES

Figure 1.1	Cultural Differences in Aging	5
Figure 2.1	Population by Age and Sex: 1905	17
Figure 2.2	Population by Age and Sex: 1975	17
Figure 2.3	Projected Population by Age and Sex: 2010	17
Figure 2.4	Projected Population by Age and Sex: 2030	17
Figure 2.5	Average Annual Percent Growth of Older Population in Developed and Developing Countries	26
Figure 2.6	Secular Trends of the Mortality Rates and Birth Rates in Europe and Brazil: 1725-2025	27
Figure 2.7	Ethnicity of Older Adults in 2000 and 2050 (United States)	33
Figure 2.8	Death Rates From All Causes for Persons Aged 65 and Over per 100,000 Population: Females	36
Figure 2.9	Death Rates From All Causes for Persons Aged 65 and Over per 100,000 Population: Males	37
Figure 2.10	Poverty Rates by Age: 1959 to 2000	39
Figure 3.1	Intellectual History of Theories of Adult Development	54
Figure 4.1	Mean-Level Change	79
Figure 4.2	Correlational Change and Stability	81
Figure 4.3	Structural Change	84
Figure 4.4	Ipsative Change	85
Figure 4.5	Cross-Lagged Panel Design	88
Figure 4.6	Fixed Effects Model	90
Figure 4.7	Random Effects Model	91
Figure 5.1	Aging of the Skin	100
Figure 5.2	Changes in Aging: Trabecular and Cortical Bone	107
Figure 5.3	Gait and Risk and Type of Fracture	111
Figure 5.4	Common Areas of Hip Fracture	113
Figure 5.5	Osteoarthritic Changes of the Knee	115
Figure 6.1	Structure of the Heart and Blood Flow Through the Chambers	122
Figure 6.2	Progression of Atherosclerosis in an Artery	127
Figure 6.3	Anatomy of the Respiratory Tract	133
Figure 6.4	Changes in Alveoli with Age	135
Figure 6.5	Anatomy of the Gastrointestinal Tract	142
Figure 6.6	Liver, Gallbladder, and Pancreatic Secretion Pathways	144
Figure 6.7	Diverticulosis	148
Figure 6.8	Anatomy of the Renal/Urinary Tract	153

Figure 6.9   Anatomy of the Male Urinary System,
              Including Prostate   158
Figure 7.1   Anatomy of the Ear   166
Figure 7.2   Anatomy of the Eye   168
Figure 7.3   Structure of the Brain   174
Figure 7.4   Structure of the Cortex   175
Figure 7.5   Endocrine Glands   186
Figure 7.6   Endocrine Actions   188
Figure 7.7   Thyroid and Thermal Regulation   189
Figure 7.8   Organs of the Immune System   200
Figure 8.1   Percentage of Older Adults Unable to Perform
              One or More ADLs: Age and Gender Differences   211
Figure 8.2   Percentage of African Americans and Non-African
              Americans Aged 65+, With Disabilities: 1982 to 1999   214
Figure 10.1   Peripheral Pathways of the Autonomic
              Nervous System   257
Figure 10.2   Activities of the Adrenal Gland   260
Figure 10.3   A Triune Model of Reactions to Stress   263

FOREWORD

Gaining understanding of aging is one of the most complex issues facing 21st-century science. This book addresses the complexity of the factors that interact and influence the course of our longer life expectancy. It attempts the difficult task of integrating information from biology, psychology, and the social sciences. The subject matter of aging is at present like an unassembled jigsaw puzzle. There are some clear pieces of information from the many relevant sciences, but fitting them together is a difficult task rarely attempted.

How we grow old is a product of our genetic background as members of our families and the human species. But the genome expresses itself in physical and social environments that modulate the appearance of hereditary traits. In a sense, aging is an ecological problem in which the dynamics are often difficult to explain. If we are to make significant progress in raising the quality of life, we must identify the many factors that interact and influence the course of life.

This book undertakes the difficult task of assembling an objective and holistic picture of human aging. This task is rarely attempted because of the relatively low interaction of the different sciences as they develop microtheories of limited aspects of aging. Research on specific aspects of aging has contributed to advances in our understanding; to be maximally useful, however, new findings must be fitted into the functions of a complex organism, the human being.

University students are educated in depth within the bounds of single disciplines, and it is not common to read across the sciences. Yet understanding aging requires a grasp of information and concepts that cut across many areas of science. This book brings information from the sciences together in a way that is seldom seen. As its chapters reveal, the regulation and management of an organism ranges from ideas to neural conduction and biochemical communication. The information presented here helps us put the organism back together and understand how it ages. It attempts to identify the dynamic factors that underlie aging, the pathways to change.

In the past, the nervous system was not often mentioned as an organ that plays a role in how we age. Now it is recognized as the primary regulatory organ of the body, with control over many important biological processes such as respiration, body temperature, metabolism, blood pressure, and the thought processes and feelings that result in decisions. It is a hierarchical organ system that has important effects on aging. And it shares with other organ systems the results of lifelong habits of diet, exercise, alcohol and drug use, and smoking. We learn that one of the shared effects that accumulate with age is the presence of oxidants that, because of their structure with free electrons, bind to proteins and become useless for their assigned biological functions.

One learns from this volume that age alone doesn't cause problems, but it is a convenient and powerful index that enables us to group data while we search for causal factors and place them in a causal chain. How our heredity at conception is expressed in late-life outcomes involves biological mechanisms that are now being identified. At the same time, we should recognize that education and socioeconomic status contribute to life expectancy and the diseases we develop. This implies long causal chains of biological, social, and psychological interactions. This book contributes to understanding how the human organism is organized and the processes of development and aging that extend from birth to late life. It integrates knowledge about the dynamics of aging and promotes ways of modifying the life course to our advantage.

—*James Birren*
University of California at Los Angeles

CHAPTER 1

INTRODUCTION AND BASIC CONCEPTS IN AGING

Is second childhood and mere oblivion
Sans teeth, sans eyes, sans taste, sans everything.

—Shakespeare
As You Like It, Act II, Scene VII

Though I look old, yet I am strong and lusty;
For in my youth I never did apply
Hot and rebellious liquors in my blood;
Nor did not with unbashful forehead woo
The means of weakness and debility;
Therefore my age is as a lusty winter,
Frosty, but kindly.

—Shakespeare
As You Like It, Act II, Scene III

From time immemorial, there have been two markedly different views of late life, illustrated nicely by the contrasting images provided by Shakespeare. Although the first, more negative, quote is widely cited, the second is less well-known but still apropos of a major focus of this book, namely, optimal aging. What is surprising about the quote is that it presages the modern recognition that aging processes are *plastic*—to a large extent, how we age and the rate at which we age are balanced between resources to which we have access and our exposure to various toxins, both of which are, in part, reflections of the choices we make.

Psychosocial gerontologists have focused more on describing what happens cognitively, emotionally, and socially as we age, with a view toward identifying factors that promote positive aging or increase the risk of negative aging. The emerging models reflect a dialectic between cumulative resources and vulnerabilities across the life span and the idea of plasticity—that there are turning points through which people can change the trajectories of their life course. Although biogerontologists have focused on describing what happens at the molecular, cellular, and organ system levels, the models emerging in that field emphasize factors that affect the rate of aging. For example, free radicals can accelerate deterioration, but antioxidants may decelerate it. At the same time, the fields of health psychology and behavioral medicine provide clear documentation that psychosocial factors can affect physical health, and we are beginning to understand the pathways through which this occurs. While the focus has been on psychosocial risk factors, we are beginning to understand that there are protective factors as well. Thus, there appears to be an emerging consensus across these three areas of study, despite their differences in language and emphases. A major purpose of this book is to synthesize these views and perspectives under the rubric of optimal aging.

The last decade or so has seen a heightened interest in optimal aging. Scientifically, we are reaping the harvest of long-term longitudinal studies started many decades ago, which have traced individual lives for as long as 60 years. These prospective studies allow us to begin understanding predictors of the rate of change in physical health, cognitive ability, and mental health in late life. From a public policy perspective, nations around the world are graying. The baby boom generation is poised to retire and start collecting pensions and health care benefits. This has forced us to seriously consider how to keep older adults healthy, if for no other reason than preventing them from bankrupting not only our national budget but also those of most other nations. From a personal perspective, there is overwhelming interest in staving off the ravages of old age. It is not surprising that cholesterol-lowering agents and Viagra are among the most commonly prescribed medications in this country. In short, there is a growing interest in how the various aging processes respond to behavioral and environmental factors that are at least partially under our control.

Birren, Butler, Greenhouse, and Yarrow (1963) first differentiated between aging per se and disease. Using comprehensive medical examinations, they divided apparently healthy older men into two groups: those with subclinical disease and those who were completely healthy. They then compared members of both groups with younger men. Birren and his colleagues found that nearly all of the deficits generally associated with aging (such as memory problems, decrease in grip strength, and decline in cardiovascular output) were found in the older men with subclinical disease, but not in the optimally healthy men. The one exception was neuronal slowing, which even the healthiest older men manifested. This groundbreaking study opened the door to the recognition that aging is not necessarily associated with unmitigated pain and suffering and that older adults can enjoy good physical and mental health and be cognitively intact.

The recognition that optimal aging is possible led to longitudinal studies such as the Normative Aging Study (Bossé & Spiro, 1995) and the MacArthur Study of Successful Aging (Rowe & Kahn, 1997), which were undertaken with the explicit goal of understanding healthy aging. Gerontology is unique among the scientific disciplines in that, since its inception, it has recognized that interdisciplinary endeavors are required for understanding the aging process. Biogerontology has greatly increased our understanding of the genetic and cellular mechanisms of aging, but the disciplines of psychology, sociology, and anthropology are also essential for understanding both the processes and ramifications of aging. We are just beginning to comprehend the transactional nature of health and to detail the interplay among mental, cognitive, and physical health as well as sociocultural processes. This realization has led to hundreds of intervention studies demonstrating that many of the cognitive and physiological declines associated with normal aging can be reversed. Clinicians are now more successful at treating the chronic illnesses of late life, such as cardiovascular disease and diabetes, leading to rapid demographic increases in the over-85 population.

This explosion in research is extremely exciting, but it is also frustrating, because our understanding is increasingly fragmented. A complex array of different and competing theories has developed. Even more frustrating is that biogerontological findings about the mechanism of aging in one species (or even in one strain) often do not hold up in others. In epidemiology and the social sciences, findings may also vary across time, and accepted results that are true for one cohort may not hold for another. Not only are we fragmented within fields, but we are also becoming fragmented across them. The study of aging has traditionally been interdisciplinary in nature, but as the field becomes more complex, researchers are becoming more specialized, with fewer lines of communication across disciplines. This dual characteristic of the explosion of information and its increasing specialization is exemplified by the separation of the *Journal of Gerontology* into two series: *Biological Sciences and Medical Sciences* and *Psychological Sciences and Social Sciences.*

This disparity in perspectives plays out in the basic assumptions of different types of gerontologists. The first author, in an interview for a tele-course on aging, was asked, "What effect does culture have on the aging process?" The answer was, "Everything!" The producer was startled, because he had just interviewed a biologist whose answer had been an emphatic "Nothing!" When asked to account for the discrepancy, the author answered that, although the biological processes underlying the aging process were universal, the rate at which we age is largely a function of culture.

This point is illustrated by Figure 1.1. The Nepalese woman looks much older with very wrinkled skin and a face which clearly reflects much suffering. In contrast, the actress is blond and curvaceous, with smooth skin and elegant stature. When the pictures were taken, however, both of these women were about 60. How we live and the resources we can use profoundly affect the way we age as much, if not more, than our genetic endowment.

Gerontology is not yet at a stage in which a unified theory can be proposed, but we feel that similar themes are emerging in the various disciplines that comprise gerontology. A major purpose of this book is to create a bridge for understanding across disciplinary boundaries. To that end, we propose that many theories and studies of aging can be understood under the rubric of aging accelerators and decelerators—factors that increase and those that decrease the rate at which we age. This theme is central throughout the book and may help to integrate findings across disciplines with a view toward understanding successful aging. Before we explain the structure of the book, however, we feel that a brief section on basic terms is important, especially for those new to gerontology.

● BASIC DEFINITIONS

Probably the most basic question in gerontology is, When does late life begin? There is often little consistency across studies. Some studies define older populations as 65 and above and others as 60 and above, but some start at ages as young as 50. A consensus is emerging that late life is not at all homogeneous and that one needs to distinguish between "young-old" and "old-old" adults (see Neugarten, 1975). Different cutoff points have been used, but it is most common to define young-old persons as those between

Figure 1.1   Cultural Differences in Aging

SOURCE: © Rune Hellestad/CORBIS and Lea Wyler.

the ages of 65 and 79, old-old individuals as those between 80 and 99, and the oldest-old, or centenarians, as those who are age 100 or older.

Although some people experience disability in their 50s or even 40s, young-old individuals are typically relatively healthy and quite functional. As we discuss later in the book, some of the stereotypes associated with impaired aging that have been proved false in the young-old may actually be characteristic of the old-old, who are more likely to be physically and cognitively frail and in need of support. Centenarians are a class unto themselves, and it is more difficult to make generalizations about them. Some are hardy and as sharp as a tack, but more are extraordinarily frail.

Another important distinction is that between age, cohort, and period. *Age* refers to the number of years a person has been alive, whereas *cohort* refers to a group of people who share the same birth year or sometimes those who shared historical events, such as the World War II generation. *Period* refers to the time at which the measurement or assessment occurred.

If a particular phenomenon always changes with age, regardless of cohort or period, then it is an age effect. If the change is specific to a particular cohort but does not occur in any other group, then it is a cohort effect. If all cohorts or ages change at a particular point in time, then it is a period effect.

It is important to understand that a person who was 70 years old in 1950 belonged to a very different cohort from that of a 70-year-old in the year 2000. The 70-year-old in 1950 was born before the turn of the 20th century; witnessed the first cars, telephones, and electric lights; and experienced two world wars (but was too old for military service in them). The 70-year-old in 2000 was born at the beginning of the Depression but was too young to serve in World War II. She may have served in a MASH unit in Korea, however, and certainly witnessed the civil rights movement and the tumultuous dissension over the Vietnam war. Thus, a cohort may well have experienced a life course that is historically unique, and this experience may not generalize to other cohorts. It is crucial to recognize that much of what we know about human aging stems from studies of the World War II generation, and we do not know whether this will generalize to the baby boomers and other future cohorts of older adults.

Period effects are also extremely important. Sometimes general shifts in the whole culture, or even temporary shifts, may be confused with aging effects. For example, Bradburn and Caplovitz (1965) first demonstrated that historical events may affect the mood of an entire population. They happened to be conducting repeated measures of positive and negative affect when the Cuban missile crisis occurred, and they found that negative affect increased at this time. If they had not been sensitive to the particular events of this period, however, they might have thought that this increase reflected aging rather than period effects.

Another important distinction is made between life span and life expectancy. *Life span* refers to the absolute length of time a member of a given species may live. In humans, that is currently about 120 years. In contrast, *life expectancy* refers to the length of time an average member of a particular cohort can expect to live. Life expectancy refers to the age at which half of a particular cohort will have died, and demographers estimate that about half of those born in the year 2000 will survive until their 77th birthdays (Anderson & DeTurk, 2002). *Age-specific life expectancy* refers to the average number of years that members of a given cohort who have reached a specific age can expect to live. For example, people who survive to age 65 can expect to live another 18 or 20 years, even if the average life expectancy for their cohort is much lower. In nearly every country, women enjoy higher life expectancies than men. In the United States, infant girls born in 1999 can expect to live 79.4 years, but their male peers can expect to live only 73.9 years (Anderson & DeTurk, 2002).

Calculating life expectancy involves a number of assumptions and cannot take into account unforeseen historical circumstances. For example, life expectancy in Russia went down when the former USSR broke up. Furthermore, it may also be difficult to accurately project for immigrant groups, especially if information is lacking about their cohort in the country of origin. If older members of the group return to their native country, tracking mortality rates is also difficult.

As gerontology and geriatrics focus so much on health, it is important to understand the distinction between mortality, morbidity, and functional health. *Mortality* refers to death; *morbidity* refers to illness. Mortality rates refer to the number of people who die during a given period of time. Epidemiological and biomedical studies may attempt to predict all-cause mortality (the total number of deaths in a population), or they may try to predict specific causes of mortality, such as heart disease or cancer. Morbidity rate refers to the *prevalence* or total number of cases of a specific disease in a population, whereas the *incidence* of illness refers to the number of new cases in a year.

Epidemiologists further distinguish between acute and chronic illness. *Acute illnesses* are often self-limiting and/or can be successfully treated with medicines, but *chronic diseases* are often incurable, and treatment focus is on the management and the delay of disability rather than cure. Before the advent of antibiotics during World War II, most people died of acute illnesses such as pneumonia, influenza, scarlet fever, smallpox, or cholera, or from complications due to childbirth, and death was much more evenly distributed across the life span. With antibiotics, better sanitation, and better nutrition, however, acute illnesses are less likely to be lethal, and most people develop chronic diseases such as cardiovascular disease (CVD), cancer, arthritis, and diabetes. Nearly 80% of people over the age of 65 have at least one chronic disease (Kramarow, Lentzner, Rooks, Weeks, & Saydah, 1999). Although some diseases such as CVD and cancer are the leading causes of death in late life, others such as arthritis are not fatal but can adversely affect quality of life.

In late life, however, the acute versus chronic distinction can become blurred. For example, people with chronic obstructive pulmonary disease are more susceptible to acute illnesses such as colds, pneumonia, and other viral infections of the lungs. Diabetics are susceptible to a variety of infections, including infections of the skin, bladder, and so on. The presence of a chronic illness may also reduce the ability to recover from an acute incident. Conversely, acute illnesses such as viral infections may give rise to chronic problems, such as viral-triggered hypersensitivity of the lungs and asthma, and it is possible that some forms of diabetes or multiple sclerosis may be triggered by viruses. Although chronic illnesses such as arthritis may not be fatal in and of themselves, they may give rise to a variety of health problems that can have very serious consequences. In other words, acute and chronic illnesses can intertwine to produce a cascade of health problems that can affect the ability to function in social roles and to care for oneself.

Thus, gerontologists and geriatricians often focus on functional health rather than specific illnesses. *Functional health* refers to the ability to perform daily tasks such as shopping, paying bills, preparing meals, or getting around, called instrumental activities of daily living (IADLs), and caring for oneself, such as bathing, dressing, and eating, which are called activities of daily life (ADLs). Many older adults have several chronic illnesses such as hypertension, arthritis, and diabetes but nonetheless are quite capable of living in the community and taking care of themselves (and, very often, taking care of others as well). Once functional health declines, however, older adults are at greater risk for dependency and institutionalization. Most dread the possibility of institutionalization; indeed, it is the negative Shakespearean fate that we all seek to avoid.

When we think of successful aging, the image of the active senior emerges, an image often touted in advertisements for expensive retirement communities. It is tempting to define successful aging in terms of good physical function, cognitive abilities, and mental health. But such a definition also implies that there is only one way to age successfully and ignores the fact that the vast majority of older adults will develop illnesses and limitations (Minkler & Fadem, 2002). Furthermore, as one commentator put it, we appear to be the only culture on earth that regards death as optional—doing our best to ignore the fact that, barring accidental death, we will all develop fatal illnesses, often involving pain and disability. Thus, we prefer to use the term *optimal aging*, which allows for the recognition that there may be different ways of aging well, that people begin with different configurations of vulnerabilities and resources that affect how they age, and that this is a process that continually unfolds. Understanding what constitutes and what promotes optimal aging is a primary function of this book, but, as we will see, such understanding is a difficult task, because it entails assumptions that reflect cultural and individual values. Nonetheless, we argue that optimal aging is a multidimensional construct that involves avoiding the accelerating agents that promote premature illness and disability, as well as developing protective factors that delay or decelerate the aging and disease processes to maintain good physical, cognitive, and mental health. At the heart of optimal aging, however, is the concept of wisdom. We propose that the development of wisdom in adulthood allows individuals to assist others (especially those in younger generations) to optimize capacities despite illness and disability, to find meaning and purpose in life, and to face disability and even death with relative equanimity.

ORGANIZATION OF THE BOOK ●

The purpose of this book is to provide an interdisciplinary understanding of the factors that affect aging. As mentioned earlier, we feel that the field is becoming increasingly fragmented, yet theories and models are emerging that can help tie together diverse perspectives. Our overall goal is to examine the biological and psychosocial aging literatures to determine if they can be organized using the aging accelerators and decelerators model, in order to enhance understanding of the many facets of aging and to promote optimal aging.

To that end, we have organized the book in four sections. Section I provides a general overview of demographic, theoretical, and methodological issues. Chapter 2 provides a detailed examination of various age-related population shifts and their causes and consequences. Much has been written about the graying of America, but the increasing age of the population is a phenomenon seen not only in the United States but also in Europe and in most developing countries as well. Drawing on the 2000 census and other national and international data, we discovered some very surprising facts that challenge long-held assumptions about the demography of aging. Chapter 2 also examines demographic factors that accelerate or decelerate the aging process, including marital status, ethnicity, and socioeconomic status.

Chapter 3 is an overview of theories of aging. The first half focuses on biological theories of aging in humans. Beginning with theories of the genetic regulation of aging, we also review cellular theories, including DNA repair mechanisms and antioxidants, as well as the effects of waste accumulation. At the systems level, some theories of aging emphasize the effects of wear and tear; others focus on problems with interorgan communication. The second half reviews psychosocial theories of aging, including classic stage theories as well as more modern approaches such as developmental systems theory, models of adaptation in late life, and the definitions and development of wisdom. We explore whether the construct of aging accelerators and decelerators is broad enough to develop a common language between biological and psychosocial theories of aging and also discuss the interface between the dialectic of cumulative and plastic models.

An overview of methodological issues is presented in Chapter 4. We review different types of longitudinal designs, including cohort, cross-, and time-sequential designs and provide a brief introduction to longitudinal statistics, especially health statistics. Much confusion exists concerning the uses and misuses of longitudinal statistics, and differences in preferred analytical strategies across fields may render interdisciplinary comparisons problematic. By providing a literate, nontechnical review, we hope to increase general understanding of longitudinal designs and statistics that will increase the uniformity of their use across disciplines. Although longitudinal statistics are difficult, understanding them is absolutely crucial for gerontology, given its inherent focus on examining the rate of change in a variety of phenomena.

Section II examines the aging of select biological systems. Much of the book focuses on biological systems, because these tend to be less well understood. For each system, we provide a brief overview of the anatomy and physiology. Following Rowe and Kahn (1998), we describe normal age-related changes, then we focus on diseases and the factors that accelerate the rate at which they occur. Finally, we describe ways of maintaining optimal aging in each system, with an emphasis on aging decelerators.

Chapter 5 looks at changes in the musculoskeletal and integumentary systems. With age, there are systematic changes in the overall body composition, including bones and muscles. Problems with the skeleton also increase with age. Most older adults have some form of arthritis, and osteoporosis is often one of the most painful diseases in later life. Muscle mass also declines with age, although weight-bearing exercise can attenuate that loss. Although not usually life threatening, aging and disease processes in the musculoskeletal system can be extremely painful and debilitating and may be one of the greatest influences on quality of life in late life.

Chapter 6 focuses on the internal organ systems, including the cardiovascular, respiratory, gastrointestinal, renal/urinary, and reproductive systems. In many ways, the functioning of the heart and lungs regulates the rate at which we age. Both systems are crucial in carrying oxygen and other nutrients to every cell in the body, as well as in carrying away waste products. Failure or deficiencies in these systems often underlie damage to other systems. Our knowledge of both normal aging processes and disease processes in these systems has greatly increased in the past two decades. Much of what we know about interventions to delay problems with aging emphasizes the maintenance of the cardiovascular and pulmonary systems.

Relatively few age-related changes occur in the gastrointestinal system, but it is responsible for overall nutrition needed to maintain the rest of the body, and disruptions can have serious systemic effects. Inadequate nutrition can also result in confusional states, as well as a host of other problems. Weight loss in very late life may result in serious risk of mortality. Because the renal system regulates fluids and electrolytes, problems in this area can also lead to a multitude of problems, including hypertension and difficulties in regulating the heart rate, as well as transitory confusional states, often confused with dementia. Urinary incontinence in later life, although extremely common, is almost always treatable, but it constitutes one of the biggest barriers to freedom of movement and social interaction and thus quality of life. Finally, age-related changes in the reproductive system are considered.

Chapter 7 addresses the regulatory systems, including the nervous, sensory, endocrine, and immune systems. In many ways, the functioning of any one system is of less importance than communication between systems in determining the rate at which we age. These four systems work in concert using a variety of electrochemical means of communication to fine-tune coordination across systems. An explosion of knowledge has occurred in both biogerontology and in the cognitive neurosciences in the past 10 years. We are much better at understanding the mechanisms of brain aging and the factors that give rise to disorders such as Alzheimer's disease. We are also much better at treating sensory problems such as glaucoma, cataracts, and hearing loss. The endocrine system is of such importance for aging that for many years the pituitary was considered the master gland that regulated all aging. Finally, we describe our growing understanding of the complexity of the immune system, which, contrary to general belief, does not necessarily decline with age (Miller, 1996a, 1996b).

Chapter 8 reviews Lawton and Nahemow's (1973) theory of environmental competence as well as functional health. This theory first hypothesized that a person's level of ability interacted with environmental facilities to create disability. This idea—that environments can be changed to accommodate mobility, sensory, and cognitive problems—resulted in radical changes in housing and facilities for older adults in the last 25 years. Thus, accelerators and decelerators of aging are not necessarily internal, nor do they inevitably affect internal processes. Rather, the configuration of the environment can affect the expression of aging processes on functional health. We discuss ways in which functional health has been conceptualized and how this concept has generally evolved into a study of health-related quality of life in later years.

Section III centers on the psychosocial factors that affect physical health, with a specific view toward understanding psychosocial accelerators and decelerators of the aging process. Dr. Michael Levenson assisted in writing Chapter 9, which addresses the interface between physical and mental health. In it, we review the evidence for and the pathways through which personality processes can affect morbidity and mortality. Most reviews focus on psychological risk factors, but we will discuss evidence for personality processes that can be protective of health, especially in late life. Health behavior habits also can affect the rate of aging. The impact of smoking, exercise,

and diet as accelerators and decelerators are addressed in Section II, but the consumption of alcohol has important implications for mental, cognitive, and physical health, albeit in a complex, nonlinear fashion. Furthermore, symptoms of common illnesses may present differently in older adults. For example, in younger adults, the primary symptom of a urinary tract infection is burning pain on urination. But in older adults, the primary symptom may be a confusional state (Ouslander, 1994). Thus, it may be very hard to distinguish between psychological and physical health problems in late life, as there are often overlapping symptoms. For example, if an older person is listless, sleeping poorly, has little appetite, and appears somewhat confused, this may be due to a number of problems such as depression, hypo- or hyperthyroidism, leukemia, congestive heart failure, pneumonia, alcoholism, or a bladder infection. Proper differentiation of symptoms and diagnoses may require both physical and psychological screening.

The next two chapters focus on other psychosocial processes that may affect health in later life. Chapter 10 addresses the evidence for the effects of stressors on health in late life. We know that older adults are more vulnerable to the physical effects of stress, but it is not clear whether they are also more vulnerable to the psychological effects of stress. How elders cope with problems, especially chronic illness, may well differentiate between those individuals who are able to live in the community and those who become institutionalized.

Chapter 11 reviews social support, which may be one of the most important predictors of health in late life. We discuss the different types of support and theories of age-related change and stability in the amount and type of support. We also review the relationship of social support to morbidity and mortality.

Section IV revisits the idea of aging accelerators and decelerators, addressing whether this construct can provide an integrating framework for biological and psychosocial theories of aging. From this perspective, Chapter 12 reviews theories of optimal aging as a framework for integrating biological and psychosocial factors in aging and argues for the centrality of wisdom.

We learned a great deal while researching material for this book. Knowledge in this field is changing rapidly, and we have done our best to present the most recent information available. More important, we hope that this book will serve as a bridge between the biological and psychosocial gerontology communities and promote a more holistic understanding of the aging process.

SECTION I

DEMOGRAPHIC, THEORETICAL, AND METHODOLOGICAL ISSUES

CHAPTER 2

DEMOGRAPHY
OF AGING

The 20th century witnessed a dramatic change in population demographics. At its beginning, most countries had pyramid-shaped population profiles, with children and young people greatly outnumbering those who were older. By the century's end, however, the pyramid shape had changed as the percentage of the population who were children decreased and the number of middle-aged and older persons increased. Although most people are aware that the United States and Europe have experienced an increase in the number of older adults, especially those over the age of 85, what is less well-known is that this is true of most nations. The increase in the number of older citizens is creating problems for developing countries that do not have adequate resources or the economic stability to support a large older adult population. In the United States, ethnic diversity in the older population is growing. No longer primarily European Americans, this group now includes substantial numbers of Asian, Latino, and African Americans. The greater number, ethnic diversity, and increasing age of the population will complicate treatment and service delivery in the areas of health and social care, as well as affecting transportation, business, education, and even recreation.

This chapter examines the dynamics of the population growth in the United States, focusing particularly on the increase in numbers of older adults, with an overview of how life expectancy has changed in the past 100 years. We will address, briefly, how increasing numbers of older people may affect the economy of the country. We also report the geographic distribution of older people. Particular attention is given to those who live in rural areas, because a large percentage of older adults live in nonmetropolitan areas. Next, we look at population changes in other parts of the world (including Europe, Africa, South America, and Asia). A focus of this discussion is the morbidity and mortality rates of these countries and the difficulties of providing resources for their aging populations.

The last part of the chapter addresses demographic factors as they relate to the rate of aging; more specifically, how do gender, marital status, ethnicity, and socioeconomic status affect the mortality and/or morbidity of an individual? Each subsection covers the demographics of a particular population and the specific risk involved in being a member of that group.

The worldwide demographic shift highlights the fact that aging is not strictly genetically determined but is plastic, or susceptible to influence. Nonetheless, the demographics of morbidity and mortality also demonstrate the opposing principle—that aging processes also exhibit cumulative effects, which can manifest either as aging acceleration or deceleration. How differences in gender, marital status, ethnicity, and socioeconomic status affect life expectancy will be reviewed with this dialectic in mind.

● AGING IN THE WORLD

In this section, we focus primarily on aging trends in the United States, but we provide an international overview as well.

Population Aging in the United States

Changing demographic profiles. In 1905, children and young people made up the largest segment of the population, with only a small percentage of people 65 years of age and older (see Figure 2.1a). This created a pyramid-shaped profile, with a broad base of infants and children and relatively few older adults. Pyramid-shaped population profiles result from high fertility rates and high mortality rates.

By 1975, the demographic profile of the country had changed (see Figure 2.1b). Infants and children were no longer the largest population groups. Instead, the largest cohort consisted of the baby boomers, who were then between the ages of 10 and 30. There was also a slight widening at the top of the pyramid as more people in their 60s and 70s survived into their 80s and 90s. On the other hand, the indentation in the middle of the 1975 pyramid characterized those between the ages of 35 and 45, the result of the low birthrate during the Depression.

The smaller Depression cohort has resulted in an interesting occurrence. For the first time in over a century, the growth rate of the older population in the 2000 census did not exceed that of the rest of the population. Although the total population increased by 13.2%, the population of older adults increased by just 12%. Furthermore, the proportion of those 65 and older in the total population dropped from 12.6% in 1990 to 12.4% in 2000 (Hetzel & Smith, 2001). This will change as the baby boomers begin to turn 65 in the year 2011.

Figure 2.1c depicts the remarkable changes that are expected to occur by the year 2010. The bottom two thirds of the pyramid will have squared off considerably by that time. There will be comparable numbers of children and young and middle-aged adults. Many more will survive into their 70s and 80s, although there will be relatively few who are 85 and older, compared with the rest of the population. By 2030, the baby boomers will have swelled the ranks of older people, becoming the grandparent boomers (see Figure 2.1d). It is projected that as many as 70 million people in the United States will be 65 or older by 2030 (Administration on Aging [AOA], 2002). The demographic profile continues to change from a pyramid shape to one that is rectangular. Atchley (2000) argues that countries with rectangular population distributions tend to be more prosperous and more politically stable than those with the classic pyramid shape.

85+ in the United States. About 100,000 people were over the age of 85 in the United States in 1900. This number has grown rapidly since that time. Although this age group represents a small proportion of the total population, currently 1.5%, it is the fastest growing segment of the older population. In fact, it increased by 38% in the 1990s, from 3.1 million in 1990 to 4.2 million in 2000 (Hetzel & Smith, 2001). Remarkably, this number is expected to quadruple in the first half of this century, nearing a projected 18.9 million by the year 2050 (Hobbs & Damon, 1996).

Accurately counting the number of centenarians in this country (or any other) is not easy, as exaggeration of reported age is common in older people who are proud of their ability to survive into later years (Medvedev, 1974). It is estimated, however, that about 14,000 centenarians lived in the United States in 1980 (Hobbs & Damon, 1996). This more than tripled in the past 20 years; the 2000 census reported 50,454 centenarians. Four out of five were women, reflecting the change in gender ratio with age. South Dakota had the highest proportion of centenarians in its population—1 of every 3,056 people (Hetzel & Smith, 2001). The chances of becoming a centenarian

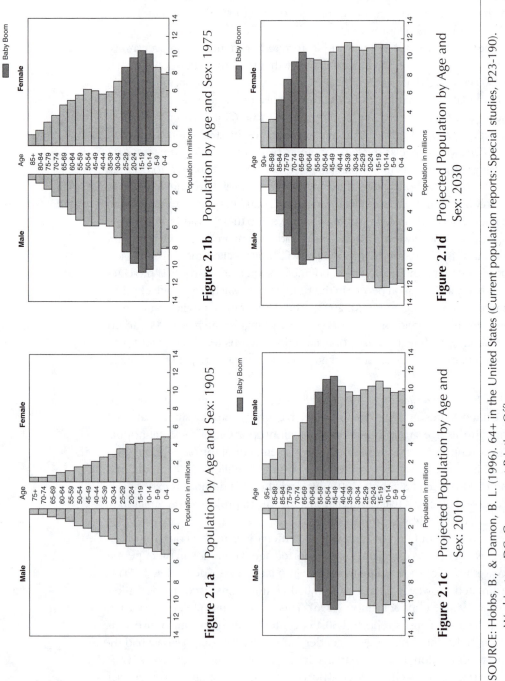

Figure 2.1a Population by Age and Sex: 1905

Figure 2.1b Population by Age and Sex: 1975

Figure 2.1c Projected Population by Age and Sex: 2010

Figure 2.1d Projected Population by Age and Sex: 2030

SOURCE: Hobbs, B., & Damon, B. L. (1996). 64+ in the United States (Current population reports: Special studies, P23-190). Washington, DC: Government Printing Office.

greatly improved during the 20th century. A person born in 1879 had a 1 in 400 chance of living to be 100 years old, but a person born in 1980 has a 1 in 87 chance of living to 100 (Hobbs & Damon, 1996).

Although it is true that the older population is healthier than ever before, there is concern about the economic stress that growing numbers of older adults may place on the country. More than any other age group, those 85 and older have the greatest health and social care needs, and an increase in their numbers may have a major impact on the resources of the nation.

Age dependency ratios. The sheer number of older adults will present daunting challenges for subsequent generations, but there still will be more younger and middle-aged than older people. Therefore, the working units of the population will outnumber those who are dependent on them. Furthermore, in many cases, older adults are beneficial to the economic health of the country rather than a burden.

A *total dependency ratio* (TDR) compares the number of economically nonproductive citizens (below age 18 and age 65 and older) with the number of working-aged adults. Although not entirely accurate (some individuals make considerable money in early or late life and some working-aged adults are disabled, unemployed, or taking time out to raise children), the age dependency ratio is a rough estimate of the number of people who need to be supported by workers. The equation is simple:

$$TDR = (a + c)/b$$

where a = children < 18, b = adults 18 to 65, and c = adults 65 and older.

A serious concern is that the growing percentage of older adults in the population will create a crisis in TDRs and place an overwhelming burden on working-aged adults. Furthermore, an increase in TDRs may result in competition for services between the old and the young. TDRs do not translate directly to dollars spent, however. The amount that children and elders cost working family members and society depends on such factors as the level of services provided and the savings, pensions, investments and other types of benefits that older adults can draw on. Older adults are healthier than ever before, which may lessen the expected burden of health care costs. Although there has been a considerable downturn in economic stability recently, with the uncertainty of the stock market and failure of some retirement funding, older people are still less likely to live in poverty than in the past (more on this later in the chapter). In poor families in the United States, Social Security payments to grandparents are often the most stable source of income for the family as a whole. Countries that have economic surpluses, such as the

United States and Europe, are able to provide sufficient resources for the dependent members of their societies. Developing nations, however, may experience much more strain, as will be explained later in this chapter.

Life expectancy. As mentioned in Chapter 1, life expectancy is the average number of years a person in a particular cohort can expect to live. There has been a remarkable change in the life expectancy of people living in the United States. A child born today can expect to live at least 30 years longer than one born a century ago. Although life expectancy in 1900 was about 47 years (Hobbs & Damon, 1996), a female born in 1999 can expect to live 79 years and a male, almost 74 years (Anderson & DeTurk, 2002).

In 1900, the leading causes of death in the United States were infectious diseases such as tuberculosis, pneumonia, influenza, and gastroenteritis (Sahyoun, Lentzner, Hoyert, & Robinson, 2001). Very few deaths were caused by heart disease, and death from lung cancer was extremely rare. Death was distributed throughout the life span; people of all ages died of smallpox and tetanus, childbirth was associated with high mortality rates, and infant mortality was quite high (about 16%, compared with less than 2% today). Treatment for bacterial infections was rudimentary and often ineffective, and vaccines against viruses had not yet been developed. The discovery of how infectious diseases spread occurred in the late 19th and early 20th centuries, leading to the development of public health measures to control the spread of communicable diseases and the research and development of vaccines and drugs (Green & Ottonson, 1994).

Since the 1930s, the primary causes of death have shifted away from infectious diseases to ones that are more chronic in nature. By the latter part of the 20th century, the five leading causes of death among those 65 years and older were heart disease, cancer, stroke, chronic obstructive pulmonary disease, and pneumonia and influenza, with slight variations depending on ethnicity (Sahyoun et al., 2001).

Age-specific life expectancy has also changed dramatically in the past 100 years, however. The conditions that have fostered this extension of life include a decrease in infant and maternal mortality rates, improved sanitation practices, better nutrition, and improved medical care. For example, in 1900, a 65-year-old would be expected to live less than 13 more years. In contrast, a person who was 65 years of age in 1999 could expect to live another 17.7 years (Anderson & DeTurk, 2002). As might be anticipated, age-specific life expectancy has changed less for the old-old over the course of the last century. In 1900, the life expectancy of an 85-year-old was about 4 years (Hobbs & Damon, 1996), and it had increased to only 6.3 years in 1999 (Anderson & DeTurk, 2002).

A French woman, Jeanne Calment, was possibly the longest-lived person in the world. At her death in 1997, she had reached the age of 122 years and

5 months (Noveck, 1997). Although there have been reports of people living beyond this time, when records are examined, these cases of longevity are not validated. For example, Medvedev (1974) visited and studied centenarians in Georgia in the former USSR, where there appeared to be a large number of the oldest-old. He found that ages were often exaggerated. Many had taken on the birth dates of siblings who died as infants but shared the same name. Of great interest was that, when he returned a couple of years later, people had often increased their stated ages by 5 or 10 years. Thus, an individual who claimed to be 125 was found to be only 104. This reflected the fact that centenarians were valued in the USSR; often, parades were held in their honor.

Longevity comes at a cost. Chronic diseases such as arthritis, diabetes, osteoporosis, hypertension, arteriosclerosis, and multiple neurological disorders have replaced the acute diseases of years ago. In general, chronic diseases are not curable, and the main goal of treatment is management of the illness to decrease its rate of progression and therefore limit disability.

Thus, this dramatic increase in life expectancy has evoked two major controversies. Fries and Crapo (1981) first argued for a phenomenon they termed the "compression of morbidity." Fries (1989) noted that survival tables showed an increased squaring of the curve, with larger numbers of people surviving until late life. Demographic trends suggested that the onset of major chronic disabling illnesses had been delayed. He proposed a fairly rosy scenario, that people would remain healthy longer, until a few months before their maximum life span (about 85) and would then die after a relatively short period of disability. Others, however, have argued that the increase in number of persons surviving until very late life translates into an extension of morbidity, with people living longer with disabilities (Roos, Havens, & Black, 1993). Still others have maintained that periods of active life expectancy exceed disability (Doblhammer & Kytir, 2001; Manton & Land, 2000).

It is likely that individual differences exist in the compression or extension of morbidity. For example, people with poor behavior habits (cigarette smoking, inactivity, and obesity) have higher levels of disability in late life and extended declines before death, whereas those with healthier lifestyles show little disability and only short periods of disability before death (Hubert, Bloch, Oehlert, & Fries, 2002). Centenarians may enjoy a compression of morbidity, but those who die in their 80s may not (Perls, 1997).

The second controversy, over whether there is a maximum life span in humans, has not been resolved. Clearly, the maximum life span is not 85; Jeanne Calment was a witness to that. Is it 122? Or not really fixed? Vaupel and his colleagues (1998; Oeppen & Vaupel, 2002) have argued that the dramatic increase in old age survival presages an increase in the maximum life span. The average life expectancy in the world has more than doubled in the past two centuries. Before 1950, most of that increase was due to a decrease in infant mortality, but in the past half century, it is because of greater survival in late life. Current projections are that the average life expectancy for women will be in the 90s by 2040.

Vaupel and his colleagues argue that the maximum life span reflects statistical forces rather than simply genetic ones. For example, suppose that the force of mortality in late life is .5—that is, half of the individuals 90 years old will die in the next year. When there are only a few individuals, their numbers rapidly diminish. If there are a million 90-year-olds, however, it will take longer for their numbers to become depleted, and the maximal life span will be extended. Others have argued that there are genetic limitations to the life span and that average life expectancy is unlikely to go over 85 (Olshansky, Carnes, & Desesquelles, 2001). This controversy has serious implications for public policy. Retirement at 60 is not feasible if people are likely to live another 60 years, to say nothing of the burden of the additional numbers of humans on the planet.

Geographic location and residence. Of the 50 states, California has the largest number of older adults: 3.6 million in the year 2000. This accounts for more than 10% of the total number of older adults in the United States. Other states have fewer numbers, but higher percentages of older adults in their populations. For example, 17.6 % of Florida's population is age 65 or older, with Pennsylvania, at nearly 16%, coming in a close second (California has only 10.6%). Only 5.7 % of Alaska residents are 65 and older (Hetzel & Smith, 2001).

Although older people tend to be residentially stable, they may move when they retire. For example, retirees may move where the cost of living is lower or the climate more temperate. From 1990 to 2000, the number of those 65 and older living in Nevada increased by an astounding 71.5%; in Arizona, this group grew by 39.5%. The District of Columbia, Iowa, and Rhode Island either lost or simply maintained their older adult population from 1990 to 2000. Alaska had the lowest proportion of older adults in 2000 (as noted above), but, surprisingly, this number increased by 59.6% from 1990 to 2000 (Hetzel & Smith, 2001). This may be explained by the tendency of many older adults to revisit and relocate to parts of the country in which they previously vacationed, such as Alaska, Arizona, or Hawaii. Some older adults maintain dual residences and are referred to as snowbirds, leaving the cold north during the winters and escaping the hot south during the summers. Retirement villages in Arizona, Florida, and New Mexico, known for their social activities and inexpensive living, attest to their desire to leave their home states for warmer ones when they retire.

In later years, after the death of a spouse or if one partner experiences poor health, older people often return to the state in which they spent their younger years, seeking a familiar environment and family members who provide social support. Thus, states that have high levels of in-migration of elders tend to host the young-old, who are relatively healthy and have a fair amount of disposable income, providing net gains. The more frail will often return home, however, and the financial burden of their care is provided by their home states.

More than 80% of older adults live independently in their homes. An additional 15% live in their homes but use outside assistance, such as help with shopping, housekeeping, cooking, or personal care. This care is usually provided by a spouse, other family member, or a paid caregiver (see Chapter 11). A very small proportion of older adults live in nursing homes, 5.4% in 1994 and 3.4% in 1999 (Manton & Gu, 2001). Fewer than 3% of older adults reside in assisted-living communities, a type of institutional residence that emerged in the past 20 years. Although some of these residents need assistance, many of them live independently (or with the help of a spouse), with the assurance that if help is needed, it will be provided by the facility. Sometimes the help is minimal, such as laundry service or two meals a day, and in other cases, personal care such as bathing is provided. The care is not as extensive as that provided in a nursing home, however. Thus, the population demographics of older adults in the United States are complex. Certainly, there are positive aspects to having older people in the population, but there are responsibilities as well. Rural areas are often attractive places for people to live in later years, but drawbacks appear when frailty and disease occur.

Graying of rural America. Population demographics in rural and urban areas have changed considerably in the past 100 years. Although nearly a third of all U.S. citizens lived on farms in the 1920s, this number had dropped to 2% by the end of the 20th century (Elder, King, & Conger, 1996). Older people still find rural areas attractive to live in, however; 23% of people 65 and older live in nonmetropolitan areas. Therefore, a large proportion of rural communities are made up of older people. In 1997, about 14% of people who lived in rural areas were 65 years of age or older, compared to 11% of the urban population (McBride & Mueller, 2002). This shift in population dynamics is due to several factors, including out-migration of younger people and in-migration of retiring older people, as well as aging in place.

Older people who live in rural areas are not a homogeneous group but a diverse population who have chosen to live outside urban areas for a variety of reasons. They are often dissimilar in resources, health, and family relationships. One group of rural older adults consists of lifelong farmers who have lived in the area all of their lives. This group usually has an adequate income and good health, although they report poorer self-perceptions of health than other rural older adults (Coward, McLaughlin, Duncan, & Bull,

1994). This may be explained by the exceptional physical demands placed on any active participant in farming. The lifelong farmers receive substantial social support from family and friends, who often live nearby and with whom they enjoy reciprocal helping relationships.

The second group consists of older people who retire to rural areas after working and raising a family in an urban or suburban environment. Generally, this group is financially secure, well educated, and enjoys relatively good health. These "new farmers" frequently relocate to rural areas at retirement in the hopes of finding a more simple but higher quality of life. Although they find country life comfortable for a number of years, health problems in later life may cause these older adults to reconsider the wisdom of leaving urban areas where health care resources are more readily available. Therefore, members of this group will often return to metropolitan areas to be closer to family and to medical facilities.

The third group of rural older adults lives in small communities rather than on farms. They are usually lifelong residents of their towns and may lack the necessary resources to leave their small communities. On average, these people are less educated, have poorer housing, and are less financially secure than other rural older adults (Longino & Haas, 1993). These nonfarm people report more health problems than other older adults and have fewer family members to provide care if it is needed.

Ethnic populations account for about 7% of rural older people. African Americans make up the greatest proportion of this group, followed by Mexican Americans. The health of both these groups is generally poorer than that of other older adults living in rural areas. Older Mexican Americans may follow their family members into the rural areas to help with harvests or to care for children. This group is almost twice as likely to live in poverty as European American older adults. Furthermore, they often have delayed and poor access to health care due to questionable residential status (and eligibility to receive benefits) in the United States, the lack of English-speaking ability, or a desire to use traditional health care (for a review, see Gilmer, Aldwin, & Ober, 1998).

Older people in rural areas are an important asset to their community. They bring financial resources to the area and often take on roles as community leaders. Scheidt and Norris-Baker (1990) report that the survival of some small communities is often dependent on the willingness and ability of older persons to take on major roles. Older adults serve on city councils and as church elders, run local businesses, and volunteer in schools, libraries, and community clinics. They play a key role in sustaining facilities that would be closed without their continued assistance. Jobs and resources are brought to the community when frail older adults need assistance in their homes

(Gilmer et al., 1998). Thus, rural older adults are a unique and important part of the aging demographics, not only in the United States but in many countries throughout the world.

International Aging

Worldwide, there were approximately 420 million people 65 years of age or over in 2000 (Kinsella & Velkoff, 2001). Demographically, the European countries and Japan have the greatest percentage of older adults in their populations; Italy is first in this respect, with more than 18% of its population aged 65 or over. The median age of the population in Italy was 40 in 2000 and is expected to increase to 52 by 2030. In contrast, the United States is a relatively young nation, as its median age was 36 in 2000 and is expected to be 39 in 2030. Developing countries have a much lower median age, mostly due to their high birthrate. For example, the median age of the population in Malawi was 17 in 2000, and it is expected in increase to 23 in 2030.

Most nations have increasing numbers of older adults in their populations. According to Kinsella and Velkoff (2001), half of the world's population of older adults live in developed countries and the other half in developing countries. This is changing, however, and by the year 2030, there will be more than twice as many older people in developing countries (686 million) as in developed nations (300 million). This unprecedented increase in number of older adults is due to the public health advances that have been introduced in developing countries, extending life expectancy.

Figure 2.2 depicts the average annual rate of population increase from 1950 to 2000 and projects it to 2030. As can be seen, the growth rate of the total world, all ages, was 2% in 1970 and is expected to decrease to less than 1% by 2030. The growth rate for those 65 and over is far greater. In the next 10 years, a dramatic increase is predicted in the growth rate of those 65 and older in both developed and developing countries, which will not decrease until 2020.

Great differences exist in the economic resources of the developed and developing countries. Developing countries often have high percentages of people living at or below the poverty level. For example, fully 89% of the people in India and Ethiopia and nearly 60% of those in China, Indonesia, and Nigeria live on less than $2 per day. In contrast, the gross national product per capita in Switzerland and Japan is more than $40,000 per year (Kalache, 2001).

The economic problems in developing countries will be confounded by changes in the population dynamics. *Demographic transition* is a term used

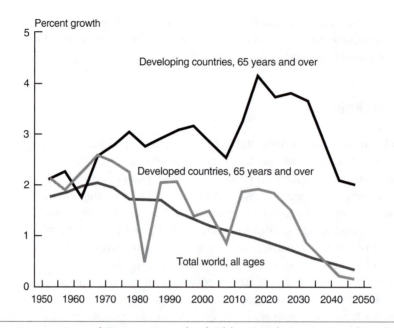

Percent growth

Developing countries, 65 years and over

Developed countries, 65 years and over

Total world, all ages

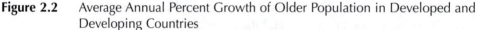

Figure 2.2   Average Annual Percent Growth of Older Population in Developed and Developing Countries

SOURCE: U.S. Census Bureau, *Aging World*, 2001. http://www.census.gov/prod/2001pubs/p95-01-1.pdf

to describe the process by which a society or nation moves from one of high birthrate and high mortality to one of low birthrate and low mortality. Figure 2.3 demonstrates differences between Europe and Brazil in demographic transition. In Europe, mortality rates began to fall in the late 1700s, followed by a slowing of birthrates in the late 1800s. This allowed Europe more than 100 years to find ways to adapt to the aging of its population. In Brazil, however, mortality rates did not begin to fall until the 1940s, with fertility rates dropping 30 years later. A rapidly aging population resulted. Thus, the demographic transition in Brazil is taking place in half the time that it occurred in Europe (Ramos, Perracini, Rosa, & Kalache, 1993). As Kalache (2001) noted, people in the developed world became rich before they became old, but people in developing nations are becoming old before they become rich.

This demographic transition may be modified by the AIDS epidemic. AIDS devastation continues in the developing world, with 95% of the world's cases found in these countries (Hopkins, 2000). In some African nations, a whole generation has been nearly wiped out. This creates a tremendous burden on older adults, who not only take care of their dying children but are often the sole support for their grandchildren, many of whom also have AIDS.

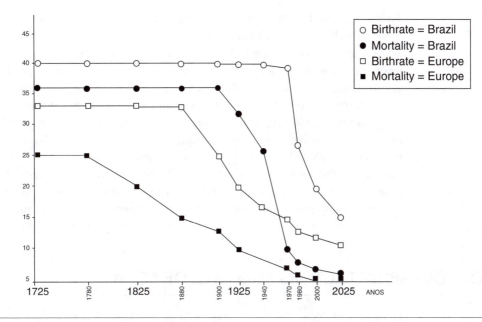

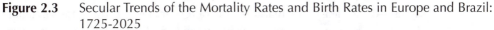

Figure 2.3   Secular Trends of the Mortality Rates and Birth Rates in Europe and Brazil: 1725-2025

SOURCE: From Ramos, L. R. "Brazil." In E. B. Pamore (Ed.), *Developments and Research on Aging: An International Handbook*. Copyright © 1993. Reproduced with permission of Greenwood Publishing Group, Inc. Westport, CT.

Although many developing regions of the world have curbed the high incidence of mortality from infectious and parasitic diseases, death still results from curable illnesses. By midlife, the most prevalent diseases in developing countries are noncommunicable, such as the chronic diseases found in Europe and the United States. It is projected that in the relatively near future, diseases of aging will account for three quarters of all deaths in developing countries. For example, the primary causes of death for those in urban areas of China are coronary vascular disease and cancer.

Chronic diseases seen first in developed countries already have had a major impact on older people in other parts of the world. For example, cataracts, which are easily cured in developed nations, cause 40% of the blindness found in Asia and Africa. The relatively simple surgery used to correct cataracts is simply not available to many people. Senile dementia is another disease that is increasingly affecting the populations of Africa, Asia, and Latin America, escalating in numbers from the current 29 million affected to a predicted 55 million in 2020 (World Health Organization [WHO], 1998).

Thus, the public health consequences of aging are being felt in the developing world as well as industrialized nations.

At a recent conference in Madrid, WHO (2002) highlighted the increasing numbers and problems of older adults in developing countries. WHO acknowledged that healthy older adults are a benefit to the community and that treatment of chronic diseases is a drain on the economy. It was recommended that developing countries promote and sponsor programs for their older adults, emphasizing a healthy lifestyle and preventive care. Suggestions included affordable health care services, control of tobacco and alcohol use throughout life, appropriate nutrition, and physical activity at all ages. WHO concluded that developing countries need to care for their older adults, as they make important contributions to the economy of their communities. Furthermore, having healthy older adults frees money for other needs.

● DEMOGRAPHIC FACTORS AND RATE OF AGING

Demographic factors play a major role as accelerators or decelerators of aging—or at least, as markers for determinants of the rate of aging. Demographic predictors of longevity include gender, marital status, ethnicity, and socioeconomic status.

Gender

In preindustrial times, men and women had similar life expectancies, largely because death was due to infectious disease. Now, one of the strongest predictors of life expectancy is gender, with women living longer than men. In the mid-1800s, life expectancy increased for both genders, but more for women than for men. For example, Cockerham (1998) reported that life expectancy in England and Wales increased by 41% for women from 1850 to 1950, but only 30% for men. This gender gap has also been evident in the United States. In 1900, women could expect to live 2 years longer than men. The gender gap reached its peak in 1975, at 7.8 years, but since that time, this difference has been decreasing, falling to 5.5 years in 1999. These fairly recent changes are mostly due to a decrease in cardiovascular disease in men and an increase in lung cancer mortality for women (Anderson & DeTurk, 2002).

Several reasons are given for historical differences between men's and women's longevity. Perhaps the most obvious are the reduced pregnancy and childbirth mortality rates that started in the late 1800s and early 1900s. Better sanitation practices and medical procedures greatly decreased the risk to women in childbirth, as did the decrease in family size that started in the 1930s. Public health measures, better nutrition, and a general improvement in socioeconomic status all had an impact on the population of the United States during the early 20th century. The benefits of these improved conditions appear to have been greater for women than for men (Cockerham, 1998).

The continued differential in life expectancy between men and women is due to a number of biological, behavioral, and environmental factors (Gold, Malmberg, McClearn, Pedersen, & Berg, 2002). More males are conceived and born than females, but male death rates exceed female death rates at every age of life, from conception through adulthood (Hazzard, 1994). Males are more likely to have prenatal and neonatal problems and are more susceptible, as infants, to infections and cardiovascular problems. In childhood, accidents cause more deaths among males than females.

In adulthood, men develop heart disease earlier than women, typically beginning in midlife. In women, however, estrogen may have a protective effect, as heart disease does not usually occur until about 10 years after menopause, at which time women's rates of heart disease accelerate and actually exceed that of men. On average, women have lower rates of smoking and alcohol abuse, less risk-taking behaviors, and greater willingness to seek medical help than men. In addition, men may have more hazardous occupations and experience greater societal and cultural pressure to engage in risky behaviors.

Despite their greater longevity, women typically report poorer health than men, take more sick days and visit health professionals more frequently. They also have higher rates of disability. If women are sicker, why are men more likely to die? For some time, it was thought that women were overreporting illnesses, but this was shown not to be true. Verbrugge (1989) argued that women report more illnesses because they have a higher incidence of nonfatal but disabling conditions such as arthritis and autoimmune disorders. On the other hand, men are more likely to experience fatal illnesses such as cancer or cardiovascular disease.

Gold et al. (2002) examined this hypothesis in a sample of older unlike-sex twins sharing similar genetic endowments and environmental exposures. They confirmed that women reported more psychological and physical symptoms because they actually did have more health problems and more non-life-threatening illnesses. Men, however, do have more cardiovascular and other life-threatening conditions, confirming Verbrugge's hypothesis.

One of the results of longer life expectancy for women is that they far outnumber men in later years. The greater number of males than females in a given cohort in earlier life ends at the age of about 36. With increasing age, the ratio of men to women grows smaller. In the 2000 census, of those 65 and over, there were 70 men to every 100 women, and by the age of 85 and over, this had dropped to 41 men to every 100 women (Hetzel & Smith, 2001). In very late life, then, there are indeed "two girls for every boy" (*pace* Brian Wilson). This excess mortality rate for males has profound implications for marital status and health in late life.

Marital Status

Marital status affects the health and longevity of adults. Data from the United States and other developed countries indicate that marriage appears to provide the greatest health benefits, divorce the most difficult problems, and widowhood mixed results.

Men are much more likely to be married than women, due in part to the just-mentioned gender imbalance. For example, in 2000, 72.6% of men aged 65 and older were married, compared to only 41.3% of women. As age increases, the percentage of both men and women who are married decreases, although less so for men. In 2000, a little over half of men 75 and over were married, compared with only about a quarter of women (Fields & Casper, 2001). In 1999, a quarter of all male centenarians were married, but only one out of 25 female centenarians (Krach & Velkoff, 1999).

Marriage appears to have a protective effect on health; married people live longer than the never-married, widowed, or divorced, although men may benefit from marriage more than women (Ben-Shlomo, Davey Smith, Shipley, & Marmot, 1993). There are two alternate pathways that may account for the positive affect of marriage. First, it may be that those who are healthier are more likely to marry, thus confounding marital status and health. Second, the state of marriage may confer health benefits. Obviously, these models are not mutually exclusive, but the general consensus is that marriage is beneficial to health, over and above baseline health status.

There are several reasons why married people are healthier and live longer (Lillard & Waite, 1995). First, married people often have better health behavior habits. They are less likely to smoke or to abuse alcohol and drugs and, in general, are less likely to engage in risk behaviors. For example, the greater mortality of single males may be due in large part to their greater tendency to indulge in risk behaviors. Married people are also more likely to have better diets and to exercise regularly. Second, married couples have higher incomes and thus higher socioeconomic status, which is also protective of health (see the last section in this chapter). Third, the social integration that accompanies marriage is important for health. For example, one reason that marriage may be more beneficial for men than for women is that single women are more likely to have extensive social networks than are single men, who tend to be social isolates. Finally, being married may also be a stress buffer. As Pearlin and Johnson (1977) stated, "Marriage does not prevent . . . problems, but it apparently can help people fend off the psychological assaults that such problems otherwise create" (p. 714). Marital status may be especially protective for those with illnesses such as heart disease (Coyne et al., 2001), cancer (Kravdal, 2001), and chronic obstructive pulmonary disease (Almagro et al., 2002). Thus, marriage can be seen as an aging decelerator, and disruptions in marital status may confer considerable risk.

Divorce is quite rare in late life; about 10% of older U.S. adults were divorced or separated in 2001 (AOA, 2002). Divorce can be a highly stressful event for any individual, increasing the risk for disease and mortality. Johnson, Backlund, Sorlie, and Loveless (2000) found an increase in cardiovascular disease among older European American men and women and African American women following divorce, although not among older African American men. In this study, older European American women were also at increased risk of cancer. The burden of an unhappy marriage and subsequent divorce can be a stressful event that affects the health of an older adult.

In contrast, the death of a spouse is a common occurrence in later years, especially for women. In 1999, more than 50% of women aged 75 to 84, and 77% of those 85 and older, were widowed. Men are much less likely to be widowed: Only 18% of men aged 75 to 84, and less than half of men 85 and older, were widowed in 1999 (Smith & Tillipman, 2000).

Men are usually widowed at a later age than women and widowed for a shorter period of time, as they tend to remarry. Women are widowed at an earlier age and widowed for a longer period of time, and they are less likely to remarry. They are also more likely to suffer from a decrease in financial status with widowhood, as their financial security in later life is often connected to having a spouse. Women can regain part of this security with remarriage, although far fewer men are available to marry in later years.

The effect of widowhood on health and mortality in later life is not well understood, but probably contingent on a number of factors including gender, age at death of spouse, ethnicity, length of widowhood, and whether death occurred suddenly or after a long illness. An early study by Parkes (1972) found an increase in mortality among widowed men, especially from heart disease, in the first year following bereavement. Johnson et al. (2000) also examined the effects of widowhood on health. In their study, older (65+) European American and African American women, but not men, were at increased risk of death from cardiovascular disease after the death of a spouse, when compared to married counterparts. Furthermore, age at widowhood affected the pattern of mortality. In mid-life (45-64) death from cardiovascular disease following bereavement was greater among European American men and women and African American men but not African American women. In this study, the younger group was generally at greater risk of illness than the older one, indicating the stress of widowhood differentially affects older and younger people. The belief that widowhood is an expected event in later years, compared to middle age, may explain some of these findings.

Both men and women appear to suffer from mental health problems after being widowed, although it may be more prominent among men than women. Many widowers suffer from depression, especially men who have been widowed for a long time (vanGrootheest, Beekman, van Groenou, Broese, & Deeg, 1999). Caserta (2002) explains that men benefit from the social support of a wife, and this helps protect them from the stresses of life (see Pearlin & Johnson, 1977, noted above). At widowhood, a man may feel this loss more acutely than a woman, who enjoys a more extensive network of family and friends.

Another factor that appears to affect the health of widowed persons is the length of illness suffered by the spouse. Smith and Zick (1996) found that younger men (aged 25 to 64) whose wives died suddenly were at greater risk of early death than those whose wives died after a long illness. This was not true of older widowers, aged 65 and over. Furthermore, and contrary to expectations, older women who expected the death of their spouses actually had greater longevity than similarly aged married women. Caregiving may be extremely stressful, and health may improve once the task of caring for a spouse during a long illness is ended.

As Lieberman (1996) pointed out, widowed men and women may find themselves free of previous obligations and experience a growth of personal awareness and ability. It can be a time for reexploration of previous interests. In the Lieberman study, such widows and widowers exhibited an understanding of themselves that made it possible to undertake challenges and risks previously denied them. As one woman said,

> I've grown so much. . . . I see myself now as a much more effective person. I'm also more serene, more generous, and calmer. I've learned to accept things much more gracefully, and I've taken on disputes and won them. (Lieberman, 1996, p. 142)

Thus, marriage may be protective of health and disruptions may contribute to significant health problems. Factors such as age and timing of the death may moderate the effect of widowhood. As the study by Johnson et al. (2000) showed, there may also be ethnic differences in the effects of marital disruption.

Ethnicity

The United States is undergoing a rapid transformation in not only the size but the composition of its older population (see Figure 2.4). In 2000, approximately 84% of older adults were European American, 8% were African American, 6% Hispanic or Latino, 2% Asian and Pacific Islander, and less than 1% American Indian and Native Alaskan. Projections indicate that by the year 2050, however, over a third (36%) of the older population will be of an ethnic background other than European American. The composition breakdown at that time is anticipated to be 64% European American, 16% Hispanic or Latino, 12% African American, 7% Asian and Pacific Islander, and less than 1% American Indian and Native Alaskan (AOA, 2000). (It should be noted that there is great diversity within all population groups, with many people claiming one or more ethnic identity. Furthermore, the designation *Hispanic or Latino* includes people from a number of different countries, such as Puerto Rico, Mexico, and Guatemala.)

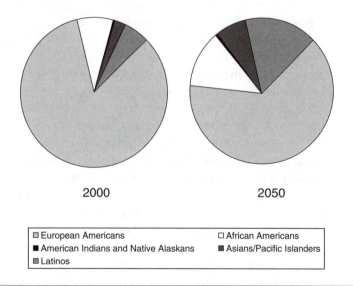

| 2000 | 2050 |

☐ European Americans   ☐ African Americans
■ American Indians and Native Alaskans   ■ Asians/Pacific Islanders
▨ Latinos

Figure 2.4 Ethnicity of Older Adults in 2000 and 2050 (United States)

SOURCE: U.S. Census Bureau, Population Projects of the United States by Age, Sex, Race, Hispanic Origin, and Nativity: 1999-2100. http://www.aoa.dhhs.gov/agingstats/chartbook2000/population.html

Mortality rates and life expectancy vary by ethnicity for a variety of reasons that are as yet poorly understood. Older adults from minority groups are less likely to be vaccinated against influenza and pneumonia, although this is improving (AOA, 2000). Older African American men and women suffer from hypertension more than European Americans (AOA, 2000), and African American men are more likely to smoke (Hobbs & Damon, 1996). Some studies have reported that African American women with breast cancer have a poorer 5-year survival rate than European American women (Kramarow, Lentzner, Rooks, Weeks, & Saydah, 1999). These findings have been disputed by others. In a recent study, African American women had no significant differences in survival rate from European American women, although they were younger when their breast cancer was diagnosed and had poorer diagnostic indicators, for example, higher stage tumor at diagnosis and greater incidence of lymph node involvement (English, Cleveland, & Barber, 2002). Fortunately, the percentage of all women 65 and older who have mammograms has steadily increased in recent years and, since 1993, African American women were most likely to have had the test of any group (Kramarow et al., 1999).

An unusually high incidence of diabetes and high blood pressure is present in the older Hispanic or Latino population, possibly due to poor nutritional intake or obesity. The health problems of American Indians have been well documented; these include tuberculosis, diabetes, and vision and hearing problems. Chronic disease and disability in this population are so extensive that almost three out of four American Indians over the age of 65 have some degree of disability or limitation in their ability to carry out normal activities of daily living (Kivett, 1993). Older Asian Americans generally enjoy good health, due in part to advantageous socioeconomic status and lower rates of smoking (Rogers, Hummer, Nam, & Peters, 1996). Therefore, it is not surprising that life expectancy varies by ethnicity.

There are inherent problems in accurately estimating life expectancy by ethnicity (Pamuk, Makuc, Heck, Reuben, & Lochner, 1998), as errors may occur in reporting age and ethnicity. For example, it is not uncommon for those aged 85 and older to inaccurately report their age, or for family members to be unsure as to exact date of birth of a deceased elderly relative. Epstein, Moreno, and Bacchetti (1997) reported that many nonreservation American Indian deaths in infants have been misreported as Hispanic infant deaths. Also, immigrants are thought to be generally healthier and to live longer than nonimmigrants, and, if they return to their native countries in late life, deaths in this group will be underreported. Despite these caveats, a consensus is growing concerning the patterns of life expectancy over the life course.

Using data from the National Mortality Followback Survey, Hahn and Eberhardt (1994) found that Asians and Pacific Islanders had the greatest life expectancy at birth, followed by European Americans, American Indians, and African Americans. The Hispanic or Latino group was not examined in this study, but some suggest that adult Hispanic or Latino life expectancy is similar to that of European Americans (Rogers et al., 1996), although studies including infant and child mortality find that it is lower (Go, Brustrom, Lynch, & Aldwin, 1996). Because immigrants tend to be healthier, as noted earlier, Hispanic or Latino immigrants enjoy slightly better life expectancy than those born in the U.S. (Rogers et al., 1996).

The most interesting aspect of ethnic differences in longevity is the crossover of age-specific life expectancy in later life. Manton, Poss, and Wing (1979) were the first to suggest that in very late life, African Americans have a longer life expectancy than European Americans. Crossover effect studies were criticized, however, due to evidence that some oldest-old African Americans exaggerated their age (Rosenwaike & Hill, 1996). To address this issue, Corti et al. (1999) used data from the Established Populations for Epidemiologic Studies of the Elderly (EPESE) study, in which age at death was confirmed, and still found a crossover effect for mortality.

Hahn and Eberhardt (1994) examined African American, American Indian, European American, and Asian and Pacific Islander populations to determine whether this crossover effect in late life existed for other ethnic groups as well. They confirmed a crossover effect starting at age 85 for African American men and women when compared to European Americans. Surprisingly, the crossover effect for American Indians began at age 25, and this advantage was maintained through the rest of the life span. According to this study, after age 85, European American males and females had the lowest life expectancy of any ethnic group in the United States. Asian Americans maintained their advantage in life expectancy over all of the groups, regardless of age.

These findings are largely supported by mortality data from the National Center for Health Statistics (Kramarow et al., 1999), with some exceptions. In this large data set, differences in death rates by age for European Americans, African Americans, Asian Americans and Pacific Islanders, American Indians and Native Alaskans, and Latinos were examined.

Death rates for women from the years 1995-1997 can be seen in Figure 2.5. In the two age groups, 65-74 and 75-84, African American women had the highest death rates, and Asian Americans and Pacific Islanders the lowest. American Indians and Native Alaskans and European American women had comparable mortality rates from age 65 to 74, changing in the 75-84 age

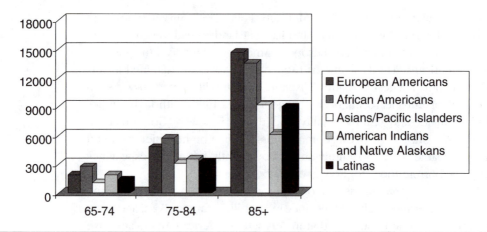

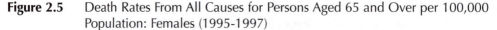

Figure 2.5 Death Rates From All Causes for Persons Aged 65 and Over per 100,000 Population: Females (1995-1997)

SOURCE: Based in part from data by Kramarow, E., Lentzner, H., Rooks, R., Weeks, J., & Sayday, S. (1999). Health, United States, 1999 (DHHS Publication No. 99-1232). Washington, DC: Government Printing Office.

group, when death rates for European Americans were greater. By the age of 85, European Americans had the highest death rates and American Indians and Native Alaskans the lowest. Latinas maintained the second lowest rate.

Similar patterns are seen among the men in the study. As shown in Figure 2.6, African American men had the highest death rates from the ages of 65-74 and 75-84, with European Americans the second highest. Asian American men maintained the lowest death rates in the age group of 65-74, but by the ages of 85 plus, had the third highest death rate. Finally, by the ages of 85 and above, the death rate was highest among European American men. At that age, American Indians and Native Alaskans had the lowest death rate and the Hispanic or Latino population the second lowest.

The data on American Indians and Native Alaskans are surprising, because data from the national Indian Health Service (IHS) reported some of the lowest life expectancies of any group in the United States: 67.3 years for men and 75.9 years for women (IHS, 1992). Hahn and Eberhardt (1994) argued that the IHS report was based primarily on life expectancies of American Indians living on reservations, whereas their own data included nonreservation American Indians as well.

Crossover effects are undoubtedly due to differential survival. Mortality rates in midlife for African Americans and American Indians and Native Alaskans are relatively high due to diseases such as diabetes, prostate and

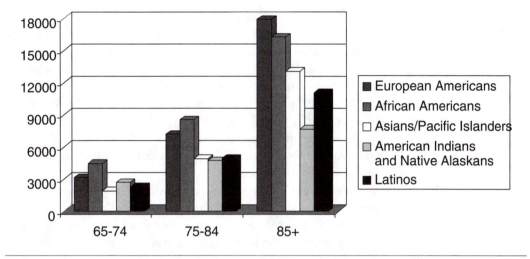

Figure 2.6   Death Rates From All Causes for Persons Aged 65 and Over per 100,000
Population: Males (1995-1997)

SOURCE: Based in part from data by Kramarow, E., Lentzner, H., Rooks, R., Weeks, J., & Sayday, S.
(1999). Health, United States, 1999 (DHHS Publication No. 99-1232). Washington, DC: Government
Printing Office.

breast cancer, and cardiovascular diseases. Having outlived the diseases of
younger years, surviving African Americans and American Indians and Native
Alaskans may be very healthy indeed.

Thus, ethnic differences in life expectancy are due to genetic factors as
well as health behavior habits and differential immigration patterns. Another
major factor in differential longevity is socioeconomic status (SES). While SES
is influenced by gender, marital status, and ethnicity, it is also likely that SES
mediates the relationship between other demographic factors and mortality.

Socioeconomic Status (SES)

SES has highly significant effects on morbidity and mortality (Lynch,
Davey Smith, Kaplan, & House, 2000). Although most older people in the
United States have adequate incomes, there are others who live in poverty or
near the poverty line at a time in life when there is little possibility of economic growth. Furthermore, health care, housing, and transportation costs
are often greater in later life.

In 2001, the median income of older men was $19,688 and $11,313 for women. Income sources included Social Security, assets, public and private pensions, and earnings. Social Security was always meant to provide a supplement to private savings and pensions, but it has become a major part of the retirement income of many. In 2000, some 90% of people reported that their major source of income was Social Security (AOA, 2002). About two thirds of the net worth of many older persons is represented by their homes; on paper, their assets may appear adequate. For those elders of modest incomes who live in older housing, however, maintenance costs may consume a fair amount of their resources.

It was once thought that economic needs decrease with retirement, as work-related expenses such as formal clothing, business lunches, and transportation to and from work are no longer necessary. We now know that increased frailty results in the need to purchase services that would not have been required at an earlier time, such as transportation to the store or to health services, and in-home care to help with cooking, personal services, medications, or home maintenance. Although most older adults do not have child care expenses, they often contribute to grandchildren's child care and college expenses, and to children's major purchases such as houses and cars.

As shown in Figure 2.7, poverty rates for older people have decreased steadily since the 1950s, when they were higher by far than those of any other age group. At that time, more than 35% of older adults lived in poverty. This has changed dramatically; in 2000, only 10.2% of the older population lived in poverty (Dalaker, 2001).

Although not living in poverty, another group of older adults at risk of having inadequate resources are those who have incomes that are low but still above the poverty level (from 100% to 200% of poverty). This group of elders has been labeled *tweeners* by Smeeding (1990); they make too much money to receive most federal and state services such as Medicaid or SSI, but too little money to have financial security. In many cases, older adults in this group are the most bereft of all, as they often have to juggle resources to pay for unexpected or increasingly expensive medications but do not have access to state resources that the poor have.

Yet, the myth persists that older people need less money, and poverty levels are set accordingly. In 2000, the poverty level was $8,259 annually for a single person 65 or older, but $8,959 for someone under the age of 65 (Dalaker, 2001). Thus, a younger person making $8,500 per year would be deemed poor, but not an older one. It is especially difficult that the types of expenses used to calculate minimal levels of income needed to survive do not include medical expenses such as medications or doctor visits, which are especially high in late life. If poverty levels were calculated for older adults

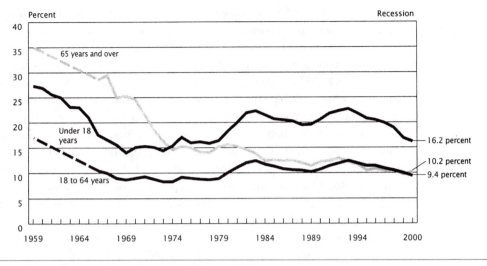

Figure 2.7 Poverty Rates by Age: 1959 to 2000

SOURCE: Dalaker, J. (2001). *Poverty in the United States: 2000* (Current population reports: Consumer income, pp. 60-214). Washington, DC: U.S. Department of Commerce.

NOTE: The data points represent the midpoints of the respective years. The latest recession began in July 1990 and ended in March 1991. Data for people 18 to 64 and 65 and older are not available from 1960 to 1965.

using the criteria applied to younger adults, their poverty rates would be closer to that of children. Although poverty rates for children are unacceptably high (see Figure 2.10), it should be noted that poverty is a temporary state for most children, because family income levels tend to increase with a child's age. In older people, however, poverty is much more likely to be permanent.

There is great diversity among individuals in education, income, and health, and some groups are more likely to live in poverty than others, for example, single women, members of certain ethnic groups, and the very old. Furthermore, membership in two or more of these categories may place a person at great jeopardy of financial insufficiency, for example, Hispanic and female (AOA, 2002).

Older American Indians and Native Alaskans have the highest rates of poverty, at 27.1% (2-year average rate). Almost a quarter (23%) of older African Americans lived at or below the poverty level in 2001 and more than 18% of older Hispanics or Latinos, although poverty rates in this population have fallen (Dalaker, 2001). The reasons for poverty among these groups are numerous. Many of these older adults earned less than their European American counterparts during their employment years and, subsequently, have lower pension benefits during retirement years than European Americans.

Older women are among the poorest people in the country, especially if they are widowed and live alone. Men, in their working years, earn annual incomes almost 80% higher than those of most women. It is therefore not surprising that 10.7% of women from age 65 to 74 and 15.1% of those 75 and older lived in poverty in 2000, compared with only a little over 7% of older men (Smith & Tillipman, 2000). As noted previously, being both female and in certain ethnic groups compounds the problem, as 55.5 % of older Latina women who live alone have incomes below the poverty line (AOA, 2002). There are numerous reasons for poverty among older women. The most important is inadequate education, resulting in low-paying jobs during their employment years. Women also frequently experience interrupted career paths, taking time out to care for family members, including children and elders.

The longer a person lives, the greater the risk of poverty. In late life, poverty rates are highest for those 85 and over, reaching 14% in 1998 (AOA, 2002). A great proportion of their income was from Social Security, as they were least likely to have pensions or adequate retirement incomes. They also may have simply outlived their savings. Social Security benefits are particularly important to those in the lowest income brackets, accounting for an average of 80% of their total income. Public assistance makes up another 10% of the income for these people (AOA, 2000).

As noted above, SES affects the health and longevity of the older person. In studies completed as long ago as the mid-19th century, those who had lower incomes, inadequate housing, poor sanitation, and insufficient nutrition had higher death rates from communicable diseases than those who could afford better amenities. Although death now occurs in later life from chronic disorders, rather than communicable or infectious diseases, a relationship still exists between SES, health, and life expectancy (Pamuk et al., 1998).

The role of SES on health has been studied extensively. Education, health behaviors, and access to health care are all important elements for a healthy life. For example, life expectancy is greater for those with more than high school degrees (AOA, 2000). In 1995, men with only high school degrees or less were almost two and a half times more likely to have chronic disease than those with some postsecondary education (Pamuk et al., 1998). Educational status also influences how long people think they will live (subjective perception of life expectancy). In a study by Mirowsky and Ross (2000), people who had more education predicted that they would live longer. Interestingly, self-perceived health is a strong indicator of health and life expectancy (see Chapter 8).

SES also affects health behaviors. In the 1950s, death from heart disease was greatest for those with high family incomes. This changed, however, as this demographic group more readily adopted better health behavior habits of exercise, low-fat diets, and smoking cessation than those with lower incomes. Currently, mortality rates from heart disease are highest among those with the lowest family incomes. In fact, among those 65 and older, European American males with the highest incomes can expect to live 3.1 years longer than their peers in the lowest income groups (Pamuk et al., 1998). Lynch, Kaplan, and Shema (1997) found that those who are poorer have a greater incidence of functional loss, including disabilities and depression. Some of this difference can be explained by health habits and access to medical care. For example, an inverse relationship exists between income and being overweight for women. Women over the age of 50 who have better incomes are more likely to have better health habits, such as yearly mammograms, than those who are poorer. Furthermore, those who are poorer are more likely to have hypertension, to have a sedentary lifestyle, and not have routine dental care (Pamuk et al., 1998)

The effect of SES on life expectancy may dissipate somewhat in the later years, although it still exists. Longino, Warheit, and Green (1989) suggested that SES in later years is not as good a predictor of health and longevity as it is in earlier years. For those under the age of 65, there is an inverse relationship between SES and access to health care; the lower the income, the fewer the health care services (Pamuk et al., 1998). Those in older age groups have greater to access to health care, however. As Cockerham (1998) noted, after Medicaid legislation was enacted, the lowest SES groups had better access to health care than the working poor. Older Americans enjoy nearly universal health care, Medicare, and thus are among a select group of people who have health insurance and access to health care. There are limits to what Medicare covers, however. It was designed to pay for acute illnesses that need medical attention and hospital care, compared to care of chronic needs or preventive care, such as dental check-ups or medications. Therefore, Medicare, although not perfect, provides an avenue for health care coverage during disease.

SUMMARY ●

A tremendous change in life expectancy has occurred throughout the world, with populations in nearly every country showing an increase in the years they can expect to live. This greater longevity is the result of better health measures, including sanitation practices, nutrition, medical care, and lifestyle changes, all of which have served to decelerate the aging process and perhaps extend the human life span. In the next 30 years, there will be a tremendous increase in the number of older adults, which may strain economic resources, especially in developing countries. On the other hand, we are living in better health than ever before, and healthy older adults are important resources to their communities, whether in developed or developing countries. In the United States, ethnic diversity will increase in the next few decades. Demographic factors such as gender, marital status, ethnicity, and SES have a surprisingly large impact on health and well-being. But it is necessary to understand why and how individuals age in order to understand how psychosocial factors can affect health.

CHAPTER 3

THEORIES OF AGING

Aging processes occur at the biological, psychological, and social levels. There are any number of different theories of aging that are generally specific to each discipline. The truth is, no one is really certain why we age, although we are beginning to identify different processes that regulate or govern the rate of aging. For the most part, though, these theories are often specific to the particular process being studied (e.g., genetic or molecular), and relatively few attempts have been made to bridge different theories or aging mechanisms (Birren, 1999).

Bengtson, Rice, and Johnson (1999) suggest two reasons for the lack of integration in theories of gerontology. First, there are three different aspects of age on which theories can focus: characteristics of the aging population, the developmental or aging process, and the way in which age is incorporated into the social structure. Second, gerontology has historically been a bottom-up discipline; it starts from facts (systematic observation) that may be grouped loosely into models (which specify categories of variables that should be related) and only rarely achieve the status of theory (which tries to explain or at least specify the processes involved in a particular phenomenon). Unfortunately, models and theories are often not carefully distinguished in the literature.

Rowe and Kahn's (1998) theory of successful aging and Ford and Lerner's (1992) developmental systems theory do attempt to cut across disciplines but are really more models than theories per se. Rowe and Kahn specify that successful aging consists of good physical and mental health, as well as good social functioning. Ford and Lerner also link biological, psychological, and social aging, although specific processes and mechanisms are not detailed. Kuypers and Bengtson's (1973) social breakdown theory argues that physical, psychological, and social health are tightly linked in later life, and problems in one area may cause (and/or accelerate) problems in another area. Exactly how this integration occurs, however, tends to be unspecified. Campisise (2000) does present an interesting theory of a possible link between caloric restriction and altered gene expression that may affect the rate of aging. This does provide specific processes but is restricted to a particular phenomenon.

Von Dras and Blumenthal (2000) present a convincing argument that psychosocial factors moderate the rate at which individuals age. Citing Martin (1997), they argue, "Although there are genetic programs that specify fetal development, postnatal growth, and sexual maturity, there is no genetic program that specifies senescence—only one that specifies maximum life span" (von Dras & Blumenthal, p. 200). This may not be quite accurate—Walker, McColl, Jenkins, Harris, and Lithgow (2000) provide an interesting discussion of the trade-off between alleles that confer extended life span versus those that confer adaptational fitness. Restating the various biological, psychological, and social theories of aging in terms of accelerating or decelerating the rate of aging (and thus their effects on quality of life in old age), however, may provide an overarching framework in which different theories and models of aging processes may be linked.

Maruyama's (1963) deviation amplification model may provide a useful way of articulating this overarching framework. Maruyama added a dynamic component to von Bertalanffy's (1969) classic systems theory model, which holds that most systems have deviation-countering mechanisms to maintain homeostasis. In other words, if change occurs, mechanisms typically exist for countering that change and returning the organism to a steady state. Classic examples include blood pressure regulation, heart rate, respiratory rate, glucose regulation, and DNA repair. Maruyama argued, however, that systems can and do change over time. Once a system is jarred out of homeostasis, then deviation amplification mechanisms can take over, accelerating the change or imbalance.

In many ways, Maruyama's (1963) theory represents an early precursor to chaos theory, which is a wonderful way of specifying nondeterminate processes—those that do not follow simple cause-and-effect processes. Nondeterminate processes occur when systems have a large number of interacting variables (e.g., weather systems). Chaos theory shows how initially small changes can result in very large differences between systems or individuals. It has been used to describe cascade effects in cardiovascular functioning problems and has been proposed as a general model for aging (Goldberger, 1996). Our contention, however, is that Maruyama's deviation amplification model may be a better framework for integrating theories of aging, because it includes mechanisms for maintaining homeostasis as well as for promoting change, both positive and negative.

Aldwin and Stokols (1988) used this model to describe the effects of environmental stress. Stress represents perturbations in the system, and most stress theories posit some sort of coping mechanism as a way of maintaining homeostasis. However, if a stressor is sudden, severe, and cuts across different domains, it is likely to provoke deviation amplification processes and result in long-term change, whether negative or positive.

The applicability of Maruyama's (1963) model to theories of developmental processes and aging is clear. Biological processes relevant to aging, we argue, fall into two categories—those that promote homeostasis and decelerate the aging process (such as DNA repair mechanisms and heat shock proteins) and those that amplify the deviations and accelerate the aging process (such as free radicals). Psychological and social theories often discuss positive changes with age, however, and it must be remembered that Maruyama's model may need to be applied to positive as well as negative changes. Many of the psychosocial theories of aging interface with biological theories and may fit loosely in this framework.

Thus, this review focuses primarily on biological and psychosocial theories of the process of aging, rather than those that address population characteristics and the relationship between age and the social structure. These types of theories may address the quality of life in late life, however, and thus will be discussed when relevant.

BIOLOGICAL THEORIES OF AGING •

There are more than a dozen different biological theories of aging (for reviews, see Cristafalo, Tresini, Francis, & Volker, 1999; DiGiovanna, 2000; Hayflick, 1996; Masoro, 1999), and we do not attempt a comprehensive review of all of these theories. Instead, we focus on those that seem to be most relevant to the deviation counter/amplification framework. There are many different ways of categorizing biological theories of aging; we find it useful to loosely group these into genetic, molecular/cellular, and system-level theories. Note that these theories are not mutually exclusive but rather provide a snapshot of the aging process at different levels of analysis.

Genetic Theories

Probably the best evidence for genetic theories of aging is the relatively fixed differences between species in length of life span. The maximum life span of a human is about 120 years, whereas that of a fruit fly is about 30 days. In general, life spans appear to be inversely related to various factors such as metabolic rate, length of time to maturation (especially sexual maturity), and response to stress (Jazwinski, 1996). The mechanism through which genes regulate aging and death, however, especially in mammalian species, is currently unknown, although there are many interesting clues.

Programmed Cell Death (Apoptosis)

Most genetic theories of aging specify what can go wrong; thus, these can be classified as deviation amplification theories. The most dramatic example proposes the existence of a death gene—a gene that regulates sudden cell death, a process that is also called apoptosis. Genetic material is not static—different segments turn on and off, depending on the need to synthesize proteins, perform other functions such as motility and transport, or to control the functions of other genes, including the complicated process of cell proliferation. Damage to these regulator proteins may be one mechanism for cancer, that is, uncontrolled cell proliferation. But cells may also be turned off, failing to produce needed substances. Apoptosis is one mechanism for the destruction of cells that have proliferated for specific purposes, such as T-cells in the immune system, and need to be destroyed after having accomplished their task. Researchers have found evidence for senescence genes, including one mortality factor simply called MORF (Campisise, 2001), which appears to control the rate of a cell's aging.

There is some evidence for programmed cell death, at least in some cell lines. In the 1960s, Hayflick and his colleagues (1977, 1996) performed a very interesting series of experiments showing that certain cell lines in vitro, that is, cultured in petri dishes, showed finite numbers of divisions and that fetal cells replicated more times than adult cells did. Clearly, there is a link of some sort between number of possible cell replications and life span. For example, there is an inverse relationship between the age of the donor and the number of cell replications; the cells of individuals with diseases characterized by accelerated aging, such as progeria, show fewer cell replications in vitro. Thus, there may be a positive correlation between the life span of a species and the number of times a cell will replicate (for a review, see Norwood, 1990).

In humans, the number of times somatic cells can replicate is partially regulated by the telomere length (for a review, see Smith & Pereira-Smith, 1996). Telomeres consist of the specialized ends of DNA strands that help hold them together during mitosis. The DNA strands do not completely unwind during mitosis, but are held together by these caps at their ends, which do not replicate and thus are lost (Masoro, 1999). About 100 base pairs per cell are lost during each replication, and when several thousand base pairs are lost, the cell stops replicating and senesces (de Lange, 1998). However, telomeres can be restored by an enzyme called telomerase, and indeed, cancer cells have much longer telomeres and more active telomerase than normal cells (except perhaps for those that need to proliferate extensively, such as epithelial cells in the intestine).

The number of times a cell replicates may also be directly controlled by genes. Recent research may have identified immortality genes that regulate cell senescence. These were often identified in the course of cancer research. Mutations in these genes may invoke immortality; that is, cells appear to replicate seemingly infinitely. The nonmutated versions of these genes appear to regulate senescence (Ehrenstein, 1998).

It is tempting to generalize the processes of apoptosis and genetically regulated cell senescence to organ failure and shortened life expectancy. But it is an open question as to whether apoptosis and cell senescence have major effects on life expectancy in humans (Smith & Pereira-Smith, 1996). The *absence* of these processes could well shorten life, as apoptosis and senescence may be one way of getting rid of damaged and cancerous cells. Indeed, Campisise (2001) has called senescence the major protection against cancer and has described it as a form of antagonistic pleiotropy—a process that is helpful and promotes reproduction in early life but may have harmful effects in later life.

Stochastic Processes

Rather than actual programmed death, geneticists such as Hayflick (1996) are now arguing that there may simply be a limited number of times that a cell can replicate without error. Thus, aging may be a function of random (or stochastic) errors. Replication error is one of the leading theories of aging. DNA is susceptible to damage by a host of environmental factors, including a variety of chemical agents (e.g., cigarette smoke) and radiation (e.g., background or cosmic radiation), as well as internal processes such as oxidation. Damage to DNA can impair a cell's ability to synthesize proteins and other substances and/or respond to regulation. For critical DNA sequences, there are often multiple backups. Cells can limit this damage by turning off the damaged segment and turning on identical backup segments or by using DNA repair mechanisms to correct the error (see below). Eventually, however, the cell runs out of backups, and it can no longer function adequately. One theory suggests that genomes may have a limited number of replications of different DNA strands. Once all of the strands are damaged or the damage overwhelms the repair mechanisms, the cell becomes impaired and may replicate with this impaired segment. If too many cells in a particular organ system fail, the system can become compromised (Selkoe, 1992).

An interesting twist is that the DNA in mitochondria may be particularly susceptible to damage (Masoro, 1999). The oxidation process is carried out in the mitochondria. The close proximity of mitochondrial DNA to reactive oxygen is part of the reason why they are susceptible to damage. Mitochondrial DNA repair mechanisms also appear to be less efficient (Cristafalo et al., 1999). Cells in highly oxidative organs (such as the heart, brain, and skeletal muscles) have the most damaged mitochondrial DNA in later life. If a cell's energy source is damaged, then the functioning of the whole cell is impaired, and it becomes a candidate for apoptosis. Thus, damaged mitochondrial DNA may be a cause of significant cell loss in late life. Although it is tempting to generate a theory of aging from these observations, direct evidence of a link between mitochondrial DNA damage and senescence in humans is as yet lacking.

DNA Repair Mechanisms

As mentioned earlier, damaged DNA can be repaired, which can be considered a deviation-countering mechanism for aging. Many different factors can damage DNA, including light, ultraviolet and other types of radiation, exposure to toxic chemicals, and the oxidation process itself. We do not know how the cell recognizes errors in the DNA structure, but we do know that damage tends to activate transcription and replication (Friedberg, 2000). In the process of replication, there are several different checkpoints through which the cell checks the integrity of the DNA strands. If an error is caught, replication is stopped so that repairs can be made.

There are several mechanisms of DNA repair. The primary ones include base excision repair, nucleotide excision repair, mismatch repair, and repair of strand breaks. Sometimes the errors escape detection, but at other times the damage can be tolerated, and the cell uses replication bypass (presumably, it simply skips over the error). If the error burden is too severe, the cell undergoes apoptosis.

Molecular/Cellular Theories of Aging

Oxidation

One of the most popular theories of aging is the free radical theory (for a review, see Sohal & Weindruch, 1996). Free radicals or reactive oxygen species (ROS) are molecules that are generated during the oxidation process in cells. Each ROS has an unpaired electron; thus, they are unstable and extremely chemically reactive. They can interfere with the functions of other molecules in the cell, including DNA replication, the metabolism of fatty acid chains, and protein synthesis. In part, free radicals such as superoxide can damage proteins by causing them to unfold; without their proper conformation (structure), proteins cannot perform their functions correctly. ROS may also interfere with DNA and DNA transcription (Cristafalo et al., 1999).

Cells produce antioxidant factors such as superoxide dismutase (SOD). Sohal and Weindruch (1996) argue that the concentration of free radicals (and thus cell damage) increases with age, because (a) more free radicals are generated in aging cells, (b) there appears to be a decrease in the ability of the cell to generate antioxidants, and (c) cellular repair mechanisms become less efficient. They also argue that the ability of caloric restriction to extend maximal life span, at least in rodents, may be due in part to decreased oxidative stress. The concentration of SOD is higher in cells of centenarians, but it is unclear whether that is a cause or a reaction to longevity.

Lipofuscin

Aging cells also accumulate waste matter called lipofuscin, a dark mixture of lipoproteins and various waste products. Normally, these waste products are disposed of via liposomal enzymes, but (for as yet unknown reasons) this process is impaired in older cells. Lipofuscin is found in nearly all cell types, from heart muscle cells to neurons, and increases with age. Early studies failed to document an association between the presence of lipofuscin and cell functioning; more recent findings, however, suggest that there may be different types of lipofuscin, one of which may be associated with Alzheimer's disease (Horie et al., 1997). Furthermore, in rats, the presence of lipofuscin in neurons may affect their functioning (Sharma & Singh, 1996), and when lipofuscin production is artificially induced in human cells in vitro, it blocks cell proliferation and induces cell death (von Zglinicki, Nilsson, Docke, & Brunk, 1995). Accumulation of lipofuscin may be a biomarker for metabolic rate, because it reflects oxidation and thus the production of free radicals (Nakano, Oenzil, Mizuno, & Gotoh, 1995). Furthermore, severe caloric restriction in rats appears to decrease the rate of production of lipofuscin (Moore, Davey, Weindruch, Walford, & Ivy, 1995).

Heat Shock Proteins

Just as there are DNA repair mechanisms to protect genes, there are many different types of cellular repair mechanisms, which can be considered aging decelerators. The most important of these for the aging processes may be heat shock proteins (Hsps), so called because they were first identified in plants undergoing heat-related stress. But they play a major role in protecting cells from nearly every kind of stressor, from radiation to infection to oxidation. The importance of Hsps is signaled by the fact that they are found in every living organism, from bacteria to humans, and in nearly all types of cells. In addition to protecting cells against the effects of stress, they also are important in promoting healthy cell growth and proliferation (Punyiczki & Fésüs, 1998).

There are several different types of Hsps, which have a variety of functions. They are also called "molecular chaperones" because they assist in protein synthesis and repair (Trent, Kagawa, & Yaoi, 1998). Small Hsps protect cells from stress and oxidative processes by regulating enzymatic processes necessary for repair and apoptosis; others refold damaged proteins into their proper configurations (Welsh & Gaestel, 1998). They also play a major role in the inflammatory process (Polla, Bachelet, Elia, & Santoro, 1998), including active recruitment of immune system cells such as macrophages and neutrophils to attack bacteria or virus-infected cells (see Chapter 7). Although the inflammatory process is usually necessary for healing, it can damage surrounding healthy tissue if unregulated. Hsps are one of the mechanisms that control inflammation. If they cannot repair a cell, they may help the cell to self-destruct, "choosing" between apoptosis and necrosis. In apoptosis, a cell systematically dismantles and repackages itself and is readily reabsorbed by the surrounding cells. But in necrosis, the cell ruptures, spewing toxic chemicals and distress signals, leading to an increase in the inflammatory process. Thus, Hsps may aid in the healing process by dismantling damaged cells, or they may contribute to chronic inflammation (and perhaps autoimmune disorders) by mechanisms that are as yet poorly understood.

Jurivich, Qiu, and Welk (1997) argue that aging in cells is defined by poorer responses to physiological stress, perhaps mediated by transcription errors in heat shock genes. Although this lessened efficiency may interfere directly with organ functioning, it may also impair the body's ability to communicate and regulate functioning at the systems level, leading to failures in homeostasis.

System-Level Theories

Homeostasis

To function, organisms must maintain a certain level of homeostasis, that is, stability in intra- and extracellular environmental conditions, such as pH balance, blood pressure, heart rate, temperature, and electrolyte and fluid balance. Nearly all conditions fluctuate in response to environmental demands but then must return to baseline levels. Homeostasis requires communication among the various organ systems and is largely regulated by the autonomic nervous system via the neuroendocrine system.

There is good evidence to suggest that, as we age, it becomes harder to maintain homeostasis (Taffett, 1996). A number of systems in the elderly show slower responses to environmental challenges but may eventually show heightened responses that take much longer to abate and return to baseline. This may be due to both disease-related and intrinsic age-related processes, which may be difficult to disentangle.

Problems in homeostatic regulation may be due to one of three factors (which also may work in combination). First, there may be a decline in the production of hormones or other type of regulatory peptides. Ovarian decrease in estrogen production is a good example of this. Second, the target organs may become less responsive, due either to fewer receptors for neuroendocrine signals or to degradation in the functioning of receptor sites on cell surfaces. For example, receptor cites for insulin may degrade with age (a process hastened by obesity).

Finally, the target organ may synthesize less than optimal amounts of its product, due either to fewer secretory cells or to less efficient production. Thus, the system may respond sluggishly, causing more difficulty in maintaining adequate homeostasis. A number of illnesses commonly associated with aging reflect these problems in homeostasis, such as orthostatic hypotension (failure to maintain sufficient blood pressure when standing up) and diabetes (failure either to produce sufficient insulin or for insulin receptor sites to respond adequately; see Chapter 7).

Aging is also associated with changes in the temporal organization of physiological rhythm. For example, there is a reduction in the circadian amplitude of processes such as sleep, plasma cortisol, body temperature, and a variety of neuroendocrine hormones (Taffett, 1996). For example, body temperatures fluctuate over a 24-hour period, with the lowest temperatures occurring in the early hours of the morning for individuals with typical circadian rhythms. In older adults, however, these lower temperature and coinciding sleep phases may occur one to two hours earlier, and elders may have difficulty adjusting to changes in time zones. For reasons that are as yet unclear, physiological rhythms also become less complex with age, showing decreased variability. The consequences of this are as yet unknown (Lipsitz & Goldberger, 1992).

Wear-and-Tear Theories

One of the earliest theories of aging was the simple wear-and-tear theory—that is, with continual use, our organs and joints simply wear out. For most organ systems, this early theory does not hold. For example, if this were true, then athletes should have shorter lives than sedentary individuals, which does not appear to be the case (Paffenbarger et al., 1993). As reviewed in a later section of this chapter, many systems such as the cardiovascular system need regular, moderate exercise to maintain function, and intellectual stimulation may be necessary to the maintenance of cognitive function (Diamond, 1993). Indeed, the most common phrase in gerontology today seems to be "Use it or lose it."

The one exception to this adage appears to be skeletal joints. One of the causes of osteoarthritis is wear and tear on the joints, and it is nearly universal in late life. However, it is also true that total bed rest in the elderly can result in stiffened, immobile joints (contracture), as well as problems with a host of other systems, including the cardiovascular, gastrointestinal, genital-urinary, respiratory, endocrine, metabolic, and neuropsychological systems (Fishburn & de Lateur, 1996). Under most conditions, then, moderate usage is far preferable for organ functioning.

Nonetheless, abuse of a system will shorten its life span. For example, athletes with high levels of injury may shorten the effective life spans of several of their organ systems. Problems with the skeletomuscular system in professional football players are legendary, as are neurological problems in professional boxers who have sustained many concussions.

Stress

Stress models of aging are a modern reincarnation of the wear-and-tear theories. There is growing evidence that prolonged exposure to stress, both physiological and psychosocial, may increase the rate of aging in various organ systems, as stress-related hormones and catecholamines can have toxic effects (see Finch & Seeman, 1999; Sapolsky, 1992). Reactivity to stress tends to have deleterious effects, because it is associated with prolonged exposure to stress-related hormones and catecholamines. Chapter 10 includes a more complete discussion of this model.

However, there is also an exciting new line of research into a phenomenon called hormesis, in which moderate exposure to toxins or stressors may promote future resistance to stress and enhance longevity (Calabrese & Baldwin, 2002). Johnson et al. (2002) note that all gene mutations that result in increased longevity in a species of worm studied extensively (*Caenorhabditis elegans*) do so by increasing the organism's resistance to stress, and will be discussed more fully in Chapter 10.

Interrelationships Among Levels of Analysis

These different levels of analysis in biological theories of aging—genetic, molecular/cellular, and systems-level—are linked. Perturbations at the genetic level affect cellular functioning, which in turn affect the ability of the system as a whole to maintain homeostasis. Similarly, problems in maintaining homeostasis, such as stress reactivity, may cause damage at the cellular and genetic levels. Thus, the rate at which organisms age is affected by a host of factors that are not necessarily linked in unidirectional causal chains but rather interact or transact in highly complex fashions. This plasticity in the system allows for intervention and the use of aging decelerants but also may result in cascades that accelerate aging. It is becoming increasingly clear that the plasticity in the system also allows for psychosocial influences, both positive and negative.

PSYCHOSOCIAL THEORIES OF AGING ●

Just as there are dozens of theories of aging, so, too, are there many psychosocial theories of aging (for reviews, see Alexander & Langer, 1990; Baltes, Lindenberger, & Staudinger, 1998; Bengtson & Schaie, 1999; Elder, 1998). Most focus on descriptors of the aging population or on the way in which age is embedded in the social structure, but the focus of this book is on developmental processes and factors that affect the rate of aging. However, given that the quality of life is also important, we briefly review some of the major psychosocial theories of aging before focusing on developmental processes.

Figure 3.1 presents a flowchart of the intellectual history of the major theories of adult development. It is not meant to be inclusive, but illustrative, tracing the origins of the major schools and their development from classical to modern theories. It is used to organize this discussion.

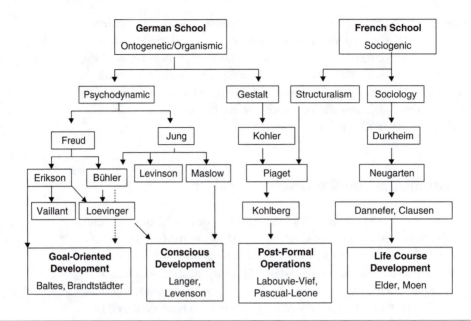

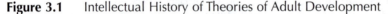

Figure 3.1   Intellectual History of Theories of Adult Development

Classical Theories

Early on, the primary tension in theories of adult development was between the ontogenetic school, which posited that developmental forces are internal and probably biologically based, and the sociogenic schools, which argued that change in adulthood is largely due to social forces. In general, ontogenetic scholars were based in Germany, whereas the sociologists who largely made up the sociogenic schools were influenced by French sociologists such as Durkheim (1951), hence the headers in Figure 3.1.

Ontogenetic Models

Classical ontogenetic models posit that development stems from internal forces and consists of stages that are universal, sequential, and irreversible. *Universal* means applicable to everyone, regardless of gender, social status, or culture. The stages are *sequential*, follow a definite order, and are thought to be *irreversible*, that is, they represent achievements. In these models, change is discontinuous and is characterized by qualitative changes (as opposed to continuous, quantitative change).

Psychodynamic schools focused largely on personality development. Ego psychologists such as Erikson (1950) modified Freud's psychosexual theory of early childhood to a psychosocial model that extended from birth through late life. Erikson posited eight stages, ranging from basic trust versus mistrust, in early infancy, to ego integrity versus despair, in late life. Adolescence and early adulthood are characterized by identity versus confusion and intimacy versus isolation, respectively, whereas midlife is characterized by generativity versus stagnation, with generativity involving caring for subsequent generations, as well as the institutions that transmit culture across generations. Each stage is characterized by a dialectic—a positive and a negative pole, and resolution of this dialectic sets the stage for positive or negative resolution of the next stage. For example, it is hard to develop generativity if you have never learned to be intimate with anyone.

Erikson's theory is thought to satisfy all the requirements of a purely ontogenetic theory—positing qualitatively distinct stages that are thought to be universal, sequential, and irreversible. However, closer reading of his original work shows that he perceived these stages more in terms of themes that are revisited at different ages in the life span. As Erikson (1950) stated,

> In fact, some writers are so intent on making an *achievement scale* out of these stages that they blithely omit all the "negative" senses (basic mistrust, etc.) which are and remain the dynamic counterpart of the "positive" ones throughout life. The assumption that at each stage a goodness is achieved which is impervious to new inner conflicts and to changing conditions, is, I believe, a [dangerous] projection. (pp. 273-274)

This can complicate analyses examining change. For example, Whitbourne and her colleagues (2002) found little aggregate change in generativity from young adulthood to midlife, because the number of individuals who increased in generativity was balanced by those who decreased and presumably were stagnating. Furthermore, some individuals increased and then decreased in response to changing life circumstances. Erikson's caveat is important and suggests more complex analyses than those examining simple aggregate change (see Chapter 4).

Other early theorists such as Peck (1968) and Vaillant (1977) elaborated in various ways on Erikson's basic paradigm. For example, Vaillant added a "career consolidation" stage, and characterized development in terms of changing defense mechanisms, whereas Peck added a further stage in late life that presaged some of the later work on transcendence (see below).

Jung's (1933) perspective on development was quite different from Freud's. He focused on adult development, believing that adolescents and young adults develop a persona, a false self developed to conform to adult social role conventions. This involves suppressing aspects of the self that are socially unacceptable and emphasizing those characteristics that are socially desirable. In Jung's highly gendered culture, young men were encouraged to emphasize masculine traits such as courage, suppressing their emotions, and focusing on career development. In contrast, women were supposed to be feminine, nurturant, and focused on family. From Jung's perspective, the goal of development in adulthood is to individuate, to abandon the persona and become more of an individual. Individuation involves the development of self-knowledge, bringing unconscious material into consciousness, and developing one's true capacities. Jung believed that people who repress their true selves will find them reemerging in midlife. Thus, men will become more feminine, and women, more masculine, to the extent that they suppressed those aspects of themselves early on. Parker and Aldwin (1997) did find partial support for this theory.

Although both Bühler (1968) and Loevinger (1977) were ego psychologists, they were also influenced by Jung and the humanistic movement in psychology. Bühler emphasized meaning and goals in development rather than strict ontogenetic stages. She defined intention as the pursuit of an objective that provides an individual with a sense of purpose in life. Loevinger viewed development as an increase in autonomy and differentiation of self from others. Like Jung, she felt that development involves a progressive freeing of the self from constraints due to contextual and social factors. Maslow (1970) called this stage self-actualization, as the endpoint of a motivational hierarchy. Although he is not traditionally considered a theorist in adult development, his theory is in many ways very similar to that of Loevinger and thus should be included. In contrast, the work of Levinson (1978) was more explicitly an amalgam of Jungian and Eriksonian theories. He posited a series of stages or life structures that are punctuated by periods of transition.

Gestalt theories also influenced theories of adult development. Early on, Wolfgang Kohler (1940) and the other Gestalt psychologists argued that the pattern of relationships among variables is more important than the absolute level of any particular variable. (For example, we can recognize the tune "Happy Birthday" no matter which key it is in, because the meaning or import of the tune is carried in the relationship among the notes rather than in any particular set of notes.) In this model, development occurs in a discontinuous series of qualitative changes. For instance, it was the Gestalt psychologists who suggested that learning occurs via insight experiences in which new patterns of relationships among variables are established. (The standard example used is the chimpanzee's insight that two sticks can be stuck together to get down the bananas that one stick alone cannot reach.)

In many ways, this type of discontinuous development is best exemplified by Piaget's (1954) model of cognitive development.[1] Like Freud, though, Piaget focused primarily on childhood.

Kohlberg (1984) drew on Piaget's theory to describe a series of stages in moral development that occurred in both childhood and adulthood. Although Loevinger's model focused on ego development and Kohlberg's on moral development, both theories described the lessening dependence on societal norms (conformism) and instead emphasized the development of autonomous reasoning capacity concerning moral issues.

Thus, the psychological adult development and aging theorists emphasized internal processes and posited that development had a goal, or *telos*. That goal was variously described but usually involved psychological integration, autonomy, and/or the development of choice in adulthood.

Sociogenic Models

The ontogenetic theorists were strongly criticized for positing one primary goal or developmental pathway and ignoring differences in life courses due to gender, social class, culture, and cohort (see Rossi, 1980). Sociogenic models eschew telos-driven development, focusing instead on change in adulthood that varies as a function of social roles and historical contexts. Thus, Neugarten and Datan (1973) presented a model that reflected the timing and acquisition of social roles as a way to structure the life course. Transitions that follow social norms are considered to be *on time*, whereas those that occur earlier or later than normal are *off time* and therefore much more difficult. For example, it is much easier for a mother to start a family when she is in her 20s than in early adolescence or midlife. This was seen as a much more flexible model, because it allowed for the influence of social factors such as socioeconomic status, as well as gender differences in life course structure (Dannefer, 1984; Moen, 1992).

This gave rise to many different theories such as disengagement theory (Cummings & Henry, 1961), which posited a mutual withdrawal between the individual and society as one ages. Disengagement theory was countered by activity theory (Havighurst, 1961), which argued that the more active the older person is, the greater the life satisfaction. Havighurst, Neugarten, and Tobin (1968) resolved this controversy by demonstrating that the moderating factor is personal desire: The activity level preferred by older adults. In other words, those who want to be active but cannot be are unhappy, whereas those who do not want to be very active but are forced to be by their circumstances are also unhappy. For example, someone who wants to keep working but is forced to retire may find retirement stressful, and someone who would like to retire but cannot due to lack of adequate pensions and savings may find working stressful.

Thus, according to these theories, change in adulthood is characterized by a succession of role transitions that are shaped by the immediate social context and larger social structure rather than by internal psychological processes. However, strict sociogenic models began to give way to those recognizing that individuals are also agents who take an active role in structuring their life course (see Clausen, 1995).

Current Theories

Most current theories take some sort of middle ground between strict sociogenic and ontogenetic stances, but they do so with varying emphases on the context, individual goals, and *agency* (the individual's choice or ability to influence the situation). Most attempt to integrate biological, psychological, and sociohistorical influences on development in adulthood.

Life Course Theory

Current theorists such as Elder (1998) have developed a much more elaborate theory of life course development, which examines the ways in which cohort and historical periods affect the life course structure of individuals. Development is seen as a series of transitions and choice points that are influenced both by the immediate social context and the larger sociohistorical period, as well as gender and social roles (Moen, 1992).

For example, Elder (1974) conducted a classic study of the effects of the Great Depression on subsequent development, using archives from what is now known as the Intergenerational Study, which followed children born in the 1920s and 1930s through their childhood and adulthood into late life. Elder showed that the Depression influenced the life course of individuals, but how it did so was modified by social class and family resources. Not everyone was equally affected by the Depression, and there was an interaction between economic deprivation and social class. Children from working-class families that were economically deprived generally had very difficult, chaotic lives. They were less likely to finish high school than their nondeprived peers and consequently had poorer work histories, less savings, troubled marital histories, and worse relationships with their children. Curiously, though, the middle-class children who were economically deprived did better than their nondeprived peers: They were more likely to achieve higher education and had better jobs and finances, more stable marriages, and better relations with their children. The stress of economic deprivation apparently motivated them to focus and achieve more in their lives. Thus, Elder (1998) argued for an interdependent life course: How individuals weather transitions, turning points, and hard times is a function of personal choices and those of others in the immediate social context, the availability or lack of resources, and larger historical events.

Goal-Oriented Models

Baltes (1987) characterized development in adulthood as a balance between gains and losses, with relatively more gains in early adulthood and more losses in later. Like Erikson (1950), Baltes proposed a life span (as opposed to life course) theory, and the dynamic between gains and losses is reminiscent of Erikson's dialectic between positive and negative outcomes. However, Baltes did not propose a series of stages but instead argued for a process approach that describes adaptation to aging. Successful aging is characterized by the selection, optimization, and compensation (SOC) model (Baltes, 1997). Assuming that older individuals have fewer resources, they must select the goals or activities they wish to pursue and optimize their performance by devoting resources to those particular goals. They may also compensate for any deficiencies that could prevent them from achieving their goals.

A classic example of the SOC process is the pianist Arthur Rubinstein, who performed well into his 80s. He was able to maintain his career by decreasing his repertoire, selecting those pieces he felt most capable of performing, and optimizing his performance by practicing these fewer pieces. To compensate for neurological slowing with age that affected the speed with which he could play demanding pieces, he would slow down the passage just before one with a fast tempo, which made it seem as though he played the following passage faster than he actually did.

Brandtstädter's (1999) self-development model also emphasizes goals but argues that there are developmental changes in goals from young adulthood to late life. The goal in early adulthood is to achieve the ideal self, which is largely culturally determined. In later life, however, the goal becomes to maintain the self as much as possible, as a means of preserving resources and counteracting developmental losses. Brandtstädter, Wentura, and Rothermund (1999) have shifted from simply describing changes in the types of goals in adulthood to hypothesizing that development in adulthood consists of self-directed development in pursuit of goals.

Postformal Operations

Piagetian theory ended with the stage of formal operations, generally described as scientific reasoning, that most (but not all) individuals achieve in adolescence and early adulthood. Theorists such as Pascual-Leone (1990) and Labouvie-Vief (1990) focus on more complex cognitive development in adulthood—postformal operations, which emphasizes relativistic and dialectical reasoning. Relativistic reasoning argues that there are very few absolutes; instead, complex thinkers understand that the context modifies decisions and thought processes, which may be carefully nuanced. Rather than an absolute such as "Lying is always wrong," a relativist thinker may realize that lying is wrong when one seeks to cover up wrongdoing or to harm someone but may be acceptable if one intends to prevent harm (e.g., concealing one's true feelings about someone else's new outfit).

In dialectical reasoning, it may be understood that there are often opposing but equally valid intellectual stances (thesis and counterthesis). Rather than choosing one to be right and the other wrong, the dialectic reasoner develops ways of synthesizing contradictory information, often by recognizing that some ideas may be better applicable in some contexts than others. For example, Newtonian and Einsteinian physics posit very different models of the universe, but one is not wrong and the other right; rather, Newtonian physics is seen as a very special and small part of Einsteinian physics, which has broader applicability. Similarly, from a dialectic viewpoint, there is no contradiction between religion and evolution, as long as one does not take a literalist view of scriptures such as the Bible or the Koran. Evolution can be seen as a process through which creation occurs.

Labouvie-Vief (2002) also argues for the necessity to integrate emotion with cognition in adult development. Not only do people become more cognitively complex with age, but they also may become more emotionally complex. Labouvie-Vief's study showed that cognitive and emotional complexity increase from young adulthood to midlife but then decrease in late life. Instead of emotional complexity, Pascual-Leone (1990) focused on ego transcendence, a construct that may form a critical element in theories of successful aging (which will be discussed in Chapter 12).

Conscious Development

There is a growing sense that adult development is something that individuals do, not something that simply occurs. Langer and her colleagues (1990) argued that development in adulthood consists of increasing mindfulness. Langer (1997) defines mindfulness as consisting of three characteristics:

the continuous creation of new categories, openness to new information, and an implicit awareness of more than one perspective. Its counterpart, mindlessness, is characterized by an entrapment in old categories, by autonomic behavior, and by awareness of only a single perspective. The development of mindfulness is not automatic with age but reflects a process of conscious attempts to increase awareness and think in more flexible ways.

Levenson and Crumpler (1996) proposed a liberative model of adult development that defined adult development as increasing freedom from social and biological conditioning. It differed from earlier models in suggesting the way in which this occurred. In the liberative model, the method of development is based on self-observation. Through self-observation, one can become aware of negative characteristics that can constrain understanding and behavior, limiting one's choices of action. (Note that positive characteristics may also be constraining.) Levenson, Aldwin, and Cupertino (2001) have argued that loss plays a central role in adult development, as it can force individuals to examine their own assumptions and develop new and more mindful ways of being. They suggest that this is the process that underlies Tornstam's (1994) observation of gerotranscendence in late life, which is similar to Peck's construct of ego transcendence and is characterized by less rigid ego boundaries (a sense of oneness or connection with the universe) coupled with a decreasing reliance on others for life satisfaction.

Interrelationships Among Theories

Thus, early theories of adult development tended to focus on one aspect of adult development (e.g., personality or social), whereas contemporary theories tend to emphasize multiple influences. Many of these theories focus more on describing the older population and/or the importance of the social context rather than on developmental processes per se and thus may not be seen as relevant to biological processes. Furthermore, it is interesting that the current models may describe changes in personality and adaptation from young adulthood to midlife. For example, Baltes (2002) reported that SOC peaks in midlife, while Labouvie-Vief (2002) found that cognitive and emotional complexity also peak in midlife. Thus, we may know less about the process of development in late life.

Most current theories emphasize some sort of agency, or conscious choice, in developmental processes. Some theories posit the opportunity for conscious choice as an outcome of developmental processes. Although biological theories seldom address choice and agency, relying primarily on causal physiological models, health psychology often addresses the impact of lifestyle choices on health and the development of disease. These choices, which are addressed in the third section of this volume, may accelerate or decelerate the aging process. These theories also may play an important role in how people adapt to biological changes with age, and thus they have relevance for quality of life in late life.

● PSYCHOSOCIAL FACTORS AND AGING

As important as genetic factors are, the best estimates are that they account for less than half of the variance in late-life illness and mortality (McClearn & Heller, 2000). The percentage varies as a function of type of illness or risk factor, but in late life, it ranges from 0% to about 40%. Clearly, environmental and psychosocial factors play a major role in how one ages. Section III of this book is devoted to examining the interplay between psychosocial factors and health, so we discuss theories relevant to aging processes only briefly here. As previously noted, biological theories can be subsumed under the deviation amplification model. One can also understand the effects of psychosocial factors on health in terms of accelerating or decelerating the aging process.

The deviation-amplification theory can also encompass the role of psychosocial factors in aging. Some factors are well-known aging accelerators, including smoking, excessive alcohol consumption, sedentary lifestyles, and poor diets leading to obesity. Lower social-class status may also play a significant role (see Chapter 2), as may personality factors such as hostility (see Chapter 9). Other factors may slow the aging process. These include healthy behavior habits such as exercise, moderate alcohol consumption, and perhaps caloric restriction (which may work very well in laboratory animals but has not as yet been proven in humans). Other factors are less obvious but nonetheless intriguing, including social support and marital status, especially for men, and personality factors such as a calm disposition (Spiro, Aldwin, Ward, & Mroczek, 1995). Meditation may also have positive effects on longevity (Alexander, Langer, Newman, Chandler, & Davies, 1989), but more research is needed to confirm this.

A very intriguing question is whether or not psychosocial factors have more or less effect in older adults (Kaplan, Haan, & Wallace, 1999). On one hand, there is fairly good presumptive evidence to argue that psychosocial factors and physical health are more tightly entwined in late life. Solomon and Benton (2000) have remarked that "there appears to be a very close correlation between physical and psychological well-being in the aged" (p. 115).

We know that older people are more vulnerable to physical stressors because they have difficulty regulating homeostasis and have more chronic illnesses. At times of massive population upheavals, it is the infants and the elderly who are most likely to die. Older people are also more susceptible to dehydration and heat stroke. However, there may also be complex interactions between physical and psychological health (see Chapter 10).

Kuypers and Bengtson's (1973) social-breakdown theory argues that relatively trivial events may snowball into serious problems for older adults because psychological, social, and physical health are so tightly intertwined. For example, a very active older woman in one of our studies broke an ankle. Her only daughter lived too far away to take care of her, and, being older, our study participant had balance problems that made it very difficult to learn to use crutches. She was forced to enter a rehabilitation center, and her progress was very slow. This older woman lost her subsidized housing because she was absent too long, and her daughter sold her furniture. She became very depressed, stopped eating, and had to remain institutionalized. So a broken ankle, which a younger person would take in stride, became ultimately a life-threatening problem for this woman. This illustrates the confluence of biological, psychological, and social factors in later life.

Others argue, however, that older adults are less vulnerable to psychosocial factors. Williams (2000) reviewed the literature on risk factors and aging, and concluded that the effects of risk factors decrease with age, primarily due to survivor effects. He presented data showing that the excess cardiovascular mortality in people with Type A personalities is seen primarily in individuals in their 20s and 30s; risk ratios are similar in the 40s and 50s, and Type Bs actually have higher rates in late life. Williams showed that this is due to differential survival—people who were vulnerable to the adverse physiological effects of the Type A personality died earlier.

Other studies have found no differential age vulnerability. Elias, Elias, D'Agostino, and Wolf (2000) found that the effects of hypertension on neuropsychological performance did not vary by age, although their sample consisted of older individuals.

Thus, the findings on relative vulnerability (or resilience) of older adults to the effects of psychosocial risk factors on health are mixed (Kaplan et al., 1999) and likely vary by type of factor, health outcome, and age of the sample. Despite his finding of less risk, Williams (2000) noted,

> Even given the decreasing relative risk associated with psychosocial risk factors as age increases, their continuing significant impact on coronary heart disease and all-cause mortality among the elderly means that

in terms of absolute numbers of deaths the psychosocial risk factors probably account for more deaths among the elderly than among younger groups. (pp. 140-141)

● SUMMARY

Biological aging is a highly complex phenomenon that can be examined at many different levels, including genetic, cellular, organ-system, and even psychosocial levels. These are not mutually exclusive. The study of aging is inherently cross-disciplinary, and some of the most fascinating findings occur across levels. Differences in methods across fields often lead to discordant findings, however, resulting in heated arguments between epidemiologists, geneticists, nutritionists, physiologists, geriatricians, psychologists, and sociologists. A first step toward resolving some of these discrepancies is finding a common language. Understanding factors in terms of accelerators or decelerators of the aging process may help to provide that common language.

Furthermore, both psychosocial and biological theories of aging are becoming more complex, attempting to integrate multiple factors while acknowledging contextual effects. New and more sophisticated ways of designing studies and analyzing data are required, as addressed in the next chapter.

● NOTE

1. Piaget considered himself to be a structuralist. Structuralism was a French school growing out of sociology, anthropology, linguistics, and Marxism. Both Gestalt psychology and structuralism hold that the whole is greater than the sum of the parts—that the relationship among the components is more important than the components themselves. Furthermore, the Gestaltists focused on sudden insight and qualitative change, elements crucial to Piagetian theory, which is why we classified him in the Gestalt school in Figure 3.1.

CHAPTER 4

UNDERSTANDING CHANGE IN AGING RESEARCH

The study of age-related changes in health, cognition, and psychosocial functioning demands new ways of designing studies and analyzing data. A tremendous amount of work has been done in the design and analysis of longitudinal studies, and the past decade has witnessed the development of new techniques that allow researchers to address more interesting and complex questions. Relatively few graduate programs offer courses in longitudinal design and statistics, however, and many researchers, students, clinicians, and applied gerontologists are intimidated by these new methods. In addition, these methods and statistics often come with their own terminology, which makes them difficult to understand. This chapter provides an overview of these types of designs and statistics as a way of introducing the concepts and familiarizing the reader with the terminology used in this book, which will make understanding individual research studies easier. We draw on our own research and that of others in illustrating these types of designs and statistics. Special attention will be paid to those used most frequently in health-related research. Readers requiring more detailed examinations of these topics should refer to texts such as Collins and

Sayer (2001), MacCallum and Austin (2000), or Raudenbush (2000). Before we review these types of longitudinal designs and statistics, however, we will start with some basic definitions for those less familiar with statistics used in health-related research.

● BASIC DEFINITIONS

Statistics answers two basic questions: (a) Is there a difference between two (or more) groups on a given variable, and (b) Is there an association between two or more variables? These two questions are often simply restatements or mirror images of each other. The question "Are low-birth-weight babies more likely to have health problems later in life than normal-birth-weight babies?" compares two groups. This question is identical to "What is the association between birth weight and subsequent health problems?" Statistics are used to establish whether the observed effects are "real" (significant) or due to chance.

Basic Statistical Terms

Different statistics are used to answer these two questions, depending on the type of data available (continuous or categorical) and, in part, which statistics are in vogue in different fields. *Continuous variables* are those that form a series, such as age or number of symptoms, whereas *categorical variables* refer to groups that cannot be added together, such as where someone was born or type of illness. In health-related research, when a study describes mean differences between the groups, it is assessing a continuous variable (e.g., number of symptoms) and describing average differences between the groups. When a study discusses the probability of developing a health problem (odds or risk ratios), the dependent variable is categorical.

Table 4.1 presents a summary of commonly used statistics and their uses, divided by whether they test differences or associations. For example, *t*-tests assess mean differences between two groups, whereas correlations examine whether two variables *covary* using a standardized metric (−1 to +1). A positive correlation between two variables means that people who are high on one measure also tend to be higher on the other one (e.g., education and income), whereas a negative correlation means that being high on one variable is associated with being low on the other.

Different statistics are used depending on whether or not the outcome variable is categorical or continuous. *Nonparametric statistics* such as

Table 4.1   Summary of Common Statistics

	Type of Question	
Type of Data	*Are There Differences?*	*Are There Associations?*
Nonparametric (categorical) bivariate (2 variables)	**Chi-square (χ^2)**—Does the observed categorical distribution differ from the expected one?	**Eta (η)**—Is there a significant association between two categorical variables?
Multivariate (> 2 variables)	**Loglinear**—Do different groups have different distributions on multiple categorical variables?	**Logistic regressions (odds ratios)**—What are the best predictors of a dichotomous outcome (e.g., death?)
Parametric (continuous) bivariate (2 variables)	**t-test**—Do these two groups differ on a continuous dependent variable y?	**Correlations (r)**—Is there a significant association between two continuous variables?
Multivariate (> 2 variables)	**Analysis of variance (ANOVA; F)**—Do these three or more groups differ on y?	**Multiple regressions (β)**—What are the best predictors of y?
	Multivariate analysis of variance (MANOVA)—Do two or more groups differ on a set of variables?	**Structural equation modeling (SEM)**—What is the pattern of associations across multiple variables?

chi-square analysis are used if both the *independent* (predictor) and *dependent* (outcome) variables are categorical. *Parametric statistics* such as *t*-tests and analyses of variance (ANOVAs) are used when the dependent variables are continuous. They compare the means between groups, depending on whether there are two or more than two groups, respectively.

Finally, MANOVAs are used when there are multiple dependent variables that are intercorrelated. MANOVAs can control for *correlated errors* that reflect systematic biases in response patterns. For example, some people fill out questionnaires very quickly, and, when confronted with a scale of several items rated from 1 to 5, they may just circle all the 5s. If they do this with several scales, high correlations between the scales may result, but these are probably spurious (hence the term, correlated errors). Thus, if a researcher has a set of dependent variables that are intercorrelated, it is much better to calculate a MANOVA that yields a multivariate F rather than calculating several different ANOVAs.

Summary of Common Statistical Techniques

Statistics can be grouped depending on whether they are *bivariate* (examining only two variables, such as *t*-tests, correlations, or chi-squares) or *multivariate* (examining more than one variable, such as multiple or logistic regression). A *partial correlation* controls for one variable *a* when correlating two other variables (*b* with *c*). For example, education, *a*, and income, *b*, are highly intercorrelated, and both are correlated with health, *c*. To determine whether income has an effect independent of education, one would partial out education. A *regression equation* is basically a series of partial correlations. It does much the same thing, but with several variables, so that one can examine the contribution of each variable independent of the others in the equation. Thus, one could construct an equation that examined the independent contributions of occupation, education, income, and job satisfaction to health outcomes. Regression can be used to decide which variables best predict a given outcome. Structural equation modeling (SEM) simultaneously estimates the relationships among several variables and will be discussed later in this chapter.

Which statistic one uses depends on the question, the research design, and the type of data available. A good question literally dictates the type of design and the statistics used in a study.

Research Designs

There are two major types of research designs (Campbell & Stanley, 1963). In an experimental design, research participants are randomly assigned to an experimental group that receives the treatment or manipulation and a control group that does not (or that receives a placebo of some sort). Random assignment to groups is absolutely critical to determine whether or not a given manipulation or treatment works. Especially in clinical trials that examine the efficacy of a drug, these should be double-blind studies in which neither the medication administrator nor the research participant knows whether or not that person has been assigned to the experimental group. Instead, an elaborate system of codes is used to track which participants receive the drug and which receive the placebo. At the end of the study, these codes are broken, and researchers can analyze the data. This controls for the *placebo effect*—the tendency for people to positively evaluate any treatment, even though there may be no physiological effects attributable to the treatment.

A good example of the importance of random assignment is the effect of combination estrogen/progesterone hormone replacement therapy (HRT) on health. Early studies showed that women who used HRT tended to be healthier than those who did not. However, women on HRT also tend to be better educated and more health conscious. Only when they were randomly assigned to the group receiving HRT or the control group could researchers establish that HRT actually resulted in slightly increased risks of heart disease and breast cancer (Rossouw et al., 2002).

Health researchers often study the effects of a treatment on symptoms. A major issue in question is what dose is adequate to significantly reduce symptom levels. A *dose-response curve* plots symptoms against amount of medication—or it can also refer to the relationship between toxic substances and symptoms. The classic finding is called a *dose-response effect* and refers to a linear relationship—the more of the toxic substance, the greater the impairment. For example, Strawbridge, Wallhagen, Shema, and Kaplan (2000) found a dose-response effect between hearing impairment and problems in other domains—that is, the greater the degree of hearing impairment, the more the respondents reported psychosocial problems. Sometimes, however, the relationship is not linear. For example, there may be an optimum dose of a particular medication—lesser amounts may not have an effect, or greater amounts may not confer any additional benefits.

Sometimes it is neither practical nor ethical to randomly assign people to experimental groups. For example, in studying the long-term health effects of parental divorce in childhood, one cannot randomly assign children to groups—after all, the parents cannot be asked to divorce just so one can study its effect on their children. Thus, the researcher must employ a *quasi-experimental*, or *cohort*, design in which one identifies people whose parents divorced when they were children and compares them to similar people whose parents did not divorce. The hitch here is "similar"—children of divorce may differ in other ways, such as exposure to an abusive or mentally ill parent or greater financial difficulties before or after divorce. Thus, it is critical to statistically control for other differences between the groups to identify those effects that could be the result of divorce. Researchers who use quasi-experimental designs are generally very careful to avoid using causal language (e.g., divorce causes behavioral problems in children) and instead talk about associations (e.g., parental divorce is associated with behavioral problems).

A special type of quasi-experimental design sometimes used in health research is called *case control* (Norman & Streiner, 2000). A quasi-experimental design may not be practical when studying a relatively rare phenomenon; huge samples would be needed to identify enough cases to analyze. In this instance, case control designs can be useful. For example, if there is a cluster of a few deaths in a particular area, one can identify who died (cases), then identify a group of living people similar to those who died (control), and then compare the two groups to see what difference between the two might account for the deaths.

Many quasi-experimental studies do not divide people into groups but instead simply examine the associations between groups of variables. To assign variables to independent or dependent status, one must have a strong theoretical rationale. For example, when studying the relationship between personality, coping, and symptoms, it may be very difficult to assign *causal directionality* (i.e., which variables cause the others). A reasonable hypothesis is that individuals who are high in hostility cope with problems by expressing negative affect (e.g., yelling), which in turn raises their blood pressure. It is entirely possible, however, that highly variable blood pressure may lead to overreacting in stressful situations, resulting in hostile behaviors and outlooks (Kasl, 1983). Thus, causal directionality cannot be determined with cross-sectional, correlational data, but one can find interesting relations that can be further investigated.

These different designs may result in very different findings. Clinical studies, especially those using case control designs, may overestimate the effect size (or magnitude of the effect). Large surveys using quasi-experimental designs that gather more random samples often underestimate the effect size, because individuals who are ill or troubled tend not to respond. Experimental studies may not find an effect because their sample sizes are too small, or because they use too little of the treatment, assess the outcomes at inappropriate times, and so on.

With any review of the scientific literature, great variability often exists in the results found across studies. It is not unusual for some studies to find positive effects, others to find negative effects, and yet others to find no effects. For example, early studies found that older adults had high rates of depression, but these were largely based on clinical or help-seeking samples. Epidemiological studies that assessed random samples sometimes found that younger adults were more likely to be depressed than older adults; others found no relationship between age and depression (see Aldwin, 1991).

Rather than throwing up one's hands in disgust when faced with this type of contradictory evidence, it is important to understand that the process of reconciling disparate findings can often provide a much more detailed and precise understanding of the phenomenon. If there are differences between studies, these must be due to the types of samples used, the types of measures assessed, and/or the types of analyses conducted.

In the problem just cited about aging and depression, all three types of problems were relevant. The results varied by the age of sample: Symptoms decreased from young adulthood to midlife, then rose in late life (see Kessler, Foster, Webster, & House, 1992). Therefore, studies that sampled primarily young adults and the middle-aged tended to find a negative relationship between age and depressive symptoms, whereas those whose samples were older often found a positive one.

Type of measure used was also important. Studies using measures of depression that included physical symptoms such as fatigue, sleep problems, or aches and pains were more likely to find that older adults were more depressed—not because they were unhappier, but because their health was poorer. Studies that focused just on negative affect often found younger adults were more likely to be depressed.

The type of analysis used was also critical. Most simple statistics examining the association between two or more variables assume that the association is linear (which is why regression is called "linear regression"). However, many associations are nonlinear, and special procedures are needed to identify nonlinear relationships (see Aldwin, Spiro, Levenson, & Cupertino, 2001). In this case, there was a nonlinear relationship, a J-shaped curve, between age and depressive symptoms.

The process of trying to reconcile findings across studies is called a *meta-analysis*. In meta-analyses, researchers identify as many studies as possible that look at a given phenomenon and try to account for the differences. Sometimes there are relatively few studies, and these have used very disparate measures, so the best one can do is to determine what proportion of the studies found the relationship in question. For example, Tennant and McLean (2001) reviewed the literature examining whether people who were recently widowed were more likely to die in the following year; they reported that 9 of 14 studies showed a positive association.

Sometimes there are many studies, and one can statistically examine effect size, depending on the type of sample or the type of measure used. For example, Miller, Smith, Turner, Guijarro, and Hallet (1996) conducted a meta-analysis of the relationship between hostility and health. They concluded that there was a general relationship between hostility and coronary heart disease but that the magnitude of the effect depended in part on the particular hostility measure used, as well as the type of study design. The structured interview provided stronger and more consistent results than self-report measures. Furthermore, studies using case control designs that contrasted sick with healthy individuals provided the strongest results, whereas those that restricted the range of illness outcomes (e.g., those that examined only patients with coronary heart disease) showed the weakest results. Meta-analyses are a powerful way of summarizing the literature and developing hypotheses to explain contradictory findings, which can lead to definitive studies to resolve contradictions in the literature.

In both developmental research and health-related research, careful attention must be paid to timing issues. One must distinguish between a *proximal*, or immediate, cause and a *distal*, or distant, one. For example, the proximal cause of having a heart attack may be eating a holiday meal loaded with fat; the distal cause may be having been a low-birth-weight baby whose liver never developed properly, resulting in chronic high cholesterol levels (Barker, 1999). When examining distal causes, it is useful to construct a plausible chain of events that links distal and proximate causes.

Finally, in health psychology research, one must distinguish between three types of effects: direct, mediated, and moderated (Aldwin & Yancura, in press). Direct effects indicate that an independent variable, x, has a *direct* (or causal) impact on the dependent variable, y. For example, hostility is associated with high blood pressure, and it is possible that this is a direct effect. Sometimes there is an association between two variables, but the effect is actually *mediated* by a third variable. For example, hostility may be associated with higher blood pressure levels because people who are high in hostility are more likely to smoke, which in turn is associated with higher blood pressure. Finally, the effect of one variable on another one may be *moderated*— that is, it may vary by some other variable such as context, age, or gender. For example, individuals high in hostility may have elevated blood pressure levels primarily in situations in which there is interpersonal conflict. Under normal conditions, their blood pressure may be similar to individuals who are low in hostility.

The distinction between mediated and moderated is subtle but perhaps can best be remembered by the differences between the associated statistical analyses. Both designs typically use hierarchical multiple regression, which enters variables in the equation in a specific order or step. To examine mediating relationships, x_1 is entered in the first step, so the direct relationship between x_1 and y is examined. In the second step, the hypothesized mediator, x_2, is added. If the β between x_1 and y is significantly decreased, then one can conclude that the effect of x_1 on y is through x_2. In the example above, smoking (x_2) mediates the relationship between hostility (x_1) on blood pressure (y).

In regressions examining moderating effects, one must first compute the interaction term, $x_1 \times x_2$. In the hierarchical regression, x_1 is entered in the first step, x_2 on the second step, and the interaction term on the third. If the interaction term is statistically significant, then one can conclude that smoking moderates the effects of hostility on blood pressure. In other words, people who are high in hostility and who smoke may be much more likely to have high blood pressure than people who smoke but who are low in hostility. In this instance, smoking *enhances* the effect of hostility on health. If a moderator *decreases* the effect, then it is said to *buffer* the effect. For example, problem-focused coping may buffer the effect of stress on health outcomes. (For more extensive discussion of this issue, see Aldwin, 1999.)

New research designs and statistics can be useful in examining these types of complex problems, in both health and age-related designs.

AGE-RELATED DESIGNS •

Many studies of the effects of aging use quasi-experimental designs, because it is not possible to randomly assign people to different ages. However, some studies examine age effects by sampling young and old subjects, randomly assigning them to experimental conditions, and then testing for interactions with age. The statistics involved with this type of design are fairly simple, usually involving *t*-tests or ANOVAs (see Table 4.1). Other studies simply use natural groupings of different ages or follow individuals over time and thus use quasi-experimental designs that often have more complex statistics. Therefore, this chapter focuses on quasi-experimental designs and the statistics required to analyze them.

Cross-Sectional Versus Longitudinal Designs

Several decades ago, researchers recognized that studying age differences is very different from studying age-related change. *Age differences* are studied using cross-sectional designs, which compare different age groups at one point in time. *Age-related changes* are examined using longitudinal designs, which follow people over time. The two designs can yield varying results. Finding age differences in a phenomenon between different age groups does not mean that there are age-related changes.

For example, nearly every cross-sectional study finds that older people have lower IQ levels. However, we know that there is a *cohort effect* of education—older people tend to have less education than younger people, which can affect IQ levels. For example, Botwinick (1977), in a classic study using the Duke Longitudinal Study of Aging (DLSA) sample, confirmed that cross-sectional differences in IQ showing an apparent decline with age, but he also conducted a longitudinal study on the same sample, which showed an *increase* in IQ with age. One could conclude that the apparent age effect was actually a cohort effect, as cross-sectional studies confound age effects with those due to cohort.

Actually, neither of these findings were accurate. The cross-sectional analysis did confound age with education, but the longitudinal analysis had a problem with *survivor effects*. In longitudinal studies, there are generally fewer respondents at each assessment, due to deaths, dropouts, and individuals who have moved and been lost to follow-up. Typically, poorer-functioning individuals tend to drop out of longitudinal studies, and the ones who remain are generally healthier, wealthier, and better educated. Thus, in the longitudinal analysis of the DLSA sample, IQ appeared to increase with age, but only because there was a more select sample at each time point. When only data from those individuals who responded at all time points were included in the analysis, then IQ was much more stable, decreasing only after age 60 or so. However, excluding individuals who have missing data still entails selection effects. In longitudinal studies, excluding individuals with even one missing data point often results in losing substantial proportions of the sample, and researchers have developed innovative ways to estimate missing data.

Longitudinal designs also confound aging effects with cohort effects, as one cohort may change in a way that other cohorts do not. This is terribly important, because nearly all of our information on aging has been gathered on the World War II cohort, and there is no guarantee that baby boomers or any subsequent cohorts will age in the same manner. For example, we can estimate the rate of hearing loss with age based on what we know about existing cohorts, but there is strong evidence to suggest that young adults today are losing their hearing at about twice the rate of previous generations (Wallhagen, Strawbridge, Cohen, & Kaplan, 1997), probably due to greater exposure to noise from rock concerts, Walkmans, and the like.

Longitudinal designs also confound *period* (historical or time of measurement) effects. This was first noted by Bradburn and Caplovitz (1965), who were conducting national studies on positive and negative affect. One longitudinal study found a marked rise in negative affect, and a simplistic interpretation would be that negative affect increases with age. However, Bradburn happened to take his second assessment at the time of the Cuban missile crisis when many thought that nuclear war was imminent, and the increase in negative affect reflected a period rather than an age effect. Thus, longitudinal researchers sometimes use sequential designs to tease apart age, cohort, and period (historical or time of measurement) effects.

Table 4.2   Sequential Designs Indicating Ages at Different Periods for Different Cohorts

Cohort (Birth Year)	A. Cohort-Sequential Design			B. Cross-Sequential Design			C. Time-Sequential Design		
	Period (Measurement Point)			Period (Measurement Point)			Period (Measurement Point)		
	1969	1979	1989	1969	1979	1989	1969	1979	1989
1947	22	32	42	22	32	42	22	32	42
1957		22	32		22	32		22	32
1967			22			22			22

Sequential Designs

There are three types of sequential designs: cohort-, cross-, and time-sequential (Schaie, 1977). Why three? Because age, cohort, and period effects are confounded and need to be teased apart, but, as we shall see, each design can address only two of these phenomena. Remember that age refers to a person's chronological age, cohort to the year in which he or she was born, and period to the time of measurement.

The differences between these three designs are depicted in Table 4.2, which is based on data from a study of change in mastery from young adulthood to midlife by Parker and Aldwin (1997). This study used data from the Davis Longitudinal Study, which follows several cohorts of college alumni (the classes of 1969, 1979, and 1989).

Cohort-Sequential Designs

Cohort-sequential designs follow two or more cohorts over the same ages but confound time (see panel A, Table 4.2). Members of the first cohort illustrated in Table 4.2, born in 1947, were 22 years old at the first time of measurement in 1969 and 32 years old in 1979. Members of the second cohort, born 10 years later in 1957, were also assessed at ages 22 and 32, but their assessments occurred in 1979 and 1989. Thus, we have two cohorts (1947 and 1957), two ages (22 and 32), but three time periods (1969, 1979, and 1989). Therefore, period is confounded, because the cells are unbalanced. The 1957 cohort had no measurements in 1969, and the 1989 assessment of the 1947 cohort was not used because the age was out of range (age 42). Therefore, cohort-sequential designs can only test age and cohort effects, not period effects.

For a phenomenon to be an age effect, both cohorts must show similar (preferably identical) changes. Parker and Aldwin (1997) found that the 1947 cohort, who graduated in 1969, increased in mastery from ages 22 to 32. To determine if this was an age or cohort effect, they also studied the 1957 cohort, who graduated in 1979, and also found that this second cohort increased in mastery nearly the identical amount from ages 22 to 32. However, it was entirely possible that this was a period effect—that there was a general increase in mastery over this time period. Therefore, Parker and Aldwin also conducted a cross-sequential study.

Cross-Sequential Designs

These designs examine cohort and period effects but confound age (see panel B, Table 4.2). The cross-sequential design shown in Table 4.2 examines two cohorts (1947 and 1957) at two periods (1979 and 1989), but it includes measurements at three different ages: 22, 32, and 42. Again, cross-sequential designs confound age; here, there are two assessments of 32-year-olds but only one assessment of 22-year-olds and one of 42-year-olds. Parker and Aldwin (1997) examined whether the two cohorts changed in similar ways in mastery from 1979 to 1989 and found that they did not. The older cohort did not change, but the younger cohort increased in mastery. Therefore, this change was probably not a period effect, because the two cohorts did not change in the same way. But to confirm this, Parker and Aldwin also performed a time-sequential design.

Time-Sequential Designs

Time-sequential designs examine two different age groups at two different time periods. To do this, however, requires three cohorts. In these designs, only one cohort is studied longitudinally (indicated by the dashed box in Table 4.2), but it is compared at two different periods with a different cohort (hence three cohorts). In other words, in the time-sequential design illustrated in Table 4.2, panel C, the 1957 cohort is followed from age 22 to age 32. In 1979, this cohort (aged 22) is compared to the 1947 cohort (aged 32). In 1989, the 1957 cohort is now aged 32, and it is compared to the 1967 cohort (aged 22). This design answers the question, Is the difference between 22- and 32-year-olds in the year 1979 similar to that between 22- and 32-year-olds in 1989? Thus, time-sequential designs have two age groups and two time periods but require three cohorts, thus confounding cohort. When Parker and Aldwin (1997) performed this time-sequential analysis, they found nearly identical differences in mastery between 22- and 32-year-olds at both time points, which suggested there was indeed an age or developmental change in mastery between the 20s and the 30s.

In summary, in two of the three sequential analyses, Parker and Aldwin (1997) had significant age effects but no cohort or period effects. They concluded that the increase in mastery in early adulthood is an age or developmental effect not restricted to a particular cohort or time period.

Values, however, were an entirely different story. Parker and Aldwin (1997) compared the primacy of family versus work values in the same sample and found massive period and cohort effects but no age effects. Although most participants at all time points said that family was more important than work, the number of people who thought work was primary increased in the 1970s, especially among women, but decreased in the 1980s. Thus, changes in personality appeared to be developmental and age related, but changes in personal values reflected the historical periods being studied.

STATISTICS FOR ASSESSING CHANGE ●

Caspi and Bem (1990) categorized change and stability into four different types: absolute or mean-level, relative, structural, and idiothetic or ipsative. Absolute change refers to changes in mean level over time, whereas relative change refers to shifts in rank order. Note that these two types of change are independent of each other. It is possible to have stable means across time but changes in rank order and vice versa. Structural change refers to whether or not the factor structure (pattern of relationships) is similar across age or time. Note also that all of these types of change refer to changes in populations. In contrast, idiothetic or ipsative change refers to changes in individuals, and different types of statistics are required for this type of assessment. These types of longitudinal statistics are summarized in Table 4.3.

Table 4.3   Summary of Longitudinal Statistics

Statistic	Type of Question
Mean-Level Change	
Paired *t*-test	Is there change from Time 1 to Time 2 in two groups?
Repeated-measures MANOVA	Is there change across multiple time periods in multiple groups?
Relative Change	
Cross-time correlation	Are two or more variables associated across time?
Residualized regression	What predicts change from Time 1 to Time 2?
Proportional-hazards model	What predicts the occurrence of an event over time?
Structural Change	
Confirmatory factor analysis	Does the pattern of relationships vary across time or groups?
Ipsative Change	
Growth curve models: random effects, HLM, GEE, latent growth curves	How do individuals change over time and what predicts that change?

Mean-Level Change

Figure 4.1 illustrates an example of mean-level change. This figure depicts a personality trait, introversion, that has a normal distribution and a mean of 5 at Time 1. At Time 2, the personality trait still has a normal distribution, but the entire distribution has shifted two points to a mean of 7. This indicates that, as a whole, the population increased in this personality trait with age.

The simplest way to assess whether there is a change in mean level over time is a paired *t*-test. A standard *t*-test compares two different groups (a *between-subjects* analysis). If individuals are followed over time, this is a *within-subjects* analysis. Thus, a paired *t-test* can determine if two groups increased or decreased on a variable over time, but it cannot tell you very much about why they changed, because it does not include any way of assessing predictors of the change.

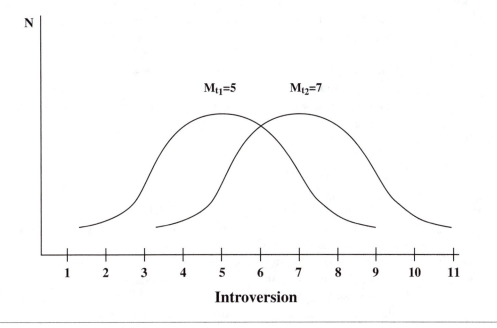

Figure 4.1   Mean-Level Change

A better way of assessing change is a repeated-measures multivariate analysis of variance (MANOVA). A repeated-measures MANOVA also assesses mean-level change over time (within-subjects analysis), but it also allows examination of whether or not different groups are changing similarly (between-subjects analysis). The MANOVA yields F statistics for time as well as for group.

The statistical significance of the interaction term between the grouping and time variables indicates whether the two groups differ in how they have changed over time. For example, a repeated-measures MANOVA can determine whether men and women show the same pattern of change or if they show different patterns over time. We could hypothesize that personality changes with age differently in men and women. Men might become less extraverted and women might become more extraverted. Thus, we would hypothesize a Gender × Time interaction.

Repeated-measures MANOVAs are used to analyze both cohort- and cross-sequential designs. In cohort-sequential designs, the independent variables are age and cohort, and in cross-sequential designs, the independent variables are cohort and period. To use a repeated-measures MANOVA, one must have a *balanced* design, that is, all respondents must have assessments at all points in time. However, simple ANOVAs must be used to analyze time-sequential designs, as only one cohort has two data points; the other two cohorts have only one data point each, and thus between-subjects statistics cannot be used. For example, in Table 4.2, only the 1957 cohort has two time points; the other cohorts have only one. Therefore, a repeated-measures MANOVA could not be used, because only one group actually was assessed twice.

Relative Change

Another way of assessing change and stability is to simply correlate two assessments across time. This indicates the extent to which individuals in the sample maintain their relative rank order. Figure 4.2A illustrates one pattern of correlational stability. Let us assume that this figure illustrates change in introversion with age. At Time 1, the scores on introversion are normally distributed, and Jill has an introversion score of 7, which is higher than Jack's, who scores at the mean (5). In turn, Jack has a higher score than Rachel (3). By Time 2, the population as a whole has increased in introversion, but there is relative stability. Everyone has increased by two points. Jill's extraversion score (9) still has a higher level than Jack's (7), who still has a higher level than Rachel (5). Thus, correlations may indicate stability of individual differences even when there actually is a mean-level change occurring.

It is also possible to have no significant mean-level change across time while there is a change in rank order. As Figure 4.2B indicates, the population mean can remain the same, but the individuals may change. In this instance, Jill has become withdrawn following a series of negative life events and has become much more introverted than the other two. Rachel is now working as a real estate agent and must become more extraverted, so has raised her score from 3 at Time 1 to 7 at Time 2. Jack has not changed; he either is in a rut or is simply happy the way he is. The net mean change, however, is zero, so the population mean is stable, but there is correlational instability: There may be a negative correlation over time, as high introversion scores at Time 1 are associated with low ones at Time 2, and vice versa.

Many researchers assume that a significant correlation indicates stability, when, in truth, stability and change are always relative, and the magnitude of the correlation should be examined to assess the degree of stability. In general, correlations over .8 indicate a high degree of stability, correlations of .4 to .6 indicate moderate stability, and .2 to .4 show weak stability (Cohen & Cohen, 1983).

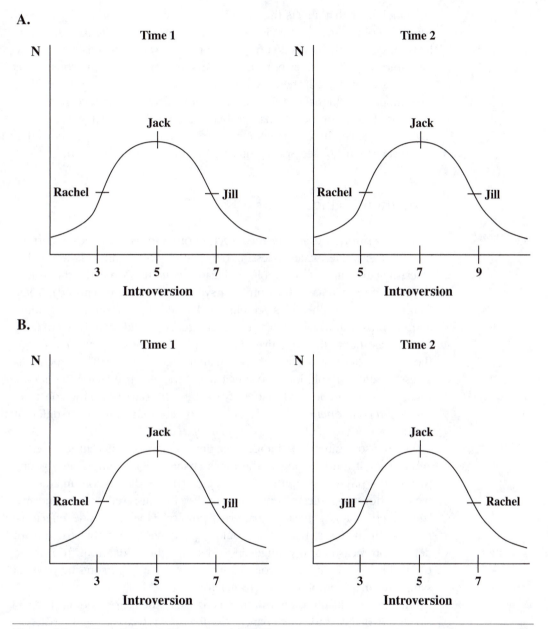

Figure 4.2   Correlational Change and Stability

One factor that affects the magnitude of the correlation is the *internal reliability* of the scale, which is a measure of how well the items in the scale intercorrelate. If the items do not "hang together" very well, reliability may be low—meaning that it does not clearly assess the construct. If the construct is not assessed very well, then the cross-time correlations may be lower than they should be. Nunnally (1978) recommends calculations that correct cross-time correlations for the internal reliability of the scales. Note that if scales are highly unreliable, these corrections may result in cross-time correlations that are greater than 1.0 (see Spiro, Butcher, Aldwin, & Levenson, 2000).

Structural Change

Factor analysis examines the structure or patterns in a series of correlations. For example, scales assessing depression typically include items that assess negative affect (feeling blue), negative cognition (thinking that everything is hopeless), as well as physical symptoms (being exhausted). Thus, factor analyzing such scales should yield three factors: affect, cognition, and symptoms. In other words, the affect items should intercorrelate fairly strongly, as should the cognitive ones and physical ones. A *factor loading* is the strength of the association between an item and a factor. Thus, the items assessing affect should load more heavily on the affective factor, and so on. Factor analysis can be used to identify the best items to assess the construct (*principal components*), or it can be used to determine if there are different dimensions or facets of a construct (*principal axis*).

Factor structures can change over time or vary in different samples or age groups, if the meaning of the items changes. For example, in a young person, the physical symptoms may be indicative of depression. In an older person, they may indicate depression, or they may also reflect either normal age-related changes in sleep patterns, physical illness, or side effects of medication. If this is true, one would expect that the factor structure of depression measures in younger individuals might be different from those used with older individuals. For example, in a younger person, the physical symptoms may load on the affective factor.

It may be difficult to tell whether a change in the factor loadings is really significant or just varies by chance. *Confirmatory factor analysis* (CFA) is used to assess structural change and stability and is a specific type of *structural equation modeling*, or SEM (Bentler, 1998; Long, 1983; MacCallum & Austin, 2000). SEM basically uses a type of factor analysis to "purify" the variance in a scale (i.e., make it more reliable) and then uses regression analysis to examine the relationship between these "purified" constructs. CFA allows a researcher to determine whether the factor loadings for a construct at Time 1 (or in one age group) are significantly different from the factor loadings for a construct at Time 2 (or in a second age group).

Figure 4.3 illustrates this. Let's assume we have a depression measure consisting of six items: two affective, two cognitive, and two physical. The indicator variables (or scale items) are represented by squares, and the latent construct (purified measure) of depression is represented by an oval. The factor loadings between the indicator variables and the latent construct are symbolized by the Greek letter lambda (λ). So λ_1 represents the strength of the association between affect 1 and depression, λ_2 between affect 2 and depression, and so on. In Figure 4.3, the first six lambdas (λ_1 through λ_6) represent the relationships between the items and the overall construct of depression in the younger group, and the second set of lambdas (λ_7 through λ_{12}) indicates the same relationships in the older group.

If there is structural stability, the λs should be comparable across the two models, that is, λ_1 should be similar to λ_6, λ_2 to λ_7, and so on. To determine this, CFA contrasts two models (Byrne, Shavelson, & Muthen, 1989). In Model 1, the Time 1 and Time 2 λs are assumed not to be equal but are allowed to vary freely, and in Model 2, the λs are assumed that they are equal and are fixed. For each model, the degree to which the hypothesized model differs from the actual data is indicated by a chi-square (χ^2): The smaller the χ^2, the better the model fits the actual data. A very good model is one in which the χ^2 is not significant—that is, the observed model is not different from the predicted model.

CFA calculates the difference between the two χ^2s to determine if the models are significantly different from each other. If the factor structure is not stable, we assume that the χ^2 for the Model 2 would be bigger than Model 1, because it is not a good fit to the data. If the χ^2 for the two models are not significantly different, then the freely estimated model is similar to (or replicates) the constrained model, so we would conclude that the factor structure is relatively stable across age groups.

CFA is a very complex technique, and it is not used very often. But it is very important, because it tests a critical assumption in developmental research. If the factor structure of a particular measure is not relatively stable across age groups or across time, you cannot use that measure to examine cross-sectional differences or change, because the meaning of the measure varies by age.

Ipsative Change

Ipsative or idiothetic change (Lamiell, 1981) refers to the process of examining change at the individual level rather than the group level. Lack of

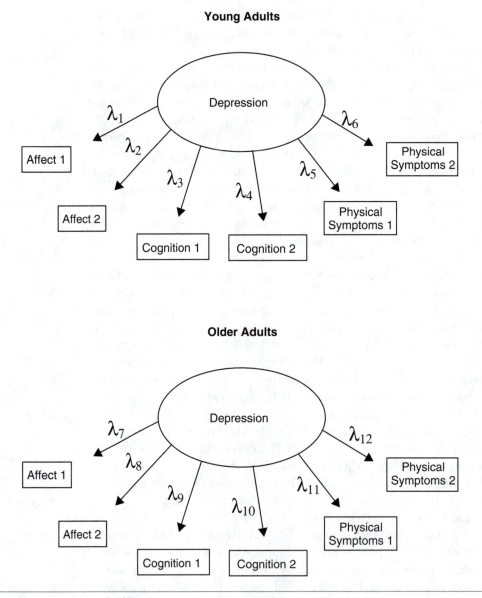

Figure 4.3   Structural Change

change at the group level does not necessarily mean that there is no change at the individual level. Figure 4.4 provides an example of two individuals who changed in different ways. Rachel had high scores on introversion at Time 1 but was low at Time 2, and Jill showed the opposite pattern. The difference

Introversion

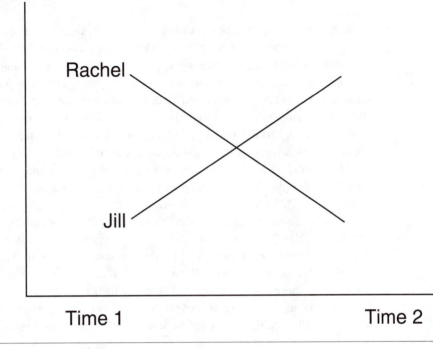

Rachel

Jill

Time 1   Time 2

Figure 4.4   Ipsative Change

between Time 1 and Time 2 for this group of two individuals would be 0—the group average did not change, but the individuals showed different and opposite trajectories.

One of the simplest ways to examine ipsative change is simply to look at *turnover rates*, or whether a person stays in the same category over time. For example, using the Normative Aging Study (NAS) alcohol data archive, Levenson, Aldwin, and Spiro (1998) showed dramatic differences between group and individual stability in problem drinking. At the group level, the percentage of NAS men who reported problem drinking remained roughly stable at about 5% at all three time points (1973, 1982, and 1991). However, there was a very high turnover rate—almost none of the men who were problem drinkers in 1973 still had problems in 1982, and most of the problem drinkers in 1982 did not report problem drinking in 1991. In fact, out of 1,056 men who had data at all three time points, only 25 (.02%) reported problem drinking at all three time points. So, although the group rates of problem drinking appeared stable, the ipsative data showed that individuals were not at all stable. Thus, one cannot generalize from group-level data to individuals.

A second way of examining change at the individual level is to calculate change or difference scores (e.g., $T_2 - T_1$). Several decades ago, Cronbach and Furby (1970) argued strenuously against the use of change scores, because they did not take into account differences in where individuals started. For example, a two-point rise in body temperature from 98°F to 100°F does not signify very much, but a change from 104°F to 106°F might well prove fatal. Cronbach and Furby argued that researchers instead should use residualized regressions to assess change (see below).

However, Rogosa (1988) argued for the utility of change scores, and sometimes simple change scores can prove very informative. For example, Spiro et al. (2000) showed how different methods of assessing change and stability in the same sample can yield dramatically different results. Over a 5-year period, MMPI-2 scores show great correlational stability, usually about .8. The standard interpretation would be that personality traits are very stable. However, change scores showed that 15% to 20% of the sample changed one standard deviation or more on each scale, which was clinically significant. Examining change over the various subscales showed that 70% of the sample had a clinically significant change on at least one of the subscales.

● STATISTICS THAT PREDICT CHANGE

Two-Point Designs

Often researchers want to use baseline data (Time 1) to predict some outcome (Time 2). The simplest way of doing this is to use either multiple regression if the dependent variable (y) is continuous, or logistic regression if it is categorical. However, two-point designs can quickly become very complicated.

In biomedical and psychosocial research, the outcome variable may occur over a period of time. For example, analyses predicting outcomes such as death or the recurrence of cancer will typically follow the sample over a period of several months or years. Not only will there be individual differences in whether the outcome variable occurs, but there may be differences in the timing of that occurrence. To analyze this type of data, researchers typically use a special form of logistic regression called Cox proportional hazards models (Cox & Oakes, 1984). In these models, occurrences of the outcome are referred to as events; cases that do not have the event by the study's end are censored. Relative risk ratios (RRs) are calculated which indicate the risk by period of time (usually years). An RR of 1.7 refers to a 70% increase in the risk of the outcome per unit increase of the independent variable relative to a comparison group, whereas .7 refers to a 30% decrease in such a risk. Epidemiologists often categorize the independent or predictor variable, in which case one of the categories is used as the reference group. For example, it is easier to comprehend a finding that pack-a-day smokers have a 70% increased risk of mortality compared to nonsmokers than a finding that there is an increased risk of 3.5% per every cigarette smoked per day.

Sometimes, however, researchers want to predict change in an outcome variable. If you have a continuous dependent variable, the easiest way to do this is simply to compute change scores $(y_2 - y_1)$ as the dependent variable. However, for reasons outlined above, change scores fell out of favor in psychological research, and residualized regressions became the most common way of examining predictors of change. *Residualized regressions* are hierarchical regressions in which the Time 1 dependent variable is entered first and thus covaried out, and other variables are used to predict the adjusted Time 2 scores.

For reasons that are not clearly understood, some researchers have begun using change scores as dependent variables in a residualized regression equation. This makes very little statistical sense, because it results in the same variable being on both sides of the equation.

$$y_2 - y_1 = y_1 + b_1 x_1 + b_2 x_2 + a$$

Solving the equation yields:

$$y_2 = 2y_1 + b_1 x_1 + b_2 x_2 + a$$

Logically, there is no reason why twice the level of the dependent variable at Time 1 should be used to predict the dependent variable at Time 2, so this may result in invalid negative betas. Thus, one should either use change scores as the dependent variable or residualized regressions, but not both.

Cross-Lagged Panel Designs and Analyses

Even with longitudinal data, causal directionality can sometimes be questionable. For example, we know that stressful life events can predict depressive symptoms, but people who are depressed may also be exposed to (or

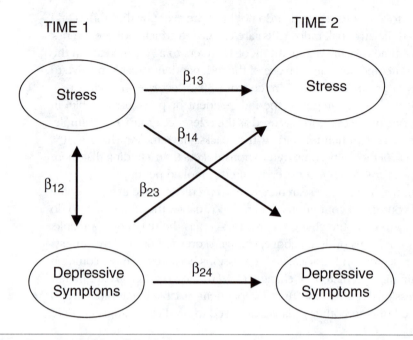

Figure 4.5   Cross-Lagged Panel Design

report) more life events. A cross-lagged panel design can be used to determine the relative strength of each pathway. Figure 4.5 depicts this cross-lagged design. Both stress and depressive symptoms are assessed at Time 1 and Time 2. The double-headed arrow between stress and symptoms at Time 1 indicates unknown causal directionality.

There are two ways of analyzing cross-lagged panel models. One is to compute two residualized regressions. The first predicts Time 2 stress, controlling for Time 1 stress (β_{13}) and examines the independent contribution of symptoms at Time 2 to stress at Time 2 (β_{23}). The second equation predicts Time 2 depressive symptoms, controlling for Time 1 symptoms (β_{24}) and then entering Time 1 stress (β_{14}). The relative sizes of the cross-lagged betas (β_{24} vs. β_{14}) reveal which path is stronger and therefore provide a clue as to causal directionality.

Another way of doing this analysis is to use structural equation modeling (SEM), which simultaneously estimates all pathways. This can provide the cross-lagged betas controlling for all the other variables in the model. To determine whether β_{24} is significantly different from β_{14}, however, one would compute four models. The first model would have only the autocorrelations

(Time 1 stress to Time 2 stress; Time 1 symptoms to Time 2 symptoms) and no lagged paths. The second would include the autocorrelations and one lagged path (e.g., β_{14}), and the third, the autocorrelations and the other lagged path (β_{23}). The fourth model would have all paths in it. One then compares the χ^2s of the different models to determine which lagged path significantly improves the goodness of fit, or if both of them do. If both lagged paths are significant, there is a *bidirectional* causal relationship.

Analyzing Multiple-Point Longitudinal Data

Longitudinal studies are becoming more sophisticated, and often they have more than two data points. Although one could use a series of correlations, regular MANOVAs, or SEMs to analyze data occurring at multiple points in time, missing data often results in unbalanced data sets, with different people having different numbers of valid follow-up assessments, making traditional analyses difficult or impossible to interpret. MANOVAs, for example, require complete data at all time points. If different people are in the sample at the different time points, the change in mean could be due to sample composition rather than time.

A number of different ways of examining multiple-point data have emerged in the past few years (for a review, see Affleck, Zautra, Tennen & Armeli, 1999). These types of analyses, called *growth curve models*, can be used to analyze ipsative data, that is, to determine change in individuals over time, as well as to predict it.

The simplest way of analyzing this data is to compute individual trajectories by fitting regression lines for each individual. This yields a predicted intercept (baseline) and slope (*B*) for each person. In a *two-stage growth modeling* approach (Raudenbush, 2000; Rogosa & Willett, 1985), the resulting intercepts and *B*s can be used as dependent variables in a second equation to predict change. Aldwin et al. (1989), again using Normative Aging Study data, computed individual trajectories, plotting age against symptoms, and showed a clear linear increase in physical symptoms over time. On average, men in the NAS sample developed one new symptom every 3 years.

As Affleck, Zautra, et al. (1999) point out, however, there are a number of problems with simply computing individual regression lines. They do not control for the correlated errors common in longitudinal data sets, and they may unduly capitalize on chance. Furthermore, the measure of the goodness of fit of the line, *root mean-squared error* (RMSE), may be inaccurate on an individual basis. RMSE measures how much the individual data points deviate from the predicted line; a large RMSE indicates that the fit is not very

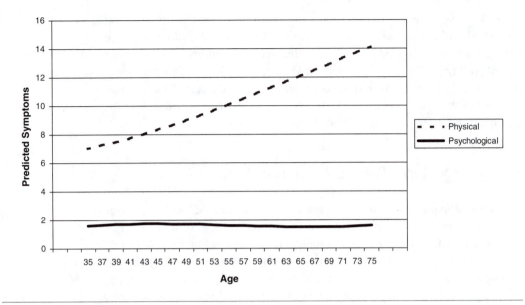

Figure 4.6   Fixed Effects Model

SOURCE: Aldwin, C. M., Spiro, A., III, Levenson, M. R., & Cupertino, A. P. (2001). Longitudinal findings from the Normative Aging Study. III. Personality, individual health trajectories, and mortality. *Psychology and Aging, 16,* 450-465. Copyright © 20012 by the American Psychological Association. Reprinted with permission.

good, a small one that the fit is good. However, if someone is stable and has an absolutely flat line, there is no (0) deviation, and the RMSE cannot be assessed accurately, as it would involve dividing by zero.

A more sophisticated way of estimating individual trajectories is to compute a *random effects model* (Willett, 1988), also called a *hierarchical linear model* (HLM; Raudenbush, 2000). In HLM models, the average trajectory is computed first (*fixed effects*), and then individual trajectories are computed as variants of the average curve, or how they differ (*random effects*). This yields an estimated curve for each individual, to avoid some of the problems with correlated errors, because these error terms can be modeled and the curves adjusted accordingly.

For example, Aldwin, Spiro, et al. (2001) examined changes in psychological and physical symptoms over time using random effects models. To examine nonlinear patterns of change over age, they included polynomials in their equations (age^2 and age^3). Using cluster analysis (similar to factor analysis, but grouping people rather than variables), they then identified patterns of change over time. As Figure 4.6 shows, the average slopes, or

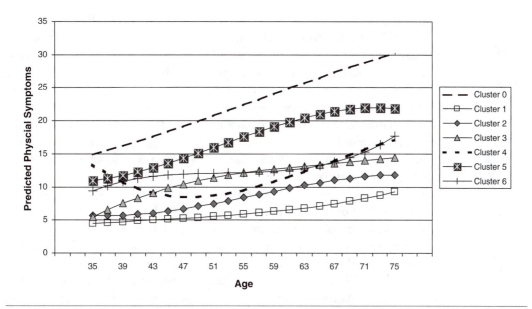

Figure 4.7   Random Effects Model

SOURCE: Aldwin, C. M., Spiro, A., III, Levenson, M. R., & Cupertino, A. P. (2001). Longitudinal findings from the Normative Aging Study. III. Personality, individual health trajectories, and mortality. *Psychology and Aging, 16,* 450-465. Copyright © 2001 by the American Psychology Association. Reprinted by permission.

fixed effects, were rather simple. Physical symptoms increased linearly, whereas there was almost no change in psychological symptoms. Figure 4.7 shows the random effects models for physical symptoms. Some individuals showed little or no change in the number of symptoms reported, but others showed exponential change. Individuals in particularly poor health showed asymptotic curves, whereas others resembled sine curves. Averaging the slopes ignored the astounding amount of individual differences in health over time.

Latent growth curve models are another way of examining multiple-point designs. This model is a variant of an SEM approach and can handle the type of missing data often found in multiple-point longitudinal designs, as well as correlated errors. It also can provide a more direct means of predicting change. A drawback, however, is that latent growth curves with more than three or four points tend to be difficult to analyze, especially if one starts examining correlated errors. (Take Figure 4.3 and multiply it by 5, for five time points, then start drawing arrows between all the different times, to generate a truly complex figure.)

In standard latent growth curve models, the goal is to determine which variables predict change rather than showing patterns in how individuals change. Thus, it is more a variable-centered than a person-centered approach. However, a new type of latent growth curve analysis, M+, does try to group trajectories (Bergman, 2001; Muthen, 2001; Nagin & Tremblay, 2001), but it has not as yet been widely used.

Generalized estimating equations, or GEEs (Diggle, Liang, & Zeger, 1994), are another way of examining trajectories over time and provide the advantage of being able to use time-varying covariates. In other words, GEEs can answer questions such as whether individuals' curves differ as a function of changes in some type of variable. For example, Schnurr, Spiro, Aldwin, and Stukel (1998) examined whether individuals' health trajectories changed as a function of exposure to trauma. They found that individuals who were exposed to both combat and noncombat trauma were likely to have steeper curves than those who were exposed to only one type of trauma (or who were lucky enough to avoid all trauma). Exposure to both combat and non-combat trauma resulted in an increased rate of symptoms change with age. The problem with GEE designs is that the metric is a little awkward. To examine symptom change, for example, a two-way interaction term—Symptoms × Time—is computed. To examine one covariate, a three-way interaction term is computed—Symptoms × Time × Trauma. Obviously, the more variables one has, the more complex the interaction terms, and power to examine multiple-level interactions can often be insufficient.

Growth curve analyses are quite new, and there are a number of problems to consider for which there are currently no set answers. For example, in examining developmental change, should one use age or time as the dependent variable? If one enters polynomial terms to examine nonlinear change with age, the age terms should be centered to control for multicollinearity. But if random effects models are used, should the mean age be used as the center, or the individual age? In latent growth curves, what criteria should be used to determine possible causal directionality? In GEEs, does one omit the outliers to smooth out the curve, or does omitting the outliers lose the rare (and possibly most interesting) cases? In estimating missing data, should the population average or the individual average be used? Or should a regression equation be computed that attempts to estimate the missing data based on what the trajectory predicts the response at that particular time should be?

● SUMMARY

The past decade has seen the emergence of new ways to analyze longitudinal data. These analytical techniques can answer more sophisticated questions, and they provide the opportunity to examine complex designs such as those needed to examine multivariate or transactional models. However, a serious problem with these types of analyses is that they are all extremely complicated and require sophisticated understanding. Interpreting the output of such programs is often more of an art than a science. Nonetheless, mastering them can help to answer some fascinating research questions, including what predicts different rates of aging.

SECTION II

AGING OF
BIOLOGICAL SYSTEMS

CHAPTER 5

AGING OF THE SKIN AND MUSCULOSKELETAL SYSTEM

This chapter covers two systems of the body, the skin and the musculoskeletal system. The skin provides the covering for the body and is the first line of defense against bacteria, viruses, and other types of environmental damage. The bones, ligaments, tendons, and muscles that make up the musculoskeletal system provide shape and support for the body, make movement and adjustments in position possible, and protect the internal vital organs from external trauma. The skin and the musculoskeletal system provide the most obvious external signs of aging, with both normal changes and disease processes.

The purpose of this chapter is to provide an anatomical overview of these systems, present normal age changes, and describe disease processes. We also address factors that accelerate aging processes and those that promote optimal aging.

● SKIN

Basic Anatomy and Physiology

The skin, or integumentary system, has several major functions. It is the front line of defense against harmful environmental influences and is an important part of our immunologic and endocrine systems. The skin is critical in temperature maintenance and, in general, aids in homeostasis. Sensory nerves in the skin allow us to monitor the environment but also warn us of danger through pain. Finally, the integumentary system has important symbolic functions in that it is a key component of our appearance and is a critical source of cues that affect social interaction. Aging of the skin is one of the most obvious clues to an individual's age.

The skin is the largest and most visible organ of the body. The outermost layer of skin is called the epidermis, and the second layer is the dermis. Beneath the epidermis and dermis is a layer of subcutaneous fat. Hair follicles, nail beds and nails, and sweat and sebaceous glands are embedded in the various layers.

The epidermis consists mostly of keratinocytes (more than 90% of all epidermal cells), cells that protect the skin from outside harm and help it heal if it is injured. As young cells, keratinocytes are found deep in the epidermis. They slowly move to the surface of the epidermis as they age, a process that takes about 30 days. If the skin is injured, the keratinocytes will reproduce and turn over at a more rapid rate, allowing the damage to be repaired. Keratinocytes are also necessary for the synthesis of vitamin D_3, which is eventually used in the absorption of calcium (Gilchrest, 1999).

Melanocytes, which make up about 2% of the cells in the epidermis, produce melanin for keratinocytes and give color to the skin. Exposure to the sun results in an increase in melanin production by these cells, which helps to protect the skin from damage. Finally, Langerhans cells, although they make up only about 1% of the cells in the epidermis, are an important part of the immune system. Along with the mast cells found in the dermal layer, they respond to toxic allergic stimuli.

The dermis consists largely of collagen and elastin tissue, which provides strength and elasticity to the skin. Blood vessels, lymphatic tissue, and nerves are imbedded in this connective tissue, as are the sweat glands and hair follicles. Cells in the dermis layer include mast cells that are responsible for the skin's ability to respond to allergens. Under the epidermis and dermis is a layer of subcutaneous fat, which consists mostly of adipocytes (fat cells). Subcutaneous fat gives shape and form to the body and provides protection and insulation.

Age-Related Changes

Changes in the skin are nearly universal with age, although there are large individual differences in the rate at which the integument ages. Changes in the hair follicles result in the graying and loss of hair. Wrinkles are partially due to a decrease in the subcutaneous fat layer and in the collagen and elastin found in the dermal layer. Some areas of the body are more likely to wrinkle than others. The skin over the nose almost always stays smooth, whereas there is usually some wrinkling around the eyes and deepening of the lines around the mouth.

In addition to cosmetic changes, there are a number of normal aging changes in the layers of the skin that affect its ability to protect itself and to maintain homeostasis (see Figure 5.1). A decrease in the size and number of keratinocytes limits the skin's ability to help the body produce vitamin D. Furthermore, the turnover rate of keratinocytes is reduced as much as 50%, limiting the skin's ability to heal (Gilchrest, 1999). A decrease in melanocytes affects the skin's ability to protect itself from the sun. Some of the remaining melanocytes clump together, leaving blotchy unpigmented areas of the skin (Goldfarb, Ellis, & Voorhees, 1997). The Langerhans cells decrease by as much as 40%, reducing the ability of the skin to respond to allergic stimuli.

The dermis is almost 20% thinner in an older person, and fewer fibroblasts in this layer make the skin less elastic and not as strong as that of younger people. These changes, in addition to fewer and increasingly thin-walled blood vessels, give the skin of an older person a fragile, almost translucent appearance. As can be seen in Figure 5.1, there is a flattening of the junction between the epidermis and dermis, which decreases the adhesion between the two layers. Because of these changes, the skin is much more likely to bruise and tear if an injury occurs, and less likely to heal. Furthermore, the decrease in blood vessel availability predisposes the older person to both hypothermia and hyperthermia (Gilchrest, 1999). Decrease in number of sensory nerves also results in decreased sensitivity to touch, injury, and to heat and cold. Thus, there is a lessened ability of the integumentary system to inform the sensory system of potential danger, which contributes to injury. Finally, a decrease in mast cells lowers antigen sensitivity.

Thinning of the subcutaneous fat layer also affects the ability of the body to maintain homeostasis with age. This thinning not only makes the skin more fragile, but the loss of insulation also increases the risk of an older person's developing hypothermia. In addition, the loss of sweat (eccrine) glands in the skin affects thermal regulation, decreasing the ability to sweat, which is one reason why elders are more vulnerable to high temperatures

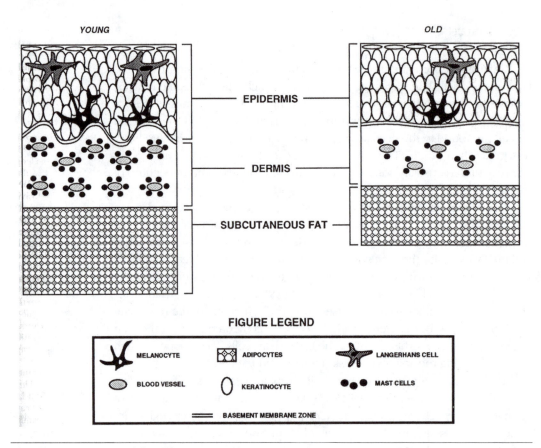

Figure 5.1 Aging of the Skin

SOURCE: Kaminar, M. S., & Gilchrest, B. A. (1994). Aging of the skin. In W. R. Hazzard, E. L. Bierman, J. P. Blass, W. H. Ettinger, Jr., & J. B. Halter (Eds.), *Principles of geriatric medicine and gerontology* (3rd ed., p. 413, Figure 41.1). New York: McGraw-Hill.

(hyperthermia) than younger people. Loss of subcutaneous fat changes the appearance of the older person, as the protruding angles of the jaw and elbows become more obvious. Thus, changes in the integumentary system not only decrease the skin's protective functions but also its appearance.

Disease-Related Processes

There are numerous skin disorders in later life. Most of these are relatively minor, creating mild discomfort or appearance problems, but some are dangerous and even deadly.

Xerosis

One of the most common dermatological problems of the older person is xerosis, or dry skin. Xerosis is characterized by red, scaly, and itchy skin on the legs, back and arms. The cause of xerosis is not known, although it may be associated with the slowing of the keratinocyte turnover rate. Xerosis is particularly troublesome during the winter months when people tend to spend a lot of time indoors in a warm and dry environment. Treatment is generally the application of skin creams (topical emollients) after bathing to slow the loss of water from the epidermis. Helpful emollients include those with lanolin, glycerin, lactic acid, and urea among their ingredients. Sometimes mild corticosteroid ointments help to heal severely affected areas (Gilchrest, 1999).

Seborrheic Keratoses

Seborrheic keratoses, or old-age spots, are benign (nonmalignant) lesions commonly found in older people. They are usually brown to black in color and have irregular edges; these can occur in young adulthood but appear more frequently with age. Because they are slightly raised, people frequently remark that they appear to be stuck on top of the skin. Although sun exposure is a risk factor for seborrheic keratoses, some people probably have a hereditary predisposition to develop them (Schleicher, 2000). It is important that they be evaluated, and possibly removed, to differentiate them from malignant growths.

Skin Cancer

Two of the most common forms of skin cancer are basal-cell and squamous-cell carcinomas. A basal-cell carcinoma appears as a small, fleshy bump or nodule (pearly in appearance), usually on the head or neck. The greatest risk factor for the development of this type of cancer is exposure to the sun. Although basal-cell carcinoma is very slow growing and metastases are rare, the lesions are generally removed in an early stage of growth to minimize further damage to the skin. It is relatively common for people with this type of a lesion to have a second primary growth.

Squamous-cell carcinomas are usually found on the face or the back of the hand. They have the appearance of a red, scaly, and hard patch, although they may become ulcerated and crusty with time. Exposure to the sun is a significant risk factor, but other risks include chronic irritations. For example, chronic dermatitis due to exposure to allergens or scarring from radiation or ulcers can increase the risk of this type of carcinoma. Squamous-cell carcinomas are always removed, and follow-up is very important as the risk of recurrence is great. These types of skin cancers can be very unattractive, and many older people wish to have them removed for this reason. Basal-cell and squamous-cell carcinomas are less likely to be found in younger people than are malignant melanomas (Schleicher, 2000).

Malignant melanomas are the most dangerous of the skin cancers. They are cancers of melanocytes, cells normally found in the epidermis of the skin. Typically, a melanoma is a red, white, blue, or black growth with an irregular border. These growths are painless, although they may ulcerate and bleed in later stages of development. Risk factors for this type of cancer include very light skin and blond or red hair, a family history of melanoma, and a history of severe intermittent sunburns, especially when young. Malignant melanoma cells may metastasize to the lymph nodes and then to other parts of the body, such as the liver or brain. Although they are usually found on the skin, a malignancy can develop as a primary site in the eye, the digestive tract, or the liver, because melanocytes are also found in these parts of the body.

Men are more likely to have malignant melanomas on the trunk of the body or the head and neck, and women on the lower legs or the soles of the feet. In recent years there has been an increase in melanomas on trunk sites in women, possibly due to changes in sun exposure among women. People with dark or black skin are less likely to develop melanomas, but when they do, these are more likely to occur under the fingernails or toenails or on the soles of the feet (National Cancer Institute, 2000).

Incidence rates of malignant melanoma have more than doubled in the United States in the past 20 years (National Cancer Institute, 2000). That said, it should be noted that there has been a drop in incidence rate in cohorts of women born in the 1930s and later and of men born after 1950 (Hall, Miller, Rogers, & Bewerse, 1999). Reasons for this slowing may include greater awareness of skin protection among these age cohorts. Malignant melanomas occur at all ages, but incidence increases with age and older people are more likely to die of the disease than those who are younger.

It is essential that malignant melanoma be detected early and treated aggressively. Those at risk for this type of cancer should have a specialist inspect their skin on a 6-month or yearly basis. Treatment options for melanomas include surgery, chemotherapy, and radiation.

Pressure Ulcers

Pressure ulcers are conditions of the skin that most often occur in those who spend long periods of time immobile in wheelchairs or beds. They are frequently called bedsores or decubitus ulcers, but the preferred name is pressure ulcer because they are caused by pressure over a susceptible tissue. This type of ulcer usually begins because an area of skin has been damaged or there is a breakdown of tissue over a bony prominence.

There are numerous risk factors for pressure ulcers in later years. The aging skin has fewer blood vessels and nerves, collagen tissue in the skin loses elasticity, and all layers of the skin are thinner, including the layer of subcutaneous fat. The ability to sense cutaneous pain decreases in later years and with disease, making people unaware that they have injured tissue (Thomas, 1997). Finally, pressure ulcers are more likely to occur in those who are unable to easily move themselves about, people with disabling illnesses such as a fractured hip, Parkinson's disease, or dementia.

Pressure ulcers are unsightly and can be very painful. Once begun, they are extremely difficult to heal, especially given the decrease in keratinocyte turnover rate, blood perfusion, and immunocompetence of the aging skin. Care of a pressure ulcer is problematic; they are often the bane of nursing homes and hospitals that care for frail older persons. Although not all patients are able to complain of the pain, many do, and it has been reported that pain medication in a significant number of cases is inadequate (Allman, 1999). Treatment includes adequate nutrition with protein, skin hydration, cleanliness, special beds (egg-crate-foam or alternating air mattresses), prevention of infection, and surgery to debride the unhealthy tissue of the ulcer. Pressure ulcers can take weeks or even months to heal, and some never heal. Therefore, prevention is far easier to accomplish than treatment.

Promoting Optimal Aging

The rate at which skin ages is influenced by genetics, disease, nutrition, smoking, socioeconomic status, and environmental conditions. People of some ethnic groups (Asian American, African American, and Latino) have fewer wrinkles and smoother skin than others. On the other hand, those who smoke or are exposed to harsh pollutants are more likely to have damaged skin.

The skin is one of the first systems to be affected by poor nutritional intake. Some of the most important elements of a healthy skin include adequate food and fluid intake. Protein is especially needed for healing and building new tissue, as the skin becomes more fragile if it does not get enough protein. Lack of vitamin A can cause xerosis, vitamin B deficiencies have been implicated in dermatitis, and vitamin C is needed for healing. Malnutrition is not an uncommon occurrence in older people, especially for those who must cook for themselves, have limited incomes, and do not have fresh fruits, vegetables, and meats available. The skin suffers when a person is chronically ill, primarily because of the toll that the illness takes on the nutritional status of the body. Therefore, general illness-prevention strategies will also help the skin.

Lifetime exposure to sunlight and inclement weather or pollutants has a major impact on the skin in later years. This can be seen in those who have worked most of their lives in the sun or in harsh environments. Smoking also has a profound effect on the skin, causing wrinkling and a leathery appearance. Although moisturizers cannot decrease wrinkles, they can mitigate their appearance. Furthermore, a topical medication, Retin-A, has been shown to improve sun-damaged skin and help increase skin smoothness (Goldfarb et al., 1997). There are a number of ways to protect the skin from the sun, including the use of hats, sunshades, and sunblock. Estrogen replacement therapy improves the appearance of aging skin and increases skin thickness in postmenopausal women (Cortes-Gallego, Villanueva, Sojo-Arnada, & Santa Cruz, 1996; Vaillant & Callens, 1996). Finally, Botox injections, face-lifts, chemical peels, and use of the laser have been successful in the removal of wrinkles and to help smooth the skin.

Healthy skin protects the body from the outside environment, helps maintain the integrity of the body systems, and is significant in how people perceive themselves. Appearance is important for most people, including those who are older. Looking good makes them feel good. Therefore, maintenance of healthy skin is important and can be maximized by both preventive and ameliorative actions.

● MUSCULOSKELETAL SYSTEM

The musculoskeletal system consists of hard tissue (the bones that constitute the skeleton) and soft tissue (including the muscles, ligaments, tendons, and cartilage). The musculoskeletal system is especially hard hit by aging, and most people have some wear and tear in this area as they get older.

Basic Anatomy and Physiology

Bones

The bones of the skeleton provide both structure and strength for the body. The size and shape of bones vary greatly, from the short, thin bones in the toes to the large, thick bones of the thigh. Regardless of size, all bones are made up of trabecular or cortical tissue. Cortical (compact) bone makes up the outer layer of all bones and constitutes the bulk of the long bones of the body (legs and arms). This type of bone is tightly packed or compact, which makes it both extremely strong and heavy, making up about 75% of the body's skeletal weight. Trabecular bone, which accounts for the remaining 25% of skeletal weight, is found largely in the vertebrae, ribs, cranium, and the ends of long bones (e.g., the end of the femur, or thigh bone). This type of bone is also extremely strong, but it is more porous than cortical bone and has a lacy or honeycomblike appearance (Meier, 1997).

Bones contain blood vessels, nerves, and bone marrow which produces and stores immature red and white blood cells. Bones also serve as storage sites for mineral salts, such as calcium, phosphorus, and magnesium, widely used for bone building and for functions such as muscle contraction and maintaining fluid and electrolyte balance. It should be emphasized that bone is not a static system but rather is dynamic, responding to internal and environmental demands. When more calcium is needed, such as for muscle contraction or during pregnancy, calcium is leached from the bones. Thus, bone tissue is constantly turning over, with old bone resorbed by osteoclasts and new bone generated by osteoblasts.

Soft Tissues

Ligaments and tendons are composed of extremely strong fibrous connective tissue. The tendons in the musculoskeletal system attach muscles to bones, and ligaments bind bones to bones and other structures of the body. These tissues work to stabilize the joints between the bones while allowing for flexibility and movement (Loeser & Delbono, 1999). The periosteum (fibrous membrane) that covers the bone serves as a place of attachment for both tendons and ligaments. Cartilage, a specialized type of connective tissue, is found on the ends of bones and acts as a cushion to protect the joints of the body, such as the knee joint. In addition, freely moveable joints, such as those found in the knee, are lined with a synovial membrane, and synovial fluid therein lubricates and protects the joints. Cartilage has no nerve or blood supply of its own, which affects the ability of this tissue to heal and renew itself. External fleshy structures such as the end of the nose are also composed of cartilage.

There are three different types of muscles. Skeletal muscles are striated, that is, the tubes of muscle fibers lie in rows. Each bundle of muscle fiber has a plate to which a motor neuron is attached. Stimulation by the nervous system either contracts or extends the muscle fibers, which pull against the skeleton, resulting in movement. Skeletal muscles make up about 40% of the body's mass. In addition to providing support and movement, friction caused by the movement of muscles helps to provide heat for the body. (Energy released by a number of metabolic processes heats the body. These processes include synthesis of proteins and other food sources and the friction of blood moving against walls of vessels.)

Smooth muscles are not attached to the skeleton but are found in the walls of internal organs and are responsible for contraction in the respiratory system and the digestive and urinary tracts. They also line the walls of the blood vessels to help with contraction and expansion. Smooth muscle is also found in all sphincters in the body, including the urinary bladder and pyloric sphincters.

The most complex muscle in the body is the cardiac muscle. These muscles contract an average of 72 times a minute, 24 hours a day, every day, for an entire lifetime. Unlike the other muscles of the body, cardiac muscle initiates its own beat, although the rate changes due to enervation by the sympathetic and parasympathetic nervous systems.

Age-Related Changes

Bones

Peak bone mass is achieved by the age of 30 and then declines, although there are factors that can accelerate or slow its loss. With increasing age, calcium metabolism is disturbed due to factors such as decreases in calcium and vitamin D intake. In addition, vitamin D is less well absorbed, in part as a function of sunlight deprivation. Serum calcium is maintained, as it is critical to ion transport and muscle contraction, but this maintenance comes at the expense of bone (Baylink et al., 1999).

As shown in Figure 5.2, there are age-related changes in both cortical and trabecular bone. The earliest and greatest bone loss occurs in the lacy or trabecular bone, increasing its porous look. Trabecular bone not only thins, but entire trabeculae (thin bars of bone) are lost and possibly not replaced, permanently weakening these areas (Baylink et al., 1999). Changes in cortical bone occur at a later time and at a slower rate, although decrease in thickness and increase in porosity eventually cause it to weaken as well. By very

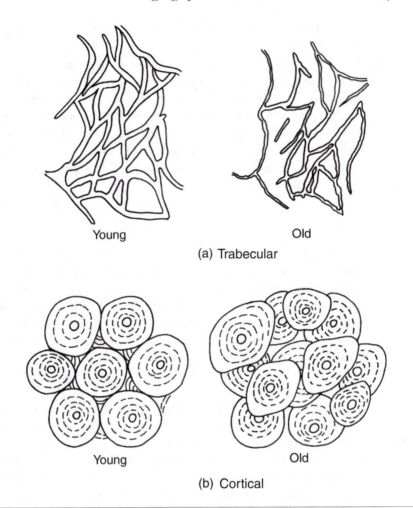

(a) Trabecular

(b) Cortical

Figure 5.2   Changes in Aging: Trabecular and Cortical Bone

SOURCE: DiGiovanna, A. G. (2000). *Human aging: Biological perspectives* (2nd ed., p. 196, Figure 9-6). Boston: McGraw-Hill.

late life, there can be a loss of as much as 50% of trabecular and 30% of cortical bone from their peak bone mass (Meier, 1997).

Women are at greater risk of bone loss than men, particularly in the years during and immediately following menopause. After menopause, there appears to be a slowing of bone loss for a few years and an increase in very late life (Black, 1995). Estrogen level, calcium intake and absorption, vitamin D status, physical activity, and genetics all have an impact on bone loss for women.

Men also lose bone mass, but at a slower rate than women. Baylink et al. (1999) suggest that this is because men are more physically active than women, even in late life, and the rate of decline of sex hormones in men is much slower than in women. Furthermore, the bones of young men are more dense, and men generally weigh more and maintain a heavier weight in later years than women. For both men and women, maintenance of adult weight may prevent some of the age-related decline in bone mass (May, Murphy, & Khaw, 1994).

Soft Tissues

Normal age-related changes in tendons and ligaments are caused by calcification, microtears, and increased cross-linking in the collagen tissue. Cross-linking causes stiffness and shortening of tendons and ligaments, which can result in as much as a 25% decrease in range of motion in the older person. The inflexible and shortened tendon or ligament can cause more than usual stress on the bone, damaging one that has been weakened by osteoporosis (Hamerman, 1994). Thus, an injury that would probably result in a torn tendon or ligament in a younger person may break a bone in an older one.

There are also changes in cartilage tissue with age, although it is difficult to determine if this is due to normal aging or to injury. As with ligaments and tendons, there appears to be an increase in cartilage stiffness, undoubtedly due to increased cross-linkages in the collagen tissue. There is no normal thinning of the cartilage with age, but there is a decrease in overall strength (Loeser & Delbono, 1999). As noted earlier, cartilage has little or no ability to heal itself, and when injuries occur, permanent damage can result in joints such as the knees (Pottenger, 1997).

Atrophy and muscle loss are inevitable with age, although the rate of decline varies across individuals (Loeser & Delbono, 1999). The receptor sites on the individual bundles of muscle fibers degrade, which results in atrophy of both the muscles and the motor neurons. The remaining muscle cells become enlarged but can only partially compensate for the loss of these cells. Age-related slowing in the nervous system further impacts muscle responsivity and the coordination that is necessary for movement, especially in those muscles responsible for fine motor control. Therefore, there is a decrease in muscle strength, endurance, and reactivity with age, although remaining active slows the rate of decline.

Normal changes in the musculoskeletal system can lead to an increase in disability. Changes in bone density, muscle strength, and joint flexibility affect the posture, sense of balance, and self-image of the older person. Decrease in muscle strength and agility will eventually affect the ability to perform both activities of daily living (ADLs) and instrumental activities of daily living (IADLs) (see Chapter 8), as it impairs walking and lifting, as well as an older adult's ability to maintain his or her body temperature. Inactivity and disuse of the musculoskeletal system can lead to a negative downhill cycle of loss of confidence in the ability to walk, decrease in mobility and physical activities, and fear of falling. This, of course, further weakens the physical ability of the older person.

Disease-Related Processes

In addition to the normal aging changes mentioned above, a number of diseases of the musculoskeletal system can lead to chronic disability, including osteoporosis, osteoarthritis, bursitis, tendinitis, and back pain. All of these disorders can have a major impact on an older person's physical and mental health.

Osteoporosis

Osteoporosis (porous bone) is characterized by bone loss and deterioration so severe that the bone can fracture. It is frequently called a silent disease, because bone loss occurs without any obvious symptoms. Both trabecular and cortical bone are affected by osteoporosis, with increased porosity of the trabecular bone and thinning of the cortical bone.

According to the Osteoporosis and Related Bone Diseases National Resource Center at the National Institutes of Health (NIH ORBD-NRC, 2000), osteoporosis affects more than 10 million men and women. In the United States, 60% of women 65 and over have some degree of osteoporosis, and 90% of otherwise healthy women over the age of 80 have abnormal bone density (Ott, 1999). European American and Asian American women, and those with low body weight and/or a family history of osteoporosis, are at higher risk of developing the illness than are African American women or those with greater body weight. Other risk factors include a diet low in calcium (especially in the teenage and young-adult years), early menopause, anorexia nervosa or bulimia, an inactive lifestyle, and excessive use of alcohol. Prescription drugs such as corticosteroids and thyroid medications can also increase the risk of osteoporosis. Although 80% of osteoporosis victims are women, men can have the disease as well. Less is known about the causes of osteoporosis in men, although calcium intake, genetics, and lifestyle options are probably risk factors.

Current predictions are that half of all women over the age of 50 will have fractures in their lifetime because of osteoporosis (NIH ORBD-NRC, 2000). Fractures can occur in virtually any part of the body, but some of the more common sites are the vertebrae, wrist, and upper part of the femur (hip).

Fractures of the lower thoracic and upper lumbar areas of the vertebrae are fairly common among people with osteoporosis. These fractures may go undiagnosed for some time, as there is frequently no specific injury to the back (sometimes just a sneeze can cause a fracture among those with severe osteoporosis). Furthermore, the pain of the fracture may be ascribed to osteoarthritis. Diagnosis is often made during a routine chest X-ray (Pottenger, 1997).

Although less common, multiple vertebral fractures (crush fractures) may also occur in those with osteoporosis, resulting in skeletal kyphosis, or dowager's hump. This is a severe and often painful condition of the spine that affects not only posture and height but other systems of the body as well. In some cases, the head and chest may be bent over to the extent that the lowest rib in the body is actually resting on the iliac crest of the pelvis. The collapse of the vertebrae can put pressure on the rib cage, which will compress the heart and the lungs, diminishing respiratory and cardiac function. The person with kyphosis may have to walk with the head downward, restricting the visual field and impairing balance and coordination. Driving becomes difficult, as does finding clothes that fit. People with this disease often have a great fear of falling, which further limits their willingness to maintain normal activities of life.

Wrist fractures are more common among those aged 50 to 60 and hip fractures among those aged 75 years and over. Reasons for these differences are age-related changes in gait and a lack of balance (see Figure 5.3). For example, whether a person falls and breaks a wrist or a hip is somewhat dependent on how fast that person walks and how he or she falls. In the first set of drawings in Figure 5.3, the older person is walking slowly and loses balance, therefore falling directly downward (or sideways) onto her hip (more on fractured hips later). The woman depicted in the second characterization is walking faster, with a more forward movement of the body. When balance is lost, she puts out her hands to catch herself (parachute reflex), risking a wrist fracture (Grisso & Kaplan, 1997). Therefore, fractures of the wrist are more common among those between the ages of 50 and 60 (Ott, 1999); hip fractures are more common in those 75 and older. Although a wrist fracture

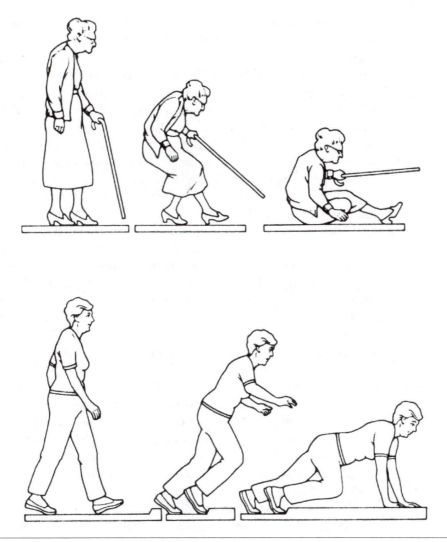

Figure 5.3   Gait and Risk and Type of Fracture

SOURCE: Grisso, J. A., & Kaplan, F. (1994). Hip fractures. In W. R. Hazzard, E. L. Bierman, J. P. Blass, W. H. Ettinger, Jr., & J. B. Halter (Eds.), *Principles of geriatric medicine and gerontology* (3rd ed., p. 1324, Figure 122-2). New York: McGraw-Hill.

is not considered life threatening, it is painful and immobilizing, and it can result in continued weakness of the affected wrist and a decrease in range of motion, even after recovery. Hip fractures, however, are usually very serious conditions.

The incidence of hip fractures differs greatly by gender and ethnic group. African American women are less likely to have hip fractures than European Americans or Asian Americans. Asian Americans, although they have lower bone density than European Americans, have fewer hip fractures. (One theory includes anatomical structure differences between ethnic groups.) Latino women have about half as many hip fractures as European American women, but more than African Americans (Ott, 1999). Socioeconomic status is also a risk factor; in one study, those who were married and had the highest incomes were less likely to experience hip fractures (Farahmand et al., 2000).

Although it is frequently suggested that a spontaneous hip fracture causes a person to fall rather than vice versa, this is only true in about 5% of cases (Ott, 1999). In addition to gait disturbances, mobility problems, and diminished visual acuity, use of psychotropic medications and visual impairment are risk factors for hip fractures.

As shown in Figure 5.4, fractures of the hip occur primarily in two areas of the upper femur, about half in the intertrochanteric area and half in the femoral neck or subcapital (intracapsular) area. Fractures in the intertrochanteric area are usually due to diminished bone density, whereas those in the femoral neck are attributed to mechanical factors, such as a bad fall. As might be expected, the proportion of fractures occurring in the intertrochanteric area increases with older years, especially among women (Ott, 1999). Surgery is almost always required to repair a fracture, and recovery can be arduous and lengthy. Rehabilitation usually takes place in nursing homes, which are called on more and more to provide physical therapy to older people in the hope that they will be able to return to their homes and live as independently as possible.

Rehabilitation from a fractured hip is moderately successful, although the subsequent fear of falling detracts from the willingness to become independent and the person may remain dependent on the use of a walker or cane. Social support can become an important part of the healing process. In one study, older women with fractured hips reported fewer depressive symptoms and greater improvement in walking skills if they had adequate social support early in the recovery period (Mutran, Reitzes, Mossey, & Fernandez, 1995). It is important that social support members encourage and facilitate mobility and independence rather than an increase in dependency (Tinetti & Powell, 1993).

Older people fear the possibility of having a fractured hip, as it is generally thought to be a harbinger of disability and death. In truth, it is one of the few skeletal disorders associated with significant mortality. About 20% of older people who have hip fractures die within a year, not necessarily because of the fracture but due to secondary causes or because the person was debilitated (Cooney, 1999; Pottenger, 1997).

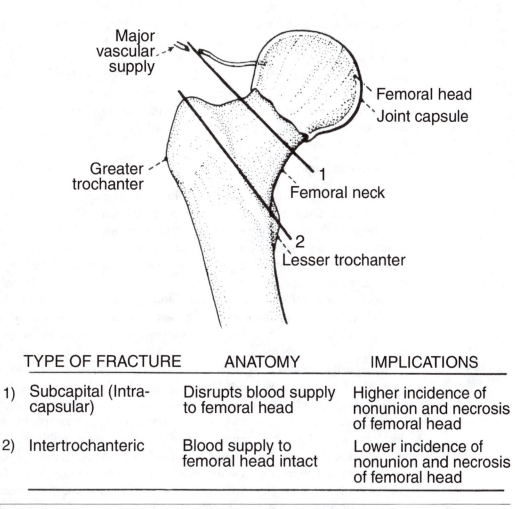

Figure 5.4   Common Areas of Hip Fracture

TYPE OF FRACTURE	ANATOMY	IMPLICATIONS
1) Subcapital (Intra-capsular)	Disrupts blood supply to femoral head	Higher incidence of nonunion and necrosis of femoral head
2) Intertrochanteric	Blood supply to femoral head intact	Lower incidence of nonunion and necrosis of femoral head

SOURCE: Adapted from Kane, R. L., Ouslander, J. G., & Abrass, I. B. (1994). *Essentials of clinical geriatrics* (3rd ed., p. 240, Figure 8-1). New York: McGraw-Hill.

A number of medications are used to treat osteoporosis. Calcitonin is a naturally occurring hormone that works directly on osteoclasts to prevent trabecular bone loss (Meier, 1997). Bisphosphonates are synthetic medications that have been used successfully to increase bone mass. Fosamax is an example of a bisphophonate which has been quite helpful in improving bone density. Estrogen has also been used extensively and, according to Ott (1999), hip fractures in older women could be cut in half by the use of estrogen replacement therapy alone. Recent data from the Women's Health Study, however, have suggested that estrogen plus progesterone replacement therapy for women should be limited due to the increased risk of heart disease and breast cancer (Rossouw et al., 2002). Other researchers have been testing the use of hormone replacement therapy at lower doses, hoping to minimize the risks while maintaining the protective aspects of the hormones (Harvard Women's Health Watch, 2002).

Osteoarthritis

It is now believed that osteoarthritis, the most common form of arthritis, is not a single disease but a group of osteoarthritic disorders (Creamer & Hochberg, 1999). In this disease, the protective cartilage thins or is damaged, allowing the bones of the joints to rub together, resulting in injury. It is unclear whether the disease starts in the cartilage or the bone. For example, if the cartilage is damaged, it can fail to protect the bone, but thickening of the bone may result in damage to the cartilage. As shown in Figure 5.5, changes in both the cartilage and the bone of the knee are evident as the disease progresses. Further, there is an increase in bone spurs and synovial fluid.

Osteoarthritis causes swelling, stiffness, and tenderness around affected joints, most often the hips, knees, fingers, or intervertebral joints, but it is seldom found in the elbows or ankles. Pain can become very severe, changing the gait and affecting the balance of the afflicted person. Osteoarthritis seldom causes problems in the young, although the disease probably starts at an earlier age than symptoms would indicate. By the age of 55, most people will have some osteoarthritis. On the other hand, not every older person has osteoarthritis and not every joint is affected in those who have the disease.

Osteoarthritis is not a result of normal aging process in the joints, as many of the changes found in the cartilage and bone in this disease are different (and sometimes opposite) from normal aging changes. The changes in osteoarthritis are also different from those found in osteoporosis; increased bone turnover in osteoarthritis thickens bones, whereas the disease processes in osteoporosis thin the bones. Thus, it is rare to find these two diseases co-occurring (Loeser & Delbono, 1999; Stewart, Black, Robins, & Reid, 1999).

Genetics, obesity, persistent wear and tear, and prior injuries may all play a role in the development of osteoarthritis (Sorensen & Blair, 1997). Overuse of joints may be one of the biggest risk factors for the disease. Lane, Hochberg, Pressman, Scott, and Nevitt (1999) found that the risk of osteoarthritis of the hip was highest in older women who were highly active as teenagers or did weight-bearing exercises in their 30s. Older participants in the Framingham

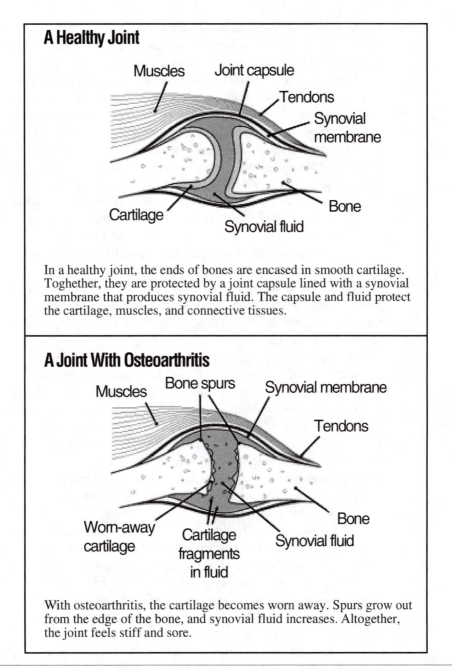

A Healthy Joint

In a healthy joint, the ends of bones are encased in smooth cartilage. Toghether, they are protected by a joint capsule lined with a synovial membrane that produces synovial fluid. The capsule and fluid protect the cartilage, muscles, and connective tissues.

A Joint With Osteoarthritis

With osteoarthritis, the cartilage becomes worn away. Spurs grow out from the edge of the bone, and synovial fluid increases. Altogether, the joint feels stiff and sore.

Figure 5.5   Osteoarthritic Changes of the Knee

SOURCE: NIH. National Arthritis and Musculoskeletal Skin Disease, National Institute of Health.

Heart Study had increases in osteoarthritis of the knee when they were involved in heavy physical activity; this was especially true among those who were obese (McAlindon, Wilson, Aliabadi, Weissman, & Felson, 1999).

Although osteoarthritis is not a disease that causes death, it is linked to high levels of disability. Many people complain of severe stiffness, especially on waking in the morning or after a long period of inactivity (e.g., sitting in a chair or sofa for an extended period of time). Those with severe osteoarthritis may suffer from depression because of the pain and immobility caused by the disease. Briggs, Scott, and Steele (1999) studied the quality of life of older people with and without osteoarthritis. Those with the disease had significantly lower quality-of-life scores—including those for vitality, social functioning, and general health—when compared to those who were unaffected.

Treatment of osteoarthritis is centered around maintenance of the joint function and pain relief. For example, physical therapy helps to maintain muscle strength and joint mobility. Exercises that minimize weight bearing (to protect the joint) are recommended, such as swimming and low-impact aerobics. Aerobic conditioning (walking or aquatics) has proven to be a well-tolerated method of maintaining strength and mobility without creating damage to the joints.

Although the mainstays of medications for osteoarthritis are the non-steroidal anti-inflammatory medications (NSAIDs), injections of corticosteroids into joints may be used for those more severely affected. Surprisingly, estrogen replacement therapy may protect against osteoarthritis as well as osteoporosis (Nevitt et al., 1996). Glucosamine sulfate, a nutritional supplement used by veterinarians in the treatment of joint diseases in animals, is now being used, with sodium chondroitin and manganese ascorbate, to treat humans who have mild osteoarthritis (Das & Hammad, 2000). Although results are not conclusive, there is some evidence that vitamins C and E and beta carotene are also beneficial (Creamer & Hochberg, 1999).

Alternative forms of health care, such as acupuncture and yoga, are also being used to treat osteoarthritis. Acupuncture is widely used in Asian countries to treat the pain of osteoarthritis, but its use has yet to be widely accepted in the United States. Yoga is often practiced in the Western world as an exercise of stretching and relaxing, and recent studies suggest that it may help to relieve some symptoms of osteoarthritis as well as other musculoskeletal diseases (Garfinkel & Schumacher, 2000).

Management of osteoarthritis can be difficult, but educational programs to help people deal with the problems of chronic disease (by controlling pain but maintaining exercise) have been successful. Lorig et al. (1999) found that participants in educational programs had a higher quality of life and fewer physician visits than those who did not. Social support is beneficial in helping people continue with exercise programs or maintain medication regimens. Those with severe disability, functional limitations, and pain from osteoarthritis may eventually choose to have surgical replacement of the injured joint (Creamer & Hochberg, 1999).

Bursitis, Tendinitis, and Back Pain

Other disorders of the musculoskeletal system include bursitis, tendinitis, and back pain. Bursitis is inflammation of the fluid-filled sacs (bursas) that are found where muscles or tendons cross over bony prominences, such as the knee or shoulder; tendinitis is inflammation of a tendon. These disorders are usually due to an injury or years of overuse of the joint, although age-related changes in these structures also puts a person at risk. Bursitis in the shoulder may limit a person's ability to reach above his or her head, and tendinitis in the elbow decreases the strength and flexibility of the arm. Thus, these relatively simple problems may greatly impact ADLs and IADLs.

Back pain, probably the most common source of discomfort and limitation in older people, has a number of different causes, including damage to the vertebrae due to degeneration of the disks and resulting compression of the nerves. Back and abdominal muscles frequently weaken with age, resulting in increased risk of muscle strain and poor posture. Although bursitis, tendinitis, and back problems are found in younger people, they occur more frequently in later years.

Treatment for problems of the back and joints usually involves rest and NSAIDs, along with an exercise program that strengthens and stretches muscles to prevent tissue atrophy. There are a number of relaxation programs, such as the Alexander technique, that teach how to relax muscles, easing the pain of the shoulders, back, and neck. Frequently, old habits and practices must be relearned, such as lifting with the leg rather than the back muscles. Even simple motions like brushing the hair can aggravate bursitis in the shoulder. Part of the problem in treating bursitis or tendinitis is the difficulty of getting older persons to change long-established patterns of behavior. In some cases, the environment needs to be modified, as in lowering cabinets for easier accessibility, substituting Velcro for buttons on clothes, and using assistive devices.

Promoting Optimal Aging

Maintenance of the musculoskeletal system into very late years is vitally important to physical, social, and mental health. Exercise and adequate protein intake can decelerate the loss of muscle mass that occurs with aging. Both men and women can gain muscle size and strength with long-term weight-training programs, even in very late life (McCartney, Hicks, Martin, & Webber, 1995; Taaffe, Pruitt, Pyka, Guido, & Marcus, 1996). This increase in muscle mass permits the performance of basic ADLs such as walking, getting up out of chairs, and carrying groceries. Greater flexibility also allows the person to get dressed more easily, move the neck and head so as drive safely, and participate in normal everyday activities in general. In addition, the greater the muscle mass, the easier it is to maintain and regulate body temperature.

The maintenance of healthy bone tissue depends on a number of factors, including adequate intake and absorption of calcium and vitamin D. In one study, more than half of Danish nursing home residents had low blood vitamin D levels, probably due to insufficient intake of this vitamin and inadequate exposure to the sun. Vitamin D supplements were recommended, as well as increase in sun exposure (Rasmussen et al., 2000). Some nursing homes in northern climates have started using tanning beds to increase vitamin D production. Smoking and excess caffeine intake can accelerate the loss of bone mass and should be avoided.

Researchers are studying the effects of herbal products and dietary sources of phytoestrogens on reducing the side effects of menopause, including minimizing bone loss. Chiechi (1999) reported that diets high in phytoestrogen (a soy-based product) may decrease postmenopausal symptoms and increase bone density. Scheiber and Rebar (1999) reviewed the still preliminary literature and suggested that isoflavones (one class of phytoestrogens) are a safe alternative to estrogen and appear to be useful in treating low bone mass. Much of this literature relies on animal models, and more testing in women is needed.

Immobility and inactivity also accelerate bone loss. Thus, movement and weight-bearing exercise are essential to the growth and maintenance of bone tissue, especially trabecular bone. Regular physical activity is important not only in preventing osteoporosis but also in reducing the incidence of fractures in those who have the disease (Forwood & Larsen, 2000). Weight-bearing exercise such as walking or lifting weights helps to increase bone density and strength, as there is a direct positive relationship between bone volume and mechanical strain on a bone. (Swimming, although it confers cardiovascular benefits, does not help to strengthen bone.) Moderate levels of weight gain in later years may protect against osteoporosis, as women who have gained weight since the age of 25 have a lower incidence of fractures (Cooney, 1999).

Exercise stimulates the synovial tissue to produce synovial fluid, helping to lubricate joints and protect them against arthritis (although extremely heavy exercise may damage the musculoskeletal system). Exercise can improve strength, endurance, and mobility and can decrease the incidence of falls among older people who have suffered previous falls; this is true for men as well as women (Rubenstein et al., 2000). Many older adults do not take part in exercise programs for fear of falling (Bruce, Devine, & Prince, 2002), yet remaining active is one of the most important protective factors for risk of falling. Finally, long-term tai chi classes have been shown to improve balance in a group of people over the age of 80 (Wolfson et al., 1996), and yoga may be beneficial in improving muscle flexibility and strength, as well as maintaining flexibility in ligaments and tendons.

SUMMARY ●

Skin, muscle, and bone are living, breathing tissue that need adequate nutrients and exercise to maintain health. The skin in particular reflects the rate of aging of the body as a whole, given that it is affected by chronic illness. The skeleton is also a very dynamic system, serving as a reservoir for calcium and other minerals needed for metabolism, nerve transmission, and movement. Damage to the musculoskeletal system greatly affects the quality of life in later years. Osteoporosis and osteoarthritis afflict well over half of the older population and are responsible for many limitations in functional ability, to say nothing of the pain and suffering that they cause. Although we are developing better treatments for these diseases, prevention is by far the better course. The primary way to maintain the health of the musculoskeletal system is through good nutrition and moderate exercise. As discussed in the next chapter, exercise is important in maintaining the health of many internal organs as well.

CHAPTER 6

AGING OF THE INTERNAL ORGAN SYSTEMS

T his chapter discusses aging of the cardiovascular, respiratory, gastrointestinal, and renal/urinary systems. These systems are extraordinarily complex, and we provide only a brief overview of the basic anatomy and physiology of each system. We focus on describing normative age-related changes (i.e., changes common enough that most older adults can expect to experience them) and discuss the common diseases and malfunctions of the individual systems that can accelerate the aging process. A section follows on how to delay or slow aging in each of the systems.

● CARDIOVASCULAR SYSTEM

Basic Anatomy and Physiology

The cardiovascular system is the body's main transportation system. It sends supplies such as fluids, nutrients, hormones, oxygen, and antibodies to tissues in the body while at the same time removing waste products such as carbon dioxide and hydrogen ions. The system is composed of the heart, blood vessels (arteries, arterioles, capillaries, veins, and venules), and blood. In general, arteries carry blood away from the heart, and veins carry blood to the heart.

Blood is a highly complex fluid composed of water, red and white blood cells, and platelets, as well as nutrients such as fat globules, carbohydrates, and proteins. It is perfused by gases such as oxygen, carbon dioxide, and nitrogen. Blood also carries electrolytes, to help maintain the acid/base balance, and a host of other chemicals, including hormones, neurotransmitters, and various other peptides necessary to regulate homeostasis, cognition, movement, and every other function of the body (Guyton & Hall, 1996).

The heart is the center of the circulatory system. It is located behind the chest wall, in a slightly canted position, with the midsection somewhat to the left of the sternum, or breastbone. It is enclosed in a fibrous sac called the pericardium. The left and right sides of the heart each have two upper chambers (atria), which collect the blood, and two lower chambers (ventricles), which pump blood to the lungs and the rest of the body (see Figure 6.1). Anatomically, the atria are thin-walled; the walls of the ventricles are thicker and more muscular, as they do the long-distance pumping.

The right and left sides of the heart each serve as a pump. Oxygen-poor blood is collected in the right atrium from the large veins of the body, the superior and inferior vena cava. From there it flows to the right ventricle and is pumped via the pulmonary arteries into the capillary system of the lungs for carbon dioxide and oxygen exchange. Oxygen-rich blood is sent via the pulmonary veins to the left atrium, from where it flows to the left ventricle and is pumped out through the aorta. The blood from the aorta flows into the large arteries and then to the smaller arteries, arterioles, and capillaries.

The capillaries are so small that they are literally only one cell wide, ensuring that all cells in the body have access to the bloodstream. Fluid, nutrients, electrolytes, hormones, and other substances are exchanged in the capillaries. Venules collect blood from the capillaries and move it into larger and larger veins until it finally reaches the superior and inferior vena cavae. Veins serve as a huge reservoir for the body's blood supply, as 64% of its volume is found in the veins (Guyton & Hall, 1996). The walls of the arteries and veins are composed of flexible smooth muscle, elastic fibers, and collagen. Nerve cells in their walls regulate the expansion and contraction of the blood vessels, helping to regulate blood pressure and blood flow.

As shown in Figure 6.1, valves from the atria to the ventricles and from the ventricles to the lungs and the rest of the body keep the blood flowing in one direction. These valves also serve to control the timing and amount of blood flow. The right and left sides of the heart have no direct connection to

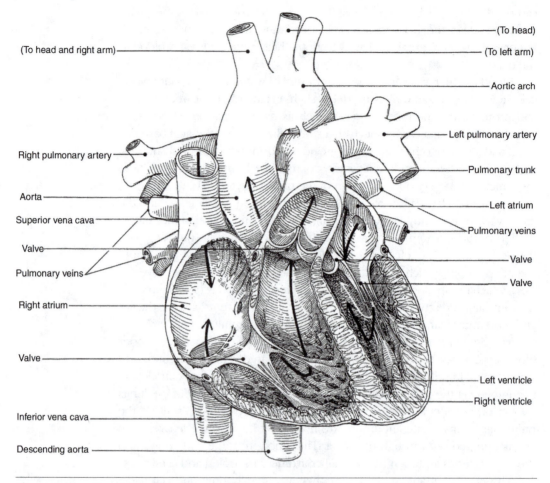

(To head and right arm)

(To head)

(To left arm)

Aortic arch

Left pulmonary artery

Right pulmonary artery

Pulmonary trunk

Aorta

Left atrium

Superior vena cava

Pulmonary veins

Valve

Valve

Pulmonary veins

Valve

Right atrium

Valve

Left ventricle

Right ventricle

Inferior vena cava

Descending aorta

Figure 6.1   Structure of the Heart and Blood Flow Through the Chambers

one another and, in a healthy heart, oxygen-poor blood is never mixed with oxygen-rich blood.

The timing of the two pumps is exquisitely coordinated. A beat is started in the sinoatrial node, or pacemaker, in the upper part of the right atrium. Once started, the signal spreads down the heart through the atrial myocardium to reach the atrioventricular node. From there the impulse is conducted to the atrioventricular bundle and to the Purkinje fibers where it is sent on to both ventricles. As the signal moves down, contraction of the cardiac or heart muscle occurs. Contraction of the heart is called systole and relaxation diastole. Asystole means there is no heartbeat. The first and loudest sound of a heartbeat ("lub") is when the valves between the atria and ventricles close and the ventricles contract. The second, softer beat ("dub") occurs with the closure of the valves between the ventricles and the large arteries (pulmonary and aorta).

The movement of arterial blood reflects the fact that it is being pumped rhythmically, which creates a pulse felt in many different areas of the body. Most people are familiar with the pulse of the carotid artery on the neck and the radial pulse on the outer edge of the wrist. The pulse can be felt in other parts of the body as well, such as the one on the top of the foot (pedal pulse) and the back of the knee (popliteal pulse).

Only the arteries reflect the heartbeat, however; veins do not have the benefit of the heart as a pump to help push the blood along. As noted earlier, the veins are more like a holding reservoir for blood than pressurized tubes. To help keep blood moving up to the heart and to prevent it from pooling in the extremities, some veins have valves, for example, the great saphenous found in the back of the legs. These valves consist of tissue inside the vein wall that extends into the vein (like a flapper valve) forcing the blood to flow in only one direction, toward the heart. In addition, skeletal muscle movement puts pressure on the vein to keep the blood moving. For example, activities such as walking cause the skeletal muscles to squeeze the veins, and, because the valves in the legs allow blood to move in only one direction, it has to flow back to the heart. This whole system is referred to as the venous pump.

Venous blood can be seen in the distended veins of the hands and feet, especially after exercise. If a person stands perfectly still for 15 minutes or more, the venous pumps are less able to work and the normal flow of blood to the upper part of the body is lost, which can cause fainting (a serious problem for Buckingham Palace guards, which is why they move periodically). Other problems can result from constriction of the veins. When a person sits for a long period of time in an airplane seat, for example, damage to a vessel can occur and possibly lead to blood clots.

The rate of blood flow is largely determined by physical demands on the body. For example, when exercising, blood flow needs to be increased not only to deliver more oxygen and other nutrients but also to remove waste, such as lactic acid. Thus, the heart alters its rate of pumping depending on both external and internal demands. Stimulation to decrease and increase the heart rate is under the direction of the autonomic nervous system, with the sympathetic nervous system increasing rate and strength of the heartbeat, and, to a lesser extent, the parasympathetic system decreasing its rate and strength (Guyton & Hall, 1996).

The value of the cardiovascular system to the functioning of every cell in the body is inestimable. As well as delivering blood and nutrients to all tissues of the body, it serves as the conduit for communication among the organs. As will be seen, the health of the cardiovascular system greatly affects the well-being of every other organ in the body. Thus, it is not surprising that the first arteries to leave the aorta go to the heart muscle, ensuring that the heart has the most oxygen-rich blood.

Age-Related Changes

There are a few normal changes in the cardiovascular system with age. Most studies, although not all, report a normal enlargement of the heart mass with age, due to increase in size of the muscle cells or myocytes. There is also a slowing of the electrical activity of the heart. By the age of 75, only about 10% of pacemaker cells that are found in younger people remain. Furthermore, there is an increase in the amount of fat tissue around the sinoatrial node, which interferes with the conduction system (Lakatta, 1999), which can lead to an abnormally slow pulse, called bradycardia. This condition is often treated by giving the person an artificial pacemaker that keeps the heart from falling below a preset rate.

Changes in the collagen in the middle layer of the large arteries of the body cause them to thicken and become stiff. These arteries widen and lengthen, providing more space for blood, which initially is helpful in controlling blood pressure. Over time, though, the larger size and rigidity of these large arteries require the heart to work harder, eventually increasing blood pressure. Interestingly, there is not a similar physical change among the smaller arteries in the body (Lakatta, 1999). There is a decreased ability of the smaller arteries to dilate or constrict when necessary, however, affecting the exercise tolerance of the older person as well as the body's ability to cool or heat itself. The capillaries become even narrower with age, which impedes the normal flow of blood at the cellular level. There are minimal changes in the veins; thus, there is little impact on their normal functioning.

Overall, heart function is less efficient with age. There is a decrease in cardiovascular responsiveness to exercise and a reduction in the maximum heart rate that can be reached. It also takes longer for the heart rate and the blood pressure to return to normal resting levels following a stressful event. On the other hand, exercise can mitigate some of these aging effects.

Most of the normal aging changes have little impact on the everyday functioning of an older person. Cardiovascular disease is very common in later life, however, and results in the majority of disability and deaths among older adults.

Disease-Related Processes

Hypertension

Optimal blood pressure for adults over the age of 18 is 120/80 or lower. (The first number refers to the systolic and the second to the diastolic pressure.) Blood pressure is still considered normal at a reading of 130/85, but at 140/90 or greater, it is classified as hypertension (although some have argued that 160/90 is normal for older adults). Hypertension is one of the most prevalent problems in the older population. About a quarter of European Americans and a third of African Americans over the age of 65 have hypertension (Applegate, 1999). Systolic hypertension (a high reading in systolic pressure only) increases throughout life, whereas an elevation in diastolic pressure tends to level off in later years.

High blood pressure affects all the major arteries of the body and the organs and tissues that they serve. Highly variable (or labile) blood pressure refers to the rapid expansion and contraction of the arteries. Both conditions damage the collagen in the arterial walls, making them stiffer. It also damages the lining of the arteries, contributing to atherosclerosis, and increases the risk of heart and kidney disease, peripheral vascular disease, and cerebral vascular accidents (strokes), which can lead to dementia (see Chapter 7). One of the dangers of hypertension is that damage from the disease occurs in the absence of symptoms. Hypertension has a number of causes, including changes in kidney function, obesity, hormonal changes, increased sensitivity to sodium, and genetic propensities. It also results from arteriosclerosis and atherosclerosis, which will be discussed below.

The first step in managing hypertension is to encourage lifestyle changes such as weight control, a decrease in sodium intake, high calcium and magnesium intake, and an increase in physical activity. Diuretics are the first drugs of choice to control hypertension, although they should be used cautiously as side effects can be severe, including low blood pressure, confusion, impotence, and depression. Because of adverse side effects, Applegate

(1999) suggests that when medications are used for the older person, the initial daily dose should be half that recommended for middle-aged people. Thus, prevention through behavior change may be preferable to pharmaceutical treatment. Health education and peer counseling are effective ways to enhance patient compliance with diet, exercise, and use of medications. For example, women with heart disease who met weekly with educators did more exercising and had fewer health complaints than a control group (Clark et al., 2000).

Arteriosclerosis and Atherosclerosis

Arteriosclerosis refers to the thickening and loss of elasticity of arterial walls. Stiffened arteries tend to be slightly contracted, raising blood pressure and leading to hypertension, which can create further damage to the walls. Thus, high blood pressure both results from and is a cause of arteriosclerosis.

One of the most common forms of arteriosclerosis is atherosclerosis, or the deposition of plaques inside the arterial wall. Atherosclerosis creates a disruption of blood supply to all systems of the body, for example, the heart and kidneys, and accounts for at least half of the mortality in Europe and North America (Chang & Chait, 1999). The disease usually starts with an injury to the inner lining of an artery, which can be caused by trauma (including high blood pressure), toxins, or viruses. Cholesterol, especially in the form of oxidized low-density lipoproteins (LDLs) and triglycerides, dead blood cells, and other materials in the blood, can adhere to these rough spots or injured areas, causing plaques to form (see Figure 6.2). Plaques are sticky; eventually they attract more dead cells, blood clots, and bacteria, further narrowing the artery and creating an inflammatory process (see Chapter 7). High-density lipoprotein (HDL) is the "good" form of cholesterol because it is not sticky and is less likely to adhere to the arterial walls.

The first visible sign of atherosclerosis is a fatty streak on the inner wall of the artery. The growth of this plaque into the middle layer of the artery causes it to stiffen and weaken. With time, the artery becomes narrower and less elastic, reducing the flow of blood to vital areas of the body including the brain, heart, and legs. Increased blood pressure results from the heart's attempt to push blood through these narrowed arteries. Blood clots or hemorrhaging can occur in these damaged blood vessels, which further disrupts blood flow to the organs of the body (Chang & Chait, 1999).

Risk factors for both arteriosclerosis and atherosclerosis include being male, having a family history of the disease, smoking, a diet high in saturated fat, diabetes, hypertension, obesity, and leading a sedentary lifestyle. High

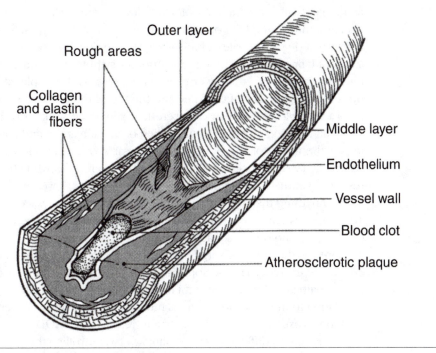

Figure 6.2   Progression of Atherosclerosis in an Artery

SOURCE: DiGiovanna, A. G. (2000). *Human aging: Biological perspectives* (2nd ed., p. 76, Figure 4.7). Boston: McGraw-Hill. Reprinted with permission of the McGraw-Hill Companies.

levels of homocystine (a non-protein-forming sulfur amino acid) associated with aging also increase the risk of cardiovascular disease (Singh & Rosenberg, 1999). Most likely, a number of these factors coexist and interact to cause the disease. Atherosclerotic processes may begin at a young age, although the incidence of the disease increases with age. The primary treatment for atherosclerosis includes a decrease in dietary cholesterol and exercise, as well as lipid-lowering medications such as the statins. Surprisingly, although the statins do lower cholesterol, they may have little effect on mortality (Newby et al., 2002). Statins are also being studied as possibly protective against Alzheimer's disease, as there is a link between cardiovascular health and dementia (see Chapter 7).

Peripheral Vascular Disease

Atherosclerosis can also damage peripheral blood vessels. In peripheral arterial occlusive disease (PAOD), arteries that carry blood to the legs and feet are partially or completely blocked due to atherosclerosis, resulting in a decrease in the supply of oxygen and nutrients to these areas. Symptoms of PAOD include pain, a pale or bluish color to the skin of the feet and legs, and a lack of hair growth in these areas. Another symptom is a weak or nonexistent arterial pulse in the lower extremities, such as the popliteal and pedal pulses felt at the back of the knee and the top of the foot, respectively.

Lack of blood flow causes severe leg pain when walking or exercising. The pain can stop a person from walking or moving about and consequently impair the ability of the older person to carry out activities of daily living (Gardner, 1999). In later stages, pain can be severe even while the person is resting. Eventually, ulcerations and gangrene of the lower extremities can result. Anything that slows the flow of blood to the legs exacerbates PAOD. This includes smoking (constriction of blood vessels), diabetes (impaired circulation), and physical inactivity.

One of the primary ways of treating peripheral vascular disease is to encourage exercise. The person with PAOD is encouraged to walk until limited by pain and then to rest until the pain diminishes. This improves blood circulation to the area and increases muscle strength, among other things. In addition to exercise, the most important treatment of PAOD is to stop smoking, an extremely difficult but important key to controlling the symptoms and progression of the disease.

Coronary Heart Disease

Coronary heart disease (CHD) results from atherosclerosis of the coronary arteries of the heart. It the leading cause of heart disease in the older population and is a major cause of disability and death. Among those over the age of 65, about 85% of deaths from heart disease are due to CHD (Wei, 1999). Heart disease typically occurs at an earlier age for men than for women, although after menopause, there is a rapid progression of the disease in women, probably due to a decrease in estrogen levels. In later years, the incidence of CHD for men and women is similar, although women are less likely to be diagnosed or treated for the disease. The arteries of women are smaller, and this may lead to differences in presentation of symptoms. The small size may also make them more vulnerable to even minor problems, as well as compromising surgical success.

African American men and women have a higher death rate from heart disease than European Americans until age 80. After 80, however, there is a crossover effect, and the death rate for European Americans is higher than that of African Americans (Kramarow, Lentzner, Rooks, Weeks, & Saydah, 1999). Risk factors for coronary artery disease include smoking, high blood pressure, high cholesterol, being overweight, and having an inactive lifestyle. Abdominal and chest fat are especially dangerous risk factors for the disease.

Angina pectoris is a common symptom of coronary heart disease. It develops when the demand for blood to the heart muscle is greater than what can be supplied. It can be a temporary, although painful, condition that resolves when the person is resting or relaxed. On the other hand, angina pectoris is one of the symptoms of an impending heart attack, especially among older people. Generally, angina is felt as pain that radiates to the left shoulder and down the left arm or to the jaw or back. However, older people may also have dyspnea (difficulty breathing), coughing, or confusion (Wei, 1999). Therapy must include a moderate, acceptable exercise level, as it is important that the older person be able to remain active. Treatment may also include nitroglycerin or other pharmaceuticals, although careful monitoring and follow-up are necessary, because side effects are common.

Coronary heart disease can lead to a myocardial infarction (MI) or heart attack. This occurs when an artery in the heart is blocked because of a blood clot. The blood clot could be lodged at the site of an atherosclerotic artery or it could move to a smaller artery and block the blood flow at that point. In either case, blood circulation to that particular heart muscle is stopped and damage to tissue occurs. Severe pain from an MI can be experienced as a crushing chest pain and often serves as an important diagnostic indicator. Symptoms in older adults, however, can be more obscure, for example, confusion, abdominal pain or a severe headache (Amendo, Brown, Kossow, & Weinberg, 2001). These symptoms can be confusing for the practitioner, making appropriate diagnosis difficult. Among older people, an MI can even be silent or occur while sleeping or at rest.

The initial goal of caring for someone with an MI is to reduce further heart damage and the risk of heart failure. Angiograms and catheterization are used to determine how occluded the arteries are, and treatment includes the administration of medications to thin the blood and control the rhythm of the heartbeat. Both coronary bypass surgery and angioplasty have been successfully used on older people, although the rate of mortality is higher, both before and during surgery, in this group. Furthermore, the 10-year survival rate among those who have been treated medically or treated surgically is very similar (Wei, 1999).

Changes in health behavior habits such as quitting smoking, improving diet, and beginning an exercise program are the keys to successful post-MI rehabilitation. One of the most popular therapies to reduce reoccurrences of MIs is to take a low dose of aspirin daily or even weekly to reduce blood clotting.

Long-term goals post-heart attack are to strengthen the heart through cardiac rehabilitation, health education, diet, and medication. Cardiac rehabilitation is an extensive physical therapy program that includes health education programs and physical exercise under close supervision. Many post-heart attack patients stay in the program for years. It has been proven to be beneficial even for the very old (Forman & Farquhar, 2000).

Heart Failure

One definition of heart failure is the cessation of a heartbeat, with death imminent. Another use of the term *heart failure* describes a heart that is no longer able to pump blood to meet the metabolic needs of the body's tissues. This is the type of heart failure addressed in this section. Unlike hypertension and coronary artery disease, which are found among younger people, heart failure is almost exclusively a disease of older people.

In heart failure, the left ventricle is less able to pump blood out through the aorta and into the arteries of the body, so the supply of oxygen and nutrition to the body's tissues is reduced. Other systems of the body are affected by this reduction in blood supply. For example, the kidneys (already affected by normal aging changes that limit their ability to respond to stress) restrict the excretion of sodium and water, which creates an excess of fluid in the body's venous system, including an increase in blood flow to the heart and lungs. Simultaneously, fluid builds up in the lungs because the left ventricle is a less effective pump (Carelock & Clark, 2001). Increased pressure in the capillaries of the lungs causes fluid to seep into the lung tissue, especially the alveoli. If the condition is severe enough, a bubbling sound can be heard in the lower part of the lungs. This excess fluid reduces the amount of oxygen and carbon dioxide that can be exchanged in the lungs (Guyton & Hall, 1996). Overt symptoms of heart failure include shortness of breath, fatigue, confusion, and lethargy.

The decrease in mortality from hypertension and CHD in recent years has led to an unfortunate increase in incidence of heart failure. In other words, people with heart disease are experiencing greater longevity, albeit with hearts that are weakened. About 10% of those over the age of 80 have some degree of heart failure (Rich, 1999), and it is a frequent reason for hospitalization among older adults. A number of factors can exacerbate heart failure, including anything that causes fluid retention, such as a diet high in sodium and the use of estrogens. Nonsteroidal anti-inflammatory medications (NSAIDs), commonly used by older people, conserve water and sodium in the system, creating abnormal fluid levels in the body (Page, 2000).

Treatment of heart failure includes smoking cessation, change in diet, and exercise, as well as medications (antihypertensives and diuretics) to reduce the edema or swelling caused by fluid intake. Many older people with heart failure find it difficult to follow a treatment plan, and they need support from both family and medical personnel to understand the illness, its treatment, and its progression. Proctor, Morrow-Howell, Li, and Dore (2000) found that self-perceived adequacy of formal and informal support while being cared for in their homes led to fewer rehospitalizations among older adults with heart failure. A randomized clinical trial also showed that education and support were successful in reducing the rate of readmission to hospitals for those with heart failure (Krumholz et al., 2002).

Promoting Optimal Aging

There are a number of ways that diseases of the cardiovascular system can be slowed or delayed, and deceleration of these disease processes can lead to many additional years of healthy life. Prevention of cardiovascular disease should begin early in life, although there can also be benefits to lifestyle changes in later life.

Especially important are changes in diet: decreasing cholesterol intake from meat and dairy products and ingesting sufficient amounts of fruits and vegetables. Folic acid may be particularly important in preventing cardiovascular disease. We are beginning to recognize that cardiovascular disease is an inflammatory process, and antioxidants such as vitamin E may also be helpful. Light to moderate alcohol use may help to prevent heart disease, although high levels can promote it.

Smoking harms the cardiovascular system by damaging arterial linings, constricting blood vessels, increasing blood pressure, and promoting atherosclerosis. Thus, not smoking is critical to maintaining good cardiovascular health. Health education programs can be of some assistance in helping people cope with nicotine dependence and withdrawal (Galvin, Webb, & Hillier, 2001). For those who have extreme difficulty in quitting, sometimes the prescription of antidepressants is helpful.

Aerobic exercise has a protective effect on the cardiovascular system, and individuals who have followed a lifelong program of exercise have better cardiovascular function than others. Exercise decreases weight, lowers cholesterol, and strengthens the heart muscle. In times of need, physically fit older adults can increase their cardiac output 50% more than can those who are not in good physical condition (Guyton & Hall, 1996). For those who have cardiovascular disease, exercise continues to be beneficial, although the heart rate needs to be carefully monitored during aerobic exercise.

Alleviating stress is also important. In a study of men with coronary artery disease, Manchanda et al. (2000) found that those who practiced yoga for a year had fewer angina attacks, decreased weight, and increased exercise capacity when compared with those in the control group.

Changing lifelong health behavior habits can be very difficult, but social support from others can help. In one cardiovascular disease prevention program, men and women rated their physicians as their most important support persons (Mosca, McGillen, & Rubenfire, 1998), although, in another study, support from the spouse was especially important for adherence to medical regimes among CHD patients (Coyne & Smith, 1994). Change can be difficult, but there are great benefits to be accrued from adopting a healthy lifestyle.

● RESPIRATORY SYSTEM

Basic Anatomy and Physiology

The primary function of the respiratory system is to transfer oxygen from the air into the bloodstream and to remove carbon dioxide. The breathing process is highly complex and involves not only the respiratory tract but also the muscles of the abdomen, chest, and diaphragm. To breathe in, the diaphragm and intercostal (rib cage) muscles of the chest contract, causing the diaphragm to lower and the thoracic cavity to expand. The decreasing pressure in the chest cavity creates a relative vacuum that forces the air to flow into the lungs. With expiration (breathing out), the relaxing diaphragm bows upward and the intercostal muscles relax, allowing the air to leave the lungs.

A pleural lining surrounds the outside of the lung tissue, and another one lines the chest wall. These two linings do not touch each other; instead, a fluid flows between them, lubricating the movement of the lungs. Constant suction of excess pleural fluid into lymphatic channels creates negative pressure between the pleural linings, which holds the lungs to the thoracic wall.

As shown in Figure 6.3, air travels from the nasal cavities into the nasopharynx, the trachea, and the bronchi. Finally air moves into the bronchioles and the alveoli. Each of these avenues for passage of air is smaller than the previous one. The alveoli are perfused by capillaries, and it is in the alveoli that blood gases are exchanged, replenishing the supply of oxygen and extracting carbon dioxide from the blood. The lungs have the most extensive capillary network surface of any organ in the body.

The respiratory system processes the air before it enters the bloodstream, warms and moisturizes the air in the nose and trachea, and guards

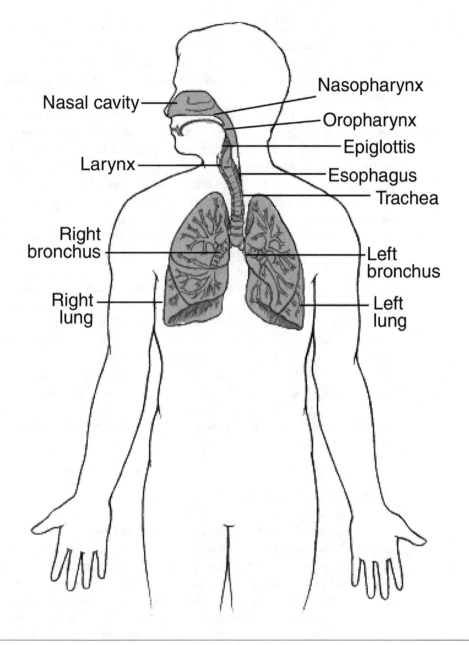

Figure 6.3   Anatomy of the Respiratory Tract

SOURCE: AMA's Current Procedural Terminology, revised 1998 edition, retrieved from http://www.medem.com/MedLB/article_detaillb.cfm?article_ID=ZZZQZDECGJC&sub_cat=522. Reprinted with permission of the American Medical Association.

the body against invasion by germs, viruses, and other toxins. Mast cells lining the respiratory tract are the immune system's first line of defense against airborne germs and viruses. Sneezing and coughing are reflexes that serve to clear the upper and lower respiratory passages, respectively. Cilia (tiny hairlike structures that line the respiratory tract) clear mucus and other detritus from the lungs with an upward sweeping motion. The control center in the brain, which governs the rate and depth of breathing, is located in the medulla oblongata and pons (Guyton & Hall, 1996). This center carefully balances the need for oxygen and the need to get rid of excess carbon dioxide. In part, the respiratory rate is governed by the lung volume (amount of air expired with each breath). When a person is resting quietly, this amount is called the tidal volume. The more active the person, the more deeply and frequently he or she must breathe. The vital capacity of the lungs is a combination of the tidal volume and the extra amounts a person can inspire (inspiratory reserve volume) and expire (expiratory reserve capacity). Vital capacity is measured by the total amount a person can expire after taking a deep breath. Even when as much air as possible is blown out, some residual air is still left in the dead spaces in the lung (residual volume). Thus, total lung capacity consists of the vital capacity and the residual volume. A common measure of lung function is forced vital capacity (FVC), which is determined by blowing as hard as possible into a spirometer, an instrument that measures the volume of air inhaled and expelled. Breathing problems such as asthma and chronic obstructive pulmonary disease are diagnosed by lower than normal forced expiratory volumes occuring in the first minute (FEV_1).

Age-Related Changes

A number of age-related changes in the respiratory system decrease the lungs' ability to exchange oxygen and carbon dioxide. Intercostal and diaphragm muscles become weaker and atrophy with age, and the chest wall becomes stiffer, reducing the ability of the lungs to expand and contract. Age-related changes in collagen and elastin cause the lung tissue to become less elastic and airways to be open for a shorter period of time. As shown in Figure 6.4, alveoli become enlarged and flattened with age. The bronchioles (small airways) that lead from the alveoli collapse, trapping the air. These physiological changes result in an uneven exchange of oxygen and carbon dioxide, a decrease in vital capacity and an increase in air left in the lungs after maximal expiration.

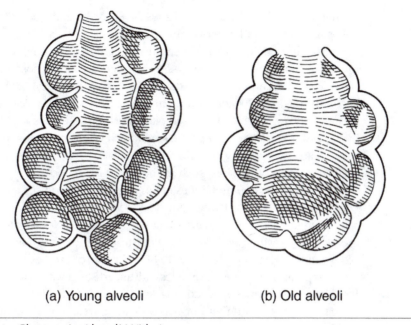

(a) Young alveoli   (b) Old alveoli

Figure 6.4   Changes in Alveoli With Age

SOURCE: DiGiovanna, A. G. (2000). *Human aging: Biological perspectives* (2nd ed., p. 104, Figure 5.8). Boston: McGraw-Hill. Reprinted with permission of the McGraw-Hill Companies.

In addition to the above aging changes, there is a normal decrease in the cough reflex, which reduces the ability of airways to clean themselves and fight infection. Furthermore, ciliary function decreases with age, as does T-cell immunity (Witta, 1997).

Normal age-related changes in the respiratory system do not have a major impact on the daily functioning of the older healthy person, although they can result in a decreased capacity for exercise and maximal exertion. Furthermore, changes in the respiratory system can make the older adult more vulnerable to illness late in life.

Disease-Related Processes

Lung Cancer

Currently, lung cancer is the leading cause of cancer death in both men and women in the United States. The rate of death from lung cancer has changed in the last decade, but varies by ethnicity and age. Since the early 1990s, when the incidence of death from lung cancer reached its peak, death rates from lung cancer have decreased among European American men aged 65 to 84, but increased among African American men, those aged 85 and older, and women (Sahyoun, Lentzner, Hoyert, & Robinson, 2001). Smoking accounts for up to 90% of all lung cancers, and risk for the disease is directly related to how much a person smokes. Furthermore, it is well-known that even passive exposure to cigarette smoke is very harmful. Most primary lung cancers are the result of smoking, but secondary lung cancers can occur as metastasis from other sites, such as the breast or the bone.

The two most common types of lung cancer are small-cell and non-small-cell cancer. The small-cell lung cancers generally grow rapidly and have a high rate of metastasis (they usually spread very quickly). Non-small-cell cancers are slower growing, less likely to metastasize, and more common among older adults (Maghfoor & Perry, 1999). Therefore, lung cancer among the older population is generally at a less advanced stage when diagnosed and is less likely to have metastasized (Blackwell & Crawford, 1997). These factors increase the likelihood that lung cancer can be treated in older adults.

Unfortunately, lung cancer is often underdiagnosed among older people. One reason is that many symptoms of the disease—such as persistent cough, shortness of breath, and weight loss—are common occurrences in late life, especially in those who have other diseases. Therefore, careful screening of older persons who present with these symptoms is critical (Maghfoor & Perry, 1999).

Lung cancer is frequently undertreated in older people, although they do well with current therapies. Santambrogio, Nosotti, Bellaviti, and Mezzetti (1996) found that surgical treatment of non-small-cell lung cancers was equally beneficial for the old as for the young. Chemotherapy is also useful in treating non-small-cell lung cancers in older people, although side effects from the chemicals used in treatment can be especially harmful for this age group. Fortunately, new chemotherapy drugs used to treat these cancers are less toxic than previous ones, which make them more acceptable for use with older adults (Manegold, 2001). Therefore, advanced age alone should not be a limiting factor for treatment of lung cancer.

As is true with all persons undergoing treatment for lung cancer, older adults and their families require extensive supportive care to maintain a reasonable quality of life. They also need emotional support and palliative care if the disease is terminal. Treatment of pain is particularly important, and medication should be used liberally without worry that it might become addictive.

Pneumonia

Although infectious diseases are not the frequent cause of death that they were at the beginning of the 20th century, pneumonia is still a serious illness for a frail older person. As might be expected, pneumonia is especially virulent among those over 80 and those who live in crowded places such as institutions. Pneumonias found in nursing homes are often caused by unusual and more virulent organisms than those circulating in the community (A. Duxbury, personal communication, August 2002). The disease can spread rather rapidly among nursing home patients, putting older residents at great risk of morbidity and death.

Frail older people are particularly vulnerable to pneumonia because of normal aging changes in the lungs, including decreased lung capacity, inadequate cough reflex, and a decline in immune function. Comorbid conditions, such as diabetes or heart failure, further limit the ability of the body to heal itself or to recover from an infectious lung disease. Finally, normal aging changes in the renal system hamper its ability to maintain homeostasis. Inactivity is particularly dangerous, as the bedridden or wheelchair-using person is less able to move about, breathe deeply, or cough productively, which makes it difficult to move secretions out of the airways. Furthermore, coughing can be very tiring and debilitating for a frail older person (Stollerman, 1997).

Aspiration pneumonia is a fairly common occurrence among the very old, especially those who have difficulty drinking, eating, or taking medications (Marrie, 2000). It is caused by the aspiration (inhalation) of substances such as food, fluids, or medications into the respiratory tract. Because the right bronchi is shorter and has a less acute angle than the left bronchi (as it leaves the trachea), aspiration of a foreign body is more likely to occur on that side (Thomas, 1993).

Pneumonia can be difficult to diagnose among older people. Young people with pneumonia typically have fever, chills, or a cough, whereas an older person may have none of these symptoms. Instead, symptoms may include confusion, poor appetite, or weakness that has resulted in a fall. In some cases, confusion and loss of ability to perform normal activities are the only symptoms (see Chapter 9).

Pneumonia is treated fairly successfully with antibiotics, but the recovery period for an older person can be lengthy and debilitating. Ambulation and mild exercise are essential in the recovery process to prevent deconditioning. It is preferable that people be treated for the disease at home, as older persons are especially vulnerable to infections acquired in hospitals.

It is important that older adults protect themselves from contracting pneumonia. Prevention includes eating a good diet, getting adequate rest, and avoiding exposure to those who may have pneumonia. The National Institute on Aging recommends that pneumococcal and influenza vaccines be given to all persons 65 years of age or older. These vaccines are most effective in those who are immunocompetent but also provide some protection for immunocompromised people (Stollerman, 1997).

Chronic Obstructive Pulmonary Disease

Chronic obstructive pulmonary disease (COPD) is a general term for several diseases of the respiratory tract, two of the most common of which are chronic bronchitis and emphysema. (The majority of people with chronic bronchitis also have emphysema.) COPD is a leading cause of both morbidity and mortality among the older population, ranking as the fourth leading cause of death in those 65 years of age and older.

COPD is often underdiagnosed among the older population because many of the symptoms, such as shortness of breath, fatigue, and coughing, are assumed to be normal signs of aging. Yet older adults are at great risk for the disease because they grew up in an era when smoking was fashionable and the public was not aware of the dangers of air pollution. COPD is strongly related to cigarette smoking, although not all people who smoke develop COPD. This generation of older adults may also have worked in dangerous environments (exposure to asbestos, lead in paints) that put them at risk for COPD.

Chronic bronchitis is the most common of the COPD disorders. In chronic bronchitis, the cells of the respiratory tract are inflamed and secrete copious amounts of thickened mucus, making it difficult for the person to clear his or her respiratory tract. With time, it becomes increasingly arduous to breath as the mucus becomes thicker and the bronchials narrow. The person tries to clear the tract by coughing and expectorating the thick mucus, but this becomes tiring over time and may produce exhaustion. A crackling sound can be heard in the chest as people with chronic bronchitis breathe in and out through the mucus that has settled there.

Emphysema is characterized by abnormal and permanent deterioration of tissue at the end of the respiratory tract, in the smallest bronchiole and alveoli. With time, there is scarring on the surface of the alveoli and they become less elastic. Over time, alveoli become flattened and unusable or are lost outright. Thus, there is increasingly limited alveoli surface area for gas exchange, causing shortness of breath. Furthermore, there is an excessive secretion of mucus, and the alveoli and bronchiole close prematurely with expiration. The person with emphysema has to work hard to exhale and get rid of trapped air.

Despite their different pathology, the diseases that comprise COPD have common characteristics. In each condition, there is difficulty in exchanging gas in the respiratory tract and a decrease in maximal expiratory flow. It is not uncommon for the person to overuse accessory respiratory muscles, such as the sternocleidomastoid muscles in the upper chest, to aid in expanding the lungs. Diaphragm and intercostal muscles are used less over time, and these muscles decline in strength, which further limits respiratory function. The chest can take on a barrel shape with the overuse of all of these muscles. In later and more severe stages, all of the person's energy goes toward breathing. Even the smallest effort to walk or to carry groceries can be difficult for the person with these diseases, and quality of life is compromised. As might be expected, people with COPD are more likely to rate their health as fair or poor than others, and twice as likely to report that there are restrictions on their activities of daily living (Webster & Cain, 1997).

Early diagnosis and treatment of COPD are important to help maintain and optimize pulmonary health, prevent further damage to the lungs, and minimize the risk of other respiratory diseases, especially pneumonia. Pharmaceutical treatment often consists of steroids to reduce the inflammation in the bronchi, bronchodilators to open them up and ease breathing, and antibiotics when appropriate. In severe cases, individuals may need to use an oxygen tank to help them breathe. Smoking cessation is critical, as many victims of these diseases are current smokers. (Nicotine is an anti-inflammatory and bronchodilator and may help to temporarily relieve symptoms, but the tars in cigarette smoke only result in further long-term damage.) Pulmonary function can be enhanced through aerobic exercises and muscle reconditioning, including flexibility and strength training. Good nutrition is extremely important in helping to maintain the energy and protein requirements needed to live with the disease. Nearly one quarter of people who have severe COPD are malnourished due to anorexia (loss of appetite), the increased metabolic demand of laboring chest muscles, fatigue, depression, and dyspnea (difficulty breathing) while eating or preparing meals (Witta, 1997). Education and family support are very important because COPD can be frightening, and assistance and understanding from caregivers are critical.

Tuberculosis

Tuberculosis (TB) is a bacterial infection that can occur in several different organs but particularly affects the lungs. The United Nations has declared this disease to be a global epidemic, although the prevalence of tuberculosis is much lower in developed countries (Rajagopalan, 2001). In the United States, the rate of tuberculosis has been decreasing steadily since the 1950s and is now negligible in the general population. Some groups continue to show high rates, however, including the homeless, prison populations, those with HIV, and some immigrant groups (Centers for Disease Control [CDC], 2000b).

The older population constitutes another vulnerable group, as more than a quarter of all cases of tuberculosis in the United States are found among those aged 65 and over (Stollerman, 1997). Older adults who live in close quarters, especially long-term care facilities, are at high risk of tuberculosis because the bacteria are airborne. Although the bacteria reside in the lung tissue and can remain dormant for many years, the disease can reactivate in a more frail person or one with reduced immunity. Furthermore, diagnosing tuberculosis may be difficult in older populations. As with many diseases, symptoms tend to be nonspecific, such as chronic fatigue, cognitive impairment, and a persistent low-grade fever (Rajagopalan, 2001).

Tuberculosis can be treated, although the regimen of three medications a day for many months can be tedious and compliance rates are often low—in fact, public health nurses often go into the community to ensure that people take their medications. Surveillance is necessary for adequate treatment and to prevent the development of resistant strains of the bacteria. Good nutrition and a moderate exercise regimen are also beneficial in helping older adults return to good health, although prevention of the disease is best.

Promoting Optimal Aging

Avoiding smoking is the most important factor in maintaining healthy lungs in later years. There are thousands of chemical compounds in cigarette smoke, many of which do great damage to the sensitive alveoli, bronchioles, and bronchi. Smoking lowers good cholesterol levels and promotes atherosclerosis by increasing blood fibrinogen and viscosity levels, which can lead to blood clots. Finally, smoking is known to cause lung cancer. In a 10-year study of men in the Normative Aging Study, Bossé et al. (1980) examined the effect of cigarette smoking on pulmonary decline. As was expected, those who had never smoked had the best pulmonary function, as measured by forced vital capacity (FVC) and forced expiratory volume (FEV_1). The greatest decline in FEV_1 was among those who had both smoked in the past and were current smokers. For those who were former smokers but had been nonsmokers for 10 or more years, however, results were fairly similar to those who never smoked. Smoking effects were greater on FEV_1 than FVC, suggesting that being able to rid the lungs of air on expiration was hampered the most by smoking.

Exercise is essential for maintaining and enhancing respiratory function. Pulmonary fitness as a young person is predictive of good respiratory function as an older person, although exercising in later years is also beneficial. Aerobic exercise increases vital capacity and VO_2 max (the maximum volume of oxygen that can be processed) even in the very old. One study of frail 85-year-old women found that walking training improved VO_2 max by 18% (Puggaard, Larsen, Stovring, & Jeune, 2000).

Exercise may also decrease the incidence of respiratory infections in older adults, further leading to respiratory health. Kostka, Berthouze, Lacour, and Bonnefoy (2000) studied the relationship between oxygen consumption, physical activity, and upper respiratory tract infections among older adult volunteers. They found that increase in pulmonary exertion capacity resulted in fewer respiratory tract infection symptoms.

Good health habits, exercise, and avoidance of respiratory infections provide optimal respiratory health. Older people should avoid exposure to those who have symptoms of respiratory disease and should be vaccinated against pneumonia and influenza. Environmental pollutants are especially damaging to their respiratory systems and also should be avoided. Good nutrition is important in healthy lung function, as it reduces the impact of infections, is good for efficient respiratory muscle strength, and is important for the maintenance of the immune system. A healthy, functional respiratory system is essential to good health in later years.

GASTROINTESTINAL SYSTEM ●

Basic Anatomy and Physiology

The gastrointestinal (GI) system consists of the organs and glands needed for processing and absorption of fluids, electrolytes, and nutrients. The digestive tract extends from the mouth to the anus and includes the teeth and mouth, esophagus, stomach, and small and large intestines. The large intestine includes the cecum; ascending, transverse, and descending colon; the sigmoid colon; and the rectum (see Figure 6.5). Organs such as the liver, pancreas, and gall bladder also are part of the digestive system. The digestive process includes the secretion of gastric acids and enzymes that break down nutrients into their component parts, which are then absorbed into the blood system for delivery throughout the body. Carbohydrates get

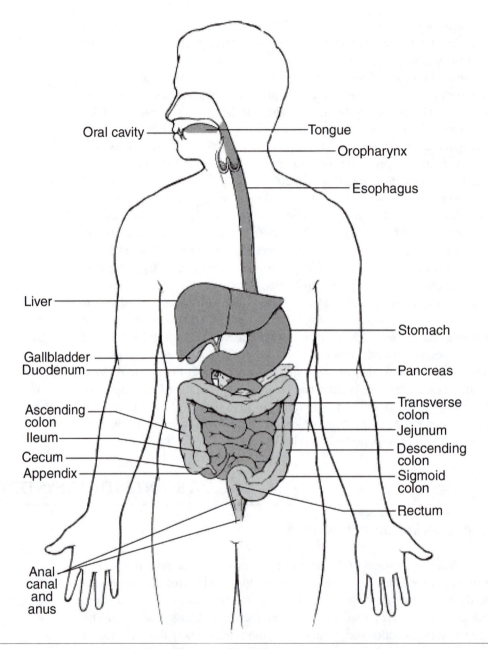

Figure 6.5   Anatomy of the Gastrointestinal Tract

SOURCE: Adapted from AMA's Current Procedural Terminology, revised 1998 edition, http://www.medem.com/MedLB/article_detaillb.cfm?article_ID=ZZZ7C4T46JC&sub_cat=511. Reprinted with permission of the American Medical Association.

broken down into sugars such as glucose and glycogen for energy use or for conversion into fats for storage. Proteins are broken down into their component amino acids that are used to construct the new proteins necessary for maintenance and growth of cells and every other body function. Fats are converted into fatty acids and glycerol, used for building cell membranes, absorption of fat soluble vitamins, and energy. The GI system also provides for the elimination of the body's waste products.

The digestive process begins in the mouth, where chewing breaks the food down into smaller particles. Enzymes in the saliva break down the nutrients and lubricate food so that it can be more easily swallowed. The act of swallowing allows food to enter the esophagus, where rhythmic muscular contractions push the food toward the stomach. The gastroesophageal sphincter at the base of the esophagus relaxes to allow the food to move into the stomach. The contractions of the esophagus and the constriction of the gastroesophageal sphincter normally prevent partially digested food from flowing back into the esophagus.

The stomach churns the food and secretes powerful gastric acids and enzymes, which begin the digestion of carbohydrates and proteins. The pyloric glands found at the entrance to the duodenum secrete thin mucus that helps to lubricate food. This mucus also serves to protect the stomach wall from the gastric juices, as does a layer of alkaline mucus cells found on the surface of the stomach. The processed food, now called chyme, moves by peristalsis through the relaxed pyloric sphincter into the first part of the small intestine, the duodenum (see Figure 6.6).

In the duodenum, enzymes are secreted from the intestinal mucosa (a membrane lining the intestine) to digest food, assisted by pancreatic and bile secretions. Glands located close to the entrance of the duodenum secrete mucus that helps to protect the wall of the duodenum from gastric juices. The second part of the small intestine is the jejunum (approximately 9 feet in length) and the third part the ileum (approximately 13 feet long). The wall mucosa of the small intestine has small fingerlike folded projections called villi. These villi increase the surface area of the intestine many-fold, adding to the area that absorption of water, electrolytes, and nutrients can take place.

Unabsorbed contents left in the small intestine pass into the large intestine. The large intestine is about 5 feet long and extends to the rectum (see Figure 6.5). The large intestine has no villa and secretes few enzymes but instead reabsorbs water and electrolytes. Cells in the intestinal wall secrete mucus that contains large amounts of bicarbonate ions, which protect the wall of the intestine from strong acids and help in forming fecal (waste) material. Feces are stored in the second half of the large intestine. Mucus secreted by the cells of the large intestine also aids in the passage of feces out through the anus.

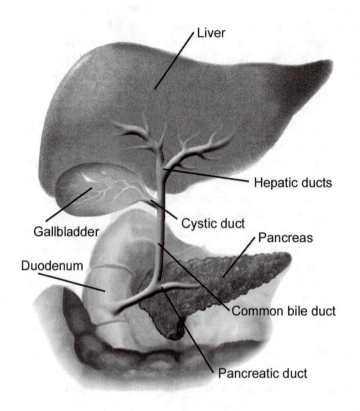

Figure 6.6   Liver, Gallbladder, and Pancreatic Secretion Pathways

SOURCE: Artist: Barry Burns. Used with permission.

The pancreas is a large gland that is tucked behind the stomach (see Figure 6.5). It secretes enzymes necessary for digestion; sodium bicarbonate to neutralize gastric acids; and insulin, which regulates blood glucose (see Chapter 7). Secretions from the pancreas enter the common bile duct before emptying into the duodenum.

The liver is situated on the right side of the body beneath the diaphragm. It regulates the metabolism of carbohydrates, fats, and proteins and breaks down toxins such as alcohol and medications. It converts the highly toxic byproduct ammonia into urea and is a storage area for iron and fat-soluble vitamins A, D, E, and K. The liver also manufactures fibrinogen and prothrombin necessary for blood clotting (Guyton & Hall, 1996). The liver secretes bile, necessary for the digestion and absorption of fats and cholesterol. A portion of bile is stored in the gallbladder and emptied into the cystic duct when digestion of food, especially fatty food, begins. Secretions from the liver and gallbladder enter the common bile duct before emptying into the small intestine (see Figure 6.6).

The liver is also responsible for the manufacture of cholesterol. Dietary cholesterol is broken down into its component parts and reassembled in the liver, a process partially under genetic control. Cholesterol is used for many functions in the body, including the manufacture of steroid hormones, and as part of the components necessary for building cell walls. Although too much cholesterol can damage the arteries and heart, it is nonetheless a key chemical for many different processes in the body.

Age-Related Changes

There are few normative changes in the digestive system with age, although some of them may affect health. The ability of the small intestine to absorb certain nutrients (such as vitamin D, vitamin B_{12}, and folic acid) may decline with age, affecting health. For example, vitamin B_{12} deficiency is the most common cause of pernicious anemia, and lack of this vitamin can cause neurologic deficits, such as gait problems and sensory and motor loss. On the other hand, there is an increase in the absorption of vitamin A although the requirement decreases with age, and toxicity can result if excessive supplements of this vitamin are taken (Lipschitz, 1997).

Older adults are more susceptible to gastrointestinal infections than are younger people, due to changes in the gastrointestinal mucosa which makes it more vulnerable to trauma (Hall & Wiley, 1999). Furthermore, the lining of the large intestine becomes thinner with age, less mucus is secreted, and the intestinal muscles can become weaker with a more sedentary life. There also may be an age-related slowing in large intestine motility, which can lead to constipation.

There is little change in the structure of the pancreas with age or its ability to function effectively (Guyton & Hall, 1996). On the other hand, an inactive lifestyle and obesity can impact pancreatic function, leading to diabetes (see Chapter 7).

Some age-related changes occur in the liver, including a decrease in the weight of the organ and the number of hepatocytes (liver cells). This has little effect on the ability of the liver to function, however, as it has a large functional reserve capacity. On the other hand, the ability of the liver to generate new cells after an injury or disease may be somewhat diminished in later years. Furthermore, due to circulatory and metabolic changes, the ability of the liver to synthesize proteins and metabolize toxins may be decreased, altering drug metabolism in the liver. Thus, it may take longer to clear medications from the system in older adults, which puts them at risk of a toxic overdose of medication. There is also an increased risk of gallstones with age, as bile becomes more concentrated and the gallbladder contracts less frequently.

Generally, the gastrointestinal system retains much of its regular function with age, and it is unclear whether the few normal changes significantly affect health. A number of gastrointestinal diseases do affect the health of the older population, however.

Disease-Related Processes

Periodontal Disease

Periodontal disease is a disease of the structures that support the teeth, including the bone that anchors the teeth. Bacterial infections damage the gums (gingivitis) and eat away at the roots of teeth, creating severe damage. Bacterial deposits form plaques at the junction of the gums and teeth, which can harden, causing periodontal disease. It is not a normal consequence of aging but reflects inadequate care of the teeth, which should include brushing, flossing, and frequent dental checkups. Older adults in the current cohort have extensive loss of teeth, mostly due to less access to dental care, although utilization of dental services by older adults has improved over the past 30 years (Ship, 1999).

Constipation

Constipation is medically defined as a bowel movement that is hard and dry. It is one of the most common gastrointestinal complaints of an older person. Although some normal aging changes in the gastrointestinal system may contribute to problems of constipation, studies generally show little difference in colon activity between healthy older and younger people. The most common causes of constipation are a diet low in fiber, inadequate fluid intake, inactivity, and a history of delayed defecation. Laxative use is also a common cause of chronic constipation, as the use of these medicines changes the normal functioning of the gastrointestinal system. Laxatives are expensive and potentially harmful, because excessive use can cause myoneural degeneration that leads to continued constipation (Wilson &

Rogers, 1997). On the other hand, there are times when constipation can be a serious problem for the older person. It can interfere with the quality of life of the person and is listed as a medical problem by many older people. Control of constipation by adequate exercise, a high-fiber diet, and a high fluid intake is preferable to the use of laxatives.

A number of medications cause constipation, including analgesics, sedatives or tranquilizers, anticholinergics, diuretics, and iron and calcium supplements. Constipation is quite common among people who have neurological diseases such as Parkinson's. Other health conditions that may contribute to constipation include depression and hypothyroidism. Furthermore, those who use wheelchairs or are bedridden, have little exercise, inadequate nutrition, and poor fluid intake are prone to constipation, as are those who are terminally ill. Finally, there is always a danger that constipation may mask a more serious illness, such as bowel cancer or hypothyroidism. In all cases, it is important to find the source of the constipation and treat accordingly.

Diverticular Disease

Diverticulosis, or the presence of diverticula in the colon, is a frequent gastrointestinal problem of older adults. In fact, from one third to two thirds of people over the age of 60 have some diverticulosis (Wilson & Rogers, 1997). As can be seen in Figure 6.7, diverticula are outpouchings of the lining of the colon. They most often occur in the descending and sigmoid colon (see Figure 6.5). In most cases, diverticulosis is caused by long-time lack of fiber in the diet. When there is not enough fluid or fiber in the stool, it becomes harder and the muscles of the colon have to strain to move it along. The extra pressure in the colon causes a weakness in its wall and a change in its elasticity, resulting in out-pouching of the tissue. Not surprisingly, since fiber plays such a big role in the development of diverticulosis, vegetarians and others with a lifelong high intake of fiber have a lower incidence of the disease (Cheskin & Schuster, 1994).

Diverticulosis becomes diverticulitis (inflammation of the diverticula) when stool becomes trapped in the diverticula. About 25% of people with diverticulosis develop diverticulitis (Hogan, 1997). If diverticulitis is particularly severe and infected, antibiotics or even surgery may be required. Diets high in fiber, fruits, vegetables, and whole grain fibers and adequate fluid intake can protect the bowel and prevent diverticulitis.

Gallbladder Disease

Another gastrointestinal disorder commonly found among older adults is gallbladder disease. About 30% to 50% of people over the age of 70 have

Diverticulosis

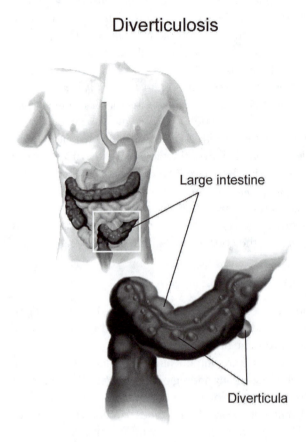

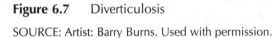

Figure 6.7   Diverticulosis

SOURCE: Artist: Barry Burns. Used with permission.

gallstones, although in most cases they are asymptomatic and do not create a problem for the individual (Hogan, 1997). Large gallstones can cause problems, however, when they move out of the gallbladder and become stuck in either the cystic or common bile duct (see Figure 6.6). Injury to either of these ducts may occur. In particular, problems can develop when the common bile duct is blocked and there is a backup of bilirubin in the system. These conditions cause pain, nausea, vomiting, and problems with digestion. Treatment of these conditions includes chemicals to dissolve the stones or surgical removal of the stone and/or the gallbladder.

Risk factors for gallstones and gallbladder disease are obesity, inactivity, a diet high in cholesterol and fat, high blood pressure, diabetes, being female, and the use of estrogen. Prevention includes a low-fat diet, exercise, and regulation of blood pressure and diabetes.

Cancer

Colorectal cancer is the third leading cause of cancer death. Although this type of cancer is found among younger people, incidence of the disease increases with age, doubling every 5 years after the age of 40 (DiGiovanna, 2000). Colorectal cancer is usually asymptomatic in very early stages of the disease, and when overt symptoms finally appear they are often vague (e.g., weight loss or slight pains in the abdominal area). Anemia is another symptom of colorectal cancer that may be overlooked, as there are numerous causes of anemia in the older person, for example, hemorrhoidal bleeding, a diet low in iron, and other disease processes. For these reasons, colorectal cancer may not be recognized until late in the disease. A very late and serious symptom is a partial or complete blockage of the colon by the growing cancerous tumor. Risk factors for this type of cancer include a diet low in fiber and high in fat, a family history of colorectal cancer or polyps, long-standing colitis or polyps, and, for women, a history of breast, ovarian, and/or endometrial cancer.

Colorectal cancer is almost always treated surgically. Older adults do quite well during and after surgery, although there is an increase in mortality and morbidity among those over the age of 80, most likely due to problems of coexisting diseases. Chemotherapy is sometimes used as an adjunct to surgery if the cancer is high risk and the person is able to undergo its rigors (Forman, 1997).

Screening for colorectal cancer should begin at about the age of 40, especially for those who have a family history of colorectal cancer or intestinal polyps. Colonoscopy and sigmoidoscopy, although expensive and invasive, are reliable methods used to detect this type of cancer. A sigmoidoscopy is an examination of the descending colon; a colonoscopy is used to view the ascending, transverse, and descending colon.

Undernutrition

The older, isolated, and chronically ill person may be at risk of being undernourished, defined as having a diet low in calcium, protein, and calories, as well as an inadequate fluid intake. Poor nutrition levels may be the result of many factors: inability to shop or cook, an inadequate income, physical problems such as poorly fitting dentures, or illnesses and medical treatment such as chemotherapy, which causes fatigue and anorexia. Sometimes the problems are psychological in nature; depression or the use of drugs or alcohol can interfere with proper nutrition. The newly bereaved may not know how to cook or may not wish to eat alone and may neglect proper nutrition.

Poor nutrition has serious consequences in the older population. It can impair immune system functioning, making older adults vulnerable to bacteria and viruses. Dehydration can cause electrolyte imbalances, leading to kidney or cardiac failure. It can also impair cognition, resulting in confusional states that may be mistaken for dementia (see Chapter 7). In turn, mental confusion can lead to forgetting whether one has eaten or not, resulting in a worsening negative cycle.

Institutionalized older adults are also at risk of undernutrition. In-hospital mortality is often related to low serum levels of albumin, indicating an inadequate intake of protein or an increased need for protein for healing of tissue. Therefore, it is not surprising that these older adults have poor wound healing, develop pressure sores, and have impaired immunity (Palmer, 1997).

Treatment of undernutrition centers on increased food and fluid consumption. Generally, diets need to be high in protein, vitamins and minerals, and calories, as well as fluids. Depending on the cause of undernutrition, dentures should be repaired, home health aides instructed on the correct diet for the older adult, and institutions made more aware of the dietary intake of their older residents. If undernutrition is due to illness or medical treatment, extra efforts should be made to improve the nutritional values of foods (e.g., making sure foods are high in proteins, vitamins, and minerals). There are times when older adults should be encouraged to eat any foods that are tempting for them, rather than to regulate their cholesterol or caloric intake. In some cases, older adults should be assisted in shopping and safely preparing meals. Those who are recently widowed may need help in menu planning or be encouraged to take part in one of the programs offered through the Older Americans Act, congregate eating sites, or the Meals on Wheels program.

Obesity

Poor nutrition includes not only undereating but overeating as well. Diets high in calories can lead to obesity, especially in sedentary individuals. Body mass index (BMI) is a calculation that takes into account weight and height. The equation is

$$BMI = (\text{Weight in pounds})/(\text{Height in inches})^2 \times 703.$$

A BMI index between 25 and 29.99 is considered overweight; an index over 30 denotes obesity.

Rates of obesity have been increasing dramatically over the last two decades. The CDC (2000a) recently declared obesity to be a major public health risk as it can lead to cardiovascular disease, diabetes, gallstones, and arthritis, among other diseases. Using data from the National Health and Nutrition Epidemiological Survey (NHANES), the CDC found that the obesity rate is highest among those aged 55 to 64 (27.2% of men and 33.7% of women), falling to about 25% in the 65- to 74-year-old age group. By age 75 and over, less than 14% of men and about 20% of women fall into this category (Krumholz et al., 1999).

A major controversy in the field of gerontology is the relationship between weight and mortality. Walford (1990) has been the major proponent of caloric restriction. Many studies in lab animals have shown that animals fed up to one third less than normal are healthier and live longer than animals who are allowed to eat normally. Various reasons for this have been discussed, including lower rates of oxidation and therefore fewer free radicals (Sohal & Weindruch, 1996). This general finding has been contradicted by epidemiological studies in humans that show a J-shaped curve between weight and mortality, with underweight and very overweight people showing the worst longevity, and those who are slightly overweight the best (Durazo-Arvizu et al., 1997). Some argue that there is a problem in causal directionality—people in poor health may be underweight, and thus the underlying illness is causing both the lower weight and higher mortality. However, some of these studies have controlled for preexisting illness and still find the J-shaped curve (Manson et al., 1995).

Although some weight loss tends to occur after age 65, this loss does not necessarily represent good health, as lean muscle mass decreases with age, and the relative proportion of body fat increases. Tully and Snowdon (1995) warned that weight loss in later life constitutes a serious risk for mortality, because reserves are depleted and not available if needed for healing.

Probably the best pattern for a healthy life is a stable, average weight over a lifetime, possibly slightly underweight in the 20s, followed by a modest gain over the next few decades (Pi-Sunyer, 2000). It is vitally important to recognize, however, that obesity places individuals at risk of numerous diseases. Furthermore, those with hypertension or high cholesterol show significant improvements when they lose weight (Williamson, 1997).

Promoting Optimal Aging

The gastrointestinal system is usually healthy in later years, but a few changes occur. Although an older person's energy or caloric needs are less, the requirements for other nutrients (protein, vitamins, and minerals) remain much the same. A healthy diet for older adults should include a slight increase in protein to help maintain muscle mass, especially if the person has an acute or chronic illness. Those who are overweight should lower their fat intake. Nutritional intake should include adequate amounts of calcium (for bone maintenance) and vitamins, such as vitamin K and B_{12}. Finally, those with chronic illnesses may need to increase their intake of zinc (a mineral that aids in wound healing and immune function), either by using supplements or preferably by increasing the intake of foods such as red meat. Exercise, a diet high in fiber, and sufficient water intake are needed to avoid constipation and diverticulitis, and perhaps colon cancer as well. Screening for diseases such as polyps and colon cancer is another way to promote health and prevent more serious outcomes.

● RENAL/URINARY SYSTEM

Basic Anatomy and Physiology

The urinary system serves to filter waste products from the blood, maintain fluids and electrolytes, and regulate osmotic pressure, acid/base balance, and blood pressure. It also helps maintain appropriate concentrations of minerals and regulate oxygen levels (DiGiovanna, 2000). Components of this system include the right and left kidneys, a ureter leading from each kidney into the urinary bladder, and the urethra that empties the urine outside the body (see Figure 6.8).

The kidneys are relatively small organs; each is about the size of a small fist. They are located at the back of the abdominal cavity, well protected by abdominal muscles and the rib cage (see Figure 6.8). The right kidney is slightly lower than the left kidney. The indented area of each kidney is the entry point for nerves and the renal artery and the exit point for the renal vein. It is also where the ureters leave the kidneys.

Each kidney contains approximately 1.2 million nephrons, all of which are capable of producing urine. These nephrons are the working units of the kidneys. Each nephron consists of a glomerulus, various tubules (proximal,

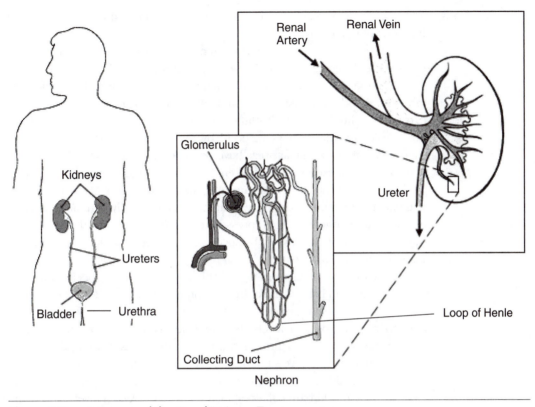

Figure 6.8 Anatomy of the Renal/Urinary Tract

distal, and a loop of Henle), and a collecting duct. The glomeruli are composed of capillaries through which the blood is filtered. The glomeruli and the tubular structures of the kidneys are responsible for the reabsorption of water and solutes such as electrolytes, glucose, and amino acids (Guyton & Hall, 1996). These substances are returned to the circulatory system to be reused by the body. The remaining fluid passes through the collecting duct, where it goes from the kidney into the ureters. From there, urine flows to the bladder, from where it is eliminated via the urethra.

The kidneys remove metabolic waste products from the blood. The metabolism of amino acids creates urea, uric acid, and ammonia, which can be highly toxic at even low levels. The kidneys also filter out other metabolic byproducts such as creatinine, which is generated from breakdown of the muscle cells and the waste products of various hormones. It also processes toxins such as dyes and heavy metals, as well as medications and pesticides.

The glomerular filtration rate (GFR) is a measure of the kidney's ability to rid the body of waste products.

The kidneys are vitally important in maintaining osmotic and blood pressures through regulation of fluids and electrolytes. To maintain homeostasis, the excretion of water and electrolytes need to match the body's intake. For example, if sodium intake is high, initially there will be a slight increase in extracellular fluid volume, leading to an increase in blood pressure. Over time, however, the kidneys respond by excreting the excess sodium and water that the extracellular areas have been holding, decreasing blood pressure. Similarly, if excess water is taken in (in the absence of excessive sodium intake), urine output will be greater. Because of the ability of the kidneys to maintain the fluid and electrolyte balance, there is usually minimal change in extracellular fluid levels. Blood pressure is also maintained by the kidneys by the secretion of vasoactive substances such as renin, which increases the vasoconstrictor angiotension.

The kidneys are responsible for the maintenance of specific minerals necessary for acid/base balance. In addition to sodium, the kidneys regulate potassium, magnesium, calcium, and phosphorus levels. Finally, the kidneys help to regulate oxygen levels. If oxygen levels are too low, the kidneys secrete the hormone erythropoietin, which stimulates red blood cell production. High oxygen levels inhibit the secretion of this hormone.

Thus, the kidneys perform vital functions in the management of fluid, electrolyte, and acid/base balances; maintenance of oxygen levels; and elimination of waste products. Unfortunately, these functions are very sensitive to the effects of age.

Age-Related Changes

There is a progressive structural and functional breakdown of the kidneys with age. Although not a normal age-related change, atherosclerosis affects arteries throughout the organs of the body, limiting the blood supply to those areas. It impacts the kidneys with its vast circulatory system as well, affecting the arterial blood supply to that organ. Therefore, it is not surprising that arterial blood flow to the kidneys begins to decrease in the fourth decade of life. Renal mass also decreases during these times as well as the size and number of nephrons and glomeruli. In fact, by the age of 70, from 30% to 50% of the body's glomeruli have been lost. Equally important is that the number of sclerotic (hardened and thickened) glomeruli and nonfunctioning glomeruli increase. The remaining ones may become more permeable with age, allowing proteins and other substances to be lost from the body (Anderson, 1997). Glomeruli filtration rate normally decreases with age, indicating less glomeruli efficiency. The decrease in GFR reduces the rate that noxious substances such as medications or toxins can be eliminated from the systems. Another measure of kidney function, serum creatinine, remains relatively constant in later years in healthy older adults. This is partially due to a decrease in muscle mass in the older person, however, and an age-related lower production of creatinine (Beck, 1999). An increase in serum creatinine is a marker for renal failure.

There is relatively normal regulation of fluid and electrolytes in healthy older people, although the response rate and adaptability to a change is slower. The aging kidneys are less able to concentrate urine to conserve water or to dilute urine to excrete excess water (Anderson, 1997). On the other hand, older kidneys are less able to regulate homeostasis when the body is under stress. Because of this, an older person is more likely to either become dehydrated or to have too much fluid in the body. For example, the kidneys of an older person are slower to respond to a loss of fluid and electrolytes during vomiting and diarrhea. When a younger person has vomiting and diarrhea, urine excretion of sodium is reduced rapidly, and fluid is saved. In older adults, the kidneys are slower to respond to the crisis, and the person can become quite ill. The dehydration problem is exacerbated by the fact that thirst recognition in later years is blunted, even among those who are healthy.

Changes in kidney function also affect potassium homeostasis, putting the older person both at risk of excess and inadequate levels of this mineral in the body. A number of medications commonly used by older adults can add to this problem. Some diuretics cause potassium to be retained in the body while others block the excretion of potassium, as do NSAIDs. It should also be kept in mind that salt substitutes frequently used by those with hypertension or heart disease are often high in potassium (Beck, 1999).

Bladder capacity and the ability to postpone voiding are reduced with age. There is also a decrease in the ability to completely empty the bladder, which may lead to bladder and kidney infections. Involuntary muscle contractions of the bladder (which can lead to leakage of urine) are also a fairly normal occurrence in the older population. The prostate gland in men enlarges normally with age, partially obstructing the outlet to the urethra so that the bladder cannot empty completely. Finally, because of changes in bladder and kidney function, both men and women can have problems with nocturia, or nighttime urination.

In most healthy older adults, changes in this system cause minimal problems and the aging renal/urinary system remains fairly competent into very old years. Yet loss in normal kidney function has a critical impact on the ability of the body to respond during times of stress, such as illness, heart failure, or surgery.

Disease-Related Processes

Urinary Incontinence

Urinary incontinence is one of the most embarrassing and annoying problems facing older adults. It affects 5% to 30% of those over the age of 65 who live at home and almost 60% of those living in nursing homes (Resnick, 1997). It is also a primary risk factor for skilled nursing placement, as caring for a person who is incontinent can easily overload a caregiver. Urinary incontinence is frequently underdiagnosed and often undertreated.

There are four major types of urinary incontinence: urge, functional, stress, and overflow (see benign prostatic hyperplasia below). Urge incontinence is characterized by an inability to delay voiding after bladder fullness is felt. In some cases, there is no warning sign of a need to urinate. This is usually due to a problem of sphincter function and an inability on the part of the person to stop involuntary bladder contractions (a normal aging change, as noted above, is less severe). Its source may be an obstruction or a neurogenic disorder, such as in a stroke, Parkinsonism, or a spinal cord injury. Although bladder training can be effective, incontinence undergarments are also frequently used.

Functional incontinence is the inability to control urination due to cognitive or physical limitations. This includes neurological disorders such as dementia or psychological ones like depression or hostility. There are times when the person is unable to reach the toilet. This may be due to a mobility problem or an environmental one, such as a toilet that is inaccessible or inconvenient for someone with cognitive or physical limitations. Behavioral therapy and incontinence undergarments can alleviate some of the problems of functional incontinence.

Stress incontinence is common among older women; it is frequently caused by estrogen deficiency, previous vaginal childbirth, or sphincter weakness. Anatomically, there is a weakness of the pelvic floor musculature, and small amounts of urine are lost when there is an increase in intra-abdominal pressure, such as when a person laughs, coughs, or sneezes. Usually this is not terribly inconvenient, although it can be bothersome. At other times, it can be severe and the woman may avoid going out in public because of the embarrassment of possibly losing urine.

Contrary to public opinion, there are a number of ways to treat this type of urinary incontinence. Women can practice Kegel exercises (repetitive tightening of the pelvic muscles) to strengthen the pelvic floor musculature. Estrogen is frequently given to older women to alleviate the symptoms of atrophic vaginitis (inflammation of the vaginal wall due to atrophy of the tissue), a cause of stress incontinence (Resnick, 1997). The changes in the pelvic floor, noted above, and atrophic vaginitis, increase the chances of bladder infections, which can cause incontinence. The success of estrogen in alleviating incontinence is mixed. Ouslander et al. (2001) found that giving oral estrogen/progestin to incontinent female nursing home patients (mean age 88) provided only a partial effect on vaginitis and no reduction in incontinence. However, the authors recommended that future studies examine the use of topical estrogen as a way to prevent urinary infections and incontinence. The new studies on the use of oral hormone replacement further suggest that topical estrogen be used as an alternative therapy.

Urinary incontinence can be a great inconvenience to the older person, interfering with daily activities, limiting social interaction, and decreasing satisfaction with life. Furthermore, it has been associated with an increase in depressive symptoms, especially among women (Dugan et al., 2000). Older adults often hesitate to talk with health professionals about the problem. Some may be embarrassed; others may believe that a degree of incontinence is a normal part of aging and that there is no treatment available. Those who want to remain active are most likely to use self-help remedies such as sanitary pads. People who think incontinence is a normal aging change are less likely to seek formal help. Health professionals know surprisingly little about how to treat incontinence, or even that it can be treated (Locher, Burgio, Goode, Roth, & Rodriguez, 2002).

Benign Prostatic Hyperplasia

One of the major causes of incontinence is enlargement of the prostrate, benign (nonmalignant) prostatic hypertrophy (BPH), an almost universal disorder in older men. As can be seen in Figure 6.9, the prostate is found at the base of the bladder circling the urethra. The causes of BPH are complex and include age-related changes in androgens (DuBeau, 1997). There is an accelerated growth of the prostate at about 50 years, changing the shape and consistency of the gland. These changes compress the opening to the urethra at the bladder, making it difficult to urinate or to completely empty the bladder. The most common signs of BPH are problems with voiding, such as nocturia, urgency, frequency, hesitancy, weak urine flow, or interrupted stream. There is also a sense of incompletely emptying the bladder. Men often wait to seek

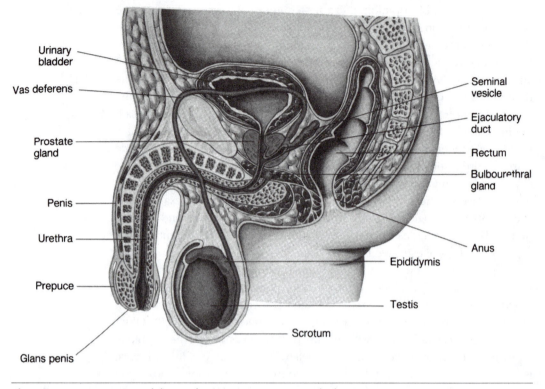

Urinary bladder

Vas deferens

Prostate gland

Penis

Urethra

Prepuce

Glans penis

Seminal vesicle

Ejaculatory duct

Rectum

Bulbourethral gland

Anus

Epididymis

Testis

Scrotum

Figure 6.9   Anatomy of the Male Urinary System, Including Prostate

SOURCE: Ferrini, A. F., & Ferrini, R. L. (2000). *Health in the later years* (3rd ed., p. 82, Figure 3.9). Boston: McGraw-Hill. Reprinted with permission of the McGraw-Hill Companies.

help for this problem until voiding symptoms become uncomfortable, worrisome, or embarrassing. BPH can affect the quality of life of the older man, interfering with sleep patterns, work, and sexual function.

There is no permanent treatment for BPH, but symptoms can be alleviated through limiting fluids a few hours before bedtime and avoiding the many medications known to cause urinary retention. If symptoms are severe, surgery to remove part of the prostate provides the greatest relief. An alternative to surgery is watchful waiting, especially for those who have mild to moderate symptoms or are quite elderly. Risk factors for the surgery include impotence, incontinence, bleeding, and infection.

BPH is a very common occurrence among older men and needs to be addressed by health care professionals to ensure the highest quality of life for the older adult. Furthermore, it is important for professionals to reassure men that there is no connection between this disorder and prostate cancer (DuBeau, 1997).

Prostate Cancer

Prostate cancer is second only to lung cancer as a cause of cancer death in men. The primary risk factors for prostate cancer are age, heredity, and lifestyle, with age being the greatest risk. The disease is seldom seen in men under the age of 50, but by the eighth decade, 70% to 90% of men will have evidence of prostate cancer at death (McClain & Gray, 2000). Men with a father or brother with the disease are at great risk, as are those with a mother or sister with breast or ovarian cancer (Smith & Trump, 1997). African American, Asian American, and European American men have the same prevalence of the disease, but African Americans are more likely to have an aggressive type of tumor (McClain & Gray, 2000). Of great concern is that African American men are also less likely to be screened for prostate cancer than those in other groups.

There are currently two methods to screen for prostate cancer. One is a digital exam of the prostate gland, checking for unusual hardened nodules and asymmetry. It is recommended that all men have annual digital rectal examinations starting at the age of 40. The second screening test is a blood test that measures prostatic-specific antigen (PSA). PSA values increase with age; normal values are 2.5 or less up to age 40 and 6.5 or less at age 70. PSA values also increase if a man has BPH, but not as high as it does for men with prostate cancer. There are indications that PSA screening identifies aggressive prostate cancer at an early stage and may thus decrease mortality. The PSA test is definitely advised for younger men (Isola et al., 2001).

Prostate cancer is frequently asymptomatic early in the disease. With time, however, symptoms resemble those of BPH (e.g., nocturia and urgency). Tumor aggressiveness is hard to determine from either symptoms or a biopsy, which makes treatment options difficult to determine (although the PSA may prove useful for this). Appropriate treatment options are surgery to remove the tumor, radiation, or hormone therapy, although all of these may have serious side effects such as incontinence and impotence. Gene therapy is in an experimental stage, and neither the efficacy nor the side effects of the treatment are known. Finally, early evidence indicates that a diet low in fat and high in vitamin D (Konety & Getzenberg, 2002) and vitamin E (Fleshner, 2002) may slow the growth of prostatic cancer.

Treatment choices are often determined by the age of the man. Prostate cancer is more virulent and death rates are higher among younger men than among older ones. Consequently, prostate cancer is treated more aggressively among younger men.

On the other hand, prostate cancer among older men is typically slower growing and, even if metastasized, takes a longer time to progress. Some health professionals believe that no treatment is warranted in the very old and that a watch-and-wait attitude should be taken instead, as these men are more likely to die of diseases other than prostate cancer (Smith & Trump, 1997). Furthermore, some suggest that PSA is an inappropriate test to use among very old men who may not be good candidates for treatment.

The value of friends and family in supporting and encouraging men who have prostate cancer cannot be underestimated. The formal and informal support systems must work together to provide optimal care and assistance, physically and emotionally, to men who undergo therapy or a watch-and-wait regimen for prostate cancer.

Promoting Optimal Aging

The renal/urinary system, more than most systems of the body, is affected by the aging process. There are a number of illnesses of the urinary tract which have been discussed. Incontinence, a common and bothersome problem in later years, can often be treated. Diagnosis, treatment, educational programs, exercise, and good nutritional and fluid intake can help the older person with bladder problems maintain a healthier and more satisfying life. Health professionals need to be aware that older people may be hesitant to talk to them about incontinence.

Men need to be encouraged to seek prostate cancer screening, to allow for early diagnosis and treatment of this disease. Diet may play a role in prostrate health. Both vitamin D (Konety & Getzenberg, 2002) and vitamin E (Fleshner, 2002) are thought to be useful both in preventing prostate cancer and in delaying its progression. Epidemiological studies also suggest that eating tomatoes and tomato products may lower the risk of prostrate cancer, presumably because lycopene, an anticancer agent, is found in tomatoes. Clinical trials are necessary to confirm this (Miller et al., 2002).

Acute and chronic kidney failure are not necessarily diseases of the old (and are not covered in this chapter), although they occur more often in later years. Nonetheless, normal aging changes in the kidneys affect the health of the older person. A number of diseases affect kidney health; in particular, atherosclerosis severely impacts the supply of arterial blood to the area, which affects the health of the kidney.

Therefore, deceleration of disease processes in the renal/urinary system must involve maintaining kidney health and protection of the kidneys from further harm. For example, normal age-related changes in renal function leave older adults extremely vulnerable to a fluid and electrolyte imbalance when they are ill. If older adults are sick, they may eat and drink very little (older people are less likely to experience thirst). Infections such as pneumonia or influenza can affect their eating habits (as well as their ability to shop and cook) at a time when they need good nutrition and fluids. Exacerbation of emphysema, a broken wrist, or diarrhea can upset the acid/base and fluid and electrolyte balance of the body. Older people need to avoid heat stress and dehydration when temperatures are high. Fluid intake is especially important during hot weather. Elderly persons and their family members need to be aware of the environmental dangers of excessive heat. Imbalances in fluid and electrolytes that result from exposure to hot temperatures can cause older persons to be confused, so they often do not realize that they are in serious trouble. In fact, hundreds of older adults die every year from heat stress, which causes dehydration, kidney failure, and cardiovascular failure.

There are numerous medications that are cleared through the kidneys, and a high risk of toxicity exists as the kidneys are less able to rid the body of these medications in later years. Some medications that are particularly toxic are also ones that are commonly used among the elderly, such as digoxin, diuretics, NSAIDs, and beta-blockers. Some classes of diuretics remove potassium from the system, but others save it, which can cause either high or low potassium levels in the older person. Appropriate management of these medications includes modification of dose and monitoring of blood levels to assess toxicity level.

Treatment of diseases that may harm the kidneys is critical in preserving the ability of the kidneys to maintain optimal function. High blood pressure should be kept under close control. Older persons should avoid a diet high in sodium if they are hypertensive, although it should be noted that salt substitutes (often used by those on a low sodium diet) are high in potassium, which can also be a problem. Furthermore, some people are much more sensitive to sodium intake than others (sodium sensitive), and these people need to be especially careful about salt intake. Diabetes should be kept under close control with a nutritious diet and appropriate medication. Both of these diseases have a negative effect on the arteries of the kidneys.

Good nutritional and fluid intake is important for the maintenance of kidney health. A diet low in protein may help reduce the sclerotic glomerular changes that occur in the aging kidneys (Beck, 1999), but protein intake is also necessary for the maintenance of many of the body's functions, especially during time of injury or illness. The older person should be encouraged to consume adequate amounts of water and avoid toxins such as excessive alcohol.

Therefore, the most important factor in maintaining optimal kidney health in later years is to protect the normal function of the kidneys. The kidneys can be protected by avoiding the ingestion of substances that can harm the kidneys, such as excessive alcohol and kidney-toxic medications, treating diseases that can harm the kidneys (atherosclerosis, hypertension, congestive heart failure, and diabetes), and monitoring kidney function when the person is ill or under extreme environmental conditions, such as heat waves or cold snaps.

● SUMMARY

This review of the internal organ systems shows that there is a heterogeneity in the degree of normative age-related changes. Some organs, such as the liver and the gastrointestinal tract, show relatively little change with age, whereas others, such as the kidneys, are much more susceptible. In all of these systems, one can identify aging accelerators and aging decelerators. The most consistent findings are that exercise and good nutrition are the primary protectors against aging of the organ systems and that obesity and disease-related processes can greatly increase the rate of aging. Another intriguing finding is the interconnectedness of the different systems. Clearly, health and illness in one organ system can have tremendous impacts on the health of the others. How these organ systems communicate and are coordinated is the concern of the regulatory systems, which are discussed in the next chapter.

CHAPTER 7

AGING AND THE REGULATORY SYSTEMS

I n order for the organs to function properly, they must recognize changes in both the external and internal environment and be able to communicate with each other to maintain homeostasis, avert dangers, and manage growth. The regulatory systems that manage this communication are the sensory, nervous, endocrine, and immune systems. Disruption in the communication among these systems plays a major role in the development of disease and in the aging process itself. Less is known about how to maintain optimal health in these systems.

SENSORY SYSTEM ●

The sensory system is composed of five senses: touch, smell, taste, hearing, and vision. Sensory organs allow the nervous system to gain information about the external environment. In the interest of brevity, we focus primarily on changes in the senses due to aging and disease rather than describing the anatomy and physiology of these highly complex organs in depth.

Age- and Disease-Related Changes

Touch

The skin is the sense organ for touch. There are age-related changes in both touch receptors (Meissner's corpuscles) and pressure receptors (Pacinian corpuscles). With age, these receptors decrease both in number and in sensitivity, resulting in a degradation of the sense of touch, with decreased ability to detect, locate, or identify objects (Desrosiers, Herbert, Bravo, & Rochette, 1999; DiGiovanna, 2000; Ranganathan, Siemionow, Sahgal, & Yue, 2001). Loss of sensitivity also impairs the ability to manipulate small objects and may be exacerbated by some of the normative aging skin changes reviewed in Chapter 5, as well as by disease-related changes such as diabetic neuropathy. Whether age-related changes in pain occur is a matter of some controversy, however, with some studies finding increased pain thresholds, others showing decreased thresholds, and some finding no change (Ferrell, 1999).

Smell

Modest changes in the sense of smell occur with age, averaging only about a 10% decline (Baker & Martin, 1997). There are decreases in both the number of sensory neurons in the nasal lining and in the olfactory pathways to the brain (DiGiovanna, 2000). Large individual differences occur in the preservation of the sense of smell, however. Smoking degrades it, although some function may return if an individual quits smoking. The olfactory bulb is very close to the hippocampus, and one of the first indicators of incipient Alzheimer's disease is a decrease in the sense of smell (Doty, 2001), indicating that there may be neurological changes in the olfactory bulb as well.

Given the importance of smell in the sense of taste, degradations in the ability to smell food may impair an older person's appetite. The ability to smell is also important in detecting whether food has gone bad. Food-borne illnesses are a risk for older adults who have lost much of their sense of smell, as they may be unable to determine whether or not food such as eggs, milk, or meat has spoiled (although not all food pathogens are detectable by smell). Decrease in the sense of smell may have other safety and behavioral implications, such as an inability to detect leaking gas or when one has unacceptable body odors.

Taste

Most of what we consider taste is actually a function of smell. The taste buds in the tongue can sense salt, sweet, sour, bitter, fat, and "umami," which is composed of glutamate, best known in the form of monosodium glutamate (MSG) often used in Chinese cuisine (Herness & Gilbertson, 1999; Lindemann, 2001). There are differing opinions on whether the sense of taste diminishes with age. Early studies suggested a drastic decline, but they were conducted on institutionalized older adults, who are often heavily medicated. At worst, aging may cause slight decreases in the sensitivity of these neurons, which may be below the sensory threshold and thus undetectable. Any gradual losses in taste may actually be due to smoking, periodontal disease, illness, or use of medications, whereas a sudden loss may be indicative of a brain tumor (Ship, 1999). Decline in the sense of taste can have serious consequences, as it is one factor that can lead to anorexia in older adults. As we saw in Chapter 6, weight loss is associated with excess mortality in late life.

Hearing

Age-related changes in the auditory structures affect not only hearing but balance as well. Sound is transmitted through the outer ear via the ear canal into the middle ear through vibrations in the eardrum (see Figure 7.1). The middle ear contains three ossicles, or little bones, that pass vibrations to the oval window, a flexible membrane that is the beginning of the inner ear. Fluid in the inner ear puts pressure on the cochlea, an organ that looks like a snail shell. This is lined with the basilar membrane, which bristles with rows of thousands of neurons that make up the organ of Corti. These "hair cells" contact nerve fibers that transmit acoustic signals to the central nervous system (Willis, 1993). A highly complex structure in the inner ear, called the vestibule, allows organisms to sense gravity and head rotation. The vestibule consists of two small, gelatin-filled sacks that have small mineral particles and hairlike sensors. The minerals press down on the sensors, transmitting information to the brain on the position of the head, and therefore whether one is upright, upside down, or tilted.

Many age-related changes can affect hearing and balance. Cells in the ear canal generate earwax, a lubricant that thickens with age and can build up, decreasing sensitivity to sound. Although the eardrum itself can become stiffer and the ossicles a bit arthritic, this does not tend to affect hearing. However, the organ of Corti may be affected by atherosclerotic changes in the capillaries that provide nutrients to it, by wear and tear, and by ototoxic medications—those that are toxic to the delicate mechanisms in the ear (Mhoon, 1997). These include some antibiotics, pain relievers, diuretics, and cancer drugs. Furthermore, the structures of the inner ear that sense gravity and head position can also degrade over time, leading to dizziness and falls.

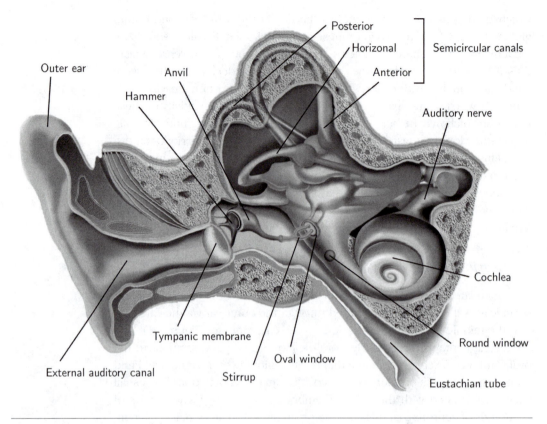

Figure 7.1 Anatomy of the Ear

SOURCE: Reprinted from Beatty, J. (2001). *The human brain: Essentials of behavioral neuroscience.* Thousand Oaks, CA: Sage. Copyright © 2001 Sage Publications. Artist: Barry Burns. Used with permission.

Presbycusis, or hearing loss with age, is the most common hearing problem. On average, men lose 80% of hearing capacity by age 90, but women lose only about 30% (Baker & Martin, 1997). Because the shorter hair cells that respond to high frequencies are located at the beginning of the cochlea, they receive the most wear and tear; thus high-pitched sounds, such as women's voices, are usually lost first. Severe loss can result from exposure to loud noises such as factory machinery, jet planes, military equipment (e.g., artillery), and even music. The damage can be temporary, as in the loss of hearing for a day or two after a rock concert, but over time such damage can become permanent. A multicohort study showed that the prevalence of hearing impairment nearly doubled between 1965 and 1994, especially for men.

Risk factors included ototoxic drug use and occupations with high noise exposure, whereas exercise was protective, probably due to its positive effects on blood flow (Wallhagen, Strawbridge, Cohen, & Kaplan, 1997). Interestingly, African American men have less hearing loss, even with equal exposure to loud noses, suggesting that genetics plays a role in accelerating or decelerating the loss of this sense (Mhoon, 1997).

Severe presbycusis can profoundly affect the life of the older person. Diminished ability to hear car horns, smoke alarms, and barking dogs negatively affects personal safety. As the ability to determine the presence of others and to hear birds singing or water running declines or disappears, one may lose a sense of connection to the environment. Furthermore, a decreased willingness to communicate with others, or to mingle in social settings, frequently accompanies diminished hearing. Use of hearing aids can mitigate hearing loss, but people often complain that aids do not allow them to focus or screen out unwanted sounds. Because they cannot focus on or follow one particular conversation, hearing-impaired people may avoid social settings, such as parties, that have multiple conversations and music. Strawbridge, Wallhagen, Shema, and Kaplan (2000) found a dose-response curve between hearing impairment and problems in other domains. That is, there was a linear increase in problems in physical health, mental health, and social functioning with each decrement in hearing ability, showing that hearing loss can have a profound effect on an older adult's quality of life.

Tinnitus, often defined as a ringing in the ears with no discernable cause, is another common problem with age. It has many sources, including ear infections, high blood pressure, diabetes, tumors, atherosclerosis, malnutrition, medications, and toxic chemicals. For most people, this is simply an annoyance that can be masked by the use of soft music. If tinnitus becomes severe, however, it can be very distracting and interfere with sleep and everyday activities.

Vision

Figure 7.2 shows the anatomy of the eye. Light passes through the cornea, a transparent structure that protects the eye. By contracting and dilating, muscles in the iris regulate the amount of light that enters the eye. At the back of the eye is the retina, which contains photoreceptors (rods and cones). The lens focuses the image on the retina, adjusting for the distance of the object. The photoreceptors then translate light energy into action potentials in the optic nerve. Cones are responsible for color vision, whereas rods only transmit information in black and white, although they are more sensitive to light. Cones are most numerous in the macula, which is in the center of gaze

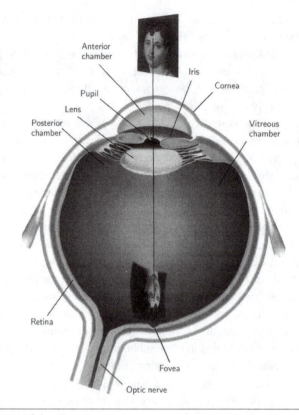

Figure 7.2   Anatomy of the Eye

SOURCE: Reprinted from Beatty, J. (2001). *The human brain: Essentials of behavioral neuroscience.* Thousand Oaks, CA: Sage. Copyright © 2001 Sage Publications. Artist: Barry Burns. Used with permission.

in a direct line from the cornea; rods are typically found in the more peripheral regions of the retina. The whole structure is supported by gel-like substances called humors in the chambers in the eye. Aqueous (watery) humor not only provides support but also transports nutrients and wastes, whereas the more gel-like vitreous humor protects the eye against shock. The conjunctiva, a clear mucus membrane inside the eyelids, also provides protection.

The complexity and sensitivity of the eye make it quite vulnerable to aging effects. The cornea, lens, and vitreous humor all diminish in transparency, reducing the amount of light entering the eye and also scattering the light that does come in, making the eye more sensitive to glare. Yellowing of the lens also decreases its transparency and makes it difficult to differentiate blues, greens, and violets. (This may first be noticed when middle-aged people discover that they cannot differentiate navy-blue socks from black ones.)

The lens loses elasticity with age, making it more difficult to focus on near objects. This is called presbyopia and is the most common age-related visual problem. (In midlife, individuals find that they need to hold reading matter increasingly farther away and that their eyes fatigue more readily.) The curvature of the cornea becomes more irregular, resulting in astigmatisms that distort vision by doubling the edges of objects and/or causing starry halos around lights (Goto et al., 2001).

The muscles in the iris decrease in number and strength with age, and its collagen stiffens, reducing the ability of the pupil to enlarge. This process begins at about age 20 and steadily reduces the amount of light available to the eye. These changes in the iris also decrease the speed at which it responds to light, so it stays open fractionally too long when the eye is exposed to bright light and does not expand quickly enough when the light dims. This makes older adults more vulnerable to glare and reduces their ability to see at night.

The fluids in the eye also show age-related changes. The lacrimal (tear) gland and conjunctiva produce less of their protective fluids, which can result in inflammation and irritation. The rate at which aqueous humor is generated also declines, and there might not be enough to properly maintain the shape of the cornea. Vitreous humor also decreases in size and becomes more liquid. As the vitreous humor moves about, it can create tension on the retina, causing flashes; too much tension can cause the retina to detach, causing blindness.

The retina also undergoes age-related changes. Cones and rods lose sensitivity progressively from adolescence through the remainder of the life span. Cones in the fovea, which is in the central area of the macula, are stable, but the rods in the central retina are vulnerable to aging (Kalina, 1999). Rods in the older person's retina may become irregular, further decreasing the ability to see in dim light. Optic nerve fibers are also lost, decreasing the quality of vision.

Age-related changes in vision may make driving problematic for an older person, especially at night. For example, the first author used to live in a small town in New England that was accessible only by one dimly lit, winding country road. A large number of older persons lived in that town. Driving home at night was often a frustrating experience; when a car passed coming the other way, the driver ahead would often slam on the brakes. This was undoubtedly due to the light scatter which increases glare, coupled with the slower rate of adaptation in the older pupil. The older driver would literally be temporarily blinded and would slow down. Of course, this problem was exacerbated by the fact that many of the older drivers were using their high beams to compensate for diminished night vision.

The four most common serious diseases of the eye in late life are cataracts, macular degeneration, glaucoma, and diabetic retinopathy (which will be covered in the endocrinology section later in this chapter). Cataracts are characterized by cloudiness or opacity of the lens; this can occur at any age but is found much more frequently in later years. Although painless, with time, cataracts can interfere with vision, particularly at night or in bright sunlight. The main risk factors for developing cataracts, besides age, are exposure to UV-B light and environmental pollutants, topical or internal steroids, diabetes, smoking, dehydration, eye trauma, and low levels of antioxidants such as vitamins A, C, and E (Kalina, 1999). Cataracts are easily treatable by surgery, which involves removal of the damaged lens and its replacement by an artificial one. Sometimes the lens is not replaced, and corrective contact lenses or eyeglasses are used instead. Cataracts are the leading cause of blindness among elders in developing countries.

In this country, glaucoma is a leading cause of blindness in adults over the age of 50. It is caused by an increasing buildup of aqueous humor in the eye, which results in an increase in intraocular pressure and damage to the retina and optic nerve. This disease can be present for many years without any symptoms. In narrow-angle or primary angle-closure glaucoma, which occurs in 10% of cases, there may be a very rapid increase in pressure that can result in blindness very quickly (DiGiovanna, 2000; Kalina, 1999). People most at risk for glaucoma include those of African American descent or with a family history of glaucoma. High blood pressure and diabetes are also risk factors. There are several ways to control the damage of glaucoma, including medications and laser therapy, but early detection is the key to prevention of retinal damage (Ernest, 1997).

One of the most deleterious retinal diseases is age-related macular degeneration (AMD), a disease that accounts for about 40% of visual impairment in people over the age of 80 and is the leading cause of severe vision loss in people over 60 (Arnold & Sarks, 2001; Kalina, 1999). There are two types, known informally as wet (or exudative) and dry (atrophic) AMD. Dry AMD, accounting for about 90% of cases (National Eye Institute, 2002), has a gradual onset. In contrast, the onset of wet AMD can be sudden, resulting in precipitous visual decline (Ernest, 1997). Although the dry form is the most common type of AMD, the wet form is responsible for most cases in which there is severe vision loss. The exact mechanism is not known, but it appears that free radicals damage the supply of nutrients to the retina, and the macula of the eye degenerates, destroying central vision.

As yet, no good treatments have been found for dry or atrophic AMD (Kalina, 1999), although high doses of antioxidants such as vitamin E are often used to try to slow its progression. Surgery may prove effective in halting the damage due to wet or exudative AMD, however. In this treatment, the eye is drained of vitreous humor, and lasers are used to repair the retina (Ciulla, Danis, & Harris, 1998; Hesse & Kroll, 1999). Exposure to UV rays and smoking are probably the major risk factors, but there is some evidence that the ingestion of vegetable fats also increases the risk of AMD (Seddon et al., 2001; Smith et al., 2001).

Promoting Optimal Aging

Some changes in the sensorium are inevitable, such as loss of acuity and decreased accommodation to changes in light levels. Probably the best way of maintaining one's sensory system is to avoid smoking tobacco, which affects the taste buds, is a risk factor for cataracts, and may accelerate hearing loss, due to its effects on the cardiovascular system. Maintaining good cardiovascular health through exercise and diet is important, because disease processes such as diabetes and atherosclerosis can hasten declines in vision and hearing. Avoiding ultraviolet light through the use of sunglasses is critical in decelerating age-related changes in vision, and protection against loud noises will help maintain hearing. Good nutrition is also important, especially avoiding diets high in fats and maintaining sufficient levels of vitamin A and antioxidants (Aksoy, Keles, Kocer, & Akcay, 2001). Regular checkups to catch diseases such as glaucoma and macular degeneration early are critical.

NERVOUS SYSTEM ●

Basic Anatomy and Physiology

The nervous system is the primary regulator of the body. It monitors and provides communication between all the systems and regulates homeostasis. It also permits voluntary movement and underlies all cognitive processes, including sensation, attention, language, memory, emotions, and problem solving. The central nervous system (CNS) consists of the brain and the spinal cord; the peripheral nervous system (PNS) consists of sensory and motor neurons. The autonomic nervous system (ANS) is responsible for all regulatory functions, including monitoring and controlling blood pressure, digestion, respiration, and temperature; it includes components of both the CNS and PNS. The ANS is further subdivided into the sympathetic (SNS) and parasympathetic nervous systems, which act in consort to stimulate and inhibit their target organs in order to respond adequately to environmental challenges and then return to baseline functioning.

There are several types of neuronal cells, but each consists of a cell body or soma, an axon, and dendrites. Each nerve cell has a single axon which can extend for far distances, but many spiky dendrites, which branch out from the soma. Neurons communicate with each other across interneuronal junctions called synapses. Communication across synapses is primarily chemical, but can be electrical, especially outside of the brain. There may be as many as 200,000 presynaptic vesicles on the dendrites and somas which can release neurotransmitters which are received by postsynaptic receptor sites on adjacent neurons (Guyton & Hall, 1996). Communication across a particular synapse is always unidirectional, and can be inhibitory or excitatory.

Each neuron generally releases only one type of neurotransmitter, and the receptor sites on the cell bodies or dendrites are specific to different types of neurotransmitters. However, a cell may have multiple kinds of receptors on its surface. Neurotransmitters can stimulate, inhibit, or modulate the receiving nerve cell, depending on the type of neurotransmitter and type of receptor. They can also modulate other neurotransmitters (Poirier & Finch, 1994).

More than 50 types of transmitter molecules have been identified (Beatty, 2001; Guyton & Hall, 1996). These include both neurotransmitters, which are small-molecule, rapidly acting transmitters, and neuropeptides, which are larger, slowly acting transmitters and include hormones and enkephalins. Some neurotransmitters have been found to be produced by the heart and the stomach, and some of the hormones clearly have neurological effects. Thus, it is now more common to divide communication molecules into those that are the small-molecule, rapidly acting transmitters and the neuropeptides, which have slower effects, but are often more potent and longer-lasting. Table 7.1 presents a list of small-molecule, rapidly acting transmitters and their functions. They are divided into four classes, based on their chemical structure. The slower neuropeptides will be discussed in the section on endocrinology.

Neuroglial cells provide support for neurons. They synthesize the myelin sheath, an insulating material around axons that speeds up the transmission of the nerve impulse. Regions which contain myelinated axons are called white matter; nonmyelinized areas such as nerve cell bodies are called gray matter and are important because they contain the synapses. Target cells produce neurotrophic factors, such as nerve growth factor (NGF) and brain-derived neurotrophic factor (BDNF), which protect neurons, regulate their

Table 7.1   Selected Small-Molecule, Rapidly Acting Transmitters and Their Functions

Category	Transmitter	Function
Amines	Acetylcholine	Used in both CNS and PNS pathways; excitatory effect on the CNS, but may be secreted by postganglionic nerves and has inhibitory effects on the heart. Massive decreases seen in Alzheimer's disease.
	Epinephrine, norepinephrine	Catecholamines; also used in both CNS and PNS pathways; largely excitatory but may inhibit some organ functions. Used to track stress effects.
	Dopamine	Secreted by cells in the substantia nigra; inhibitory, especially in motor neurons. Large decreases seen in Parkinson's disease.
	Serotonin	Secreted by cells in the brain stem; inhibits pain pathways and mediates mood.
Amino Acids	γ-amninobutyric acid (GABA)	Secreted by nerves in the CNS and spinal cord; inhibitory functions.
	Glutamate	Excitatory transmitter used in sensory pathways and the cortex.
Peptides	Endorphins, enkephalins	Opioid peptides; substantial role as natural painkillers
	Somatostatin	Important in regulating blood pressure.
Other	Nitric oxide	Long-acting excitatory transmitter; may be involved in long-term behavior and memory.

NOTE: Based in part on data from Beatty (2001) and Guyton and Hall (1996).

growth and function, and can contribute to CNS plasticity by promoting dendrification (Cotman & Neeper, 1996).

Cerebrospinal fluid (CSF) also provides support for the brain. The brain and the spinal column are bathed in and partially supported by CSF, which has protective functions, including cushioning the brain and regulating its extracellular environment. CSF is generated at a relatively constant rate by the choroid plexuses in the ventricular system, a series of spaces filled with CSF in the bottom and center of the brain. The ventricles serve as a type of internal cushion for the brain, protecting it from injury.

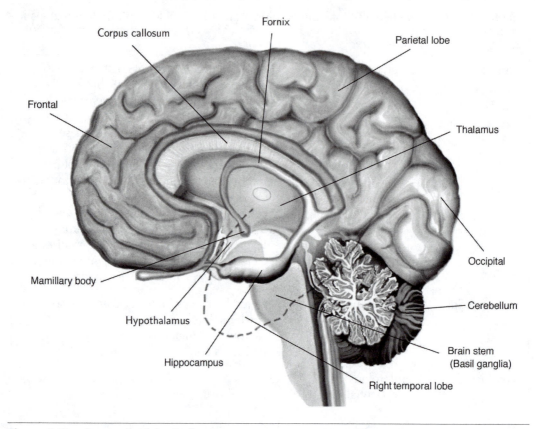

Figure 7.3   Structure of the Brain

SOURCE: Artist: Barry Burns. Used with permission.

The brain is a highly complex organization of different substructures that may have specific cell types, depending on their functions (see Figure 7.3). The phylogenetically oldest part of the brain is the brain stem, which regulates heart rate and respiration. The reticular formation within the brain stem mediates basic alertness. Wrapped around the brain stem is the cerebellum, which controls balance, body position, and movement in space and may store certain types of procedural memory related to movement, such as riding a bicycle. Sitting on top of the brain stem is the limbic system, which regulates many important functions, such as homeostasis (regulated by the hypothalamus and the pituitary gland), memory consolidation (mediated by the hippocampus), and emotions (mediated by the amygdala and pituitary).

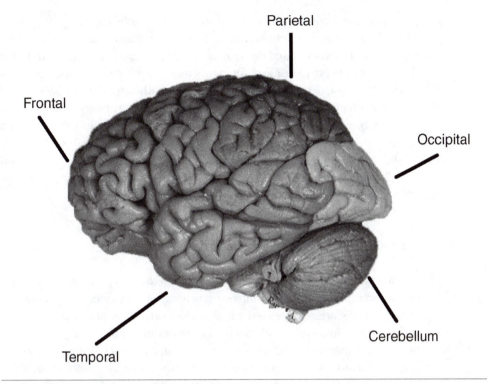

Figure 7.4   Structure of the Cortex

The limbic system is wrapped around the thalamus, which helps initiate consciousness and sort incoming information.

The cerebrum is by far the largest part of the brain and is divided into two hemispheres connected by the corpus callosum. The cerebrum consists largely of white matter and is covered by the cortex, which consists of gray matter. To increase its size and surface area, the cortex is folded into ridges called gyri. The spaces between gyri are called sulci. Each half of the cortex is divided into several lobes, including the occipital, parietal, temporal, and frontal lobes (see Figure 7.4). In simple terms, the occipital lobe processes visual information; the parietal lobe processes somatosensory information; the frontal lobes control voluntary motor behavior, language production, and higher-order cognitive and emotional processing, and the temporal lobes process hearing, recognition of faces, and higher-order visual processing and may be involved in emotional control.

Highly complex pathways connect all parts of the brain, and many researchers do not believe in a strict localization of function theory but rather posit that the brain functions as an integrated whole (Eccles, 1994). John (2001) makes a very cogent argument that presentation of a stimulus sets off temporal patterns of neural discharges throughout the brain, suggesting that the brain (and consciousness) functions more as a dispersed field, perhaps guided by constructs in quantum mechanics, rather than as a collection of simple mechanisms. In other words, consciousness may be mediated, not by simple mechanical connections in the brain, but by processes that occur at a more elementary physical level. Rather than the proverbial switchboard model of the brain, the appropriate metaphor may instead be a hologram (see Pribram, 2001). To our knowledge, however, no one has applied this construct to the aging brain.

Age-Related Changes

Whether or not normative changes occur in the morphology or structure of the brain with age is a controversial issue. As reviewed by Wickelgren (1996), early studies suggested a major loss of neurons with age. But these were often postmortem studies which did not differentiate between normal brains and those with diseases such as dementia, in which there is a massive loss of neurons. More recent magnetic resonance imaging (MRI) studies suggest a 10% to 15% decrease in brain matter with age. MRI is a precise imaging technique that allows examination of the structural integrity of the body. Unlike X-rays, which show images of the skeleton, MRIs can image soft tissue as well.

Even if brain mass does decrease, controversies exist as to what exactly is lost in normal aging. Some argue that there is a loss of large neurons, which is compensated for by the greater relative efficiency of the remaining small neurons. Some MRI studies argue that the loss consists primarily of gray matter, and others that white matter is what is lost. Still others suggest that any loss is focal, and is probably much smaller than previously thought (Albert & Moss, 1996). Poirier and Finch (1994) caution that neural tissue is highly plastic. The brain can compensate for neuronal loss with extra dendritic branching to maintain neural pathways, and a substantial number of neurons must be lost to affect functioning.

Nonetheless, being structurally intact is not necessarily equivalent to being functionally intact. Functional magnetic resonance imaging (FMRI) studies allow researchers to examine how well the particular brain regions process nutrients such as glucose or oxygen. Older neurons, especially those which do not get sufficient blood flow (perfusion), may not process glucose as effectively as younger neurons, suggesting a degree of impairment

(Sapolsky, 1999). Although it is clear that damaged neurons do not process glucose efficiently, it should be noted that more efficient neurons also use less glucose (Haier et al., 1988). Thus, if older individuals' neurons are using less glucose, this may be due either to impairment or to increased efficiency.

We do know that the speed of action potentials decreases with age in both the PNS and the CNS. This is likely due to poorer vascular perfusion of the cell body as well as damage to the myelin sheath. Whether or not the speed and integrity of neural transmission are affected by age-related changes in neurotransmitters and receptors, however, is also highly complex and varies by species as well as by site within the CNS and PNS (Poirier & Finch, 1994).

Changes also occur in neurotransmitters in the aging brain (Mattson, 1999). There is a decrease of acetylcholine in some, but not all, areas of the brain. Both pre- and postsynaptic dopamine levels decrease. There appears to be an increase of norepinephrine in some areas of the brain but a decrease in serotonin. These changes are much more evident in diseased brains.

Stress-related increases in norepinephrine appear to be heightened and return to baseline levels less quickly in the aging brain. This may underlie problems in maintaining homeostasis with age. Problems in ANS mainte-nance of homeostasis may be most noticeable in cardiovascular function. Many older adults suffer from orthostatic hypotension, a dramatic decrease in blood pressure when changing from a supine to a standing position, which can result in dizziness and falls. Normally, the SNS maintains adequate levels of blood pressure by stimulating cardiac activity and constricting blood ves-sels. However, the norepinephrine receptors may be less responsive to SNS stimulation (perhaps accounting for the higher levels of blood norepineph-rine), and thus the heart and the blood vessels do not respond rapidly enough to maintain blood pressure. There also appears to be a decrease in the number of motor neurons, as well as a decline in the speed of transmis-sion from the neurons to the muscle cells. This means that fewer muscle cells can be innervated adequately, resulting in a decrease in muscle strength, both in the heart and the skeletal muscles.

Changes in the blood-brain barrier (BBB) also occur with age (Shah & Mooradian, 1997). The BBB is an interesting structure composed primarily of glial and other supporting cells that serve as a buffer between the nerve cells in the brain and the circulating blood, protecting the nerve cells from many harmful chemicals. With age, however, the BBB can become more porous, permitting greater exposure to toxic chemicals as well as medications, drugs, or alcohol. There are some suggestions that changes in the BBB can precede the onset of Alzheimer's or Parkinson's disease (Skoog et al., 1998).

One of the more interesting constructs in the study of aging brains is the notion of brain reserve capacity (Satz, 1993). Like the genes, the brain has many redundancies built in to protect against damage. There are billions of neurons and undoubtedly trillions of connections between them. The density of neuronal cells may be one source of reserve capacity, as are the neurons' ability to metabolize glucose, the extent of dendrification (e.g., the number of connections between neurons), and even the overall size of the brain. The brain reserve capacity hypothesis suggests that the brain can absorb a fair amount of damage and still function relatively normally, given its redundant pathways. With age, this reserve capacity decreases until brains are left very vulnerable to damage and disease.

Disease-Related Processes

The incidence of diseases of the brain greatly increases with age. The most common are cerebrovascular accidents (CVAs), or strokes, but the incidence of other diseases, such as dementias and Parkinson's, also increases dramatically.

Strokes

CVAs result from the same ischemic problems as do myocardial infarctions or heart attacks (see Chapter 6), which is why they are also called brain attacks. Hypertension, arteriosclerosis, and atherosclerosis cause damage not only to the coronary arteries but also to other arteries, arterioles, and capillaries in the brain. Small, temporary ischemic blockages are called transitory ischemic attacks, or TIAs. These "ministrokes" are surprisingly prevalent, especially among African Americans, and are major risk factors for subsequent strokes (Woo et al., 1999). CVAs result from more permanent blockages in the blood delivery system in the brain, which can cause the vessel to be blocked or, less frequently, to rupture (Caplan, 1997). Aneurisms (weakened areas of blood vessels) can also cause vessels to rupture and create serious damage. These blockages or ruptures result in the death of nerve cells, and neuronal loss can have serious implications.

Which symptoms occur following a CVA depends in large part on the location of the stroke and the extent of the damage. Given that the right side of the brain controls the left side of the body (at least in right-handed people), a stroke to the right motor strip can result in paralysis of the left arm or leg, whereas a CVA on the left interrupts functioning on the right. Ruptures in the occipital cortex or disruptions of occipital nerves can result in blindness. More frequently, language is profoundly impaired. An individual with damage to Broca's area in the frontal cortex may have difficulty producing speech, but comprehension and other skills such as reading and writing may be preserved. Conversely, an individual with damage in Wernicke's area in the temporal lobe may "talk a blue streak" (which may be more or less intelligible) but be unable to comprehend language. Other types of damage may interfere with sequencing, memory, reading, writing, telling time, balance, and so on. Many neuropsychological batteries can help to pinpoint cognitive processes that have been affected, thus providing clues as to which areas of the brain have been damaged.

Ischemia and hemorrhaging are not the only sources of damage in strokes. As with any injury, CVAs are accompanied by inflammation, and cerebral edema (swelling) can occur, usually about 3 days after the initial stroke. This can result in further deterioration of brain functioning, as the additional pressure on the brain can further damage tissues (Ancheta & Reding, 1999).

If the neuronal loss is relatively minor, however, recovery of function can be achieved. Axons are capable of self-repair (Willis, 1993), and increased dendritic branching may occur to restore neuronal pathways. NGF may assist in recovery of function processes in part by stimulating dendritic branching.

Treatment for strokes depends upon whether there is a blockage or a hemorrhage. In the case of a blockage, an anticoagulant (blood thinner) such as heparin is administered to lower blood pressure. A new treatment involves tissue plasminogen activator (TPA), which, if administered within 3 hours of the stroke, helps to dissolve the clot (Guyton & Hall, 1996). TPA can improve functioning by about 30% (Ancheta & Reding, 1999), but it cannot be used for hemorrhages or if the patient has been on anticoagulants. If a patient is hemorrhaging, antihypertensives are administered. If there is massive bleeding, surgery may be required. Speech, physical, and occupational therapy can help to restore lost function. Strokes may also lead to dementia.

Dementia

The incidence of dementia also increases with age, and there are many different types. Relatively rare among the young-old, it increases rapidly in very late life, and nearly a third of people over the age of 85 suffer from some form of cognitive impairment (Backman et al., 1993). Dementias may result from several different types of disease. Vascular dementia is caused by a series of TIAs. Brain tumors in older adults may clinically present as dementia (Litchman & Posner, 1994), and also appear to be increasing. Pick's disease and Creuztfeldt-Jakob disease are particularly virulent dementias characterized by very rapid declines. However, by far the most common of the dementias is Alzheimer's disease (AD).

AD is characterized by an increase in neuritic plaques and neurofibrillary tangles. Neuritic plaques are composed of beta-amyloid proteins and dead neurons; neurofibrillary tangles consist of tau protein fibers twisted into a helix and lipoproteins called apolipoprotein E (APOE). Neuritic plaques are formed outside neurons, whereas the tangles may exist inside neuronal cell bodies, axons, and dendrites. It is currently a matter of debate whether the plaques and tangles cause massive neuronal death or are merely symptoms of an underlying process.

The hallmark of AD is a massive loss of neurons, especially cholinergic neurons. The brain atrophies and the ventricles become enlarged, as do the sulci. The symptoms of AD vary, due in part to the distribution of neurofibrillary tangles and plaques in the brain. The formation of plaques and tangles begins in the hippocampus and the innermost regions of the temporal lobes. It then spreads to the posterior regions of the cortex before eventually infiltrating the frontal lobes. Eventually, the plaques and tangles infiltrate subcortical structures, including the brain stem, making simple acts of eating, swallowing, and even breathing impossible (Scheibel, 1996).

Symptoms of AD include memory impairment and at least one other neurological deficit, such as difficulty in concentrating or confusional states. AD manifests first in a loss of short-term (recent) memory. A common complaint by caregivers is repetitive questioning—a person with AD may not remember that they have already asked the same question two minutes earlier, and two minutes before that, and so on. How much of this is driven by anxiety as well as loss of short-term memory is an open question. For example, one of our interns at a local assisted-living center for memory-impaired adults related the case of an elderly gentleman who was placed at the facility by his son. The old man was at a loss to understand where he was or why he was there. He followed the staff around, repeatedly asking what type of place this was. Despite repeated assurances, he persisted in this behavior, driving the staff to distraction.

Our intern finally asked a few of the other residents to sit down with this client. Curiously, each of them had a completely different idea of what the place was. The retired nurse thought it was a type of nursing facility, the former gambler that it was a prison, and so on. All of them continually reassured the man that the people were extremely nice there and that he would be cared for very well. He calmed down and stopped his questioning.

Management of repetitive questioning is a major concern for both family and institutional caregivers. For example, a patient may persistently ask whether her daughter is coming to visit that day. Camp, Foss, O'Hanlon, and Stevens (1996) devised a classical conditioning scheme in which they successfully taught Alzheimer's patients to orient to a board containing information whenever they start repetitive questioning. For example, a common question AD patients ask of staff is when their relatives will visit. The board will contain information about when the next visits are scheduled. The staff rewards the patients for orienting to the board and then reading the board.

In later stages, AD also affects longer-term memory. Memory losses become so extensive that the individual may fail to recognize loved ones, mistaking daughters for friends or spouses for parents, which can be devastating to both the patient and family members. Memory, however, is not a unitary construct. Rather, there are many different types of memory. One widely accepted distinction is that between episodic, semantic, and procedural forms of long-term memory (Schacter & Tulving, 1994). Episodic memory refers to memory for specific events, usually personal activities. Loss of episodic memory is most noticeable in AD, even in the early stages. Semantic memory refers to world knowledge, including knowledge of words, objects, and social customs, whereas procedural memory refers to praxis—the knowledge of how to do things. Semantic and procedural memory are relatively well preserved in the mild to moderate stages of AD but eventually become impaired in the later stages of the disease. For example, a late-stage patient may forget how to use a fork or even how to eat food.

Some interesting work by Ober and her colleagues (Ober & Shenaut, 1999; Shenaut & Ober, 1996) suggests that there may be preservation of some storage processes which are masked by performance deficits. For example, AD patients may not be able to remember many words from a list they were previously exposed to (or even remember that they had seen a list of words), but in subsequent tasks, they may respond more quickly to those words, indicating that the semantic network may be more intact than previously thought.

Memory loss is only one symptom of AD. There may also be impairments in abstract thinking and judgment, problems concentrating, and difficulty in finding and defining words or in copying three-dimensional figures. There may also be visuospatial disturbances that make it difficult to orient oneself in space. Although losing one's car in a parking lot is quite normal, the visuospatial disturbances in AD can result in an inability to find one's way around the neighborhood and sometimes even one's own house. Some patients with AD also exhibit rapid personality change, often characterized by increases in aggression and inappropriate social behavior. Eventually, in late-stage AD, the patient is unable to perform such basic tasks as feeding and toileting and may lose all sense of self. Infiltration of the pathology into the brain stem results in difficulty swallowing and even breathing, finally resulting in death. It is more common, however, for secondary causes such as pneumonia to be the cause of death in AD patients.

Not surprisingly, AD is the most widely feared of all diseases faced by older adults. Nonetheless, the progress of AD is often very slow, and patients in the early stages may have a good quality of life for a number of years.

Despite more than a decade of intensive research, we still do not understand the etiology of AD. There is a genetic component, and some of the latest research is focused on different alleles associated with APOE found in neurofibrillary tangles. There are four types of alleles, and individuals who have two copies of the fourth kind, $APOE_4$, are at increased risk of AD (Jarvik et al., 1996). $APOE_4$ may create a particularly "sticky" form of the lipoprotein, which may help to create neurofibrillary tangles. However, the largest genetic component is primarily in early-onset AD, which occurs in middle age and accounts for only about 5% of cases (Cole & Frautschy, 2001). $APOE_4$ also predisposes individuals to stroke (Zhu et al., 2000), and there is increasing evidence that TIAs and strokes may also predispose individuals to AD (Desmond et al., 2000). The co-occurrence of infarcts with plaques and tangles increases the severity of symptoms of AD (Snowdon et al., 1997). Heavy metals such as lead may also create neurofibrillary tangles (Haraguchi et al., 2001), and serum lead levels have been associated with memory deficits (Payton, Riggs, Spiro, Weiss, & Hu, 1998).

Because we do not understand the etiology of AD, there are as yet no good treatments for it. The drugs currently approved for treatment work by blocking the uptake of acetylcholine (ACh), thereby increasing the amount of ACh available. These have shown modest results at best, but there are several promising clinical trials for new treatments, including monoamine oxidase inhibitors, nonsteroidal anti-inflammatory drugs (NSAIDs), antioxidants, and estrogen (Cutler & Sramek, 2001). Recent studies have suggested that estrogen replacement therapy may reduce the risk of AD (Kawas et al., 1997) and may slow declines once they appear (Costa, Reus, Wolkowitz, Manfredi, & Lieberman, 1999). Preliminary results suggest that estrogen may also help treat it. Asthana et al. (2001) found that women with AD who were given skin patches containing estradiol demonstrated enhanced cognitive performance compared to controls. Presumably, the mechanism is through the protective effect of estrogen on vascular disease (Birge, 1997), but there may be other pathways as well, such as protection against oxidizing agents. However, combination estrogen and progestin may nearly double the incidence of dementia (Rapp, 2003).

One of the more interesting theories of the etiology of AD involves oxidative stress (Smith, Rottkamp, Nunomura, Raina, & Perry, 2000), and one of the promising approaches involves the NSAIDs. It is slowly being recognized that AD is an inflammatory disease, and new research has shown that individuals who took NSAIDs for 2 years had a lower risk for AD (Stewart, Kawas, Corrada, & Metter, 1997). Possible reasons are that some NSAIDS, such as aspirin and indomethacin, are antioxidants (Asanuma, Nishibayashi-Asanuma, Miyazaki, Kohno, & Ogawa, 2001), and also that NSAIDS may help to regulate apoptosis (Deigner, Haberkorn, & Kinscherf, 2000).

One of the most controversial potential treatments for AD involves nicotine (Newhouse, Potter, Kelton, & Corwin, 2001). There are nicotine receptor sites in the brain, especially the entorhinal cortex, which is important in memory formation. Treatment with nicotine increases blood flow after about 3 weeks, and laboratory studies have demonstrated improvement in memory performance with modest amounts of nicotine. However, nicotine is a double-edged sword: Smoking damages the cardiovascular system and is a risk factor for stroke, and, as previously mentioned, vascular damage increases not only the probability of dementia but also worsens its manifestation. Nicotine injections, although safer than smoking cigarettes, still have the potential to damage arteries.

Parkinson's Disease

The third most common neurological disorder in older adults, Parkinson's disease, is characterized by a loss of cells in the substantia nigra, an area in the brainstem which regulates dopamine levels. Loss of cells results in lower dopamine levels (McDowell, 1994). Movement is controlled through a balance of several neurotransmitters, including ACh, which governs contraction, and its antagonist, dopamine. Too much ACh results in overcontraction of the muscles. There are several different kinds of Parkinson's, but all are characterized by motor tremors of the hands, arms, and legs, which decrease when performing voluntary tasks and during sleep. Increased muscle stiffness and decrease in the control of muscle contractions results in balance and gait problems, as well as difficulty in completing voluntary movements. Some individuals with long-term Parkinson's may also develop dementia. Treatment with L-Dopa, a dopamine precursor, can mitigate the effects of Parkinson's but does not slow its progression (Moore & Clarke, 2001).

Treatment of Parkinson's includes physical therapy and occupational therapy. Although fetal tissue implants have engendered a lot of interest, they are still experimental and do not seem to be terribly successful. One of the most frustrating aspects of Parkinson's is "freezing"—a miscommunication between the nerves and the muscles that can make it difficult or even impossible to take a step forward. The more the person tries to move, the more difficult this becomes. Sometimes gently touching the individual is effective in breaking this cycle and restoring voluntary movement. Some patient groups are experimenting with the use of helper dogs, which can be trained to nudge the patient forward if he or she freezes.

Pseudodementia and Delirium

Not all cognitive impairment in late life is due to dementias. Depression can be associated with memory problems and result in a pseudodementia. Delirium is also characterized by cognitive impairments in memory and attention, but may include hallucinations and delusional states as well. It can be caused by a variety of factors that interfere with normal brain functioning, including inadequate nutrition, medication side effects, anesthesia, alcohol consumption, bladder infections, and so on. Pseudodementias and deliriums may be reversible if adequately diagnosed, but unfortunately the tendency is to attribute all memory problems or confusional states to dementia. Clinicians should first check for dehydration, malnutrition, overmedication, and changes in living conditions, such as bereavement. Note that even mild cognitive impairment can lead to mismanagement of drugs, creating more confusional states, which can result in a rapid downward spiral. Failure to recognize delirium can have serious consequences, including increased risk of morbidity and mortality (Tune, 1999).

Promoting Optimal Aging

Given that strokes are the leading cause of brain injury in late life, care of the cardiovascular system through exercise, diet, and perhaps a daily aspirin is also important for cognitive health. There is evidence in animal models that exercise directly benefits neurological functioning through an increase in the production of neurotrophic factors such as nerve growth factor, which can decrease neuronal death (Cotman & Neeper, 1996). Whether exercise directly affects cognitive function in older humans is still a matter of debate, however. Exercise does improve cognitive function for the extremely sedentary, and long-term exercisers exhibit better cognitive function, but short-term interventions in the elderly have generally shown little effect (Stones & Kozma, 1996). Longitudinal studies do suggest that older individuals who are very sedentary (maximum of one hour of any sort of physical activity per day) are twice as likely to exhibit cognitive declines over a 3-year period than are people who are more active. Sedentary individuals with the $APOE_4$ allele showed nearly four times the risk of cognitive decline (Schuit, Feskens, Launer, & Kromhout, 2001).

Nutrition is also very important in maintaining neural health. B vitamins are critical in promoting neural transmission, and there is evidence that, with age, the small intestines in mammals are less able to absorb B_{12} (Saltzman & Russell, 1998), leading not only to anemia but possibly impairing neurological functioning as well (Dharmarajan & Norkus, 2001). Antioxidants may also be important in maintaining neural health. Foods such as blueberries, strawberries, and spinach are very high in antioxidants. Bickford et al. (2000) have found that blueberries improve cognitive functioning in mice, in part by reversing age-related declines.

There is also the intriguing suggestion that cognitive stimulation may help to maintain cognitive function in late life. Enriched environments, in which animals receive extra stimulation, have been shown to increase the size of the cortex, even in elderly rats (Diamond, 1993). Education appears to be a protective factor for AD (Butler, Ashford, & Snowdon, 1996); Shimamura, Berry, Mangels, and Rusting (1995) found that emeritus professors at Berkeley who did not have serious chronic diseases showed few cognitive decrements with age. However, memory training for older adults in general has shown disappointing results (Woodruff-Pak & Hanson, 1995), and Pedersen, Reynolds, and Gatz (1996) caution that higher education may reflect better initial neurological functioning rather than function as a protective factor per se. Nonetheless, brain reserve capacity may also be important. In a landmark study of cognitive aging in nuns, Snowdon (1997) found that one nun who lived to a very advanced age was cognitively quite sharp, even though autopsy results showed that she had extensive tangles and plaques in her brain (see also Katzman et al., 1988).

One of the more intriguing hypotheses in aging research concerns the effect of stress on neurological aging. The hippocampus is particularly susceptible to neuronal loss with age, which Sapolsky (1992) suggests may be partially stress-related. Glucocorticoids released by the adrenal cortex as part of the stress response do appear to have detrimental effects on neuronal loss in the hippocampus in animals (which in turn results in increasing levels of glucocorticoid, resulting in a cascade effect). One hypothesis about the protective effects of estrogen for dementia is that it may block the neurotoxic consequences of the stress response (Henderson, 1997; see Chapter 10). Nonetheless, given that the exact etiology of AD and Parkinson's disease are poorly understood, it is difficult to specify behaviors that might avoid or defer onset of these disorders. In general, however, factors which maintain cardiovascular health often are useful for neurological health as well, if only because adequate perfusion of the brain is critical to maintaining health of the neurons and their supporting structures.

ENDOCRINE SYSTEM ●

Basic Anatomy and Physiology

The endocrine system is also a complex communication system that regulates growth, maturation, reproduction, metabolism, and body mass, as well

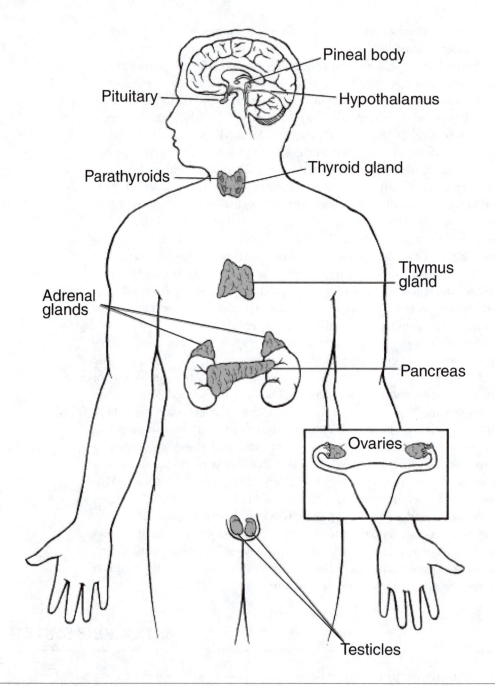

Figure 7.5 Endocrine Glands

SOURCE: American Medical Association. Http://www.medem.com/medlb/article_detailb.cfm?article_ID=ZZZW5TZ46JC7sub_cat=514. Reprinted with permission of the American Medical Association.

Table 7.2	Selected Large-Molecule, Slow-Acting Neuropeptides and Their Functions	
Class	*Transmitter*	*Regulatory Functions*
Class A: Hypothalamic releasing hormones	Thyrotrophic-releasing hormone (TRH)	Thyroid function and metabolism
Class B: Pituitary peptides	Growth hormone	Metabolism and lean muscle mass
Group C: Peptides which act on the GI system and the brain	Insulin and glucagon	Glucose and fat metabolism
	Glucocorticoids	Stress response; glucose, fat, and mineral metabolism
Group D: Miscellaneous neuropeptides	Calcitonin	Bone growth
	Melatonin	Diurnal cycle
	Sex steroids	Fertility, fat distribution, and lean muscle mass

NOTE: Based in part on data from Guyton and Hall (1996).

as senescence. Working together, the nervous and the endocrine systems integrate the organism's response to a changing environment. Clearly, there is much more overlap between the two systems than was earlier thought, and distinction between the two systems is being reassessed (Genuth, 1993).

Endocrine glands include the hypothalamus, the pituitary (anterior and posterior), the pancreas, the thymus, and the thyroid, parathyroid, pineal, adrenal, and reproductive glands (see Figure 7.5). We now know that organs such as the heart, as well as the stomach and kidneys, produce neuropeptides.

There are dozens of hormones, or large-molecule, slow-acting neuropeptide transmitters. Guyton and Hall (1996) group them into four classes, depending either on where they are released or what they act on, including hypothalamic releasing hormones, pituitary hormones, those that act on the brain and the gut, and miscellaneous. The classes and examples of these hormones most relevant for the aging process are included in Table 7.2.

Classic endocrine function involves the release of a hormone into the bloodstream for action on a distant target cell, as is illustrated in the top part of Figure 7.6. However, it is now known that hormones can also be transmitted

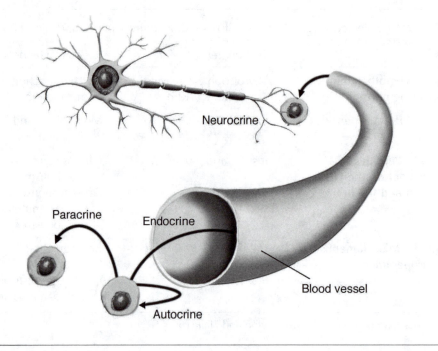

Figure 7.6   Endocrine Actions

through interstitial fluid to different cells within a tissue or organ (paracrine function) or to similar cells that produce the endocrine (autocrine function). In addition, neurocrine function refers to the transmission of a hormone (neuropeptide) from a nerve cell through the blood system to a target cell.

Although the pituitary has been called the "master gland," that distinction actually belongs to the hypothalamus, because the hypothalamus regulates pituitary function. The hypothalamus collects and integrates information from various parts of the brain and also monitors blood levels of various substances so that it knows what steps are needed to maintain homeostasis throughout the body. The hypothalamus communicates with the anterior pituitary gland by releasing hormones (in classic endocrine manner), and with the posterior pituitary through axonal (nervous) communication (much like the rest of the nervous system). The pituitary in turn produces other hormones that then regulate cells in distant target organs (long loops), and it also provides feedback information to the hypothalamus (short loops). The pituitary also monitors blood levels of various hormones and other substances. Hormone secretion is thus controlled by nervous impulses and

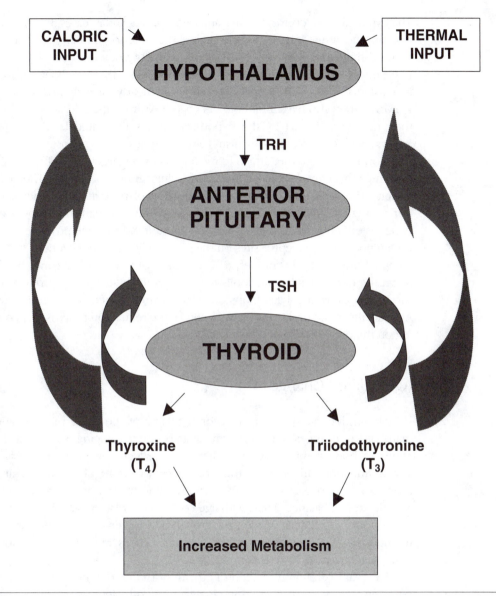

Figure 7.7   Thyroid and Thermal Regulation

other hormones, as well as by levels of the substances being regulated, which is called substrate regulation.

For example, thyroid hormones regulate energy production and utilization, increasing metabolic rates in response to cold or caloric needs often generated by exercise. Regulation of metabolic rate is illustrated in Figure 7.7.

The hypothalamus receives thermal and caloric input, and releases thyrotropin-releasing hormone (TRH), which causes the anterior pituitary to release thyroid-stimulating hormone (TSH), causing the thyroid to release thyroxine (T_4) and triiodothyronine (T_3). In turn, these raise the metabolic rate by increasing the rates of chemical reactions in nearly all cells in the body. However, they also have inhibitory effects primarily on the release of TSH by the pituitary and TRH by the hypothalamus (as illustrated by the larger arrows), which enable the organism to return quickly to homeostasis.

Hormones can either attach to receptor sites on target cell walls, or they can enter through cell walls and act on cellular function directly. They can inhibit, stimulate, or modulate the production of proteins and other substances that are lipid (fat) soluble. The effectiveness of regulation processes depends on a number of factors: (a) the amount of hormone produced, (b) the number of the receptor sites on the target cells, (c) the receptivity of the receptor sites to the hormones, (d) the length of time until enzymes break down the hormones for metabolism, and (e) the ability to stop production through negative feedback loops once the environmental challenge is met. Age can affect one or more of these facets of the regulation process, depending on the particular system being regulated.

Age-Related Changes

The endocrine system is a major regulator of the aging process, and many of the changes that we normally associate with aging, such as alterations in body composition and skin tone, reflect changes in endocrine system function. In general, the hormones which regulate growth and anabolism decrease, as do the sex hormones and those which regulate fluid and electrolyte balance. Thus, with age comes a decrease in anabolism—the synthesis of substances needed for growth and repair—and an increase in catabolism—the breakdown of complex substances into simpler components (DiGiovanna, 2000; Halter, 1999).

For example, the production of growth hormone (GH) peaks in adolescence and starts decreasing during early adulthood. Men demonstrate a linear decrease, whereas for women, growth hormone declines after menopause. Decreasing GH levels can contribute to lower bone density and less lean muscle mass. GH is produced in response to exercise, and it is likely that being sedentary contributes to declines in GH. Insulin growth factor is the primary mediator of GH action on soft tissue and muscle function. It also decreases with age, although not as dramatically as GH.

Calcitonin, a hormone secreted by the parathyroid gland, also declines with age. It is responsible for the maintenance of calcium levels in the blood. Calcitonin stimulates the osteoclasts to deposit calcium in the bone matrix and generally serves to inhibit the release of calcium from bone fluid. Dihydroepiandrosterone (DHEA) has many effects similar to other steroid hormones, and it also declines substantially with age. All of these hormones are responsible for much of the change in body composition with age, including decrease in lean muscle mass, increase in fat (especially abdominal fat), and decrease in bone mass (Tenover, 1999).

Not only are there changes in the amount of hormone secreted with age, but there are also changes in diurnal rhythms, or daily patterns of ebb and flow. For example, the elderly tend to be most alert in the morning, when levels of some hormones are highest. In general, the amplitude (differences between the highest and lowest levels secreted during the day) of these hormones decreases with age. Melatonin, a hormone secreted by the pineal gland, influences diurnal rhythms such as daily changes in the amplitude of ACTH and other hormones. Its own amplitude decreases with age, which appears to result in age-related changes in other diurnal rhythms of hormones and may affect sleep patterns.

Reproductive hormones also decrease with age but show fewer changes in men than in women. Testosterone and its derivative, dih drotestosterone (DHT), stimulate sperm production and regulate fat distribution, body hair, and libido. Testosterone and DHT also thicken and strengthen bones and muscle, resulting in a higher basal metabolic rate. Although testosterone may decrease with age, there are marked individual differences, and only 10% of older men have blood levels low enough to be considered clinically abnormal (DiGiovanna, 2000). Decreases in testosterone levels may be associated with obesity, alcohol consumption, medications, and poor health, and testosterone receptors may also decrease in sensitivity with age.

In contrast, there is a dramatic decline in sex hormones for women. In the reproductive years, the hypothalamus secretes gonadotrophin-releasing hormone (GnRH), which stimulates the anterior pituitary to release follicle-stimulating hormone (FSH) and luteinizing hormone (LH). These, in turn, stimulate the ovaries to mature a follicle. The follicle releases estrogen and progesterone, which in turn signal the pituitary to release more FSH and LH. After the follicle releases an öocyte (ovulation), the follicle grows into a mass called the corpus luteum. This in turn produces estrogen and a large amount of progesterone, which causes the pituitary hormones to decline. When the blood levels decline far enough, menstruation occurs, and the ovulatory cycle starts again.

The menopause process typically begins around age 45 and takes several years to complete. In the first (perimenopausal) stage, the menstrual cycle shortens, due to a decrease in the responsiveness of the ovaries to LH and FSH, resulting in decreasing estrogen and progesterone levels. Because there are fewer ovarian follicular cells that are responsive to FSH and LH, the levels of these hormones can increase dramatically, causing peripheral blood vessels to dilate, which results in hot flashes.

By age 51 or so, estrogen and progesterone levels become low, there is a depletion of responsive öocytes, and menses and ovulation cease, resulting in menopause. The ovaries still secrete some estrogen, although this stops by the fourth year after menopause. The adrenal cortex continues to produce small amounts of estrogen. In addition, testosterone and androstenedione (stored in fat cells) can be converted to estradiol and estrone, respectively. Consequently, there is still some circulating estrogen, although in the less potent form, as estradiol has weaker effects than estrogen.

The origin and regulating mechanisms of menopause are currently a matter of debate. One position is that menopause is driven by the decreasing numbers of follicles in the ovaries, the other that it is centrally regulated by the hypothalamus. In animal models, both mechanisms play a role in some sort of interactive fashion (Wise, Krajnak, & Kashon, 1996). But in women, evidence suggests that hypothalamic-pituitary function retains its ability to respond to steroid feedback (M. Barkeley, personal communication, September 2002).

At the turn of the century, the average postmenopausal life expectancy was 6 years. Now it is 23 years (Matthews, Wing, Kuller, Mailahn, & Owens, 2000). The drop in estrogen levels has serious health consequences. Estrogen and other sex hormones affect many functions, including such diverse ones as cardiovascular function, urinary tract function, nutrient absorption and metabolism, bone and mineral metabolism, and memory and cognition. The decline of estrogen also leads to many changes in appearance, including body fat distribution and skin wrinkling. Women who have more fat reserves may have more circulating estrogen. This is not necessarily beneficial, because higher estrogen levels and delayed menses may be associated with higher risks of breast and uterine cancers. Thus, estrogen is a good example of antagonistic pleiotropy—it has positive benefits earlier in life, primarily in regulating reproduction, but may increase the risk of cancer later in life.

Not all hormones decrease with age. Some hormones such as antidiuretic hormone (ADH) increase, usually because the sensitivity of the receptor cites on their target organs decrease. For example, ADH increases because renal responsiveness to it decreases, resulting in a reduced ability to concentrate urine and an increased frequency of urination. This can be dangerous, as decreases in aldosterone and plasma renin combine to increase sodium elimination and to decrease thirst. Thus, older people can become dehydrated, because they do not maintain adequate sodium levels and do not know they are thirsty (Gruenewald & Matsumoto, 1999). This can be exacerbated if an older person restricts sodium intake due to high blood pressure or restricts fluid intake due to urinary incontinence.

As Table 7.3 indicates, some hormones do not show normal age-related changes, including ACTH, thyroid hormones, and insulin. Levels of hormones in the blood reflect both production and clearance (breakdown or metabolism) rates, so levels can be stable either because there is no change or because both production and clearance rates decrease. Increasing or decreasing end organ sensitivity can also modify rates of production. There are many factors besides age, such as obesity and a sedentary lifestyle, that can alter these levels. Diseases may also result in changes in hormonal functioning.

Disease-Related Processes

Diabetes

The most important of the endocrine-related diseases is diabetes mellitus. Type I diabetes often occurs early in life and is linked to a lack of insulin production. Normally, insulin and glucagon are produced by the islets of Langerhans in the pancreas. Insulin regulates the conversion of glucose to glycogen for storage in various cells, including muscle and fat cells as well as those in the liver. Insulin also regulates glucose utilization by the liver. Its antagonist is glucagon, which stimulates liver cells to release glucose into the blood. It is very important to keep the levels of glucose in the blood within normal limits, as too much glucose can have toxic effects. Elevated blood glucose levels increase osmotic pressure, resulting in dehydration in cells, increased urination, and mineral loss. The inability of the target cells to utilize blood glucose results in a dramatic weight loss, as the cells are forced to metabolize fat for energy. Thus, the classic symptoms of Type I diabetes are being thirsty and extremely hungry, increased frequency of urination, and a decrease in weight. Very elevated blood glucose levels can result in brain malfunction, circulatory failure, coma, and death. Type I diabetes is treated by insulin injections and diet regulation, as well as subcutaneous insulin pumps (Halter, 1999).

Type II diabetes is defined as resistance to the metabolic effects of insulin, and thus it is sometimes called insulin-resistant diabetes. Type II diabetes is a metabolic disease in which glucose is not removed—or is removed at a slower rate—from the blood for utilization and/or storage in muscle, fat,

Table 7.3   Illustrative Changes in the Neuropeptide Transmitters With Age

	Level	Response to Stimulation	Production	Clearance	Sensitivity to Feedback	End Organ Responsiveness
Dopamine	⇔	⇑				
Norepinephrine	⇑	⇑	⇑	⇓		
Epinephrine	⇔	⇔	⇑	⇑		
Endogenous opioid peptides	⇔	⇑				
Melatonin	⇓		⇓			
Growth hormone	⇓		⇓			
IGF-1	⇓		⇓			
DHEA	⇓	⇓	⇓			
ACTH	⇔	⇓⇑	⇔			
Cortisol	⇔	⇑	⇓	⇓	⇓	⇓
ADH	⇑	⇑⇓				⇓
Aldosterone	⇓	⇓				
ANH	⇑	⇑				
FSH	⇓					
LH		⇓				
Estrogen	⇓					
Testosterone	⇓					
Insulin	??					⇓
TSH	??					⇓
Thyroxine (T$_4$)	⇔			⇓	⇓	
Triiodothyronine (T$_3$)	⇓					
Calcitonin	⇓					

NOTE: ⇑ = increased; ⇓ = decreased; ⇔ = no change; ?? = contradictory findings.

IGF-1 = insulin growth factor; DHEA = dehydroepiandrosterone; ACTH = adrenocorticotropic hormone; ADH = antidiuretic hormone; ANH = atrial natriuretic hormone; FSH = follicle-stimulating hormone; LH = luteinizing hormone; TSH = thyroid-stimulating hormone. Based on data from Gruenewald and Matsumoto (1999), Halter (1999), and Hassani and Hershman (1999).

or liver cells. This form of diabetes is linked to obesity and physical inactivity as well as genetics. Diets high in fats and carbohydrates lead to an increase in body fat, especially in the abdomen, which can interfere with the proper metabolic functioning of insulin, as does physical inactivity. Ingestion of large amounts of simple carbohydrates can lead to spiking of glucose in the blood, resulting in dramatic increases in insulin. Eventually, this decreases target cell responsiveness, which leads to higher levels of insulin production. At early stages, this is called insulin resistance, which can be readily reversed by diet and exercise but, if not controlled, can lead to outright diabetes, which may need to be controlled with oral hypoglycemics or insulin, or some combination thereof.

Type II diabetes increases dramatically with age. Some 12% to 18% of people over the age of 65 have been diagnosed with Type II diabetes, and an additional 20% have glucose intolerance, which is defined as delays in clearing excess glucose from the bloodstream (Halter, 1999; Stolk et al., 1997). African Americans have rates up to 60% higher than whites, and the greater prevalence of obesity does not fully explain this difference. At ideal weights, African Americans are 70% more likely to be diabetic; obese African American women are seven times as likely to have diabetes than obese European American women (Cowie, Harris, Silverman, Johnson, & Rust, 1993).

Nearly 40% of Americans over the age of 65 have some form of insulin resistance, and some have suggested that insulin resistance should not be designated as a disease, with the implication of abnormality. However, diabetes, if uncontrolled, greatly increases the rate of aging in three ways. First, it is a major risk factor for atherosclerosis. Second, it promotes the manufacture of sorbitol, which damages blood vessels and causes degeneration of the nerves, resulting in peripheral neuropathy. Third, high blood glucose levels also promote a process called glycosylation, which creates cross-linkages in proteins such as collagen fibers. Cross-linked collagen is stiffer and less pliable than normal. Together, these processes promote disease in many different parts of the body (Strachan, Deary, Ewing, & Frier, 1997).

Sorbitol and glycosylated proteins cause cataracts and diabetic retinopathy. In the retina, the capillaries can become so damaged that they burst, causing ischemic damage. The glycation process can also damage the lens, leading to cataracts. Although diabetic retinopathy is preventable by regulating blood sugar levels, over 60% of those with diabetes for more than 15 years develop this disease (DiGiovanna, 2000).

Sugar in the urine provides a good medium for the growth of bacteria; thus, urinary tract infections are common. Degeneration of the nerves can lead to urinary and fecal incontinence.

Sorbitol and glycosylated proteins can lead to skin breakdowns and infections. They also impair recovery from injury and lead to gangrene of the lower extremities. Amputation of limbs is only one of the serious consequences of diabetes. Diabetes impairs the circulatory system, leading to heart attacks, strokes, kidney failure, and cognitive impairment. Diabetics have twice the risk of CHD, stroke, and renal disease, and 10 times the risk of amputation (Halter, 1999). Thus, it is especially crucial that diabetics refrain from smoking.

Proper management of glucose intolerance and diabetes is extremely important and involves maintaining blood glucose within normal levels to prevent the production of sorbitol and glycosylated proteins. In many cases, glucose intolerance can be decreased through diet and exercise. Insulin sensitivity increases after only 3 days of exercise, although the exercise program must be maintained for this improvement to persist (DiGiovanna, 2000; Halter, 1999). However, compliance rates with exercise programs tend to be low. If diet and exercise do not keep blood glucose within normal limits, oral hypoglycemics can be used. The treatment of last resort involves insulin injections.

It appears to be difficult for people to make the connection between dietary habits, such as the ingestion of sweets, and the consequences of this disease, perhaps because so many different systems are affected, resulting in highly disparate problems, such as blindness, gangrene, heart disease, and urinary incontinence. Simple carbohydrates provide bursts of energy and may help to regulate moods, at least temporarily. High-fat foods are dense in calories, and preference for these types of food was undoubtedly evolutionarily advantageous. As Lev-Ran (2001) pointed out, food was often scarce throughout both our recorded history and prehistoric times, and energy accumulation was necessary for survival. Thus, genetic programming for the selection of nutritionally dense foods was critical for staving off starvation and promoting adequate fat reserves for warmth, fertility, and proper immune functioning, Again, a type of antagonistic pleiotropy seems to be at work—what may have been advantageous at an earlier time has negative consequences at a later one.

Thyroid Problems

Older adults also seem susceptible to both hypo- and hyperthyroidism, which are defined as under- and overactivity of the thyroid gland (Gregerman & Katz, 1994). Given the role of the thyroid in regulating metabolism, both of these conditions can result in fatigue and apathy. In both the young and the old, hyperthyroidism is associated with weight loss, nervousness, tremors, and heart palpitations. However, in older adults the thyroid glands are not enlarged, unlike in younger adults.

Hypothyroidism in older adults is most likely an autoimmune disorder and often results in atrophy of the thyroid gland. In the young, the classical symptoms are cold intolerance; slowness of speech, thought, and movement; and a coarsening of the hair and skin. Hypothyroidism in late life may be associated with ataxia (poor balance and gait problems), arthritic conditions, and depression, but many older adults only report fatigue. Vague symptoms such as these should not be dismissed as simply part of getting older, but require screening for hypothyroidism, as drug therapy is often effective.

Promoting Optimal Aging

Exercise and diet are important for the health of the endocrine system, especially for insulin and growth hormone levels and their effectiveness. As mentioned earlier, even among the very old, vigorous exercise and weight loss improve insulin sensitivity within days. The effect is temporary, however, and must be continued to be maintained.

Various kinds of hormone replacement therapy (HRT) have generated much interest but also much concern. Administration of growth hormones, DHEA-S, and testosterone can improve body weight and lean muscle mass in older adults. Unfortunately, this may not result in improved functional ability and may be accompanied by harmful side effects (Papadakis et al., 1996; Villareal & Morley, 1994). Not only does their administration result in relatively minor conditions such as acne and hirsutism, but they may also promote neoplasms (Dorgan et al., 1997; Tenover, 1999). Exercise is effective in increasing the body's production of growth hormone and DHEA-S, however, and is not associated with an increased incidence of cancer.

Other forms of HRT may be more beneficial. Synthetic calcitonin, often administered in nasal sprays, is effective in preventing or delaying the onset of osteoporosis and may even increase bone density slightly. Although it does not appear to affect bone density once osteoporosis is established, it may decrease pain and reduce the risk of fracture (Plosker & McTavish, 1996). Newer treatments such as Fosamax may increase bone density but can result in esophageal erosion and must be carefully monitored.

The most common form of HRT is estrogen or estrogen-progesterone combinations in postmenopausal women. Neither of these is produced by the human ovary. Early studies suggested that HRT delays the onset of osteoporosis and decreases the risk of heart disease and Alzheimer's disease (Kawas et al., 1997; Marshburn & Carr, 1994). Estrogen can decrease harmful lipids and cardiovascular reactivity to stress (Matthews et al., 2000). However, some recent research has cautioned that combination HRT may be associated with a slightly increased greater risk of heart disease, breast cancer, and dementia (Alexander et al., 2001; Rapp et al., 2003; Rossouw et al., 2002). The use of ovarian steroids such as estradiol is not as widespread and has not been studied extensively, but these may be a possible alternative to estrogen/progesterone therapy (M. Barkeley, personal communication, September 2002).

Some plants such as soy contain phytoestrogens, which some evidence has shown to be beneficial in combating the symptoms of menopause. The American College of Obstetricians and Gynecologists (ACOG, 2001) recently reviewed the evidence on the efficacy of botanicals in relieving symptoms of menopause. They found that soy and isoflavones may be helpful in the treatment of vasomotor symptoms, at least in the short term, and may improve lipoprotein profiles and protect against osteoporosis. Black cohosh may also relieve vasomotor symptoms, and St. John's wort may be helpful in the treatment of mild to moderate depression. ACOG emphasized that there is a problem with lack of standardization of products and insufficient clinical data, especially for long-term outcomes. Nonetheless, these may be helpful alternative treatments.

● IMMUNE SYSTEM

Basic Anatomy and Physiology

The basic function of the immune system is to distinguish between self and nonself. It interacts with the nervous and endocrine systems to help regulate the body and defends against invaders such as bacteria, viruses, and even parasites. The immune system is composed primarily of leukocytes, or white blood cells, that are divided into three major categories: granulocytes, monocytes, and lymphocytes, including T- and B-cells. Table 7.4 provides a useful summary of these cells and their functions.

The primary organs of the immune system include the bone marrow, lymph glands, thymus, spleen, and tonsils. The bone marrow produces granulocytes and monocytes and stores immature T- and B-cells. These lymphocytes are produced by the lymph glands, spleen, thymus, and tonsils. Lymph glands are found throughout the body but are most prominent in the neck, the armpits, and the groin area. The thymus is a small organ in the chest that also matures T-cells, and the tonsils are found in the back of the mouth, just in front of the throat. The leukocytes circulate not only through the blood but also through a parallel lymph circulatory system. Some immune cells

Table 7.4   Leukocyte Types, Locations, and Functions

Cell Type	Anatomic Location	Function
Granulocytes:		
Neutrophils	Blood, marrow, tissues	Phagocytosis
Eosinophils	Blood, marrow, tissues	Phagocytosis, resistance to parasites, modulation of hypersensitivity reactions
Basophils	Blood, marrow, tissues	Allergic reactions (source of histamine)
Monocytes and macrophages	Blood, marrow, lymph nodes	Destruction of intracellular pathogens, cytokine production, antigen presentation
Lymphocytes:		
B-cells	Blood, marrow, lymph nodes, tissues	Humoral immunity (antibody production)
T-cells	Blood, thymus, lymph nodes assistance, cytokine production	Cell-mediated immunity (B-cell immune functioning suppression)
Natural killer cells	Blood, marrow, lymph nodes	Cytotoxicity

NOTE: Based on data from Guyton and Hall (1996), Murasko and Bernstein (1999), and Rothstein (1999).

circulate, but others have fixed positions and are embedded in the tissue around the capillaries, the skin, and the liver.

Nearly every cell in the body has human leukocyte-associated (HLA) molecules on the cell membrane. These are genetically determined and are unique to each individual. HLA proteins are the primary way in which the immune system distinguishes self from nonself, with nonself including bacteria, viruses, parasites, and other noxious agents. However, the immune system can be activated by nonliving molecules as well, such as pollen or dust (which cause allergies, or hypersensitivity reactions). Anything that activates the immune system is called an *antigen*. The immune system also monitors the body for cells that have started malfunctioning, such as precancerous and tumor cells.

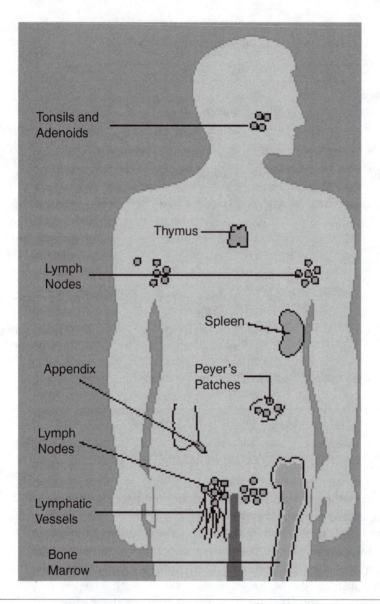

Figure 7.8 Organs of the Immune System

SOURCE: Based on artwork originally created for the National Cancer Institute. Reprinted with permission of the artist, Jeanne Kelly. Copyright © 1996.

The immune system is highly complex and has many components that interact. These can broadly be divided into two types: innate immunity and acquired immunity (Guyton & Hall, 1996).

Innate Immunity

The phylogenetically and developmentally earliest manifestations of immune functioning are called *nonspecific defenses*. Some components of this innate immunity include fevers, vomiting, defecation, and urination, which purge the body of pathogens. The immune system must communicate very closely with the neuroendocrine system in order to activate these defenses. However, they are very costly—fevers which are too high can result in brain damage or even death, and vomiting and diarrhea can result in massive imbalances in fluids and electrolytes, which can also be fatal. (Diarrhea is one of the leading causes of infant mortality in developing nations.) The immune system develops much more efficient means of defense that are specific to individual pathogens, and it continues to develop throughout the life span. Consequently, adults are less likely to run fevers than very young children, in part because their immune systems become more effective with age—at least until late life, when they may become less effective.

Innate immunity also includes the granulocytes and monocytes. The most important of these are the neutrophils and macrophages, which are responsible for most of the action against invading bacteria and viruses. These cells are phagocytes, that is, they literally eat other cells—especially those which do not have the protective coating that most indigenous cells have. Unlike the lymphocytes, they are not specific to particular types of antigens. A neutrophil can eat 5 to 20 bacteria before it dies. A macrophage is much more powerful. It can be directed by the lymphocytes to target particular bacteria or viruses and can eat as many as 100 bacteria (Guyton & Hall, 1996). The pus that is generated at the site of an infection is largely composed of dead bacteria, neutrophils, and macrophages. Basinophils are fairly weak, but they can attack parasites, which are much larger than bacteria, by attaching themselves and secreting noxious chemicals, a process called *chemotaxis*.

Acquired Immunity

In acquired immunity, the immune system "learns" to produce antibodies that can target specific types of invaders. These defenses are typically divided into cell-mediated and humoral immunity (Miller, 1996a, 1996b).

Cell-mediated immunity refers to activated T-cells. Immature or naive T-cells which have not as yet learned to become specific to a particular antigen are called rosettes. Through a process not yet understood, the thymus processes these immature T-cells, differentiates them, and "teaches" them to recognize specific antigens, or, more precisely, selects those which can recognize the antigen. Destruction of T-cells that would self-react is also a major role for the thymus.

When an organism is exposed to antigens, there is a massive increase in the number of T-cells (as well as other components of the immune system). One way this occurs is that macrophages release cytokines (a class of communicator peptides) called interleukin-1 (IL-1), which causes T-cells to proliferate in order to combat antigens.

There are several different types of T-cells (DiGiovanna, 2000). Cytotoxic T-cells (cT- or effector cells) recognize and lyse (split open) abnormal cells, such as those infected with bacteria, viruses, or fungi, cancer cells, or cells with the "wrong" HLA complex, such as those from transplanted organs. Helper T-cells, also known as CD4+ cells, generate cytokines that stimulate other parts of the immune system. Cytokines such as interleukin-4 (IL-4) stimulate B-cells to produce antibodies (see below), whereas interleukin-2 (IL-2) can assist in cell maturation. IL-4 also causes suppressor (or CD8+) T-cells, to proliferate. Suppressor T-cells serve to dampen immune reactions. This is critically important to stop inflammatory reactions.

Memory T-cells are the way the immune system remembers which antibodies work against which types of invaders. One reason the immune system becomes more efficient with age is because it does not have to spend precious time trying to figure out how to kill invading pathogens but rather simply consults its "library" of previous ways that worked. Thus, cell proliferation can take place much more rapidly, and usually the immune system can dispatch the invaders before they get a chance to multiply and take over too many cells.

Natural killer (NK) cells are an important component of cell-mediated immunity. They survey the body and can independently and quickly attack viruses and parasites without requiring presensitization, unlike most T- and B-cells (Murasko & Bernstein, 1999). They are also an important defense against cancer, because they can lyse precancerous cells, and they may be particularly important in fighting chronic viral infections (Spector, 1996).

Delayed hypersensitivity reactions are another component of cell-mediated immunity. These take longer to occur but grow in strength with repeated exposure. Delayed hypersensitivity T-cells can attract other immune cells such as macrophages or neutrophils to the site of an infection (Miller, 1996a), which takes longer, but can eventually generate a very strong inflammatory reaction. Allergic reactions to bee stings, nuts, and poison oak are examples of delayed hypersensitivity. Repeated exposure strengthens the delayed hypersensitivity reaction. This type of immune response mediates anaphylaxis, an extreme allergic response which can result in death, primarily due to swelling and closure of the airways and a dramatic drop in blood pressure. Immediate hypersensitive reactions (allergies) are mediated by an antibody called IgE that directs the mast cells to release massive amounts of histamine, causing the surrounding tissue to swell. People with allergies may sneeze and have watery eyes; in asthma, the tissue lining the airways may swell, creating difficulty breathing.

Humoral immunity refers to B-cells and their functions. B-cells do not directly destroy cells but instead generate antibodies or immunoglobulins. These are complex protein chains that specifically bind antigens and clump together (agglutinate) cells to help clear them from the body. Others simply identify antigens to the components of cellular immunity or to basinophils, which then destroy the invaders by lysing their cells. Conversely, sometimes macrophages lyse cells and then present the fragments to helper T-cells, which stimulate B-cells to produce antibodies.

There are five major types of antibodies: IgA, IgD, IgE, IgG, and IgM. (The acronym MADGE is useful in remembering them, despite the change in order.) Each of these antibodies has multiple subtypes, which in turn have different functions. For example, IgG, also known as gamma globulin, targets hepatitis, whereas IgE fights parasitic infections. As mentioned earlier, the overproduction of IgE is involved in allergic reactions and asthma. Antibodies are usually specific to particular antigens, but some antibodies can react to more than one antigen, which is called *multispecificity*. If the molecular shapes of antigens are similar enough, some *cross-reactivity* may occur, and more than one type of cell may be targeted.

One theory of autoimmune disorders is that the antibodies generated to target and destroy some viruses may inadvertently start attacking normal cells because of cross-reactivity. For example, diabetes may result from autoimmune attacks on the beta cells in the islets of Langerhans in the pancreas that produce insulin, or multiple sclerosis may be an autoimmune attack on the myelin sheaths of nerves. Thus, the immune system must be deactivated once the invaders are defeated, to reduce the risk of autoimmune problems or those associated with prolonged inflammation (see Chapter 3).

Age-Related Changes

Increases in infection and cancer rates point to impaired immunity in very late life, but there are large discrepancies in the literature about age-related changes (Khanna & Markham, 1999). The immune system is affected by nutritional status, stress levels, exercise, and disease, all of which change with age. Thus, it is often difficult to differentiate between age-related changes and those due to secondary aging. Furthermore, it is difficult to link decreased immune function with diseases such as cancer (Burns & Leventhal, 2000), and there are marked inconsistencies in the literature (Miller, 1996b), which can cause great confusion. For example, the thymus involutes, or gets smaller, with age (Aspinwall & Andrew, 2000). DiGiovanna (2000) asserts that the level of thymic hormones decline with age, and "circulating levels of these hormones reach zero by age 60" (p. 323). However, Rabin (2000, p. 67) states that thymic hormones increase with age. Whether or not thymic hormones increase or decrease with age is critical, because they help to mature, differentiate, and proliferate T-cells.

Further complicating the issue is the fact that there may be individual differences in how the immune system changes with age. According to DiGiovanna (2000), "Up to 25% of older people may show no decrease in T-cell functioning, while approximately 50% have moderate declines. The remaining 25% experience major decreases in T-cell responses to an antigen" (p. 323).

Nonetheless, there is a growing consensus that there are some age-related changes in immune functioning (Burns & Leventhal, 2000; DiGiovanna, 2000; Miller, 1996a, 1996b; Rabin, 2000). In general, the numbers of circulating B-, T-, and NK cells show little change with age, with two major exceptions. There are fewer circulating immature lymphocytes but more memory T-cells, and there may be a decrease in the diversity of both B- and T-cells. The lack of immature lymphocytes means that it may be more difficult to respond adequately to new antigens and also that vaccines may not work as well in very late life (Weksler & Szabo, 2000). On the positive side, the greater number of memory T-cells means that the older person's immune system may actually be more efficient, at least for antigens that it has already experienced. Another positive change is that delayed hypersensitivity weakens with age, which means that older people may be less sensitive to bee stings and poison oak and thus are at lower risk for anaphylaxis.

The more important changes may be in responsivity. In older organisms, there is reduced cell proliferation in response to antigens (Bruunsgaard & Pedersen, 2000). T-cells decrease in their ability both to produce and respond to cytokines. B-cells produce fewer antigens, but this may be due to a decrease in cytokines rather than any intrinsic age-related changes in the B-cells themselves. Macrophages also decrease in sensitivity. NK cells are less able to lyse cells, but they may compensate for this by increasing concentrations in the blood (Franceschi, Monti, Sansoni, & Cossarizza, 1995). Older immune systems may respond less well to vaccines, and there is some indication that vaccinations may temporarily impair immune response to other pathogens. Less work has been done on granulocytes and monocytes. Although the number of neutrophils remains the same, their responsivity may decline (Murasko & Bernstein, 1999).

Disease-Related Processes

Leukemias

With age, there is an increase in the incidence of leukemias (cancers of white blood cells), including multiple myeloma, chronic lymphatic leukemia, and chronic myelocytic leukemia (Rothstein, 1999). Early recognition of the onset of these leukemias is often missed, because the symptoms (such as general fatigue) are often vague and can be easily confused with more common problems in older adults. For example, the primary symptom of multiple myeloma may be bone pain, which can be misdiagnosed as arthritis. Sometimes the primary symptom is a series of upper and lower respiratory system infections due to the immune system's weakened ability to fight off infections. Not only are these leukemias serious and often fatal health problems, but they may create anemias which can aggravate other chronic conditions, such as cardiovascular disease. As with most cancers, early detection is critical for survival.

HIV/AIDS

Infection with the human immunodeficiency virus (HIV+) and acquired immune deficiency syndrome (AIDS) are typically associated with younger people. Yet studies consistently show that about 10% of the AIDS population consists of individuals over the age of 65. In 1997, some 60,000 older adults had AIDS (Ory & Mack, 1998). This may be due to transfusion with infected blood (less common now that blood donations are heavily screened), through sexual contact, or through intravenous drug use (Levy, 1998). There is some indication in the literature that the progression to death is faster in older AIDS patients, due in part to delayed recognition, comorbidity, and perhaps aging of the immune system (Crystal & Sambamoorth, 1998). Thus, older adults need to take the same precautions as younger adults if they engage in risky behaviors.

Promoting Optimal Aging

Current thinking suggests three ways to enhance immune functioning: hormone replacement, nutritional supplements, and exercise. Although studies in animals have suggested that hormones such as growth hormone or DHEA improve immune function, these findings are often inconsistent and have not been shown to work in humans (Miller, 1996a).

The immune system is very sensitive to nutritional deficiencies, especially to micronutrients. For example, zinc deficiency is associated with higher levels of autoimmune cells (Rabin, 2000). Vitamins E and B_6 may be helpful in boosting immune systems in older adults (Sone, 1996), as is a daily vitamin supplement (Chandra, 1992). Meydani and Ha (2000) reviewed the literature on the immunoenhancement properties of yogurt. Although many of the studies were of poor quality, they concluded that yogurt may be beneficial, especially in immune compromised populations such as the elderly, and called for more rigorously designed studies.

Exercise has some interesting paradoxical effects on the body. Different effects occur depending on the level of physical exertion. Exercise increases oxygen consumption, and, as noted in Chapter 3, oxygen consumption generates free radicals. However, moderate (but not strenuous) exercise enhances the production of superoxide dismutase and other antioxidants (Evans, 2000), even in patients with chronic heart failure (Ennezat et al., 2000). Moderate exercise may increase production of endocrine hormones (Venjatraman & Fernandes, 1997) and thus may enhance immune function, whereas very heavy exercise may impair immune function (Nieman, 2000).

The duration of the exercise program may also have an effect. Older adults who have a history of fairly high-level athletic activity have better immune functioning and fewer upper respiratory tract infections than sedentary older adults (Nieman et al., 1993; Gueldner et al., 1997; Shinkai et al., 1995; Venjatraman & Fernandes, 1997). However, short-term training programs in sedentary older adults often show little effect on immune function and may sometimes impair it (Nieman et al., 1993; Rall et al., 1996; Rincon, Solomon, Benton, & Rubenstein, 1996). Strenuous exercise can cause microtears in muscle tissues, triggering an inflammatory response (Shepard & Shek, 1996). Interestingly, Bruunsgaard and Pedersen's (2000) review suggests that a combination of exercise and dietary supplements such as vitamin E may enhance immune functioning. Although some studies found enhanced NK-cell cytotoxicity with exercise, exercise may impair NK cytotoxicity in very frail older adults. Thus, long-term moderate exercise appears to be beneficial for immune functioning, especially in the presence of sufficient antioxidants, but strenuous exercise or too much activity in nutritionally impaired or very frail older adults may harm the ability of the immune system to respond to antigens.

Finally, stress affects immunocompetence (Kiecolt-Glaser & Glaser, 1995), although studies in humans often show contradictory results, depending on the type of stressor (McIntosh, Kaplan, Kubena, & Landmann, 1993). For example, chronic stress such as marital conflict may result in impaired function (Kiecolt-Glaser et al., 1997). In contrast, caregiver stress does not affect the number of circulating immune cells, but it does affect their responsiveness to antigens and cytokines (Robinson-Whelan, Kiecolt-Glaser, & Glaser, 2000). Sadly, these effects seem to linger even after the loved one has died. Caregivers do not necessarily have more illnesses than others, but they tend to stay sick longer. Older adults who report higher levels of depressive symptoms under stress may show marked impairment in immune function (Aldwin, Spiro, Clark, & Hall, 1991; Tricerri et al., 1995). It is as yet unknown whether avoiding stress or participating in activities that can decrease stress, such as yoga, can enhance immune functioning.

SUMMARY ●

Communication among organ systems is extremely critical to the aging process. Neuroendocrine, metabolic, and immune functions play a critical role in the development of disease in the organ systems, and healthy functioning of these regulators can delay disease onset. Changes in these systems are often subtle and may (or may not) be reflected either in cell numbers, or in their functioning and/or responsivity to regulators. Maintaining the health of these critical systems is largely behavioral and includes adequate nutrition, exercise, and the avoidance of damaging behaviors such as smoking and overeating, as well as the avoidance of toxic environments (including those with very loud noise levels) and exposure to ultraviolet light.

Accelerated aging is characterized by the development of disease, and decelerated aging by the maintenance of good health. The final chapter in this section considers functional health. In many ways, successful aging cannot be judged by the presence or absence of disease; rather, it must be judged by how well an individual can function in society, which is generally referred to as functional health.

CHAPTER 8

FUNCTIONAL HEALTH, HEALTH PROMOTION, AND QUALITY OF LIFE

A person's state of health is more than the simple sum of physical illnesses and problems. Nearly everyone over the age of 65 has some form of chronic illness (Furner, Brody, & Jankowski, 1997; Jette, 1996), yet simply having an illness tells very little about how well one can function on a daily basis. Therefore, researchers and clinicians have developed various ways of conceptualizing and determining how individuals function in their social roles and enjoy life as well. The three primary constructs addressed in this chapter are functional health, health promotion, and quality of life.

Functional health refers to the ability to take care of personal needs such as bathing, toileting, and dressing, as well as tending to other tasks of everyday life, including shopping, paying bills, using the telephone, and navigating the physical and social environment. Health promotion programs optimize health and health behaviors and intervene in illness, therefore decelerating the effects of disease and functional losses. Quality of life is an overarching construct that includes optimal health and maintenance of independence, but it also has affective and cognitive components.

FUNCTIONAL HEALTH •

Older adults are healthier today than ever before, and most have an independent lifestyle. As a general rule, normative aging changes do not interfere with everyday functioning of the older adult. Indeed, most illnesses do not result in permanent disabilities or impairment—at least, not at first. There is a heightened chance of having a disability in later life, however, especially among those 85 years of age and older.

In advanced stages, chronic diseases affect many of the everyday activities of the older person. For example, sensory problems make it difficult to see or hear, impairing mobility and social interaction. Cognitive problems can limit the ability to complete simple tasks such as balancing a checkbook or making change in a store. Congestive heart failure often makes it difficult for a person to move rapidly, lift small bags of groceries, or even make a bed. Other disabling illnesses, such as arthritis or osteoporosis, can impact older adults' abilities to drive their cars and dress or even groom themselves.

Deterioration in balance and gait is a predictor of worsening health, and decline of these abilities has a major impact on the sensory, social, and mental functions of the older person. The loss of sense of balance is a major contributor to falls and fractured hips. Functional decline can also result from the cumulative effects of multiple organ dysfunctions; even modest losses, if they occur in multiple sites, can add to the stress load on the body (Karlamangla, Singer, McEwen, Rowe, & Seeman, 2002). This section describes how functional health is evaluated, the effect of functional limitations on the health and morbidity of the older person, and ways of promoting optimal health.

Assessing Functional Health

There are numerous ways of assessing functional health. Two of the most common are measures of daily living skills, activities of daily living (ADLs) and instrumental activities of daily living (IADLs), but gait and balance and cognitive function can be assessed as well.

Activities of Daily Living (ADLs)

In 1963, Katz, Ford, Moskowitz, Jackson, and Jaffe developed the first ADL scale to measure a person's ability to complete six basic functions: bathing, dressing, toileting, transferring from a bed to a chair, continence, and eating. Since that time, the scale has remained basically the same, with few modifications. It has been used extensively by health professionals to assess current status of a person, changes in a patient from one time to another (i.e., improvement or decline in condition), or level of assistance a person needs to remain independent in the home, such as help with bathing or eating.

In general, ADLs are measured by asking either the person or the caregiver whether a task can be completed. For example, the person is asked, "Can you dress yourself?" or the caregiver is asked, "Can the patient get dressed without assistance?" The answers are rated for interpretation, generally into three levels: (1) ability to perform the task independently (may need to use a walker or other assistive device); (2) ability to perform the task with some assistance (unable to cut meat, but otherwise can feed self); and (3) inability to complete a task, even with assistance (does not get out of bed without help) (Beck, Freedman, & Warshaw, 1994). At other times, it is more appropriate to observe the person completing a task (Guralnik, Branch, Cummings, & Curb, 1989). For example, an older woman may say that she can dress herself, but on observing her, it may be clear that she can pull a dress over her head but is completely unable to put on socks or shoes. Health professionals often find that observing patients completing ADL tasks in their homes is the best way to get an accurate assessment of functional ability.

Although few older adults have ADL limitations, these numbers increase with age, especially for women. Figure 8.1 shows data from a national sample of noninstitutionalized older adults (Kramarow, Lentzner, Rooks, Weeks, & Saydah, 1999). In this particular data set, the ADLs included bathing, dressing, using the toilet, and getting in and out of bed or a chair. As can be seen, fewer than 5% of people aged 70 to 74 had difficulty performing any ADLs. However, this changed with age, especially among women. ADL limitations increased to 11.8% of women and 9.9% of men in the 80- to 84-year-old group, and 22.6% of women and 19.3% of men at age 85 or older.

In general, older people are more likely to need assistance with bathing than any other ADL. Ability to feed oneself indicates the greatest dependency but is the least likely to be required. ADLs are an excellent measure of self-care ability; however, the ability to provide for one's basic needs is not all that is necessary for a life of independence. There are times when a higher order of self-sufficiency needs to be addressed. ADLs and IADLs are generally considered to be on a continuum from dependence to independence, with the latter including more complex tasks of daily living.

Instrumental Activities of Daily Living (IADLs)

Lawton and Brody introduced the IADL scale in 1969. To complete IADLs, a person has to have the physical and mental abilities to perform a

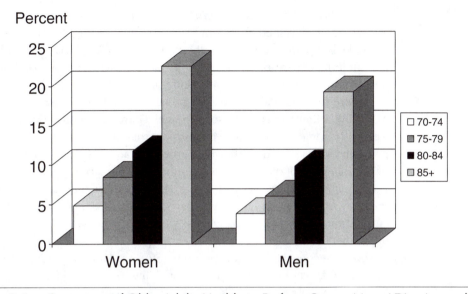

Percent

Women   Men

Figure 8.1   Percentage of Older Adults Unable to Perform One or More ADLs: Age and
Gender Differences

SOURCE: Based on Centers for Disease Control data presented by Kramarow, E., Lentzner, H., Rooks,
R., Weeks, J., & Saydah, S. (1999). *Health, United States, 1999* (DHHS Publication No. 99-1232).
Washington, DC: Government Printing Office.

task, as well as motivation. The first IADL instrument included the following:
using the telephone, shopping, food preparation, housekeeping, laundry,
independent travel, taking scheduled medications, and being able to handle
finances. Some modifications in the scale are occasionally added, such as an
item related to getting around outside, but the basic idea remains the same.

Questions evaluating IADLs are commonly addressed to the person
rather than the caregiver, as the scale is used to assess those who live fairly
independently. The questions are generally worded, "Can you go shopping
for groceries?" or "Can you prepare a meal?" The responses are rated "without help," "with some help," or "completely unable" (Beck et al., 1994).
There are a number of reasons why a person may be unable to perform a
task, such as physical limitations, environmental barriers, social constraints,
and cognitive impairment or mental illness. For example, a person may not
be able to shop because he or she can no longer get to the store or because
the local grocery store has been closed. Some men may have never learned
to clean house or to cook. Others may say that they can do something, but
prefer not to do it. Bootsma-van der Wiel et al. (2001) found a discrepancy

between those who said they *could* do a task and those who said they *did* do a task. They explained that some people could do light housework, for example, but preferred not to. It should be remembered that ADL and IADL are often dependent on not only the physical ability of the person but their mental and social function as well (Kane, 1997).

There are age and gender differences in IADL performances. As with ADLs, IADL limitations increase with age. There are gender differences as well, with women having more impairment than men. Few older adults have problems with IADLs until they reach their 70s and 80s. However, by the age of 85+, almost half of all women and more than a quarter of men have some IADL limitation (Kramarow et al., 1999). Many of these differences are due to the fact that men are more likely to have mortal illnesses and women to have chronic ones, such as osteoporosis, which are associated with functional impairment (see Chapter 2). The most frequently lost function is the ability to shop, affecting 11.1% of older adults (Stone & Murtaugh, 1990). Not surprisingly, relatively few people lose their ability to use the telephone.

Older people are more likely to have limitations in IADLs than ADLs, as they are more complex and are also more physically demanding to complete (Hoyer, Rybash, & Roodin, 1999). For example, shopping and doing light housekeeping (IADLs) call for a higher level of behavior than bathing and moving from the bed to a chair (ADLs).

In general, there has been a decrease in the rate of impairment in ADLs and IADLs among older adults in the past two decades. In a recent report, Manton and Gu (2001) compared the results of the 1982 and 1999 National Long-Term Care Surveys. In 1982, about 7% of those over the age of 65 had difficulty performing one to two ADLs, and this decreased to 6% in 1999. Similarly, those unable to complete five to six ADLs decreased from almost 4% in 1982 to about 3% in 1999. Manton and Gu suggested several reasons for this change: better health care, a more user-friendly environment for people with handicaps, and a decrease in number and a slowing of the progression of some chronic degenerative diseases (such as dementia, strokes, and heart disease). Furthermore, changes in diet and health behavior habits, such as avoiding smoking, have helped decrease functional losses.

In the above study, Manton and Gu (2001) also compared differences between African Americans and non-African Americans at two time points, 1982 and 1999 (see Figure 8.2). They pointed out that although older African Americans generally had greater rates of disability than non-African Americans, their rate of improvement over the time of the study was greater. For example, in 1982, more than 9% of older African Americans had one to two ADL limitations, compared to 6.7% of non-African Americans. By 1999, the two groups were very similar in this degree of functional loss. The

Percent

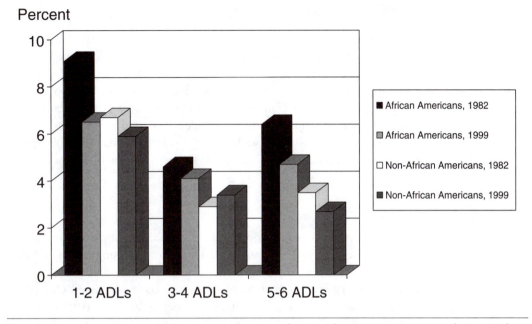

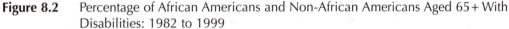

Figure 8.2   Percentage of African Americans and Non-African Americans Aged 65+ With Disabilities: 1982 to 1999

SOURCE: Reprinted with permission from *PNAS, 98*(11), "Changes in the prevalence of chronic disability in the United States black and nonblack population above age 65 from 1982 to 1999" by Manton, K. G., & Gu, X. Copyright © 2001 National Academy of Sciences, U.S.A.

pattern is similar for those with three to four ADL limitations, with non-African Americans actually increasing in percentage. The authors suggested that this improvement might be due to the increase in educational level of African Americans between 1982 and 1999. Socioeconomic status and functional losses are closely entwined.

There has been a concomitant decrease in nursing home residency over the past two decades, as noted in the Manton and Gu (2001) survey. Overall, 6.8% of older adults lived in nursing homes in 1982, declining to 3.4% in 1999. Older African Americans were even less likely than others to be residents of nursing homes (4.3% in 1982 vs. 4.2% in 1999). Manton and Gu suggested that this decrease in nursing home residency may be due to the increased use of home health care and the growth of the assisted-living industry. However, it represents the decrease in functional limitations among the elderly as well.

Balance and Gait

Another way to measure functional ability is to assess the balance and gait of the person. Loss of coordination is a risk factor for declining health in later years, and balance and gait scales are frequently used by clinicians to evaluate an older person's risk of falling. (For a complete review of balance and gait measures, see Duncan & Studenski, 1994). One frequently used scale, developed by Tinetti in 1986, includes observing a person rising from a chair to a standing position, walking and turning, and standing and leaning forward or backward. These items assess strength, flexibility, and balance.

Cognition

Another measure of functional health is cognitive ability, in particular, ability to care for oneself. There are several tools for assessing mental abilities. Some of them evaluate memory; others evaluate functional limitations, judgment, and social appropriateness of those with cognitive losses. One of the most commonly used tools to evaluate memory is the Short Portable Mental Status Questionnaire developed in 1975 by Pfeiffer. This 10-item scale measures both recent and remote memory (e.g., the current date, time, mother's birthday). It has been used extensively as a data collection instrument for epidemiological studies and also as means of screening for dementia in health clinics.

Measuring the functional status of those with dementia requires a different sort of tool than the usual ADL and IADL scales. Loewenstein et al. (1989) developed one of the first tools for this purpose, the Direct Assessment of Functional Status (DAFS) scale. Their instrument was designed to directly observe a person's ability to complete a function. For example, a person would be verbally given a grocery list and taken to a mock grocery store to find the items.

There are other challenges in measuring the functional ability of those with dementia, such as how to assess their environment for safety and their need for supervision, or management of behavior. For example, a person may wander, making it unsafe for him or her to be left alone in the home or yard (although he or she can walk with no difficulty). The person may also exhibit behavioral problems, such as aggressiveness, uncooperative behavior, agitation, and depression, that make caregiving difficult. Caregiving for those with dementia is often a complex and frustrating challenge.

Functional losses are closely entwined with the psychological, social, and physical health of the older adult. The following section describes some results of these losses.

Functional Losses, Morbidity, and Mortality

The consequences of functional losses can be severe, affecting the person's perception of self and the ability to maintain normal daily life. Losses can also foreshadow future physical and mental problems. If functional losses are great, family, friends, and other members of the informal network may be called upon to assist the older adult, although the formal network generally provides care for those with extensive needs.

Functional limitations can impact the lifestyle of the older person. Older adults who have compromised mobility can have a great fear of falling and therefore limit their activities, which causes further muscle weakness and instability in movement. Others may have sensory losses, such as vision or hearing, that confine them to their homes. The process can be cyclic in nature, and having one impairment can signal the beginning of a downward trend. For example, those who are unable to shop may have to pay others to do it for them or subsist on a lower quality of food. The spiral of loss continues downward as the person becomes more housebound, isolated, and less financially secure, with increasing feelings of loss of control and lowered self-esteem.

In 1983, Branch and Jette reported a relationship between poor ADL scores and need for help from family, friends, and neighbors. A later study by Branch et al. (1988) revealed that receiving help with at least one ADL was predictive of needing even more help, including long-term care in the home. Hager and Nennmann (1997) also found that older hospitalized patients with poor ADL scores at hospital admission were at significant risk of not being able to return to their homes.

Functional losses can affect mental health. Lawton (1983) found that poor health and difficulty with ADLs were associated with lower feelings of well-being. In another study, Japanese older adults who suffered losses in functional abilities had declines in social relationships, life satisfaction, and depression, as well as a lower quality of life (Asakawa, Koyano, Ando, & Shibata, 2000).

The relationship between functional losses, age, and mortality is not completely clear. Rudberg, Parzen, Leonard, and Cassel (1996), reporting on data from the Longitudinal Study on Aging, noted that although ADL limitation was related to a decline in life expectancy, half of the participants in their study died without ever having reported any ADL limitations, and even among those with five or more ADL limitations, death was not imminent. Furthermore, although functional losses were significantly related to mortality, age was an important modifying variable. To add to the controversy of age versus disability and mortality, Diehr, Williamson, Burke, and Psaty (2002) warned that it is the disease process that is predictive of functional losses and death, not age alone.

One of the major consequences of functional loss is the need for long-term care, either in the home or an institution. Increasing ADL impairment is often a precursor of nursing home placement, occurring after the informal network has exhausted its resources (Guralnik & Simonsick, 1993). Most nursing home residents are in need of extensive care, as more than 50% of them are dependent in the tasks of mobility, eating, toileting, and bed-to-chair transfer (Fries, Ribbe, & InterRAI Group, 1999).

Provision of extensive and long-term care has major implications for health care financing such as Medicare and Medicaid. Home care can be provided for a few older adults, as there is some payment from Medicare and more complete assistance from Medicaid. Still, there are times when the most efficient and safe environment for the older adult may be in residential care or a skilled nursing facility.

Promoting Optimal Functional Health

Positive and negative health behaviors have a major impact on functional health. Negative health behaviors, such as smoking, alcohol abuse, and obesity, accelerate the disease process and add to functional losses. On the other hand, exercise, moderate alcohol use, and tobacco avoidance lead to fewer functional limitations and greater longevity (Kahana et al., 2002). Even in later years, exercise has a positive impact on psychological and functional health (Yasunaga & Tokunaga, 2001). Other protective behaviors, such as good nutrition and having medical checkups and immunizations, can significantly reduce functional losses, compressing years of disability (Hubert, Bloch, Oehlert, & Fries, 2002).

Mental health also has an impact on functional health. Depression and low self-esteem can lead to neglect of health, including poor eating habits, social isolation, and physical inactivity (Lenze et al., 2001). Positive mental health, on the other hand, impacts functional health as well, through exercise, good nutrition, and use of a support system. In a study by Forthofer, Janz, Dodge, and Clark (2001), women with cardiovascular disease who had high levels of self-esteem were more likely to maintain or improve functioning than those with lower self-esteem.

Another indicator and predictor of one's health is the personal attitude of the person. Self-rated health is a major predictor of health status as well as mortality, over and above physicians' ratings or other objective indicators of poor health (George, 1996). Most older Americans report their health as good, very good, or excellent, even in the face of chronic illness. Not surprisingly, these ratings decrease with age (Administration on Aging, 2000). Johnson and Barer (1993) provide insight into ways that older adults maintain positive beliefs about their health, even when very frail. For example, they may minimize their problems or use positive comparisons. An older woman with severe breathing problems, for example, may feel that her health is better than someone with mobility problems who cannot lift herself out of bed. It is not unusual to hear older people say that their health is pretty good, "considering the alternative" (death). Thus, positive health behavior habits play a major role in the deferral and management of chronic illnesses, but, to a certain extent, the degree to which an individual is functionally impaired depends upon personal characteristics such as optimism, self-esteem, and coping strategies.

HEALTH PROMOTION IN OLDER ADULTS ●

Promoting good health behavior habits is critical to decelerating the rate of aging, but changing unhealthy habits (such as smoking, drinking, poor diet, and being sedentary) is often extremely difficult. Furthermore, chronic illness that causes pain and fatigue may make it difficult to exercise, or older individuals with terminal illnesses may see little benefit in changing, despite the fact that changes might enhance their functional ability and increase their quality of life. There is also an unfortunate perception, which is not supported by the literature, that interventions may not be as effective in late life. This section describes theories of behavior change and reviews some programs that have been shown to be successful in older adults.

Models of Health Behavior Change

Early models of behavior change tended to be relatively simple and to emphasize behavioral or cognitive interventions. Behavioral models focused primarily on reward and punishment. An early example was the recommendation that a smoker fasten a rubber band around one wrist and snap it whenever he or she felt the urge to have a cigarette. Health belief models emphasized cognitive processes concerning the impact of health behaviors and focused on education (e.g., the dangers of smoking). Programs based on these models had only limited success, especially with regard to long-term change (Stunkard, 1975). Most current models are more complex, including behavioral, motivational, cognitive, and social components. There are several models of health change, but here we focus on two of the most widely used, self-efficacy and self-regulation models.

Self-Efficacy Model

This model is based on social cognition theory, which details the relationships among personal characteristics, behavior, and the social environment. This model posits that people change behavior by setting goals, giving rewards or incentives, using problem-solving techniques to overcome obstacles, and engaging the social environment in achieving goals. Self-efficacy (the belief that one is capable of making and mastering desired changes) plays a key role in success of health behavior change in this model (Bandura, 2000). Change should be incremental, and the goal must not exceed the ability of the person (see DeVellis & DeVellis, 2001).

For example, the goal of quitting smoking may be best achieved through incremental steps. Individuals may not believe that they are capable of quitting, because earlier attempts at stopping all at once were unsuccessful. They may feel that they can achieve more modest goals, however, such as delaying lighting up for 5 or 10 minutes, or decreasing the number of cigarettes smoked each day. Success with achieving a minor goal increases an individual's feeling of self-efficacy and can encourage the person to gradually increase the difficulty of the goal over time. A reward system may be coupled with this. For example, some people might save the money they would have spent on cigarettes and use it for a vacation or other treat. Encouragement from the social environment is also important, and individuals may need to avoid people who are still engaging in the habit they are trying to break.

Sometimes outside interventions are necessary, especially with problems such as alcohol or drug abuse, which often involve large amounts of denial about the seriousness or magnitude of the problem. The transtheoretical model suggests that behaviors can be changed, but that attempts to change are most successful when interventions from outside sources mesh with the individual's level of readiness for change (Wilcox & King, 1999).

Self-Regulation Model

Leventhal, Rabin, Leventhal, and Burns (2001) suggest that the self-regulation model may be particularly appropriate to use with older adults, as it is built around the motivational characteristics of the participant for health promotion and disease prevention. There are several steps in the self-regulation model; in general, a person sets goals, monitors his or her own progress, and receives rewards for positive actions. The progress is detailed and encouraged by an implementer who provides guidance and support. The sociocultural context of change is also important, and the proposed change needs to be sensitive to the person's age, social influences, culture, and community (Leventhal,

Leventhal, & Cameron, 2001; Leventhal, Rabin, et al., 2001). Although there are similarities between the self-efficacy and self-regulation models, the latter focuses more on historical and social influences that may be relevant to particular cohorts of older persons, as well as the process by which change occurs.

For example, an older woman who has never exercised might hesitate to attend an exercise program after fracturing a hip, although she knows, intellectually, that she would benefit from attending. The barrier to her partaking is that she is not perceived as an exerciser, either by her immediate community or by herself. Therefore, a plan of health behavior change needs to be developed for her, one that connects to her history and her place in her community. The solution may be to have her join a small group of peers for a session of gentle sitting exercises and to incorporate it into a social session as well. Meetings twice weekly with a health educator would provide encouragement and support. A prescription by her doctor to attend such classes would also be a motivating factor.

A self-regulation-based program was used by Clark et al. (2000) to compare two groups of women who had heart disease. Women in the study group met several times with a health educator to learn disease management skills (medication management, ways to reduce stress, etc.). Although each woman selected the area of health that she wanted to work on, such as diet or stress management, increase in activity was encouraged for all. Following the self-regulation model, the women were provided information on heart disease and encouraged to evaluate their activities and to keep a journal of their progress. Weekly motivational phone calls were made to the participants, who also received occasional motivational letters. At the end of 12 months, women in the study group had lost more weight, had fewer heart symptoms, and had greater improvement in physical functioning than those in the control group. The authors concluded that participants had benefited by management of their diseases through this self-regulation program.

According to Leventhal, Rabin, et al. (2001), health behavior change reflects an ongoing process, including interactions between the facilitator and the individual and revision of goals based on intermediate outcomes. Careful attention to the process is important for its success.

Health Promotion Programs for Older Adults

There are hundreds of health promotion programs, many of which are directed at specific demographic groups, such as adolescents, preteens, women, or members of particular ethnic groups (Evans, 2001; Landrine & Klonoff, 2001; Rimer, McBride, & Crump, 2001). Given that many of the programs are targeted at diseases that affect people in midlife or late life, it is surprising that there does not appear to be a coherent literature on how programs should be altered to fit the needs of the older person. Many studies present interventions for adults aged 40 and over, but there may be huge differences between those in midlife, young-old adults, and frail elders. Individual programs often use innovative approaches, however, and a few of these are reviewed in this section.

For example, exercise has been shown to benefit muscular and skeletal strength and flexibility in older adults (see Chapter 5). Cardiovascular, pulmonary, and cognitive function can also improve with exercise, especially in the more sedentary older adult (see Chapters 6 and 7). Furthermore, early intervention in chronic disease can limit functional losses, as evidenced by Seeman and Chen (2002) in their study of older adults with cardiovascular disease, hypertension, and cancer: Those who engaged in physical activity had better physical functioning than those who did not.

Older adults are more prone to injury than younger adults, however, and exercise programs need to be modified with this caveat in mind. Rehabilitation, muscle strengthening exercises, and programs to improve balance have been very successful in maintaining mobility and reducing the incidence of injury and disability. For example, several studies have shown an increase in muscle strength when older people are in programs that use exercise bands—flexible rubber or plastic bands of varying resistance that can gradually develop strength (Capodaglio et al., 2002; Damush & Damush, 1999). Tai chi, with its emphasis on slow movements and balance, may be particularly well suited to older adults. Taggart (2001) reported improvement in self-assessed health after 3 months of participation in a tai chi program. Many older adults have been encouraged to do aerobic exercise in swimming pools to reduce the strain on weakened muscles and joints. To our knowledge, however, there have been no systematic evaluations to determine the differential benefit of this type of exercise for different age groups, or whether older adults are more likely to adhere to such programs.

One study did compare the relative efficacy of two different types of exercise (A. C. King et al., 2000). Older adults were randomly assigned to either an endurance and strengthening program or one that focused on stretching and flexibility. The endurance and strengthening program produced greater increases in upper body strength and endurance, and the stretching produced greater flexibility and relief from pain, especially for men. Adherence rates were high during the program, due to fairly intensive reminders, but dropped off once the programs ended. At the 6-month follow-up, only one difference between the groups remained significant: The endurance group had slightly better cardiovascular function. This study indicates both the benefits of participating in an exercise program and the problems of long-term adherence.

Another benefit of health education programs is that they may help delay or minimize the effects of emotional stress. For example, those recently bereaved have an increase in cardiovascular disease, presumably due to stress and a lack of self-care (see Chapter 2). Caserta, Lund, and Rice (1999) developed a self-care and health education program for men and women (aged 50 and older) who had been recently widowed. The program was designed to encourage positive behavior changes (e.g., immunizations, recognition of stress, value of exercise). Although the meetings were led by professionals, members were also asked to share their skills and expertise. The strength of the program was in the development of a support system of similarly widowed older people that helped to sustain participants in their goal of improved self-care and, ultimately, better health.

Health promotion includes health screening programs as well as out-reach. The second author worked for many years in the statewide Preventive Health Care for Older Adults (PHCA) program in California. The program is free—staffed by public health nurses and funded by the California State Department of Health. Public health nurses screen older adults for glaucoma, hearing loss, diabetes, cardiovascular disease, psychological or social prob-lems, and so on. People are screened annually and return to the clinics for educational programs or reevaluation, if needed. When a problem is evident, referrals are made to appropriate agencies. As an adjunct to this program, public health nurses go door to door in neighborhoods with high concen-trations of older adults, receiving referrals from senior centers, apartment managers, and the like. In many cases, this outreach is the primary connec-tion of the older person to a health care professional.

In another community-sponsored program, questionnaires about health status were mailed to older residents. After the questionnaires were evalu-ated, a public health nurse made a visit to the home of each person deemed at risk. If needed, a referral was made to an appropriate health care agency. In many cases, outside assistance was given that made it possible for older adults to continue living at home (Robichaud, Hebert, Roy, & Roy, 2000).

Educational programs in a community can be successful, but they will only be accepted among certain groups if attention is paid to cultural diver-sity in health beliefs and practices (Landrine & Klonoff, 2001). To reach eth-nic groups, it is necessary to recognize sociocultural differences, including values and health beliefs, such as those concerning forbidden foods, medici-nal use of opium, folk cures, and harmony of physical, spiritual, and social forces. Some older adults may not trust information from members of other ethnic groups, because it may be counter to established beliefs. When health professionals work with ethnic groups other than their own, it is helpful to include family members in health education programs or to solicit the advice of community leaders. Particularly successful programs may be those that involve collaborations between traditional healers and health care workers.

Thus, for older adults, health promotion programs with substantial amounts of outreach and individual contact may be necessary to optimize functional health and prevent institutionalization.

Environmental Competence

Environmental competence refers to the interaction between an individual's capabilities and disabilities and the characteristics of the environment in which he or she lives (Lawton & Brody, 1969). The goal of optimal health is to provide a fit between individuals and their environment. A person who has problems functioning in one environment may be much more comfortable in one that is less challenging. For example, someone with arthritis in the knees may have severe mobility problems living in an apartment with many stairs. Such a person may be perfectly capable of living in a ranch-style house, though. Lawton and Brody's seminal insight in this area triggered research into how environments can affect individual competencies. This gave rise to a whole field of elder design in housing, transportation, institutions, and streets, making them safer and more usable for individuals with disabilities. The goal in adapting the environment is to maximize the individual's independence.

Functional assessments can be used to help in modifying the environment and maximizing an older person's abilities. For example, a limitation in walking may be minimized if the environment is changed. Ramps can be installed instead of stairs. For those who have difficulty lifting themselves from a sitting position, rails can be put on bathtubs and toilets. People who are in wheelchairs may need to have counters lowered. These environmental changes can enable older persons to live fairly independently in their homes. Nursing homes and independent living homes also benefit from environmental adaptations. An innovative program called the "Wandering Gardens" in some nursing homes and adult day centers has enabled cognitively impaired older adults to continue to go for walks in an interesting, diverting, and soothing manner. These planned outdoor walking spaces help to keep older adults active in a safe environment. Walking may also reduce anxiety and can be calming.

There are times, however, when individuals must adapt to the environment or living situation following changes in their health. For example, after hip surgery, many older adults must use a walker or cane and a ramp rather than stairs. They may even have to relearn how to put on shoes and socks. Older adults with lung disease may have to take oxygen wherever they go and learn that when air quality is poor, they need to remain in their homes. Occupational therapists have developed a broad array of devices that facilitate independence even for whose who are severely impaired. For example, oversized spoons and weighted mugs can help individuals with tremors such as those caused by Parkinson's disease. Even simple devices like enlarged print can help older people read signs and labels so that they can negotiate their environment.

In assessing the well-being of older adults and others with chronic illnesses, it is apparent that health encompasses more than just the ability to perform daily tasks. Ideally, a healthy person also enjoys good mental as well as physical health and has a certain joie de vivre. Thus, researchers and clinicians focus on the broader construct of quality of life.

QUALITY OF LIFE ●

Quality of life describes the well-being and life satisfaction of an individual. It is a multifactorial construct including, but not limited to, interpersonal relationships and social support, physical and mental health, environmental comfort, and a host of psychological factors such as locus of control, emotions, usefulness, and personality, as well as meaning in life (Kaplan & Erickson, 2000). Sometimes even simple interventions can dramatically improve the quality of life for older adults. In a study of older adults in Israel (Isralowitz, 2000), providing eyeglasses to Ethiopian immigrants improved physical function, allowed individuals to better perform their personal needs, and increased their daily interaction with others, thus improving quality of life.

Quality of life can generally be divided into environmental, physical, social, and psychological well-being domains. The environmental aspect includes the everyday environment, both home and community, of the person. Older adults often want to remain in their homes and their communities as they get older. In many cases, this "aging in place" occurs in an environment that once was a desirable place to live but is no longer safe, or may not provide the resources necessary for maintaining independence. Increases in crime, old homes that are not handicapped accessible, problems with transportation, minimizing of community resources such as grocery stores or pharmacies, and loss of long-term neighbors may adversely affect quality of life of the older person. On the other hand, there are a growing number of community resources that can mitigate environmental problems, including senior citizens vans, senior handyman/-women (frequently older adults themselves), Meals on Wheels, and telephone reassurance. Sometimes older adults may find it necessary to change environments to maintain some degree of independence, either by moving to retirement communities, senior apartments, or a relative's home.

Social well-being generally refers to interrelationships and social support, or role fulfillment. Social well-being includes participating in activities with family and friends, to the degree that is comfortable to the individual. As people become more frail and unable to move about their communities, they may interact less with family, friends, and community members. Lawton, Moss, and Duhamel (1995) studied the relationship of activities and contacts with others to quality of life of frail housebound elders. They concluded that continuing activity was a result of cognitive as well as physical health and that frail older adults could be better served if they had activities that were more stimulating (e.g., being taken out of the house and having more verbal contact with caregivers). In a study of older women with heart disease, those who maintained or improved their satisfaction with social activities after a cardiac event reported significantly better quality of life than those whose satisfaction with social activities declined (Janz et al., 2001). Rowe and Kahn (1998) placed engagement with life as one of the main components of successful aging. The authors maintain that, rather than disengaging from life, older adults should retain close relationships with others and pursue activities that are purposeful.

Psychological well-being refers to an individual's mental and emotional health. Ryff, Kwan, and Singer (2001) identified six elements of psychological health: self-acceptance, positive relations with others, environmental mastery, autonomy, purpose in life, and personal growth. Meaning in life is an extremely important aspect of well-being that is not studied as much in late life. Simone de Beauvoir wrote, "The greatest good fortune, even greater than health, for the old person is to have his world still inhabited by projects: then, busy and useful, he escapes both boredom and decay" (cited in Moody, 2000, p. 422). This can be interpreted in the broadest sense, caring for family members, continued professional activities, volunteer activities, or spiritual pursuits. Ekerdt (1986) described the "busy ethic." Many retired adults claim that they are busier after retirement than they were while working. It is unclear to what extent that is because retirement frees them to pursue long-neglected avocations, or whether work expands to fill the time allotted, as the old adage goes. Regardless of the source, feeling busy is one way of maintaining one's self-worth.

On the other hand, life fulfillment can be evaluated only from the perspective of the individual Strawbridge, Wallhagen, and Cohen (2002) found that nearly half of their respondents who did not meet Rowe and Kahn's criteria for successful aging did consider themselves to be successful. Despite adverse changes in physical health and ability, older adults generally have a feeling of positive affect, well-being, and life satisfaction, in addition to a sense of continued growth and purpose in life (Ryff et al., 2001). Among many older individuals, a pulling away from community activities and social events is not necessarily negative, but the result of a desire to focus on remaining resources to save energy and to pursue other goals, such as life review. When multiple social roles are diminished, there is also a decrease in responsibility for the problems of others, which can relieve stress.

Quality of life is usually a person's value judgment of his or her life. Furthermore, an individual may perceive his or her own quality of life very differently from how others perceive it. For example, someone with a history of living in a certain part of town may find comfort in staying there even though it has become rundown and unsafe. Yet, from an outsider's point of view, the quality of life in that environment would not seem very satisfactory. Indeed, according to Lawton (1983), those who live in what appear to be unpleasant living environments can have a high perceived quality of life; in the eyes of such individuals, the greater value is to maintain autonomy and reside in their own communities.

Although self- and other-perceived quality of life may decline in later years for numerous reasons, it may not seem like a loss for the older person. For example, an older woman may need a walker to get around yet welcome each day with gladness, because she is alive and can still read her cherished newspaper. In contrast, another woman may be in relatively good physical health but feel that her life is empty and useless. What encompasses quality of life may change with age and added wisdom.

In 2001, shortly before his death, Lawton wrote a chapter for the *Handbook of the Psychology of Aging* (2001) called "Quality of Life and the End of Life." In it, he reminded us that we need to study quality-of-life issues from the perspective of the person. Therefore, when studying the quality of life of those who are dying, it is necessary to question dying persons, not those who are healthy. Quality of life at the time of dying needs to be measured as a physical, social, and psychological construct, as it is at all times of life. Lawton suggested that the social entities of continuing relationships with family and friends (during the dying process) may override physical care requirements. It is most likely true that social space becomes smaller and control of life is endangered during this time. Psychological health must also be considered, including emotional satisfaction and well-being, as well as spirituality. Lawton was requesting forthcoming studies on these issues and that the information gathered be used to help people plan for dying and for death—with quality.

● SUMMARY

This chapter addressed functional health, health promotion, and quality of life. Risk factors for functional loss, measurement, and the impact of limitations on the biological, social, and psychological health of older persons were reviewed. We also reported on some health programs that help to maintain good health in the older population through health prevention and intervention programs and changing health behaviors. With disease and functional loss, there is an increase in need to adapt to the environment and vice versa. These changes are usually made to enhance the life of the older person.

Finally, quality of life in the elder years was discussed. Psychosocial factors play an important role in accelerating and decelerating aging processes and affect functional health and the quality of life in later years. These are addressed in the next section.

SECTION III

PSYCHOSOCIAL FACTORS AFFECTING PHYSICAL HEALTH

CHAPTER 9

THE INTERFACE BETWEEN PHYSICAL AND MENTAL HEALTH

CAROLYN M. ALDWIN

MICHAEL R. LEVENSON

DIANE F. GILMER

This chapter reviews the literature on the interface between physical and mental health. We examine whether personality and affective characteristics such as hostility, anxiety, and depression constitute risk factors for morbidity and mortality, and whether the risk changes with age. We also discuss other personality processes such as control, self-efficacy, optimism, and emotional stability, and whether these can protect health, thus slowing the aging process. However, health behavior habits also have major effects on health. Although smoking and dietary factors are addressed in previous chapters, the effects of alcohol on health have not been as extensively considered, and thus issues of aging and alcohol consumption will be addressed here. Alcohol increases the risk of physical, psychological, and cognitive problems in late life, but it also may confer some protective effects. Finally, we look at the similarities between mental, cognitive, and physical health symptoms in late life and how easily they can be confused. For example, if an older adult complains of serious memory problems, is it incipient dementia or depression? Are heart palpitations related to anxiety or problems with arrhythmias? Disentangling mental, physical, and cognitive health problems can present major problems for clinicians treating older patients.

● PERSONALITY PROCESSES AND DISEASE

The idea that personality characteristics are related to health and illness is not new, by any means. The ancient Greek philosopher and physician Hippocrates developed a system of medicine based on the belief that substances called humors influenced both personality and health. As extended by Galen, the four primary humors were blood, melancholy (black bile), choler (yellow bile), and phlegm. People with an excess of bile were thought to be prone to depression and degenerative disease, whereas those with too much choler were angry and bitter. Blood led to a ruddy, sanguine personality, and phlegm was thought to cause apathy (see Friedman, 1991). As physicians learned more about how organ systems work, the importance of blood circulation, and the existence of microbes, the study of the mind and the body became separated. In the 18th century, René Descartes, eponymous author of the famed Cartesian dualism, posited that the mind and the body were separate entities, connected only tenuously through the pineal gland. In some ways, this was a way of reconciling Church doctrine and nascent scientific practice, with science concerning itself with the body, and leaving the mind (and soul) to philosophy and the Church.

Sigmund Freud is credited with developing the first Western scientific theory of mind, and he believed that eventually psychological phenomena would be traced back to neurophysiological events (Sulloway, 1983). Various psychodynamic clinicians noted a relationship between different types of psychological distress and illnesses and developed theories of psychosomatic illnesses (see Weiner, 1977). For example, these theories held that heart disease was related to repressed hostility and that asthma was linked to overprotective mothering. There were a number of problems with these somewhat simplistic theories. Most of these studies either had no controls or compared people who had preexisting illnesses with controls who were healthy. Thus, there were serious problems with causal directionality, as illnesses can cause psychological and behavioral change, both in the individual and in family members. For example, mothers of asthmatic children are often overprotective because their children are quite ill, not the other way around. Furthermore, having a serious chronic illness can lead to depression and frustration. There was also a sense of blaming the victim, and the unfortunate connotation that so-called psychosomatic illnesses were not real but rather were "in a person's head"—despite the fact that asthma and heart disease can be quite fatal. This, and the increased understanding of the pathophysiological underpinnings of disease, led psychosomatic medicine to fall briefly into disfavor.

More recent research has reinstated the relationship between personality and disease outcomes, albeit in a more sophisticated fashion. The closely linked fields of health psychology and behavioral medicine are founded on the notion that the mind and the body are intimately connected in a bidirectional or even transactional manner. Health psychology tends to be oriented toward basic research, whereas behavioral medicine focuses more on clinical applications, but, in truth, the distinction between the two is blurred. *Bidirectional* refers to a reciprocal relationship between physical and psychological health; *transactional* refers to a continuous process of change among multiple variables. Cumulative processes such as downward spirals are good examples of transactional processes (Aldwin, 1999; Caspi & Bem, 1990). For example, a person with emphysema may continue to smoke because the stimulating effect of nicotine helps to combat the fatigue associated with the disease and because nicotine may combat the depression he or she feels. In the short run, smoking may help, but, in the long run, it increases scarring of the lung tissue, worsening the emphysema, and perhaps also the related depression.

In keeping with a transactional perspective, we use the term *personality processes* to acknowledge that the psychological factors studied in connection with health and aging include traits, affective states, psychological symptoms, and beliefs and attitudes. For example, hostility is sometimes considered a personality trait and at other times a negative affect. Similarly, optimism is sometimes treated as a personality characteristic and at other times as a cognitive explanatory style. The term *personality processes* acknowledges the blurring of these traditional distinctions and allows for a greater flexibility in the review of this material.

Regardless of the terminology used, in the past three decades a strong relationship has emerged between personality processes and diseases such as coronary heart disease (CHD) and overall mortality. As risk factors, the three primary negative emotions that have been linked to the development of disease and its progression are hostility, depression, and anxiety, while control, self-efficacy, optimism, and emotional stability may have protective effects. If negative emotions can exacerbate disease and therefore aging, can positive affect and other protective factors buffer or slow down the aging process?

Psychological Risk Factors and Health

Hostility

We have known for nearly a quarter of a century that the effect sizes for the personality characteristic of hostility as a risk factor for CHD are comparable to those of more traditional risk factors such as high cholesterol, high blood pressure, and cigarette smoking (Review Panel on Coronary-Prone Behavior and Coronary Heart Disease, 1978). Thus, it is surprising that there are no public health campaigns urging people to be less hostile in their everyday lives. How the relationship between hostility and CHD came to be established is highly interesting.

The notion of Type A personality grew out of an observation that a patient's wife related to cardiologists Friedman and Rosenman (1974). She pointed out that the chairs in the waiting room had a very distinctive pattern—they were all worn at the front edge. The cardiologists then noted that their patients often sat on the edge of their chairs (hence the wear pattern) and manifested several other distinctive characteristics, including extreme, easily aroused hostility; achievement motivation; time urgency; and explosive speech patterns, which they dubbed Type A personality, later changed to Type A Behavior Pattern (TABP).

There are two primary ways of assessing TABP. The first is through the Structured Interview (SI; Rosenman, 1978). Type A people are easily aggravated and express hostility in some rather standardized ways. They are quite annoyed by people whom they perceive to be slow and tend to interrupt and finish sentences. They also get very angry and hostile when challenged, especially in social situations. The interviewer administering the SI tries to provoke these responses by asking questions slowly and challenging the responses. On the basis of their way of responding, people are categorized as either Type As or Type Bs.

The second way of assessing TABP is through self-report questionnaires, such as the Jenkins Activity Survey (JAS; Jenkins, Rosenman, & Friedman, 1967). It was found that the JAS did not predict heart disease very well, so researchers went back to the SI to determine what part of TABP was most associated with CHD. After a great deal of research, the general consensus was that the hostility component is the best predictor of CHD (Siegman, 1994). Thus, other scales, such as the Cooke–Medley (1954) Hostility Index from the MMPI, began to be used to predict CHD.

Miller, Smith, Turner, Guijarro, and Hallet (1996) conducted a meta-analysis of the relationship between hostility and health. They showed conclusively that individuals higher in hostility are more likely to develop CHD and also exhibit higher rates of overall mortality. For example, in the Normative Aging Study, men who were high in anger and hostility were two-and-one-half times more likely to develop CHD than those who had low scores on those emotions (Kawachi, Sparrow, Spiro, Vokonas, & Weiss, 1996). In the Determinants of Myocardial Infarction Onset Study, a significant number of individuals with heart attacks had experienced an episode of anger shortly before their heart attacks. (Mittleman, Maclure, Nachnani, Sherwood, & Muller, 1997; Mittleman et al., 1995).

However, Miller et al. (1996) found that the magnitude of the effect depends in part on the particular hostility measure used, as well as the type of study design. In general, the structured interview provided stronger and more consistent results than self-report measures. This is not surprising, given that many people tend to underreport negative traits on self-report measures. Furthermore, studies using case control designs which contrasted sick with healthy individuals, either matching or controlling for any demographic differences, tended to provide the strongest results, whereas those which restricted the range of illness outcomes (e.g., those which examined only CHD patients) tended to show the weakest results. Studies with shorter follow-up periods tended to show stronger effects than longer ones, in part because hostility may not be a stable personality trait, as discussed later in this chapter.

Demographic differences also exist. The relationship between hostility and CHD is stronger for men than for women and may be stronger for younger than for older people, although the results are inconsistent. Williams (2000) presented some interesting data showing that the relationship between Type A and coronary artery disease (CAD) was strongest for those in their 30s and early 40s. From ages 46 to age 55, Type A and Type B individuals had about equal rates of CAD. After age 56, Type Bs were actually higher, probably due to survivor effects. People who are most vulnerable to the effects of hostility tend to die earlier; those who are left are the survivors, a population whose members are presumably a little less vulnerable. This is also confounded by the fact that hostility tends to decrease with age (McCrae et al., 1999). The instability of hostility may be one reason why hostility in shorter studies tends to be a better predictor than in longer studies.

There are a number of possibilities why hostility may lead to higher levels of CHD and overall mortality. People high in hostility tend to have poorer health behavior habits: They are more likely to smoke, to drink excessively, to weigh more, and to be less active. Covarying out these factors does not necessarily reduce the effect size between hostility and CHD (Miller et al., 1996), however, suggesting that there are independent effects as well.

A number of laboratory studies have shown that people who are high in hostility exhibit greater cardiovascular reactivity to stress (Krantz & McCeney,

2002). That is, when subjected to stressors, especially interpersonal stressors such as criticism, they respond with larger increases in blood pressure and more elevated heart rates. There is also some indication that they also exhibit higher levels of serum lipids such as low-density lipoproteins (LDLs) and triglycerides (Niaura et al., 2000), especially under stress (Vögele, 1998) or when treated unfairly (Richards, Hof, & Alvarenga, 2000). However, results across studies are not always consistent (van Doornen, 1997), and it is likely that the relationship is moderated by a number of factors, including genetics, gender, ethnicity, diet, smoking, and stress levels (Stoney & West, 1997).

Finally, there may also be indirect pathways between hostility and CHD. People who are high in hostility tend to be low in social support, and there is some indication that individuals low in support are also at higher risk for CHD (Miller et al., 1996).

The picture becomes even more complicated when trying to extrapolate these results to a consideration of the effects of hostility on aging. The effects of hostility are very age dependent. Hostility levels tend to be highest in adolescence, and measures taken in adolescence tend not to predict future health outcomes very well (I. Siegler, personal communication, November 1998). However, hostility does have negative outcomes on cardiovascular health for people in midlife. Unfortunately, a certain proportion of those individuals may not survive until late life (Williams, 2000), so it would be difficult to determine what effect it has on aging per se. Complicating this is the fact that hostility tends to decrease from early adulthood to midlife, although it may rise again in late life (Barefoot, Beckham, Haney, Siegler, & Lipkus, 1993). One study even suggests that hostility in very late life may be protective. Lieberman and Tobin (1983) followed individuals admitted to nursing homes and found that older adults who were perceived by the staff as "ornery" or "cantankerous" were likely to live longer than more passive patients. Their negative behavior resulted in greater attention from the staff and perhaps served to stave off feelings of helplessness and hopelessness, which may have deleterious consequences for health, especially in later life.

Anxiety

Friedman and Booth-Kewley (1987), in their review of personality and health outcomes, found relatively consistent effects of anxiety on heart disease and overall mortality. Researchers have studied several different types of anxiety, including phobias, self-report anxiety, and worries (see Kubzansky & Kawachi, 2000). In the Normative Aging Study, men who reported worrying were nearly two-and-one-half times more likely to develop CHD (Kubzansky et al., 1997); those who were high in anxiety had four-and-one-half times the risk for sudden cardiac death (Kawachi, Sparrow, Vokonas, & Weiss, 1994). In a national study, phobics had six times the risk for sudden cardiac death (Kawachi, Colditz, et al., 1994). In the Framingham Heart Study, women who were homemakers (but not employed women) who were high in anxiety had nearly eight times the risk of death from heart attacks and other CHD-related mortality (Eaker, Pinsky, & Castelli, 1992). Although not all studies found a relationship between anxiety and CHD mortality, Kubzansky and Kawachi (2000) argue that this is because sudden deaths tend to be relatively rare, and studies with null findings tend to be smaller studies with design flaws. Tennant and McLean's (2001) review also concluded that anxiety significantly predicted CHD.

A number of authors have speculated on the mechanisms between anxiety and CHD. Tennant and McLean (2001) reviewed evidence showing that emotional distress, especially anxiety, is associated with a release of catecholamines, which stimulates the heart rate. Acute emotional distress and hyperventilation can be associated with vasospasm, which cuts off blood flow to the heart muscles. This is especially true in those with underlying ischemic disease. Vasospasm can lead to acute ischemic problems and changes in blood platelets, which may promote blood clots. The increased heart rate associated with acute emotional arousal can increase demands for oxygen, also leading to ischemia. Thus, anxiety may set off a cascade of events resulting in CHD.

Gorman and Sloan (2000) also summarized the literature on anxiety and CHD, providing an alternative insight into the underlying pathophysiology. Remember that the heart rate is under control of both the sympathetic and the parasympathetic nervous system (see Chapter 6). With heart disease, there is a loss of normal autonomic nervous system control of the heart rate and rhythm. Decrease in parasympathetic control results in a loss of beat-to-beat heart rate variability and may leave the heart vulnerable to sympathetic nervous system stimulation via catecholamines. In other words, the decreased heart rate variability indicates a lack of regulation of the heartbeat, and thus it can overreact to stimulation. Individuals high in anxiety may show significant arrhythmias under stress, leading to arrest and sudden death.

Heart rate variability also decreases with normal aging but is especially marked among those with diabetic neuropathy and vascular disease. Chronic anxiety and depression are also associated with decreased heart rate variability. Thus, one could speculate that the combination of aging, disease, and chronic anxiety may place older individuals in particular at higher risk for arrhythmias and sudden death. Less work has been done on what happens to anxiety with age; it is possible that anxiety, like hostility, also takes its toll in midlife. More research is needed to determine whether the proposed pathway between anxiety and CHD is correct and if this relationship varies significantly by age.

Depression

Perhaps the strongest association between negative affect and health in late life is found with depression. As noted in Chapter 2, a classic study by Parkes (1972) found that widowed men were more likely to die of coronary heart disease in the first year of bereavement, with the risk decreasing after about 1 year. Tennant and McLean (2001) also reviewed the mortality and bereavement literature, reporting that 9 of 14 studies showed a positive association. The studies with the strongest results tended to utilize younger samples and to examine the early bereavement period. Johnson, Backlund, Sorlie, and Loveless (2000) explicitly compared the effects of bereavement in middle-aged and older samples. They found that the relationship between bereavement and mortality was stronger among the middle-aged than among older adults. This is surprising, because we tend to assume that mortality is tightly linked in older couples (e.g., the classic image of the pining elderly widower who dies only a few months after his beloved wife). However, it appears that mortality is more strongly linked to bereavement in middle-aged couples, for reasons that are not clear. One could speculate that perhaps the couple shared poor health behavior habits, but that does not seem to account for this phenomenon (Lichtenstein, Gatz, & Berg, 1998). Perhaps Williams's (2000) caution about hostility and survivor effects also applies to bereavement.

The association between depression and mortality is well established in the general population (Zheng et al., 1997), and the association is not simply due to higher rates of suicide (Tsuang & Woolson, 1978). Studies of older adults, however, have been less consistent. Blazer, Hybels, and Pieper (2001) argued that this is because health problems in older adults both reflect and cause depression. It is likely that there is a reciprocal relationship, with depressed individuals more likely to have a higher rate of impaired functional and cognitive health than their nondepressed peers (Bruce, Seeman, Merrill, & Blazer, 1994). In turn, impairment may lead to greater depression. Thus, carefully controlling for the existence of other health problems may obscure a relationship between depression and mortality in older samples.

Furthermore, just as with bereavement, the impact of depression on mortality may be short-lived. Blazer et al. (2001) assessed a panel of older persons three times at approximately 3-year intervals. They found that depressive symptoms were very unstable: Most individuals who were depressed at one time point were not necessarily depressed at the next assessment. Thus, it is not surprising that depression significantly predicted mortality only for the next follow-up period, that is, Time 1 depressive symptoms predicted mortality only at Time 2, and Time 2 symptoms predicted mortality only at Time 3.

Many studies have also shown a link between depression and CHD morbidity (e.g., Anda et al., 1993; Barefoot & Schroll, 1996). This may be especially true in men (Ford et al., 1998; Hippisley-Cox, Fielding, & Pringle, 1998; Sesso, Kawachi, Vokonas, & Sparrow, 1998). In general, people with high levels of depression have one-and-one-half to two times the risk of developing CHD than their nondepressed peers (Kubzansky & Kawachi, 2000).

The relationship between depression and cardiovascular morbidity and mortality appears to be strongest among cardiac patients. Among those with preexisting CHD, depression predicts subsequent arrhythmias (Ladwig et al., 1992) and deaths (Carney et al., 1988). In the latter study, depression was the strongest of all of the predictors. Frasure-Smith and his colleagues examined depression and mortality in CHD patients at 6 months (Frasure-Smith, Lesperance, & Talajic, 1993), 12 months (Frasure-Smith, Lesperance, Juneau, Talajic, & Bourassa, 1999), 18 months (Frasure-Smith, Lesperance, & Talajic, 1995), and 5 years (Lesperance, Frasure-Smith, Talajic, & Bourassa, 2002). They found that depressed individuals were four times as likely to die, that depression was a stronger predictor of mortality than physiological factors such as a previous myocardial infarction (MI) or left ventricular function, and that the effect was present in women as well as men. This effect can last up to 10 years (Welin, Lappas, & Wilhelmsen, 2000) and has also been documented with chronic congestive heart failure patients (Murberg, Bru, Svebak, Tveteras, & Aarsland, 1999).

The reason for the association between depression and CHD morbidity and mortality is a matter of some controversy. Some have argued that the effect is largely mediated by health behavior habits. People who are depressed are more likely to be smokers, have a poor diet, and are less likely to exercise (Hayward, 1995). Researchers such as Blazer et al. (2001) argue that multiple pathways exist through which depression can affect mortality, including health behavior habits, functional health, and cognitive impairment. Pulska, Pahkala, Laippala, and Kivelä (2000) examined standard depression inventories to see which symptoms were most consistently associated with mortality. The primary differences between the depressed older adults who had died and those who survived after 6 years were anorexia and weight loss. Loss of appetite is a classic symptom of depression, and weight loss can have very serious consequences in older adults (see Chapter 8).

There is also evidence for a direct effect of depression on physiological processes. Depression is linked to atherogenesis (Appels, Bar, Bar, Bruggeman, &

de Baets, 2000). Depression also predicts subsequent arrhythmias (Ladwig, Kieser, & Konigh, 1992), perhaps because it decreases heart rate variability or responsiveness (Light, Kothandapani, & Allen, 1998; Nemeroff, Musselman, & Evans 1998). As with anxiety, decreased heart rate variability can leave the heart vulnerable to overstimulation by the sympathetic nervous system, which reacts to stress. Decreased heart rate variability has been associated with pathophysiological processes such as atherogenesis and ischemia, as well as frank disease such as arrhythmias, MIs, and sudden death (Tennant & McLean, 2001).

The effects of depression on other illnesses such as cancer are less clear. More than 100 years ago, H. L. Snow attributed cancer to "a general liability to the buffets of ill fortune" (cited in McGee, Williams, & Elwood, 1994, p. 187). That depression and other psychosocial factors are strongly linked with cancer is widely believed in the general population (Baghurst, Baghurst, & Record, 1992). Presumably, the mechanism is through depressed immune function, although this relationship has as yet to be empirically shown (Stein, Miller, & Trestman, 1991). Retrospective studies show a link, but they are subject to recall bias—that is, individuals with any disease are likely to attribute them to some recent stressor or feeling state; thus, prospective studies are needed to definitely show a link.

In their meta-analysis, McGee et al. (1994) identified seven prospective studies of depression and cancer but eliminated one (a Yugoslavian study), because the findings were extremely variant from the other studies. Overall, the relationship between depression and cancer was surprisingly weak, with an excess cancer rate of only 1% to 2%. Studies that showed the strongest results tended to have older populations with larger number of smokers. Depressed people are more likely to have poorer behavior habits which are associated with the risk of cancer, such as smoking (Covey, Glassman, & Dalack, 1991) and weight gain (DiPietro, Anda, Williamson, & Stunkard, 1992). Given the relatively few studies, no systematic attempt was made to assess the risk of cancer due to depression by age.

A related construct, Type C personality, has been linked with cancer in preliminary studies. Temoshok and her colleagues (1985) hypothesized that women with rather passive personalities who suppressed emotional expression were more likely to develop cancer. Furthermore, a related construct, helplessness, may also result in poorer prognoses in cervical cancer (Goodkin, Antoni, & Bloom, 1986). However, Cooper and Fagher (1992) demonstrated a link between Type C personality and age—older women were more likely to exhibit this personality and also more likely to develop breast cancer. Controlling for age eliminated the significance of the relationship between Type C personality and breast cancer.

In summary, there is clear evidence for the impact of anxiety, hostility, and depression on coronary heart disease. Some of these effects are mediated by health behavior habits, but there is also a growing body of evidence to suggest that negative affect may have direct effects on cardiovascular function. The relationship between personality and cancer is much weaker. There is another way in which psychological and physical factors are intertwined in late life, however. Many physical illnesses manifest in psychological symptoms such as anxiety, depression, or confusion, or in vague symptoms such as lethargy, making diagnosis somewhat difficult.

Psychological Protective Factors and Health

Most of the attention in health psychology has been on factors that increase vulnerability to stress. As noted in the previous sections, this relationship is often complex and is mediated and/or moderated by a variety of factors. Less attention has been paid to protective factors, but it is reasonable to suppose that if negative affect has adverse effects on the cardiovascular system, then positive affect should have protective effects. However, most of the research on protective factors has not focused on affect per se but rather attitudes, beliefs, and personality dispositions that can foster positive affect, such as optimism and internal locus of control. A handful of studies have examined the protective effects of emotional stability and health. There are other constructs as well, such as hardiness (Kobasa, Maddi, & Kahn, 1982) and a sense of coherence (Antonovsky, 1993), that are not addressed here, because most of the studies have associated them with either mental health or self-reported symptoms rather than morbidity and mortality, which is the focus here. (See Ouellette & DiPlacido, 2001, for a review of these constructs.)

Control and Self-Efficacy

In the 1970s, Langer and Rodin (1976; Rodin & Langer, 1977) performed a classic experiment which investigated the potentially protective effects of internal locus of control. In the previous decade, there had been a fair amount of research on the adverse consequences of learned helplessness (Seligman, 1975), and Langer and Rodin reasoned that if lack of control had negative effects on health, then perhaps enhancing a sense of control would have positive effects. At that time, nursing homes were extremely difficult environments that essentially promoted learned helplessness. Residents had very little choice about anything, even about such basics as when and what to eat, what to wear, and when to sleep. The intervention that Langer and

Rodin designed was very simple. In one wing of the nursing home, residents were given choices such as which movie to see. They were also given enhanced responsibility, which included taking care of plants in their rooms. In the other wing, residents were not given choices. Although they were also given plants, they were told that the staff would take care of these for them.

The effects were quite dramatic. Residents in the experimental condition were more alert and had better self-rated health. The staff also rated these patients' health as better (Langer & Rodin, 1976). After 18 months, these residents also had much lower rates of mortality (Rodin & Langer, 1977). Baltes (1996) has continued work in this tradition, demonstrating how skilled nursing facilities foster dependence in patients, harming not only their ability to function independently but perhaps their health as well.

Many early studies showed the protective effect of control (for a review, see Gatchel & Baum, 1983). Individuals who were given control over aversive stimuli in laboratory settings showed less adverse physiological arousal (Glass & Singer, 1972). The distress associated with medical procedures was reduced when patients were given information about the procedure and coping strategies as well, which presumably enhanced their feelings of control (Johnson & Leventhal, 1974). A series of classic studies by Frankenhaeuser and her colleagues reported that workers given control over the pace of their assembly lines showed lower neuroendocrine responses to stress (Frankenhaeuser, 1978).

Recent studies have provided a more refined examination of this topic. For example, Bandura (1997) differentiated between control beliefs and self-efficacy. The classic definition of locus of control focused on generalized expectancies about outcomes. An individual with an internal locus of control would expect to be able to affect the outcome of a given situation (Rotter, 1954). However, Bandura reasoned that there is a subtle difference between thinking that a situation can be under one's control and the belief that one can actually perform the behaviors required to affect the outcome. Thus, a person could believe that the responsibility to quit smoking lies with an individual but not think that he or she personally is capable of stopping (DeVellis & DeVellis, 2001). Self-efficacy has been a very important construct in health promotion programs (see Chapter 8).

Karasek and Theorell (1990) hypothesized that there is an interaction effect between control and responsibility in occupational settings. Workers with a great deal of responsibility but also a fair amount of control, like executives, had lower levels of work-related stress, but those with responsibility but little control, such as secretaries, reported the greatest amount of stress. In contrast, individuals who had little control but relatively few responsibilities, such as janitors, reported low amounts of stress. Indeed, subsequent work has shown that individuals with high responsibility but little control are more likely to develop cardiovascular disease.

Having a sense of control may be especially important for more disadvantaged groups. Lachman and Weaver (1998) showed that a sense of control moderates the effects of social class on health. Using national data from the MacArthur Studies of Midlife, they found that individuals with lower socioeconomic status (SES) who had a strong sense of control had self-rated health as high as more prosperous SES groups, but those with a low sense of control reported much worse health. Controlling for perceived control reduced the relationship between social class and mortality by about 50% (Bosma, Schrijvers, & Mackenbach, 1999).

Control can be a double-edged sword, however. Most control is rather illusory, and when that sense of control is shattered, people may give up, sometimes with quite devastating consequences. For example, Seligman (1975) related a relevant anecdote of a prisoner of war (POW) in Vietnam. This strong young man was in relatively good physical and mental shape, despite the horrors of the conditions under which the POWs were kept. He firmly believed that if he did everything his captors requested, he would be given an early release. Gradually, however, he realized that this promise was, in fact, a lie. He became profoundly depressed and refused to eat or drink. He curled up in a fetal position, lying in his own waste, and died shortly thereafter.

In addition, there are many different types of control measures. Some assess control in specific domains, such as work or health, while others assess more global feelings. Thus, it is not surprising that the literature on control and mortality is somewhat contradictory. For example, low work control is associated with cardiovascular mortality (Johnson, Stewart, Hall, Fredlund, & Theorell, 1996). An external locus of control has been associated with increased overall mortality (Dalgard & Lund Haheim, 1998), but health locus of control was not significantly related to all-cause mortality after an MI (Welin et al., 2000). Krause and Shaw (2000) suggest that part of the inconsistency in the literature is due to a failure to look at control with regard to an individual's most important social role. For example, some people are most invested in work, others in their families, and some in avocations or financial security. In a nationwide survey of older adults, they found that global measures of control were unrelated to mortality, but feelings of control over the most important role reduced the odds of dying during the study period.

Feelings of control change in some interesting ways with age. Lachman (1986) reviewed the rather mixed literature on aging and locus of control and concluded that control is a multidimensional construct. Although some aspects appear to change with age, others do not. Older adults begin to realize that they do not have the sort of control over the external environment that they thought they had when they were younger, but they do maintain other types of control. Aldwin (1991) investigated this and found that older individuals were less likely to say they felt responsibility for either the occurrence or the management of problems they faced. Nonetheless, they did just as much problem-focused coping as younger individuals. In some ways, acknowledging lack of control is protective, as long as one does what one can to mitigate problems. Acknowledging that circumstances are often beyond control allows one to avoid self-blame, but this is very different from a sense of helplessness. Schulz and Heckhausen (1998) have made the shift from primary to secondary control a key element of their life span theory of change in control, with primary referring to control over the environment and secondary referring to control over one's reactions to it.

One permutation of the construct of control has been mindfulness (Langer, 1989). Mindfulness is defined as the process of becoming aware of the environment and one's reactions to it, as well as one's internal states, which presumably allows a person to exercise better control. In Langer's model, it includes being able to generate new categories, being open to new information, and being able to take a new perspective. This allows individuals to examine assumptions that may turn out to be false and to avoid committing the fallacy of premature closure (making a decision before one has adequate information). This is very relevant to aging, because we often make many assumptions about what older adults can and cannot do that may limit their ability to function (see also Baltes, 1996).

Langer (1989) described a fascinating study conducted by her and her students in which older adults were taken to a "camp" for a week. The camp was a location in the country outfitted with magazines, music, and other materials from 20 years earlier. The participants were required to take responsibility in various ways, such as carrying their own luggage, and discussed issues from earlier eras. At the end of the week, not only had their self-reported mental and physical health improved, but objective physiological indices such as grip strength had also improved. In part, one's functioning may reflect assumptions about what one could or should be able to do. Satchel Paige, the inimitable baseball player, played for many years past the age when most players retire. He dodged questions about his age by saying, "How old would you be if you didn't know how old you was?"

Langer and her colleagues (Alexander, Langer, Newman, Chandler, & Davies, 1989) conducted another intervention for older adults living in various institutional settings. They randomly assigned individuals to one of four conditions: meditation, mindfulness training, relaxation, and a control group. Both the meditation and mindfulness training groups showed significant increases in cardiovascular and cognitive function, as well as mental health. The intervention also affected mortality rates. After 3 years, all members of the meditation group and 87% of the mindfulness group were still alive, compared to only about two thirds of the control group. This study was conducted on a relatively small number of subjects (81), but showed intriguing results that need to be replicated.

Optimism

The construct of optimism is one of the primary foci in the current emphasis on positive psychology (Seligman & Csikszentmihalyi, 2000). There are two different ways of defining this construct (Tomakowsky, Lumley, Markowitz, & Frank, 2001). The first is as an explanatory style in contrast to learned helplessness (Abramson, Seligman, & Teasdale, 1978; Peterson & Seligman, 1984). An optimistic explanatory style has three dimensions: internality, stability, and globality. *Internality* refers to whether one attributes the cause of an event to an internal or external source. For example, when faced with job loss, optimists might say that the cause was due to a poor economy, but pessimists would blame themselves. *Stability* refers to the temporal dimension of the attribute: An optimist would believe that the poor economy was temporary, whereas a pessimist would probably believe that things would only get worse. Finally, *globality* refers to the specificity of the cause: An optimist would believe that only a particular sector of the economy was bad, but a pessimist would believe that most, if not all, sectors were weak. Generally, optimism is assessed either through a questionnaire such as the Attributional Style Questionnaire (ASQ; Peterson et al., 1982) or via content analysis of interviews or transcriptions (Peterson, Luborsky, & Seligman, 1983).

The second way of conceptualizing optimism is as a personality disposition (Scheier & Carver, 1985). This emphasizes generalized expectancies concerning future outcomes. For example, the optimist in the previous example would believe that the job loss was only temporary and that a better job would be found, whereas the pessimist might be very negative about the possibility of future employment. Dispositional optimism is generally assessed through the Life Orientation Test (LOT; Scheier & Carver, 1985).

The primary difference between the two conceptualizations is that the ASQ refers to attributions for past events, whereas the LOT assesses expectations for future events (Tomakowsky et al., 2001). Surprisingly, the two are only modestly correlated. Another major methodological concern is whether optimism is simply the inverse of neuroticism or is an independent

244 PSYCHOSOCIAL FACTORS AFFECTING PHYSICAL HEALTH

construct. A handful of studies have examined this and are split equally as to whether it is confounded or independent. Two studies found that the relationship between optimism and self-reported health symptoms disappears when controlling for neuroticism (Robbins, Spence, & Clark, 1991; Smith, Pope, Rhodewalt, & Poulton, 1989), and two found independent effects (Mroczek, Spiro, Aldwin, Ozer, & Bossé, 1993; Scheier & Carver, 1992).

Both measures have been used to predict health outcomes. Individuals with an optimistic explanatory style report fewer illnesses (Peterson, 1988) and fewer contacts with physicians (Lin & Peterson, 1990). In general, they have fewer illnesses over the life span (Peterson, Seligman, & Vaillant, 1988) and are at lower risk for premature mortality (Peterson & Seligman, 1987). Optimistic older individuals also have better cell-mediated immunity (Kamen-Siegel, Rodin, Seligman, & Dwyer, 1991).

Dispositional optimism has also been linked to better health, including self-reported health (Scheier & Carver, 1985) and fewer influenza symptoms (Hamid, 1990). Scheier and his colleagues have done a series of studies showing that optimistic individuals recover better from coronary artery bypass surgery, both in the short term and in the long term, as indexed by fewer hospitalizations (Scheier & Carver, 1992; Scheier et al., 1989; Scheier et al., 1999). Helgeson and Fritz (1999) also found that optimism predicted fewer coronary events after angioplasty.

However, optimism is not always protective. After 18 months of unemployment, optimists were more depressed than pessimists (Frese, 1992), suggesting that they have a harder time coping with chronic stress. Although optimism may have positive effects on immune functioning for acute stressors, it may have adverse immune consequences for persistent stress (Cohen et al., 1999). It also predicts lower natural-killer-cell activity for uncontrollable stress (Sieber et al., 1992). Tomakowsky et al. (2001) found that HIV patients who were optimistic had lower CD4+ counts and that these worsened more rapidly over a 2-year follow-up. Pessimists' CD4+ counts actually increased slightly. Finally, Isaacowitz and Seligman (2002) found that optimism in older adults was associated with increased depression after negative life events.

Some of the effects of optimism on health outcomes are mediated by better health behavior habits and perhaps coping strategies (Scheier & Carver, 1992). However, other studies find independent effects (see Tomakowsky et al., 2001). The adverse effects of optimism are especially noteworthy. Perhaps optimism, like control, has more beneficial effects for short-term, controllable stressors. For long-term, uncontrollable stressors, however, optimists may be at increased risk of depression and poorer immune functioning. These studies also need to be replicated.

Emotional Stability

Clearly, part of the negative effect of anxiety, hostility, and depression is related to emotional lability. Thus, it would make sense that emotional stability would be protective. However, only a handful of studies have examined this possibility. Spiro, Aldwin, Ward, and Mroczek (1995) examined the relationship between personality and the development of hypertension (HT) in the Normative Aging Study. They hypothesized that hostility would be positively associated with the incidence of HT but found only marginal results. Instead, the strongest personality predictor was emotional stability, and it was inversely associated with the development of HT.

A second study examined personality and the self-reported symptom trajectories across 25 years. Aldwin, Spiro, Levenson, and Cupertino (2001) identified different patterns of symptom trajectories. Two patterns had very low levels of symptoms that increased only slightly from midlife to late life. The men in these trajectory groups reported the highest level of emotional stability and also had among the highest survival rates of any of the groups. Although limited by the reliance on self-report, this study raises the possibility that emotional stability is protective of health in midlife and later.

Alcohol and Aging

The past several decades have witnessed a dramatic increase in our understanding of how personality processes affect health. Sometimes there appear to be direct physiological effects, as in the relationship between hostility and increased cholesterol levels under stress, whereas in other cases, those effects are mediated by health behavior habits such as smoking, diet, or alcohol consumption. The effects of smoking and poor diet were addressed in previous chapters, but alcohol use has not been given as much attention, although it is an important factor in how individuals age. Thus, this section addresses how alcohol consumption changes with age and its effects on health outcomes, both in terms of increased risk and in terms of protective factors.

Important questions in the literature are whether or not alcohol consumption changes with age and whether older adults are particularly vulnerable to the effects of alcohol. We review the literature on the effect of alcohol on physical and mental health, as well as cognitive functioning.

Consumption Patterns With Age

The relationship between alcohol consumption and age is complex. The traditional finding that alcohol consumption decreases with age is empirically supported primarily by cross-sectional studies, which compare different age groups at one time point (for a review, see Cahalan, Cisin, & Crossley, 1969). Most of these studies simply combined adults 65 and older, and very little published information exists, even cross-sectionally, for those 75 and older. However, Schoenborn and Adams (2001) recently presented cross-sectional data from the National Health Interview Survey and found that about 45% of men 75 and older continued to drink (compared to 67% for 18- to 24-year-olds and 56% of those aged 65 to 74). The difference in drinking across ages varied by consumption category. The biggest difference was seen in abstention (55% of the old-old vs. 33% of the young adults). However, percentages of moderate drinking were very similar (16.4% vs. 19.7%), suggesting that moderate drinkers continue to drink over the age of 75. Those who abstain from drinking tend to be heavier drinkers and lighter drinkers. The percentage of heavier drinkers decreased from 6% to 2%, but the biggest difference was seen in the light drinkers (32% to 16%). This suggests that it is primarily the lighter drinkers and the heavier drinkers who become abstainers in late life. Similar patterns are seen among women, although far fewer of them use alcohol. The percentages of heavier drinkers are very similar for men and women, and women show the same pattern of differences across ages (Schoenborn & Adams, 2001).

In gerontology, however, it has long been acknowledged that cross-sectional studies are inadequate to examine age effects, as these are necessarily confounded with both cohort (birth year) and period effects (historical influences at the time of measurement; see Schaie, 1977). For example, we might speculate that individuals who grew up during Prohibition may have consumed less alcohol across the life span; cross-sectional studies in which these now-elderly individuals are compared with younger cohorts might erroneously conclude that the lower alcohol consumption of older adults is due to age rather than historical differences in cohorts. In general, longitudinal studies are considered a more efficacious way to examine whether or not a given phenomenon changes with age (see Chapter 4).

There remains a relative paucity of longitudinal studies of alcohol consumption and problem drinking across the life span. The studies that do exist have reported contradictory results. In a review of the literature, Fillmore (1988) found age declines in heavy drinking and problem drinking with only very small cohort effects. Fillmore et al. (1991) conducted meta-analyses on extant longitudinal data sets and also found age-related declines in alcohol consumption. A larger, follow-up analysis of 27 longitudinal studies also found age effects, but these appeared to be primarily concentrated in early life (Johnstone, Leino, Ager, Ferrer, & Fillmore, 1996). A retrospective study of 70 Canadian veterans (Chaikelson, Arbuckle, Lapidus, & Gold, 1994) showed large decreases in consumption in the 1970s and 1980s.

None of these studies statistically examined possible cohort and period effects. Glynn, Bouchard, LoCastro, and Laird (1985), working with the Normative Aging Study at two time points, found that age-related declines in drinking were actually due to cohort effects, with older cohorts drinking consistently less than younger ones, regardless of age. In one of the few studies to examine age, cohort, and period effects in alcohol consumption, Neve, Diederiks, Knibbe, and Drop (1993) found an increase in alcohol consumption across 30 years in five 10-year cohorts of Dutch men and women. Although abstinence was positively related to age, age and cohort had no relationship to consumption among those who did drink. Instead, consumption appeared to be governed by period effects.

Levenson, Aldwin, and Spiro (1998) conducted the first sequential study that statistically tested the differential effects of age, cohort, and period on alcohol consumption and problem drinking. By following several different age cohorts over an 18-year period, they found that the effect of age on alcohol consumption was at best modest. Although some older adults stopped consuming alcohol in late life, those who continued to drink did not appear to decrease the amount of their drinking. Levenson, Aldwin, and Spiro concluded that adult alcohol consumption is more strongly influenced by period effects. Specifically, alcohol consumption and problem drinking increased in the 1970s, regardless of age, and decreased in the 1980s. For the younger cohorts, self-reported problem drinking increased even though alcohol consumption levels decreased.

Another way of conceptualizing and analyzing change in alcohol consumption is to study trajectories of change. Using a retrospective design in 70 World War II veterans, Chaikelson et al. (1994) described a normative trajectory of alcohol consumption in adulthood in which drinking increased from young adulthood to midlife, plateaued, and then decreased sharply in the 70s and 80s. This is likely due to the fact that some older individuals quit drinking alcohol altogether.

Furthermore, there are individual differences in patterns of alcohol use across the life span. Levenson, Aldwin, Spiro, and Friedman (1998) categorized the Normative Aging Study men according to the consumption levels and the existence of problem drinking at three time points. The most typical pattern was lifetime moderate, nonproblem drinking. Other patterns included chronic or episodic heavy drinking, chronic or episodic problem drinking, episodic or permanent cessation of drinking, or (rarely) lifetime abstention. Cross-sectional studies have also suggested that there are ethnic differences in trajectories of alcohol consumption across the life span, with whites peaking in early adulthood, whereas African Americans and Latinos are more likely to develop heavy or problem drinking later in life (see Jackson, Williams, & Gomberg, 1998).

In a review of recent epidemiological research on problem drinking in older people, I. Johnson (2000) found that prevalence rates reported in the different studies varied widely, ranging from 2% to 45.5%. Moreover, age cut-offs for "older adults" ranged from 50 to 66; none of the studies he reviewed specifically examined the old-old. Zucker (1998) reviewed a handful of studies of alcohol consumption and problem drinking in very late life, and found substantial variability in daily alcohol consumption, as well as gender and regional differences. Little work has been done on drinking among ethnic minorities in very late life, however, usually due to inadequate sample sizes. Rigler's (2000) review suggests that one third of the older adults defined as alcoholic had the onset of their problems in late life.

Perhaps the most intriguing research concerns the possibility of increased problematic drinking with the sleep disturbances that are so common in older people. J. E. Johnson (1996, 1997) found that nearly all of her samples of urban ($N = 156$) and rural ($N = 175$) women over the age of 85 had problems sleeping; about two thirds used alcohol and/or drugs to cope with sleep disturbances. Alcohol consumption may decline among the young-old, but there is some possibility that it increases in very late life.

Effects on Physical Health

It has long been known that excess alcohol consumption has very deleterious effects on health. It causes cirrhosis of the liver, a scarring of the tissue that can lead to liver failure. The inability of the liver to process blood quickly enough can result in peripheral artery disease. For example, long-term alcoholics typically develop rather bulbous, red noses, due to damage to the arterioles and small veins. Excess alcohol consumption also results in hypertension and cardiac myopathy (damage to the heart muscle). It can also contribute to diabetes and colon cancer; in general, it increases the risk of premature mortality (Criqui, 2000).

There is a large body of research suggesting that moderate consumption of alcohol may be protective of health. Moderate alcohol consumption has been shown to be protective for coronary heart disease (Kannel & Ellison, 1996) and congestive heart failure (Abramson, Berger, Krumholz, & Vaccarino, 2001). One of the most consistent findings in the epidemiological literature is the J-shaped curve between alcohol consumption and mortality. That is, teetotalers and heavy drinkers have higher mortality rates than moderate drinkers (for reviews see Gronbaek et al., 2000; Liao, McGee, Cao, &

Cooper, 2000; Poikolainen, 1995). The protective effects of alcohol have been demonstrated both in general and in older populations, especially for men (Simons, McCallum, Friedlander, Ortiz, & Simons 2000). Recent evidence suggests that this effect may be stronger for cardiovascular-related mortality than for cancer mortality (Gaziano et al., 2000). Moderate consumption is also negatively associated with mortality in late life (de Labry et al., 1992; Simons et al., 2000).

Most reviews of the relationship between alcohol consumption and mortality have concentrated on mean consumption levels. However, Britton and McKee (2000) reviewed literature and suggested that the patterns of alcohol drinking, such as binge or episodic heavier drinking (EHD) and the frequency of hangovers, may also affect mortality. In particular, EHD drinkers had higher cardiovascular mortality rates than regular heavy drinkers.

Alcohol consumption may present special problems for older adults. Physiological changes with age can decrease alcohol tolerance. Although normal aging does not affect the ability of the liver to process alcohol, older people tend to be smaller, and the percentage of body mass due to water decreases. This results in a decreased volume of distribution for alcohol, causing higher blood levels and increased central nervous system (CNS) sensitivity to alcohol (Vestal et al., 1977; Vogel-Sprott & Barrett, 1984).

The effects of alcohol on the body may be potentiated by the use of prescription and nonprescription medication. There may be additive or synergistic effects for organ toxicity. For example, the combination of alcohol and aspirin and other nonsteroidal anti-inflammatory medications (NSAIDs) has erosive effects on the stomach (Fraser, 1997). The combination of alcohol and acetaminophen destroys cells in the liver (Schiodt, Rochling, Casey, & Lee, 1997); overdoses can result in a slow and painful death. Adverse alcohol-drug interactions may also be due to metabolic processes. Alcohol can change hepatic enzymes or compete directly for metabolic sites, which may either increase or decrease the availabilities and activities of drugs in the antiseizure, antidiabetic, antihypertensive, anticoagulant, and antidepressant categories (Lieber, 1992; National Institute on Alcohol Abuse and Alcoholism [NIAAA], 1995). Two studies of community samples of older samples showed that 38% and 25% of the populations studied were at risk of adverse alcohol-medication interactions (Adams, 1995a, 1995b; Forster, Pollow, & Stoller, 1993).

Effects on Mental Health

Another well-established relationship is between alcohol and Korsakoff's psychosis, which is characterized by hallucinations, mood disturbances, and cognitive impairment. This may be due not only to vascular problems but to inadequate nutrition as well. Serious alcoholics tend to have very poor diets, and alcohol also inhibits uptake of vitamin B_{12} in the gut. This vitamin is crucial to maintaining neural health.

Alcohol is well known for its sedative properties, and older people may use it to cope with sleep disturbances. Unfortunately, alcohol disrupts sleep patterns. In particular, it suppresses REM sleep and may actually increase insomnia, especially in older adults (Neubauer, 1999). The CNS sedative effects of alcohol may be potentiated by those of sedatives, tranquilizers, antihistamines, or opioid analgesics, increasing the risk of intoxication or oversedation (Hollister, 1990; NIAAA, 1995).

Finally, there is a relationship between excess alcohol consumption and depression that is likely bidirectional. That is, individuals may use alcohol to combat depressive symptoms (such as mood disturbances and insomnia), but alcohol itself depresses CNS function and can lead to depression (Vaillant, 1983). Moderate alcohol consumption in older populations, however, may be associated with lower levels of depression (Schulz et al., 2000).

Effects on Cognition

The CNS may be particularly vulnerable to the effects of alcohol consumption. Excess alcohol consumption is a risk factor for stroke, undoubtedly due to the adverse effects of alcohol on the cardiovascular system. It is also a risk factor for Alzheimer's disease, independent of its effects on vascularization (Ruitenberg et al., 2002; Zuccala et al., 2001).

The effects of alcohol on psychomotor tasks are also well known. Hand-eye coordination is impaired, as are balance and the ability to operate machinery such as automobiles. Studies in young and middle-aged men have shown an increase in alcohol-induced CNS impairment in performance of certain psychomotor tasks with aging, even controlling for blood alcohol levels (Linnoila, Erwin, Ramm, & Cleveland, 1980; Vogel-Sprott & Barrett, 1984). If indeed there is more alcohol-induced psychomotor performance impairment in older adults, the added burden of musculoskeletal, neurological, visual, or hearing disabilities, or simply general frailty, would likely increase the probability of falls.

Other cognitive tasks may not be affected by alcohol consumption, however (Collins & Mertens, 1988; Yesavage, Dolhert, & Taylor, 1994). Two studies have also shown that older individuals with moderate alcohol consumption actually have better overall cognitive functioning (Christian et al., 1995; Galanis et al., 2000). Furthermore, major studies by Ruitenberg et al. (2002) and Zuccala et al. (2001) reported protective effects of moderate alcohol consumption for both cognitive impairment and dementia in late life. It should be emphasized that moderate amounts of alcohol consumption have beneficial effects on cardiovascular and psychological health, as well as cognitive function. Many elderly individuals may use alcohol for its therapeutic or medication effects, such as for anxiety, pain, or insomnia, or to stimulate appetite, with overall beneficial effects both physically and psychologically (Dufour Archer, & Gordis, 1992). Excessive use of alcohol, however, may result in a variety of psychological and physical health problems, highlighting the interaction between physical and mental health in late life.

DIFFERENTIATING BETWEEN MENTAL AND PHYSICAL HEALTH PROBLEMS •

As discussed in previous chapters, illnesses may manifest differently in older adults than in younger persons. In middle-aged men, a classic symptom of an MI is a crushing chest pain radiating down the left arm, as well as pallor and perspiration. In an older person, the symptoms may be abdominal pain, confusion, weakness, and vertigo (Wei, 1994). In younger women, bladder infections are accompanied by a burning sensation with urination; in older women, the primary symptom may be confusion. On the other hand, psychological problems may have concomitant physiological symptoms: Anxiety may be accompanied by rapid and irregular heart rates, depression by fatigue and sleep problems. Again, the patterns of the symptoms may change with age. Thus, it may be difficult to differentiate between mental and physical health problems in late life, but the correct identification is vital to appropriate treatment.

Aldwin and Levenson (1998) reviewed the literature addressing this problem. Surprisingly, older individuals with illnesses such as vitamin deficiencies, pneumonia, MIs, and hyper- and hypothyroidism may present with anxiety. Illnesses that are fairly frequent in older adults—such as cardiovascular disease, chronic obstructive pulmonary disorder (COPD), and, to a lesser extent, hypothyroidism—often result in fatigue, sleep disturbances, and negative affect. Thus, they may be very difficult to differentiate from depression. Some commonly prescribed medications such as antihypertensives or cholesterol-lowering drugs may also result in depression. On the other hand, symptoms such as fatigue, headaches, back pain, constipation, and sleep disturbances, which are indicative of depression in younger individuals, may reflect age- or disease-related physical health problems in older adults. For this reason, any physical assessment of an older adult with nonspecific symptoms should include a psychological assessment of recent changes in life events or living circumstances, to rule out psychosocial factors.

A serious problem is the potential confusion between depression and cognitive impairment. Older people who are depressed often complain of memory problems that can be mistaken for dementia. Newman and Sweet (1992) developed a list of characteristics that can easily distinguish between memory problems due to depression and those due to dementia. The memory problems due to depression generally have a rapid onset, but those due to dementia usually start very gradually. Generally, family members are more aware of memory problems in relatives with dementia than in depressed loved ones. There is also a difference in long-term and short-term memory. Depressed older adults report poor memory for both recent events and those in the past, whereas those with dementia are often quite voluble about their past histories but can remember very little about what happened that day.

Finally, depressed older adults usually are quite distressed over their memory problems and can provide great detail about it. In contrast, those with dementia may not be aware that their memories are failing, or, if they suspect there is a problem, they may go to great lengths to hide it. An interesting exercise is to ask individuals with mild to moderate Alzheimer's disease whether they ate breakfast and what they had. Typically, they will confabulate, often at great length. If you ask if they had breakfast, they will nod and say, "Oh yes." If you ask them what they had, they will say something like "Oh, it was very good." If you get more insistent and say, "But what did you have?" the likely response is, "Oh, you know, the usual. I really enjoyed it." In truth, they have no idea what they ate and often not even whether or not they did eat.

The situation can be made even more complicated by the fact that people in the initial stages of Alzheimer's disease may become quite depressed. Sometimes, the only way one can differentiate memory problems due to depression or dementia is to administer a course of antidepressives and see if the problem is diminished.

Finally, it is important to differentiate between dementia and confusional states. Dementias are typically irreversible, whereas confusional states (deleriums or pseudodementias) can be reversed if properly diagnosed. Confusional states can result from surgeries and anesthesia, or they may be due to inadequate nutrition or dehydration. Some illnesses such as bladder infections may create confusional states because they disrupt the electrolytic balance, among other things. As we have seen, psychotropic medications and alcohol consumption may also adversely affect cognitive function.

SUMMARY ●

As noted in this and the preceding chapters, the interface between physical and mental health in later life is complex. On one hand, some studies of age-related differences in the effects of psychosocial risk factors on health suggest that individuals in midlife are more vulnerable to the effects of hostility and bereavement than are older adults. Presumably, this reflects survival bias—people who survive to late life tend to be hardy. On the other hand, it is clear that some factors such as excess alcohol consumption do have detrimental effects in late life, and older adults may be more vulnerable to them than are younger adults. This relationship is not straightforward or linear, however; moderate alcohol consumption maybe be protective of cardiovascular and cognitive health and even decrease overall mortality. Hostility, depression, and anxiety clearly have adverse effects, especially in individuals with preexisting illnesses, and we are getting a better understanding of the pathophysiology underlying these effects.

Other psychological factors, such as mindfulness and emotional stability, may be protective of health in late life. Some of these factors, such as control and optimism, may be most protective with acute stressors but may enhance vulnerability in conditions of chronic stress, which older adults may be more likely to face in late life (Aldwin & Levenson, 2001).

CHAPTER 10

STRESS, COPING, AND HEALTH

Stress is a major pathway through which psychosocial factors affect physiology and the aging process. Through the neuroendocrine system, psychosocial stress can have adverse effects on the cardiovascular and immune systems. Luckily, humans are relatively resilient to the effects of stress, in part because we have developed complex ways of coping with stress that can reduce or buffer its effects. As Pearlin and Schooler (1978) noted 25 years ago, there is no magic bullet, no one coping strategy that will instantly solve any problem. We are beginning to understand which coping strategies work in different types of situations, however, and are also investigating the pathways through which coping can affect physiology and health outcomes. Older adults may be particularly vulnerable to the effects of physical stress.

The types of stressors individuals face change over time. Problems with work and starting a family in early adulthood give way to coping with health problems and caregiving for sick parents and spouses in midlife. Loss of loved ones through bereavement becomes much more common in late life, and eventually we must all face our own deaths. We may become more adept at coping with problems as we age, although each stage of life provides new challenges, and new strategies must be learned.

It would be a mistake to believe that the effects of stress are exclusively negative, however. There is also a growing body of evidence that stress can have "toughening" or strengthening effects on everything from heat shock proteins to social ties. Whether stress has positive or negative effects may depend on its temporal patterning and also on how we cope with it.

Some have argued that resistance to the adverse effects of stress may be the key to longevity, as all of the antiaging genes appear to regulate cell-based stress resistance (Johnson et al., 2002). As detailed in Chapter 3, a variety of genetically based mechanisms protect against stress at the cellular level, including DNA repair mechanisms, antioxidants, and heat shock proteins. Although we are beginning to understand how these mechanisms protect the cell from mechanical, radiation, and chemical stressors, to our knowledge, only one study (Lewthwaite, Owen, Coates, Henderson, & Steptoe, 2002) has examined whether there are cellular responses to psychosocial stress. Most of the research, especially that in humans, has focused on how the neuroendocrine system mediates psychosocial stress and health outcomes, and it is unlikely that there are direct effects at the cellular level. As Sapolsky (1998) pointed out, however, neuroendocrine stress reactions can be very toxic, and it is likely that they may affect cellular functioning, perhaps triggering the cell-based defense mechanisms mentioned above. This chapter focuses on the effects of stress at the systems level, as well as individual differences in coping responses and how these develop over the life course.

STRESS ●

There are three major ways of defining stress (Mason, 1975). The first is as a physiological state of the organism (sometimes referred to as strain). The second is to define stress as a characteristic of the environment (or stressor). The third is to view stress as a transaction between the person and the environment.

Stress as a Physiological State

Classic Theories

Cannon (1915) was the first physiologist to systematically describe the physiological effects of stress. He noted that cats exposed to barking dogs would respond with a rush of epinephrine or adrenaline into their systems.

Cannon posited that the perception of a threat activated the sympathetic nervous system (SNS), which readies the organism for fight or flight. (He believed that threat activates the thalamus; we now know that it is the hypothalamus that responds to stress.)

The SNS reacts to stress in two ways (Gevirtz, 2000). The sympathetic nerves originate in the spinal column (preganglionic nerves) and radiate to the target organs (postganglionic nerves). The preganglionic nerves are cholinergic, that is, they secrete the neurotransmitter acetylcholine. The postganglionic nerves use norepinephrine. The sympathetic nerves directly enervate the heart, the bronchi in the lungs, the gut, and the kidney; they also influence the blood vessels, sweat glands, and piloerector muscles in the skin.

The second type of SNS response to stress is a little less direct. In the sympathetic/adrenal medulla (SAM) system, the sympathetic nerves radiate to the adrenal medulla, which is a small structure lying atop of the kidneys. The adrenal medulla, or center, secretes both epinephrine (also called adrenaline) and norepinephrine (noradrenaline) into the blood, which also stimulates the organs' muscles and blood vessels (see Figure 10.1). These two neurotransmitters have similar effects, but epinephrine is a more powerful cardiac stimulant and also increases the metabolic rate, whereas norepinephrine more strongly stimulates the peripheral vascular system and raises blood pressure. The effect of direct innervation on the various systems is faster, but the route through the medulla can last up to 10 times as long. The two systems (direct innervation and SAM) are redundant—an indicator of the importance of stress-related SNS activation.

Sympathetic activation increases heart and respiration rates, dilates the pupils, diverts blood flow from digestion to the striated muscles, and increases blood sugar. This increased activation readies an organism for physical activity. Indeed, individuals under stress can often run faster or farther or respond more quickly than they had thought possible. The phenomenological experience of SNS activation is relatively straightforward. The heart pounds, and the breath becomes faster and heavier. The "butterflies" in the stomach reflect the diverted blood flow from the gut to the muscles. Sweat-gland activation can cause the palms to become clammy or beads of sweat to appear on the forehead. The hair on the arms or the back of the neck may stand up (the piloerection response), and peripheral blood vessel constriction results in facial pallor. This state is usually temporary. Once the threat is resolved, parasympathetic nervous system (PNS) activation returns the body to homeostasis by decreasing heart rate and respiratory rates, as well as blood pressure, and returning blood flow to the internal organs, which promotes gastrointestinal activity.

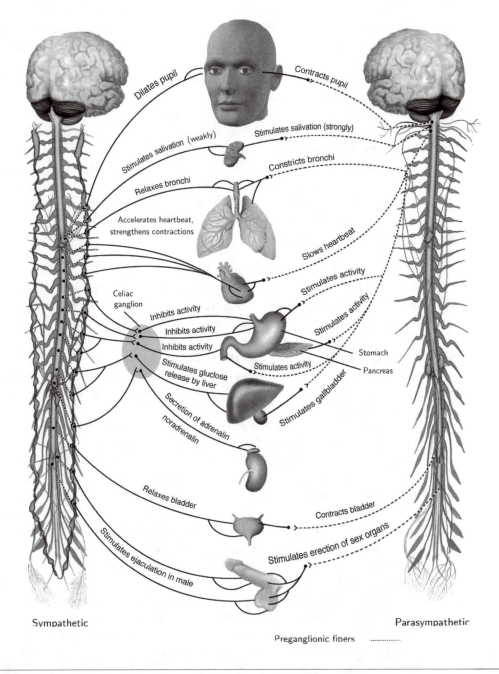

Figure 10.1 Peripheral Pathways of the Autonomic Nervous System

SOURCE: Reprinted from Beatty, J. (2001). *The human brain: Essentials of behavioral neuroscience.* Thousand Oaks, CA: Sage. Copyright © 2001 Sage Publications. Artist: Barry Burns. Used with permission.

Cannon (1929) argued that this fight/flight reaction, although adaptive in the short run, could have very harmful effects if prolonged. He used the example of what he termed "voodoo death."[1] Australian aborigines have a tradition of bone pointing, which is a way for a shaman to condemn a tribesperson to death, usually for breaking a taboo. Cannon described a case in which an Australian aborigine so cursed died a few days later, with no obvious organic cause. He reasoned that overactivation of the sympathetic nervous system can result in a state of shock. Increased blood pressure forces liquids out of the vascular system into the surrounding tissues. If prolonged, this process decreases circulating blood volume. Eventually, the blood volume is insufficient to sustain adequate blood pressure levels. In an attempt to increase blood pressure and blood flow, the arterioles dilate. This can cause the blood pressure to drop dramatically, leading to shock and cardiac arrest. Cursed aborigines may stop eating and drinking, which can hasten this process.

It is not only humans who can be frightened to death; this is a fairly common problem among animals. For example, there is a phenomenon called porcine stress syndrome in which a certain percentage of pigs being shipped to market die simply from the stress of being transported (Backstrom & Kauffman, 1995). Even relatively benign phenomena may be interpreted as stressful by animals. A few years ago, the *London Times* printed a story about an okapi (a cousin of the zebra) that lived in the Berlin zoo. During a Wagner music festival at the zoo, the okapi quite literally died of fright when the orchestra played "Ride of the Valkyries."

Cannon (1929) believed that the fight/flight reaction is a general response to any stressor, physical or social. In reacting to sudden physical threats, it is advantageous to be able to put up an aggressive defense or to run away very quickly. (For example, most joggers have found that being chased by a dog greatly increases their sprinting ability.) However, prolonged sympathetic activation in response to psychosocial stress is thought to be maladaptive and to underlie the "diseases of adaptation" (Dubos, 1965). Without the physical release of running or fighting, Dubos reasoned that prolonged increases in blood pressure and blood clotting would eventually result in hypertension and cardiovascular disease. As we shall see, chronic psychosocial stress may have adverse cardiovascular and immune effects.

Selye (1956) expanded on Cannon's conceptions in two ways. First, he noticed that corticosteroids, which are released by the adrenal cortex (or top layer of the adrenal glands), are also elevated in response to a wide variety of stressors. Even injecting dirt into a rat's veins resulted in corticosteroid increases, so Selye jokingly referred to his work as "the physiology of dirt." While Cannon initially thought that the perception of threat led the thalamus to initiate a cascade of events, we now know that it is actually the hypothalamus. The hypothalamus secretes corticotropin-releasing hormone (CHA), which activates the posterior lobe of the pituitary. The pituitary, in turn, releases adrenocorticotropin hormone (ACTH) into the blood stream. ACTH stimulates the cortex of adrenal glands to release corticosteroids, including glucocorticoids and mineral corticoids (see Figure 10.2). This hypothalamic-pituitary-adrenal (HPA) activation is a slower but more sustained response to a wide variety of stressors, including mechanical stress (such as heat, cold, or physical exertion), chemical toxins, and psychosocial problems.

Glucocorticoids are fat-soluble molecules, which enables them to cross cell membranes in every organ system in the body. Thus, they have a wide range of effects. Cortisol suppresses the inflammatory responses associated with immune-system activation. Other glucocorticoids stimulate the release of glucose into the blood system and raise metabolic rates. Some suppress fertility, others decrease the level of growth hormone, and yet others can interfere with calcium metabolism and a host of other metabolic functions. Thus, stress can affect the functioning of nearly every organ system in the body, either through SNS or HPA activation.

Second, Selye (1956) expanded Cannon's (1929) dualistic process (SNS vs. PNS activation) by describing three stages in reaction to stress. The alarm stage is similar to Cannon's fight/flight reaction but involves the adrenal glands as well as SNS activation. However, Selye noticed that some of the rats he studied seemed to become used to the stressor. For example, some rats might stop shivering in response to cold. He called this second-stage adaptation, in which there is a return to physiological homeostasis (due in part to PNS activation), or sometimes even enhanced functioning. In the third stage, exhaustion, the organism may fall ill or die if the stress continues. Selye posited that this was a result of the body's supplies of hormones becoming depleted.

Modern Theories

Modern conceptions of the stress response differ in several important ways. Both Cannon (1929) and Selye (1956) argued that there are general responses to stress, but it is now widely recognized that there are individual differences in stress reactions. From a psychosocial perspective, Lazarus, Averill, and Opton (1974) reviewed a number of studies they and their colleagues conducted investigating the effect of stress on sympathetic arousal, including heart rate, respiratory rate, and galvanic skin response (a measure of the degree to which the electrical conductance of the skin is affected by sweating). These studies consistently found individual differences in the

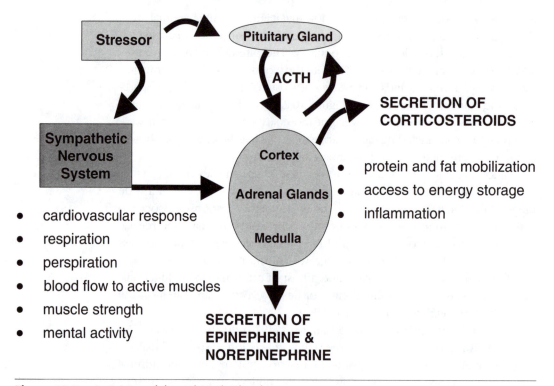

- cardiovascular response
- respiration
- perspiration
- blood flow to active muscles
- muscle strength
- mental activity

Figure 10.2 Activities of the Adrenal Gland

patterning of sympathetic arousal. For example, some individuals' heart rates increased in response to stress, but others' heart rates decreased, although they perspired more. This observation has been supported by physiological studies showing that there are different subsystems within the SNS that can be activated independently (Jänig & McLachlan, 1992). Mason (1971) also argued that there are stressor profiles (e.g., that different neuroendocrine reactions vary as a function of types of stress). Thus, physiological responses to stress can be much more differentiated than previously thought.

In addition, it is now recognized that activation of the HPA axis is an attempt to buffer the rather damaging influence of prolonged SNS activation (Gevirtz, 2000). Thus, the SNS activates immune system responses, encouraging inflammation; HPA activation suppresses the immune/inflammatory response (which is why individuals with severe inflammations are given corticosteroids). Sapolsky (1998) proposed that Selye was incorrect—stressed organisms do not die because their hormones become depleted, but because of the toxic effects of the stress response itself (see the discussion of "voodoo death" above). In contrast, Yehuda (2000) argued that chronic stress, such as that found in posttraumatic stress disorder (PTSD), is associated with *lower* levels of cortisol. Thus, chronic stress can deplete, if it does not totally exhaust, glucocorticoids. Individuals with low levels of cortisol may be unable to mount any sort of response to a challenge. For example, they may be unable to exercise, because they cannot sufficiently increase blood pressure or mobilize blood glucose and thus may be chronically fatigued (Gruenewald & Matsumoto, 1999).

In addition, we now know that most, if not all, of the endocrine hormones are affected by stress, increasing or decreasing in fairly complex temporal patterns. In general, stress activates those hormones that increase metabolic functioning and suppresses those involved in long-term growth and maintenance. Sapolsky (1998) has pointed out, however, that growth hormone in humans initially *increases* in response to stress. This may be because growth hormone helps to stimulate metabolism, and its actions on cell division are mediated by somatomedins. These are suppressed during stress, at least initially, so the body can use the metabolic effects of growth hormone without "wasting" energy on growth. With longer-term stress, however, growth hormone is suppressed. This can account for the failure-to-thrive syndrome in institutionalized infants. In severely neglected infants, lack of adequate growth hormone levels and somatomedins makes it impossible for them to utilize food in an optimal manner, even if they are receiving sufficient nutrition. Interestingly, stroking the skin appears to stimulate growth hormone and can reverse these effects (Field, 1998).

The recognition of broader endocrine responses to stress has led Taylor and her colleagues (2000) to argue for a third stress pathway, through oxytocin. Oxytocin is a hormone that is very important in reproductive activities such as breast-feeding. It may also mediate social relations, and Taylor et al. provide evidence that it might underlie sex differences in stress reactions.

Laboratory studies have shown a curious sex difference in response to stress. A series of studies reviewed by Taylor et al. (2000) showed that men and women differ in their preference for company or solitude while awaiting a stressful procedure. Overwhelmingly, men choose to wait alone, while women choose to be with other people. Based on this research, Taylor and her colleagues hypothesized that women's response to stress is mediated more by oxytocin and can be characterized by a "tend and befriend" response as opposed to the male flight-or-fight reaction mediated by the SNS. In a stressful situation, women's reaction may be to protect their children and cling to their mates or friends.

It would be a mistake to interpret this model as advocating completely different stress pathways for men and women, however. Obviously, women as well as men have SAMs and HPAs, and women have been known to run away from stressful situations and to fight, both verbally and physically. Men also protect their children, spouses, and friends from harm. Furthermore, the laboratory studies cited all observed college-aged males in artificial situations. Field studies on community samples show that men do use social support to cope in stressful situations, albeit less frequently than women (Aldwin, 1999). Nonetheless, Taylor's important observation of social responses to stress does suggest that a third axis may need to be added to Cannon's original two-dimensional response. Rather than fight-flight, perhaps it should be characterized as fight-flight-affiliate, a three-dimensional reaction to stress. Figure 10.3 illustrates this. This allows for a more complex depiction of stress responses. Furthermore, it allows for the influence of such factors as gender, age, personality, and environmental factors in the patterning of the stress response. Some people's dominant tendency may be to affiliate. For example, most toddlers and small children who feel threatened cling to their mothers (or fathers) for safety. Men, especially those high in hostility, may be more likely to fight when they feel threatened (see Chapter 9). Many people who experience an extremely traumatic event, such as the collapse of the World Trade Center towers during the September 2001 attack on the United States, find themselves simply running—without any conscious decision or, seemingly, any ability to stop before they become exhausted. In addition to personality and gender differences, it would be interesting to determine if older adults show systematic change in their pattern of stress responses using this scheme.

Stress and the Development of Chronic Illness

Studies in animal models show that stress can result in heart disease (Björntorp, 1997; Kaplan et al., 1996; Rozanski, Blumenthal, & Kaplan, 1999) and cancer (Sapolsky, 1998). Stress does cause temporary increases in cardiovascular disease (CVD) risk factors such as blood pressure and cholesterol (Rozanski et al., 1999), promotes atherosclerotic and arteriosclerotic processes, and impairs immune functioning, all of which are known risk factors for CVD (Black & Garbutt, 2002). However, empirical evidence supporting the relationship between stress and CVD in humans is surprisingly equivocal (Eliott, 1995; Greenwood, Muir, Packham, & Madeley, 1996; Karmarck & Jennings, 1991; Pickering, 1999).

Similarly, an early study showed that some 80% of rats that were genetically vulnerable and that were subjected to stress developed breast cancer (Ader, Felten, & Cohen, 1991). Subsequent studies showed that stress

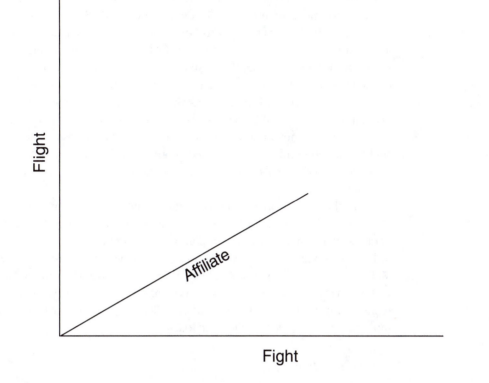

Figure 10.3 A Triune Model of Reactions to Stress

can promote tumor proliferation through pathways such as angiogenesis (development of blood vessels that feed the tumor) and by shunting glucose preferentially to tumors (Romero et al., 1992). Stress has been shown to suppress natural killer (NK) cells in humans (Cohen & Herbert, 1996). Given that a primary function of NK cells is cancer cell surveillance, it is surprising that the overall relationship between stress and cancer in humans is relatively weak (Fox, 1983), although stress does appear to play a role in the development of certain types of tumors such as breast cancer (McKenna, Zevon, Corn, & Rounds, 1999).

Some researchers have tried to create more complex models of the interplay between stress and genetic factors. For example, McEwen and Stellar (1993) proposed that there are cascading relationships between genetic and environmental factors that result in individual differences in vulnerability to stress and risk of disease. Allostasis refers to the fluctuation in physiological systems to meet external demands (McEwen, 1998, 2000; McEwen & Seeman, 1999). Taylor and Repetti (1997) define allostatic load as "the physiological costs of chronic exposure to fluctuating or heightened neural or neuroendocrine responses that result from repeated chronic environmental challenges" (p. 415). This construct is very similar to the metabolic syndrome (Björntorp, 2001; Reaven, 1998; Timor, Sestier, & Levy, 2000), which posits that stress can affect various components of the neuroendocrine system, leading to metabolic imbalances, increased fat deposits, and diseases such as diabetes and atherosclerosis. In other words, these models posit cascade effects of stress on cardiovascular, neuroendocrine, and metabolic systems.

The theoretical presentations of these highly complex models make a strong case, but the evidence for them is often pieced together from disparate studies linking stress to the individual components of these models. Although summary measures of allostatic load have predicted CVD (Seeman, McEwen, Rowe, & Singer, 2001; Seeman, Singer, Rowe, Horwitz, & McEwen 1997), it has not yet been demonstrated that *psychosocial* stress is in fact correlated with these summary biomarker indices of *physiological* stress across multiple systems (such as allostatic load).

Positive Physiological Changes

Researchers have been so focused on the negative consequences of stress that possible positive outcomes tend to be overlooked. Early work by Denenberg (1964) and Levine and his colleagues (Levine, 1966; Levine, Haltmeyer, Karas, & Denenberg, 1967) showed that infant mice and rats subjected to mild electric shock or handling matured more quickly than their nonstressed peers. They developed hair and opened their eyes earlier, had better nerve myelinization and locomotion, and reached puberty at younger ages. As adults, they showed better neuroendocrine responses to stress, showing quicker and larger increases in epinephrine and norepinephrine but returning to baseline more quickly as well. A well-controlled study by Hilakivi-Clark, Wright, and Lippman (1993) confirmed that infant handling in rats led to better growth patterns and resistance to future stress.

In humans, this work was paralleled by anthropologists Landauer and Whiting (1981), who found that adults tend to be taller in cultures in which infants are subjected to stressors in the first 2 years of life (stressors such as circumcision, sleeping apart from parents, and scarification) than in those cultures in which infants and toddlers are less stressed. Belsky, Steinberg, and

Draper (1991) also found that childhood stress was related to earlier onset of puberty.

There are a number of possible reasons for this phenomenon. Dienstbier (1989, 1992) suggested that stress can induce physiological toughness if it is followed by an adequate recovery period: "Regular exposure to challenges and stressors followed by adequate recovery periods can cause peripheral and central physiological changes that increase one's future capacity for more positive forms of arousal and the suppression of more costly forms of arousal" (1992, p. 367). Basically, Dienstbier argued that SAM activation is associated with better performance on cognitive and physical tasks, as well as emotional stability, whereas HPA axis arousal is less beneficial and may interfere with performance. Short-term depletion of central catecholamines is associated with an increased ability to generate catecholamines for future stressors, as well as resistance to future depletion.

Another mechanism may be growth hormone production, which may be stimulated by stress in humans. Perhaps in infants, the mechanism that suppresses somatomedins is not yet operative, resulting in growth enhancement. In infant rats, however, Levine (2001) argued that it is the subsequent response of the mother that promotes growth. Typically, infant pups separated from their mother for a short time are greeted on their return by extensive bathing and nurturing by the mother. In contrast, pups absent too long may be ignored or shunned. As noted earlier such stroking and touching can also stimulate growth hormone. However, this explanation does not fully account for the changes in the neuroendocrine system that Dienstbier and others have noted, and it is likely that multiple mechanisms are in effect.

Similar phenomena may also be at work at the cellular level. Holtzman (1995) reviewed the phenomenon of hormesis mentioned in Chapter 3, in which low levels of exposure to a stressor can result in resistance to more lethal levels. For example, low levels of exposure to radiation have been associated with lower levels of subsequent deaths due to cancer in humans. Low levels of radiation can stimulate the production of DNA repair mechanisms, which presumably can protect against future exposure. While this hypothesis is not without controversy, hormesis is a promising new development that may help to explain the role of stress in longevity (Calabrese & Baldwin, 2002). Other mechanisms may be involved as well. Insects exposed to low levels of radiation tend to have lower death rates (Allen & Sohal, 1982). A series of experiments led Cristafalo, Tresini, Francis, and Volker (1999) to argue that low levels of radiation can also result in a lowered metabolic rate, which can extend the life span.

Flatworms exposed to nonlethal heat stressors developed resistance to future heat stress. They were able to live through temperatures that kill flatworms without this stress-induced resistance (Lithgow, White, Hinerfeld, & Johnson, 1994; Lithgow, White, Melov, & Johnson, 1995). Presumably, the mechanisms here work through the greater production of heat shock proteins, which protect against the adverse effects of stress on the cellular level. Thus, moderate exposure to toxins can result in increased resiliency to stress on a number of different levels, and perhaps greater longevity.

Physiological Stress and Aging

The optimal stress response is a sharp increase in cortisol and other stress-related hormones and peptides, followed by a quick return to baseline. In aging rats, the response degrades—that is, there is a much slower increase in cortisol, and it takes much longer to return to baseline. Thus, the toxic elements in the stress response stay in the system longer and can create a number of problems. For example, too much epinephrine can cause microtears in the blood vessels, which promote the deposition of plaque and, eventually, atherosclerosis. Sapolsky (1992) suggested that too much cortisol can damage receptors in the hippocampus, which is one of the primary regulators of cortisol. He proposed a positive feedback loop in which too much cortisol damages the hippocampus, which leads to deregulation problems, resulting in even more cortisol in the system. Sapolsky hypothesized that this may be one mechanism for hippocampal damage and memory problems in late life.

In humans, the findings on age-related changes in the stress response are quite variable and somewhat contradictory (Wilkinson, Peskind, & Raskind, 1997). Part of the problem is that HPA responses are greatly affected by chronic illnesses and many medications, so it is difficult to disentangle normal aging from disease-related effects. Some studies show age-related increases in baseline levels of cortisol in healthy older adults (Seeman, Singer, Wilkinson, & McEwen, 2001), but others do not (Kudielka, Schmidt-Reinwald, Hellhammer, & Kirschbaum, 1999). Artificially inducing cortisol responses, by using a cortisol releasing hormone (CRH) challenge, does show greater increases in cortisol in older adults (Kudielka et al., 1999). In general, older adults also take longer to clear infused cortisol (Wilkinson et al., 1997).

Older adults do not necessarily show increased cortisol responses to psychosocial stress, however, and there are some suggestions that there may be gender differences. Kudielka et al. (1998) showed that older men had greater responses to a public speaking task, but Seeman, Singer, and Charpentier (1995) showed that women had greater responses to a driving simulation task. Seeman et al. (2001) showed that young men and older women showed heightened cortisol responses to cognitive testing. In these studies, though, the sample sizes tend to be small and many of the results marginal. Thus, in healthy older adults, there is little consistency in naturalistic responses to psychosocial stress, although they may have more difficulty clearing artificially induced cortisol.

There is no doubt that illness and the types of age-related changes detailed in Section II do make older adults more vulnerable to physical stressors. Sedentary middle-aged men who suddenly undertake strenuous physical labor are vulnerable to heart attacks. During earthquakes in California, often the only fatalities are elderly people with coronary heart disease. Difficulty in regulating body temperature renders the elderly very vulnerable to both heat and cold stress. For example, hundreds of frail elders died in a heat wave in Chicago in the 1990s. Whenever there is a massive population disruption, such as a famine or war-related refugee exodus, it is the very old and the infants who are most likely to die. Thus, when examining the effect of aging on the stress response, it is very important to differentiate between healthy aging and vulnerability due to disease as well as the type of stressor faced.

Stress as a Characteristic of the Environment

While physiologists such as Cannon and Selye were defining stress as a characteristic of the organism, behavioral and social scientists (as well as physicians) were examining stress as a characteristic of the environment. These fall roughly into four different groups: trauma, stressful life events, chronic role strain, and daily stressors or hassles. There is a fair amount of overlap between these types of stressors, but they do have some distinctive qualities.

Trauma

Traumatic stress is defined by the *DSM-IV-TR* (American Psychiatric Association [APA], 2000) as direct personal experience of an event that involves serious threat to the life or physical integrity of self or significant others, or learning about such an experience of a family member or close associate. Traumatic stress generally evokes feelings of extreme terror and helplessness, followed by emotional numbness. Eventually, 20% to 30% of trauma victims may go on to develop PTSD, which is characterized by affective disturbances including anxiety, depression, suicidal ideas, startle reactions, nightmares, and flashbacks. It may be difficult to concentrate or to complete tasks, and traumatized individuals often have difficulty in their social relationships. Traumas are difficult because they often destroy individuals' worldviews, or fundamental assumption systems (Epstein, 1991)—such as beliefs that they are safe and that really bad things will not happen to them.

Traumatic events can be loosely grouped into three general categories. Natural or technological disasters include earthquakes, tornadoes, volcanoes, floods, and nuclear accidents. These typically occur with little or no warning and, to qualify as traumatic, must include serious threat to life and limb, usually to whole communities. They usually have a relatively short duration, although the aftermath of disasters may last for years. Baum and Fleming (1993) have argued that technological disasters tend to have worse psychological effects than natural disasters, in part because they involve a sense of betrayal by and blaming of the perceived perpetrators of these disasters (which are often large, multinational companies with tenuous ties to the local community).

The second type of trauma category includes wars and related disasters such as famine. The devastation of war is well known. PTSD typically affects about 20% to 30% of combat veterans, although war affects civilians as well. Prisoners of war (POWs) and torture victims are often the most adversely affected, with high rates of PTSD (up to 50%) and lifelong mental and physical consequences (APA, 2000).

Finally, individual traumas are usually life-threatening events that happen to particular individuals, such as crimes or serious accidents. Simple muggings or fender-benders do not generally qualify as trauma, but accidents involving fatalities or serious bodily harm, as well as life-threatening crimes such as rape and incest, often have lifelong effects. Norris (1992) did a survey of lifelong exposure to trauma among older men and women and found that car accidents were the most frequent source of trauma.

The effects of trauma can last a lifetime. Several studies have shown that combat exposure is associated with PTSD symptoms as long as 50 years later (Aldwin, Levenson, & Spiro, 1994; Kahana, 1992). Spiro, Schnurr, and Aldwin (1994) estimate that approximately a quarter of men over the age of 55 had been exposed to combat in World War, II, Korea, or the Vietnam War. We know very little about how such trauma affects the aging process, however. There is some indication, though, that combat exposure can interact with subsequent exposure to trauma and accelerate the aging process (Schnurr, Spiro, Aldwin, & Stukel, 1998).

Stressful Life Events

There is some overlap between life events and individual trauma. Stressful life events are major disruptions in individuals' lives due to specific occurrences such as marriage, divorce, widowhood, and job loss. In 1950,

Wolff reported on a study in which he asked his cardiac patients to maintain diaries. Analysis of this data revealed that the patients often reported experiencing a stressful life event 6 months to a year before becoming ill. Holmes and Rahe (1967) developed a list of life events, the Schedule of Readjustment Rating Scale, that sought to specify the life change units (LCUs) associated with each event, whether positive or negative. For example, death of a spouse was considered to require the most LCUs and was set at 100. The LCU ratings were criticized as fairly arbitrary, so they also developed a checklist, the Schedule of Recent Events (SRE).

Literally thousands of studies have been done using life events scales, either the SRE or scales developed for specific populations, and it is beyond the scope of this book to review all of them. Aldwin (1999), however, provided some general observations. Negative life events do tend to show modest correlations with self-reported mental and physical health outcomes, generally in the .2 to .3 range. In general, though, positive life events show little relationship to health outcomes. Furthermore, the impact of the event varies as a function of controllability. That is, uncontrollable stressors generally have more adverse impacts than those perceived to be under an individual's control. In general, the impact of stressful life events tends to diminish after 6 to 18 months (Depue & Monroe, 1986). Furthermore, stressful life events tend to be fairly rare, and their relationship to discrete physical outcomes such as CVD is often fairly weak in humans Thus, researchers have sought alternative means of conceptualizing and measuring stress.

Chronic Role Strain

Sociologists Pearlin and Schooler (1978) developed the construct of chronic role strain, which refers to enduring problems linked to social roles such as marriage, work, parenting, finances, and health. Pearlin and Schooler argued that enduring problems were much more likely to have adverse effects than single life events. A subsequent study by Pearlin, Lieberman, Menaghan, and Mullan (1981) found that the effect of stressful life events was primarily mediated by changes in role strain. In other words, life events have adverse effects on physical and mental health because they cause disruptions in ongoing relations with spouses, children, jobs, and/or finances. Other researchers focus on stress related to particular roles. Hundreds of studies have been conducted on occupational stress (see Karasek & Theorell, 1990), and, more relevant to the elderly, on caregiver burden (see Chapter 11).

Often, a combination of problems in several roles may contribute to difficulties in individual adaptation, more so than a single event. For example, Brown and Harris (1978) found that women who were most likely to be depressed were single parents with financial difficulties and young children under the age of 5. Sometimes a number of factors may combine to make a particular role stressful. For example, retirement is generally an eagerly antic- ipated event, and many have plans to travel, move to warmer climates, enjoy their grandchildren, or seriously pursue hobbies. But retirees with insuffi- cient financial resources and those whose poor health prevents them from participating in desirable activities may find retirement stressful, as may those who find themselves caring for ill parents or spouses (Bossé, Aldwin, Levenson, & Workman-Daniels, 1991).

Pearlin, Aneshensel, Mullan, and Whitlatch (1996) argued that a chronic role strain becomes stressful when it spreads into another domain, a phe- nomenon they termed "stress proliferation." They used the example of care- giving, which can be very stressful, especially for spouses or parents with cognitive impairment or if the preexisting relationship between the caregiver and patient was strained. If problems in the caregiving role proliferate into other domains, then more adverse health effects can be expected. For example, caregiving often requires taking patients to frequent doctors' appointments, which can require time off from work. Additional time can be missed due to medical emergencies, exhaustion from being up all night, and so on. At some point, one's work role may begin to be affected. It is also not unusual for caregiving to create a strain in relationships with one's spouse or children. An early study of stress contagion found that work stress affects marital relations for men, whereas marital stress creates problems at work for women (Coyne & DeLongis, 1986).

Daily Stressors

Daily stressors or "hassles" are in many ways similar to chronic role strain. Lazarus and Folkman (1984) argued that day-to-day problems may have more generalized effects on health status than relatively rare life events. These problems range from minor disagreements with coworkers, friends, and family to traffic jams to air pollution. In general, hassles are not neces- sarily systematically linked to any particular role, and indeed, may not neces- sarily be indicative of role strain. For example, a job that one greatly enjoys may also on any given day also have a lot of hassles, such as a copier break- down shortly before a grant proposal deadline. As with chronic role strain, the effects of life events on health outcomes may be mediated by an increase in hassles (Aldwin, Levenson, Spiro, & Bossé, 1989; Wagner, Compas, & Howell, 1988). For example, a divorce may create more daily stress at home, because one must cope with all of the housekeeping chores, car mainte- nance, and the like. Although the memory for and reporting of life events is notoriously unreliable (Raphael, Cloitre, & Dohrenwend, 1991), daily stressors tend to be assessed using a daily diary in which respondents recount what happened during that day (DeLongis, Folkman, & Lazarus, 1988). Some researchers recommend event moment sampling (EMS) techniques, in which respondents are given small computers in the form of watches. When the computers beep, the respondents fill out (necessarily brief) question-naires about the types of stressors they are experiencing at that moment (Stone, Neale, & Shiffman, 1993). Daily diaries and EMS may be most useful in tracking health-related phenomena that fluctuate daily, such as chronic pain (Affleck, Zautra, Tennen, & Armeli, 1999).

Stress as a Transaction Between the Person and the Environment

From a transactionalist point of view, stress arises from an individual's experience of the environment. Stress cannot be said to be a characteristic of the environment or a response of the individual but rather arises from a com-bination of environmental demands and individual vulnerabilities and resources (Lazarus & Folkman, 1994). In this system, cognitive appraisal is central. An individual appraises a situation in terms of whether it is benign or involves a threat, harm, loss, or challenge. Thus, there are individual differ-ences in whether or not a situation is appraised as stressful, as well as the degree of stress involved. For example, being laid off from a summer job when one is 16 is not generally perceived as very serious, but for a 50-year-old single mom with two children in college, losing a job is extremely serious. Thus, the appraisal of stress depends on the match between environmental demands and individual vulnerabilities. The 16-year-old does not have a lot at stake in the matter; usually, teenagers are financially supported by their parents, and it is fairly easy to obtain entry-level positions. On the other hand, the 50-year-old has many responsibilities and thus has high stakes, and it may be very difficult for her to find a similar position.

Not only are there individual and contextual factors, but cultural factors may also play a role. For example, the first author often uses the example of individual differences in response to a car breaking down. For working adults with well-paying jobs, car problems may be a hassle, but they have sufficient financial resources to pay the garage. For graduate students, however, a car repair may be a major problem, because they tend to have limited resources. But when the first author used this example in a lecture in Brazil, the students laughed, because not one of them owned a car!

Psychosocial Stress and Aging

Whether and how stress changes across the life span is a matter of some debate. One must distinguish between the amount and types of stress, as well as their relationship to health outcomes. For example, early studies found very little relationship between stressful life events and health in older adults (Paykel, 1983). Aldwin (1990) argued that the reason for this null finding was not that adults were immune to the adverse effects of stress; instead, she proposed that the inventories then in use did not tap problems likely to occur to older adults. For example, life event inventories typically include questions about marriage, having children, starting new jobs, or getting fired—all of which are more typical of early adulthood than later life. Using a participant-observation approach, Aldwin found that elders' concerns did center more around losses, but they also seemed to focus on problems of their family members. In informal conversations, the residents in a retirement community would often discount their own problems and focus instead on those of their loved ones.

Aldwin (1990) developed an inventory to reflect these types of concerns, the Elders Life Stress Inventory (ELSI). This includes items such as death of parent, spouse, friends, and children; institutionalization of parent or spouse; declining health of spouse; and retirement, but it also includes network stressors that older adults are likely to find extremely distressing, such as the divorce of child. Aldwin found relatively little correlation between stress and age in her samples and also found that the correlation between stress and self-reported health outcomes was fairly similar to that reported in younger groups. However, a subsequent 6-year longitudinal study of the Normative Aging men found evidence of a nonlinear change over time. The number of life events increased from midlife to about age 65 and then decreased in later life (Yancura, Aldwin, & Spiro, 1999).

Using data from the Transitions Study, Chiriboga (1997) also found no cross-sectional differences in the number of life events between midlife and late life. Younger adults did report more life events, which undoubtedly reflects the fact that young people are initiating major new roles in life such as marriage, parenting, and careers. Young adults also reported more positive events than older adults, probably for similar reasons. However, Chiriboga also presented longitudinal analyses over a 12-year period that did not show a linear decrease in stressful life events with age, Rather, the apparent age differences were actually cohort effects: The younger cohorts always reported more stressful life events, regardless of age at measurement, and there was evidence of both cohort and period effects on the occurrence of stressful life events.

The types of hassles also change with age. Aldwin, Sutton, Chiara, and Spiro (1996) found that people in midlife are much more likely to report problems with children and work, whereas older adults are more likely to report problems with health and retirement. Thus, hassles are linked to social roles, which do change systematically over the life course, so it is not surprising that the types of hassles reported change as well. What is unexpected is that the number of hassles seems to decrease throughout adulthood, which is counterintuitive (Aldwin et al., 1996; Chiriboga, 1997). Middle-aged adults often have multiple social roles and great responsibilities, both for children and for aging parents. They often have managerial roles at work. Thus, it would seem plausible that older adults would report more hassles than younger adults rather than fewer. Adults in late life may have great difficulty in negotiating everyday environmental demands, especially with increasing frailty. Yet they report even fewer hassles.

The most likely explanation deals with age-related changes in the appraisal of stress. Older people may be less likely to appraise a situation as stressful. Aldwin et al. (1996) conducted more than 1,000 interviews with older men, who were often reluctant to discuss problems and would simply deny that they had any. The 80-year-olds would sometimes express "concerns," yet even these were relatively few. Aldwin et al. speculated that part of the difference is a shift from acute to chronic stress. For example, older adults with known health problems such as high blood pressure or chronic diabetes would only report these as problems if they had had acute flare-ups requiring hospitalization. As long as a chronic health problem was managed, it was no longer appraised as a "problem"

Older people may also have a different viewpoint as to what constitutes a problem due to the perspective that can come from having lived a long life. Many of the men had experienced extremely serious or even traumatic problems, such as combat or the death of a loved child. This allowed them to face relatively minor problems with equanimity. One man interviewed by Aldwin et al. (1996) had been a Navy pilot during World War II and had been downed in the Pacific Ocean. He clung to a raft for several days, a battle raging around him. He promised himself that if he got out alive, nothing would ever be a problem again! Another man sadly remarked that, having watched a 20-year-old daughter die of cancer, nothing else ever seemed particularly serious. A Gallup poll taken shortly after September 11, 2001, found that older people were the least likely to be upset by the fall of the World Trade Center. Of course, it is also possible that older people are more likely to cope by using denial (Johnson & Barer, 1993). Perhaps age differences in coping strategies may account for this phenomenon.

● COPING WITH STRESS

The relationship between stress and health in humans is fairly weak, leading researchers to examine how individuals cope as a possible moderator of the effects of stress. McEwen (1998) stated that perceived stress, and appraisals such as helplessness and threats, are the proximal agents that have their greatest impact on allostatic load in the context of chronic stressors or major life events. However, individual differences and behavioral responses influence the perception of stress as well as moderate the physiological responses leading to allostatic load. In other words, a possible reason that the relationship between stress and disease in humans is weak is our ability to cope with stress and mitigate its negative impact.

Theoretical Approaches to Coping

In the coping literature, there are three basic approaches to the study of coping. The first derives from psychoanalysis and focuses on defense mechanisms. The second approach is personality-based coping styles, and the third defines coping as a process driven by both environmental demands and personal characteristics such as beliefs, values, and preferences.

Defense Mechanisms

Anna Freud (1966) expanded on her father's original conceptions of defense mechanisms, which are defined as unconscious attempts by the ego to ward off anxiety resulting from conflicts between the id (desires) and the super ego (restraints or prohibitions). In Freud's view, defense mechanisms are a priori maladaptive, since they invariably result in a distortion of reality. According to Cramer (2000), defense mechanisms are unconscious, unintentional, and dispositional, in that individuals are characterized by defensive styles that they may exhibit on a relatively consistent basis.

Current conceptions also characterize defense mechanisms as hierarchical, based on degree of pathology. The *DSM-IV-TR* (APA, 2000) describes seven major types of defense mechanisms, ordering them from less to more adaptive. The least adaptive defense mechanisms (severe or frankly psychotic processes) are projection, denial, and delusion. For example, a woman who routinely sets a place at the dinner table for her dead daughter and really believes her child will come to dinner is in a massive state of denial and probably delusional as well. At the other end of the spectrum, the adaptive or "mature" defense mechanisms are altruism, humor, and sublimation.

Mothers Against Drunk Driving (MADD) provides an example of the use of altruism as a defense mechanism. Founded by mothers whose children had been killed by intoxicated drivers, MADD has worked very hard to change state laws regulating driving under the influence, to decrease the number of people killed.

Defense mechanisms are usually studied using qualitative data such as interviews. Although self-report inventories have been developed, they often exhibit poor psychometric properties (Cramer, 1991; Davidson & MacGregor, 1998). As Cramer (2000) observed, there is a certain amount of logical inconsistency in asking individuals to report on unconscious processes. Nonetheless, many of the early studies on individual differences in responses to stress and biomedical outcomes used these type of inventories.

Vaillant (1977) examined changes in defense mechanisms over the life course. Using long-term longitudinal data, he found that defenses used by young adults shift from neurotic mechanisms (such as displacement) to mature mechanisms (humor, sublimation, altruism) in middle and late life. An early criticism was that the first study consisted primarily of privileged young men, so Vaillant (1993) demonstrated that this sample pattern held in a sample of women and also in inner-city men. Furthermore, the use of mature mechanisms in midlife seems to promote successful aging and even longevity in late life (Vaillant, 2002).

Coping Styles

The coping styles approach focuses on how people process information. For example, repressors avoid or suppress information, whereas sensitizers seek or augment information (Byrne, 1964). Current manifestations of the dichotomy are blunting-monitoring (Miller, 1980) and approach-avoidance (Roth & Cohen, 1986). Dichotomizing coping strategies into two broad modalities can be psychometrically appealing. Like defensive styles, coping styles are thought to be based in dispositional personality characteristics and used in a variety of situations. The factor structure of coping-style inventories is more stable than process measures and often correlates reasonably well with psychological symptom inventories (Endler & Parker, 1990). Folkman and Lazarus (1980), however, have shown that both types of coping were used in over 80% of episodes; in highly stressful situations, individuals often alternate between approaching and avoiding the problem. Furthermore, individuals are markedly inconsistent across situations, suggesting that environmental as well as personality factors play a role in coping (Schwarz & Daltroy, 1999). Again, early studies linking coping to physical health often used these types of inventories.

Coping Processes

Cramer (2000) characterized coping processes as conscious strategies that are used intentionally. They are often situationally determined, nonhierarchical, and not associated with pathology. In Lazarus and Folkman's (1984) model, appraisal is the primary determinant of how individuals cope with a problem. Appraisals are influenced by environmental demands and by individual beliefs, values, and commitments, and thus are flexible. Ideally, individuals monitor the outcomes of their strategies and modify them to achieve their goals in the situation.

There are many different characterizations of coping processes, but most inventories identify five basic types. These include problem-focused coping, emotion-focused coping, social support, religious coping, and making meaning. Problem-focused strategies include cognitions and behaviors that are directed at analyzing and solving or managing a problem. Behaviors include direct action and seeking information and may include "chunking" (breaking a problem into more manageable pieces). Cognitive strategies include making a plan of action and considering alternatives.

There are several different types of emotion-focused coping. Venting and expressing emotions are one type; avoidance and withdrawal are another. One can suppress emotions in order to focus better on the problem, or one can use alcohol or other substances to regulate emotion. Avoidance, withdrawal, and substance use are usually associated with poor outcomes (Aldwin & Revenson, 1987).

Seeking social support includes asking for advice and emotional support, as well as concrete aid (Thoits, 1986). Similarly, religious coping, which includes prayer, is generally considered a form of emotion-focused coping but may involve asking for advice or even concrete aid (Pargament, 1997). Making meaning (also called cognitive reframing) involves trying to make sense of the problem and/or reinterpreting it. Strategies include trying to understand the reason it occurred or trying to find positive aspects of the current problem. Making meaning is often used in coping with a trauma or major loss (Mikulincer & Florian, 1996).

Coping and Physical Health

Coping is generally considered to be positive, but it should be emphasized that people can and do cope in ways that can adversely affect their health. For example, individuals under stress may smoke or use drugs or alcohol in an attempt to decrease anxiety or depressive feelings—strategies that may work temporarily but can have devastating long-term consequences. What types of strategies work under which circumstances is a matter for empirical investigation.

There are several different models of the way in which coping can affect health outcomes (Aldwin & Yancura, in press). First, coping may have direct effects on physiology. Although this stance may be hard to justify on a theoretical basis, the handful of studies that have examined coping and physiological outcomes examine simple correlations between strategies used and usually neuroendocrine or immune outcomes, statistically assuming a direct effect. Not surprisingly, the results tend to be mixed. Coping style measures of defensiveness, avoidance, and repression are sometimes associated with higher cortisol levels (Biondi & Picardi, 1999), but other studies have found no relationship between coping styles and cortisol (Bossert et al., 1988; Van Eck, Nicholson, Berkhof, & Sulon, 1996). Bohnen, Nicholson, Sulon, and Jones (1991) reported that cognitive reframing was negatively associated with cortisol response. Avoidance coping is also related to cardiovascular responsiveness (Vitaliano, Russo, & Niaura, 1995; Vitaliano, Russo, Paulsen, & Bailey, 1995), but the relationship between repression and cardiovascular responsiveness disappears once social desirability is controlled (Tomaka, Blascovich, & Kelsey, 1992). Among HIV+ men, problem-focused coping was positively associated with CD4+ cells, whereas venting emotions was associated with lower numbers of NK cells (Goodkin, Fuchs, Feaster, Leeka, & Rishel, 1992).

Coping strategies also affect the progression of illnesses (Stein & Spiegel, 2000). In general, avoidant strategies are associated with more symptoms and worse prognoses in cancer patients (Shapiro et al., 1997; Weihs, Enright, Simmens, & Reiss, 2000), while those using problem-focused coping or active, confrontational styles appear to live longer (Buddeberg et al., 1996; Greer, 1991; Greer & Morris, 1975; Morris, Greer, Pettingale, & Watson, 1981). Intervention studies that teach good coping skills have demonstrated better immune functioning and greater longevity with melanoma patients (Fawzy, Cousins, Fawzy, Kemeny, & Morton, 1990; Fawzy & Fawzy, 1994; Fawzy et al., 1993; Fawzy, Kemeny, et al., 1990). There is also good evidence showing the benefit of coping interventions on pain control (Devine, 1992).

The second model of coping and health outcomes reflects the way most theories of stress assume that it works—as a stress buffer or moderator. In other words, there is an interaction between stress and coping such that certain strategies may decrease the adverse effects of stress. However, Aldwin and Revenson (1987) found that some strategies may enhance the negative effects of stress, or have different effects depending on how well they worked in a particular situation. For example, negotiating with others may decrease psychological symptoms if it is effective but increase symptoms if the strategy does not work. Surprisingly, very few studies of physiological outcomes have examined the stress-buffering hypothesis, and the ones that do tend to find equivocal results (see Goodkin et al., 1992). Because the assays are costly, the sample size tends to be fairly small in such research, and Barron and Kenny (1986) have cautioned that large sample sizes are needed to definitively test stress-buffering hypotheses in field settings.

A third model is the contextual model, which posits that the effects of coping may vary as a function of situational variables such as type or severity of illness. For example, social support (relying on others) increased psychological distress among women with rheumatoid arthritis who were in relatively good health, but it was related to lower levels of distress for those in poorer health (Reich & Zautra, 1995). Similarly, social support groups had the most positive effect on physical functioning for breast cancer patients with few personal resources but were actually harmful for those women who had high levels of support (Helgeson, Cohen, Schulz, & Yasko, 2000). Seeking social support and venting were associated with increased pain in rheumatoid arthritis patients but with decreased pain in osteoarthritis patients. Tennen and Affleck (1996) suggested that these differences were due to the caregivers' responses and understandings of the illness. Osteoarthritis pain occurs whenever the patient moves, and caregivers may find the pain comprehensible. However, the pain involved in rheumatoid arthritis—swollen joints and fatigue—is more general and may evoke fewer sympathetic responses.

Aldwin and Yancura (in press) found most support for the mediated or indirect model—that is, the effect of coping strategies on physiological outcomes depends on whether they have affected an individual's sense of well-being. For example, emotion-focused coping was indirectly related to cortisol via its effect on mastery (Arnetz et al., 1991). Among men who were caregivers for AIDS patients, the effect of coping was mediated by affect. Structural-equation models showed that social support predicted an increase in positive affect, which in turn was inversely associated with physical symptoms. Avoidant coping, however, was related to an increase in negative affect, which was positively associated with physical symptoms (Billings, Folkman, Acree, & Moskowitz, 2000).

The effect of coping on the progression of disease may also be indirect. One prospective study of a sample of HIV+ men and women who were initially asymptomatic found that avoidance and passive coping increased the likelihood of developing HIV symptoms, whereas planful coping decreased the likelihood (Vassend, Eskild, & Halvorsen, 1997). Individuals diagnosed with AIDS were lower in planful problem-solving than HIV+ individuals (Krikorian, Kay, & Liang, 1995). Presumably, individuals who are good at solving problems are more likely to take steps to avoid illnesses and comply better with treatment regimes. Active confrontational coping predicted slower disease progression in HIV+ men over the course of a year (Mulder, Antoni, Duivenvoorden, & Kauffmann, 1995), which suggests that these individuals may be better at negotiating for better care. In this light, it is not surprising that individuals who used avoidant coping had a more rapid deterioration of CD4 cell counts over 7 years (Mulder, de Vroome, van Griensven, Antoni, & Sandfort, 1999).

In short, the ways individuals cope with stress may affect their physical health and may be a reason why the relationship between stress and the development of disease is weaker in humans than it is in animal models. The relationship between coping and the development of diseases such as cancer is also weak (Garssen & Goodkin, 1999), but this may be because research has generally failed to examine the more complicated buffering and mediational models. Coping strategies clearly affect the progression of disease, however, presumably through their effects on affect and/or compliance to medical regimes. Given the high prevalence of chronic illnesses in the elderly, it makes sense that coping has important effects on the quality of their lives.

Coping and Aging

There is little agreement in the literature as to whether or how coping changes with age. Early TAT studies by Gutmann (1974) suggested that older individuals become more passive copers; participants told stories in response to the TAT stimuli that bore little relationship to the pictures (which Gutmann termed "magical mastery"). In contrast, Vaillant's (1977, 1993) position, as mentioned earlier, held that coping improves with age, as adults shift from neurotic or immature defenses in early life to more mature ones such as altruism in later life. Both of these approaches are based on qualitative data, and studies using quantitative measures show different results.

On standardized measures of coping, cross-sectional studies suggest that older adults use fewer escapism or avoidant coping strategies but use similar levels of problem-focused coping (Aldwin, 1991; Felton & Revenson, 1987; Irion & Blanchard-Fields, 1987), especially once controlling for the type of problem being faced (McCrae, 1982, 1989). Folkman, Lazarus, Pimley, and Novacek (1987) found that older people used less planful problem solving and more escape avoidance; this study, however, examined the relative use of these strategies, dividing the subscales by the total number of strategies used.

Aldwin et al. (1996) explicitly compared qualitative and quantitative approaches to assessing age-related differences in coping strategies, using nearly 1,000 interviews on middle-aged and older men. They found that older adults reported less escapism (e.g., drug and alcohol use) and fewer problem-focused strategies on quantitative measures. However, there were no age differences in problem-focused coping in the qualitative assessments of interviews, nor were there age differences in the self-rated efficacy of the coping strategies. Examining the interviews provided clues to the discrepancy between the two ways of assessing coping.

In this sample, middle-aged and young-old adults reported several problem-focused strategies to solve one problem. For example, a common problem was flooding in the basement. Men in their 50s and 60s often don rubber boots, go down into the cellar to investigate and analyze the problem, make a trip to the hardware store to get the necessary parts, and then go back down and fix the problem. A man in his 80s, however, is unlikely to risk a fall in a flooded basement. He is more likely to call a plumber (or his 60-year-old son) to come and fix the problem. Thus, old-old men would use fewer strategies, but the problem would be resolved just the same. Thus, older people may be more likely to conserve resources when coping with problems (see Hobfoll, 1989), but that does not necessarily mean that they become more passive or are less efficacious copers.

There may be other types of age-related changes as well. Labouvie-Vief and her colleagues (Labouvie-Vief, DeVoe, & Bulka, 1989; Labouvie-Vief, Hakim-Larson, DeVoe, & Schoeberlein, 1989; Labouvie-Vief, Hakim-Larson, & Hobart, 1987) have suggested that both cognitive and emotional complexity increase with age, which influences the way in which older individuals both appraise and cope with stress. Older people may have very different motives and goals for their coping behaviors than do younger people. For example, older individuals talk to their friends and family about problems in order get feedback about the appropriateness of their coping strategies, but younger people appear to seek social support primarily for self-validation (Labouvie-Vief et al., 1987). Furthermore, in younger adults, stress is a stronger predictor of life satisfaction, but in midlife and late life, coping resources are better predictors of well-being (Hamarat et al., 2001).

Aldwin (1991) investigated age differences in attributions of responsibility for problems as well as coping strategies. Controlling for type of problem, she found that older adults were less likely to attribute responsibility to themselves for either causing the problem or for managing it, and they rated their problems as less stressful than younger adults. However, they were just as likely to use problem-focused coping as were younger adults, and again, there were no age differences in efficacy. She surmised that older adults were less likely to waste emotional energy blaming themselves for problems and that they distanced themselves from responsibility for solving them. Nonetheless, they appeared to go ahead and do what needed to be done. They also used less escape/avoidance coping. More important, path analysis showed that the relationship between age and depressive symptoms was indirect and mediated by appraisal and coping processes. In other words, older adults maintain their mental health, even in the face of health problems and major losses, because they have learned to avoid coping strategies that have harmful effects, such as the use of alcohol and drugs. They may have learned to differentiate between controllable and uncontrollable stressors, an important developmental task (Altschuler & Ruble, 1989), and they report no longer letting themselves get upset about minor problems or things they cannot do anything about (Aldwin et al., 1996).

Anthropologists Johnson and Barer (1993) also observed marked differences in how the old-old appraise and cope with problems. They actively compensate for disabilities through the use of canes, hearing aids, and glasses and often arrange their environment to compensate for mobility problems. They also routinize their daily lives, which conserves energy. They tend to minimize their health problems by making positive comparisons to other elders who may be more disabled and dissociating their sense of self from their bodies. This may allow them to maintain a sense of well-being. As one elderly woman stated, "What can I say, I've had bypass surgery, I now have shingles, I'm isolated and lonely, I'm losing my strength and my confidence in myself. But glory to God, I'm feeling well" (Johnson & Barer, 1993, p. 75).

SUMMARY ●

Stress and coping research has blossomed in the past two decades. Stress has effects at the genetic, cellular, and systems levels, and stress resistance is rapidly coming to the fore as a possible mechanism for longevity. Older people are more vulnerable to the physical effects of stress because they are less able to maintain homeostasis, and chronic stress may play an important role in the development of chronic illness in late life. There are marked individual differences in the effects of stress, however, which may be due in part to how individuals cope with problems. There is little evidence to suggest that relatively healthy older adults are more affected by psychosocial stress, although it is possible that those with serious chronic illnesses may be more vulnerable. Preliminary research suggests that older individuals may cope in ways that protect their resources and may be less likely to perceive problems as stressful. Social support, another important factor in dealing with stress, is addressed in the next chapter.

● NOTE

1. Vodun (voodoo) is actually practiced in the Caribbean and Brazil; application of the term to Australian culture is a rather gross misnomer.

CHAPTER **11**

SOCIAL SUPPORT, HEALTH, AND AGING

S ocial support is important for both mental and physical health throughout the life span, but it may be especially important in late life. An early negative stereotype was that the elderly were social isolated, but the past three decades have painted a much more complex picture of how social support changes in both structure and function with age.

This chapter describes the characteristics of the social support network including function, composition, and change with age. Studies in the sociological and psychological literature frequently focus on support given by the informal network (friends, family, and neighbors), but we review that provided by the formal support network as well. This includes individuals who are paid for their services, including physicians, nurses, physical therapists, and senior center and nursing home staff. We also briefly review the literature on how social support affects health and illness. Finally, caregiving in later years is discussed, especially that which takes place between spouses.

CHARACTERISTICS OF THE
SOCIAL SUPPORT NETWORK ●

In this section, we describe the functions of social support. The members of the social support network and type of assistance that they provide are also discussed. Next, we review qualitative and quantitative aspects of social support, as well as the ways in which the social support network changes with age. We describe reciprocity of support, including social exchange theory. Finally, we address the ways in which social interactions can be negative, including enforced dependency.

Functions of Social Support

Antonucci (1985, 2001) identified three functions of social support: aid (instrumental help), affect (emotional support), and affirmation (acknowledgment of one's values or agreement with one's attitudes). Generally, instrumental support includes tangible aid. For older people, this may be as simple as providing a ride to the grocery store or mowing the lawn and often takes the form of help with the tasks of daily living, such as activities of daily living (ADLs) and instrumental activities of daily living (IADLs), as discussed in Chapter 8. Emotional support refers to the quality of a person's relationships with others, including empathy, caring, companionship, love, and trust. The intention of social support is often to alleviate the psychological distress of the person. Finally, affirmation is the knowledge and understanding that one's beliefs and attitudes are similar to others, therefore providing membership and acceptance in a group.

Thoits (1982) argues that a major function of social support is to provide information and advice in times of stress. Network members may provide advice on how to cope with problems, or how to regulate the perception of the stressfulness of the situation and help individuals regulate their emotions.

These types of support are often tightly intertwined. Those who provide tangible support may also be providing reassurance and emotional support. Furthermore, different network members provide different types of support. People tend to turn to their families for instrumental support, friends for emotional support, and, during times of illness, health care workers for advice and aid (Dakof & Taylor, 1990).

Social Support Networks

Cantor and Little (1985) describe three levels of social support: informal, quasi-formal, and formal. Each of these levels has different network members and provides unique assistance and care to the older person.

Informal Support

Informal support network members consist of family, friends, and neighbors. This group provides instrumental and emotional support, companionship, acceptance, love, understanding, and respect.

Antonucci and Akiyama (1987), in their classic work on social relationships and life span development, describe the interrelatedness of people throughout life. Using a convoy model of relationships, the individual is described as surrounded by family and friends. The inner circle is usually composed of family and perhaps very close friends. Members of the other concentric circles in Antonucci and Akiyama's model typically include people who are progressively less close, such as other family members, friends, neighbors, and coworkers, with the outermost circle consisting of those who are only acquaintances.

Those in the innermost circle are the most stable members of the group; there may be a fair amount of turnover in the members in the less central circles. The innermost circle members provide safety and comfort for the person that helps in meeting the challenges of life. As the person ages, these people continue to provide them with support (Pearlin, Aneshensel, Mullan, & Whitlatch, 1996). Even people in very late life retain positive ties to family members and friends (Field & Gueldner, 2001).

Informal support members are generally the primary caregivers to the older adult who needs assistance. Family and friends provide emotional support and companionship, and help with shopping, cooking, gardening, laundry, personal care, information and advice, and in making major decisions, especially those related to health care. Daughters provide extensive care to their older parents, such as bathing or assistance with eating. Sons are generally not as involved in personal care as daughters, unless it is the father who is ill. Instead, sons tend to do other instrumental tasks, such as home repair, financial management, and transportation (Stone, Cafferata, & Sangle, 1987). Peters-Davis, Moss, and Pruchno (1999) found that children-in-law were also active caregivers for their spouses' parents, depending on the quality of the relationship. In many cases, the children-in-law felt that their relationship with their in-laws was just as valuable to them as those with their own kin.

Siblings, grandchildren, nephews, and nieces also provide support to their older relatives. In fact, siblings appear to take on increasing importance in later years, and this is particularly true of sisters after widowhood. Among people who have no children, siblings provide not only emotional support but instrumental help as well (Antonucci, 2001). Couples without children may intentionally develop strong relationships with relatives such as nephews and nieces. These relatives serve as informal support to them when they need assistance. Some unmarried people may have difficulty in finding someone to provide assistance, especially emotional support (Wu & Pollard, 1998). Living alone can place a person at risk of unavailable support, as there is no one in the home to care for the person. Thompson and Krause (1998) found that older adults who lived alone and in deteriorated neighborhoods were at double jeopardy; these older people had very low expectations of receiving support if it was needed.

Neighbors and friends are valued members of the social network, perhaps especially for older adults. Cantor (1979) called this network of neighbors and friends an overlooked resource for the older person. In her study of older people living in an inner-city neighborhood in New York City, Cantor found that neighbors and friends were important in providing socialization and "tension reduction." For example, these older people sought out neighbors and friends when they were lonely or isolated or when they wanted to talk about family problems, and in this way relieve the worries that they had. Older adults often lack means of transportation, and they may be restricted to their own neighborhoods and the socialization that takes place there.

Neighbors and friends provide not only socialization and emotional support but, at times, instrumental help. Chores that neighbors and friends undertake include shopping, mailing letters, and lending assistance during a crisis. Barker (2002) reported on the value of neighbors in providing caregiving to frail elders. In her study, neighbors of long-time older residents provided social opportunities and instrumental care, including transportation, visiting, and assistance with ADLs. Some men, at retirement, take on the responsibility of checking up and caring for older people living in their neighborhoods.

Some studies have found that positive support from friends is more important to health than support from relatives, although others have shown that support from family and friends is of equal importance (DuPertuis, Aldwin, & Bossé, 2001; George, 1996). Friends share similar histories that provide them with opportunities to talk about remembered events without the encumbrance of family dynamics. Although older persons may have excellent relationships with their children, there will always be a generational divide (Antonucci, 2001). Furthermore, relationships with friends may be particularly valued because they are voluntary, and their quality may be higher, which may account for the positive effect of friendship on health (George, 1996). Loss of friends, especially lifelong ones, is very difficult for the older person, as friends and siblings are the cohorts with whom they have shared their lives.

There are gender differences in how men and women relate to their social network members. Women frequently have many close and intimate relationships that help them cope with various problems. Yet women feel the burden of such relationships as well, because they must reciprocate and help members of their network. Relationships of men are usually less personal, and although they are not as burdensome, they are also not as helpful (Antonucci, 2001). Men typically have their wives as their main confidants, but women often have numerous people in whom they can confide.

It has been suggested that European Americans have less informal support in later years than other ethnic or racial group members. For example, African Americans are more likely to live in extended families rather than alone and to receive substantial amounts of care in their homes. Often African American families (as well as Southern ones) include fictive kin, people who are not related by blood but whose long-term relationships give them the status of family members. Mexican Americans also have large social networks to which they can turn for support (Williams & Wilson, 2001).

Caregiving burden among ethnic groups is varied. Navaie-Waliser et al. (2001) compared caregiving across a number of ethnic and racial groups. They found that African American caregivers provided higher-intensity care than either European Americans or Mexican Americans. They were also less likely to report difficulties with caregiving than European Americans. Interestingly, Mexican American caregivers were more likely to receive outside assistance than either of the other groups. Indeed, Williams and Dilworth-Anderson (2002) found that African American caregivers were at risk of poorer health than others, because they did not use formal support when the needs of the older adult increased.

There are numerous ethnic groups in our country, but there is only limited research on how some of the newer ethnic groups either provide or cope with caregiving tasks to their older relatives. For example, in California there are a number of recent immigrant groups who have come to this country with older family members, such as the Hmong and Lao from Southeast Asia. Such groups tend to have strong traditions of family care but, over time, and with acculturation and assimilation, there is some expectation that filial responsibility and general expectations of the younger generation toward their family members may change (Markides & Black, 1996). As the ethnic make-up of older adults change, further research is needed to understand cultural variance in caregiving patterns.

Quasi-Formal Support

The quasi-formal support system includes community organizations and service workers. These are religious organizations, neighborhoods, and volunteer community interest groups such as Lions clubs and Masons.

Community workers such as letter carriers and store owners can also serve as quasi-formal support members. The quasi-formal support system provides unpaid services to older persons, often as a voluntary link between individuals or families and communities, providing information, helping with transportation, or doing home repairs. These quasi-formal groups serve as watchdogs for the older person, noting when mail is not picked up or a customary shopping trip missed. For example, an older woman in our town who worked as a grocery store checkout clerk kept track of dozens of older people in the community. She would often tell the second author of this book, a public health nurse at the time, if an old-timer did not show up to shop at the usual time. This would allow formal services to check on the elder and intercede if necessary.

Places of worship are an important source of quasi-formal support. Synagogues, churches, temples, and mosques provide emotional support for their members, through spiritual connections and a sense of community. They also provide instrumental support, such as meals for someone who may not be eligible for Meals on Wheels. Others have parish nurses who watch over their congregational members. Older adults have usually been long-term members of these organizations, which makes it easier for them to accept aid.

Formal Support

The formal support system consists of members of professional organizations who are hired to provide care to the individual. These can be either private or public organizations. Examples of agencies that provide formal help are adult day health care centers, health clinics, respite facilities, home health care agencies, skilled nursing homes, social services agencies, assisted-living facilities, and public health departments.

Formal support network members give a wide spectrum of care, most of it instrumental in nature. The formal support system provides highly technical skills, including in-home care, nursing home care, health care screening, preventive care, education, support for the patient and the informal caregiver, transportation, and nutritional programs. Formal support providers organize support groups for both older persons and their caregivers. The relationship with formal support systems may be ambivalent. On the one hand, the formal system often takes control of various aspects of the older person's life, which initially may be uncomfortable or even frightening. Over time, however, the individual may rely more and more on a few key individuals, who may become "family."

Formal support can be very expensive, depending on the type of care that is provided. Many of the tasks done by this group cannot be done by the informal or the quasi-formal system because of the need for professional care. For example, physical therapy, complex medication management, and 24-hour custodial care are typically beyond an individual's or a family's resources.

Nursing home care is a type of formal support that deserves special attention. It is uncomfortable for most people to think about living in a skilled nursing facility (SNF), or having a loved one as a resident in one, but there are times when such care may be the only alternative. Individuals who need 24-hour nursing care typically cannot be cared for at home by a single caregiver, and hiring private duty nurses is beyond the financial means of most families. At some point, individuals who are in the late stages of illnesses such as Alzheimer's or other forms of dementia may simply be too difficult to care for at home. This can create the misconception that American families do not provide for their elders.

A Guatemalan student in one of the first author's classes was expressing this misconception by saying that her mother had taken care of her grandmother at home until the day she died. When asked, however, she admitted that her grandmother had died at the age of 65 after a 2-year illness. This is a very different circumstance from that faced by a 70-year-old daughter whose 90-year old parent has had Alzheimer's for 12 years. Very frail older people who require extensive care for long periods of time may receive better care in a nursing home than in their own homes.

Although some SNFs provide excellent care, this is not always the case. This is unfortunate, as the frailest, most vulnerable people are the usual residents in SNFs, and they have little voice in the policies of the institution. Recently, the U.S. Senate held hearings on the condition of California's nursing homes. Reports from these sessions indicated that 10% of facilities in California placed their patients at risk in some way, including abuse and neglect.

There are a number of factors used to judge if a nursing home is good or not, including the turnover rate of nursing assistants and nurses and the education and ability of the director. Smaller, nonprofit nursing homes appear to provide better care than others, particularly when such nonprofit homes are locally owned and managed or serve particular religious or ethnic groups (especially if they have substantial funding).

An interesting trend in nursing home care is represented by Denmark's commitment to close all nursing homes and provide home-based or communal care (Gottschalk, 1995). In the United States, many SNF residents would not have to be in institutions if they had adequate informal care backed by formal support. One of the primary reasons for nursing home admission is lack of a primary caregiver. The wave of the future appears to be in-home care, the fastest-growing of the health services, and assisted-living facilities, which permit a much more homelike atmosphere for later life. These changes may already be evident, as residency in skilled nursing homes has decreased in the past two decades (see Chapter 8).

Interface of Formal and Informal Support

There has been an ongoing debate as to whether involvement in formal support decreases the amount of work, time, and energy that the informal caregiver provides to the older person. This is fueled by the concern that if the formal system takes over the care of the older person, the informal support group will drop out of the picture. Others have postulated that using the formal support system is a sign of weakening ties with family and friends. Both past and recent research indicates that reliance on the formal support system does not substitute for help received from the informal support system. In 1990, Chappell found that informal caregivers provided the majority of care to their older relatives, even when the formal support was assisting. Recent studies substantiate that the use of formal support has minimal impact on the amount of care given by the informal system. In a study by Penning (2002), addition of formal in-home support (e.g., personal care and bathing) to older adults with chronic illnesses was not associated with less informal care or self-care. Families continue to provide care for their family members, even with outside help.

For those older people who are truly frail, both formal and informal services are frequently needed. In this case, the formal system is designed to give instrumental and hands-on care, whereas the informal system provides emotional support, socializing, community continuity, and links to the formal network. Shanas (1979) notes that, although the bureaucracy provides specialized health care for the sick and frail, the older person still needs the family. Even when older people do not live in their homes but in assisted-living facilities or board-and-care homes, there is a need for informal support from the family. In such cases, the formal support personnel assist with ADL tasks and the informal system provides other opportunities, such as shopping and community interaction (Hopp, 1999).

Assessment of Social Support

Social support can be measured by looking at both quantity and quality. Quantity is an objective measure (e.g., number of visits from friends, how they helped), whereas quality is deemed to be more subjective, assessing perceived availability of help or satisfaction with help.

Measures of quantity of support assess the number of people in a person's network, the frequency of interaction with them, and the types of assistance they provide (Rook, 1994). Density of a network refers to the degree of overlap between network members. Some people have very diffuse networks; others have very tight and close-knit ones. The size and extensiveness of the network does not necessarily say anything about its quality. Quality of support measures a person's satisfaction with friends, the number of confidants he or she has, and whether the individual can rely on others in a crisis. Simply knowing people does not mean being satisfied with the qualitative aspects of the relationship. For example, a foreign student of ours often complained of loneliness. To our surprise, for her son's first birthday, she threw a party for 100 people, which indicated that she had a very large network—especially for someone who had lived in the area for only 2 years. But these people did not provide the level of support that she would receive from her network in her home country, so she perceived herself as having relatively little support.

According to Krause (2001), perceived or anticipated support is of greater value to the older person than received support. In other words, it is not what is provided that is important, but the belief and understanding that if there is a need, help will be available. Knowing that help is available frees the individual to try to cope or solve the problem on his or her own, rather than to immediately seek help from others. In this way, self-worth and personal control are enhanced.

Change in Network Size With Age

There has been an ongoing controversy as to whether the informal network size of an older person decreases over time. Several studies have shown decreases in the size of social networks with age, as well as decreases in frequency of social contact, especially after retirement (Antonucci, 1990; Bossé, Aldwin, Levenson, Spiro, & Mroczek, 1993). This does not mean, however, that older people are bereft of support. Although numbers of people in the network may decrease slightly, the network members that do remain provide increasing amounts of care (Antonucci, 1990). Bossé et al. (1993) also found no change in the quality of support with age; that is, older people were just as satisfied with the availability and closeness of their support as were middle-aged people.

Furthermore, network membership appears to change with age. Tilburg (1998), in a study of older Dutch people, found an increasing number of close relatives in the support network during the 4 years of the study, but fewer friends. Contact frequency with members of the network decreased although instrumental support increased. Carstensen (1995) argued that the network size of the older person may decrease in size because people become more selective concerning those with whom they want a relationship. Lang (2001) added to this argument, reporting that close emotional relationships are stable in later life but peripheral ones are relinquished. Therefore, there may be judicious pruning of the social network in late life. In the Bossé et al. study, for instance, many of the men were quite happy that they no longer had to socialize with their bosses but instead could spend time with people they really cared about.

Reciprocity

Reciprocity refers to the give and take of assistance from one person to another. Older adults in particular have long histories of reciprocal relationships with their informal support networks (Antonucci & Akiyama, 1987). Family members give and receive support over the years, and many adult children feel that they want to give something back in return for the help they received from their parents. Similarly, adults invest considerable resources in their children with the understanding that they will receive support in later years (Silverstein, Conroy, Wang, Giarrusso, & Bengtson, 2002). Antonucci (1985) describes this as a support bank: Deposits are made early in expectation that a withdrawal will be made later.

It would be a mistake, however, to think that social support in later years is unidirectional. Older adults continue to provide substantial amounts of aid to their children and to others in their social network. Older adults baby-sit for their grandchildren, bake cookies for church gatherings, and provide transportation for friends who no longer are able to drive. Many provide financial support, such as help with a down payment on a house, vacation, or college tuition for grandchildren.

Social exchange theory holds that the goal of a healthy relationship is to maintain an equitable exchange in giving and receiving help; most people want to avoid feelings of indebtedness to another person. Dowd (1975) hypothesized that an imbalance of power exists when the older person is no longer able to reciprocate equally to those who give him or her care. This theory assumes, however, that support is primarily material in nature, for example, goods and services are exchanged. In a reciprocal relationship of giving and receiving, one type of support may be given but another received. People in later years provide friendship and emotional support to family and friends and, in this way, reciprocate for the instrumental care that is being given to them. In a 4-year study, Tilburg (1998) found that older people provided increasing levels of emotional support to family and friends but received more instrumental support. In this way, the older person is able to maintain reciprocity with those who give them assistance.

Furthermore, reciprocity also can exist across time. Older people who have worked as volunteers through their churches or other voluntary organizations feel comfortable receiving support from these organizations when they are in need. Medicare and health care insurance pay for physician and hospital care, but recipients are entitled to these benefits, because they have worked in careers and paid into pension funds and health insurance. Therefore, the care that comes to older persons is often a payback for what they have provided in the past.

Negative Effects of Social Support

Social support is generally considered to be helpful, but it can have negative results as well. For example, excessive formal and informal support can lead to unwarranted dependency in late life (Silverstein, Chen, & Heller, 1996). Staff in SNFs can unknowingly promote dependency by performing activities that the older person may be capable of doing independently (such as dressing or eating) in the interest of saving time (Baltes, 1996). It is not uncommon for support network members (informal, quasi-formal, and formal) to treat an elderly adult as a child, a process called infantilization. This is particularly noticeable if the person has dementia, is hard of hearing, or has to walk slowly and use a walker. There can be a tendency on the part of others to treat these older adults as if they cannot do even the simplest of tasks, such as opening doors or answering questions for themselves. A caregiver may speak loudly to someone who has dementia, as if that would help the person understand. Family members sometimes encourage the use of a wheelchair rather than a walker after someone has fallen, for fear of another fall, when the better course is to encourage walking to strengthen muscles and bones. Dependency is a downward spiral of requiring more and more help, placing a burden on the caregiver and the older person, as well.

The most frail elderly can be encouraged to exercise, eat well, be involved in activities, and take care of themselves. Staff members in SNFs sometimes encourage their patients with dementia to help fold towels or clean off tables. In a nursing home study, one group of residents was randomly assigned to receive encouragement and support from staff to complete their own ADL activities. On follow-up, members of the experimental group could perform more self-care ADLs and ranked themselves higher in self-esteem than members of the control group (Blair, 1999). The support network can help older people remain as independent as possible, even if they have fairly low levels of ability.

Negative Relationships

As noted above, social support does not always have a positive outcome. Poor social interactions can cause distress and disappointment, placing stress on the individual and affecting well-being. Rook (1994) found that negative interchanges can be more damaging to emotional health than positive ones are to promoting emotional health, and George (1996), in her review of the literature, noted that "the degree to which social ties are beneficial to health depends on their quality" (pp. 244).

Even long-time marriages can be unhealthy. Although many older couples have close, positive relationships, other marriages may be characterized by strife and negative interactions, either of long standing or due to new stressors such as caregiving (Levenson, Carstensen, & Gottman, 1994). For example, one older couple with whom the second author worked had a troubled relationship. The husband suffered from dementia, and the wife had severe hearing loss. Their relationship was characterized by substantial verbal abuse. She became so frustrated by his dementia that one day she started beating him with her cane while he slept. The neighbors had to intercede, and the husband was institutionalized.

Note that dependency may also be used to manipulate, and therefore control, the support system. For example, an older person may use dependency as leverage for visits from family members. Some may feign helplessness in order to control others. More commonly, however, older people are so determined to do things on their own that they may endanger themselves or others, such as driving when they no longer have the sensory or cognitive capacity to do so. Often individuals are so afraid of institutionalization that they may deny the existence of problems and thus do not get the help that they need in order to remain safely in the community, paradoxically increasing their risk of institutionalization (see Chapter 12). Thus, it may be difficult for a caregiver to accurately determine what level of help an older person needs.

● SOCIAL SUPPORT, MORBIDITY, AND MORTALITY

Social support is important for both mental and physical well-being. Those who have a strong social support system often enjoy greater longevity and better health. For the older person, social support may be critical to remaining in the community and avoiding institutionalization. The mechanisms by which social support and social integration are related to physical health are not well understood but probably include better adaptation to stress, instrumental help, connection to resources, and enhanced coping mechanisms.

Social Support, Mortality, and Physical Health

In 1979, Berkman and Syme published one of the first studies linking social integration and mortality. Using the Alameda County Study, they found that simple measures of social integration—including marital status, number of friends, participation in social organizations, and religious attendance—predicted mortality. Individuals who were relatively socially isolated had higher rates of early mortality than those who were more firmly integrated into their communities. In such quasi-experimental research, there are always concerns with causal directionality—perhaps individuals in poorer health are more socially isolated. Berkman and Syme reran the analyses, covarying out baseline health, and still found that lower levels of social support predicted early mortality over a 9-year period. A number of studies have replicated this finding, both here and in Europe (Wills & Fegan, 2001). In general, the effects are stronger for men than for women but seem fairly robust, given the variety of measures of social integration that have been used.

A major issue is whether there is a gradient between social integration and health, or a threshold effect. House, Robbins, and Metzner (1982) found a threshold effect (even one close social tie appeared to be enough to be protective). In other words, the stress of social isolation may have adverse effects on health rather than social support being protective. In contrast, other studies show gradient effects, with a continuous decline in early mortality rates with higher levels of support (Berkman & Syme, 1979; Kaplan et al., 1988). Interestingly, the type of effect may vary by disease. Welin, Larsson, Svärdsudd, Tibblin, and Tibblin (1992) found gradient effects for mortality due to cardiovascular disease but threshold effects for cancer mortality.

There are fewer studies examining the ability of social support to predict the development of disease, and findings are decidedly mixed. The Honolulu Heart Study found that the relationship between social integration and development of heart disease disappeared when the effects of biomedical risk factors were controlled (Reed, McGee, Yano, & Feinleib, 1983). The rate of heart disease in this sample was very low, however. A Swedish sample found that both social integration and emotional support predicted the development of cardiovascular disease, after controlling for biomedical risk factors

(Orth-Gomer, Rosengren, & Wilhelmsen, 1993). Vogt, Mullooly, Ernst, Pope, and Hollis (1992) contrasted the ability of social support to predict both mortality and the development of cardiovascular disease and cancer. The results were quite strong for social network measures and mortality, with the highest risk ratio being 6.7 for those with better networks. Surprisingly, the results predicting the development of disease were much weaker.

These findings parallel those reported in Chapter 9 on personality, morbidity, and mortality and help to explain the curious finding that the relationship between psychosocial factors and mortality may be stronger than that between social support and development of disease. In general, psychosocial factors only weakly predict the development of disease; genetics, health behavior habits, and exposure to environmental toxins may play more important roles. Once individuals are weakened by disease, though, personality and social support may play a pivotal role in recovery and decline. This suggests that social support may be particularly important for older adults.

Social Support and Recovery From Illness

Other studies have found that social support is important for recovery from disease. For example, socially isolated men and those who live alone are at greater risk of recurrent disease and death than married men or those with confidants (Case, Moss, Case, McDermott, & Eberly, 1992; Ruberman, Weinblatt, Goldberg, & Chaudhary, 1984; Williams et al., 1992). Reasons for this are unclear, but Berkman, Leo-Summers, and Horwitz (1992) suggested that the primary culprit may be lack of emotional support during illness. Controlling for age, comorbidity, and severity of the myocardial infarction, patients with no emotional support had a three times greater risk of death after a heart attack than individuals with even one source of emotional support.

The literature on recovery from cancer is mixed (Wills & Fegan, 2001). Several large-scale studies have found that various measures of social integration predict survival after cancer treatments, including marital status (Neale, Tilley, & Vernon, 1986; Goodwin, Hunt, Key, & Samet, 1987) and social network size (Funch & Marshall, 1983; Reynolds & Kaplan, 1990), as well as contact with friends (Waxlery-Morrison, Hislop, Mears, & Kan, 1991) and general social integration (Ell, Nishimoto, Mediansky, Mantell, & Hamovitch, 1992). Vogt et al. (1992) also examined recovery from illness and found that network scores predicted survival after the development of heart disease, cancer, and stroke. Not all studies found significant results, but Wills and Fegan (2001) argued that the ones that did not find significant results tended to be smaller ones with shorter follow-up times.

Organizational Memberships and Health

In her review of the literature, George (1996) found that three measures of social integration have been linked to better health: number of social roles, church attendance, and participation in voluntary organizations. She reported that social involvement and multiple social roles are significantly associated with better self-rated health. For example, religious association was associated with lower functional impairment and reduced depressive symptoms, and volunteering was related to better self-assessed health. Krause, Herzog, and Baker (1992) also found that volunteerism in late life was beneficial. In their study of people 60 years of age and older, providing assistance to others (such as transportation, shopping, or baby-sitting) led to increased feelings of control and well-being in later life and was related to lower levels of depression.

Social Support, Stressful Events, and Mental Health

Social support may be most important for older individuals in the context of a specific stressor (Wills & Fegan, 2001). For example, Silverstein and Bengtson (1991) showed that intimacy of family ties was related to greater longevity only among those who had recently lost a spouse or a family member, suggesting an important buffering role of social support. Social support has also been shown to have a protective effect against depression, primarily for those elders who had experienced high numbers of stressful life events (Cutrona, Russell, & Rose, 1986) and those with considerable financial strain (Krause, 1987). Furthermore, it appears to reduce problem drinking among elders with high levels of stress (Peirce, Frone, Russell, & Cooper, 1996).

Research studies on support systems frequently look at the direct link between social support and well-being, such as emotional support and improved health. Yet there may be indirect effects as well. Social support may provide increased access to resources. Network members may encourage individuals to stop smoking or to use alcohol more moderately. Furthermore, formal support networks provide health care educational programs on caregiver coping or support groups for those with cancer. Thus, it is likely that social support has direct, buffering, and indirect effects on health.

● CAREGIVING

Families provide most of the care to their older relatives, and assistance is given out of concern and love for parents and family members, reciprocity for care given at a different time, or because it is the thing to do. As noted earlier in the chapter, extensive caregiving is provided by daughters and sons, other family members, and the quasi-formal and formal support system. Another area of caregiving, that by spouses to their wives and husbands, has not been covered as completely. Yet the majority of caregiving to married older adults is done by their spouses. We will address caregiving by elderly couples to one another in great detail, particularly the very old who are still caring for one another in late years.

Spouse Caregiving

Spouses are the preferred source of help by both men and women in later years. The care they give is often extensive, intensive, and physically and mentally difficult. Older spouses may give care for many years, often unaware that the needs of their partner are increasing. Extensive caregiving is often provided by husbands and wives who have limitations of their own, sometimes as severe as those of the person for whom they are caring (Ory, 1985; Johnson, 1983). Many spouse caregivers are in their 60s and 70s, but some are quite elderly, in their 80s and even 90s. The old-old may be providing care to very frail spouses while they themselves may have significant levels of disability. Indeed, it is sometimes difficult to determine who the caregiver is and who is the recipient in older couples, as they often provide mutual assistance and compensate for each other's deficits.

Although caregiving for an older spouse can be stressful, it is not all negative, and many older caregivers enjoy caring for their spouses. It is hypothesized that changes in relationships with age, and age itself, help the caregivers of the older person cope with their caregiving tasks. Antonucci (2001) reported that people become more positive about their relationships over time. Erikson, Erikson, and Kivnick (1986) suggested that acceptance of receiving help is a normal task in later years. Indeed, caregiving can increase an individual's feeling of self-worth and compensate for the loss of other social roles such as work or parenting.

In a study of older caregivers, a number of husbands said that they provided care in repayment for the nurturing they had received throughout their marriage (Gilmer & Aldwin, 2002). As one elderly man said, "She cared for me all those years, I can care for her now." Many elderly couples find joy in talking, walking to shops together, sitting on a front porch holding hands, or going to the local laundromat to wash clothes. Many talk about the past and have photo albums and pictures that help them describe the history they have shared.

Both men and women provide care to their sick or disabled spouses, although methods of caregiving differ somewhat. Women care for their spouses in much the same ways they have always cared for their families, undertaking instrumental tasks. Men take on these duties in a more businesslike fashion, keeping records, following schedules, doing everything by the book (Bengtson, Rosenthal, & Burton, 1996). Medications are given at exact times, visits are kept to a minimum, and doctor appointments are on time. Although the caregiving tasks are similar for men and women, male caregivers report fewer stresses and less depressive symptoms than do women (Bookwala & Schulz, 2000). Part of this may be that men receive more outside (secondary) support, such as that provided by daughters and sons, than women (Tennstedt, McKinlay, & Sullivan, 1989). On the other hand, outside help is not always desired by the older couple; this may be especially true of the very old. Although they need help, they may not want to interrupt the lives of their children or be a burden to them.

The issue of caring for a loved one with dementia is very complex. Caregiving in this case is almost always a long arduous task with responsibilities that far exceed other caregiving roles (Pearlin et al., 1996). The caregiver has to accept the diminishing personality of the spouse he or she once knew and the loss of companionship. Furthermore, all hope of reciprocity, even a thank-you, may be lost in the later stages of this disease (Miller, Longino, Anderson, James, & Worley, 1999). Sadly, there are times when the relationship can be confrontational in couples with a history of discord or as the result of paranoid or disruptive behavior of the part of the sick spouse. Nonetheless, there are some positive sides to caregiving, even to those with dementia, and recent studies of spouse caregivers have added to this knowledge. An observational study by Jansson, Nordberg, and Grafstrom (2001) noted that, although caregiving to a spouse with dementia was laborious and time-consuming, it was done by the caregiver with concern and care. In another study, caregiving was viewed as difficult but also self-affirming (Narayan, Lewis, Tornatore, Hepburn, & Corcoran-Perry, 2001). These findings suggest that there is value in providing care, even to an elderly spouse who has dementia.

Caregiving can be rewarding for very old couples, especially at the end of a long, happy marriage. They may be grateful that they are both alive. Caring for one another is an avocation for some of these older couples—doing the shopping, preparing the medications, helping the spouse get out of bed. An elderly gentleman in the Gilmer and Aldwin (2002) study said that the highlight of his day was giving his wife a bath (although he had difficulty putting her hair up in curlers). In the case of a rural couple, the husband was cognitively intact, but he was recovering from hip surgery and unable to drive to the physician's office for his weekly visit. He was able to give directions to his wife (who had dementia), however, and together they drove the 180-mile round-trip to the doctor's office. Long-term couple dyads often depend on each other, and caring for a frail spouse is just part of that role.

Even during terminal illnesses, caregiving among the very old may be preferable to separation through institutionalization in a nursing home. Much has been written about the stressfulness of caregiving (Pearlin, Pioli, & McLaughlin, 2001), but institutionalization does not always provide relief. For example, Lieberman and Fisher (2001) found that the health and well-being of spouse caregivers of patients with dementia actually declined after placing their partners in nursing homes. It is very difficult for some of these caregivers to release the responsibility they feel is their own. One elderly husband visited his wife in the nursing home one week per month for more than two years, traveling from southern Texas to northern Minnesota. Her death was a relief for him, holding little of the intense grief that he felt at placing her in a nursing home. Pearlin, Mullan, Semple, and Skaff (1990) wrote of the loss of self that occurs when the caregiver can no longer care for the spouse.

These older couples often know that death is near and have accepted that fact. In a study of older caregivers (Gilmer & Aldwin, 2002), one older women delayed calling the physician. She knew that her husband was very ill and that he should be hospitalized, but also that he would not live long. She saw no reason for them to be separated during those last few days. The attachment of couple dyads may be particularly strong in these later years, with a feeling that they are really only one person. The woman just mentioned said, "I won't live in the future; if he dies, I will die shortly after." This was not a sad statement, just one that was true.

● SUMMARY

Overall, the literature on social support and health is positive. Most older adults have adequate support networks, although these decrease with age. The old-old in particular may have outlived spouses, friends, and often children, putting them at high risk of institutionalization. Thus, quasi-formal and formal support networks become increasingly important in later years. Although not all social interactions are positive, social support plays a major role in adaptation to disease and stressors in late life, and it is clearly associated with greater longevity. Thus, social support may serve as a way of decelerating the aging process and may be a key component in successful aging.

SECTION IV

AGING ACCELERATORS
AND DECELERATORS

CHAPTER 12

WHAT IS
OPTIMAL AGING?

D efining optimal aging has been a challenge for both medicine and psychology. We are much better at identifying illness or pathological processes than health. There is increased interest in positive psychology (Seligman & Csikszentmihalyi, 2000), as well as constructs such as wisdom. Optimal aging is more than just good health; it must include notions of adult development as well.

This chapter reviews the current models of optimal aging, using them as a framework for summarizing and extending some findings discussed in previous chapters. We focus on factors that accelerate the aging process as well as those that decelerate it.

MODELS OF OPTIMAL AGING ●

There has been a spate of publications in the last few years with titles such as *Successful Aging* (Rowe & Kahn, 1998), *Aging With Grace* (Snowdon, 2001), and *Aging Well* (Vaillant, 2002). Many of these terms are interchangeable. We chose to use optimal aging rather than successful aging, primarily to avoid the connotations of competition that the word *success* may bring, and also because too literal an interpretation may lead one to believe that there is only one way to age successfully. Furthermore, Erikson (1950) cautioned against attributing "success" to his stages of psychosocial development in adulthood, because he felt that the developmental issues underlying each stage were never totally resolved but rather continually revisited. Thus, one is not either integrated or despairing in late life; instead, the struggle to resolve these issues begins anew with each challenge that emerges. The term *optimal aging* allows for the recognition that there may be different ways of aging well, that people start with different configurations of vulnerabilities and resources that affect how they age, and that this is a process that continually unfolds, depending in part on choices that individuals make.

Defining optimal aging is an extremely difficult task. The overwhelming majority of studies predicting health in late life use unidimensional outcome measures such as longevity, avoidance of particular illnesses such as cardiovascular disease or depression, and self-reported health. Although these studies provide valuable information, most gerontologists feel that more complex models are needed. We all know individuals who live to advanced old age but are miserable and complaining, whereas others seem healthy and satisfied but somehow shallow and narcissistic. Still others have a zest for life and sense of purpose that may override any illnesses or disabilities they face. Thus, most models of optimal or successful aging are multidimensional.

Models of optimal aging are also teleological, in that they specify a desirable outcome or *telos* (goal). By definition, a telos reflects the assumptions of the dominant paradigm, as well as cultural values. For example, in all of the models in the scientific literature, longevity is considered desirable, in large part because our culture values it very highly. In some villages in ancient Japan, however, it was considered disgraceful to live too long. Once a great-grandchild was born, an elder was expected to go to the mountains to die of exposure. The problem was simple—if old people consumed too many resources, the survival of future generations might be threatened. Thus, it is not surprising that some 20% of cultures in the world practiced some form of geronticide, either active or passive (Glascock, 1997). Therefore, all models reflect assumptions and values, and it is necessary to clearly specify what those assumptions are and acknowledge their limitations.

Rowe and Kahn's Model of Successful Aging

Rowe and Kahn (1998) identified three components of successful aging: avoidance of disease, maintenance of high cognitive and physical function, and an active engagement with life. The model is hierarchical: Good health is thought to enable the other two. Avoiding disease is defined not only as the absence of overt disease but includes other risk factors as well. Absence of disease allows for the maintenance of good cognitive and physical function. In turn, good cognitive and physical function is necessary (but not sufficient) for active engagement with life. Rowe and Kahn defined active engagement as relationships with other people and productive behavior.

Avoiding Disease

Most research has been done on etiology and therefore prevention of common chronic illnesses such as cardiovascular disease, cancer, and diabetes. As reviewed extensively in this book, there are three critical elements in the prevention of chronic illnesses in late life, all of which are related to health behavior habits: avoidance of toxins such as cigarette smoke, good nutrition, and exercise. The absence of genetic endowment in this definition may be surprising, but it would appear that genetic defects play a role primarily in premature death from conditions such as Huntington's disease, and hypercholesteremia, the abnormally high production of cholesterol. Once individuals have survived into later life, their own behavior plays a much greater role in future longevity.

Exposure to toxins accelerates the aging process. Toxins that can be regulated by individuals include smoking, excessive alcohol consumption and other substance abuse, and UV radiation. Chronic methamphetamine users and those who abuse alcohol often look two or three decades older than they really are; heavy smokers, even if they avoid early deaths due to cancer, usually have deep furrows and wrinkles in their skin and very poor cardiopulmonary function. Excessive exposure to sun also promotes cancer and wrinkles and may promote cataracts and blindness. Unfortunately, many are exposed to toxins in their work environments—including agricultural pesticides, benzenes in cleaning solutions, coal dust, and asbestos—that constitute major risk factors for disease and can accelerate aging.

As has also been shown throughout this book, nutrition is extremely important. Unfortunately, it is much easier to specify what is bad nutrition than what constitutes good nutrition. Bad nutrition is simple. It is generally agreed that diets too high in fats, simple sugars, and protein, without fresh fruits or vegetables, and with too many calories promote cardiovascular disease, diabetes, and cancer. (Some are now making the argument that the fare in fast-food restaurants should come with health warnings as dire as those on packs of cigarettes.) The supersizing of portions, combined with increasing inactivity, are considered to be factors in the obesity epidemic we are currently experiencing. If the baby boomers and Generation X-ers do not improve their nutrition, we could see a reversal of the recent increase in longevity.

But what constitutes good nutrition? Should one adhere to a Mediterranean diet, low in fats and proteins but high in carbohydrates? Or follow the glycemic index, which avoids carbohydrates and starches but allows moderate levels of fat and protein as a way of regulating insulin levels? Are vitamin and mineral supplements critical or just a way of generating expensive urine, as one prominent nutrition colleague of ours claims? Clearly, too much food is harmful, but is caloric restriction a panacea or a risk?

The answer is that what constitutes good nutrition for any particular individual depends on a variety of factors, including age, gender, family history of illness, body type, and a host of other factors. For example, men whose fathers and uncles died of heart disease in their 50s would do well to severely restrict fat intake. Young, active people may flourish on Mediterranean diets, but those who are menopausal and prone to weight gain may do better avoiding pasta. People who are recovering from serious illnesses or injuries may need increased protein and calcium in their diets; those with dietary allergies may need to avoid lactose, peanuts, or glutens. Individuals prone to anemia may need to eat red meat (or to use iron and zinc supplements), and so on.

Caloric restriction clearly decelerates the aging process in lab animals (especially those that are cancer-prone), and obesity equally clearly accelerates aging in humans. The benefits of severe caloric restriction in humans have yet to be demonstrated, however. An average weight seems to be most protective of good health in later years, and losing weight in late life has been associated with heightened risk of mortality. Nonetheless, diabetics, hypertensives, and those with other risk factors for heart disease, cancer, and arthritis need to lose weight to help prevent and/or regulate illness.

The need for supplements may also depend on age, genetic endowment, and health behavior habits. Individuals with a family history of heart disease or dementia may benefit from folic acid. Women at risk of osteoporosis may need to supplement with calcium and vitamin D. Vitamin C and other antioxidants may help smokers and perhaps asthmatics; individuals who drink alcohol frequently may benefit from vitamin B supplements, as alcohol tends to block the uptake of B_{12}. Hormone supplements should be viewed more cautiously, due to their side effects. The important thing is to recognize individual differences in nutritional requirements and act accordingly.

Finally, the significance of moderate exercise as an aging decelerator cannot be overstated. Aerobic exercise maintains or improves cardiovascular function and regulates weight. Weight-bearing exercise maintains muscle and skeletal mass, preventing (or at least delaying) osteoporosis. Exercise may also regulate endocrine and immune function (although excessive exercise may have adverse effects). Older adults with a regular exercise program have fewer respiratory illnesses.

At an international conference, a geriatrician from Peru was heard criticizing theories of successful aging for being too culture bound. He was particularly annoyed by the advice about exercise, arguing that the poor elderly in the villages in his country cannot afford to go to expensive gyms. Yet older adults in mountainous villages get a tremendous amount of exercise simply from walking up and down the hills where they live. In fact, enhanced cardiovascular function from such activities has been suggested as one reason why individuals in some mountainous areas appear to enjoy longevity. Daily exertion as part of normal routines is more beneficial than occasional strenuous exercise.

Maintenance of High Cognitive and Physical Function

Less is known about the maintenance of good cognitive function in later life, in part because neural aging and the etiology of dementias are still somewhat of a mystery. It is becoming clear, however, that the same factors that maintain good cardiovascular function in late life also maintain good cognitive function—that is, good diet, exercise, and avoiding toxins. In this instance, exercise includes not only physical activity but cognitive activity as well. Older adults with active mental lives, such as emeritus professors, champion *go* players, and even those fond of bridge and crossword puzzles, are much more likely to maintain cognitive function than less active individuals (Masunaga & Horn, 2001).

Obviously, there is a fair amount of overlap between avoiding disease and maintenance of physical function. Tremendous advances have been made in the management of chronic illnesses and in recovery of function after injury. Exercise programs can improve cardiopulmonary and musculoskeletal function even in old-old and very frail elders. It may take older adults a little longer, but physical therapy can improve the function of the musculoskeletal system. Similarly, physical, speech, and occupational therapy can help with the sequelae of strokes and cancer treatment. Thus, older adults recovering from even serious illnesses can regain high levels of physical functioning.

Active Engagement With Life

Rowe and Kahn (1998) define active engagement with life as a high level of social support as well as productive work. The benefits of social support, as reviewed in Chapter 11, include helping to maintain good mental and physical health, both directly and indirectly. Marital satisfaction tends to increase in late life; as noted in Chapter 2, marriage tends to promote longevity, especially for men. Being surrounded by family and friends can protect against depression, help people adhere to medical regimes and get medical treatment when needed, improve health behavior habits, and may decrease stress hormones. Caregiving from family and friends can help to mitigate disability and allow elders to remain in the community.

In elderly couples, it is often very difficult to tell who is the caregiver and who is the care recipient. Often spouses help each other with tasks that may be beyond the other's capabilities. For example, one couple known to the first author lived into their 80s. The woman had difficulty seeing; the man had difficulty hearing. The husband took over household tasks that required eyesight, including much of the cooking; the wife dutifully repeated everything anyone said to them, shouting into his ear so he could hear. It wasn't until after her death that he could be persuaded to get a hearing aid; they died within a year of each other. Dixon (1999; Dixon & Gould, 1996) has done some wonderful work showing that dyadic memory in older couples is often quite as good as that in younger people. In other words, an older couple, especially an older married couple, working together on a memory task can perform as well as a younger person. By collaborating, they can compensate for faulty memories.

Yet social support is not always beneficial. Not only do negative interactions take a toll on physical and mental health, but people may provide poor or bad advice. In old-old dyads, we have observed something we term *dysfunctional autonomy* (Gilmer & Aldwin, 2002). When one member of such a couple is released from the hospital, it is generally assumed that the spouse will provide the primary caregiving. Yet often the other member of the dyad is nearly as disabled as the "patient" and simply may not be up to rigorous caregiving duties. We found that old-old couples would often "fake good" in order to avoid closer scrutiny from medical professionals. They were often very dependent on each other and terrified of being split up by one being institutionalized, so they would deny the existence of any problems. Unfortunately, this often meant that they did not seek the help that would allow them to remain in the community, increasing their risk of institutionalization and even death. When they did seek help, it was often from senior centers rather than medical professionals. Thus, home visits to frail elders may be essential in order to determine the level of services required.

Older adults do a great deal of the unpaid activities that sustain families and communities and, in doing so, sustain their own lives. Caregiving is one form of productive work engaged in by elders. Grandparents often provide child care for grandchildren and sometimes great-grandchildren. They often continue to provide support for their own children and often help other seniors as well. Older adults who can still drive may take more frail elders to medical appointments or shopping. In retirement communities, they may keep tabs on each other in very simple ways. A common practice is a pre-arranged signal, such as raising the kitchen blinds in the morning. If some-one has not opened the blinds by the requisite time, a neighbor will go and make sure that person has not fallen or does not need assistance in some way. Phone circles are also common: If someone does not call at a certain time, a member of the circle will go over to find out why.

Older adults also engage in organized volunteer work. They are often elders and deacons in churches; many work in food banks, orphanages, libraries, and hospitals. One older group arranged to be foster grandparents for babies with AIDS born in local hospitals. They set up a schedule of people who would simply hold and rock the infants, many of whom had been abandoned by their mothers. The Senior Gleaners in the Sacramento area is a good example of a productive, charitable organization run by seniors. About 20 years ago, a group of 12 senior citizens noticed that farmers would often leave behind some crops after harvesting or sometimes would not harvest a particular crop at all if the prices were too low. They decided to approach the farmers and ask if they could glean their fields and donate the produce to food banks. They now have trucks, their own printing press, and a few thousand volunteers, all over the age of 55. They provide thousands of meals each month through local food banks.

In rural areas, elders often are the lifeblood of the community. Through a combination of out-migration of young people going to cities for jobs and in-migration of retirees, many rural communities have disproportionate numbers of older people. The willingness of the elderly to maintain small businesses such as hardware or grocery stores, gas stations, and post offices allows the town to avoid their closure altogether (Norris-Baker & Scheidt, 1994). Thus, elders contribute not only to their families but to the larger community as well. By doing so, they maintain their own well-being.

The notion of what is productive work in late life should not be restricted to paid or even volunteer positions. As discussed later in this chapter, the task of late life may be inner development, whether this is Erikson's life review leading to ego integrity (1950; Erikson, Erikson, & Kivnick, 1986) or Tornstam's (1994) notion of gerotranscendence.

Vaillant's Model of Aging Well

Vaillant (2002) proposed a model that is similar to Rowe and Kahn's model but has six criteria instead of three. Three of the criteria involve physical health:

1. No physical disability at age 75 (physician-rated)

2. Good subjective physical health (no problems with instrumental activities of daily living)

3. Length of undisabled life

The other three concern social engagement and productive activity:

4. Good mental health (interviewer-rated; includes career, marriage, visits to psychiatrists and use of psychotropic medications, vacations, and the ability to play—to engage in social activities or games)

5. Objective social support (marriage, play, siblings, religious attendance, children, confidants, and social network)

6. Self-rated life satisfaction in eight domains: marriage, income-producing work, children, friendships and social contacts, hobbies, community service activities, religion, and recreation/sports

In deriving these (somewhat redundant) criteria, Vaillant (2002) drew on three long-term longitudinal studies: his Grant Study of Harvard men (Vaillant, 1977), a study of inner-city men at risk for delinquency (Glueck & Glueck, 1950), and women from the Terman study of gifted children (Terman, 1925). All of these studies followed their participants from childhood or adolescence to the present; average dates of birth ranged from 1911 for women in the Terman study to 1930 for the inner-city men. This study is particularly valuable because it permits examination of the predictors of healthy aging.

In many ways, what did not predict healthy aging was as important as the factors that did predict it. In Vaillant's (2002) study, ancestral longevity was a predictor of mortality before age 60 but not thereafter. In other words, premature death was predicted by genetic endowment, but once having achieved late life, individual health behavior habits were more important. Neither cholesterol level at age 50 nor the existence of stress-related illnesses before 50 predicted mortality after age 65. Childhood temperament was not important, nor was level of ego development. Early childhood environment was predictive of health at age 40, but not at age 75. This supports the conclusions in earlier chapters of this book that the variables that predict morbidity and mortality in midlife may not remain predictors in later life.

Vaillant (2002) did find predictors of successful aging. As is to be expected, four of them reflected health behavior habits: No heavy smoking or alcohol abuse before 50, some exercise, and no obesity. A stable marriage was also predictive of aging well. Other potential predictors, such as education and depression, were not included in this list, because they were mediated by health behavior habits. As reviewed in Chapter 9, individuals who are depressed often smoke and drink; Vaillant argues that these actually may cause depression rather than reflect them. Of course, poor childhood environments can lead to problems with depression and other types of mental illness, an inability to play, lack of trust, and social isolation. Of those with poor mental health at age 50, half were dead by 75, but only one out of six men who were emotionally stable had died.

There were interesting contrasts between the Harvard men in Vaillant's (2002) study, most of whom were upper class, and the inner-city men, most of whom were from lower social classes. Not surprisingly, health in the latter group was much poorer overall, in large part due to poor health behavior habits. It is intriguing, though, that the inner-city men who graduated from college enjoyed the same level of good health in later life as the Harvard men, despite what Vaillant called their "inferior" colleges.

More interesting, though, was that Vaillant argued that the use of mature defenses, including altruism, humor, suppression, and sublimation, was an important component of successful aging (see Chapter 10). Nearly half (48%) of the men classified as happy-well at 75 used mature defenses at age 50, as compared with 4% of the men who were classified as "sad-sick" at age 75. Vaillant described mature defenses not only as coping strategies but also as virtues:

> These four coping strategies are not only associated with maturity, but they can be reframed as virtues. Such virtues include doing as one would be done by (*altruism*); artistic creation to resolve conflict and spinning straw into gold (*sublimation*); a stiff upper lip, patience, seeing the bright side (*suppression*); and the ability not to take oneself too seriously (*humor*). These strategies . . . provide the antidote to narcissism. (Vaillant, 2002, p. 64)

In many ways, Vaillant's conceptualization is very similar to what Aldwin (1999) called transformational coping: the ability to perceive benefit in stressful situations and to resolve them in a manner that maximizes whatever gain can be derived from the problem and that facilitates the growth of positive characteristics such as empathy, altruism, and an increase in mastery.

Vaillant's model is similar to that proposed by Rowe and Kahn (1998) in its emphasis on physical health, social integration, and productivity. Yet the founders of gerontology have warned that these types of models are nonetheless incomplete. Vaillant (2002) cites a personal communication by Birren, who warned against characterizing successful aging as simply the deferral of decline. Lawton (1999) was even more explicit, arguing that such models held successful aging to be simply the continuation of the vitality of midlife. Physical decline comes to all, yet Rowe and Kahn, as well as Vaillant, cited examples of extraordinary individuals who demonstrate major accomplishments despite disabilities, such as Franklin Delano Roosevelt, John F. Kennedy, Stephen Hawking, and Mother Teresa. The critical question is, what is qualitatively different about optimal aging in late life that distinguishes it from good functioning in midlife?

Vaillant's engaging clinical descriptions of those he considered to be successful agers provide a hint. Clearly, many of the people in his study demonstrated what can only be called wisdom. Vaillant concluded that wisdom could be equated with the use of mature defenses. Aldwin (1999) also linked transformational coping with wisdom but argued that this is just one path toward wisdom.

● WISDOM AND OPTIMAL AGING

The past 10 years has seen a marked increase in the study of wisdom. The most common definition focuses on the cognitive aspects. Baltes and Smith (1990), for example, focus on what they call "fundamental life pragmatics," which include a rich factual-knowledge base and the ability to think contextually and relativistically. When giving advice, for example, the wise person is able to listen to the nuances of a problem and help in thinking through the ramifications of any course of action, rather than providing absolutist maxims. McKee and Barber (1999) focus on perspicacity (the ability to see through illusions), whereas Sternberg (1990) equates wisdom with reasoning ability and perspicacity.

The growing consensus, though, is that wisdom is more than just cognition, but may include other dimensions as well (Baltes & Staudinger, 2000; Sternberg, 1998). For example, Labouvie-Vief (1990) defined wisdom as encompassing both cognitive and emotional complexity. Birren and Fisher (1990) identify three aspects: cognitive, affective, and conative, which refers to motivation. Orwoll and Perlmutter (1990) suggest a personological approach that encompasses the integration of cognition with affect, affiliation, and social concerns. Wisdom thus reflects an advanced development of personality. Holliday and Chandler (1986) asked individuals to describe people they thought were wise. Frequent descriptors included kindness, compassion, and fairness—suggesting that the personality characteristics of wise individuals may be as salient as their cognitive characteristics.

Wisdom is a multidimensional construct that includes three domains: cognition, personality, and interpersonal processes. The cognitive component can be loosely defined as perspicacity or insightfulness, which is based on both knowledge and higher-order cognitive processes, such as the ability to comprehend complex constructs and to use dialectical and relativistic modes of thinking. The personality aspects of wisdom may be best thought of in terms of ego processes, including emotional balance, detachment, and integrity, which are all based on self-knowledge. The interpersonal modes of being are typified by justice, generosity, and compassion, which some cultures refer to as "character."

These three domains are not separate but rather support and inform each other in the wise person. Thus, the ability to be calm and detached can facilitate both perspicacity and moral behavior. Similarly, adhering to a strong moral core can promote calmness and detachment. Thus, wisdom cannot be defined only in terms of cognition, personality, or interpersonal processes but must be seen as the integration of these domains.

Wisdom is not necessarily a stable personality characteristic, however, but may be contextual, depending on the domain of knowledge. Also, it may be culturally specific, in that different cultures may emphasize one or more domains and may vary in their construct of character. However, aspects of wisdom transcend cultural bounds, either because there are core constructs within wisdom (e.g., insightfulness, generosity) or because wise people can detach from cultural constraints and assumptions.

Finally, wisdom has an action component that is not limited to advice-giving. Rather, wise action is that which is focused on long-term goals rather than immediate gain or gratification. Furthermore, wise action is not self-serving or self-promoting but is based on a recognition of what would be most beneficial for the community, whether this consists of families, social organizations, humankind, or the ecosphere as a whole. Given the inherent ambiguities in situations and the focus on long-term or higher-order goals, whether or not an action can be considered wise may sometimes only be determined long after the fact.

Levenson, Aldwin, and Cupertino (2001) argued that there is a much simpler process at the foundation of these changes, reflecting a more fundamental shift in the self, such as that proposed by Tornstam (1994) in his theory of "gerotranscendence." Tornstam observed that aging can be associated with a metatheoretical shift toward "a picture of the world that a Zen Buddhist would probably have" (p. 207). In direct contrast to the social engagement models reviewed earlier, he noted that gerontologists misinterpret older persons' lack of interest in social busyness as a sign of pathological disengagement rather than an increased propensity for contemplation.

314 • AGING ACCELERATORS AND DECELERATORS

Tornstam also distinguished gerotranscendence from Erikson's (1950) ego integrity. The latter is concerned with integrating one's life retrospectively and can really only be achieved near life's end. Gerotranscendence involves a forward-looking redefinition of reality that treats one's development as a work still in progress. It is a new opening rather than a closing.

Gerotranscendence does not necessarily involve withdrawal from the world, but it does imply a certain level of detachment (see also Kramer, 1990). Preliminary empirical studies suggest that elders high in gerotranscendence use more problem-focused coping. With increasing gerotranscendence, one's identity and life satisfaction are less dependent on social activity, yet satisfaction with social activity also increases. In other words, the source of one's self and one's satisfaction are less dependent on external, material objects. Vaillant (2002) also noted something similar. "Successful aging means the mastery of decay. . . . The task of integrity forces us to reflect upon human dignity in the face of disability. Indeed, to achieve positive aging at the end of life necessitates an almost Buddhist acceptance" (p. 159).

Levenson et al. (2001) argued that transcendence of self is the *sine qua non* of adult development. Most theories characterize development in terms of gains—the ego becomes more cognitively and emotionally complex (Labouvie-Vief, 1990; Loevinger, 1977); one achieves integrity (Erikson, 1950) or develops the self through goals (Brandtstädter, 1999). The problem with this perspective in late life is that there are arguably more losses than gains. Baltes (1987) characterizes development as a balance of losses and gains, but the implication is that gains compensate for losses. Loss can also be an integral part of development, however. Just as brain development in early childhood necessitates pruning of neurons, losses in adulthood allow for the transcendence of self (Levenson et al., 2001).

People often define themselves in terms of their social roles. But with age, those social roles tend to be lost. Who are we if we are no longer our work role, our parenting role, or our spousal role? Certainly, our appearances change—people who identify themselves as having youthful bodies may not be able to recognize the "stranger" in the mirror. Losses such as bereavement can present opportunities for self-observation and self-knowledge (Aldwin, 1999; Aldwin & Levenson, 2001). Lieberman (1996) studied widows and widowers and found that people often grew and developed in new ways after the death of a spouse. This increased self-knowledge can form the basis for coping strategies that promote decreases in attachment and self-deception. In this context, loss of self should not be confused with trauma-induced depersonalization; rather, it refers to transcending the ego through such practices as nonattachment, patience, and self-knowledge.

Vaillant (2002, p. 250) asked the men in the Harvard study to define wisdom. Their answers were quite instructive and included the following:

Empathy, through which one must synthesize both care and justice.

Tolerance and a capacity to appreciate paradox and irony even as one learns to manage uncertainty.

Self-awareness combined with an absence of self-absorption.

The capacity to "hear" what others say.

Perspective, sense of the larger context of life, realization that there are two sides to everything, nothing is black or white. Patience. Sense of the irony of life.

A sense of the connectedness of all things.

Vaillant (2002) observed that wisdom is the opposite of narcissism, which is characterized by self-absorption and attachment to desires. The losses and problems that one must cope with in late life can result in an increase in self-absorption and attachment, but that is a recipe for despair and social isolation in late life. Sad examples include the aging diva who cannot accept the loss of her looks or the widow who sees only her own grief and cannot attend to that of her children. Coping with loss can provide a sense of perspective, allowing one to be more tolerant of one's own and others' shortcomings. One can develop a sense of humility and willingness to listen and learn from others. For example, Vaillant found that his successful agers were able to detail what they had learned from their children, but apparently it had never occurred to the "sad-sick" that this was even possible. Decreasing egocentricity also leads to increasing compassion and underlies the emotional balance thought by both Sternberg (1998) and Baltes and Staudinger (2000) to be essential to wisdom.

Perhaps most important, loss or transcendence of self allows one an intuitive grasp of the interconnectedness of all things. Narcissists believe that they are the focus of everything. In contrast, transcending the self loosens and blurs ego boundaries, which can lead to a recognition of interconnectedness and a lack of focus on the self. Understanding this interconnectedness is the foundation for empathy and fairness and allows for a humbling perspective on one's own problems. Paradoxically, this loss of self may allow for productive activity in late life. Narcissistic attachment to previous work roles may not allow a switch to new ones that may be less prestigious in retirement. A focus on one's own problems may not allow the more satisfying work of doing for others. Snowdon (2001) provides a humbling example from his Nun Study:

> Once when Sharon Ostwald and I were visiting the convent together, we walked into a room where a half dozen sisters were busily assembling stuffed animals. One elderly nun, who appeared to be in her late eighties, sat in a wheelchair stuffing cotton balls into a cloth giraffe. Osteoporosis had thinned her bones to the point that the vertebrae in her spine had collapsed, leaving her so bent over that her face was just above her knees. I froze; how could this woman function at all?
>
> Sharon walked over to her, got down on both knees, and positioned her head within a few inches of the sister's face. "How're you doing, Sister?" she called out.
>
> "Oh, just fine," the sister piped back in a surprisingly audible voice. "They've got me slaving away here for our holiday crafts sale. Forced labor, I call it." All the sisters in the room laughed—and a light went on for me. I should not be so concerned about disability. (p. 35)

For Snowdon, the nuns' deep spirituality was a key component not only of their extraordinary longevity but also of their positive adaptation to extreme old age. Several recent studies have supported a relationship between religiosity and well-being, especially later in life.

● RELIGIOUSNESS, SPIRITUALITY, AND OPTIMAL AGING

There is a complex relationship between well-being and religiosity, which includes religious beliefs and practices. Koenig, Smiley, and Gonzales (1988) argue that participation in religious practices, especially group practices, is negatively related to mental illness, including depression. Various types of religious practices may have different relations with health, however. In a study of religiosity, depression, social support, and health in a large sample of African American and white Southerners, Koenig et al. (1997) found that religious attendance was negatively related to depression; however, listening to or watching religious radio or television programs was positively related to depression, while private prayer and Bible reading were apparently unrelated. These relationships appeared to be independent of social support and physical health, as well as age, sex, and race. Other studies, though, have shown that prayer tends to alleviate depressive symptoms caused by stress (Veroff, Douvan, & Kulka, 1981). People who are higher in intrinsic religiosity recover from depression more quickly (Koenig, George, & Peterson, 1998).

Kennedy, Kelman, Thomas, and Chen (1996) found that religious preference was also differentially associated with depressive symptoms. At baseline, elderly Catholics were less depressed than their elderly Jewish counterparts, and the latter were more likely to become depressed over time. Interestingly, though, religious attendees were less likely to be depressed in both religious groups, although this only reached significance among Catholics. Again, this was independent of health, disability, and social support. Among women, traditional sex roles and religious fundamentalism are significant risk factors for depression (Bridges & Spilka, 1992). In summary, religiosity in general may have a protective effect against depression, but some forms of religiosity may be associated with poorer mental health.

But what of positive mental health? The strongest relationship between religious behaviors and happiness is seen with the frequency of prayer, especially meditative prayer (Poloma & Pendleton, 1991). The intensity of religious experiences is also associated with happiness, although transcendental experiences showed a small negative relationship (Hills & Argyle, 1998). Interestingly, Ellison (1991) found that neither religious attendance nor a measure of divine interaction related to happiness, but existential certainty was significantly and positively related to happiness. As Argyle (2000) pointed out, social support in a religious context can include love as well as shared beliefs and emotions. Thus, the effect of religiosity on well-being may be mediated by social support (Moberg & Taves, 1965). In addition, prayer is strongly associated with forgiveness, which may also increase happiness (see Poloma & Gallup, 1991). Hood, Spilka, Hunsberger, and Gorsuch (1996) stated, "In most instances . . . faith buttresses people's sense of control and self-esteem, offers meanings that oppose anxiety, provides hope, sanctions socially facilitating behavior, enhances personal well-being, and promotes social integration" (pp. 436-437).

The relationship between religiosity and physical health is also complex. As Levin (1994) pointed out, a number of confounding factors should be taken into account. For example, religious service attendance is often correlated with good health in late life, but it may be that individuals who are well enough to travel outside of their homes may also be more likely to go to church, temple, or mosque. Also, many religions have restrictions that can promote good health behaviors, such as the Seventh Day Adventists' ban on smoking, alcohol, and eating meat. As noted earlier, participation in organized religion also provides a source of social support. Nonetheless, Levin (1994) found that religion had an effect on morbidity and mortality, independent of preexisting health, health behavior habits, and social support.

Some of the effect of religiosity on physical health may be mediated by affect and mental health. Strong religious belief was a predictor of positive affect among caregivers under chronic stress (Rabbins, Fitting, Eastham, & Fetting, 1990). Braan, Beekman, Deeg, Smit, and Tilburg (1997) also found that religiosity may function as a stress-buffer, as it protects caregivers from depression in the presence of chronic stress or strain. Chronicity and incidence of depression were higher in the nonreligious groups, particularly those in poorer health and under greater stress. There may be direct effects as well. Hixson, Gruchow, and Morgan (1998) reported that religiosity has a direct effect on blood pressure not mediated by change in health behaviors and attitudes. Religiosity may be particularly protective for lower socioeconomic groups (Ljungquist & Sundstrom, 1996).

Nonetheless, religiosity may not be an absolute requirement for optimal aging. Many of the most successful agers in Vaillant's (2002) study found religion to be irrelevant to their lives. There is a difference between religiosity and spirituality, with the former more closely associated with organized religion. In contrast, spirituality is more intrinsic and tied to being centered, as well as to the experience of the numinous. Vaillant found that the most spiritual people in his study were often those who had had very difficult childhoods; their religious experiences allowed them contentment and a sense of purpose. These people were not necessarily among the most successful agers, however. This is not surprising, given that Vaillant's definition of successful aging has a major focus on social activities and extraversion; those given to more introverted activities may not be identified in this model as successful agers.

If wisdom is a *sine qua non* for successful aging, one must ask whether religiosity is necessary for the development of wisdom. The answer is, not necessarily. As noted above, there are different types of religious experiences and practices. A famous quote by Muhammad has him saying, "My back has been broken by pious fools." If Tornstam (1994) is correct, spirituality may increase simply as a process of aging. With age, people may turn inward and focus on larger meanings, especially as they face death.

● *ARS MORIENDI*—THE ART OF DYING

No book on health, illness, and optimal aging would be complete without discussion of death and dying. Certainly, death is a physiological process, but it is a psychological and spiritual process as well. *Ars moriendi* is a term dating from the Middle Ages, when it was understood that "how a patient dies will, in any case, reflect at least in part how that patient has lived a life and what kind of character is brought to the dying" (Callahan, 1997, p. 1035). A peaceful death is an ideal to which many people aspire, but it may be difficult to achieve. Although some might prefer to die "with their boots on," as it were, certainly no one would desire a death with intractable pain such as that described in Tolstoy's (1900) *The Death of Ivan Ilych*. How do people die in late life?

Nuland (1994) wrote a fascinating book called *How We Die: Reflections on Life's Final Chapter*. Every death requires a death certificate, and that certificate lists the primary, secondary, and tertiary causes of death. As noted in Chapter 2, the primary cause of death in late life is heart disease, the second is cancer, and stroke is the third. But as Nuland pointed out, assigning causes of death in very late life is often quite arbitrary, because so often there is multiple organ system failure. Although cardiac arrest may be the official cause of death, in actuality the elderly person may have been suffering from pneumonia, emphysema, and kidney failure secondary to diabetes. The heart always stops with death, as do respiration, circulation, and kidney function—to say nothing of brain function. Thus, assigning the cause of death in very late life can be somewhat arbitrary. Cessation of brain function is generally the absolute marker of death, because cardiopulmonary function can be sustained using a ventilator. As Nuland (1994) said, "The very old do not succumb to disease—they implode their way into eternity" (p. 83).

Deaths in midlife, especially those due to myocardial infarction, tend to be rapid. In late life, however, death is much more likely to be a slow and gradual process. Although young people may prefer death to be sudden and quick, or at best, to die in their sleep, old people may express gratitude for the time left to them, so that they can prepare financially, emotionally, and spiritually. The local hospice director gave an interesting anecdote in one of our classes. Before undergoing hospice training, most volunteers say they want a quick and relatively painless death, such as a sudden heart attack or a fatal car accident. After training, though, they express a preference for slower deaths, such as that due to cancer, precisely so they will have time to finish tasks, mend relationships, if necessary, and savor time with their loved ones.

Most people prefer to die at home (King, Mackenzie, Smith, & Clark, 2000), yet the majority of deaths occur in hospitals and nursing homes (Bear, 2000). Changes in Medicare regulations regarding hospice funding has allowed more people to die in their homes (McMillan, Mentnech, Lubitz, McBean, & Russell, 1990), but the poor may be more likely to die in institutional settings (Higginson, Jarman, Astin, & Dolan, 1999). Fortunately, there has been a dramatic decrease in the use of life support systems in terminal illnesses (Prendergast & Luce, 1997), reflecting a retreat from the use of heroic measures to try to save the terminally ill.

Hospice and palliative care have had a positive impact on the way in which people die. Although adequate pain management is still problematic for some physicians who fear to give "addicting" doses of morphine to terminally ill patients (Emanuel et al., 2000), substantial pain relief can be achieved for most people. For example, one study of pain relief in hospice care found that nearly all patients were free of pain; only 9% said the pain was troublesome and annoying (Dobratz, 2001).

Engle, Fox-Hill, and Graney (1998) studied the interval between living and dying in a small multi-ethnic sample of nursing home residents who knew that death was imminent. This is obviously a difficult time; African American residents in particular complained of inadequate pain relief. However, most of the residents interviewed focused more on the quality of living rather than the dying process per se. Most were appreciative of respectful and prompt care, valued caring for others, and welcomed religious activities.

As difficult as it may be for younger people to understand, death may be welcome in very late life. People who have outlived spouses, friends, and even children may feel that it is "their time to go." They may be exhausted from fighting the infirmities of chronic disease. It is particularly sad when elders feel that they have lived too long. Seale and Addington-Hall (1995) studied the desirability of timing of death. They found that sometimes the old-old, especially women, felt that they had lived "past their time." Sometimes such people express concerns that "God has forgotten them."

Most cultures have some concept of what constitutes a good death. In traditional Irish culture, for example, one often chooses one's time to die (Scheper-Hughes, 1983). Elders who feel the time is right will announce this to their families, take to their beds, and stop eating and drinking. Family and friends come and visit; old quarrels are resolved, debts paid, and farewells taken. In many ways, this is a living wake, with plentiful libations in true Irish tradition. Celebrating the end of life with friends is certainly a good death.

Some Buddhist monks believe that one should die sitting up and meditating. This allows for a smooth transition to the *bardo*, the state after death in which one makes critical decisions that affect whether and how one is reborn (Rinpoche, 1996). Thus, meditation toward the end of life focuses on how to maintain conscious awareness through the death experience.

For some, witnessing the death of others can be a deeply spiritual experience. Collett (1996) described his experience at the Zen hospice in San Francisco, which often takes care of AIDS patients, the indigent, and the elderly. As a new hospice worker, he was, like most of us, afraid to witness the death of others. But he found that this was often a moving experience, and he was grateful that these people would share their deaths with him. Chah (1993) described death as "going home." In our experience, elders who believe in an afterlife often speak of rejoining their loved ones, which helps to mitigate their fear of death. Even those without such beliefs, however, may feel that they are old enough, that they have done what they wanted to do, and therefore accepted their imminent deaths. Truly, wisdom helps us face death.

SUMMARY ●

Figure 1.1 in Chapter 1 contrasts two women who are about 60. One is tall, blond, curvaceous, and apparently healthy; the other has deep wrinkles and has clearly lived a very hard life. From most standard theories of successful aging, Faye Dunaway (the first woman) would be considered an exemplar of delaying the ravages of aging. In the photo, she looks 20 years younger than her age, has had a very successful career, and undoubtedly has an extensive social network. In contrast, the Nepalese woman looks like a person who has experienced accelerated aging. Within her culture, however, she may be relatively hale and hearty, and she has very kindly eyes. Nothing in their appearance tells us anything about how much wisdom they have developed.

The maintenance of good health is clearly a desirable state, but it is not the most critical component of successful aging. Absent sudden death, we will all develop chronic illnesses, and a substantial proportion of us will become disabled. Theories of successful aging should include positive adaptation in the face of disability as the key element. Developing the equanimity to face the daunting adversity of disability in late life, and the development of wisdom, are the central components of optimal aging.

SUMMARY

REFERENCES

Abramson, J., Berger, A., Krumholz, H. M., & Vaccarino, V. (2001). Depression and risk of heart failure among older persons with isolated systolic hypertension. *Archives of Internal Medicine, 161,* 1725-1730.

Abramson, L. Y., Seligman, M. E. P., & Teasdale, J. D. (1978). Learned helplessness in humans: Critique and reformulation. *Journal of Abnormal Psychology, 87,* 49-74.

Adams, W. L. (1995a). Interactions between alcohol and other drugs. *International Journal of Addictions, 30,* 1903-1905.

Adams, W. L. (1995b). Potential for adverse drug-alcohol interactions among community residents. *Journal of the American Geriatric Society, 43,* 1021-1025.

Ader, R., Felten, D. L., & Cohen, N. (1991). *Psychoneuroimmunology* (2nd ed.). San Diego, CA: Academic Press.

Administration on Aging. (2000). *Older Americans 2000: Key indicators of well-being.* Retrieved from www.aoa.dhhs.gov/agingstats/chartbook2000/

Administration on Aging. (2002). *Profile of older Americans: 1999.* Retrieved from www.aoa.dhhs.gov/aoa/stats/profile/2.html

Affleck, G., Zautra, A., Tennen, H., & Armeli, S. (1999). Multilevel daily process designs for consulting and clinical psychology: A preface for the perplexed. *Journal of Consulting & Clinical Psychology, 67,* 746-754.

Aksoy, H., Keles, S., Kocer, I., & Akcay, F. (2001). Diabetic cataract and the total antioxidant status in aqueous humor. *Clinical Chemistry and Laboratory Medicine, 39,* 143-145.

Albert, M. S., & Moss, M. B. (1996). Neuropsychology of aging: Findings in humans and monkeys. In E. L. Schneider & J. W. Rowe (Eds.), *Handbook of the biology of aging* (4th ed., pp. 217-233). San Diego, CA: Academic Press.

Aldwin, C. M. (1990). The Elders Life Stress Inventory (ELSI): Egocentric and nonegocentric stress. In M. A. P. Stephens, S. E. Hobfoll, J. H. Crowther, & D. L. Tennenbaum (Eds.), *Stress and coping in later-life families* (pp. 49-69). New York: Hemisphere.

Aldwin, C. M. (1991). Does age affect the stress and coping process? The implications of age differences in perceived locus of control. *Journals of Gerontology: Psychological Sciences, 46,* P174-P180.

Aldwin, C. M. (1999). *Stress, coping, and development: An integrative approach.* New York: Guilford.

Aldwin, C. M., & Levenson, M. R. (1998). Assessment of mental health in older adults. In H. S. Friedman (Ed.), *Encyclopedia of mental health* (pp. 149-156). San Diego, CA: Academic Press.

Aldwin, C. M., & Levenson, M. R. (2001). Stress, coping, and health at midlife: A developmental perspective. In M. E. Lachman (Ed.), *The handbook of midlife development* (pp. 188-214). New York: Wiley.

Aldwin, C. M., Levenson, M. R., & Spiro, A., III. (1994). Vulnerability and resilience to combat exposure: Can stress have lifelong effects? *Psychology and Aging, 9,* 34-44.

Aldwin, C. M., Levenson, M. R., Spiro, A., III, & Bossé, R. (1989). Does emotionality predict stress? Findings from the Normative Aging Study. *Journal of Personality and Social Psychology, 56,* 618-624.

Aldwin, C. M., & Revenson, T. A. (1987). Does coping help? A reexamination of the relationship between coping and mental health. *Journal of Personality and Social Psychology, 53,* 337-348.

Aldwin, C. M., Spiro, A., III, Clark, G., & Hall, N. (1991). Thymic hormones, stress, and psychological symptoms in older men: A comparison of different statistical techniques for small samples. *Brain, Behavior, and Immunity, 5,* 206-218.

Aldwin, C. M., Spiro, A., III, Levenson, M. R., & Bossé, R. (1989). Longitudinal findings from the Normative Aging Study. I. Does mental health change with age? *Psychology and Aging, 4,* 295-306

Aldwin, C. M., Spiro, A., III, Levenson, M. R., & Cupertino, A. P. (2001). Longitudinal findings from the Normative Aging Study. III. Personality, individual health trajectories, and mortality. *Psychology and Aging, 16,* 450-465.

Aldwin, C., & Stokols, D. (1988). The effects of environmental change on individuals and groups: Some neglected issues in stress research. *Journal of Environmental Psychology, 8,* 57-75.

Aldwin, C. M., Sutton, K. J., Chiara, G., & Spiro, A., III. (1996). Age differences in stress, coping, and appraisal: Findings from the Normative Aging Study. *Journals of Gerontology: Psychological Sciences, 51B,* P179.

Aldwin, C. M., & Yancura, L. A. (in press). Coping and health: A comparison of the stress and trauma literatures. In P. P. Schnurr & B. L. Green (Eds.), *Physical health consequences of exposure to extreme stress.* Washington, DC: American Psychological Association

Alexander, C. N., & Langer, E. J. (1990). *Higher stages of human development.* Oxford, UK: Oxford University Press.

Alexander, C. N., Langer, E. J., Newman, R. I., Chandler, H. M., & Davies, J. (1989). Transcendental meditation, mindfulness, and longevity: An experimental study with the elderly. *Journal of Personality & Social Psychology, 57,* 950-964.

Alexander, K. P., Newby, L. K., Hellkamp, A. S., Harrington, R. A., Peterson, E. D., Kopecky, S., Langer, A., O'Gara, P., O'Connor, C. M., Daly, R. N., Califf, R. M., Khan, S., & Fuster, V. (2001). Initiation of hormone replacement therapy after acute myocardial infarction is associated with more cardiac events during follow-up. *Journal of the American College of Cardiology, 38,* 8-10.

Allen, R. G., & Sohal, R. S. (1982). Life-lengthening effects of ã-irradiation on the adult house fly, *Musca domestica. Mechanisms of Aging and Development, 20,* 369-375.

Allman, R. M. (1999). Pressure ulcers. In W. R. Hazzard, J. P. Blass, W. H. Ettinger, Jr., J. B. Halter, & J. G. Ouslander (Eds.), *Principles of geriatric medicine and gerontology* (4th ed., pp. 1577-1583). New York: McGraw-Hill.

Almagro, P., Calbo, E., Ochoa de Echaguen, A., Barreiro, B., Quintana, S., Heredia, J. L., & Garau, J. (2002). Mortality after hospitalization for COPD. *Chest, 121,* 1441-1448.

Altschuler, J. L., & Ruble, D. N. (1989). Developmental changes in children's awareness of strategies for coping with uncontrollable stress. *Child Development, 60,* 1337-1349.

Amendo, M. T., Brown, B. A., Kossow, L. B., & Weinberg, F. M. (2001). Headache as the sole presentation of acute myocardial infarction in two elderly patients. *American Journal of Geriatric Cardiology, 10,* 100-101.

American College of Obstetricians and Gynecologists. (2001). Use of botanicals for management of menopausal symptoms. *ACOG Practice Bulletin, 28.* Retrieved December 26, 2002, from ww.acog.org/from_home/publications/misc/pb028.htm

American Psychiatric Association (2000). *Diagnostic and statistical manual of mental disorders: DSM-IV-TR* (4th ed., text revision). Washington, DC: Author.

Ancheta, J. I., & Reding, M. R. (1999). Stroke diagnosis and treatment: A multidisciplinary effort. In W. R. Hazzard, J. P. Blass, W. H. Ettinger, Jr., J. B. Halter, & J. G. Ouslander (Eds.), *Principles of geriatric medicine and gerontology* (4th ed., pp. 1239-1256). New York: McGraw-Hill.

Anda, R., Williamson, D., Jones, D., Macea, C., Eaker, E., Glassman, A., & Marks, J. (1993). Depressed affect, hopelessness, and the risk of ischemic heart disease in a cohort of U.S. adults. *Epidemiology, 4,* 285-294.

Anderson, R. N., & DeTurk, P. B. (2002). *United States life tables 1999* (National Vital Statistics Report 50[6]). Hyattsville, MD: National Center for Health Statistics. Retrieved December 26, 2002, from www.cdc.gov/nchs/data/nvsr/nvsr50/ nvsr50_06.pdf

Anderson, S. (1997). Nephrology/fluid and electrolyte disorders. In C. K. Cassel, H. J. Cohen, E. B. Larson, D. E. Meier, N. M. Resnick, L. Z. Rubenstein, & L. B. Sorensen (Eds.), *Geriatric medicine* (3rd ed., pp. 571-583). New York: Springer-Verlag.

Antonovsky, A. (1993). The structure and properties of the sense of coherence scale. *Social Science & Medicine, 36,* 725-733.

Antonucci, T. C. (1985). Personal characteristics, social support, and social behavior. In R. H. Binstock & E. Shanas (Eds.), *Handbook of aging and the social sciences* (2nd ed., pp. 94-128). New York: Van Nostrand Reinhold.

Antonucci, T. C. (1990). Social supports and social relationships. In R. H. Binstock & L. K. George (Eds.), *Handbook of aging and the social sciences* (3rd ed., pp. 205-226). San Diego, CA: Academic Press.

Antonucci, T. C. (2001). Social relations: An examination of social networks, social support, and sense of control. In J. E. Birren & K. W. Schaie (Eds.), *Handbook of the psychology of aging* (5th ed., pp. 427-453). San Diego, CA: Academic Press.

Antonucci, T. C., & Akiyama, H. (1987). Social networks in adult life and a preliminary examination of the Convoy model. *Journals of Gerontology, 42,* 519-527.

Appels, A., Bar, F. W., Bar. J., Bruggeman, C., & de Baets, M. (2000). Inflammation, depressive symptomatology, and coronary artery disease. *Psychosomatic Medicine, 62,* 601-605.

Applegate, W. B. (1999). Hypertension. In W. R. Hazzard, J. P. Blass, W. H. Ettinger, Jr., J. B. Halter, & J. G. Ouslander (Eds.), *Principles of geriatric medicine and gerontology* (4th ed., pp. 713-720). New York: McGraw-Hill.

Argyle, M. (2000). Psychology and religion: An introduction. London: Routledge

Arnetz, B. B., Brenner, S. O., Levi, L., Hjelm, R., Petterson, I. L., Wasserman, J., et al. (1991). Neuroendocrine and immunologic effects of unemployment and job insecurity. *Psychotherapy and Psychosomatics, 55,* 76-80.

Arnold, J., & Sarks, S. (2001). Age-related macular degeneration. *Clinical Evidence, 6,* 476-486.

Asakawa, T., Koyano, W., Ando, T., & Shibata, H. (2000). Effects of functional decline on quality of life among the Japanese elderly. *International Journal of Aging and Human Development, 50,* 319-328.

Asanuma, M., Nishibayashi-Asanuma, S., Miyazaki, I., Kohno, M., & Ogawa, N. (2001). Neuroprotective effects of non-steroidal anti-inflammatory drugs by direct scavenging of nitric oxide radicals. *Journal of Neurochemistry, 76,* 1895-1904.

Aspinwall, R., & Andrew, D. (2000). Thymic involution in aging. *Journal of Clinical Immunology, 20,* 250-256.

Asthana, S., Baker, L. D., Craft, S., Stanczyk, F. Z., Veith, R. C., Raskind, M. A., & Plymate, S. R. (2001). High-dose estradiol improves cognition for women with AD: Results of a randomized study. *Neurology, 28,* 605-612.

Atchley, R. (2000). *Social forces and aging: An introduction to social gerontology* (9th ed.). Belmont, CA: Wadsworth.

Backman, D. L., Wolf, P. A., Linn, R. T., Knoefel, J. E., Cobb, J. L., Belanger, A. J., White, L. R., & D'Agostino, R. B. (1993). Incidence of dementia and probably Alzheimer's disease in a general population: The Framingham Study. *Neurology, 43,* 515-519.

Backstrom, L., & Kauffman, R. (1995). The porcine stress syndrome: A review of genetics, environmental factors, and animal well-being implications. *Agri-Practice, 16,* 24-30.

Baghurst, K. I., Baghurst, P. A., & Record, S. J. (1992). Public perceptions in the role of dietary and other environmental factors in cancer causation or prevention. *Journal of Epidemiology & Community Health, 46,* 120-126.

Baker, G. T., III, & Martin, G. R. (1997). Molecular and biological factors in aging: The origin, causes, and prevention of senescence. In C. K. Cassel, H. J. Cohen, E. B. Larson, D. E. Meier, N. M. Resnick, L. Z. Rubenstein, & L. B. Sorenson (Eds.), *Geriatric Medicine* (3rd ed., pp. 3-28). New York: Springer-Verlag.

Baltes, M. M. (1996). The many faces of dependency in old age. New York: Cambridge University Press.

Baltes, P. B. (1987). Theoretical propositions of life-span developmental psychology: On the dynamics between growth and decline. *Developmental Psychology, 24,* 611-626.

Baltes, P. B. (1997). On the incomplete architecture of human ontogeny: Selection, optimization, and compensation as foundation of developmental theory. *American Psychologist, 52,* 366-380.

Baltes, P. B. (2002, August). Successful aging: The role of wisdom and a strategy of life management. Invited address to the American Psychological Association, Chicago.

Baltes, P. B., Lindenberger, U., & Staudinger, U. M. (1998). Life-span theory in developmental psychology. In W. Damon (Series Ed.) & R. M. Lerner (Vol. Ed.), *Handbook of child psychology, Vol. 1. Theoretical models of human development* (5th ed., pp. 1029-1143). New York: Wiley.

Baltes, P. B., & Smith, J. (1990). Toward a psychology of wisdom and its ontogenesis. In R. J. Sternberg (Ed.), *Wisdom: Its nature, origins, and development* (pp. 317-332). Cambridge, UK: Cambridge University Press.

Baltes, P. B., & Staudinger, U. M. (2000). Wisdom: A metaheuristic (pragmatic) to orchestrate mind and virtue toward excellence. *American Psychologist, 55,* 122-136.

Bandura, A. (1997). *Self-efficacy: The exercise of control.* New York: Freeman.

Bandura, A. (2000). Health promotion from the perspective of social cognitive theory. In P. Norman, C. Abraham, & M. Conner (Eds.), *Understanding and changing health behaviour: From health beliefs to self-regulation* (pp. 299-339). Amsterdam: Harwood.

Barefoot, J. C., Beckham, J. C., Haney, T. L., Siegler, I. C., & Lipkus, I. M. (1993). Age differences in hostility among middle-aged and older adults. *Psychology and Aging, 8,* 3-9.

Barefoot, J. C., & Schroll, M. (1996). Symptoms of depression, acute myocardial infarction, and total mortality in a community sample, *Circulation, 93,* 1976-1980.

Barker, D. J. (1999). Fetal origins of cardiovascular disease. *Annals of Medicine, 31,* 3-6.

Barker, J. C. (2002). Neighbors, friends, and other nonkin caregivers of community-living dependent elders. *Journals of Gerontology, 57B,* S158-S167.

Barron, R. M., & Kenny, D. A. (1986). The mediator-moderator variable distinction in social psychological research: Conceptual, strategic, and statistical considerations. *Journal of Personality and Social Psychology, 51,* 1173-1182.

Baum, A., & Fleming, I. (1993). Implications of psychological research on stress and technological accidents. *American Psychologist, 48,* 665-672.

Baylink, D. J., Jennings, J. C., & Mohan, S. (1999). Calcium and bone homeostasis and changes with aging. In W. R. Hazzard, J. P. Blass, W. H. Ettinger, Jr., J. B. Halter, & J. G. Ouslander (Eds.), *Principles of geriatric medicine and gerontology* (4th ed., pp. 1041-1056). New York: McGraw-Hill.

Bear, E. (2000). Going home. *Caring, 20,* 40.

Beatty, J. (2001). *The human brain: Essentials of behavioral neuroscience.* Thousand Oaks, CA: Sage.

Beck, J. C., Freedman, M. L., & Warshaw, G. A. (1994, February 28). Geriatric assessment: Focus on function. *Patient Care,* pp. 1-14.

Beck, L. H. (1999). Aging changes in renal function. In W. R. Hazzard, J. P. Blass, W. H. Ettinger, Jr., J. B. Halter, & J. G. Ouslander (Eds.), *Principles of geriatric medicine and gerontology* (4th ed., pp. 767-776). New York: McGraw-Hill.

Belsky, J., Steinberg, L., & Draper, P. (1991). Childhood experience, interpersonal development, and reproductive strategy: An evolutionary theory of socialization. *Child Development, 62,* 647-670.

Bengtson, V. L., Rice, C. J., & Johnson, M. L. (1999). Are theories of aging important? Models and explanations in gerontology at the turn of the century. In V. L. Bengtson & K. W. Schaie (Eds.), Handbook of theories of aging (pp. 3-20). New York: Springer.

Bengtson, V. L., Rosenthal, C., & Burton, L. (1996). Paradoxes of families and aging. In R. H. Binstock & L. K. George (Eds.), Handbook of aging and the social sciences (4th ed., pp. 253-282). San Diego, CA: Academic Press.

Bengtson, V. L., & Schaie, K. W. (1999). Handbook of theories of aging. New York: Springer.

Ben-Shlomo, Y., Davey Smith, G., Shipley, M., & Marmot, M. G. (1993). Magnitude and causes of mortality differences between married and unmarried men. Journal of Epidemiology and Community Health, 47, 200-205.

Bentler, P. M. (1998). Causal modeling: New interfaces and new statistics. In J. G. Adair & D. Belanger (Eds.), Advances in psychological science, Vol. 1: Social, personal, and cultural aspects (pp. 353-370). Hove, UK: Taylor and Francis.

Bergman, L. R. (2001). A person approach in research on adolescence: Some methodological challenges. *Journal of Adolescent Research, 16*, 28-53.

Berkman, L. F., Leo-Summers, L., & Horwitz, R. I. (1992). Emotional support and survival after myocardial infarction: A prospective, population-based study of the elderly. *Annals of Internal Medicine, 117*, 1003-1009.

Berkman, L. F., & Syme, S. L. (1979). Social networks, host resistance, and mortality: A nine-year follow-up study of Alameda County residents. *American Journal of Epidemiology, 109*, 186-204.

Bickford, P. C., Gould, T., Briederick, L., Chadman, K., Pollock, A., Young, D., Shukitt-Hale, B., & Joseph, J. (2000). Antioxidant-rich diets improve cerebellar physiology and motor learning in aged rats. *Brain Research, 866,* 211-217.

Billings, D. W., Folkman, S., Acree, M., & Moskowitz, J. T. (2000). Coping and physical health during caregiving: The roles of positive and negative affect. *Journal of Personality and Social Psychology, 79,* 131-142.

Biondi, M., & Picardi, A. (1999). Psychological stress and neuroendocrine function in humans: The last two decades of research. *Psychotherapy and Psychosomatics, 68,* 114-150.

Birge, S. J. (1997). The role of estrogen in the treatment of Alzheimer's disease. *Neurology, 48*(Suppl. 7), S36-S41.

Birren, J. E. (1999). Theories of aging: A personal perspective. In V. L. Bengtson & K. W. Schaie (Eds.), *Handbook of theories of aging* (pp. 459-472). New York: Springer.

Birren, J. E., Butler, R. N., Greenhouse, S. W., & Yarrow, M. R. (Eds.). (1963). *Human aging: A biological and behavioral study.* Bethesda, MD: U.S. Department of Health, Education, and Welfare.

Birren, J. E., & Fisher, L. E. (1990). The elements of wisdom: Overview and integration. In R. J. Sternberg (Ed.), *Wisdom: Its nature, origins, and development* (pp. 317-332). Cambridge, UK: Cambridge University Press.

Björntorp, P. (1997). Stress and cardiovascular disease. *Acta Physiologica Scandinavica, 640,* 144-148.

Björntorp, P. (2001). Heart and soul: Stress and the metabolic syndrome. *Scandinavian Cardiovascular Journal, 35,* 172-177.

Black, D. M. (1995). Why elderly women should be screened and treated to prevent osteoporosis. *American Journal of Medicine, 98,* 67S-75S.

Black, P. S., & Garbutt, L. D. (2000). Stress, inflammation, and cardiovascular disease. *Journal of Psychosomatic Research, 52,* 1-23.

Blackwell, S., & Crawford, J. (1997). Lung cancer. In C. K. Cassel, H. J. Cohen, E. B. Larson, D. E. Meier, N. M. Resnick, L. Z. Rubenstein, & L. B. Sorensen (Eds.), *Geriatric medicine* (3rd ed., pp. 293-303). New York: Springer-Verlag.

Blair, C. E. (1999). Effect of self-care ADLs on self-esteem of intact nursing home residents. *Issues in Mental Health Nursing, 20,* 559-570.

Blazer, D. G., Hybels, C. F., & Pieper, C. F. (2001). The association of depression and mortality in elderly persons: A case for multiple, independent pathways. *Journals of Gerontology: Medical Sciences, 65A,* M505-M509.

Bohnen, N., Nicholson, N., Sulon, J., & Jones, J. (1991). Coping style, trait anxiety and cortisol reactivity during mental stress. *Journal of Psychosomatic Research, 35,* 141-147.

Bookwala, J., & Schulz, R. (2000). A comparison of primary stressors, secondary stressors, and depressive symptoms between elderly caregiving husbands and wives: The Caregiver Health Effects Study. *Psychological Aging, 15,* 607-616.

Bootsma-van der Wiel, A., Gussekloo, J., de Craen, A. J., van Exel, D., Knook, D. L., Lagaay, A. M., & Westendorp, R. G. (2001). Disability in the oldest old: "Can do" or "do do?" *Journal of the American Geriatrics Society, 49,* 909-914.

Bosma, H., Schrijvers, C., & Mackenbach, J. P. (1999). Socioeconomic inequalities in mortality and importance of perceived control: Cohort study. *British Medical Journal, 319,* 1469-1470.

Bossé, R., Aldwin, C. M., Levenson, M. R., Spiro, A., III, & Mroczek, D. K. (1993). Change in social support after retirement: Longitudinal findings from the Normative Aging Study. *Journals of Gerontology: Psychological Sciences, 48,* P210.

Bossé, R., Aldwin, C. M., Levenson, M. R., & Workman-Daniels, K. (1991). How stressful is retirement? Findings from the Normative Aging Study. *Journal of Gerontology, 46,* 9-14.

Bossé, R., Sparrow, D., Garvey, A. J., Costa, P. T., Weiss, S. T., & Rowe, J. W. (1980). Cigarette smoking, aging, and decline in pulmonary function: A longitudinal study. *Archives of Environmental Health, 35,* 247-252.

Bossé, R., & Spiro, A., III (1995). The Normative Aging Study. In G. Maddox (Ed.), *Encyclopedia of aging* (2nd ed., pp. 688-690). New York: Springer.

Bossert, S., Berger, M., Krieg, J. C., Schrieber, W., Junker, M., & von Zerssen, S. (1988). Cortisol response to various stressful situations: Relationship to personality variables and coping styles. *Neuropsychobiology, 20,* 36-42.

Botwinick, J. (1977). Intellectual abilities. In J. E. Birren & K. W. Schaie (Eds.) *Handbook of the psychology of aging* (1st ed., pp. 580-605). New York: Nostrand Reinhold.

Braan, A. W., Beekman, A. T. F., Deeg, D. J. H., Smit, J. H., & Tilburg, W. V. (1997). Religiosity as a protective or prognostic factor of depression in later life, results from a community survey in the Netherlands. *Acta Psychiatrica Scandinavica, 96,* 199-205.

Bradburn, N., & Caplovitz, D. (1965). *Reports on happiness: A pilot study of behavior related to mental health.* Chicago: Aldine.

Branch, L. G., & Jette, A. M. (1983). Elders' use of informal long-term care assistance. *The Gerontologist, 23,* 51-56.

Branch, L. G., Wetle, T. T., Scherr, P. A., Cook, N. R., Evans, D. A., Hebert, L. E., Masland, E. N., Keough, M. E., & Taylor, J. O. (1988). A prospective study of incident comprehensive medical home care use among the elderly. *American Journal of Public Health, 78,* 255-259.

Brandtstädter, J. (1999). The self in action and development: Cultural, biosocial, and ontogenetic bases of intentional self-development. In J. Brandtstädter & R. M. Lerner (Eds.), *Action and self-development: Theory and research through the life span* (pp. 37-66). Thousand Oaks, CA: Sage.

Brandtstädter, J., Wentura, D., & Rothermund, K. (1999). Intentional self-development through adulthood and later life: Tenacious pursuit and flexible adjustment of goals. In J. Brandtstädter & R. M. Lerner (Eds.), *Action and self-development: Theory and research through the life span* (pp. 373-400). Thousand Oaks, CA: Sage.

Bridges, R. A., & Spilka, B. (1992). Religion and the mental health of women. In J. F. Schmacher (Ed.), *Religion and mental health* (pp. 43-53). New York: Oxford University Press.

Briggs, A., Scott, E., & Steele, K. (1999). Impact of osteoarthritis and analgesic treatment on quality of life of an elderly population. *Annals of Pharmacotherapy, 33,* 1154-1159.

Britton, A., & McKee, M. (2000). The relation between alcohol and cardiovascular disease in Eastern Europe: Explaining the paradox. *Journal of Epidemiology & Community Health, 54,* 328-332.

Brown, G., & Harris, T. (1978). *Social origins of depression: A study of psychiatric disorder in women.* New York: Free Press.

Bruce, D. G., Devine, A., & Prince, R. L. (2002). Recreational physical activity levels in healthy older women: The importance of fear of falling. *Journal of the American Geriatrics Society, 50,* 84-89.

Bruce, M., Seeman, T., Merrill, S., & Blazer, D. (1994). The impact of depressive symptomatology on physical disability: MacArthur studies of successful aging. *American Journal of Public Health, 84,* 1796-1799.

Bruunsgaard, H., & Pedersen, B. K. (2000). Effects of exercise on the immune system in the elderly population. *Immunology and Cell Biology, 28,* 523-531.

Buddeberg, C., Sieber, M., Wolf, C., Laudolt-Ritter, C., Richter, D., & Steiner, R. (1996). Are coping strategies related to disease outcome in early breast cancer? *Journal of Psychosomatic Research, 40,* 255-264.

Bühler, C. (1968). The general structure of the human life cycle. In C. Bühler & F. Massarik (Eds.), *The course of human life: A study of goals in the humanistic perspective* (pp. 12-16). New York: Springer.

Burns, E. A., & Leventhal, E. A. (2000). Aging, immunity, and cancer. *Cancer Control, 7,* 513-522.

Butler, S. M., Ashford, J. W., & Snowdon, D. A. (1996). Age, education, and changes in the Mini-Mental State Exam scores of older women: Findings from the Nun Study. *Journal of the American Geriatrics Society, 44,* 675-681.

Byrne, B. M., Shavelson, R. J., & Muthen, B. (1989). Testing for the equivalence of factor covariance and mean structures: The issue of partial measurement invariance. *Psychological Bulletin, 105,* 456-466.

Byrne, D. (1964). Repression-sensitization as a dimension of personality. In B. A. Maher (Ed.), *Progress in experimental personality research* (Vol. 1, pp. 169-220). New York: Academic Press.

Cahalan, D., Cisin, I. H., & Crossley, H. M. (1969). *American drinking practices.* New Brunswick, NJ: Rutgers Center for Alcohol Studies.

Calabrese, E. J., & Baldwin, L. A. (2002). Hormesis: The dose-response revolution. *Annual Review of Pharmacology and Toxicology, 43,* 175-197.

Callahan, D. (1997). The value of achieving a peaceful death. In C. K Cassel, H. J. Cohen, E. B. Larson, D. E. Meier, N. M. Resnick, L. Z. Rubenstein, & L. B. Sorensen (Eds.), *Geriatric medicine* (3rd ed., pp. 1035-1042). New York: Springer-Verlag.

Camp, C. J., Foss, J. W., O'Hanlon, A. M., &, Stevens, A. B. (1996). Memory interventions for persons with dementia. *Applied Cognitive Psychology, 10,* 193-210.

Campbell, D. T., & Stanley, J. C. (1963). *Experimental and quasi-experimental designs for research.* Chicago: Rand McNally.

Campisise, J. (2000). Aging, chromatin, and food restriction: Connecting the dots. *Science, 289,* 2062-2063.

Campisise, J. (2001). Causes and consequences of cellular senescence. *The Gerontologist, 41,* 311.

Cannon, W. B. (1915). *Bodily changes in pain, hunger, fear, and rage: An account of recent researches into the function of emotional excitement.* New York: D. Appleton.

Cannon, W. B. (1929). *Bodily changes in pain, hunger, fear and rage: An account of recent researches into the function of emotional excitement* (2nd ed.). New York: Appleton-Century-Crofts.

Cantor, M. H. (1979). Neighbors and friends: An overlooked resource in the informal support system. *Research on Aging, 1,* 434-463.

Caplan, L. (1997). Cerebrovascular disease and stroke. In C. K. Cassel, H. J. Cohen, E. B. Larson, D. E. Meier, N. M. Resnick, L. Z. Rubenstein, & L. B. Sorensen (Eds.), *Geriatric medicine* (3rd ed., pp. 923-938). New York: Springer-Verlag.

Capodaglio, P., Facioli, M., Burroni, E., Giordano A., Ferri, A., & Scaglioni, G. (2002). Effectiveness of a home-based strengthening program for elderly males in Italy. *Aging, 14,* 28-34.

Carelock, J., & Clark, A. P. (2001). Heart failure: Pathophysiologic mechanisms. *American Journal of Nursing, 101,* 26-33.

Carney, R., Rich, M., Freedland, K., Saini, J., Tel Velder, A., & Simeone, I. (1988). Major depressive disorder predicts cardiac events in patients with coronary artery disease. *Psychosomatic Medicine, 59,* 627-633.

Carstensen, L. L. (1995). Evidence for a life-span theory of socioemotional selectivity. *Current Directions in Psychological Science, 4,* 151-156.

Case, R. B., Moss, A. J., Case, N., McDermott, M., & Eberly, S. (1992). Living alone after myocardial infarction: Impact on prognosis. *Journal of the American Medical Association, 267,* 515-519.

Caserta, M. S. (2002). Widows. In R. Kastenbaum (Ed.), *Macmillan encyclopedia of death and dying.* New York: Macmillan.

Caserta, M. S., Lund, D. A., & Rice, S. J. (1999). Pathfinders: A self-care and health education program for older widows and widowers. *The Gerontologist, 39,* 615-620.

Caspi, A., & Bem, D. J. (1990). Personality continuity and change across the life course. In L. A. Pervin (Ed.), *Handbook of personality: Theory and research* (pp. 549-575). New York: Guilford.

Centers for Disease Control. (2000a). *Obesity continues to climb in 1999 among American adults.* Retrieved from www.cdc.gov/nccophp/dnpa/press/archieves/ obesity

Centers for Disease Control. (2000b). *Surveillance reports: Reported tuberculosis in the United States, 2000.* Retrieved December 26, 2002, from www.cdc.gov/nchstp/ tb/surv/surv2000/

Chah, A. (1993). Our real home. In S. Bercholz & S. C. Kohn (Eds.), *Entering the stream* (pp. 87-94). Boston: Shambala.

Chaikelson, J. S., Arbuckle, T. Y., Lapidus, S., & Gold, D. P. (1994). Measurement of lifetime alcohol consumption. *Journal of Studies on Alcohol, 55,* 133-140.

Chandra, R. K. (1992). Effect of vitamin and trace-element supplementation on immune responses and infection in elderly subjects. *Lancet, 340,* 1124-1127.

Chang, M. Y., & Chait, A. (1999). Atherosclerosis and aging. In W. R. Hazzard, J. P. Blass, W. H. Ettinger, Jr., J. B. Halter, & J. G. Ouslander (Eds.), *Principles of geriatric medicine and gerontology* (4th ed., pp. 61-68). New York: McGraw-Hill.

Chappell, N. L. (1990). Aging and social care. In R. H. Binstock & L. K. George (Eds.), *Handbook of aging and the social sciences* (pp. 438-454). San Diego, CA: Academic Press.

Cheskin, L. J., & Schuster, M. M. (1994). Colonic disorders. In W. R. Hazzard, E. L. Bierman, J. P. Blass, W. H. Ettinger, Jr., & J. B. Halter (Eds.), *Principles of geriatric medicine and gerontology* (3rd ed., pp. 723-732). New York: McGraw-Hill.

Chiechi, L. M. (1999). Dietary phytoestrogens in the prevention of long-term postmenopausal diseases. *International Journal of Gynaecology and Obstetrics, 67,* 39-40.

Chiriboga, D. A. (1997). Crisis, challenge, and stability in the middle years. In M. E. Lachman & J. B. James (Eds.), *Multiple paths of midlife development* (pp. 293-343). Chicago: University of Chicago Press.

Christian, J. C., Reed, T., Carmelli, D., Page, W. F., Norton, J. A., & Breitner, J. C. S. (1995). Self-reported alcohol intake and cognition in aging twins. *Journal of Studies on Alcohol, 56,* 414-416.

Ciulla, T. A., Danis, R. P., & Harris, A. (1998). Age-related macular degeneration: A review of experimental treatments. *Survey of Ophthalmology, 43,* 134-46.

Clark, N. M., Janz, N. K., Dodge, J. A., Schork, M. A., Fingerlin, T. E., Wheeler, John, R. C., Liang, J., Keteyian, S. J., & Santinga, J. T. (2000). Changes in functional health status of older women with heart disease: Evaluation of a program based on self-regulation. *Journals of Gerontology: Social Science, 55B*, S117-126.

Clausen, J. A. (1995). *American lives: Looking back at the children of the Great Depression*. Berkeley: University of California Press.

Cockerham, W. C. (1998). *Medical sociology* (4th ed.). New Jersey: Prentice Hall.

Cohen, F., Kearney, K. A., Zegans, L. S., Kemeny, M. E., Neuhaus, J. M., & Stites, D. P. (1999). Differential immune system changes with acute and persistent stress for optimists vs. pessimists. *Brain, Behavior, and Immunity, 13*, 155-174.

Cohen, J., & Cohen, P. (1983). *Applied multiple regression/correlation analysis for the behavioral sciences* (2nd ed.). Hillsdale, NJ: Lawrence Erlbaum.

Cohen, S., & Herbert, T. (1996). Health psychology: Physiological factors and physical disease from the perspective of human psychoneuroimmunology. *Annual Review of Psychology, 47*, 113-142.

Cole, G. M., & Frautschy, S. A. (2001). Church baptizes Joseph and Perry: Eccentric views absolved. *Neurobiology of Aging, 22*, 147-150.

Collett, M. (1996, March/April). Stay close and do nothing. *Yoga Journal*, pp. 34-42.

Collins, L. M., & Sayer, A. G. (Eds.). (2001). *New methods for the analysis of change*. Washington, DC: American Psychological Association.

Collins, W. E., & Mertens, H. W. (1988). Age, alcohol, and simulated altitude: effects on performance and breathalyzer scores. *Aviation, Space, and Environmental Medicine, 59*, 1026.

Cooke, W., & Medley, D. (1954). Proposed hostility and pharisaic-virtue scales for the MMPI. *Journal of Applied Psychology, 38*, 414-418.

Cooney, L. M. (1999). Hip fractures. In W. R. Hazzard, J. P. Blass, W. H. Ettinger, Jr., J. B. Halter, & J. G. Ouslander (Eds.), *Principles of geriatric medicine and gerontology* (4th ed., pp. 1547-1551). New York: McGraw-Hill.

Cooper, C., & Fagher, E. (1992). Coping strategies and breast disorders/cancer. *Psychological Medicine, 22*, 447-455.

Cortes-Gallego, V., Villanueva, G. L., Sojo-Arnada, I., & Santa Cruz, F. J. (1996). Inverted skin changes induced by estrogen and estrogen/glucocorticoid on aging dermis. *Gynecological Endocrinology, 10*, 125-128.

Corti, M., Guralnik, J. M., Ferrucci, L., Ismirlian, G., Leveille, S. G., Pahor, M., Cohen, H. J., Pieper, C., & Havlik, R. J. (1999). Evidence for a black-white crossover in all-cause and coronary heart disease mortality in an older population: The North Carolina EPESE. *American Journal of Public Health, 89*, 308-314.

Costa, M. M., Reus, V. I., Wolkowitz, O. M., Manfredi, F., & Lieberman, M. (1999). Estrogen replacement therapy and cognitive decline in memory-impaired post-menopausal women. *Biological Psychiatry, 46*, 182-188.

Cotman, C., & Neeper, S. (1996). Activity-dependent plasticity and the aging brain. In E. L. Schneider & J. W. Rowe (Eds.), *Handbook of the biology of aging* (4th ed., pp. 284-299). San Diego, CA: Academic Press.

Covey, L. A., Glassman, A., & Dalack, G. W. (1991). Re: Depressed mood and the development of cancer. *American Journal of Epidemiology, 134,* 324-326.

Coward, R. T., McLaughlin, D. K., Duncan, R. P., & Bull, C. N. (1994). An overview of health and aging in rural America. In R. T. Coward, C. N. Bull, G. Chuckle, & J. M. Galliher (Eds.), *Health services for rural elders* (pp. 1-32). New York: Springer.

Cowie, C. C., Harris, M. I., Silverman, R. E., Johnson, E. W., & Rust, K. F. (1993). Effect of multiple risk factors on differences between blacks and whites in the prevalence of non-insulin-dependent diabetes mellitus in the United States. *American Journal of Epidemiology, 137,* 719-732.

Cox, D. R., & Oakes, D. (1984). *Analysis of survival data.* London: Chapman & Hall.

Coyne, J. C., & DeLongis, A. (1986). Going beyond social support: The role of social relationships in adaptation. *Journal of Consulting and Clinical Psychology, 54,* 454-460.

Coyne, J. C., Rohrbaugh, M. J., Shoham, V., Sonnega, J. S., Nicklas, J. M., & Cranford, J. A. (2001). Prognostic importance of marital quality for survival of congestive heart failure. *American Journal of Cardiology, 88,* 526-529.

Coyne, J. C., & Smith, D. A. F. (1994). Couples coping with a myocardial infarction: Contextual perspective on patient self-efficacy. *Journal of Family Psychology, 8,* 43-54.

Cramer, P. (1991). Anger and the use of defense mechanisms in college students. *Journal of Personality, 59,* 39-55.

Cramer, P. (2000). Defense mechanisms in psychology today: Further processes for adaptation. *American Psychologist, 55,* 637-646.

Creamer, P., & Hochberg, M. C. (1999). Management of osteoarthritis. In W. R. Hazzard, J. P. Blass, W. H. Ettinger, Jr., J. B. Halter, & J. G. Ouslander (Eds.), *Principles of geriatric medicine and gerontology* (4th ed., pp. 1155-1161). New York: McGraw-Hill.

Criqui, M. H. (2000). Epidemiology of cardiovascular disease. In L. Goldman & J. C. Bennett (Eds.), *Textbook of medicine* (21st ed., pp. 167-170). Philadelphia: W. B. Saunders.

Cristafalo, V. J., Tresini, M., Francis, M. K., & Volker, C. (1999). Biological theories of senescence. In V. L. Bengtson & K. W. Schaie (Eds.), *Handbook of theories of aging* (pp. 98-112). New York: Springer.

Cronbach, L. J., & Furby, L. (1970). How we should measure "change": Or should we? *Psychological Bulletin, 74,* 68-80.

Crystal, S., & Sambamoorth, U. (1998). Health care needs and services delivery for older people with HIV/AIDS. *Research on Aging, 20,* 739-759.

Cummings, E., & Henry, W. E. (1961). *Growing old: The process of disengagement.* New York: Basic Books.

Cutler, N. R., & Sramek, J. J. (2001). Review of the next generation of Alzheimer's disease therapeutics: Challenges for drug development. *Progress in Neuro-Psychopharmacology and Biological Psychiatry, 25,* 27-57.

Cutrona, C., Russell, D., & Rose, J. (1986). Social support and adaptation to stress by the elderly. *Psychology and Aging, 1,* 47-54.

Dakof, G. A., & Taylor, S. E. (1990). Victims' perceptions of social support: What is helpful from whom? *Journal of Personality and Social Personality, 58,* 80-89.

Dalaker, J. (2001). *Poverty in the United States: 2000* (Current population reports: Consumer income, pp. 60-214). Washington, DC: U.S. Department of Commerce. Retrieved December 19, 2002, from www.census.gov/prod/2001pubs/p60-214.pdf

Dalgard, O. S., & Lund Haheim, L. (1998). Psychosocial risk factors and mortality: A prospective study with special focus on social support, social participation, and locus of control in Norway. *Journal of Epidemiology & Community Health, 52,* 476-481.

Damush, T. M., & Damush, J. G., Jr. (1999). The effects of strength training on strength and health-related quality of life in older adult women. *The Gerontologist, 39,* 705-710.

Dannefer, D. (1984). The role of the social in lifespan developmental psychology: Past and future. Rejoinder to Baltes & Nesselroade. *American Sociological Review, 49,* 847-850.

Das, A., Jr., & Hammad, T. A. (2000). Efficacy of a combination of FCHG49 glucosamine hydrochloride, TRH122 low molecular weight sodium chondroitin sulfate, and manganese ascorbate in the management of knee osteoarthritis. *Osteoarthritis and Cartilage, 8,* 343-350.

Davidson, K., & MacGregor, M. (1998). A critical appraisal of self-report defense mechanism measures. *Journal of Personality, 66,* 965-992.

Deigner, H. P., Haberkorn, U., & Kinscherf, R. (2000). Apoptosis modulators in the therapy of neurodegenerative diseases. *Expert Opinions on Investigational Drugs, 9,* 747-64.

De Labry, L., Glynn, R., Levenson, M. R., Hermos, J., LoCastro, J., & Vokonas, P. (1992). Alcohol and mortality in an aging male population: Recovering the U-shaped function. *Journal of Studies on Alcohol, 53,* 25-32.

de Lange, T. (1998). Telomeres and senescence: Ending the debate [Comment]. *Science, 279,* 334-335.

DeLongis, A., Folkman, S., & Lazarus, R. S. (1988). The impact of daily stress on health and mood: Psychology and social resources as mediators. *Journal of Personality and Social Psychology, 54,* 486-495.

Denenberg, V. H. (1964). Critical periods, stimulus input, and emotional reactivity: A theory of infantile stimulation. *Psychological Review, 71,* 335-357.

Depue, R. A., & Monroe, S. M. (1986). Conceptualization and measurement of human disorder in life stress research: The problem of chronic disturbance. *Psychological Bulletin, 99,* 36-51.

Desmond, D. W., Moroney, J. T., Paik, M. C., Sano, M., Mohr, J. P., Aboumatar, S., Tseng, C.-L., Chan, S., Williams, J. B. W., Remien, R. H., Hauser, W. A., & Stern, Y. (2000). Frequency and clinical determinants of dementia after ischemic stroke. *Neurology, 54,* 1124-1131.

Desrosiers, J., Herbert, R., Bravo, G., Rochette, A. (1999). Age-related changes in upper extremity performance of elderly people: A longitudinal study. *Experimental Gerontology, 341,* 393-405.

DeVellis, B. M., & DeVellis, R. F. (2001). Self-efficacy and health. In A. Baum, T. A. Revenson, & J. E. Singer (Eds.), *Handbook of health psychology* (pp. 235-248). Mahwah, NJ: Lawrence Erlbaum.

Devine, E. C. (1992). Effects of psychoeducational care for adult surgical patients: A meta-analysis of 191 studies. *Patient Education and Counseling, 19,* 129-142.

Dharmarajan, T. S., & Norkus, E. P. (2001). Approaches to vitamin B12 deficiency: Early treatment may prevent devastating complications. *Postgraduate Medicine, 110,* 99-105.

Diamond, M. C. (1993). An optimistic view of the aging brain. *Generations, 17,* 31-33.

Diehr, P., Williamson, D. P., Burke, G. L., & Psaty, B. M. (2002). The aging and dying processes and the health of older adults. *Journal of Clinical Epidemiology, 55,* 269-278.

Dienstbier, R. A. (1989). Arousal and physiological toughness: Implications for mental and physical health. *Psychological Bulletin, 96,* 84-100.

Dienstbier, R. A. (1992). Mutual impacts of toughening on crises and losses. In L. Montada, S.-H. Filipp, & M. J. Lerner (Eds.), *Life crises and experience of loss in adulthood.* Hillsdale, NJ: Lawrence Erlbaum.

Diggle, P. J., Liang, K.-Y., & Zeger, S. C. (1994). *Analysis of longitudinal data.* New York: Oxford University Press.

DiGiovanna, A. G. (2000). *Human aging: Biological perspectives* (2nd ed.). Boston: McGraw-Hill.

DiPietro, L., Anda, R. F., Williamson, D. F., & Stunkard, A. J. (1992). Depressive symptoms and weight change in a national cohort of adults. *Internal Journal of Obesity, 16,* 745-753.

Dixon, R. A. (1999). Exploring cognition in interactive situations: The aging of N + 1 minds. In T. M. Hess & F. Blanchard-Fields (Eds.), *Social cognition and aging* (pp. 267-290). San Diego, CA: Academic Press.

Dixon, R. A., & Gould, O. N. (1996). Adults telling and retelling stories collaboratively. In P. B. Baltes & U. M. Staudinger (Eds.), *Interactive minds: Life-span perspectives on the social foundation of cognition* (pp. 221-241). New York: Cambridge University Press.

Doblhammer, G., & Kytir, J. (2001). Compression or expansion of morbidity? Trends in healthy-life expectancy in the elderly Austrian population between 1978 and 1998. *Social Science & Medicine, 52,* 385-391.

Dobratz, M. C. (2001). Patterns of advanced cancer pain in home hospice patients. *Cancer Nursing, 24,* 294-299.

Dorgan, J. F., Stanczyk, F. Z., Longcope, C., Stephenson, H. E., Jr., Chang, L., Miller, R., Franz, C., Falk, R. T., & Kahle, L. (1997). Relationship of serum dehydroepiandrosterone (DHEA), DHEA sulfate, and 5-androstene-3 beta, 17 beta-diol to risk of breast cancer in postmenopausal women. *Cancer Epidemiology, Biomarkers and Prevention, 6,* 177-181.

Doty, R. L. (2001). Olfaction. *Annual Review of Psychology, 52,* 423-452.

Dowd, J. J. (1975). Aging as exchange: A preface to theory. *Journal of Gerontology, 30,* 584-594.

DuBeau, C. E. (1997). Benign prostatic hyperplasia. In C. K. Cassel, H. J. Cohen, E. B. Larson, D. E. Meier, N. M. Resnick, L. Z. Rubenstein, & L. B. Sorensen (Eds.), *Geriatric medicine* (3rd ed., pp. 557-569). New York: Springer-Verlag.

Dubos, R. (1965). *Man adapting*. New Haven: Yale University Press.

Dufour, M. C., Archer, L., & Gordis, E. (1992). Alcohol and the elderly. *Clinics in Geriatric Medicine, 8,* 127-141.

Dugan, E., Cohen, S. J., Bland, D. R., Preisser, J. S., Davis, C. C., Suggs, P. K., & McGann, P. (2000). The association of depressive symptoms and urinary incontinence among older adults. *Journal of the American Geriatric Society*, 48, 414-416.

Duncan, P. W., & Studenski, S. (1994). Balance and gait measures. In M. P. Lawton & J. A. Teresi (Eds.), *Annual review of gerontology and geriatrics* (Vol. 14, pp. 76-92). New York: Springer.

DuPertuis, L. L., Aldwin, C. M., & Bossé, R. (2001). Does the source of support matter for different health outcomes? Findings from the Normative Aging Study. *Journal of Aging and Health, 13,* 494-510.

Durazo-Arvizu, R., Cooper, R., Luke, A., Prewitt, T., Liao, Y., & McGee, D. (1997). Relative weight and mortality in U.S. blacks and whites: Findings from representative national population samples. *Annals of Epidemiology, 7,* 383-395.

Durkheim, E. (1951). *Suicide, a study in sociology*. Glencoe, IL: Free Press.

Eaker, E. D., Pinsky, J., & Castelli, W. P. (1992). Myocardial infarction and coronary death among women: Psychosocial predictors from a 20-year follow-up of women in the Framingham Study. *American Journal of Epidemiology, 135,* 854-864.

Eccles, J. (1994). *How the self controls the brain*. Berlin, Germany: Springer-Verlag.

Ehrenstein, D. (1998). Immortality gene discovered. *Science, 279,* 177.

Ekerdt, D. J. (1986). The busy ethic: Moral continuity between work and retirement. *The Gerontologist, 26,* 239-244.

Elder, G. H., Jr. (1974). *Children of the Great Depression*. Chicago: University of Chicago Press.

Elder, G. H., Jr. (1998). The life course and human development. In W. Damon (Series Ed.) & R. M. Lerner (Vol. Ed.), *Handbook of Child Psychology, Vol. 1. Theoretical models of human development* (5th ed., pp. 939-991). New York: Wiley.

Elder, G. H., King, V., & Conger, R. D. (1996). Intergenerational continuity and change in rural lives: Historical and developmental insights. *International Journal of Behavioural Development, 19,* 443-455.

Elias, M. F., Elias, P. K., D'Agostino, R. B., & Wolf, P. A. (2000). Comparative effects of age and blood pressure on neuropsychological test performance: The Framingham Study. In S. B. Manuck, R. Jennings, B. S. Rabin, & A. Baum (Eds.), *Behavior, health, and aging* (pp. 199-244). Mahwah, NJ: Lawrence Erlbaum.

Eliott, S. J. (1995). Psychosocial stress, women, and heart health. *Social Science & Medicine, 40,* 105-115.

Ell, K., Nishimoto, R., Mediansky, L., Mantell, J., & Hamovitch, M. (1992). Social relationships, social support and survival among patients with cancer. *Journal of Psychosomatic Research, 36,* 531-541.

Ellison, C. G. (1991). Religious involvement and subjective well-being. *Journal of Health and Social Behavior, 32,* 80-99.

Emanuel, E. J., Fairclough, D., Clarridge, B. C., Blum, D., Bruera, E., Penley, W. C., Schnipper, L. E., & Mayer, R. J. (2000). Attitudes and practices of U.S. oncologists regarding euthanasia and physician-assisted suicide. *Annals of Internal Medicine, 133,* 527-532.

Endler, N. S., & Parker, J. D. (1990). Multidimensional assessment of coping: A critical evaluation. *Journal of Personality and Social Psychology, 58,* 844-854.

Engle, V. F., Fox-Hill, E., & Graney. J. (1998). The experience of living-dying in a nursing home: Self-reports of black and white older adults. *Journal of the American Geriatric Society, 46,* 1091-1096.

English, W. P., Cleveland, K. E., & Barber, W. H. (2002). There is no difference in survival between African-American and white women with breast cancer. *American Surgery, 8,* 594-597.

Ennezat, P. V, Malendowicz, S. L., Testa, M., Colombo, P. C., Cohen-Solal, A., Evans, T., & LeJemtel, T. H. (2001). Physical training in patients with chronic heart failure enhances the expression of genes encoding antioxidative enzymes. *Journal of the American College of Cardiology, 38,* 194-198.

Epstein, M., Moreno, R., & Bacchetti, P. (1997). The underreporting of deaths of American Indian children in California, 1979 through 1993. *American Journal of Public Health, 87,* 1363-1366.

Epstein, S. (1991). The self-concept, the traumatic neurosis, and the structure of personality. In D. Ozer, J. H. Healy, & A. J. Stewart (Eds.), *Perspectives in personality* (Vol. 3, pp. 63-98). Bristol, PA: Jessica Kingsley.

Erikson, E. H. (1950). *Childhood and society*. New York: Norton.

Erikson, E., Erikson, J., & Kivnick, H. (1986). *Vital involvement in old age*. New York: Norton.

Ernest, J. E. (1997). Changes and diseases of the aging eye. In C. K. Cassel, H. J. Cohen, E. B. Larsen, D. E. Meier, N. M. Resnick, L. Z. Rubenstein, & L. B. Sorensen (Eds.), *Geriatric medicine* (3rd ed., pp. 683-697). New York: Springer-Verlag.

Evans, R. I. (2001). Social influences in etiology and prevention of smoking and other health threatening behaviors in children and adolescents. In A. Baum, T. A. Revenson, & J. E. Singer (Eds.), *Handbook of health psychology* (pp. 459-468). Mahwah, NJ: Lawrence Erlbaum.

Evans, W. J. (2000). Vitamin E, vitamin C, and exercise. *American Journal of Clinical Nutrition, 72*(Suppl. 2), 647S-652S.

Farahmand, B. Y., Persson, P. G., Michaelsson, K., Baron, J. A., Parker, M. G., Ljunghall, S., & Swedish hip fracture group. (2000). Socioeconomic status, marital status and hip fracture risk: A population-based case-control study. *Osteoporosis International, 11,* 803-808.

Fawzy, F. I., Cousins, N., Fawzy, N. W., Kemeny, M., & Morton, D. I. (1990). A structured psychiatric intervention for cancer patients. I. Changes over time in methods of coping and affective disturbance. *Archives of General Psychiatry, 47,* 720-725.

Fawzy, F. I., & Fawzy, N. W. (1994). Psychoeducational interventions and health outcomes. In R. Glaser & J. K. Kiecolt-Glaser (Eds.), *Handbook of human stress and immunity* (pp. 365-402). San Diego, CA: Academic Press.

Fawzy, F. I., Fawzy, N. W., Hyun, C., Elashoff, R., Guthrie, D., Fahey, J. L., & Morton, D. L. (1993). Malignant melanoma: Effects on early structured psychiatric intervention, coping, and affective state on recurrence and survival six years later. *Archives of General Psychiatry, 50,* 681-689.

Fawzy, F. I., Kemeny, M., Fawzy, N. W., Elashoff, R., Morton, D., Cousins, N., & Fahey, J. L. (1990). A structured psychiatric intervention for cancer patients. II. Changes over time in immunological measures. *Archives of General Psychiatry, 47,* 720-725.

Felton, B. J., & Revenson, T. A. (1987). Age differences in coping with chronic illness. *Psychology and Aging, 2,* 164-170.

Ferrell, B. A. (1999). Pain management. In W. R. Hazzard, J. P. Blass, W. H. Ettinger, Jr., J. B. Halter, & J. G. Ouslander (Eds.), *Principles of geriatric medicine and gerontology* (4th ed., pp. 413-434). New York: McGraw-Hill.

Ferrini, A. F., & Ferrini, R. L. (2000). *Health in the later years* (3rd ed.). Boston: McGraw-Hill.

Field, T. M. (1998). Massage therapy effects. *American Psychologist, 53,* 1270-1281.

Fields, D., & Gueldner, S. H. (2001). The oldest-old: How do they differ from the old-old? *Journal of Gerontological Nursing, 27,* 20-27.

Fields, J., & Casper, L. M. (2001). *America's families and living arrangements* (Economics and Statistics Administration, P20-537). Washington DC: U.S. Department of Commerce.

Fillmore, K. M. (1988). *Alcohol use across the life course: A critical review of 70 years of Int. longitudinal research.* Toronto: Addiction Research Foundation.

Fillmore, K. M., Harka, E., Johnstone, B. M., Leino, E. V., Motoyoshi, M., & Temple, M. T. (1991). The collaborative alcohol-related longitudinal project. *British Journal of Addiction, 86,* 1221-1268.

Finch, C. E., & Seeman, T. E. (1999). Stress theories of aging. In V. L. Bengtson & K. W. Schaie (Eds.), *Handbook of theories of aging* (pp. 81-97). New York: Springer.

Fishburn, M. J., & de Lateur, B. J. (1996). Rehabilitation. In D. B. Reuben, T. T. Yoshikawa, & R. W. Besdine (Eds.), *Geriatrics review syllabus* (3rd ed., pp. 93-103). Dubuque, IA: Kendall/Hunt.

Fleshner, N. E. (2002). Vitamin E and prostate cancer. *Urological Clinics of North America, 29,* 107-113.

Folkman, S., & Lazarus, R. S. (1980). An analysis of coping in a middle-aged community sample. *Journal of Health and Social Behavior, 21,* 219-239.

Folkman, S., Lazarus, R. S., Pimley, S., & Novacek, J. (1987). Age differences in stress and coping processes. *Psychology and Aging, 2,* 171-184.

Ford, D. E., Mead, L. A., Chang, P. P., Cooper-Patrick, L., Wang, N.-Y., & Klag, M. J. (1998). Depression is a risk factor for coronary artery disease in men. *Archives of Internal Medicine, 158,* 1422-1426.

Ford, D. H., & Lerner, R. M. (1992). *Developmental systems theory: An integrative approach*. Newbury Park, CA: Sage.

Forman, D. E., & Farquhar, W. (2000). Cardiac rehabilitation and secondary prevention programs for elderly cardiac patients. *Clinics in Geriatric Medicine, 16,* 619-629.

Forman, W. B. (1997). Colon cancer and other gastrointestinal malignancies. In C. K. Cassel, H. J. Cohen, E. B. Larson, D. E. Meier, N. M. Resnick, L. Z. Rubenstein, & L. B. Sorensen (Eds.), *Geriatric medicine* (3rd ed., pp. 281-291). New York: Springer-Verlag.

Forster, L. E., Pollow, R., & Stoller, E. P. (1993). Alcohol use and potential risk for alcohol-related adverse drug reactions among community-based elderly. *Journal of Community Health, 18,* 225-239.

Forthofer, M. S., Janz, N. K., Dodge, J. A., & Clark, N. M. (2001). Gender differences in the associations of self-esteem, stress and social support with functional health status among older adults with heart disease. *Journal of Women Aging, 13,* 19-37.

Forwood, M. R., & Larsen, J. A. (2000). Exercise recommendations for osteoporosis. A position statement of the Australian and New Zealand bone and mineral society. *Australian Family Physician, 29,* 761-764.

Fox, B. H. (1983). Current theory of psychogenic effects on cancer incidence and prognosis. *Journal of Psychosocial Oncology, 1,* 17-31.

Franceschi, C., Monti, D., Sansoni, P., & Cossarizza, A. (1995). The immunology of exceptional individuals: The lesson of centenarians. *Immunology Today, 16,* 12-16.

Frankenhaeuser, M. (1978). Coping with job stress: A psychobiological approach. Stockholm, Sweden: University of Stockholm.

Fraser, A. G. (1997). Pharmacokinetic interactions between alcohol and other drugs. *Clinical Pharmacokinetics, 33,* 79-90.

Frasure-Smith, N., Lesperance, F., Juneau, M., Talajic, M., & Bourassa, M. G. (1999). Gender, depression, and one-year prognosis after myocardial infarction. *Psychosomatic Medicine, 61,* 26-37.

Frasure-Smith, N., Lesperance, F., & Talajic, M. (1993). Depression following myocardial infarction. *Journal of the American Medical Association, 270,* 1819-1825.

Frasure-Smith, N., Lesperance, F., & Talajic, M. (1995). Depression and 18-month prognosis after myocardial infarction. *Circulation, 91,* 999-1005.

Frese, M. (1992). A plea for realistic pessimism: On objective reality, coping with stress, and psychological dysfunction. In L. Montada, S.-H. Filipp, & M. J. Lerner (Eds.), *Life crises and experiences of loss in adulthood* (pp. 81-94). Hillsdale, NJ: Lawrence Erlbaum.

Freud, A. (1966). *The ego and the mechanisms of defense* (Rev. ed.). New York: International Universities Press.

Friedberg, E. G. (2000). Biological responses to DNA damage: A perspective in the new millennium. *Cold Spring Harbor Symposium on Quantitative Biology, 65,* 593-602.

Friedman, H. S. (1991). *The self-healing personality: Why some people achieve health and others succumb to illness.* New York: Henry Holt.

Friedman, H. S., & Booth-Kewley, S. (1987). The "disease-prone personality": A meta-analytic view of the construct. *American Psychologist, 42,* 539-555.

Friedman, M., & Rosenman, R. H. (1974). *Type A behavior and your heart.* New York: Knopf.

Fries, B. E., Ribbe, M., & InterRAI Group. (1999). Cross-national aspects of geriatrics: Comparisons of nursing home patients. In W. R. Hazzard, J. P. Blass, W. H. Ettinger, Jr., J. B. Halter, & J. G. Ouslander (Eds.), *Principles of geriatric medicine and gerontology* (4th ed., pp. 227-238). New York: McGraw-Hill.

Fries, J. F. (1989). The compression of morbidity. *Milbank Memorial Foundation Quarterly/Health and Society, 67,* 208-232.

Fries, J. F., & Crapo, L. M. (1981). *Vitality and aging: Implications for a rectangular curve.* San Francisco: W. H. Freeman.

Funch, D. P., & Marshall, J. (1983). The role of stress, social support and age in survival from breast cancer. *Journal of Psychosomatic Research, 27,* 77-83.

Furner, S. E., Brody, J. A., & Jankowski, L. M. (1997). Epidemiology and aging. In C. K. Cassel, H. J. Cohen, E. B. Larson, D. E. Meier, N. M. Resnick, L. Z. Rubenstein, & L. B. Sorensen (Eds.), *Geriatric medicine* (3rd ed., pp. 37-43). New York: Springer-Verlag.

Galanis, D. J., Joseph, C., Masaki, K. H., Petrovich, H., Ross, G. W., & White, L. (2000). A longitudinal study of drinking and cognitive performance in elderly Japanese American men: The Honolulu–Asian Aging Study. *American Journal of Public Health, 90,* 1254-1259.

Galvin, K., Webb, C., & Hillier, V. (2001). Assessing the impact of a nurse-led health education intervention for people with peripheral vascular disease who smoke: The use of physiological markers, nicotine dependence and withdrawal. *International Journal of Nursing Studies, 38,* 91-105.

Gardner, A. W. (1999). Peripheral vascular disease. In W. R. Hazzard, J. P. Blass, W. H. Ettinger, Jr., J. B. Halter, & J. G. Ouslander (Eds.), *Principles of geriatric medicine and gerontology* (4th ed., pp. 705-712). New York: McGraw-Hill.

Garfinkel, M., & Schumacher, H. R. (2000). Yoga. *Rheumatic Diseases Clinics of North America, 26,* 125-132.

Garssen, B., & Goodkin, K. (1999). On the role of immunological factors as mediators between psychosocial factors and cancer progression. *Psychiatry Research, 85,* 51-61.

Gatchel, R. J., & Baum, A. (1983). *An introduction to health psychology.* Reading, MA: Addison Wesley.

Gaziano, J. M., Gaziano, T. A., Glynn, R. J., Sesso, H. D., Ajani, U. A., Stampfer, M. J., Manson, J. E., Hennekens, C. H., & Buring, J. E. (2000). Light-to-moderate alcohol consumption and mortality in the Physicians' Health Study enrollment cohort. *Journal of the American College of Cardiology, 35,* 96-105.

Genuth, S. M. (1993). The endocrine system. In R. M. Berne & M. N. Levy (Eds.), *Physiology* (3rd ed., pp. 813-1024). St. Louis, MO: Mosby Year Book.

George, L. K. (1996). Social factors and illness. In R. H. Binstock & L. K. George (Eds.), *Handbook of aging and the social sciences* (pp. 229-252). San Diego, CA: Academic Press.

Gevirtz, R. (2000). The physiology of stress. In D. T. Kenny, J. G. Carson, F. J. McGuigan, & J. L. Sheppard (Eds.), *Stress and health: Research and clinical applications* (pp. 53-72). Amsterdam: Harwood.

Gilchrest, B. A. (1999). Aging of the skin. In W. R. Hazzard, J. P. Blass, W. H. Ettinger, Jr., J. B. Halter, & J. G. Ouslander (Eds.), *Principles of geriatric medicine and gerontology* (4th ed., pp. 573-590). New York: McGraw-Hill.

Gilmer, D. F., & Aldwin, C. M. (2002). Trajectories of health and social support in frail young-old and old-old patients after hospitalization. *Journal of the Aging Family System, 1,* 4-20.

Gilmer, D. F., Aldwin, C. M., & Ober, B. A. (1998). The greying of rural America. *Youth Development Focus: A Monograph of the 4-H Center for Youth Development, 4.* Davis: University of California, Davis.

Glascock, A. P. (1997). When is killing acceptable? The moral dilemmas surrounding assisted suicide in America and other societies. In J. Sokolovsky (Ed.), *The cultural context of aging* (pp. 43-56). New York: Bergin & Garvey.

Glass, D. C., & Singer, J. E. (1972). *Urban stress: Experiments on noise and social stressors*. New York: Academic Press.

Glueck, S., & Glueck, E. (1950). *Delinquents and nondelinquents in perspective.* Cambridge, MA: Harvard University Press.

Glynn, R. J., Bouchard, G. R., LoCastro, J. S., & Laird, N. M. (1985). Aging and generational effects on drinking behaviors in men: Results from the Normative Aging Study. *American Journal of Public Health, 75,* 1413-1419.

Go, C. G., Brustrom, J. E., Lynch, M. F., & Aldwin, C. M. (1995). Ethnic trends in survival curves and mortality. *The Gerontologist, 35,* 318-326.

Gold, C. H., Malmberg, B., McClearn, G. E., Pedersen, N. L., & Berg, S. (2002). Gender and health: A study of older unlike-sex twins. *Journals of Gerontology: Psychological and Social Sciences, 57B,* S168-S176.

Goldberger, A. L. (1996). Non-linear dynamics for clinicians: Chaos theory, fractals, and complexity at the bedside. *Lancet, 347,* 1312-1314.

Goldfarb, M. T., Ellis, C. N., & Voorhees, J. J. (1997). Dermatologic disease and problems. In C. K. Cassel, H. J. Cohen, E. B. Larson, D. E. Meier, N. M. Resnick, L. Z. Rubenstein, & L. B. Sorensen (Eds.), *Geriatric medicine* (3rd ed., pp. 667-681). New York: Springer-Verlag.

Goodkin, K., Antoni, M., & Bloom, P. (1986). Stress and hopelessness in the promotion of cervical intraepithelial neoplasm to invasive squamous cell carcinoma of the cervix. *Journal of Psychosomatic Research, 30,* 67-76.

Goodkin, K., Fuchs, I., Feaster, D., Leeka, J., & Rishel, L. (1992). Life stressors and coping style are associated with immune measures in HIV-1 infection: A preliminary report. *International Journal of Psychiatry in Medicine, 22,* 155-172.

Goodwin, J. S., Hunt, W. C., Key, C. R., & Samet, J. M. (1987). The effect of marital status on stage, treatment, and survival of cancer patients. *Journal of the American Medical Association, 258,* 3125-3130.

Gorman, J. M., & Sloan, R. P. (2000). Heart rate variability in depression and anxiety disorders. *American Heart Journal, 140*(Suppl. 4), 77-83.

Goto, T., Klyce, S. D., Zheng, X., Maedam, N., Kuroda, T., & Ide, C. (2001). Gender- and age-related differences in corneal topography. *Cornea, 20,* 270-276.

Gottschalk, G. (1995). Housing and supportive services for frail elders in Denmark. In J. Pynoos & P. S. Liebig (Eds.), *Housing frail elders: International policies, perspectives, and prospects* (pp. 19-44). Baltimore: Johns Hopkins University Press.

Green, L. W., & Ottonson, J. M. (1994). *Community health* (7th ed.). St. Louis, MO: Mosby.

Greenwood, D. C., Muir, K. R., Packham, C. J., & Madeley, R. J. (1996). Coronary heart disease: A review of the role of psychosocial stress and social support. *Journal of Public Health Medicine, 18,* 221-31.

Greer, S. (1991). Psychological response to cancer and survival. *Psychological Medicine, 21,* 43-49.

Greer, S., & Morris, T. (1975). Psychological attributes of women who develop breast cancer. *Journal of Psychosomatic Research, 19,* 147-153.

Gregerman, R. I., & Katz, M. S. (1994). Thyroid diseases. In W. R. Hazzard, E. L. Bierman, J. P. Blass, W. H Ettinger, Jr., & J. B. Halter (Eds.), *Geriatric medicine and gerontology* (3rd ed., pp. 807-824). New York: McGraw-Hill.

Grisso, J. A., & Kaplan, F. (1997). Hip fractures. In C. K. Cassel, H. J. Cohen, E. B. Larson, D. E. Meier, N. M. Resnick, L. Z. Rubenstein, & L. B. Sorensen (Eds.), *Geriatric medicine* (3rd ed., pp. 1321-1327). New York: Springer-Verlag.

Gronbaek, M., Becker, U., Johansen, D., Gottschau, A., Schnohr, P., Hein, H. O., Jensen, G., & Sorensen, T. I. (2000). Type of alcohol consumed and mortality from all causes, coronary heart disease, and cancer. *Annals of Internal Medicine, 133,* 411-419.

Gruenewald, D. A., & Matsumoto, A. M. (1999). Aging of the endocrine system. In W. R. Hazzard, J. P. Blass, W. H. Ettinger, Jr., J. B. Halter, & J. G. Ouslander (Eds.), *Principles of geriatric medicine and gerontology* (4th ed., pp. 949-965). New York: McGraw-Hill.

Gueldner, S. H., Poon, L. W., La Via, M., Virella, G., Michel, Y., Bramlett, M. H., Noble, C.A., & Paulling, E. (1997). Long-term exercise patterns and immune function in healthy older women. A report of preliminary findings. *Mechanisms of Aging and Development, 93,* 215-222.

Guralnik, J. M., Branch, L. G., Cummings, S. R., & Curb, J. D. (1989). Physical performance measures in aging research. *Journals of Gerontology: Medical Sciences, 44,* M141-M146.

Guralnik, J. M., & Simonsick, E. M. (1993). Physical disability in older Americans [Special issue]. *Journals of Gerontology: Social Sciences, 48,* S3-S10.

Gutmann, D. L. (1974). Alternatives to disengagement: The old men of the Highland Druze. In R. A. LeVine (Ed.), *Culture and personality: Contemporary readings* (pp. 232-245). Chicago: Aldine.

Guyton, A. C., & Hall, J. E. (1996). *Textbook of medical physiology* (9th ed.). Philadelphia: W. B. Saunders.

Hager, K., & Nennmann, U. (1997). Rehabilitation of the elderly: Influence of age, sex, main diagnosis, and activities of daily living (ADL) on the elderly patients' return to their previous living conditions. *Archives of Gerontology and Geriatrics, 25,* 131-139.

Hahn, R. A., & Eberhardt, S. (1994). Life expectancy in four U.S. racial/ethnic populations: 1990. *Epidemiology, 6,* 350-355.

Haier, R. J., Siegel, A. V., Nuechterlein, K. H., Hazlett, E., Wu, J. C., Pack, J., Browning, H. L., & Buchsbaum, M. (1988). Cortical glucose metabolic rate correlates of abstract reasoning and attention studied with positron emission tomography. *Intelligence, 12,* 199-217.

Hall, H. I., Miller, D. R., Rogers, J. D., & Bewerse, B. (1999). Update on the incidence and mortality from melanoma in the United States. *Journal of the American Academy of Dermatology, 40,* 35-42.

Hall, K. E., & Wiley, J. W. (1999). Age-associated changes in gastrointestinal function. In W. R. Hazzard, J. P. Blass, W. H. Ettinger, Jr., J. B. Halter, & J. G. Ouslander (Eds.), *Principles of geriatric medicine and gerontology* (4th ed., pp. 835-842). New York: McGraw-Hill.

Halter, J. B. (1999). Diabetes mellitus. In W. R. Hazzard, J. P. Blass, W. H. Ettinger, Jr., J. B. Halter, & J. G. Ouslander (Eds.), *Principles of geriatric medicine and gerontology* (4th ed., pp. 991-1011). New York: McGraw-Hill.

Hamarat, E., Thompson, D., Zabrucky, K. M., Steele, D., Matheny, K. B., & Aysan, F. (2001). Perceived stress and coping resources availability as predictors of life satisfaction in young, middle-aged, and older adults. *Experimental Aging Research, 27,* 181-196.

Hamerman, D. (1994). Aging and the musculoskeletal system. In W. R. Hazzard, E. L. Bierman, J. P. Blass, W. H. Ettinger, Jr., & J. B. Halter (Eds.), *Principles of geriatric medicine and gerontology* (3rd ed., pp. 935-945). New York: McGraw-Hill.

Hamid, P. N. (1990). Optimism and the reporting of flu episodes. *Social Behavior & Personality, 18,* 224-234.

Haraguchi, T., Ishizu, H., Kawai, K., Tanabe, Y., Uehira, K., Takehisa, Y., Terada, S., Tsuchiya, K., Ikeda, K., & Kuroda, S. (2001). Diffuse neurofibrillary tangles with calcification (a form of dementia): X-ray spectrometric evidence of lead accumulation in calcified regions. *Clinical Neuroscience and Neuropathology, 12,* 1257-1260.

Harvard Women's Health Watch. (2002). Has lower-dose HRT come of age? *Harvard Medical School: Harvard Health Publications.* Retrieved from medline/women/W0602a.html

Hassani, S., & Hershman, J. M. (1999). Thyroid diseases. In W. R. Hazzard, J. P. Blass, W. H. Ettinger, Jr., J. B. Halter, & J. G. Ouslander (Eds.), *Principles of geriatric medicine and gerontology* (4th ed., pp. 973-989). New York: McGraw-Hill.

Havighurst, R. J. (1961). Successful aging. *The Gerontologist, 1,* 8-13.

Havighurst, R. J., Neugarten, B. L., & Tobin, S. S. (1968). Disengagement and patterns of aging. In B. L. Neugarten (Ed.), *Middle age and aging: A reader in social psychology* (pp. 17-177). Chicago: University of Chicago Press.

Hayflick, L. (1977). The cellular basis for biological aging. In C. E. Finch & L. Hayflick (Eds.), *Handbook of the biology of aging* (pp. 159-186). New York: Van Nostrand Reinhold.

Hayflick, L. (1996). *How and why we age*. New York: Ballantine.

Hayward, C. (1995). Psychiatric illness and cardiovascular disease risk. *Epidemiological Review, 17,* 129-138.

Hazzard, W. R. (1994). The sex differential in longevity. In W. R. Hazzard, E. L. Bierman, J. P. Blass, W. H. Ettinger, Jr., & J. B. Halter (Eds.), *Principles of geriatric medicine and gerontology* (4th ed., pp. 37-47). New York: McGraw-Hill.

Helgeson, V. S., Cohen, S., Schulz, R., & Yasko, J. (2000). Group support interventions for women with breast cancer: Who benefits from what? *Health Psychology, 19,* 107-114.

Helgeson, V. S., & Fritz, H. L. (1999). Cognitive adaptation as a predictor of new coronary events after percutaneous transluminal coronary angioplasty. *Psychosomatic Medicine, 61,* 488-495.

Henderson, V. W. (1997). The epidemiology of estrogen replacement therapy and Alzheimer's disease. *Neurology, 48*(Suppl. 7), S27-S35.

Herness, M. S., & Gilbertson, T. A. (1999). Cellular mechanisms of taste transduction. *Annual Review of Physiology, 61,* 873-900.

Hesse, L., & Kroll, P. (1999). Successful treatment of acute subretinal hemorrhage in age-related macular degeneration by combined intravitreal injection of recombinant tissue plasminogen activator and gas. *Graefes Archives for Clinical & Experimental Ophthalmology, 237,* 273-277.

Hetzel, L., & Smith, A. (2001). *The 65 years and over population: 2000* (Department of Commerce Publication No. C2KBR/-1-10). Washington, DC: Government Printing Office.

Higginson, I. J., Jarman, B., Astin, P., & Dolan, S. (1999). Do social factors affect where patients die: An analysis of 10 years of cancer deaths in England. *Journal of Public Health Medicine, 21,* 22-28.

Hilakivi-Clark, L., Wright, A., and Lippman, M. E. (1993). DMBA-induced mammary tumor growths in rats exhibiting increased or decreased ability to cope with stress due to early postnatal handling or antidepressant treatment. *Physiology and Behavior, 54,* 229-236.

Hills, P., & Argyle, M. (1998). Musical and religious experiences and their relationship to happiness. *Personality and Individual Differences, 25,* 91-102.

Hippisley-Cox, J., Fielding, K., & Pringle, M. (1998). Depression as a risk factor for ischaemic heart disease in men: Population based case-control study. *British Medical Journal, 316,* 1714-1719.

Hixson, K. A., Gruchow, H. W., & Morgan, D. W. (1998). The relation between religiosity, selected health behaviors and blood pressure among adult females. *Preventive Medicine: An International Journal Devoted to Practice and Theory, 27,* 545-552.

Hobbs, B., & Damon, B. L. (1996). *65+ in the United States* (Current population reports: Special studies, P23-190). Washington, DC: Government Printing Office.

Hobfoll, S. E. (1989). Conservation of resources: A new attempt at conceptualizing stress. *American Psychologist, 44,* 513-524.

Hogan, T. M. (1997). Geriatric emergencies. In C. K. Cassel, H. J. Cohen, E. B. Larson, D. E. Meier, N. M. Resnick, L. Z. Rubenstein, & L. B. Sorensen (Eds.), *Geriatric medicine* (3rd ed., pp. 131-151). New York: Springer-Verlag.

Holliday, M., & Chandler, J. (1986). *Wisdom: Explorations in adult competence*. New York: Karger.

Hollister, L. E. (1990). Interactions between alcohol and benzodiazepines. In M. Galanter (Ed.), *Recent developments in alcoholism, Vol. 8. Combined alcohol and other drug dependence* (pp. 233-239). New York: Plenum.

Holmes, D., & Rahe, R. (1967). The Social Readjustment Rating Scale. *Journal of Psychosomatic Research, 11,* 213-218.

Holtzman, D. (1995). Hormesis: Fact or fiction? *Journal of Nuclear Medicine, 36,* 13-16.

Hood, R. W., Jr., Spilka, B., Hunsberger, B., & Gorsuch, R. (1996). *The psychology of religion: An empirical approach.* New York: Guilford.

Hopkins, M. E. (2000). Mission: Possible. *NurseWeek, 13,* 8-9.

Hopp, F. P. (1999). Patterns and predictors of formal and informal care among elderly persons living in board and care homes. *The Gerontologist, 39,* 167-176.

Horie, K., Miyata, T., Yasuda, T., Takeda, A., Yasuda, Y., Maeda, K., Sobue, G., & Kurokawa, K. (1997). Immunohistochemical localization of advanced glycation end products, pentosidine, and carboxymethyllysine in lipofuscin pigments of Alzheimer's disease and aged neurons. *Biochemical and Biophysical Research Communications, 236,* 327-332.

House, J. S., Robbins, C., & Metzner, H. L. (1982). The association of social relationships and activities with mortality. *American Journal of Epidemiology, 116,* 123-140.

Hoyer, W. J., Rybash, J. M., & Roodin, P.A. (1999). *Adult development and aging* (4th ed.). Boston: McGraw-Hill.

Hubert, H. B., Bloch, D. A., Oehlert, J. W., & Fries, J. F. (2002). Lifestyle habits and compression of morbidity. *Journals of Gerontology: Biological and Medical Sciences, 57,* M347-M351.

Indian Health Service. (1992). *Trends in Indian Health 1992.* Rockville, MD: Indian Health Service.

Irion, J. C., & Blanchard-Fields, F. (1987). A cross-sectional comparison of adaptive coping in adulthood. *Journal of Gerontology, 42,* 502-504.

Isaacowitz, D. M., & Seligman, M. E. P. (2002). Is pessimism a risk factor for depressive mood among community dwelling older adults? *Behavioral Research & Therapy, 39,* 255-72.

Isola, J., Auvinen, A., Poutiainen, M., Kakkola, L., Jarvinen, T. A., Maattanen, L., Stenman, U. H., Tammela, T., Hakama, M., & Visakorpi, T. (2001). Predictors of biological aggressiveness of prostate specific antigen screening detected prostate cancer. *Journal of Urology, 165,* 1569-1574.

Isralowitz, R. E. (2000). Vision change and quality of life among Ethiopian elderly immigrants in Israel. *Journal of Gerontological Social Work, 33,* 89-96.

Jackson, J. S., Williams, D. R., & Gomberg, E. S. L. (1998). Aging and alcohol use and abuse among African Americans: A life course perspective. In E. S. L. Gomberg,

A. M. Hegedus, & R. A. Zucker (Eds.), *Alcohol problems and aging* (pp. 63-90, NIAAA Research Monograph Series). Bethesda, MD: U.S. Department of Health and Human Services, National Institutes of Health, National Institute on Alcohol Abuse and Alcoholism.

Jänig, W., & McLachlan, E. (1992). Specialized functional pathways are building blocks of the autonomic nervous system. *Journal of the Autonomic Nervous System, 41,* 3-14.

Jansson, W., Nordberg, G., & Grafstrom, M. (2001). Patterns of elderly spousal caregiving in dementia care: An observational study. *Journal of Advanced Nursing, 34,* 804-812.

Janz, N. K., Janevic, M. R., Dodge, J. A., Fingerlin, T. E., Schork, M. A., Mosca, L. J., & Clark, N. M. (2001). Factors influencing quality of life in older women with heart disease. *Medical Care, 39,* 588-598.

Jarvik, G. P., Larson, E. B., Goddard, K., Kukull, W. A., Schellenberg, G. D., & Wijsman, E. M. (1996). Influence of apoplipoprotein E genotype on the transmission of Alzheimer disease in a community-based sample. *American Journal of Human Genetics, 58,* 191-200.

Jazwinski, S. M. (1996). Longevity, genes, and aging. *Science, 273,* 54-59.

Jenkins, C. D., Rosenman, R. H., & Friedman, M. (1967). Development of an objective psychological test for the determination of the coronary-prone behavior pattern in employed men. *Journal of Chronic Diseases, 20,* 371-379.

Jette, A. M. (1996). Disability trends and transitions. In R. H. Binstock & L. K. George (Eds.), *Handbook of aging and the social sciences* (4th ed., pp. 94-116). San Diego, CA: Academic Press.

John, E. R. (2001). A field theory of consciousness. *Consciousness and Cognition, 10,* 184-213.

Johnson, C. L. (1983). Dyadic family relations and social support. *The Gerontologist, 23,* 377-383.

Johnson, C. L., & Barer, B. M. (1993). Coping and a sense of control among the oldest old. *Journal of Aging Studies, 7,* 67-80.

Johnson, I. (2000). Alcohol problems in old age: A review of recent epidemiological research. *International Journal of Geriatric Psychiatry, 15,* 575-581.

Johnson, J. E. (1996). Sleep problems and self-care in very old rural women. *Geriatric Nursing, 17,* 72-74.

Johnson, J. E. (1997). Insomnia, alcohol, and over-the-counter drug use in old-old urban women. *Journal of Community Health Nursing, 14,* 181-188.

Johnson, J. E., & Leventhal, H. (1974). Effects of accurate expectations and behavioral instructions on reactions during a noxious medical examination. *Journal of Personality and Social Psychology, 29,* 710-718.

Johnson, J. V., Stewart, W., Hall, E. M., Fredlund, P., & Theorell, T. (1996). Long-term psychosocial work environment and cardiovascular mortality among Swedish men. *American Journal of Public Health, 86,* 324-31.

Johnson, N. J., Backlund, E., Sorlie, P. D., & Loveless, C. A. (2000). Marital status and mortality: The National Longitudinal Mortality Study. *Annals of Epidemiology, 10,* 224-238.

Johnson, T. E., Henderson S., Murakami, S., de Castro, E., de Castro, S. H., Cypser, J., Rikke, B., Tedesco, P., & Link, C. (2002). Longevity genes in the nematode Caenorhabditis elegans also mediate increased resistance to stress and prevent disease. *Journal of Inherited and Metabolic Disease, 25,* 197-206.

Johnstone, B. M., Leino, E. V., Ager, C. R., Ferrer, H., & Fillmore, K. M. (1996). Determinants of life-course variation in the frequency of alcohol consumption: Meta-analysis of studies from the collaborative alcohol-related longitudinal project. *Journal of Studies on Alcohol, 57,* 494-506.

Jung, C. G. (1933). *Modern man in search of a soul.* New York: Harcourt Press & World.

Jurivich, D. A., Qiu, L., & Welk, J. F. (1997). Attenuated stress responses in young and old human lymphocytes. *Mechanisms of Ageing and Development, 94,* 233-249.

Kahana, B. (1992). Late-life adaptation in the aftermath of extreme stress. In M. Wykel, E. Kahana, & J. Kowal (Eds.), *Stress and health among the elderly* (pp. 5-34). New York: Springer.

Kahana, E., Lawrence, R. H., Kahana, B., Kercher, K., Wisniewski, A., Stoller, E., Tobin, J., & Stange, K. (2002). Long-term impact of preventive proactivity on quality of life of the old-old. *Psychosomatic Medicine, 64,* 382-394.

Kalache, A. (2001). Rural aging: Reduction of existing inequities—Keynote address, June 10, 2000. *Journal of Rural Health, 17,* 312-313.

Kalina, R. A. (1999). Aging and visual function. In W. R. Hazzard, J. P. Blass, W. H. Ettinger, Jr., J. B. Halter, & J. G. Ouslander (Eds.), *Principles of geriatric medicine and gerontology* (4th ed., pp. 603-615). New York: McGraw-Hill.

Kamen-Siegel, L., Rodin, J., Seligman, M. E., & Dwyer, J. (1991). Explanatory style and cell-mediated immunity in elderly men and women. *Health Psychology, 10,* 229-235.

Kaminar, M. S., & Gilchrest, B. A. (1994). Aging of the skin. In W. R. Hazzard, E. L. Bierman, J. P. Blass, W. H. Ettinger, Jr., & J. B. Halter (Eds.), *Principles of geriatric medicine and gerontology* (3rd ed.). New York: McGraw-Hill.

Kane, R. A. (1997). Instruments to assess functional status. In C. K. Cassel, H. J. Cohen, E. B. Larson, D. E. Meier, N. M. Resnick, L. Z. Rubenstein, & L. B. Sorensen (Eds.), *Geriatric medicine* (3rd ed., pp. 169-179). New York: Springer-Verlag.

Kane, R. L., Ouslander, J. G., & Abrass, I. B. (1994). *Essentials of clinical geriatrics* (3rd ed.). New York: McGraw-Hill.

Kannel, W. B., & Ellison, R. C. (1996). Alcohol and coronary heart disease: The evidence for a protective effect. *Clinica Chimica Acta, 246,* 59-76.

Kaplan, G. A., & Haan, M. N., & Wallace, R. B. (1999). Understanding changing risk factor associations with increasing age in adults. *Annual Review of Public Health, 20,* 89-108.

Kaplan, G. A., Salonen, J. T., Cohen, R. D., Brand, R. J., Syme, S. L., & Puska, P. (1988). Social connections and mortality: Prospective evidence from Finland. *American Journal of Epidemiology, 128,* 370-380.

Kaplan, J. R., Adams, M. R., Clarkson, T. B., Manuck, S. B., Shively, C. A, & Williams, J. K. (1996). Psychosocial factors, sex differences and atherosclerosis. *Psychosomatic Medicine, 58,* 598-611.

Kaplan, R., & Erickson, J. (2000). Quality adjusted life expectancy for men and women in the United States. In S. B. Manuck (Ed.), *Behavior, health, and aging.* Mahwah, NJ: Lawrence Erlbaum.

Karasek, R., & Theorell, T. (1990). *Healthy work: Stress, productivity, and the reconstruction of working life.* New York: Basic Books.

Karlamangla, A., Singer, B., McEwen, B., Rowe, J., & Seeman, T. (2001). Allostatic load as a predictor of functional decline. MacArthur studies of successful aging. *Journal of Clinical Epidemiology, 55,* 696.

Karmarck, T. W., & Jennings, J. R. (1991). Biobehavioral factors in sudden cardiac death. *Psychological Bulletin, 109,* 42-75.

Kasl, S. (1983). Pursuing the link between stressful life experiences and disease: A time for reappraisal. In C. I. Cooper (Ed.), *Stress research* (pp. 79-102). New York: Mentor Books.

Katz, S., Ford, A. B., Moskowitz, R. W., Jackson, B. A., & Jaffe, M. W. (1963). Studies of illness in the aged. The index of ADL: A standardized measure of biological and psychosocial function. *Journal of the American Medical Association, 185,* 914-919.

Katzman, R., Terry, R., De Teresa, R. F., Brown, T., Davies, P., Fuld, P., Renbing, X., & Peck, A. (1988). Clinical, pathological and neurochemical changes in dementia: A subgroup with preserved mental status and numerous neocortical plaques. *Annals of Neurology, 23,* 138-144.

Kawachi, I., Colditz, G. A., Ascherio, A., Rimm, E. B., Giovannucci, E., Stampfer, M. J., & Willett, W. C. (1994). Prospective study of phobic anxiety and risk of coronary heart disease in men. *Circulation, 89,* 1992-1997.

Kawachi, I., Sparrow, D., Spiro, A., Vokonas, P., & Weiss, S. T. (1996). A prospective study of anger and coronary heart disease. The Normative Aging Study. *Circulation, 94,* 2090-2095.

Kawachi, I., Sparrow, D., Vokonas, P. S., & Weiss, S. T. (1994). Symptoms of anxiety and risk of coronary heart disease. The Normative Aging Study. *Circulation, 90,* 2225-2229.

Kawas, C., Resnick, S., Morrison, A., Brookmeyer, R., Corrada, M., Zonderman, A., Bacal, C., Lingle, D. C., & Metter E. (1997). A prospective study of estrogen replacement therapy and the risk of developing Alzheimer's disease: The Baltimore Longitudinal Study of Aging. *Neurology, 48,* 1517-1521.

Kennedy, G. J., Kelman, C. T., Thomas, C., & Chen, J. (1996). The relation of religious preference and practice to depressive symptoms among 1,855 older adults. *Journals of Gerontology: Psychological Sciences, 51B,* P301.

Kessler R. C., Foster, C. Webster, P. S., & House, J. S. (1992). The relationship between age and depressive symptoms in two national surveys. *Psychology and Aging, 7,* 119-126.

Khanna, K. V., & Markham, R. B. (1999). A perspective on cellular immunity in the elderly. *Clinical Infectious Diseases, 28,* 710-13.

Kiecolt-Glaser, J. K., & Glaser, R. (1995). Psychoneuroimmunology and health consequences: Data and shared mechanisms. *Psychosomatic Medicine, 57,* 269-74.

Kiecolt-Glaser, J. K., Glaser, R., Cacioppo, J. T., MacCallum, R. C., Snydersmith, M., Kim, C., & Malarkey, W. B. (1997). Marital conflict in older adults: Endocrinological and immunological correlates [Comments]. *Psychosomatic Medicine, 59,* 339-349.

King, A. C., Pruitt, L. A., Phillips, W., Oka, R., Rodenburg, A., & Haskell, W. L. (2000). Comparative effects of two physical activity programs on measured and perceived physical functioning and other health-related quality of life outcomes in older adults. *Journals of Gerontology: Medical Sciences, 55,* M74-M83.

King, G., Mackenzie, J., Smith, H., & Clark, D. (2000). Dying at home: Evaluation of a hospice rapid-response service. *International Journal of Palliative Nursing, 6,* 280-287.

Kinsella, K., & Velkoff, V. A. (2001). *An aging world: 2001* (U.S. Census Bureau, Series P95-01-1). Washington DC: Government Printing Office.

Kivett, V. R. (1993). Informal supports among older rural minorities. In C. N. Bull (Ed.), *Aging in rural America* (pp. 204-215). Newbury Park, CA: Sage.

Kobasa, S. C., Maddi, S. R., & Kahn, S. (1982). Hardiness and health: A prospective study. *Journal of Personality and Social Psychology, 42,* 168-177.

Koenig, H. G., George, L. K., & Peterson, B. L. (1998). Religiosity and remission of depression in medically-ill older adults. *American Journal of Psychiatry, 155,* 536-542.

Koenig, H. G., Smiley, M., & Gonzales, J. A. P. (1988). *Religion, health, and aging.* New York: Greenwood.

Koenig, H. G., Hays, J. C., George, L. K., Blazer, D. G., Larson, D. B., & Landerman, L. R. (1997). *American Journal of Geriatric Psychiatry, 5,* 131-144.

Kohlberg, L. (1984). *The psychology of moral development, Vol. 2. Essays on moral development.* San Francisco: Harper & Row.

Kohler, W. (1940). *Dynamics in psychology.* New York: Liveright Publishing.

Konety, B. R., & Getzenberg, R. H. (2002). Vitamin D and prostate cancer. *Urological Clinics of North America, 29,* 95-106.

Kostka, T., Berthouze, S. E., Lacour, J., & Bonnefoy, M. (2000). The symptomatology of upper respiratory tract infections and exercise in elderly people. *Medicine and Science in Sports and Exercise, 32,* 46-51.

Krach, C. A., & Velkoff, V. A. (1999). *Centenarians in the United States* (U.S. Bureau of the Census, Current Population Reports, Series P23-199RV). Washington, DC: Government Printing Office.

Kramarow, E., Lentzner, H., Rooks, R., Weeks, J., & Saydah, S. (1999). *Health, United States, 1999* (DHHS Publication No. 99-1232). Washington, DC: Government Printing Office.

Kramer, D. A. (1990). Conceptualizing wisdom: The primacy of affect-cognition relationships. In R. J. Sternberg (Ed.), *Wisdom: Its nature, origins, and development* (pp. 279-316). Cambridge, UK: Cambridge University Press.

Krantz, D. S., & McCeney, M. K. (2002). Effects of psychological and social factors on organic disease: A critical assessment of research on coronary heart disease. *Annual Review of Psychology, 53,* 341-369.

Krause, N. (1987). Chronic financial strain, social support, and depressive symptoms among older adults. *Psychology and Aging, 2,* 185-192.

Krause, N. (2001). Social supports. In R. H. Binstock & L. K. George (Eds.), *Handbook of aging and the social sciences* (5th ed., pp. 272-294). San Diego, CA: Academic Press.

Krause, N., Herzog, A. R., & Baker, E. (1992). Providing support to others and well-being in later life. *Journals of Gerontology: Psychological Sciences, 47,* P300-P311.

Krause, N., & Shaw, B. A. (2000). Role-specific feelings of control and mortality. *Psychology of Aging, 15,* 617-26.

Kravdal, O. (2001). The impact of marital status on cancer survival. *Social Science and Medicine, 52,* 357-368.

Krikorian, R., Kay, J., & Liang, W. M. (1995). Emotional distress, coping, and adjustment in human immunodeficiency virus infection and acquired immune deficiency syndrome. *Journal of Nervous and Mental Disease, 183,* 293-298.

Krumholz, H. M., Amatruda, J., Smith, G. L., Materra, J. A., Roumanis, S. A., Radford, M. J., Crombie, P., & Vaccarino, V. (2002). Randomized trial of an education and support intervention to prevent readmission of patients with heart failure. *Journal of American Collegiate Cardiology, 39,* 83-89.

Kubzansky, L. D., & Kawachi, I. (2000). Going to the heart of the matter: Do negative emotions cause coronary heart disease? *Journal of Psychosomatic Research, 48,* 323-337.

Kubzansky, L. D., Kawachi, I., Spiro, A., III, Weiss, S. T., Vokonas, P. S., & Sparrow, D. (1997). Is worrying bad for your heart? A prospective study of worry and coronary heart disease in the Normative Aging Study. *Circulation, 95,* 818-824.

Kudielka, B. M., Hellhammer, J., Hellhammer, D. H., Wolf, O. T., Pirke, K. M., Varadi, E., Pilz, J., & Kirschbaum, C. (1998). Sex differences in endocrine and psychological responses to psychosocial stress in healthy elderly subjects and the impact of a two-week dehydroepiandrosterone treatment. *Journal of Clinical Endocrinology Metabolism, 83,* 1756-1762.

Kudielka, B. M., Schmidt-Reinwald, A. K., Hellhammer, D. H., & Kirschbaum, C. (1999). Psychological and endocrine responses to psychosocial stress and dexamethasone/corticotropin-releasing hormone in healthy postmenopausal women and young controls: The impact of age and a two-week estradiol treatment. *Neuroendocrinology, 70,* 422-30.

Kuypers, J. A., & Bengtson, V. L. (1973). Social breakdown and competence: A model of normal aging. *Human Development, 16,* 181-201.

Labouvie-Vief, G. (1990). Wisdom as integrated thought: historical and developmental perspectives. In R. J. Sternberg (Ed.), *Wisdom: Its nature, origins, and development* (pp. 52-86). Cambridge, UK: Cambridge University Press.

Labouvie-Vief, G. (August, 2002). Dynamic integration: Affect, cognition, and the self in adulthood. Invited address to the American Psychological Association, Chicago.

Labouvie-Vief, G., DeVoe, M., & Bulka, D. (1989). Speaking about feelings: Conceptions of emotion across the life span. *Psychology and Aging, 4,* 425-437.

Labouvie-Vief, G., Hakim-Larson, J., DeVoe, M., & Schoeberlein, S. (1989). Emotions and self-regulation: A life span view. *Human Development, 32,* 279-299.

Labouvie-Vief, G., Hakim-Larson, J., & Hobart, C. (1987). Age, ego level, and the life-span development of coping and defense processes. *Psychology and Aging, 2,* 286-293.

Lachman, M. E. (1986). Locus of control in aging research: A case for multidimensional and domain-specific assessment. *Psychology and Aging, 1,* 34-40.

Lachman, M. E., & Weaver, S. L. (1998). The sense of control as a moderator of social class differences in health and well-being. *Journal of Personality and Social Psychology, 74,* 763-73.

Ladwig, K. H., Kieser, M., & Konigh, J. (1991). Affective diseases and survival after acute myocardial infarction. *European Health Journal, 12,* 959-964.

Ladwig, K. H., Lehmacher, W., Rorth, R., Breithardt, G., Budde, T. H., & Borggrefe, M. (1992). Factors which provoke post infarction depression: Results from the post infarction late potential study (PILP). *Journal of Psychosomatic Research, 36,* 723-729.

Lakatta, E. G. (1999). Circulatory function in younger and older humans in health. In W. R. Hazzard, J. P. Blass, W. H. Ettinger, Jr., J. B. Halter, & J. G. Ouslander (Eds.), *Principles of geriatric medicine and gerontology* (4th ed., pp. 645-660). New York: McGraw-Hill.

Lamiell, J. T. (1981). Toward an idiothetic psychology of personality. *American Psychologist, 36,* 276-289.

Landauer, R. K., & Whiting, J. W. M. (1981). Correlates and consequences of stress in infancy. In R. H. Munroe, R. L. Munroe, & B. B. Whiting (Eds.), *Handbook of cross-cultural human development* (pp. 355-375). New York: Garland.

Landrine, H., & Klonoff, E. A. (2001). Cultural diversity and health psychology. In A. Baum, T. A., Revenson, & J. E. Singer (Eds.), *Handbook of health psychology* (pp. 851-891). Mahwah, NJ: Lawrence Erlbaum.

Lane, N. E., Hochberg, M. C., Pressman, A., Scott, J. C., & Nevitt, M. C. (1999). Recreational physical activity and the risk of osteoarthritis of the hip in elderly women. *Journal of Rheumatology, 26,* 849-854.

Lang, F. R. (2001). Regulation of social relationships in later adulthood. *Journals of Gerontology: Psychological Sciences, Social Sciences, 56,* P321-P326.

Langer, E. J. (1989). *Mindfulness.* Reading, MA: Addison-Wesley.

Langer, E. J. (1997). *The power of mindful learning.* Reading, MA: Addison-Wesley.

Langer, E. J., Chanowitz, B., Palmerino, M., Jacobs, S., Rhodes, M., & Thayer, P. (1990). Nonsequential development and aging. In C. N. Alexander & E. J. Langer, *Higher stages of human development* (pp. 114-138). Oxford, UK: Oxford University Press.

Langer, E. J., & Rodin, J. (1976). The effects of choice and enhanced personality responsibility for the aged: A field experiment in an institutional setting. *Journal of Personality and Social Psychology, 34,* 191-198.

Lawton, M. P. (1983). Environment and other determinants of well-being in older people. *The Gerontologist, 23,* 349-357.

Lawton, M. P. (1999). Quality of life in chronic illness. *Gerontology, 45,* 181-183.

Lawton, M. P. (2001). Quality of life and the end of life. In J. E. Birren & K. W. Schaie (Eds.), *Handbook of the psychology of aging* (5th ed., pp. 592-616). San Diego, CA: Academic Press.

Lawton, M. P., & Brody, E. M. (1969). Assessment of older people: Self-maintaining and instrumental activities of daily living. *The Gerontologist, 9,* 179-186.

Lawton, M. P., Moss, M., & Duhamel, L. M. (1995). The quality of daily life among elderly care receivers. *Journal of Applied Gerontology, 14,* 150-171.

Lawton, M. P., & Nahemow, L. (1973). Ecology and the aging process. In C. Eisdorfer & M. P. Lawton (Eds.), *Psychology of adult development & aging* (pp. 660-676). Washington: American Psychological Association.

Lazarus, R. S., Averill, J. R., & Opton, E. M., Jr. (1974). The psychology of coping: Issues of research and assessment. In G. V. Coelho, D. A. Hamburg, & J. E. Adams, *Coping and adaptation* (pp. 249-315). New York: Basic Books.

Lazarus, R. S., & Folkman, S. (1984). *Stress, appraisal, and coping.* New York: Springer.

Lenze, E. J., Rogers, J. C., Martire, L. M., Mulsant, B. H., Rollman, B. L., Dew, M. A., Schulz, R., & Reynolds, C. F. (2001). The association of late-life depression and anxiety with physical disability. *American Journal of Geriatric Psychiatry, 9,* 113-135.

Lesperance, F., Frasure-Smith, N., Talajic, M., & Bourassa, M. G. (2002). Five-year risk of cardiac mortality in relation to initial severity and one-year changes in depression symptoms after myocardial infarction. *Circulation, 105,* 1049-53.

Levenson, M. R., Aldwin, C. M., & Cupertino, A. P. (2001). Transcending the self: Towards a liberative model of adult development. In A. L. Neri (Ed.), *Maturidade & Velhice: Um enfoque multidisciplinar* (pp. 99-116). São Paulo, Brazil: Papirus.

Levenson, M. R., Aldwin, C. M., & Spiro, A., III. (1998). Age, cohort and period effects on alcohol consumption and problem drinking: Findings from the Normative Aging Study. *Journal of Studies on Alcohol, 59,* 712-722.

Levenson, M. R., Aldwin, C. M., Spiro, A., III, & Friedman, L. J. (1998). Personality and problem drinking in middle-aged and older men: Longitudinal findings from the Normative Aging Study. In E. S. L. Gomberg, A. M Hegedus, & R. A. Zucker (Eds.), *Alcohol problems and aging* (pp. 247-260). (NIAAA Research Monograph Series). Bethesda, MD: U.S. Department of Health and Human Services (NIH), National Institute on Alcohol Abuse and Alcoholism.

Levenson, M. R., & Crumpler, C. (1996). Three models of adult development. *Human Development, 39,* 135-149.

Levenson, R. W., Carstensen, L. L., & Gottman, J. M (1994). The influence of age and gender of affect, physiology, and their interrelations: A study of long-term marriage. *Journal of Personality and Social Psychology, 67,* 56-68.

Leventhal, H., Leventhal, E. A., & Cameron, L. (2001). Representations, procedures, and affect in illness self-regulation: A perceptual-cognitive model. In A. Baum, T. A., Revenson, & J. E. Singer (Eds.), *Handbook of health psychology* (pp. 19-47). Mahwah, NJ: Lawrence Erlbaum.

Leventhal, H., Rabin, C., Leventhal, E. A., & Burns, E. (2001). Health risk behaviors and aging. In J. E. Birren & K. W. Schaie (Eds.), *Handbook of the psychology of aging* (5th ed., pp. 186-214). San Diego, CA: Academic Press.

Levin, J. W. (1994). Religion and health: Is there an association, is it valid, and is it causal? *Social Science & Medicine, 38,* 1475-1484.

Levine, S. (1966). Sex differences in the brain. *Scientific American, 498,* 84-91.

Levine, S. (2001). Primary social relationships influence the development of the hypothalamic-pituitary-adrenal axis in the rat. *Physiology & Behavior, 73,* 255-260.

Levine, S., Haltmeyer, G. G., Karas, C. G., & Denenberg, V. H. (1967). Physiological and behavioral effects of infant stimulation. *Physiology and Behavior, 2,* 55-59.

Levinson, D. (1978). *Seasons of a man's life.* New York: Knopf.

Lev-Ran, A. (2001). Human obesity: An evolutionary approach to understanding our bulging waistline. *Diabetes Metabolism Research Review, 17,* 347-362.

Lewthwaite, J., Owen, N., Coates, A., Henderson, B., & Steptoe, A. (2002). Circulating human heat shock protein 60 in the plasma of British civil servants: Relationship to physiological and psychosocial stress. *Circulation. 106,* 196-201.

Levy, J. A. (1998). AIDS and injecting drug use in later life. *Research on Aging, 20,* 776-797.

Liao, Y., McGee, D. L., Cao, G., & Cooper, R. S. (2000). Alcohol intake and mortality: Findings from the National Health Interview Surveys (1998 and 1990). *American Journal of Epidemiology, 151,* 651-9.

Lichtenstein, P., Gatz, M., & Berg, S. A. (1998). Twin study of mortality after spousal bereavement. *Psychological Medicine, 28,* 635-643.

Lieber, C. S. (1992). Interactions of ethanol with other drugs. In C. S. Lieber (Ed.), *Medical and nutritional consequences of alcoholism: Mechanisms and management* (pp. 165-183). New York: Plenum.

Lieberman, M. A. (1996). *Doors close, doors open: Widows, grieving and growing.* New York: G. P. Putnam.

Lieberman, M.A., & Fisher, L. (2001). The effects of nursing home placement on family caregivers of patients with Alzheimer's disease. *The Gerontologist, 41,* 819-826.

Lieberman, M. A., & Tobin, S. (1983). *The experience of old age: Stress, coping, and survival.* New York: Basic Books.

Light, K. C., Kothandapani, R. V., & Allen, M. T. (1998). Enhanced cardiovascular and catecholamine responses in women with depressive symptoms. *International Journal of Psychophysiology, 28,* 157-166.

Lillard, L. J., & Waite, L. J. (1995). 'Til death do us part: Marital disruption and mortality. *American Journal of Sociology, 100,* 1131-1156.

Lin, E. H., & Peterson, C. (1990). Pessimistic explanatory style and response to illness. *Behavior Research and Therapy, 28,* 243-248.

Lindemann, B. (2001). Receptors and transduction in taste. *Nature, 413,* 219-225.

Linnoila, M., Erwin, C. W., Ramm, D., & Cleveland, W. P. (1980). Effects of age and alcohol on psychomotor performance of men. *Journal Studies on Alcohol, 41,* 488-495.

Lipschitz, D. A. (1997). Nutrition. In C. K. Cassel, H. J. Cohen, E. B. Larson, D. E. Meier, N. M. Resnick, L. Z. Rubenstein, & L. B. Sorensen (Eds.), *Geriatric medicine* (3rd ed., pp. 801-813). New York: Springer-Verlag.

Lipsitz, L. A., & Goldberger, A. L. (1992). Loss of "complexity" and aging: Potential applications of fractals and chaos theory to senescence. *Journal of the American Medical Association, 267,* 1807.

Litchman, C. D., & Posner, J. B. (1994). Brain tumors in the elderly. In W. R. Hazzard, E. L. Bierman, J. P. Blass, W. H. Ettinger, Jr., & J. B. Halter (Eds.), *Geriatric medicine and gerontology* (3rd ed., pp. 1095-1103). New York: McGraw-Hill.

Lithgow, G. J., White, T. M., Hinerfeld, D. A., & Johnson, T. E. (1994). Thermotolerance of a long-lived mutant of Caenorhabditis elegans. *Journals of Gerontology: Biological Sciences, 49,* B270-B276.

Lithgow, G. J., White, T. M., Melov, A., & Johnson, T. E. (1995). Thermotolerance and extended life span conferred by single-gene mutations and induced by thermal stress. *Proceedings of the National Academy of Sciences, 92,* 7540-7544.

Ljungquist, B., & Sundstrom, G. (1996). Health and social networks as predictors of survival in old age. *Scandinavian Journal of Social Medicine, 24,* 90-101.

Locher, J. L., Burgio, K. L., Goode, P. S., Roth, D. L., & Rodriquez, E. (2002). Effects of age and causal attribution to aging on health-related behaviors associated with urinary incontinence in older women. *The Gerontologist, 42,* 515-521.

Loeser, R. F., & Delbono, O. (1999). Aging and the musculoskeletal system. In W. R. Hazzard, J. P. Blass, W. H. Ettinger, Jr., J. B. Halter, & J. G. Ouslander (Eds.), *Principles of geriatric medicine and gerontology* (4th ed., pp. 1097-1111). New York: McGraw-Hill.

Loevinger, J. (1977). *Ego development: Conceptions and theories.* San Francisco: Jossey-Bass.

Loewenstein, D. A., Amigo, E., Durara, R., Guterman, A., Hurwitz, D., Berkowitz, N., Wilkie, F., Weinberg, G., Black, B., Gittelman, B., & Eisdorfer, D. (1989). A new scale for the assessment of functional status in Alzheimer's disease and related disorders. *Journals of Gerontology: Psychological Sciences, 44,* P114-P121.

Long, J. S. (1983). *Confirmatory factor analysis: A preface to LISREL.* Beverly Hills, CA: Sage.

Longino, C. F., & Haas, W. H., III. (1993). Migration and the rural elderly. In C. N. Bull (Ed.), *Aging in rural America* (pp. 17-29). Newbury Park, CA: Sage.

Longino, C. F., Warheit, G. J., & Green, J. A. (1989). Class, aging, and health. In K. S. Markides (Ed.), *Aging and health* (pp. 79-109). Newbury Park, CA: Sage.

Lorig, K. R., Sobel, D. S., Stewart, A. L., Brown, B. W., Jr., Bandura, A., Ritter, P., Gonzalez, V. M., Laurent, D. D., & Holman, H. R. (1999). Evidence suggesting that a chronic disease self-management program can improve health status while reducing hospitalization: A randomized trial. *Medical Care, 37,* 5-14.

Lynch, J. W., Davey Smith, G., Kaplan, G. A., & House, J. S. (2000). Income inequality and mortality: Importance to health of individual income, psychosocial environment, or material conditions. *British Medical Journal, 320,* 1200-1204.

Lynch, J. W., Kaplan, G. A., & Shema, S. J. (1997). Cumulative impact of sustained economic hardship on physical, cognitive, psychological, and social functioning. *New England Journal of Medicine, 337,* 1889-1895.

MacCallum, R. C., & Austin, J. T. (2000). Applications of structural equation modeling in psychological research. *Annual Review of Psychology, 51,* 201-226.

Maghfoor, I., & Perry, M. C. (1999). Lung cancer. In W. R. Hazzard, J. P. Blass, W. H. Ettinger, Jr., J. B. Halter, & J. G. Ouslander (Eds.), *Principles of geriatric medicine and gerontology* (4th ed., pp. 757-765). New York: McGraw-Hill.

Manchanda, S. C., Narang, R., Reddy, K. S., Sachdeva, U., Prabhakaran, D., Dharmanand, S., Rajani, M., & Bijlani, R. (2000). Retardation of coronary atherosclerosis with yoga lifestyle intervention. *Journal of the Association of Physicians of India, 48*I, 687-694.

Manegold, C. (2001). Treatment of elderly patients with non-small-cell lung cancer. *Oncology, 15,* 46-51.

Manson, J., Willett, W., Sampfer, M., Colditz, G. A., Hunter, D. J., Hankinson, S. E., Hennekens, C. H., & Speizer, F. E. (1995). Body weight and mortality among women. *New England Journal of Medicine, 333,* 677-685.

Manton, K. G., & Gu, X. (2001). Changes in the prevalence of chronic disability in the United States black and non-black population above age 65 from 1982 to 1999. *Proceedings of the National Academy of Sciences, 98,* 6354-6359.

Manton, K. G., & Land, K. C. (2000). Active life expectancy estimates for the U.S. elderly population: A multidimensional continuous-mixture model of functional change applied to completed cohorts, 1982-1996. *Demography, 37,* 253-65.

Manton, K. G., Poss, S. S., & Wing, S. (1979). The black/white mortality crossover: Investigation from the perspective of the components of aging. *Gerontologist, 19,* 291-300.

Markides, K. S., & Black, S. A. (1996). Race, ethnicity, and aging: The impact of inequality. In R. H. Binstock & L. K. George (Eds.), *Handbook of aging and the social sciences* (pp. 153-170). San Diego, CA: Academic Press.

Marrie, T. J. (2000). Community-acquired pneumonia in the elderly. *Clinical Infectious Diseases, 31,* 1066-1078.

Martin, G. A. (1997). The genetics of aging. *Hospital Practice, 32,* 47-55.

Marshburn, P. B., & Carr, B. R. (1994). The menopause and hormone replacement therapy. In W. R. Hazzard, E. L. Bierman, J. P. Blass, W. H. Ettinger, & J. B. Halter (Eds.), *Principles of geriatric medicine and gerontology* (3rd ed., pp. 867-878). New York: McGraw-Hill.

Maruyama, M. (1963). The second cybernetics: Deviation-amplifying mutual causal processes. *American Scientist, 51,* 164-179.

Maslow, A. H. (1970). *Motivation and personality.* New York: Harper & Row.

Mason, J. W. (1971). A re-evaluation of the concept of "non-specificity" in stress theory. *Journal of Psychiatric Research, 8,* 323-333.

Mason, J. W. (1975). A historical view of the stress field. *Journal of Human Stress, 1,* 6-27.

Masoro, E. J. (1999). *Challenges of biological aging.* New York: Springer.

Masunaga, H., & Horn, J. (2001). Expertise and age-related changes in components of intelligence. *Psychology and Aging, 16,* 293-311.

Matthews, K A., Wing, R. R., Kuller, L. H., Mailahn, E. N., & Owens, J. F. (2000). Menopause as a turning point in midlife. In S. B. Manuck, R. Jennings, B. S. Rabin, & A. Baum (Eds.), *Behavior, health, and aging* (pp. 43-57). Mahwah, NJ: Lawrence Erlbaum.

Mattson, M. P. (1999). Cellular and neurochemical aspects of the aging brain. In W. R. Hazzard, J. P. Blass, W. H. Ettinger, Jr., J. B. Halter, & J. G. Ouslander (Eds.), *Principles of geriatric medicine and gerontology* (4th ed., pp. 1193-1217). New York: McGraw-Hill.

May, H., Murphy, S., & Khaw, K. T. (1994). Age-associated bone loss in men and women and its relationship to weight. *Age and Aging, 23,* 235-240.

McAlindon, T. E., Wilson, P. W., Aliabadi, P., Weissman, B., & Felson, D. T. (1999). Level of physical activity and the risk of radiographic and symptomatic knee osteoarthritis in the elderly: The Framingham Study. *American Journal of Medicine, 106,* 151-157.

McBride, T. D., & Mueller, K. J. (2002). Effect of Medicare payment on rural health care systems. *Journal of Rural Health, 18,* 147-163.

McCartney, N., Hicks, A. L., Martin, J., & Webber, C. E. (1995). Long-term resistance training in the elderly: Effects on dynamic strength, exercise capacity, muscle, and bone. *Journals of Gerontology: Biological Sciences and Medical Sciences, 50,* B97-B104.

McClain, R., & Gray, M. L. (2000). Prostate cancer: A primer. *Clinical Advisor, 3,* 37-48.

McClearn, G. E., & Heller, D. A. (2000). Genetics and aging. In S. B. Manuck, R. Jennings, B. S. Rabin, & A. Baum (Eds.), *Behavior, health, and aging* (pp. 1-14). Mahwah, NJ: Lawrence Erlbaum.

McCrae, R. R. (1982). Age differences in the use of coping mechanisms. *Journal of Gerontology, 37,* 454-460.

McCrae, R. R. (1989). Age differences and changes in the use of coping mechanisms. *Journals of Gerontology: Psychological Sciences, 44,* P161-P169.

McCrae, R. R., Costa, P. T., Jr., Pedroso de Lima, M., Simoes, A., Ostendorf, F., Angleitner, A., Marusic, I., Bratko, D., Caprara, G. V., Barbaranelli, C., Chae, J. H., & Piedmont, R. L. (1999). Age differences in personality across the adult life span: Parallels in five cultures. *Developmental Psychology, 35,* 466-477.

McDowell, F. H. (1994). Parkinson's disease and related disorders. In W. R. Hazzard, E. L. Bierman, J. P. Blass, W. H. Ettinger, Jr., & J. B. Halter (Eds.), *Geriatric medicine and gerontology* (3rd ed., pp. 1051-1062). New York: McGraw-Hill.

McEwen, B. S. (1998). Stress, adaptation, and disease. *Annals of the New York Academy of Sciences, 840,* 33-44.

McEwen, B. S. (2000). From molecules to mind: Stress, individual differences, and the social environment. In A. R. Damasio, & A. Harrington (Eds.), *Unity of knowledge: The convergence of natural and human science* (pp. 42-49). New York: New York Academy of Sciences.

McEwen, B. S., & Seeman, T. (1999). Protective and damaging effects of mediators of stress. *Annals of the New York Academy of Sciences, 896,* 30-47.

McEwen, B. S., & Stellar, E. (1993). Stress and the individual. *Archives of Internal Medicine, 153,* 2093-2101.

McGee, R., Williams, S., & Elwood, M. (1994). Depression and the development of cancer: A meta-analysis. *Social Science & Medicine, 38,* 187-192.

McIntosh, W. A., Kaplan, H. B., Kubena, K. S., & Landmann, W. A. (1993). Life events, social support, and immune response in elderly individuals. *International Journal of Aging and Human Development, 37,* 23-36.

McKee, P., & Barber, C. (1999). On defining wisdom. *International Journal of Aging and Human Development, 249,* 149-164.

McKenna, M. C., Zevon, M. A., Corn, B., & Rounds, J. (1999). Psychosocial factors and the development of breast cancer: A meta-analysis. *Health Psychology, 18,* 520-531.

McMillan, A., Mentnech, R. M., Lubitz, J., McBean, A. M., & Russell, D. (1990). Trends and patterns in place of death for Medicare enrollees. *Health Care Finance Review, 12,* 1-7.

Medvedev, Z. A. (1974). Caucasus and Altay longevity: A biological or social problem? *The Gerontologist, 14,* 381-387.

Meier, D. (1997). Osteoporosis and other disorders of skeletal aging. In C. K. Cassel, H. J. Cohen, E. B. Larson, D. E. Meier, N. M. Resnick, L. Z. Rubenstein, & L. B. Sorensen (Eds.), *Geriatric medicine* (3rd ed., pp. 442-432). New York: Springer-Verlag.

Meydani, S. N., & Ha, W. K. (2000). Immunologic effects of yogurt. *American Journal of Clinical Nutrition, 71,* 861-872.

Mhoon, E. (1997). Otologic changes and disorders. In C. K. Cassel, H. J. Cohen, E. B. Larsen, D. E. Meier, N. M. Resnick, L. Z. Rubenstein, & L. B. Sorensen (Eds.), *Geriatric medicine* (3rd ed., pp. 699-715). New York: Springer-Verlag.

Mikulincer, M., & Florian, V. (1996). Coping and adaptation to trauma and loss. In M. Zeidner & N. S. Endler (Eds.), *Handbook of coping: Theory, research, applications* (pp. 554-572). New York: Wiley.

Miller, E. C., Giovannucci, E., Erdman, J. W., Jr., Bahnson, R., Schwartz, S. J., & Clinton, S. K. (2002). Tomato products, lycopene, and prostate cancer risk. *Urological Clinics of North America, 29,* 83-93.

Miller, M. E., Longino, C. F., Anderson, R. T., James, M. K., & Worley, A. S. (1999). Functional status, assistance, and the risk of a community-based move. *Gerontologist, 39,* 187-200.

Miller, R. A (1996a). Aging and the immune response. In E. L. Schneider & J. W. Rowe (Eds.), *Handbook of the biology of aging* (4th ed., pp. 355-392). San Diego, CA: Academic Press.

Miller, R. A. (1996b). The aging immune system: Primer and prospectus. *Science, 273,* 70-74.

Miller, S. (1980). When is a little information is a dangerous thing? Coping with stressful events by monitoring vs. blunting. In S. Levine & H. Ursin (Eds.), *Coping and health* (pp. 145-170). New York: Plenum.

Miller, T. D., Smith, T. W., Turner, C. W., Guijarro, M. L., & Hallet, A. J. (1996). A meta-analytic review of research on hostility and physical health. *Psychological Bulletin, 119,* 322-348.

Minkler, M., & Fadem, P. (2002). "Successful aging": A disability perspective. *Journal of Disability Policy Studies, 12,* 229-235.

Mirowsky, J., & Ross, C. E. (2000). Socioeconomic status and subjective life expectancy. *Social Psychology Quarterly, 63,* 133-151.

Mittleman, M. A., Maclure, M., Nachnani, M., Sherwood, J. B., & Muller, J. E. (1997). Educational attainment, anger, and the risk of triggering myocardial infarction onset: determinants of myocardial infarction onset study investigators. *Archives of Internal Medicine, 157,* 769-775.

Mittleman, M. A., Maclure, M., Sherwood, J. B., Mulry, R. P., Tofler, G. H., Jacobs, S. C., Friedman, R., Benson, H., & Muller, J. E. (1995). Triggering of acute myocardial infarction onset by episodes of anger: Determinants of myocardial infarction onset study. *Circulation, 92,* 1720-1725.

Moberg, D. O., & Taves, M. J. (1965). Church participation and adjustment in old age. In A. M. Rose & W. A. Peterson (Eds.), *Older people and their social world.* Philadelphia: F. A. Davis.

Moen, P. (1992). *Women's two roles: A contemporary dilemma.* New York: Auburn House.

Moody, H. R. (2000). *Aging: Concepts and controversies.* Thousand Oaks, CA: Pine Forge.

Moore, A. P., & Clarke, C. (2001). Parkinson's disease. *Clinical Evidence, 6,* 1019-1028.

Moore, W. A., Davey, V. A., Weindruch, R., Walford, R., & Ivy, G. O. (1995). The effect of caloric restriction on lipofuscin accumulation in mouse brain with age. *Gerontology, 41*(Suppl. 2)*,* 173-85.

Morris, T., Greer, S., Pettingale, K. W., & Watson, M. (1981). Patterns of expression of anger and their psychological correlates in women with breast cancer. *Journal of Psychosomatic Research, 25,* 111-117.

Mosca, L., McGillen, C., & Rubenfire, M. (1998). Gender differences in barriers to lifestyle change for cardiovascular disease prevention. *Journal of Women's Health, 7,* 711-715.

Mroczek, D. K., Spiro, A., III, Aldwin, C. M., Ozer, D. J., & Bossé, R. (1993). Construct validation of optimism and pessimism: Findings from the Normative Aging Study. *Health Psychology, 12,* 406-409.

Mulder, C. L., Antoni, M. H., Duivenvoorden, H. J., & Kauffmann, R. H. (1995). Active confrontational coping predicts decreased clinical progression over a one-year period in HIV-infected homosexual men. *Journal of Psychosomatic Research, 39,* 957-965.

Mulder, C. L., de Vroome, E. M. M., van Griensven, G. J. P., Antoni, M H., & Sandfort, T. G. M. (1999). Avoidance as a predictor of the biological course of HIV infection over a 7-year period in gay men. *Health Psychology, 18,* 107-113.

Murasko, D. M., & Bernstein, E. D. (1999). Immunology of aging. In W. R. Hazzard, J. P. Blass, W. H. Ettinger, Jr., J. B. Halter, & J. G. Ouslander (Eds.), *Principles of geriatric medicine and gerontology* (4th ed., pp. 97-116). New York: McGraw-Hill.

Murberg, T. A., Bru, E., Svebak, S., Tveteras, R., & Aarsland, T. (1999). Depressed mood and subjective health symptoms as predictors of mortality in patients with congestive heart failure: A two-year follow-up study. *International Journal of Psychiatry and Medicine, 29,* 311-26.

Muthen, B. (2001). Second-generation structural equation modeling with a combination of categorical and continuous latent variables: New opportunities for latent class/latent growth modeling. In L. M. Collins & A. G. Sayer (Eds.), *New methods for the analysis of change* (pp. 291-322). Washington, DC: American Psychological Association.

Mutran, E. J., Reitzes, D. C., Mossey, J., & Fernandez, M. E. (1995). Social support, depression, and recovery of walking ability following hip fracture surgery. *Journals of Gerontology: Social Sciences, 50B,* S354-S361.

Nagin, D. S., & Tremblay, R. E. (2001). Analyzing developmental trajectories of distinct but related behaviors: A group-based method. *Psychological Methods, 6,* 18-34.

Nakano, M., Oenzil, F., Mizuno, T., & Gotoh, S. (1995). Age-related changes in the lipofuscin accumulation of brain and heart. *Gerontology, 41*(Suppl. 2), 69-79.

Narayan, S., Lewis, M., Tornatore, J., Hepburn, K., & Corcoran-Perry, S. (2001). Subjective responses to caregiving for a spouse with dementia. *Journal of Gerontological Nursing, 27,* 19-28.

National Cancer Institute (1999). *Melanoma.* Cancer Net: A service of the national cancer institute, NIH Publication No. 99-1563. Updated September 16, 2002. Retrieved December 26, 2002, from www.cancer.gov/cancerinfo/wyntk/melanoma

National Eye Institute (2002). *Facts about age-related macular degeneration.* Retrieved December 13, 2002, from www.nei.nih.gov/health/maculardegen/armd_facts.htm

National Institute on Alcohol Abuse and Alcoholism. (January, 1995). Alcohol Alert: Alcohol-Medication Interactions. *NIAAA, No. 27.*

National Institutes of Health Osteoporosis and Related Bone Diseases National Resource Center. (2000). *Fast facts on osteoporosis.* Retrieved December 23, 2002, from www.osteo.org/osteofastfact.html

Navaie-Waliser, M., Feldman, P. H., Gould, D. A., Levine, C., Kuerbis, A. N., & Donelan, K. (2001). The experiences and challenges of informal caregivers: Common themes and differences among whites, blacks, and Hispanics. *Gerontologist, 42,* 733-741.

Neale, A. V., Tilley, B. C., & Vernon, S. W. (1986). Marital status, delay in seeking treatment, and survival from breast cancer. *Social Science and Medicine, 23,* 305-312.

Nemeroff, C. B., Musselman, D. L., & Evans, D. L. (1998). Depression and cardiac disease. *Depression and Anxiety, 8*(Suppl. 1), 71-79.

Neubauer, D. N. (1999). Sleep problems in the elderly. *American Family Physician, 59,* 2551-8, 2259-60.

Neugarten, B. L. (1975). The future and the young-old. *Gerontologist, 15,* 4-9.

Neugarten, B. L., & Datan, N. (1973). Sociological perspectives on the life cycle. In P. B. Baltes and K. W. Schaie (Eds.), *Life-span developmental psychology: Personality and socialization* (pp. 53-69). New York: Academic Press.

Neve, R. J., Diederiks, J. P., Knibbe, R. A., & Drop, M, J. (1993). Developments in drinking behavior in The Netherlands from 1958 to 1989, a cohort analysis. *Addiction, 88,* 611-21.

Nevitt, M. C., Cummings, S. R., Lane, N. E., Hochberg, M. C., Scott, J. C., Pressman, A. R., Genant, H. K., & Cauley, J. A. (1996). Association of estrogen replacement therapy with the risk of osteoarthritis of the hip in elderly white women. Study of osteoporotic fractures research group. *Archives of Internal Medicine, 156,* 2073-2080.

Newby, L. K., Kristinsson, A., Bhapkar, M. V., Aylward, P. E., Dimas, A. P., Klein, W. W, McGuire, D. K., Moliterno, D. J., Verheugt, F. W., Weaver, W. D., & Califf, R. M.,

SYMPHONY & 2nd SYMPHONY Investigators. (2002). Early statin initiation and outcomes inpatients with acute coronary syndromes. *Journal of the American Medical Association, 287,* 3130-3132.

Newhouse, P. A., Potter, A., Kelton, M., & Corwin, J. (2001). Nicotinic treatment of Alzheimer's disease. *Biological Psychiatry, 49,* 268-278.

Newman, P. J., & Sweet, J. J. (1992). Depressive disorders. In A. E. Puente & R. J. McCaffrey (Eds.), *Handbook of neuropsychological assessment: A bio-psychosocial perspective* (pp. 263-307). New York: Plenum.

Niaura, R., Banks, S. M., Ward, K. D., Stoney, C. M., Spiro, A., III, Aldwin, C. M., Landsberg, M.D., & Weiss, S. T. (2000). Hostility and the metabolic syndrome in older males: The Normative Aging Study. *Psychosomatic Medicine, 62,* 7-16.

Nieman, D. C., Henson, D. A., Gusewitch, G., Warren, B. J., Dotson, R. C., & Butterworth, D. E., & Nehlsen-Cannarella, S. L. (1993). Physical activity and immune function in elderly women. *Medicine and Science in Sports and Exercise, 25,* 823-31.

Nieman, D. C. (2000). Exercise immunology: Future directions for research related to athletes, nutrition, and the elderly. *International Journal of Sports Medicine, 21*(Suppl. 1), S61-S68.

Norman, G. R., & Streiner, D. L. (2000). *Biostatistics: The bare essentials* (2nd ed.). Hamilton, Ontario: B. C. Decker.

Norris, F. H. (1992). Epidemiology of trauma: Frequency and impact of different potentially traumatic events on different demographic groups. *Journal of Consulting and Clinical Psychology, 60,* 409-418.

Norris-Baker, C., & Scheidt, R. J. (1994). From "Our Town" to "Ghost Town"? The changing context of home for rural elders. *International Journal of Aging and Human Development, 38,* 181-202.

Norwood, T. H. (1990). Cellular aging. In C. K. Cassel, D. E. Riesenberg, L. B. Sorensen, & J. R. Walsh (Eds.), *Geriatric medicine* (2nd ed., pp. 1-15). New York: Springer-Verlag.

Noveck, J. (1997, August 4). Jeanne Calment, world's oldest person, dies at 122. *The Detroit News.* Retrieved from http://www.lauralewis.com/article_1100b.htm (Laura Lewis, *Houston Chronicle*)

Nuland, S. B. (1994). *How we die: Reflections on life's final chapter.* New York: Alfred A. Knopf.

Nunnally, J. C. (1978). *Psychometric theory* (2nd ed.). New York: McGraw-Hill.

Ober, B. A., & Shenaut, G. K. (1999). Well-organized conceptual domains in Alzheimer's disease. *Journal of the International Neuropsychological Society, 5,* 676-684.

Oeppen, J., & Vaupel, J. W. (2002). Broken limits to life expectancy. *Science, 296,* 1029-1031.

Olshansky, S. J., Carnes, B. A., & Desesquelles, A. (2001). Demography. Prospects for human longevity. *Science, 291,* 1491-1492.

Orth-Gomer, K., Rosengren, A., & Wilhelmsen, L. (1993). Lack of social support and incidence of coronary heart disease in middle-aged Swedish men. *Psychosomatic Medicine, 55,* 37-43.

Orwoll, L., & Perlmutter, M. (1990). The study of wise persons: Integrating a personality perspective. In R. J. Sternberg (Ed.), *Wisdom: Its nature, origins, and development* (pp. 160-177). Cambridge, UK: Cambridge University Press.

Ory, M. (1985, Fall). The burden of care. *Generations,* pp. 14-18.

Ory, M. G., & Mack, K. A. (1998). Middle-aged and older people with AIDS. *Research on Aging, 20,* 653-654.

Ott, S. M. (1999). Osteoporosis and osteomalacia. In W. R. Hazzard, J. P. Blass, W. H. Ettinger, Jr., J. B. Halter, & J. G. Ouslander (Eds.), *Principles of geriatric medicine and gerontology* (4th ed., pp. 1057-1084). New York: McGraw-Hill.

Ouellette, S. C., & DiPlacido, J. (2001). Personality's role in the protection and enhancement of health: Where the research has been, where it is stuck, how it might move. In A. Baum, T. A. Revenson, & J. E. Singer (Eds.), *Handbook of health psychology* (pp. 175-194). New York: Guilford.

Ouslander, J. G. (1994). Incontinence. In W. R. Hazzard, E. L. Bierman, J. P. Blass, W. H. Ettinger, Jr., & J. B. Halter (Eds.), *Principles of geriatric medicine and gerontology* (3rd ed., pp. 1229-1249). New York: McGraw-Hill.

Ouslander, J. G., Greendale, G. A., Uman, G., Lee, C., Paul, W., & Schnelle, J. (2001). Effects of oral estrogen and progestin on the lower urinary tract among female nursing home residents. *Journal of the American Geriatric Society, 49,* 803-807.

Paffenbarger, R. S., Hyde, R. T., Wing, A. L., Lee, I. M., Jung, D. L., & Kampert, J. B. (1993). The association of changes in physical-activity level and other lifestyle characteristics with mortality among men. *New England Journal of Medicine, 328,* 538-545.

Page, J. (2000). Consumption of NSAIDs and the development of congestive heart failure in elderly patients. *Archives of Internal Medicine, 160,* 777-784.

Palmer, R. M. (1997). Acute hospital care. In C. K. Cassel, H. J. Cohen, E. B. Larson, D. E. Meier, N. M. Resnick, L. Z. Rubenstein, & L. B. Sorensen (Eds.), *Geriatric medicine* (3rd ed., pp. 119-129). New York: Springer-Verlag.

Pamuk, E., Makuc, D., Heck, K., Reuben, C., & Lochner, K. (1998). *Health, United States, 1998* (DHHS Publication No. 98-1232). Washington, DC: Government Printing Office.

Papadakis, M. A., Grady, D., Black, D., Tierney, M. J., Gooding, G. A., Schambelan, M., & Grunfeld, C. (1996). Growth hormone replacement in healthy older men improves body composition but not functional ability. *Annals of Internal Medicine, 124,* 708-16.

Pargament, K. (1997). *The psychology of religion and coping: Theory, research, and practice.* New York: Guilford.

Parker, R., & Aldwin, C. M. (1997). Do aspects of gender identity change from early to middle adulthood? Disentangling age, cohort, and period effects. In M. Lachman & J. James (Eds.), *Multiple paths of mid-life development* (pp. 67-107). Chicago: University of Chicago Press.

Parkes, C. M. (1972). *Bereavement: Studies of grief in adult life.* New York: International Universities Press.

Pascual-Leone, J. (1990). Reflections on life-span intelligence, consciousness, and ego development. In C. N. Alexander & E. J. Langer (Eds.), *Higher stages of human development* (pp. 258-341). Oxford: Oxford University Press.

Paykel, E. S. (1983). Methodological aspects of life events research. *Journal of Psychosomatic Research, 27,* 341-352.

Payton, M., Riggs, K. M., Spiro, A., III, Weiss, S. T., & Hu, H. (1998). Relations of bone and blood lead to cognitive function: The VA Normative Aging Study. *Neurotoxicology & Teratology, 20,* 19-27.

Pearlin, L. I., Aneshensel, C. S., Mullan, J. T., & Whitlatch, C. J. (1996). Caregiving and its social support. In R. H. Binstock and L. K. George (Eds.), *Handbook of Aging and the Social Science* (4th ed., pp. 283-302). San Diego, CA: Academic Press.

Pearlin, L. I., & Johnson, J. S. (1977). Marital status, life-strains and depression. *American Sociological Review, 42,* 704-715.

Pearlin, L. I., Lieberman, M. A., Menaghan, E. G., & Mullan, J. T. (1981). The stress process. *Journal of Health and Social Behavior, 22,* 337-356.

Pearlin, L. I., Mullan, J. T., Semple, S. J., & Skaff, M. M. (1990). Caregiving and the stress process: An overview of concepts and their measures. *The Gerontologist, 30,* 583-594.

Pearlin, L. I., Pioli, M. F., & McLaughlin, A. E. (2001). Caregiving by adult children: Involvement, role disruption, and health. In R. H. Binstock & L. K. George (Eds.), *Handbook of aging and the social sciences* (5th ed., pp. 238-254). San Diego, CA: Academic Press.

Pearlin, L. I., & Schooler, C. (1978). The structure of coping. *Journal of Health and Social Behavior, 19,* 2-21.

Peck, R. C. (1968). Psychological developments in the second half of life. In B. L. Neugarten (Ed.), *Middle age and aging: A reader in social psychology* (pp. 88-92). Chicago: University of Chicago Press.

Pedersen, N. L., Reynolds, C. A., & Gatz, M. (1996). Sources of covariation among mini-mental state examination scores, education, and cognitive abilities. *Journals of Gerontology: Psychological Sciences, 51B,* P55.

Peirce, R. S., Frone, M. R., Russell, M., & Cooper, M. L. (1996). Financial stress, social support, and alcohol involvement: A longitudinal test of the buffering hypothesis in a general population survey. *Health Psychology, 15,* 38-47.

Penning, M. J. (2002). Hydra revisited: Substituting formal for self- and informal in-home care among older adults with disabilities. *The Gerontologist, 42,* 4-16.

Perls, T. T. (1997). Centenarians prove the compression of morbidity hypothesis, but what about the rest of us who are genetically less fortunate? *Medical Hypotheses, 49,* 405-407.

Peters-Davis, N. D., Moss, M. S., & Pruchno, R. A. (1999). Children-in-law in caregiving families. *The Gerontologist, 39,* 66-75.

Peterson, C. (1988). Explanatory style as a risk factor for illness. *Cognitive Therapy and Research, 12,* 117-130.

Peterson, C., Luborsky, L., & Seligman, M. E. P. (1983). Attributions and depressive mood shifts: A case study using the symptom-context method. *Journal of Abnormal Psychology, 29,* 96-103.

Peterson, C., & Seligman, M. E. P. (1984). Causal explanations as a risk factor for depression: Theory and evidence. *Psychological Review, 91,* 347-374.

Peterson, C., & Seligman, M. E. P. (1987). Explanatory style and illness. *Journal of Personality, 55,* 237-265.

Peterson, C., Seligman, M. E. P., & Vaillant, G. E. (1988). Pessimistic explanatory style is a risk factor for physical illness: A thirty-five-year longitudinal study. *Journal of Personality and Social Psychology, 55,* 23-27.

Peterson, C., Semmel, A., vonBaeyer, C., Abramson, L. Y., Metalsky, G. I., & Seligman, M. E. P. (1982). The Attributional Style Questionnaire. *Cognitive Therapy Research, 6,* 287-299.

Pfeiffer, E. (1975). A short portable mental status questionnaire for the assessment of organic brain deficiencies in elderly patients. *Journal of American Geriatrics Society, 23,* 433-441.

Piaget, J. (1954). *The construction of reality in the child* (Trans. M. Cook). New York: Basic Books.

Pickering, T. (1999). Cardiovascular pathways: Socioeconomic status and stress effects on hypertension and cardiovascular function. *Annals of the New York Academy of Sciences, 896,* 262-277.

Pi-Sunyer, R. X. (2000). Obesity. In L. Goldman & J. C. Bennett (Eds.), *Textbook of medicine* (21st ed., pp. 1155-1162). Philadelphia: W. B. Saunders.

Plosker, G. L., & McTavish, D. (1996). Intranasal salcatonin (salmon calcitonin). A review of its pharmacological properties and role in the management of post-menopausal osteoporosis. *Drugs and Aging, 8,* 378-400.

Poikolainen, K. (1995). Alcohol and mortality: A review. *Journal of Clinical Epidemiology, 48,* 455-65.

Poirier, J., & Finch, C. E. (1994). Neurochemistry of the aging human brain. In W. R. Hazzard, E. L. Bierman, J. P. Blass, W. H. Ettinger, Jr., & J. B. Halter (Eds.), *Geriatric medicine and gerontology* (3rd ed., pp. 1005-1012). New York: McGraw-Hill.

Polla, B. A., Bachelet, M., Elia, G., & Santoro, M. G. (1998). Stress proteins in inflammation. In P. Csermeley (Ed.), *Stress of life: From molecules to man. Annals of the New York Academy of Sciences, 851,* 75-85.

Poloma, M. M., & Gallup, G. H. (1991). *The varieties of prayer: A survey report.* Philadelphia: Trinity Press International.

Poloma, M. M., & Pendleton, B. F. (1991). *Religiosity and well-being: Exploring neglected dimensions of quality of life research.* Lewiston, NY: Edwin Mellen.

Pottenger, L. A. (1997). Orthopedic problems. In C. K. Cassel, H. J. Cohen, E. B. Larson, D. E. Meier, N. M. Resnick, L. Z. Rubenstein, & L. B. Sorensen (Eds.), *Geriatric medicine* (3rd ed., pp. 433-448). New York: Springer-Verlag.

Prendergast, T. J., & Luce, J. M. (1997). Increasing incidence of withholding and withdrawal of life support from the critically ill. *American Journal of Respiratory & Critical Care Medicine, 155,* 15-20.

Pribram, K. (2001). Commentary on E. R. John et al. "Invariant reversible QEEG effects of anesthetics" and E. R. John "A field theory of consciousness," *Conscious Cognition, 10,* 246-258.

Proctor, E. K., Morrow-Howell, N., Li, H., & Dore, P. (2000). Adequacy of home care and hospital readmission for elderly congestive heart failure patients. *Health and Social Work, 25,* 87-96.

Puggaard, L., Larsen, J. B., Stovring, H., & Jeune, B. (2000). Maximal oxygen uptake, muscle strength and walking speed in 85-year-old women: Effects of increased physical activity. *Aging (Milano), 12*, 180-189.

Pulska, T., Pahkala, K., Laippala, P., & Kivelä, S.-L. (2000). Depressive symptoms predicting six-year mortality in depressed elderly Finns. *International Journal of Geriatric Psychiatry, 15*, 940-946.

Punyiczki, M., & Fésüs, L. (1998). Heat shock and apoptosis. In P. Csermeley (Ed.), Stress of life: From molecules to man. *Annals of the New York Academy of Sciences, 851*, 67-74.

Rabbins, P. V., Fitting, M. D., Eastham, J., & Fetting, J. (1990). The emotional impact of caring for the chronically ill. *Psychosomatics, 31*, 331-336.

Rabin, B. S. (2000). Changes in the immune system during aging. In S. B. Manuck, R. Jennings, B. S. Rabin, & A. Baum (Eds.), *Behavior, health, and aging* (pp. 59-68). Mahwah, NJ: Lawrence Erlbaum.

Rajagopalan, S. (2001). Tuberculosis and aging: A global health problem. *Clinical Infectious Diseases, 33*, 1034-1039.

Rall, L. C., Roubenoff, R., Cannon, J. G., Abad, L. W., Dinarello, C. A., & Meydani, S. N. (1996). Effects of progressive resistance training on immune response in aging and chronic inflammation. *Medicine and Science in Sports and Exercise, 28*, 1356-1365.

Ramos, L. R. (1993). Brazil. In E. B. Palmore (Ed.), *Developments and research on aging: An international handbook* (pp. 25-40). Westport, CT: Greenwood.

Ramos, L. R., Perracini, M., Rosa, T. E., & Kalache, A. (1993). Significance and management of disability among urban elderly residents in Brazil. *Journal of Cross-Cultural Gerontology, 8*, 313-332.

Ranganathan, V. K., Siemionow, V., Sahgal, V., & Yue, G. H. (2001). Effects of aging on hand function. *Journal of the American Geriatric Society, 49*, 1478-1484.

Raphael, K. G., Cloitre, M., & Dohrenwend, B. P. (1991). Problems of recall and misclassification with checklist methods of measuring stressful life events. *Health Psychology, 10*, 62-74.

Rapp, S. R., Espeland, M. A., Shumaker, S. A., Henderson, V. W., Brunner, R. L., Manson, J. E., Gass, M.L.S., Stefanick, M. L., Lane, D. S., Hays, J., Johnson, K. C., Coker, L. H., Dailey, M., & Bowen, D. (2003). Effect of estrogen plus progestin on global cognitive function in postmenopausal women. The Women's Health Initiative Memory Study: A randomized controlled trial. *Journal of the American Medical Association, 289*, 2663-2672.

Rasmussen, L. B., Hansen, G. L., Hansen, E., Koch, B., Mosekilde, L., Molgaard, C., Sorensen, O. H., & Ovesen, L. (2000). Vitamin D: Should the supply in the Danish population be increased? *International Journal of Food Sciences and Nutrition, 51*, 209-215.

Raudenbush, S. W. (2000). Comparing personal trajectories and drawing causal inferences from longitudinal data. *Annual Review of Psychology, 52*, 501-525.

Reaven, G. M. (1998). Banting lecture 1988: Role of insulin resistance in human disease. *Diabetes, 37*, 1595-1607.

Reed, D., McGee, D., Yano, K., & Feinleib, M. (1983). Social networks and coronary heart disease among Japanese men in Hawaii. *American Journal of Epidemiology, 117,* 384-396.

Reich, J. W., & Zautra, A. J. (1995). Other-reliance encouragement effects in female rheumatoid arthritis patients. *Journal of Social and Clinical Psychology, 14,* 119-133.

Resnick, N. M. (1997). Urinary incontinence. In C. K. Cassel, H. J. Cohen, E. B. Larson, D. E. Meier, N. M. Resnick, L. Z. Rubenstein, & L. B. Sorensen (Eds.), *Geriatric medicine* (3rd ed., pp. 735-756). New York: Springer-Verlag.

Review Panel on Coronary-Prone Behavior and Coronary Heart Disease. (1978). Coronary-prone behavior and coronary heart disease: A critical review. *Circulation, 65,* 1199-1215.

Reynolds, P., & Kaplan, G. A. (1990). Social connections and risk for cancer: Prospective evidence from the Alameda County study. *Journal of Behavioral Medicine, 16,* 101-110.

Rich, M. W. (1999). Heart failure. In W. R. Hazzard, J. P. Blass, W. H. Ettinger, Jr., J. B. Halter, & J. G. Ouslander (Eds.), *Principles of geriatric medicine and gerontology* (4th ed., pp. 679-700). New York: McGraw-Hill.

Richards, J. C., Hof, A., & Alvarenga, M. (2000). Serum lipids and their relationships with hostility and angry affect and behaviors in men. *Health Psychology, 19,* 393-398.

Rigler, S. K. (2000). Alcoholism in the elderly. *American Family Physician, 61,* 1710-1716, 1883-1884, 1887-1888.

Rimer, B. K., McBride, C. M., & Crump, C. (2001). Women's health promotion. In A. Baum, T. A., Revenson, & J. E. Singer (Eds.), *Handbook of health psychology* (pp. 519-539). Mahwah, NJ: Lawrence Erlbaum.

Rincon, H. G., Solomon, G. F., Benton, D., & Rubenstein, L. Z. (1996). Exercise in frail elderly men decreases natural killer cell activity. *Aging, 8,* 109-112.

Rinpoche, K. (1996). *Luminous mind: The way of the Buddha.* Boston: Wisdom.

Robbins, A. S., Spence, J. T., & Clark, H. (1991). Psychological determinants of health and performance: The tangled web of desirable and undesirable characteristics. *Journal of Personality & Social Psychology, 61,* 755-765.

Robichaud, L., Hebert, R., Roy, P., & Roy, C. (2000). A preventive program for community-dwelling elderly at risk of functional decline: A pilot study. *Archives of Gerontology and Geriatrics, 30,* 73-84.

Robinson-Whelan, S., Kiecolt-Glaser, J., & Glaser (2000). Effects of chronic stress on immune function and health in the elderly. In S. B. Manuck, R. Jennings, B. S. Rabin, & A. Baum (Eds.), *Behavior, health, and aging* (pp. 69-82). Mahwah, NJ: Lawrence Erlbaum.

Rodin, J., & Langer, E. J. (1977). Long-term effects of a control-relevant intervention with institutionalized aged. *Journal of Personality and Social Psychology, 35,* 897-902.

Rogers, R. G., Hummer, R. A., Nam, C. B., & Peters, K. (1996). Demographic, socioeconomic, and behavioral factors affecting ethnic mortality by cause. *Social Forces, 74,* 1419-1438.

Rogosa, D. (1988). Myths about longitudinal research. In K. W. Schaie & R. T. Campbell (Eds.), *Methodological issues in aging research* (pp. 171-209). New York: Springer.

Rogosa, D., & Willett, J. (1985). Understanding correlates of change by modeling individual differences in growth. *Psychometrika, 50,* 203-28.

Romero, L. M., Raley-Susman, I. M., Redish, D. M., Brooke, S. M., Horner, H. C., & Sapolsky, R. (1992). Possible mechanism by which stress accelerates growth of virally derived tumors. *Proceedings of the National Academy of Sciences, 89,* 11084-11087.

Rook, K. S. (1994). Assessing the health-related dimensions of older adults' social relationships. In M. P. Lawton & J. A. Teresi (Eds.), *Annual review of gerontology and geriatrics* (Vol. 14, pp. 142-181).New York: Springer.

Roos, N. P., Havens, B., & Black, C. (1993). Living longer but doing worse: Assessing health status in elderly persons at two points in time in Manitoba, Canada, 1971 and 1983. *Social Science and Medicine, 36,* 273-282.

Rosenman, R. H. (1978). The interview method of assessment of the coronary-prone behavior pattern. In T. M. Dembrowski, S. M. Weiss, J. L. Siehlds, S. G. Hayes, & M. Feinleib (Eds.), *Coronary-prone behavior.* New York: Springer-Verlag.

Rosenwaike, I., & Hill, M. E. (1996). The accuracy of age reporting among elderly African Americans. *Research on Aging, 18,* 311-324.

Rossi, A. (1980). Life-span theories and women's lives. *Signs, 6,* 4-32.

Rossouw, J. E., Anderson, G. L., Prentice, R. L., LaCroix, A. Z., Kooperberg, C., Stefanik, M. L., Jackson, R. D., Beresford, S. A. A., Howard, B. V., Johnson, K. C., Kotchen, J. M., & Ockene, J. (2002). Risks and benefits of estrogen plus progestin in healthy postmenopausal women: Principal results from the Women's Health Initiative randomized controlled trial. *Journal of the American Medical Association, 288,* 321-333.

Roth, S., & Cohen, L. J. (1986). Approach, avoidance, and coping with stress. *American Psychologist, 41,* 813-819.

Rothstein, G. (1999). White cell disorders. In W. R. Hazzard, J. P. Blass, W. H. Ettinger, Jr., J. B. Halter, & J. G. Ouslander (Eds.), *Principles of geriatric medicine and gerontology* (4th ed., pp. 907-918). New York: McGraw-Hill.

Rotter, J. B. (1954). *Social learning theory and clinical psychology.* Englewood Cliffs, NJ: Prentice Hall.

Rowe, J. W., & Kahn, R. L. (1998). *Successful aging.* New York: Pantheon.

Rozanski, A., Blumenthal, J. A., & Kaplan, J. (1999). Impact of psychological factors on the pathogenesis of cardiovascular disease and implications for therapy. *Circulation, 99,* 2192-217.

Rubenstein, L. Z., Josephson, K. R., Trueblood, P. R., Loy, S., Harker, J. O., Pietruszka, F. M., & Robbins, A. S. (2000). Effects of a group exercise program on strength, mobility, and falls among fall-prone elderly men. *Journals of Gerontology: Biological Sciences and Medical Sciences, 55,* M317-M321.

Ruberman, W., Weinblatt, E., Goldberg, J. D., & Chaudhary, B. S (1984). Psychosocial influences on mortality after myocardial infarction. *New England Journal of Medicine, 311,* 552-559.

Rudberg, M. A., Parzen, M. I., Leonard, L. A., & Cassel, C. K. (1996). Functional limitation pathways and transitions in community-dwelling older persons. *The Gerontologist, 36,* 430-440.

Ruitenberg, A., van Swieten, J. C., Witteman, J. C., Mehta, K. M., van Duijn, C. M., Hofman, A, & Breteler, M. M. (2002). Alcohol consumption and risk of dementia: The Rotterdam study. *Lancet, 359,* 281-286.

Ryff, C. D., Kwan, C. M. L., & Singer, B. H. (2001). Personality and aging: Flourishing agendas and future challenges. In J. E. Birren & K. W. Schaie (Eds.), *Handbook of the psychology of aging* (5th ed., pp. 477-499). San Diego, CA: Academic Press.

Sahyoun, N. R., Lentzner, H., Hoyert, D., & Robinson, K. N. (2001). Trends in the causes of death among the elderly. (Aging Trends 1). Hyattsville, MD: National Center for Health Statistics.

Saltzman, J. R, & Russell, R. M. (1998). The aging gut. Nutritional issues. *Gastroenterology Clinics of North America, 27,* 309-324.

Santambrogio, L., Nosotti, M., Bellaviti, N., & Mezzetti, M. (1996). Prospective study of surgical treatment of lung cancer in the elderly patient. *Journals of Gerontology: Biological Sciences and Medical Sciences, 51,* M267-M269.

Sapolsky, R. M. (1992). *Stress, the aging brain, and the mechanisms of neuron death.* Cambridge, MA: MIT Press.

Sapolsky, R. M. (1998). *Why zebras don't get ulcers: An updated guide to stress, stress-related diseases, and coping.* New York: W. H. Freeman.

Sapolsky, R. M. (1999). Glucocorticoids, stress, and their adverse neurological effects: Relevance to aging. *Experimental Gerontology, 34,* 721-732.

Satz, P. (1993). Brain reserve capacity on symptom onset after brain injury: A formulation and review of evidence for threshold theory. *Neuropsychology, 7,* 273-295.

Schacter, D. L., & Tulving, E. (1994). What are the memory systems of 1994? In D. L. Schacter & E. Tulving (Eds.), *Memory systems 1994* (pp. 1-38). Cambridge, MA: MIT Press.

Schaie, K. W. (1977). Quasi-experimental designs in the psychology of aging. In J. E. Birren & K. W. Schaie (Eds.), *Handbook of the psychology of aging* (1st ed., pp. 39-58). New York: Van Nostrand Reinhold.

Scheibel, A. B. (1996). Structural and functional changes in the aging brain. In J. E. Birren & K. W. Schaie (Eds.), *Handbook of the psychology of aging* (4th ed., pp. 105-128). San Diego, CA: Academic Press.

Scheiber, M. D., & Rebar, R. W. (1999). Isoflavones and postmenopausal bone health: A viable alternative to estrogen therapy? *Menopause, 6,* 233-241.

Scheidt, R. J., & Norris-Baker, C. (1990). A transactional approach to environmental stress among older residents of rural communities: Introduction to a special issue. *Journal of Rural Community Psychology, 11,* 5-30.

Scheier, M. F., & Carver, C. S. (1985). Optimism, coping, and health: Assessment and implications of generalized outcome expectancies. *Health Psychology, 4,* 219-247.

Scheier, M. F., & Carver, C. S. (1992). Effects of optimism on psychological and physical well-being: Theoretical overview and empirical update. *Cognitive Therapy Research, 16,* 201-228.

Scheier, M. F., Matthews, K., Owens, J. F., Magovern, G. J., Lefebvre, R. C., Abbott, R. A., & Carver, C. S. (1989). Dispositional optimism and recovery from coronary artery bypass surgery: The beneficial effects on physical and psychological well-being. *Journal of Personality and Social Psychology, 57,* 1024-1040.

Scheier, M. F., Matthews, K., Owens, J. F., Schulz, R., Bridges, M. W., Magovern, G. J., & Carver, C. S. (1999). Optimism and rehospitalization after coronary artery bypass graft surgery. *Archives of Internal Medicine, 159,* 829-835.

Sheper-Hughes, N. (1983). Deposed kings: The demise of the rural Irish gerontocracy. In J. Sokolovsky (Ed.), *Growing old in different societies: Cross-cultural perspectives* (pp. 130-146). Belmont, CA: Wadsworth.

Schiodt, F. V., Rochling, F. A., Casey, D. L., & Lee, W. M. (1997). Acetaminophen toxicity in an urban county hospital. *New England Journal of Medicine, 337,* 1112-1117.

Schleicher, S. M. (2000). A pair of pigmented lesions. *Clinical Advisor for Nurse Practitioners, 3,* 29-32.

Schnurr, P., Spiro, A., III, Aldwin, C. M., & Stukel, T. A. (1998). Symptom trajectories following trauma exposure: Longitudinal findings from the Normative Aging Study. *Journal of Nervous and Mental Disorders, 186,* 522-528.

Schoenborn, C. A., & Adams, P. F. (2001). Alcohol use among adults: United States, 1997-1998. *Advanced Data From Vital and Health Statistics, #324,* whole issue.

Schuit, A. J., Feskens, E. J. M., Launer, L. J., & Kromhout, D. (2001). Physical activity and cognitive decline, the role of the apolipoprotein e4 allele. *Medicine & Science in Sports & Exercise, 33,* 772-777.

Schulz, R., Beach, S. R., Ives, D. G., Martire, L. M., Ariyo, A. A., & Kop, W. J. (2000). Association between depression and mortality in older adults: The cardiovascular health study. *Archives of Internal Medicine, 160,* 1761-1968.

Schulz, R., & Heckhausen, J. (1998). Emotion and control: A life-span perspective. In K. W. Schaie & M. P. Lawton (Eds.), *Annual review of gerontology and geriatrics. Vol. 17: Focus on emotion and adult development* (pp. 185-205). New York: Springer.

Schwarz, C. E., & Daltroy, L. H. (1999). Learning from unreliability: The importance of inconsistency in coping dynamics. *Social Science & Medicine, 48,* 619-631.

Seale, C., & Addington-Hall, J. (1995). Dying at the best time. *Social Science & Medicine, 40,* 589-595.

Seddon, J. M., Rosner, B., Sperduto, R. D., Yannuzzi, L., Haller, J. A., Blair, N. P., & Willett, W. (2001). Dietary fat and risk for advanced age-related macular degeneration. *Archives of Ophthalmology, 119,* 1191-1199.

Seeman, T., & Chen, W. (2002). Risk and protective factors for physical functioning in older adults with and without chronic conditions: MacArthur studies of successful aging. *Journals of Gerontology: Social Sciences, 57,* S135-S144.

Seeman, T. E., McEwen, B. S., Rowe, J. W., & Singer, B. H. (2001). Allostatic load as a marker of cumulative biological risk: MacArthur studies of successful aging. *Proceedings of the National Academy of Sciences, 98,* 4770-4775.

Seeman, T. E., Singer, B. H., & Charpentier, P. (1995). Gender differences in HPA response to challenge: MacArthur studies of successful aging. *Psychoneuroendocrinology, 20,* 711-725.

Seeman, T. E., Singer, B. H., Rowe, J. W., Horwitz, R. I., & McEwen, B. S. (1997). Price of adaptation–allostatic load and its health consequences. *Archives of Internal Medicine, 157,* 2259-2268.

Seeman, T. E., Singer, B. H., Wilkinson, C. W., & McEwen, B. (2001). Gender differences in age-related changes in HPA axis reactivity. *Psychoneuroendocrinology, 26,* 225-240.

Seligman, M. E. P. (1975). *Helplessness: On depression, development, and death.* San Francisco: W. H. Freeman.

Seligman, M. E. P., & Csikszentmihalyi, M. (2000). Positive psychology: An introduction. *American Psychologist, 55,* 5-14.

Selkoe, D. J. (1992). Aging brain, aging mind. *Scientific American, 267,* 134-42.

Selye, H. (1956). *The stress of life.* New York: McGraw-Hill.

Sesso, H. D., Kawachi, I., Vokonas, P. S., & Sparrow, D. (1998). Depression and the risk of coronary heart disease in the Normative Aging Study. *American Journal of Cardiology, 82,* 851-856.

Shah, G. N., & Mooradian, A. D. (1997). Age-related changes in the blood-brain barrier. *Experimental Gerontology, 32,* 501-519.

Shanas, E. (1979). The family as a social support system in old age. *The Gerontologist, 2,* 169-175.

Shapiro, D. E., Boggs, S. R., Rodrigue, J. R., Urrya, H. L, Algina, J. J., Hellman, R., & Ewen, F. (1997). Stage II breast cancer: Differences between four coping patterns in side effects during chemotherapy. *Journal of Psychosomatic Research, 43,* 143-157.

Sharma, D., & Singh, R. (1996). Age-related decline in multiple unit action potentials of cerebral cortex correlates with the number of lipofuscin-containing neurons. *Indian Journal of Experimental Biology, 34,* 776-781.

Shenaut, G. K., & Ober, B. A. (1996). Methodological control of semantic priming in Alzheimer's disease. *Psychology and Aging, 11,* 443-448.

Shepard, R. J., & Shek, P. N. (1996). Impact of physical activity and sport on the immune system. *Reviews on Environmental Health, 11,* 133-147.

Shimamura, A. P., Berry, J. M., Mangels, J. A., & Rusting, C. L. (1995). Memory and cognitive abilities in university professors: Evidence for successful aging. *Psychological Science, 6,* 271-277.

Shinkai, S., Kohno, H., Kimura, K., Komura, T., Asai, H., Inai, R., Oka, K., Kurokawa Y., & Shepard, R. (1995). Physical activity and immune senescence in men. *Medicine and Science in Sports and Exercise, 27,* 1516-1526.

Ship, J. A. (1999). The oral cavity. In W. R. Hazzard, J. P. Blass, W. H. Ettinger, Jr., J. B. Halter, & J. G. Ouslander (Eds.), *Principles of geriatric medicine and gerontology* (4th ed., pp. 591-602). New York: McGraw-Hill.

Sieber, W. J., Rodin, J., Larson, L., Ortega, N., Cummings, N., Levy, S., Whiteside, T., & Herberman, R. (1992). Modulation of human natural killer cell activity by exposure to uncontrollable stress. *Brain, Behavior, & Immunity, 6,* 141-156.

Siegman, A. W. (1994). From Type A to hostility to anger: Reflections on the history of coronary prone behavior. In A. W. Siegman & T. W. Smith (Eds.), *Anger, hostility and the heart* (pp. 1-21). Hillsdale, NJ: Lawrence Erlbaum.

Silverstein, M., & Bengtson, V. L. (1991). Does intergenerational social support influence the psychological well-being of older parents? The contingencies of declining health and widowhood. *Social Science and Medicine, 38,* 943-957.

Silverstein, M., Chen, X., & Heller, K. (1996). Too much of a good thing? Intergenerational social support and the psychological well-being of older parents. *Journal of Marriage and the Family, 58,* 970-982.

Silverstein, M., Conroy, S. J., Wang, H., Giarrusso, R., & Bengtson, V. L. (2002). Reciprocity in parent-child relations over the adult life course. *Journals of Gerontology: Social Sciences, 57B,* S3-S13.

Simons, L. A., McCallum, J., Friedlander, Y., Ortiz, M., & Simons, J. (2000). Moderate alcohol intake is associated with survival in the elderly: The Dubbo Study. *Medical Journal of Australia, 173,* 121-124.

Singh, M. A. F., & Rosenberg, I. H. (1999). Nutrition and aging. In W. R. Hazzard, J. P. Blass, W. H. Ettinger, Jr., J. B. Halter, & J. G. Ouslander (Eds.), *Principles of geriatric medicine and gerontology* (4th ed., pp. 81-96). New York: McGraw-Hill.

Skoog, I., Wallin, A., Fredman, P., Hesse, C., Aevarsson, O., Karlsson, I., Gottfries, C. G., & Blennow, K. (1998). A population study on blood-brain barrier function in 85-year-olds: Relation to Alzheimer's disease and vascular dementia. *Neurology, 50,* 966-971.

Smeeding, T. M. (1990). Economic status of the elderly. In R. H. Binstock & L. K. George (Eds.), *Handbook of aging and the social sciences* (4th ed., pp. 362-380). San Diego, CA: Academic Press.

Smith, D., & Tillipman, H. (2000). *The older population in the United States* (U.S. Census Bureau, P20-532). Washington, DC: U.S. Department of Commerce, Economics and Statistics Administration.

Smith, D. C., & Trump, D. L. (1997). Prostate cancer. In C. K. Cassel, H. J. Cohen, E. B. Larson, D. E. Meier, N. M. Resnick, L. Z. Rubenstein, & L. B. Sorensen (Eds.), *Geriatric medicine* (3rd ed., pp. 305-315). New York: Springer-Verlag.

Smith, J. R., & Pereira-Smith, O. M. (1996). Replicative senescence: Implications for in vivo aging and tumor suppression. *Science, 273,* 63-67.

Smith, K. R., & Zick, C. D. (1996). Risk of mortality following widowhood: Age and sex difference by mode of death. *Social Biology, 43,* 59-71.

Smith, M. A., Rottkamp, C. A., Nunomura, A., Raina, A. K., & Perry, G. (2000). Oxidative stress in Alzheimer's disease. *Biochimica et Biophysical Acta, 1502,* 139-144.

Smith, T. W., Pope, M. K., Rhodewalt, F., & Poulton, J. L. (1989). Optimism, neuroticism, coping, and symptom reports: An alternative interpretation of the Life Orientation Test. *Journal of Personality and Social Psychology, 56,* 640-648.

Smith, W., Assink, J., Klein, R., Mitchell, P., Klaver, C. C. W., Klein, B. E. K., Hofman, A., Jensen, S., Wang, J. J., & de Jong, P. T. V. M. (2001). Risk factors for age-related macular degeneration: Pooled findings from three continents. *Ophthalmology, 108,* 697-704.

Snowdon, D. A. (1997). Aging and Alzheimer's Disease: Lessons from the Nun Study. *The Gerontologist, 37,* 160-156.

Snowdon, D. A. (2001). *Aging with grace: What the Nun Study teaches us about leading longer, healthier, and more meaningful lives.* New York: Bantam.

Snowdon, D. A., Greiner, L. H., Mortimer, J. A., Riley, K. P., Greinder, P. A., & Markesbery, W. R. (1997). Brain infarction and the clinical expression of Alzheimer disease: The nun study. *Journal of the American Medication Association, 277,* 813-817.

Sohal, S. S., & Weindruch, R. (1996). Oxidative stress, caloric restriction, and aging. *Science, 273,* 59-63.

Solomon, G. F., & Benton, D. (2000). Immune functions, their psychological correlates, and health. In S. B. Manuck, R. Jennings, B. S. Rabin, & A. Baum (Eds.), *Behavior, health, and aging* (pp. 109-117). Mahwah, NJ: Lawrence Erlbaum.

Sone, Y. (1996). Age-associated problems in nutrition. *Applied Human Science, 14,* 201-210.

Sorensen, L. B., & Blair, J. M. (1997). Rheumatologic diseases. In C. K. Cassel, H. J. Cohen, E. B. Larson, D. E. Meier, N. M. Resnick, L. Z. Rubenstein, & L. B. Sorensen (Eds.), *Geriatric medicine* (3rd ed., pp. 449-479). New York: Springer-Verlag.

Spector, N. H. (1996). Neuroimmunodulation: A brief review. Can conditioning of natural killer cell activity reverse cancer and/or aging? *Regulatory Toxicology and Pharmacology, 24,* S32-S38.

Spiro, A., III, Aldwin, C. M., Ward, K. D., & Mroczek, D. K. (1995). Personality and the incidence of hypertension among older men: Longitudinal findings from the Normative Aging Study. *Health Psychology, 14,* 563-569.

Spiro, A., III, Butcher, J. E., Aldwin, C. M., & Levenson, M. R. (2000). Change and stability in personality: A 5-year study of the MMPI-2 in older men. In J. E. Butcher (Ed.), *Basic sources on the MMPI-2* (pp. 443-462). Minneapolis: University of Minnesota Press.

Spiro, A., III, Schnurr, P., & Aldwin, C. M. (1994). Combat-related PTSD in older men. *Psychology and Aging, 9,* 17-26.

Stein, M., Miller, A. H., & Trestman, R. L. (1991). Depression: The immune system, and health and illness. *Archives of General Psychiatry, 48,* 171-177.

Stein, S., & Spiegel, D. (2000). Psychoneuroimmune and endocrine effects on cancer progression. In K. Goodkin & A. P. Visser (Eds.), *Psychoneuroimmunology: Stress, mental disorders, and health* (pp. 105-151). Washington, DC: American Psychiatric Press.

Sternberg, R. J. (1990). Understanding wisdom. In R. J. Sternberg (Ed.), *Wisdom: Its nature, origins, and development* (pp. 3-12). Cambridge, UK: Cambridge University Press.

Sternberg, R. J. (1998). A balance theory of wisdom. *Review of General Psychology, 2,* 347-365.

Stewart, A., Black, A., Robins, S. P., & Reid, D. M. (1999). Bone density and bone turnover in patients with osteoarthritis and osteoporosis. *Journal of Rheumatology, 26,* 622-626.

Stewart, W. F., Kawas, C., Corrada, M., & Metter, J. (1997). Risk of Alzheimer's disease and duration of NSAID use. *Neurology, 48,* 626-632.

Stolk, R. P., Pols, H. A., Lamberts, S. W., de Jong, P. T., Hofman, A., & Grobbee, D. E. (1997). Diabetes mellitus, impaired glucose tolerance, and hyperinsulinemia in an elderly population: The Rotterdam study. *American Journal of Epidemiology, 145,* 24-32.

Stollerman, G. H. (1997). Infectious diseases. In C. K. Cassel, H. J. Cohen, E. B. Larson, D. E. Meier, N. M. Resnick, L. Z. Rubenstein, & L. B. Sorensen (Eds.), *Geriatric medicine* (3rd ed., pp. 599-626). New York: Springer-Verlag.

Stone, A. A., Neale, J. M., & Shiffman, S. (1993). Daily assessments of stress and coping and their association with mood. *Annals of Behavioral Medicine, 15,* 8-16

Stone, R. I., Cafferata, G., L., & Sangle, J. (1987). Caregivers of the frail elderly: A national profile. *The Gerontologist, 27,* 616-626.

Stone, R. I., & Murtaugh, C. M. (1990). The elderly population with chronic functional disability: Implications for home care eligibility. *The Gerontologist, 4,* 491-496.

Stones, M. J., & Kozma, A. (1996). Activity, exercise, and behavior. In J. E. Birren & K. W. Schaie (Eds.), *Handbook of the psychology of aging* (4th ed., pp. 338-352). San Diego, CA: Academic Press.

Stoney, C., & West, S. (1997). Lipids, personality, and stress: Mechanisms and modulators. In. M. Hillbrand & R. T. Spitz (Eds.), *Lipids, health, and behavior* (pp. 47-68). Washington, DC: American Psychological Association.

Strachan, M. W., Deary, I. J., Ewing, F. M., & Frier, B. M. (1997). Is type II diabetes associated with an increased risk of cognitive dysfunction? A critical review of published studies. *Diabetes Care, 20,* 438-445.

Strawbridge, W. J., Wallhagen, M. I., Shema, S. J., & Kaplan, G. A. (2000). Negative consequences of hearing impairment in old age: A longitudinal analysis. *Gerontologist, 40,* 320-326.

Strawbridge W. J., Wallhagen, M. I., & Cohen, R. D. (2002). Successful aging and well-being: Self-rated compared with Rowe and Kahn. *The Gerontologist, 42,* 727-733.

Stunkard, A. J. (1975). From explanation to action in psychosomatic medicine: The case of obesity. *Psychosomatic Medicine, 37,* 195-236.

Sulloway, F. J. (1983). *Freud: Biologist of the Mind.* New York: Basic Books.

Taaffe, D. R., Pruitt, L., Pyka, G., Guido, D., & Marcus, R. (1996). Comparative effects of high- and low-intensity resistance training on thigh muscle strength, fiber area, and tissue composition in elderly women. *Clinical Physiology, 16,* 381-392.

Taffett, G. E. (1996). Age-related physiologic changes. In D. B. Reuben, T. T. Yoshikawa, & R. W. Besdine (Eds.), *Geriatrics review syllabus* (3rd ed., pp. 11-15). Dubuque, IA: Kendall/Hunt.

Taggart, H. M. (2001). Self-reported benefits of t'ai chi practice by older women. *Holistic Nursing, 19,* 233-237.

Taylor, S. E, Klein, L. C., Lewis, B. P., Gruenewald, T. L., Gurung, R. A., & Updegraff, J. A. (2000). Biobehavioral responses to stress in females: tend-and-befriend, not fight-or-flight. *Psychological Review, 107,* 411-429.

Taylor, S. E., & Repetti, R. L. (1997). Health psychology: What is an unhealthy environment and how does it get under the skin? *Annual Review of Psychology, 48,* 411-447.

Temoshok, L., Heller, B., Sagebiel, R., Blois, M., Sweet, D., Diclemete, R., & Gold, M. (1985). The relationship of psychosocial factors to prognostic indicators in cutaneous melanoma. *Journal of Psychosomatic Research, 29,* 137-155.

Tennant, C., & McLean, L. (2001). The impact of emotions on coronary heart disease risk. *Journal of Cardiovascular Risk, 8,* 175-183.

Tennen, H., & Affleck, G. (1996). Daily processes in coping with chronic pain: Methods and analytic strategies. In M. Zeidner and N. S. Endler (Eds.), *Handbook of coping: Theory, research, applications* (pp. 151-177). New York: John Wiley.

Tennstedt, S. L., McKinlay, J. M., & Sullivan, L. M. (1989. Informal care for frail elders: The role of secondary caregivers. *The Gerontologist, 29,* 677-683.

Tenover, J. L. (1999). Trophic factors and male hormone replacement. In W. R. Hazzard, J. P. Blass, W. H. Ettinger, Jr., J. B. Halter, & J. G. Ouslander (Eds.), *Principles of geriatric medicine and gerontology* (4th ed., pp. 1029-1040). New York: McGraw-Hill.

Terman, L. M. (1925). *Mental and physical traits of a thousand gifted children. Vol. 1: Genetic studies of genius.* Stanford, CA: Stanford University Press.

Thoits, P. (1986). Social support as coping assistance. *Journal of Consulting and Clinical Psychology, 54,* 416-423.

Thoits, P. A. (1982). Conceptual, methodological, and theoretical problems in studying social support as a buffer against life stress. *Journal of Health and Social Behavior, 23,* 145-159.

Thomas, C. L. (1993). *Taber's cyclopedic medical dictionary.* Philadelphia: F. A. Davis.

Thomas, D. R. (1997). Pressure ulcers. In C. K. Cassel, H. J. Cohen, E. B. Larson, D. E. Meier, N. M. Resnick, L. Z. Rubenstein, & L. B. Sorensen (Eds.), *Geriatric medicine* (3rd ed., pp. 767-785). New York: Springer-Verlag.

Thompson, E. E., & Krause, N. (1998). Living alone and neighborhood characteristics as predictors of social support in late life. *Journals of Gerontology: Social Sciences, 53B,* S354-S363.

Tilburg, T. V. (1998). Losing and gaining in old age: Changes in personal network size and social support in a four-year longitudinal study. *Journals of Gerontology: Social Sciences, 53B,* S313-S323.

Timor, O., Sestier, F., & Levy, E. (2000). Metabolic syndrome X. *Canadian Journal of Cardiology, 16,* 779-789.

Tinetti, M. E. (1986). Performance-oriented assessment of mobility problems in elderly patients. *Journal of the American Geriatrics Society,* 119-126.

Tinetti, M. E., & Powell, L. (1993). Fear of falling and low self-efficacy: A cause of dependence in elderly persons. *Journals of Gerontology, 48,* 35-38.

Tolstoy, L. (1900). *The death of Ivan Ilych.* New York: H. Wolff.

Tomaka, J., Blascovich, J., & Kelsey, R. M. (1992). Effects of self-deception, social desirability, and repressive coping on psychophysiological reactivity to stress. *Personality and Social Psychology Bulletin, 18,* 616-624.

Tomakowsky, J., Lumley, M. A., Markowitz, N., & Frank, C. (2001). Optimistic explanatory style and dispositional optimism in HIV-infected men. *Journal of Psychosomatic Research, 51,* 577-587.

Tornstam, L. (1994). Gero-transcendence: A theoretical and empirical exploration. In L. E. Thomas & S. A. Eisenhandler (Eds.), *Aging and the religious dimension* (pp. 203-225). Westport, CT: Auburn House.

Trent, J. D., Kagawa, H. K., & Yaoi, T. (1998). The role of chaperonins *in vivo*: The next frontier. In P. Csermeley (Ed.), *Stress of life: From molecules to man. Annals of the New York Academy of Sciences, 851,* 36-47.

Tricerri, A., Errani, A. R., Vangeli, M., Guidi, L., Pavese, I., Antico, L., & Bartoloni, C. (1995). Neuroimmunomodulation and psychoneuroendocrinology: Recent findings in adults and aged. *Panminerva Medica, 37,* 77-83.

Tsuang, M., & Woolson, R. (1978). Excess mortality in schizophrenia and affective disorders: Do suicides and accidental deaths solely account for this excess? *Archives of General Psychiatry, 35,* 1181-1185.

Tully, C. L., & Snowdon, D. A. (1995). Weight change and physical function in older women: Findings from the Nun Study. *Journal of the American Geriatric Society, 43,* 1394-1397.

Tune, L. E. (1999). Delirium. In W. R. Hazzard, J. P. Blass, W. H. Ettinger, Jr., J. B. Halter, & J. G. Ouslander (Eds.), *Principles of geriatric medicine and gerontology* (4th ed., pp. 1229-1237). New York: McGraw-Hill.

Vaillant, G. (1977). *Adaptation to life: How the best and the brightest came of age.* Boston: Little, Brown.

Vaillant, G. E. (1983). *The natural history of alcoholism.* Cambridge, MA: Harvard University Press.

Vaillant, G. E. (1993). *The wisdom of the ego.* Cambridge, MA: Harvard University Press.

Vaillant, G. E. (2002). *Aging well: Surprising guideposts to a happier life.* Boston: Little, Brown.

Vaillant, L., & Callens, A. (1996). Hormone replacement treatment and skin aging. *Therapie, 51,* 67-70.

van Doornen, L. J. P. (1997). Lipids and the coronary-prone personality. In M. Hillbrand & R. T. Spitz (Eds.), *Lipids, health, and behavior* (pp. 81-98). Washington, DC: American Psychological Association.

Van Eck, M. M., Nicholson, A. A., Berkhof, H., & Sulon, J. (1996). Individual differences in cortisol responses to a laboratory speech task and their relationship to responses to stressful daily events. *Biological Psychology, 43,* 69-84.

van Grootheest, D. S., Beekman, A. T. F., van Groenou, Broese, M. I., & Deeg, D. J. H. (1999). Sex differences in depression after widowhood: Do men suffer more? *Social Psychiatry & Psychiatric Epidemiology, 34,* 391-398.

Vassend, O., Eskild, A., & Halvorsen, R. (1997). Negative affectivity, coping, immune status, and disease progression in HIV infected individuals. *Psychology and Health, 12,* 375-388.

Vaupel, J. W., Carey, J. R., Christensen, K., Johnson, T. E., Yashin, A. I., Holm, N. V., Iachine, I. A., Kannisto, V., Khazaeli, A. A., Liedo, P., Longo, V. D., Zeng, Y., Manton, K. G., & Curtsinger, J. W. (1998). Biodemographic trajectories of longevity. *Science, 288,* 855-860.

Venjatraman, J. T., & Fernandes, G. (1997). Exercise, immunity and aging. *Aging (Milano), 9,* 42-56.

Verbrugge, L. M. (1989). The twain meet: Empirical explanation of sex differences in health and mortality. *Journal of Health and Social Behavior, 30,* 282-304.

Veroff, J., Douvan, E., & Kulka, R. A. (1981). *The inner American: A self-portrait.* New York: Basic Books.

Vestal, R. E., McGuire, E. A., Tobin, J. D., Andres, R., Norris, A. N., & Mezey, E. (1977). Aging and alcohol metabolism. *Clinical Pharmaceutical Therapeutics, 21,* 343-354.

Villareal, D. T., & Morley, J. E. (1994). Trophic factors in aging. Should older people receive hormonal replacement therapy? *Drugs and Aging, 4,* 492-509.

Vitaliano, P. P., Russo, J., & Niaura, R. (1995). Plasma lipids and their relationships with psychosocial factors in older adults. *Journals of Gerontology: Psychological Sciences & Social Sciences, 50,* P18-P24.

Vitaliano, P. P., Russo, J., Paulsen, V. M., & Bailey, S. L. (1995). Cardiovascular recovery from laboratory stress: Biopsychosocial concomitants in older adults. *Journal of Psychosomatic Research, S39,* 361-377.

Vogel-Sprott, M., & Barrett, B. (1984). Age, drinking habits and the effects of alcohol. *Journal of Studies on Alcohol, 45,* 517-521.

Vögele, C. (1998). Serum lipid concentrations, hostility, and cardiovascular reactions to mental stress. *International Journal of Psychophysiology, 28,* 167-179.

Vogt, T. M., Mullooly, J. P., Ernst, D., Pope, C. R., & Hollis, J. F. (1992). Social networks as predictors of ischemic heart disease, cancer, stroke and hypertension: Incidence, survival and mortality. *Journal of Clinical Epidemiology, 45,* 659-666.

von Bertalanffy, L. (1969). *General systems theory: Foundations, development, applications.* New York: G. Brazilier.

Von Dras, D. D., & Blumenthal, H. T. (2000). Biological, social-environmental, and psychological dialecticism: An integrated model of aging. *Basic and Applied Social Psychology, 22,* 199-212.

von Zglinicki, T., Nilsson, E., Docke, W. D., & Brunk, U. T. (1995). Lipofuscin accumulation and aging of fibroblasts. *Gerontology, 41* (Suppl. 2), 95-108.

Wagner, B. M., Compas, B. E., & Howell, D. C. (1988). Daily and major life events: A test of an integrative model of psychosocial stress. *American Journal of Community Psychology, 16,* 189-205.

Walford, R. L. (1990). The clinical promise of diet restriction. *Geriatrics, 45,* 81-83, 86-87.

Walker, D. W., McColl, G., Jenkins, N. L., Harris, J., & Lithgow, G. J. (2000). Evolution of lifespan in *C. elegans. Nature, 405,* 296-297.

Wallhagen, M. I., Strawbridge, W. J., Cohen, R. D., & Kaplan, G. A. (1997). An increasing prevalence of hearing impairment and associated risk factors over three decades of the Alameda County Study. *American Journal of Public Health, 87,* 440-442.

Waxlery-Morrison, N., Hislop, T. G., Mears, B., & Kan, L. (1991). Effects of social relationships on survival for women with breast cancer: A prospective study. *Social Science and Medicine, 33,* 177-183.

Webster, J. R., Jr., & Cain, T. (1997). Pulmonary disease. In C. K. Cassel, H. J. Cohen, E. B. Larson, D. E. Meier, N. M. Resnick, L. Z. Rubenstein, & L. B. Sorensen (Eds.), *Geriatric medicine* (3rd ed., pp. 653-665). New York: Springer-Verlag.

Wei, J. Y. (1994). Aging and atherosclerosis. In W. R. Hazzard, E. L. Bierman, J. P. Blass, W. H. Ettinger, Jr., & J. B. Halter (Eds.), *Principles of geriatric medicine and gerontology* (3rd ed., pp. 517-532). New York: McGraw-Hill.

Wei, J. Y. (1999). Coronary heart disease. In W. R. Hazzard, J. P. Blass, W. H. Ettinger, Jr., J. B. Halter, & J. G. Ouslander (Eds.), *Principles of geriatric medicine and geron-tology* (4th ed., pp. 661-668). New York: McGraw-Hill.

Weihs, K. L., Enright, T. M., Simmens, S. J., & Reiss, D. (2000). Negative affectivity, restriction of emotions, and site of metastases predict mortality in recurrent breast cancer. *Journal of Psychosomatic Research, 49,* 59-68.

Weiner, H. (1977). *Psychobiology and human disease.* New York: Elsevier.

Weksler, M. E., & Szabo, P. (2000). The effect of age on the B-cell repertoire. *Journal of Clinical Immunology, 20,* 240-9.

Welin, C., Lappas, G., & Wilhelmsen, L. (2000). Independent importance of psychosocial factors for prognosis after myocardial infarction. *Journal of Internal Medicine, 247,* 629-39.

Welin, L., Larsson, B., Svärdsudd, K., Tibblin, B., & Tibblin, G. (1992). Social network and activities in relation to mortality from cardiovascular disease, cancer, and other causes: A 12-year follow-up of the study of men born in 1013 and 1923. *Journal of Epidemiology and community Health, 46, 127*-132.

Welsh, M. J., & Gaestel, M. (1998). Small heat-shock protein family: Function in health and disease. In P. Csermeley (Ed.), *Stress of life: From molecules to man. Annals of the New York Academy of Sciences, 851,* 28-35.

Whitbourne, S. K. (2002, August). *Personality at midlife in the baby boomers: Individual patterns of change.* Paper presented at the annual meeting of the American Psychological Association, Chicago.

Wickelgren, I. (1996). For the cortex, neuron loss may be less than thought. *Science, 273,* 48-50.

Wilcox, S., & King, A. C. (1999). Health behaviors and aging. In W. R. Hazzard, J. P. Blass, W. H. Ettinger, Jr., J. B. Halter, & J. G. Ouslander (Eds.), *Principles of geriatric medicine and gerontology* (4th ed., pp. 287-302). New York: McGraw-Hill.

Wilkinson, C. W., Peskind, E. R., & Raskind, M. A. (1997). Decreased hypothalamic-pituitary-adrenal axis sensitivity to cortisol feedback inhibition in human aging. *Neuroendocrinology, 65,* 79-90.

Willett, J. (1988). Questions and answers in the measurement of change. *Review of Research in Education, 15,* 345-422.

Williams, E. R., & Wilson, C. M. (2001). Race, ethnicity, and aging. In R. H. Binstock & L. K. George (Eds.), *Handbook of aging and the social sciences* (pp. 160-178). San Diego, CA: Academic Press.

Williams, M. E. (1991). Aging of tissues and organs. In J. C. Beck (Ed.), *Geriatrics review syllabus* (pp. 15-29). New York: American Geriatrics Society.

Williams, R. B. (2000). Psychological factors, health, and disease: The impact of aging and the life cycle. In S. B. Manuck, R. Jennings, B. S. Rabin, & A. Baum (Eds.), *Behavior, health, and aging* (pp. 135-151). Mahwah, NJ: Lawrence Erlbaum.

Williams, R. B., Barefoot, J. C., Califf, R. M., Haney, T. L., Saunders, W. B., Pryor, D. B., Hlatky, M. A., Siegler, I. C., & Mark, D. B. (1992). Prognostic importance of social resources among patients with CAD. *Journal of the American Medical Association, 267,* 520-524.

Williams, S. W., & Dilworth-Anderson, P. (2002). Systems of social support in families who care for dependent African American Elders. *The Gerontologist, 42*, 224-236.

Williamson, D. F. (1997). Intentional weight loss: patterns in the general population and its association with morbidity and mortality. *International Journal of Obesity-Related Metabolic Disorders, 21*(Suppl. 1), S14-19.

Willis, W. D., Jr. (1993). The nervous system. In R. M. Berne & M. N. Levy (Eds.), *Physiology* (3rd ed., pp. 93-278). St. Louis, MO: Mosby Year Book.

Wills, T. A., & Fegan, M. F. (2001). Social networks and social support. In A. Baum, T. A., Revenson, & J. E. Singer (Eds.), *Handbook of health psychology* (pp. 209-234). Mahwah, NJ: Lawrence Erlbaum.

Wilson, J. A. P., & Rogers, E. L. (1997). Gastroenterologic disorders. In C. K. Cassel, H. J. Cohen, E. B. Larson, D. E. Meier, N. M. Resnick, L. Z. Rubenstein, & L. B. Sorensen (Eds.), *Geriatric medicine* (3rd ed., pp. 637-652). New York: Springer-Verlag.

Wise, P. M., Krajnak, K. M., & Kashon, M. L. (1996). Menopause: The aging of multiple pacemakers. *Science, 273*, 67-70.

Witta, K. M. (1997). COPD in the elderly. *Advance for Nurse Practitioners, 5*, 18-27, 72.

Wolff, H. G. (1950). Life stress and cardiovascular disorders. *Circulation, 1*, 187-203.

Wolfson, L., Whipple, R., Derby, C., Judge, J., King, M., Amerman, P., Schmidt, J., & Smyers, D. (1996). Balance and strength training in older adults: Intervention gains and tai chi maintenance. *Journal of the American Geriatrics Society, 44*, 498-506.

Woo, D., Gebel, J., Miller, R., Kothari, R., Brott, T., Khoury, J., Salisbury, S., Shukla, R., Pancioli, A., Jauch, E., & Broderick, J. (1999). Incidence rates of first-ever ischemic stroke: Subtypes among blacks: A population-based study. *Stroke, 30*, 2517-2522.

Woodruff-Pak, D., & Hanson, C. (1995). Plasticity and compensation in brain memory systems in aging. In R. A. Dixon & L. Backman (Eds.), *Compensating for psychological deficits and declines: Managing losses and promoting gains* (pp. 191-218). Mahwah, NJ: Lawrence Erlbaum.

World Health Organization. (1998). *Population aging: A public health challenge.* Fact Sheet N 135. Retrieved December 10, 2002, from www.who.int/inf-fs/en/fact135.html

World Health Organization. (2002). *Healthy ageing is vital for development* Press Release WHO/24. Retrieved December 10, 2002, from www.who.int/inf/en/pr-2002-24.html

Wu, Z., & Pollard, W. S. (1998). Social support among unmarried childless elderly persons. *Journals of Gerontology: Social Sciences, 53B*, S324-W335.

Yancura, L. A., Aldwin, C. M., & Spiro, A., III. (1999). Does stress decrease with age? A longitudinal examination of stress in the Normative Aging Study [Abstract]. *The Gerontologist, 39*, 212.

Yasunaga, A., & Tokunaga, M. (2001). The relationships among exercise behavior, functional ADL, and psychological health in the elderly. *Journal of Physiological Anthropology Applied Human Science, 20*, 339-343.

Yehuda, R. (2000). Cortisol alterations in PTSD. In A. Y. Shalev, R. Yehuda, & A. C. McFarlane (Eds.), *International handbook of human response to trauma* (pp. 265-283). New York: Kluwer/Plenum.

Yesavage, J. A., Dolhert, N., & Taylor, J. L. (1994). Flight simulator performance of younger and older aircraft pilots: Effects of age and alcohol. *Journal of the American Gerontological Society, 42,* 577.

Zheng., D., Macera, C., Croft, J., Giles, W., Davis, D., & Scott, W. (1997). Major depression and all-cause mortality among white adults in the United States. *Annuals of Epidemiology, 7,* 213-218.

Zhu, L., Fratiglioni, L., Cuo, Z., Basun, H., Corder, E. H., Winblad, B., & Viitanen, M. (2000). APOE4, are at increased risk. *Stroke, 31,* 53-60.

Zuccala, G., Onder, G., Pedone, C., Cesari, M., Landi, F., Bernabei, R., & Cocchi, A. (2001). Dose-related impact of alcohol consumption on cognitive function in advanced age: results of a multicenter survey. *Alcohol Clinical & Experimental Research, 25,* 1743-8.

Zucker, R. A. (1998). Developmental aspects of aging, alcohol involvement, and their interrelationship. In E. S. L. Gomberg, A. M Hegedus, & R. A. Zucker (Eds.), *Alcohol problems and aging* (pp. 3-23). (NIAAA Research Monograph Series). Bethesda, MD: U.S. Department of Health and Human Services (NIH), National Institute on Alcohol Abuse and Alcoholism.

AUTHOR INDEX

Aarsland, T., 237
Abad, L. W., 206
Abbott, R. A., 244
Aboumatar, S., 182
Abramson, J., 248
Abramson, L. Y., 243
Abrass, I. B., 113
Achroll, M., 237
Acree, M., 278
Adams, M. R., 262
Adams, P. F., 246
Adams, W. L., 249
Addington-Hall, J., 320
Ader, R., 262
Aevarsson, O., 177
Affleck, G., 89, 271, 278
Ager, C. R., 246
Ajani, U. A., 249
Akcay, F., 171
Akiyama, H., 285, 292
Aksoy, H., 171
Albert, M. S., 176
Aldwin, C. M., 24, 25, 35, 45, 56, 61, 62, 70, 71,
        72, 73, 75, 76, 77, 82, 85, 86, 89, 90, 91,
        92, 207, 231, 234, 242, 244, 245, 247, 251,
        253, 262, 268, 269, 270, 272, 273, 276,
        277, 278, 279, 280, 281, 286, 291, 298,
        299, 300, 308, 311, 312, 313, 314
Alexander, C. N., 53, 62, 242
Alexander, K. P., 198
Algina, J. J., 277
Aliabadi, P., 116
Allen, M. T., 238
Allen, R. G., 265
Allman, R. M., 103

Almagro, P., 31
Altschuler, J. L., 281
Alvarenga, M., 234
Amatruda, J., 131, 151
Amerman, P., 119
Amigo, E., 214
Ancheta, J. I., 179
Anda, R. F., 237, 238
Anderson, G. L., 69, 114, 198
Anderson, R. N., 6, 20, 28
Anderson, R. T., 299
Anderson, S., 155
Ando, T., 215
Andres, R., 249
Andrew, D., 204
Aneshensel, C. S., 270, 285, 299
Angleitner, A., 233
Antico, L., 207
Antoni, M., 238
Antoni, M. H., 279
Antonovsky, A., 239
Antonucci, T. C., 284, 285, 286, 287,
        291, 292, 298
Appels, A., 237
Applegate, W. B., 125
Arbuckle, T. Y., 247
Archer, L., 251
Argyle, M., 317
Ariyo, A. A., 250
Armeli, S., 89, 271
Arnetz, B. B., 278
Asai, H., 206
Asakawa, T., 215
Asanuma, M., 182
Ascherio, A., 235

Ashford, J. W., 185
Aspinwall, R., 204
Asthana, S., 182
Astin, P., 319
Atchley, R., 17
Austin, J. T., 66, 82
Auvinen, A., 159
Averill, J. R., 259
Aylward, P. E., 127
Aysan, F., 280

Bacal, C., 182, 197
Bacchetti, P., 34
Bachelet, M., 50
Backlund, E., 31, 33, 236
Backstrom, L., 258
Baghurst, P. A., 238
Bagjurst, K. I., 238
Bailey, S. L., 277
Baker, E., 297
Baker, G. T., III, 164, 166
Baker, L. D., 182
Baldwin, L. A., 53, 265
Baltes, P. B., 53, 59, 61, 242, 293, 312, 315
Bandura, A., 116, 218, 240
Banks, S. M., 234
Bar, F. W., 237
Bar, J., 237
Barbaranelli, C., 233
Barber, C., 312
Barber, W. H., 34
Barefoot, J. C., 234, 237, 296
Barer, B. M., 216, 273, 281
Barker, D. J., 72
Barker, J. C., 286
Baron, J. A., 112
Barreiro, B., 31
Barrett, B., 249, 250
Barron, R. M., 278
Bartoloni, C., 207
Basun, H., 182
Baum, A., 240, 268
Baylink, D. J., 106, 108
Beach, S. R., 250

Beatty, J., 166, 172, 173, 257
Beck, J. C., 155, 210, 211
Beck, L. H., 161
Becker, U., 248
Beckham, J. C., 234
Beekman, A. T. F., 32, 318
Bellaviti, N., 136
Belsky, J., 264
Bem, D. J., 77, 231
Bengtson, V. L., 43, 53, 63, 292, 297, 299
Ben-Shlomo, Y., 30
Benson, H., 233
Benstson, V. L., 44
Bentler, P. M., 82
Benton, D., 62, 206
Beresford, S. A. A., 69, 114, 198
Berg, S., 29
Berg, S. A., 236
Berger, A., 248
Berger, M., 277
Bergman, L. R., 92
Berkhof, H., 277
Berkman, l. F., 295, 296
Berkowitz, N., 214
Bernabei, R., 250
Bernstein, E. D., 202, 204
Berry, J. M., 185
Berthouze, S. E., 141
Bewerse, B., 102
Bhapkar, M. V., 127
Bickford, P. C., 184
Bijlani, R., 131
Bilka, D., 280
Billings, D. W., 278
Biondi, M., 277
Birge, S. J., 182
Birren, J. E., 3, 43
Björntorp, P., 262, 264
Black, A., 114
Black, B., 214
Black, C., 21
Black, D., 197
Black, D. M., 106
Black, P. S., 262

Black, S. A., 287
Blackwell, S., 136
Blair, C. E., 294
Blair, J. M., 114
Blanchard-Fields, F., 279
Bland, D. R., 157
Blascovich, J., 277
Blazer, D., 236
Blazer, D. G., 236, 237, 316
Blennow, K., 177
Bloch, D. A., 21, 216
Blois, M., 238
Bloom, P., 238
Blum, D., 320
Blumenthal, H. T., 44
Blumenthal, J. A., 262
Boggs, S. R., 277
Bohnen, N., 277
Bonnefoy, M., 141
Bookwala, J., 299
Booth-Kewley, S., 234
Bootsma-van der Wiel, A., 211
Borggrefe, M., 237
Bosma, H., 241
Bossé, R., 3, 89, 140, 244, 270, 286, 291
Bossert, S., 277
Botwinick, J., 73
Bouchard, G. R., 247
Bourassa, M. G., 237
Braan, A. W., 318
Bradburn, N., 6
Bramlett, M. H., 206
Branch, L. G., 210, 215
Brand, R. J., 295
Brandstädter, J., 59, 314
Bratko, D., 233
Bravo, G., 164
Breithardt, G., 237
Breitner, J. C. S., 250
Brenner, S. O., 278
Breteler, M. M., 250
Bridges, M. W., 244
Bridges, R. A., 317
Briederick, L., 184

Briggs, A., 116
Britton, A., 249
Broderick, J., 178
Brody, E. M., 222
Brody, J. A., 208
Broese, M. I., 32
Brooke, S. M., 263
Brookmeyer, R., 182, 197
Brott, T., 178
Brown, B. W., Jr., 116
Brown, G., 269
Brown, T., 185
Browning, H. L., 177
Bru, E., 237
Bruce, D. G., 119
Bruce, M., 236
Bruera, E., 320
Bruggeman, C., 237
Brunk, U. T., 49
Brustrom, J. E., 35
Bruunsgaard, H., 204, 206
Buchsbaum, M., 177
Budde, T. H., 237
Buddeberg, C., 277
Bühler, C., 56
Bull, C. N., 23
Burgio, K. L., 157
Buring, J. E., 249
Burke, G. L., 215
Burns, E., 218, 219
Burns, E. A., 204
Burroni, E., 220
Burton, L., 299
Butcher, J. E., 82, 86
Butler, R. N., 3
Butler, S. M., 185
Butterworth, D. E., 206
Byrne, B. M., 83
Byrne, D., 275

Cacioppo, J. T., 206
Cafferata, G., 285
Cahalan, D., 246
Cain, T., 139

Calabrese, E. J., 53, 265
Calbo, E., 31
Califf, R. M., 127, 198, 296
Callahan, D., 318
Callens, A., 104
Cameron, L., 219
Camp, C. J., 180
Campbell, D. T., 68
Campisise, J., 44, 46, 47
Cannon, J. G., 206
Cannon, W. B., 255, 258, 259
Canta Cruz, F. J., 104
Cantor, M. H., 286
Cao, G., 248
Caplan, L., 178
Caplovitz, D., 6
Capodaglio, P., 220
Caprara, G. V., 233
Carelock, J., 130
Carmelli, D., 250
Carnes, B. A., 22
Carney, R., 237
Carr, B. R., 197
Carstensen, L. L., 292, 294
Carver, C. S., 243, 244
Case, N., 296
Case, R. B., 296
Caserta, M. S., 32, 221
Casey, D. L., 249
Casper, L. M., 30
Caspi, A., 77, 231
Cassel, C. K., 215
Castelli, W. P., 235
Cauley, J. A., 116
Cesari, M., 250
Chadman, K., 184
Chae, J. H., 233
Chah, A., 320
Chaikelson, J. S., 247
Chait, A., 126
Chan, S., 182
Chandler, H. M., 62, 242
Chandler, J., 312
Chandra, R. K., 206

Chang, L., 197
Chang, M. Y., 126
Chang, P. P., 237
Chanowitz, B., 60
Charpentier, P., 266
Chaudhary, B. S., 296
Chen, J., 317
Chen, W., 220
Chen, X., 293
Cheskin, L. J., 147
Chiara, G., 273, 280, 281
Chiechi, L. M., 118
Chiriboga, D. A., 272, 273
Christian, J. C., 250
Cisin, I. H., 246
Ciulla, T. A., 171
Clark, A. P., 130
Clark, D., 319
Clark, G., 207
Clark, H., 244
Clark, N. M., 126, 216, 219, 224
Clarke, C., 183
Clarkson, T. B., 262
Clarridge, B. C., 320
Clausen, J. A., 58
Cleveland, K. E., 34
Cleveland, W. P., 250
Cloitre, M., 271
Cocchi, A., 250
Cockerham, W. C., 28, 41
Cohen, F., 244
Cohen, H. J., 35
Cohen, J., 80
Cohen, L. J., 275
Cohen, N., 262
Cohen, P., 80
Cohen, R. D., 69, 74, 167, 295
Cohen, S., 263, 278
Cohen, S. J., 157
Cohen-Solal, A., 206
Colditz, G. A., 151, 235
Cole, G. M., 182
Collett, M., 320
Collins, L. M., 65

Collins, W. E., 250
Colombo, P. C., 206
Compas, B. E., 270
Conger, R. D., 23
Conroy, S. J., 292
Cook, N. R., 215
Cooney, L. M., 112, 118
Cooper, C., 238
Cooper, M. L., 297
Cooper, R., 151
Cooper, R. S., 248
Cooper-Patrick, L., 237
Corcoran-Perry, S., 299
Corder, E. H., 182
Corn, B., 263
Corrada, M., 182, 197
Cortes-Gallego, V., 104
Corti, M., 35
Corwin, J., 183
Cossarizza, A., 204
Costa, M. M., 182
Costa, P. T., Jr., 140, 233
Cotman, C., 173, 184
Cousins, N., 277
Covey, L. A., 238
Coward, R. T., 23
Cowie, C. C., 195
Cox, D. R., 86
Coyne, J. C., 31, 132, 270
Craft, S., 182
Cramer, P., 274, 275, 276
Cranford, J. A., 31
Crapo, L. M., 21
Crawford, J., 136
Creamer, P., 114, 116, 117
Criqui, M. H., 248
Cristafalo, V. J., 45, 48, 49, 265
Croft, J., 236
Crombie, P., 131, 151
Cronbach, L. J., 86
Crossley, H. M., 246
Crump, C., 219
Crumpler, C., 61
Crystal, S., 205

Csikszentmihalyi, M., 243, 303
Cummings, E., 57
Cummings, N., 244
Cummings, S. R., 116, 210
Cuo, Z., 182
Cupertino, A. P., 61, 71, 90, 245, 313, 314
Curb, J. D., 210
Cutler, N. R., 182
Cutrona, C., 297
Cypser, J., 53, 255

D'Agostino, R. B., 63
Dakof, G. A., 284
Dalack, G. W., 238
Dalaker, J., 38, 39
Dalgard, O. S., 241
Daltroy, L. H., 275
Daly, R. N., 198
Damon, B. L., 17, 19, 20, 34
Damush, J. G., Jr., 220
Damush, T. M., 220
Danis, R. P., 171
Dannefer, D., 57
Das, A., Jr., 116
Datan, N., 57
Davey Smith, G., 30, 37
Davey, V. A., 50
Davidson, K., 275
Davies, J., 62, 242
Davies, P., 185
Davis, C. C., 157
Davis, D., 236
Deary, I. J., 195
de Baets, M., 237
de Castro, E., 53, 255
de Castro, S. H., 53, 255
de Craen, A. J., 211
Deeg, D. J. H., 32, 318
Deigner, H. P., 183
de Jong, P. T., 195
De Labry, L., 249
de Lange, T., 47
de Lateur, B. J., 52
Delbono, O., 105, 108, 114

DeLongis, A., 270

Denenberg, V. H., 264

Depue, R. A., 269

Derby, C., 119

Desesquelles, A., 22

Desmond, D. W., 182

Desrosiers, J., 164

DeTurk, P. B., 6, 20, 28

DeVellis, B. M., 240

DeVellis, R. F., 240

Devine, A., 119

Devine, E. C., 277

DeVoe, M., 280

de Vroome, E. M. M., 279

Dew, M. A., 216

Dharmanand, S., 131

Dharmarajan, T. S., 184

Diamond, M. C., 52, 185

Diclemente, R., 238

Diehr, P., 215

Dienstbier, R. A., 265

Diggle, P. J., 92

DiGiovanna, A. G., 45, 107, 122, 127, 135, 149, 152, 164, 170, 190, 191, 195, 196, 202, 204

Dilworth-Anderson, P., 287

Dimas, A. P., 127

Dinarello, C. A., 206

DiPeitro, L., 238

DiPlacido, J., 239

Dixon, R. A., 308

Doblhammer, G., 21

Dobratz, M. C., 320

Docke, W. D., 49

Dodge, J. A., 126, 216, 219, 224

Dohrenwend, B. P., 271

Dolan, S., 319

Dolhert, N., 250

Donelan, K., 287

Dore, P., 131

Dorgan, J. F., 197

Dotson, R. C., 206

Doty, R. L., 164

Dowd, J. J., 292

Draper, P., 264

Drop, M. J., 247

DuBeau, C. E., 157, 159

Dubos, R., 258

Dufour, M. C., 251

Dugan, E., 157

Duhamel, L. M., 224

Duncan, P. W., 214

Duncan, R. P., 23

DuPertuis, L. L., 286

Durara, R., 214

Durazo-Arvizu, R., 151

Durkheim, E., 54

Dwyer, J., 244

Eaker, E. D., 235, 237

Eastham, J., 318

Eberhardt, S., 35, 36

Eberly, S., 296

Eccles, J., 176

Ehrenstein, D., 47

Eisdorfer, D., 214

Ekerdt, D. J., 224

Elashoff, R., 277

Elder, G. H., Jr., 23, 53, 58, 59

Elia, G., 50

Elias, M. F., 63

Elias, P. K., 63

Eliott, S. J., 262

Ell, K., 296

Ellis, C. N., 99, 104

Ellison, R. C., 248

Elwood, M., 238

Emanuel, E. J., 320

Endler, N. S., 275

Engle, V. F., 320

English, W. P., 34

Ennezat, P. V., 206

Enright, T. M., 277

Epstein, M., 34

Epstein, S., 268

Erickson, J., 223

Erikson, E., 55, 298, 309

Erikson, E. H., 304, 314

Erikson, J., 298, 309
Ernest, J. E., 170
Ernst, D., 296
Errani, A. R., 207
Erwin, C. W., 250
Eskild, A., 279
Evans, D. A., 215
Evans, D. L., 238
Evans, R. I., 219
Evans, T., 206
Evans, W. J., 206
Ewen, F., 277
Ewing, F. M., 195

Facioli, M., 220
Fadem, P., 8
Fagher, E., 238
Fahey, J. L., 277
Fairclough, D., 320
Falk, R. T., 197
Farahmand, B. Y., 112
Farquhar, W., 130
Fawzy, F. I., 277
Fawzy, N. W., 277
Feaster, D., 277, 278
Fegan, M. F., 295, 296, 297
Feinleib, M., 295
Feldman, P. H., 287
Felson, D. T., 116
Felten, D. L., 262
Felton, B. J., 279
Fernandes, G., 206
Fernandez, M. E., 112
Ferrell, B. A., 164
Ferrer, H., 246
Ferri, A., 220
Ferrini, A. F., 158
Ferrini, R. L., 158
Ferrucci, L., 35
Feskens, E. J. M., 184
Fésüs, L., 50
Fetting, J., 318
Field, T. M., 261
Fielding, K., 237

Fields, D., 285
Fields, J., 30
Fillmore, K. M., 246
Finch, C. E., 52, 172, 176, 177
Fingerlin, T. E., 126, 219, 224
Fishburn, M. J., 52
Fisher, L., 300
Fitting, M. D., 318
Fleming, I., 268
Fleshner, N. E., 159
Florian, V., 276
Folkman, S., 270, 271, 275, 276, 278, 279
Ford, A. B., 209
Ford, D. E., 237
Ford, D. H., 43, 44
Forman, D. E., 130
Forman, W. B., 149
Forster, L. E., 249
Forthofer, M. S., 216
Forwood, M. R., 118
Foss, J. W., 180
Foster, C., 71
Fox, B. H., 263
Fox-Hill, E., 320
Franceschi, I., 204
Francis, M. K., 45, 48, 49, 265
Frank, C., 243, 244
Frankenhaeuser, M., 240
Franz, C., 197
Fraser, A. G., 249
Frasure-Smith, N., 237
Fratiglioni, L., 182
Frautschy, S. A., 182
Fredlund, P., 241
Fredman, P., 177
Freedland, K., 237
Freedman, M. L., 210, 211
Frese, M., 244
Friedberg, E. G., 48
Friedlander, Y., 249
Friedman, H. S., 230, 234
Friedman, L. J., 247
Friedman, M., 232
Friedman, R., 233

Frier, B. M., 195
Fries, B. E., 216
Fries, J. F., 21, 216
Fritz, H. L., 244
Frone, M. R., 297
Fuchs, I., 277, 278
Fuld, P., 185
Funch, D. P., 296
Furby, L., 86
Furner, S. E., 208
Fuster, V., 198

Gaestel, M., 50
Galanis, D. J., 250
Gallup, G. H., 317
Galvin, K., 131
Garau, J., 31
Garbutt, L. D., 262
Gardner, A. W., 128
Garfinkel, M., 116
Garssen, B., 279
Garvey, A. J., 140
Gatchel, R. J., 240
Gatz, M., 185, 236
Gaziano, J. M., 249
Gaziano, T. A., 249
Gebel, J., 178
Genant, H. K., 116
George, L. K., 216, 286, 294, 297, 316
Getzenberg, R. H., 159
Gevirtz, R., 256, 260
Giarrusso, R., 292
Gilbertson, T. A., 165
Gilchrest, B. A., 98, 99, 100, 101
Giles, W., 236
Gilmer, D. F., 24, 25, 298, 299, 300, 308
Giordano, A., 220
Giottelman, B., 214
Giovannucci, E., 235
Glascock, A. P., 304
Glaser, R., 206, 207
Glass, D. C., 240
Glassman, A., 237, 238
Glueck, E., 310

Glueck, S., 310
Glynn, R. J., 247, 249
Go, C. G., 35
Goddard, K., 182
Gold, C. H., 29
Gold, D. P., 247
Gold, M., 238
Goldberg, J. D., 296
Goldberger, A. L., 45, 52
Goldfarb, M. T., 99, 104
Gomberg, E. S. L., 248
Gonzales, J. A. P., 316
Gonzalez, V. M., 116
Goode, P. S., 157
Gooding, G. A., 197
Goodkin, K., 238, 277, 278, 279
Goodwin, J. S., 296
Gordis, E., 251
Gorman, J. M., 235
Gorsuch, R., 317
Goto, T., 169
Gotoh, S., 49
Gottfries, C. G., 177
Gottman, J. M., 294
Gottschalk, G., 289
Gottschau, A., 248
Gould, D. A., 287
Gould, O. N., 308
Gould, T., 184
Grady, D., 197
Grafstrom, M., 299
Graney, J., 320
Gray, M. L., 159
Green, J. A., 41
Green, L. W., 20
Greendale, G. A., 157
Greenhouse, S. W., 3
Greenwood, D. C., 262
Greer, S., 277
Gregerman, R. I., 196
Greinder, P. A., 182
Greiner, L. H., 182
Grisso, J. A., 110, 111
Grobbee, D. E., 195

Gronbaek, M., 248
Gruchow, H. W., 318
Gruenewald, D. A., 193, 194, 261
Grunfeld, C., 197
Gu, X., 23, 212, 213
Gueldner, S. H., 206, 285
Guidi, L., 207
Guido, D., 118
Guijarro, M. I., 71, 232, 233, 234
Guralnik, J. M., 35, 210, 216
Gurung, R. A., 261
Gusewitch, G., 206
Gussekloo, J., 211
Guterman, A., 214
Guthrie, D., 277
Gutmann, D. L., 279
Guyton, A. C., 121, 123, 130, 131, 134, 145, 153, 172, 173, 179, 187, 199, 201

Ha, W. K., 206
Haan, M. N., 62, 63
Hager, K., 215
Hahn, R. A., 35, 36
Haier, R. J., 177
Hakama, M., 159
Hakim-Larson, J., 280
Hall, E. M., 241
Hall, H. I., 102
Hall, J. E., 121, 123, 130, 131, 134, 145, 153, 172, 173, 179, 187, 199, 201
Hall, K. E., 145
Hall, N., 207
Hallet, A. J., 71, 232, 233, 234
Halter, J. B., 190, 193, 194, 195, 196
Haltmeyer, G. G., 264
Halvorsen, R., 279
Hamarat, E., 280
Hamerman, D., 108
Hamid, P. N., 244
Hammad, T. A., 116
Hamovitch, M., 296
Haney, T. L., 234, 296
Hankinson, S. E., 151
Hansen, E., 118

Hansen, G. L., 118
Hanson, C., 185
Haraguchi, T., 182
Harka, E., 246
Harker, J. O., 119
Harrington, R. A., 198
Harris, A., 171
Harris, J., 44
Harris, M. I., 195
Harris, T., 269
Haskell, W. L., 220
Hass, W. H., III, 24
Hassani, S., 194
Hauser, W. A., 182
Havens, B., 21
Haverkorn, U., 183
Havighurst, R. J., 57
Havlik, R. J., 35
Hayflick, L., 45, 46
Hays, J. C., 316
Hayward, C., 237
Hazlett, E., 177
Hazzard, W. R., 29, 100, 111
Heckhausen, J., 242
Heck, K., 34, 40, 41
Hein, H. O., 248
Helgeson, V. S., 244, 278
Heller, B., 238
Heller, D. A., 62
Heller, K., 293
Hellhammer, D. H., 266
Hellhammer, J., 266
Hellkamp, A. S., 198
Hellman, R., 277
Henderson, S., 53, 255
Henderson, V. W., 185
Hennekens, C. H., 249
Henry, W. E., 57
Henson, D. A., 206
Hepburn, K., 299
Herberman, R., 244
Herbert, L. E., 215
Herbert, R., 164, 221
Herbert, T., 263

Heredia, J. L., 31
Hermos, J., 249
Herness, M. S., 165
Hershman, J. M., 194
Herzog, A. R., 297
Hesse, C., 177
Hesse, L., 171
Hetzel, L., 17, 22
Hicks, A. L., 118
Higginson, I. J., 319
Hilakivi-Clark, L., 264
Hill, M. E., 35
Hillier, V., 131
Hills, P., 317
Hinerfeld, D. A., 266
Hippisley-Cox, J., 237
Hislop, T. G., 296
Hixson, K. A., 318
Hjelm, R., 278
Hlatky, M. A., 296
Hobart, C., 280
Hobbs, B., 17, 19, 20, 34
Hobfoll, S. E., 280
Hochberg, M. C., 114, 116, 117
Hof, A., 234
Hofman, A., 195, 250
Hogan, T. M., 147, 148
Holliday, M., 312
Hollis, J. F., 296
Hollister, L. E., 250
Holman, H. R., 116
Holmes, D., 269
Holtzman, D., 265
Hood, R. W., Jr., 317
Hopkins, M. W., 26
Hopp, F. P., 290
Horie, K., 49
Horn, J., 307
Horner, H. C., 263
Horwitz, R. I., 264, 296
House, J. S., 37, 71, 295
Howard, B. V., 69, 114, 198
Howell, D. C., 270
Hoyert, D., 20, 136

Hoyer, W. J., 212
Hu, H., 182
Hubert, H. B., 21, 216
Hummer, R. A., 34, 35
Hunsberger, B., 317
Hunt, W. C., 296
Hunter, D. J., 151
Hurwitz, D., 214
Hybels, C. F., 236, 237
Hyde, R. T., 52
Hyun, C., 277

Ide, C., 169
Ikeda, K., 182
Inai, R., 206
Irion, J. C., 279
Ishizu, H., 182
Ismirlian, G., 35
Isola, J., 159
Isralowitz, R. E., 223
Ives, D. G., 250
Ivy, G. O., 50

Jackson, B. A., 209
Jackson, J. S., 248
Jackson, R. D., 69, 114, 198
Jacobs, S. C., 60, 233
Jaffe, M. W., 209
James, M. K., 299
Janevic, M. R., 224
Jänig, W., 260
Jankowski, L. M., 208
Jansson, W., 299
Janz, N. K., 126, 216, 219, 224
Jarman, B., 319
Jarvik, G. P., 182
Jarvinen, T. A., 159
Jauch, E., 178
Jazwinski, S. M., 46
Jenkins, C. D., 232
Jenkins, N. L., 44
Jennings, J. C., 106, 108
Jennings, J. R., 262
Jensen, G., 248

Jeune, B., 141
Johansen, D., 248
John, R. C., 126, 219
Johnson, C. L., 216, 273, 281, 298
Johnson, E. W., 195
Johnson, I., 248
Johnson, J. E., 240, 248
Johnson, J. S., 31, 32
Johnson, J. V., 241
Johnson, K. C., 69, 114, 198
Johnson, M. L., 43
Johnson, N. J., 31, 33, 236
Johnson, T. E., 53, 255, 266
Johnstone, B. M., 246
Jones, D., 237
Jones, J., 277
Joseph, C., 250
Joseph, J., 184
Josephson, K. R., 119
Judge, J., 119
Juneau, M., 237
Jung, C., 55
Jung, D. L., 52
Junker, M., 277
Jurivich, D. A., 50

Kagawa, H. K., 50
Kahana, B., 216, 268
Kahana, E., 216
Kahle, L., 197
Kahn, R. L., 3, 10, 43, 224, 303, 304, 307, 311
Kahn, S., 239
Kakkola, L., 159
Kalache, A., 25, 26
Kalina, R. A., 169, 170, 171
Kamen-Siegel, L., 244
Kaminar, M. S., 100
Kampert, J. B., 52
Kan, L., 296
Kane, R. A., 212
Kane, R. L., 113
Kannel, W. B., 248
Kaplan, F., 110, 111

Kaplan, G. A., 37, 41, 62, 63, 69, 74, 167, 295, 296
Kaplan, H. B., 206
Kaplan, J. R., 262
Kaplan, R., 223
Karas, C. G., 264
Karasek, R., 240, 269
Karlamangla, A., 209
Karlsson, I., 177
Karmarck, T. W., 262
Kashon, M. I., 192
Kasl, S., 70
Katz, M. S., 196
Katz, S., 209
Katzman, R., 185
Kauffman, R., 258
Kawachi, I., 233, 234, 235, 237
Kawai, K., 182
Kawas, C., 182, 197
Kay, J., 279
Kearney, K. A., 244
Keles, S., 171
Kelman, C. T., 317
Kelsey, R. M., 277
Kelton, M., 183
Kemeny, M. E., 244, 277
Kennedy, G. J., 317
Kenny, D. A., 278
Keough, M. E., 215
Kercher, K., 216
Kessler, R. C., 71
Keteyian, S. J., 126, 219
Key, C. R., 296
Khanna, K. V., 203
Khan, S., 198
Khaw, K. T., 108
Khoury, J., 178
Kiecolt-Glaser, J. K., 206, 207
Kiederiks, J. P., 247
Kieser, M., 238
Kim, C., 206
Kimura, K., 206
King, A. C., 218, 220
King, G., 319

King, M., 119
King, V., 23
Kinscherf, R., 183
Kinsella, K., 25
Kirschbaum, C., 266
Kivelä, S. -L., 237
Kivett, V. R., 34
Kivnick, H., 298, 309
Klag, M. J., 237
Klein, L. C., 261
Klein, W. W., 127
Klonoff, E. A., 219, 221
Klyce, S. D., 169
Knibbe, R. A., 247
Knook, D. L., 211
Kobasa, S. C., 239
Kocer, I., 171
Koch, B., 118
Koenig, H. G., 316
Kohlberg, L., 57
Kohno, H., 206
Kohno, M., 182
Konety, B. R., 159
Konigh, J., 238
Kooperberg, C., 69, 114, 198
Kop, W. J., 250
Kopecky, S., 198
Kostka, T., 141
Kotchen, J. M., 69, 114, 198
Kothandapani, R. V., 238
Kothari, R., 178
Koyano, W., 215
Kozma, A., 184
Krach, C. A., 30
Krajnak, K. M., 192
Kramarow, E., 7, 34, 35, 128, 210, 211, 212
Kramer, D. A., 314
Krantz, D. S., 233
Krause, N., 241, 286, 291, 297
Kravdal, O., 31
Krieg, J. C., 277
Krikorian, R., 279
Kristinsson, A., 127
Kroll, P., 171

Kromhout, D., 184
Krumholz, H. M., 131, 151, 248
Kubena, K. S., 206
Kubzansky, L. D., 234, 235, 237
Kudielka, B. M., 266
Kuerbis, A. N., 287
Kukull, W. A., 182
Kuller, L. H., 192, 197
Kuroda, S., 182
Kuroda, T., 169
Kurokawa, K., 49
Kurokawa, Y., 206
Kuypers, J. A., 44, 63
Kwan, C. M. L., 224, 225
Kytir, J., 21

Labouvie-Vief, G., 60, 61, 280, 312, 314
Lachman, M. E., 241
Lacour, J., 141
LaCroix, A. Z., 69, 114, 198
Ladwig, K. H., 237, 238
Lagaay, A. M., 211
Laippala, P., 237
Laird, N. M., 247
Lakatta, E. G., 124
Lamberts, S. W., 195
Lameill, J. T., 83
Land, K. C., 21
Landauer, R. K., 264
Landi, F., 250
Landmann, W. A., 206
Landrine, H., 219, 221
Landsberg, M. D., 234
Lane, N. E., 114, 116
Lang, F. R., 292
Langer, A., 198
Langer, E. J., 53, 60, 62, 239, 240, 242
Lapidus, S., 247
Lappas, G., 237, 241
Larsen, J. A., 118
Larsen, J. B., 141
Larson, E. B., 182
Larson, L., 244
Larsson, B., 295

Laudolt-Ritter, C., 277
Launer, L. J., 184
Laurent, D. D., 116
La Via, M., 206
Lawrence, R. H., 216
Lawton, M. P., 11, 215, 222, 224, 225, 312
Lazarus, R. S., 259, 270, 271, 275, 276, 279
Lee, C., 157
Lee, I. M., 52
Lee, W. M., 249
Leeka, J., 277, 278
Lefebvre, R. C., 244
Lehmacher, W., 237
Leino, E. V., 246
LeJemtel, T. H., 206
Lentzner, H., 7, 20, 34, 35, 128, 136, 210, 211, 212
Lenze, E. J., 216
Leonard, L. A., 215
Leo-Summers, L., 296
Lerner, R. M., 43, 44
Lesperance, F., 237
Leveille, S. G., 35
Levenson, M. R., 61, 71, 82, 85, 86, 89, 90, 91, 245, 247, 249, 251, 253, 268, 270, 291, 313, 314
Levenson, R. W., 294
Leventhal, E. A., 204, 218, 219
Leventhal, H., 218, 219, 240
Levi, L., 278
Levin, J. W., 317
Levine, C., 287
Levine, S., 264, 265
Levinson, D., 56
Lev-Ran, A., 196
Levy, E., 264
Levy, J. A., 205
Levy, S., 244
Lewis, B. P., 261
Lewis, M., 299
Li, H., 131
Liang, J., 126, 219
Liang, K. -Y., 92
Liang, W. M., 279

Liao, Y., 151, 248
Lichtenstein, P., 236
Lieberman, M. A., 32, 182, 234, 269, 300, 314
Light, K. C., 238
Lillard, L. J., 30
Lin, E. H., 244
Lindemann, B., 165
Lindenberger, U., 53
Ling, C., 53
Lingle, D. C., 182, 197
Link, C., 53, 255
Linnoila, M., 250
Lipkus, I. M., 234
Lippman, M. E., 264
Lipschitz, D. A., 145
Lipsitz, L. A., 52
Lithgow, G. J., 44, 266
Ljunghall, S., 112
Ljungquist, B., 318
LoCastro, J. S., 247, 249
Locher, J. L., 157
Lochner, K., 34, 40, 41
Loeser, R. F., 105, 108, 114
Loevinger, J., 56, 314
Loewenstein, D. A., 214
Long, J. S., 82
Longcope, C., 197
Longino, C. F., 24, 41, 299
Lorig, K. R., 116
Loveless, C. A., 31, 33, 236
Loy, S., 119
Lubitz, J., 319
Luborsky, L., 243
Luce, J. M., 319
Luke, A., 151
Lumley, M. A., 243, 244
Lund, D. A., 221
Lund Haheim, L., 241
Lynch, J. W., 37, 41
Lynch, M. F., 35

Maattanen, L., 159
MacCallum, R. C., 66, 82, 206
Macera, C., 236, 237

MacGregor, M., 275
Mack, K. A., 205
Mackenbach, J. P., 241
Mackenzie, J., 319
Maclure, M., 233
Maddi, S. R., 239
Madeley, R. J., 262
Maeda, K., 49
Maedam, N., 169
Maghfoor, I., 136
Magovern, G. J., 244
Mailahn, E. N., 192, 197
Makuc, C., 34, 40, 41
Malarkey, W. B., 206
Malendowicz, S. L., 206
Malmberg, B., 29
Manchanda, S. C., 131
Manegold, C., 136
Manfredi, F., 182
Mangels, J. A., 185
Manson, J., 151
Manson, J. E., 249
Mantell, J., 296
Manton, K. G., 21, 23, 35, 212, 213
Manuck, S. B., 262
Marcus, R., 118
Mark, D. B., 296
Markesbery, W. R., 182
Markham, R. B., 203
Markides, K. S., 287
Markovitz, N., 243, 244
Marks, J., 237
Marmot, M. G., 30
Marrie, T. J., 137
Marshall, J., 296
Marshburn, P. B., 197
Martin, G. A., 44
Martin, G. R., 164, 166
Martin, J., 118
Martire, L. M., 216, 250
Marusic, I., 233
Maruyama, M., 44, 45
Masaki, K. H., 250
Masland, E. N., 215

Maslow, A. H., 56
Mason, J. W., 255, 260
Masoro, E. J., 45, 47, 48
Masunaga, H., 307
Materra, J. A., 131, 151
Matheny, K. B., 280
Matsumoto, A. M., 193, 194, 261
Matthews, K. A., 192, 197, 244
Mattson, M. P., 177
May, H., 108
Mayer, R. J., 320
McAlindon, T. E., 116
McBean, A. M., 319
McBride, C. M., 219
McBride, T. D., 23
McCallum, J., 249
McCartney, N., 118
McCeney, M. K., 233
McClain, R., 159
McClearn, G. E., 29, 62
McColl, G., 44
McCrae, R. R., 233, 279
McDermott, M., 296
McDowell, F. H., 183
McEwen, B. S., 209, 263, 264, 266, 274
McGann, P., 157
McGee, D. L., 151, 248, 295
McGee, R., 238
McGillen, C., 132
McGuire, D. K., 127
McGuire, E. A., 249
McIntosh, W. A., 206
McKee, M., 249
McKee, P., 312
McKenna, M. C., 263
McKinlay, J. M., 299
McLachlan, E., 260
McLaughlin, A. E., 300
McLaughlin, D. K., 23
McLean, L., 71, 235, 236, 238
McMillan, A., 319
McTavish, D., 197
Mead, L. A., 237
Mears, B., 296

Mediansky, L., 296
Medvedev, Z. A., 17, 21
Mehta, K. M., 250
Meier, D., 105, 106, 113
Melov, A., 266
Menaghan, E. G., 269
Mentnech, R. M., 319
Merrill, S., 236
Mertens, H. W., 250
Metalsky, G. I., 243
Metter, E., 182, 197
Metter, J., 182
Metzner, H. L., 295
Meydani, S. N., 206
Mezey, E., 249
Mezzetti, M., 136
Mhoon, E., 167
Michaelsson, K., 112
Michel, Y., 206
Mikulincer, M., 276
Miller, A. H., 238
Miller, D. R., 102
Miller, M. E., 299
Miller, R., 178, 197
Miller, R. A., 11, 201, 202, 204, 205
Miller, S., 275
Miller, T. D., 71, 232, 233, 234
Minkler, M., 8
Mirowsky, J., 40
Mittleman, M. A., 233
Miyata, T., 49
Miyazaki, I., 182
Mizuno, T., 49
Moberg, D. O., 317
Moen, P., 57
Mohan, S., 106, 108
Mohr, J. P., 182
Molgaard, C., 118
Moliterno, D. J., 127
Monroe, S. M., 269
Monti, D., 204
Moody, H. R., 224
Mooradian, A. D., 177
Moore, A. P., 183

Moore, W. A., 50
Moreno, R., 34
Morgan, D. W., 318
Morley, J. E., 197
Moroney, J. T., 182
Morris, T., 277
Morrison, A., 182, 197
Morrow-Howell, N., 131
Mortimer, J. A., 182
Morton, D. L., 277
Mosca, L. J., 132, 224
Mosekilde, L., 118
Moskowitz, J. T., 278
Moskowitz, R. W., 209
Moss, A. J., 296
Moss, M. B., 176, 224
Moss, M. S., 285
Mossey, J., 112
Motoyoshi, M., 246
Mroczek, D. K., 62, 244, 245, 291
Mueller, K. J., 23
Muir, K. R., 262
Mulder, C. L., 279
Mullan, J. T., 269, 270, 285, 299, 300
Muller, J. E., 233
Mullooly, J. P., 296
Mulry, R. P., 233
Mulsant, B. H., 216
Murakami, S., 53, 255
Murasko, D. M., 202, 204
Murberg, T. A., 237
Murphy, S., 108
Murtaugh, C. M., 212
Musselman, D. L., 238
Muthen, B., 83, 92
Mutran, E. J., 112

Nachnani, M., 233
Nagin, D. S., 92
Nahemow, L., 11
Nakano,M., 49
Nam, C. B., 34, 35
Narang, R., 131
Narayan, S., 299

Navaie-Waliser, M., 287
Neale, A. V., 296
Neale, J. M., 271
Neeper, S., 173, 184
Nehlsen-Cannarella, S. L., 206
Nemeroff, C. B., 238
Nennmann, U., 215
Neubauer, D. N., 250
Neugarten, B. L., 4, 57
Neuhaus, J. M., 244
Neve, R. J., 247
Nevitt, M. C., 114, 116
Newby, L. K., 127, 198
Newhouse, P. A., 183
Newman, P. J., 252
Newman, R. I., 62, 242
Niaura, R., 234, 277
Nicholson, A. A., 277
Nicholson, N., 277
Nicklas, J. M., 31
Nieman, D. C., 206
Nilsson, E., 49
Nishibayashi-Asanuma, S., 182
Nishimoto, R., 296
Noble, C. A., 206
Nordberg, G., 299
Norkus, E. P., 184
Norman, G. R., 69
Norris, A. N., 249
Norris, F. H., 268
Norris-Baker, C., 24
Norton, J. A., 250
Norwood, T. H., 46
Nosotti, M., 136
Novacek, J., 279
Noveck, J., 21
Nuechterlein, K. H., 177
Nuland, S. B., 319
Nunnally, J. C., 82
Nunomura, A., 182

Oakes, D., 86
Ober, B. A., 24, 25, 181
Ochoa de Echaguen, A., 31

Ockene, J., 69, 114, 198
O'Connor, C. M., 198
Oehlert, J. W., 21, 22, 216
Oenzil, F., 49
Oeppen, J., 21
O'Gara, P., 198
Ogawa, N., 182
O'Hanlon, A. M., 180
Oka, K., 206
Oka, R., 220
Olshansky, S. J., 22
Onder, G., 250
Opton, E. M., Jr., 259
Ortega, N., 244
Orth-Gomer, K., 296
Ortiz, M., 249
Orwoll, L., 312
Ory, M. G., 205, 298
Ostendorf, F., 233
Ott, S. M., 109, 110, 112, 113
Ottonson, J. M., 20
Ouellette, S. C., 239
Ouslander, J. G., 113, 157
Ovesen, L., 118
Owens, J. F., 192, 197, 244
Ozer, D. J., 244

Pack, J., 177
Packham, C. J., 262
Paffenbarger, R. S., 52
Page, J., 130
Page, W. F., 250
Pahkala, K., 237
Pahor, M., 35
Paik, M. C., 182
Palmer, R. M., 150
Palmerino, M., 60
Pamuk, E., 34, 40, 41
Pancioli, A., 178
Papadakis, M. A., 197
Pargament, K., 276
Parker, J. D., 275
Parker, M. G., 112
Parker, R., 56, 75, 76, 77

Parkes, C. M., 31, 236
Parzen, M. I., 215
Pascual-Leone, J., 60
Paul, W., 157
Paulling, E., 206
Paulsen, V. M., 277
Pavese, I., 207
Paykel, E. S., 272
Payton, M., 182
Pearlin, L. I., 31, 32, 254, 269, 270, 285, 299, 300
Peck, A., 185
Peck, R. C., 55
Pedersen, B. K., 204, 206
Pedersen, N. L., 29, 185
Pedone, C., 250
Pedroso de Lima, M., 233
Peirce, R. S., 297
Pendleton, B. F., 317
Penley, W. C., 320
Penning, M. J., 290
Pereira-Smith, O. M., 47
Perlmutter, M., 312
Perls, T. T., 21
Perracini, M., 26
Perry, G., 182
Perry, M. C., 136
Persson, P. G., 112
Peskind, E. R., 266
Peters, K., 34, 35
Peters-Davis, N. D., 285
Peterson, B. L., 316
Peterson, C., 243, 244
Peterson, E. D., 198
Petrovich, H., 250
Petterson, I. L., 278
Pettingale, K. W., 277
Pfeiffer, E., 214
Phillips, W., 220
Picardi, A., 277
Pickering, T., 262
Piedmont, R. L., 233
Pieper, C. F., 35, 236, 237
Pietruszka, F. M., 119

Pilz, J., 266
Pimley, S., 279
Pinsky, J., 235
Pioli, M. F., 300
Pirke, K. M., 266
Pi-Sunyer, R. X., 151
Plosker, G. L., 197
Plymate, S. R., 182
Poikolainen, K., 249
Poirier, J., 172, 176, 177
Polla, B. A., 50
Pollard, W. S., 286
Pollock, A., 184
Pollow, R., 249
Poloma, M. M., 317
Pols, H. A., 195
Poon, L. W., 206
Pope, C. R., 296
Pope, M. K., 244
Poss, S. S., 35
Pottenger, L. A., 108, 110, 112
Potter, A., 183
Poulton, J. L., 244
Poutiainen, M., 159
Powell, L., 112
Prabhakaran, D., 131
Preisser, J. S., 157
Prendergast, T. J., 319
Prentice, R. L., 69, 114, 198
Pressman, A. R., 114, 116
Prewitt, T., 151
Pribram, K., 176
Prince, R. I., 119
Pringle, M., 237
Proctor, E. K., 131
Pruchno, R. A., 285
Pruitt, L. A., 118, 220
Pryor, D. B., 296
Psaty, B. M., 215
Puggaard, L., 141
Pulska, T., 237
Punyiczki, M., 50
Puska, P., 295
Pyka, G., 118

Qiu, L., 50
Quintana, S., 31

Rabbins, P. V., 318
Rabin, B. S., 204, 206
Rabin, C., 218, 219
Radford, M. J., 131, 151
Rahe, R., 269
Raina, A. K., 182
Rajagopalan, S., 140
Rajani, M., 131
Raley-Susman, I. M., 263
Rall, L. C., 206
Ramm, D., 250
Ramos, L. R., 26
Ranganathan, V. K., 164
Raphael, K. G., 271
Raskind, M. A., 182, 266
Rasmussen, L. B., 118
Raudenbush, S. W., 66, 89, 90, 91
Reaven, G. M., 264
Rebar, R. W., 118
Record, S. J., 238
Reddy, K. S., 131
Reding, M. R., 179
Redish, D. M., 263
Reed, D., 295
Reed, T., 250
Reich, J. W., 278
Reid, D. M., 114
Reiss, D., 277
Reitzes, D. C., 112
Remien, R. H., 182
Renbing, X., 185
Repetti, R. L., 264
Resnick, N. M., 156, 157
Resnick, S., 182, 197
Ressell, R. M., 136
Reuben, C., 34, 40, 41
Reus, V. I., 182
Revenson, T. A., 276, 277, 279
Reynolds, C. A., 185
Reynolds, C. F., 216
Reynolds, P., 296

Rhodes, M., 60
Rhodewalt, F., 244
Ribbe, M., 216
Rice, C. J., 43
Rice, S. J., 221
Rich, M. W., 130, 237
Richards, J. C., 234
Richter, D., 277
Riggs, K. M., 182
Rigler, S. K., 248
Rikke, B., 53, 255
Riley, K. P., 182
Rimer, B. K., 219
Rimm, E. B., 235
Rinpoche, K., 320
Rinson, H. G., 206
Rishel, L., 277, 278
Ritter, P., 116
Robbins, A. S., 119, 244
Robbins, C., 295
Robichaud, L., 221
Robins, S. P., 114
Robinson, K. N., 20, 136
Robinson-Whelan, S., 207
Rochette, A., 164
Rochling, F. A., 249
Rodenburg, A., 220
Rodin, J., 239, 240, 244
Rodrigue, J. R., 277
Rodriguez, E., 157
Rogers, E. L., 146, 147
Rogers, J. C., 216
Rogers, J. D., 102
Rogers, R. G., 34, 35
Rogosa, D., 86, 89
Rohrbaugh, M. J., 31
Rollman, B. L., 216
Romero, L. M., 263
Roodin, P. A., 212
Rook, K. S., 291, 294
Rooks, R., 7, 34, 35, 128, 210, 211, 212
Roos, N. P., 21
Rorth, R., 237
Rosa, T. E., 26

Rose, J., 297
Rosenberg, I. H., 126
Rosengren, A., 296
Rosenman, R. H., 232
Rosenthal, C., 299
Rosenwaike, I., 35
Ross, C. E., 40
Ross, G. W., 250
Rossi, A., 57
Rossouw, J. E., 69, 114, 198
Roth, D. L., 157
Roth, S., 275
Rothermund, K., 59
Rothstein, G., 205
Rottkamp, C. A., 182
Roubenoff, R., 206
Roumanis, S. A., 131, 151
Rounds, J., 263
Rowe, J. W., 3, 10, 43, 140, 209, 224, 264, 266, 303, 304, 307, 311
Roy, C., 221
Roy, P., 221
Rozanski, A., 262
Rubenfire, M., 132
Rubenstein, L. Z., 119, 206
Ruberman, W., 296
Ruble, D. N., 281
Rudberg, M. A., 215
Ruitenberg, A., 250
Russell, D., 297, 319
Russell, M., 297
Russell, R. M., 184
Russo, J., 277
Rusting, C. L., 185
Rust, K. F., 195
Rybash, J. M., 212
Ryff, C. D., 224, 225

Sachdeva, U., 131
Sagebiel, R., 238
Sahgal, V., 164
Sahyoun, N. R., 20, 136
Saini, J., 237
Salisbury, S., 178

Salonen, J. T., 295
Saltzman, J. R., 184
Sambamoorth, U., 205
Samet, J. M., 296
Sampfer, M., 151
Sandfort, T. G. M., 279
Sangle, J., 285
Sano, M., 182
Sansoni, P., 204
Santambrogio, L., 136
Santinga, J. T., 126, 219
Santoro, M. G., 50
Sapolsky, R. M., 52, 177, 185, 255, 260, 261, 262, 263, 266
Satz, P., 178
Saunders, W. B., 296
Saydah, S., 7, 34, 35, 128, 210, 211, 212
Sayer, A. G., 66
Scaglioni, G., 220
Schacter, D. L., 181
Schaie, K. W., 53, 246
Schambelan, M., 197
Scheibel, A. B., 180
Scheiber, M. D., 118
Scheidt, R. J., 24
Scheier, M. F., 243, 244
Schellenberg, G. D., 182
Scheper-Hughes, N., 320
Scherr, P. A., 215
Schiodt, F. V., 249
Schleicher, S. M., 101, 102
Schmidt, J., 119
Schmidt-Reinwald, A. K., 266
Schnelle, J., 157
Schnipper, L. E., 320
Schnohr, P., 248
Schnurr, P., 92, 268
Schoeberlein, S., 280
Schoenborn, C. A., 246
Schooler,C., 254, 269
Schork, M. A., 126, 219, 224
Schrieber, W., 277
Schrijvers, C., 241
Schuit, A. J., 184

Schulz, R., 216, 242, 244, 250, 278, 299

Schumacher, H. R., 116

Schuster, M. M., 147

Schwarz, C. E., 275

Scott, E., 116

Scott, J. C., 114

Scott, W., 236

Seale, C., 320

Seeman, T. E., 52, 209, 220, 236, 264, 266

Seligman, M. E. P., 239, 241, 243, 244, 303

Selkoe, D. J., 48

Selye, H., 258, 259

Semmel, A., 243

Semple, S. J., 300

Sesso, H. D., 237, 249

Sestier, F., 264

Shah, G. N., 177

Shanas, E., 290

Shapiro, D. E., 277

Sharma, D., 49

Shavelson, R. J., 83

Shaw, B. A., 241

Shek, P. N., 206

Shema, S. J., 37, 41, 69, 167

Shenaut, G. K., 181

Shepard, R. J., 206

Sherwood, J. B., 233

Shibata, H., 215

Shiffman, S., 271

Shimamura, A. P., 185

Shinkai, S., 206

Ship, J. A., 146, 165

Shipley, M., 30

Shively, C. A., 262

Shoham, V., 31

Shukitt-Hale, B., 184

Shukla, R., 178

Sieber, M., 277

Sieber, W. J., 244

Siegel, A. V., 177

Siegler, I. C., 234, 296

Siegman, A. W., 232

Siemionow, V., 164

Silverman, R. E., 195

Silverstein, M., 292, 293, 297

Simeone, I., 237

Simmens, S. J., 277

Simoes, A., 233

Simonsick, E. M., 216

Simons, J., 249

Simons, L. A., 249

Singer, B. H., 209, 224, 225, 264, 266

Singer, J. E., 240

Singh, M. A. F., 126

Singh, R., 49

Skaff, M., 300

Skoog, I., 177

Sloan, R. P., 235

Smeeding, T. M., 38

Smiley, M., 316

Smit, J. H., 318

Smith, A., 17, 22

Smith, D., 31, 40

Smith, D. A. F., 132

Smith, D. C., 159, 160

Smith, G. L., 131, 151

Smith, H., 319

Smith, J., 312

Smith, J. R., 47

Smith, K. R., 32

Smith, M. A., 182

Smith, T. W., 71, 232, 233, 234, 244

Smyers, D., 119

Snowdon, D. A., 151, 182, 185, 303, 316

Snydersmith, M., 206

Sobel, D. S., 116

Sobue, G., 49

Sohal, R. S., 265

Sohal, S. S., 49, 151

Soho-Arnada, I., 104

Solomon, G. F., 62, 206

Sonnega, J. S., 31

Sorensen, L. B., 114

Sorensen, O. H., 118

Sorensen, T. I., 248

Sorlie, P. D., 31, 33, 236

Sparrow, D., 140, 233, 234, 235, 237

Spector, N. H., 202
Spence, J. T., 244
Spiegel, D., 277
Spilka, B., 317
Spiro, A., III, 3, 62, 71, 82, 85, 86, 89,
    90, 91, 92, 182, 207, 233, 234, 244,
    245, 247, 268, 270, 272, 273, 280,
    281, 291
Sramek, J. J., 182
Stampfer, M. J., 235, 249
Stanczyk, F. Z., 182, 197
Stange, K., 216
Stanley, J. C., 68
Staudinger, U. M., 53, 315
Steele, D., 280
Steele, K., 116
Stefanik, M. L., 69, 114, 198
Stein, M., 238
Stein, S., 277
Steinberg, L., 264
Steiner, R., 277
Stellar, E., 263
Stenman, U. H., 159
Stephenson, H. E., Jr., 197
Stern, Y., 182
Sternberg, R. J., 312, 315
Stevens, A. B., 180
Stewart, A. L., 114, 116
Stewart, W., 241
Stewart, W. F., 182
Stites, D. P., 244
Stokols, D., 45
Stolk, R. P., 195
Stoller, E. P., 216, 249
Stollerman, G. H., 137, 138, 140
Stone, A. A., 271
Stone, R. I., 212, 285
Stones, M. J., 184
Stoney, C. M., 234
Stovring, H., 141
Strachan, M. W., 195
Strawbridge, W. J., 69, 74, 167
Streiner, D. L., 69
Studenski, S., 214

Stukel, T. A., 92
Stunkard, A. J., 217, 238
Suggs, P. K., 157
Sullivan, L. M., 299
Sulloway, F. J., 230
Sulon, J., 277
Sundstrom, G., 318
Sutton, K. J., 273, 280, 281
Svärdsudd, K., 295
Svebak, S., 237
Sweet, D., 238
Sweet, J. J., 252
Syme, S. L., 295
Szabo, P., 204

Taaffe, D. R., 118
Taffett, G. E., 51
Taggart, H. M., 220
Takeda, A., 49
Takehisa, Y., 182
Talajic, M., 237
Tammela, T., 159
Tanabe, Y., 182
Taves, M. J., 317
Taylor, J. L., 250
Taylor, J. O., 215
Taylor, S. E., 261, 263, 284
Teasdale, J. D., 243
Tedesco, P., 53, 255
Tel Velder, A., 237
Temoshok, L., 238
Temple, M. T., 246
Tennant, C., 71, 235, 236, 238
Tennen, H., 89, 271, 278
Tennstedt, S. L., 299
Tenover, J. L., 191, 197
Terada, S., 182
Teresa, R. F., 185
Terman, L. M., 310
Terry, R., 185
Testa, M., 206
Thayer, P., 60
Theorell, T., 240, 241, 269
Thoits, P. A., 276, 284

Thomas, C., 317
Thomas, C. L., 137
Thomas, D. R., 103
Thompson, D., 280
Thompson, E. E., 286
Tibblin, B., 295
Tibblin, G., 295
Tierney, M. J., 197
Tilburg, T. V., 291, 293
Tilburg, W. V., 318
Tilley, B. C., 296
Tillipman, H., 31, 40
Timor, O., 264
Tinetti, M. E., 112, 214
Tobin, J. D., 216, 249
Tobin, S. S., 57, 234
Tofler, G. H., 233
Tokunaga, M., 216
Tolstoy, L., 319
Tomaka, J., 277
Tomakowsky, J., 243, 244
Tornatore, J., 299
Tornstam, L., 309, 313, 318
Tremblay, R. E., 92
Trent, J. D., 50
Tresini, M., 45, 48, 49, 265
Trestman, R. L., 238
Tricerri, A., 207
Tronstam, L., 61
Trueblood, R. P., 119
Trump, D. L., 159, 160
Tseng, C. -L., 182
Tsuang, M., 236
Tsuchiya, K., 182
Tully, C. L., 151
Tulving, E., 181
Tune, L. E., 184
Turner, C. W., 71, 232, 233, 234
Tverteras, R., 237

Uehira, K., 182
Uman, G., 157
Updegraff, J. A., 261
Urrya, H. L., 277

Vaccarino, V., 131, 151, 248
Vaillant, G. E., 55, 150, 244, 275, 279, 303, 309, 310, 311, 314, 315, 318
Vaillant, L., 104
van Doornen, L. J. P., 234
van Duijn, C. M., 250
Van Eck, M. M., 277
van Exel, D., 211
Vangeli, M., 207
van Griensven, G. J. P., 279
van Groenou, 32
van Grootheest, D. S., 32
van Swieten, J. C., 250
Varadi, E., 266
Vassend, O., 279
Vaupel, J. W., 21, 22
Veith, R. C., 182
Velkoff, V. A., 25, 30
Venjatraman, J. T., 206
Verbrugge, L. M., 29
Verheugt, F. W., 127
Vernon, S. W., 296
Vestal, R. E., 249
Viitanen, M., 182
Villanueva, G. L., 104
Villareal, D. T., 197
Virella, G., 206
Visakorpi, T., 159
Vitaliano, P. P., 277
Vögele, C., 234
Vogel-Sprott, M., 249, 250
Vogt, T. M., 296
Vokonas, P. S., 233, 234, 235, 237, 249
Volker, C., 45, 48, 49, 265
vonBaeyer, C., 243
von Bertalanffy, L., 44
Von Dras, D. D., 44
von Zerssen, S., 277
von Zglinicki, T., 49
Voorhees, J. J., 99, 104

Wagner, B. M., 270
Waite, L. J., 30
Walford, R. L., 50, 151

Walker, D. W., 44

Wallace, R. B., 62, 63

Wallhagen, M. I., 69, 74, 167

Wallin, A., 177

Wang, H., 292

Wang, N. -Y., 237

Ward, K. D., 62, 234, 245

Warheit, G. J., 41

Warren, B. J., 206

Warshaw, G. A., 210, 211

Wasserman, J., 278

Watson, M., 277

Waxlery-Morrison, N., 296

Weaver, S. L., 241

Weaver, W. D., 127

Webb, C., 131

Webber, C. E., 118

Webster, J. R., Jr., 139

Webster, P. S., 71

Weeks, J., 7, 34, 35, 128, 210, 211, 212

Wei, J. Y., 128, 129, 251

Weihs, K. L., 277

Weinberg, G., 214

Weinblatt, E., 296

Weindruch, R., 49, 50, 151

Weiner, H., 230

Weiss, S. T., 140, 182, 233, 234, 235

Weissman,B., 116

Weksler, M. E., 204

Welin, C., 237, 241

Welin, L., 295

Welk, J. F., 50

Welsh, M. J., 50

Wentura, D., 59

West, S., 234

Westendorp, R. G., 211

Wetle, T. T., 215

Wheeler, 126, 219

Whipple, R., 119

Whitbourne, S. K., 55

White, L., 250

White, T. M., 266

Whiteside, T., 244

Whiting, J. W. M., 264

Whitlatch, C. J., 270, 285, 299

Wickelgren, I., 176

Wijsman, E. M., 182

Wilcox, S., 218

Wiley, J. W., 145

Wilhelmsen, L., 237, 241, 296

Wilkie, F., 214

Wilkinson, C. W., 266

Willett, J., 89, 90

Willett, W. C., 151, 235

Williams, D. R., 248

Williams, E. R., 287

Williams, J. B. W., 182

Williams, J. K., 262

Williams, R. B., 63, 233, 234, 236, 296

Williams, S., 238

Williams, S. W., 287

Williamson, D., 237

Williamson, D. F., 151, 238

Williamson, D. P., 215

Willis, W. D., Jr., 165, 179

Wills, T. A., 295, 296, 297

Wilson, C. M., 287

Wilson, J. A. P., 146, 147

Wilson, P. W., 116

Winblad, B., 182

Wing, A. L., 52

Wing, R. R., 192, 197

Wing, S., 35

Wise, P. M., 192

Wisniewski, A., 216

Witta, K. M., 134, 139

Witteman, J. C., 250

Wolf, C., 277

Wolf, O. T., 266

Wolf, P. A., 63

Wolfson, L., 119

Wolkoqitz, O. M., 182

Woo, D., 178

Woodruff-Pak, D., 185

Woolson, R., 236

Workman-Daniels, K., 270

Worley, A. S., 299

Wright, A., 264

Wu, J. C., 177
Wu, Z., 286

Yancura, L. A., 72, 272, 277, 278
Yano, K., 295
Yaoi, T., 50
Yarrow, M. R., 3
Yasko, J., 278
Yasuda, T., 49
Yasuda, Y., 49
Yasunaga, A., 216
Yehuda, R., 261
Yesavage, J. A., 250
Young, D., 184
Yue, G. H., 164

Zabrucky, K. M., 280
Zautra, A. J., 89, 271, 278
Zegans, L. S., 244
Zeger, S. C., 92
Zevon, M. A., 263
Zheng, D., 236
Zheng, X., 169
Zhu, L., 182
Zick, C. D., 32
Zonderman, A., 182, 197
Zuccala, G., 250
Zucker, R. A., 248

SUBJECT INDEX

Activities of Daily life (ADLs), 8, 109, 209-210, 211 (figure)
  chronic obstructive pulmonary disease and, 139
  hearing loss and, 167
  support networks and, 284, 293-294
Acute illness, 7-8, 21
Adult development. *See* Psychosocial theories
Age dependency ratios, 19
Age-specific life expectancy, 6, 20-21
Aging:
age/cohort/period distinctions, 5-6
  biological processes of, 45-53
  control, feelings of, 241-243
  disease and, 3, 7-8
  late life, definition of, 4-5
  life span/expectancy, 6-7
  optimal progression of, 2-3, 8
  plasticity and, 2
  psychosocial theories of, 2, 53-62
  rate of, 4, 5 (figure)
  See also Alcohol consumption;
     Demographics of aging; Theories of aging
Aging research. *See* Research
AIDS, 26-27, 205, 278-279
Alcohol consumption, 62, 245
  age, consumption patterns and, 245-248
  cognitive function and, 250-251
  Korsakoff's psychosis, 249
  medication efficacy and, 249
  mental health and, 249-250
  physical health and, 248-249
  psychomotor tasks and, 250
  sleep disturbances and, 248, 250

Alexander Technique, 117
Allergic reactions. *See* Immune system
Allostasis, 264
Alzheimer's disease (AD), 180
  alcohol consumption and, 250
  blood-brain barrier and, 177
  cognitive disturbances in, 181
  etiology of, 182-183
  long-term memory and, 181
  memory problems and, 252
  nicotine treatment for, 183
  repetitive questioning in, 180-181
  sense of smell and, 164
  symptoms of, 180
Anaphylaxis, 202-203
Aneurisms, 178
Anxiety, 234-236
Apoptosis, 46-47
Arrhythmias, 235-236, 237, 238
Ars moriendi, 318-321
Arteriosclerosis, 126-127, 127 (figure)
Arthritis, 7-8, 21
  coping with, 278
  gender and, 29
  osteoarthritis, 114-117, 115 (figure)
Assisted-living communities, 23, 290
Atherosclerosis, 126-127, 127 (figure), 128
  hearing and, 165
  kidney function and, 154-155
Attributional Style Questionnaire (ASQ), 243
Autoimmune disorders:
  acquired immune deficiency syndrome, 205
  hypothyroidism, 197
  mechanisms of, 203
Automobile driving, 169-170

Autonomic nervous system (ANS), 171-172, 256-258, 257 (figure)

Balance, 165, 183, 197, 214
Benign prostatic hyperplasia, 157-159, 158 (figure)
Bereavement, 236
Biogerontology, 3
Biological processes, 45
　DNA repair mechanisms, 48
　genetic theories, 46-48
　heat shock proteins, 50
　homeostasis, 51-52
　interrelationships among, 53
　lipofuscin, 49-50
　molecular/cellular theories, 49-50
　oxidation, 49
　programmed cell death/apoptosis, 46-47
　stochastic processes, 47-48
　stress models, 52-53
　systems-level theories, 51-53
　wear-and-tear theories, 52
Bladder function, 155
Blood-brain barrier (BBB), 177
Body mass index (BMI), 150-151
Bone loss, 106-108, 107 (figure)
Botox injections, 104
Brain function. See Alzheimer's disease (AD); Nervous system
Breast cancer, 198, 238, 262-263
Bronchitis, 138
Bursitis, 117

Calment, Jeanne, 20-21
Cancer, 7, 34, 36-37
　breast cancer, 198, 238, 262-263
　cervical cancer, 238
　colorectal cancer, 149
　depression and, 238
　lung cancer, 135-136, 140
　prostate cancer, 159-160
　skin cancer, 101-102
Cardiovascular disease (CVD), 7, 37
　arteriosclerosis/atherosclerosis, 126-127, 127 (figure)

coronary heart disease, 128-130
　heart failure, 130-131
　hypertension, 125-126
　peripheral vascular disease, 127-128
　stress and, 262
　widowhood and, 31-32
Cardiovascular system:
　age-related changes in, 124-125
　anatomy/physiology of, 120-124, 122 (figure)
　blood, components of, 121
　disease-related processes, 125-131
　optimal aging and, 131-132
Caregiving, 298
　dementia and, 299
　gender and, 299
　pleasure of, 299-300
　religious belief and, 317-318
　spouse caregiving, 298-299
　terminal illness and, 300
Cataracts, 170, 195
Centenarians, 5, 17, 19, 20-21, 30
Central nervous system (CNS), 171-172, 177
Cerebrovascular accidents (CVAs), 178-179
Change research. See Research
Choice, 239-243
Cholesterol, 126, 234
Chronic illness, 3, 7-8, 20, 21
　chronic obstructive pulmonary disease, 138-139
　developing nations and, 27-28
　environmental competence and, 222-223
　ethnicity and, 34
　positive health behavior habits and, 216-217
　stress and, 262-264
　See also Functional health
Chronic obstructive pulmonary disease (COPD), 138-139, 251
Chronic role strain, 269-270
Climatic factors, 22
Cognitive decline, 3
　alcohol consumption and, 250-251
　Alzheimer's disease, 180-183
　cognitive stimulation and, 185
　confusional states, 252
　depression and, 252

estrogen and, 185
    functional health measures, 214
    pseudodementia, 184
Cohorts, 5-6, 246, 247
Colorectal cancer, 149
Compression of morbidity, 21
Confusional states, 252
Conscious development, 60-61
Constipation, 145, 146-147
Control, 239-243
Coping, 274
    aging process and, 279-281
    defense mechanisms, 274-275
    emotion-focused coping, 276, 278
    optimism and, 244
    physical health and, 276-279
    problem-focused coping, 242, 276, 281
    processes of, 276
    religiosity and, 318
    social support and, 276
    styles of, 275
    See also Social support
Coronary heart disease (CHD):
    angina pectoris, 129
    anxiety and, 235
    ethnicity and, 128
    gender and, 128
    heart failure and, 130-131
    hostility and, 232-234
    myocardial infarction, 129
    personality processes and, 231
    rehabilitation and, 129-130
    risk factors for, 128-129
    widowhood and, 236
Creuztfeldt-Jakob disease, 179

Death, 8
    art of dying, 318-321
    causes of, 20
    disability preceding, 21
    widowhood, 31-33
Delirium, 184
Delusional states, 184
Dementia, 179, 252, 299
Demographics of aging, 15-16

compression of morbidity, 21
demographic profiles, changes in, 16-17,
    18 (figures)
demographic transition, 25-26, 27 (figure)
dependency ratios, 19-20
ethnicity, 33-37, 33 (figure), 36-37 (figures)
extreme old age, 17, 19, 21-22
gender and, 28-30
geographic location, 22-23
international aging, 25-28
life expectancy, 20-22
marital status and, 30-33
rate of aging, factors in, 28-41
residential arrangements, 23
rural vs. urban living, 23-25
socioeconomic status and, 37-41, 39 (figure)
Dependency:
    activities of daily living and, 210, 211 (figure)
    dysfunctional autonomy, 308
    economic dependency, 19-20
    living arrangements and, 23
    social support and, 293, 294
    See also Socioeconomic status (SES)
Depression:
    bereavement and, 236
    cancer and, 238
    cognitive impairment and, 252
    coronary heart disease and, 237
    functional losses and, 215, 216
    helplessness, 238
    hypothyroidism and, 197
    memory problems and, 252
    mortality and, 236-237
    physiological processes and, 237-239
    pseudodementia and, 184
    urinary incontinence and, 157
Determinants of Myocardial Infarction Onset
    Study, 233
Developing nations, 25-26
Developmental models. *See* Psychosocial
    theories
Deviation amplification model, 44-45, 62
Diabetes, 7, 8, 21, 34, 36, 51
    aging and, 195
    diabetic neuropathy, 164, 235

ethnicity and, 195
healing process and, 196
kidney function and, 161
management of, 196
retinopathy, 170, 195
Type I, 193
Type II, 193-194
Diabetic retinopathy, 170
Digestion. *See* Gastrointestinal system (GI)
Direct Assessment of Functional Status
(DAFS), 214
Disability levels, 21
activities of daily living, 209-210, 211 (figure)
instrumental activities of daily living and,
210-213, 213 (figure)
Disease, 2-3
Diverticular disease, 147, 148 (figure)
Divorce, 30, 31
DNA repair mechanisms, 45, 48
Duke Longitudinal Study of Aging (DLSA),
73-74
Dying process, 225-226, 300
Dysfunctional autonomy, 308

Economic dependency, 19-20, 25-26
Educational status, 40
Elders Life Stress Inventory (ELSI), 272
Emotional stability, 245
Emphysema, 138-139
Endocrine system:
age-related changes in, 190-193
anatomy/physiology of, 185-190
antidiuretic hormone, 192-193
calcium serum levels, 191
diabetes, 193-196
disease-related processes, 193-197
diurnal rhythms and, 191
endocrine function, 187-190, 188 (figure)
growth hormone, 190
hormone replacement therapy, 197-198
menopause, 192
neuropeptide transmitters, 187-193, 187
(table), 194 (table)
optimal aging and, 197-198

reproductive hormones, 191-192
thermal regulation, thyroid and, 189-190,
189 (figure)
thyroid problems, 196-197
Environmental competence, 222-223
Established Populations for Epidemiologic
Studies of the Elderly (EPESE), 35
Ethnicity:
chronic illness and, 34
diabetes incidence and, 195
divorce effects and, 31
heart disease deaths and, 128
instrumental activities of daily living and,
212-213, 213 (figure)
mortality rates, 34, 35-37, 36-37 (figures)
population statistics, 33, 33 (figure)
poverty rates and, 39-40
prostate cancer and, 159
rural populations and, 24
social support and, 287
widowhood and, 31-32
Exercise, 41, 62
cardiovascular system and, 131
health promotion programs, 220-221
immune system functioning and, 206
musculoskeletal system and, 117-119
pulmonary function and, 139, 141
Eyes. *See* Vision

Fight-or-flight response, 258, 261-262
Fluid intake, 161
Forced expiratory volume (FEV), 134, 140-141
Forced vital capacity (FVC), 134, 140-141
Fractures, 110-112, 111 (figure), 113 (figure)
Framingham Heart Study, 116, 235
Functional health, 8, 208-209
activities of daily living, 209-210, 211 (figure)
assessment of, 209-214
balance/gait disturbances, 214
cognitive ability measures, 214
functional incontinence, 156
instrumental activities of daily living,
210-213, 213 (figure)
morbidity/mortality and, 215-216

optimal functional health, 216-217
    See also Health promotion
Functional magnetic resonance imaging
    (FMRI), 176-177

Gait disturbances, 165, 183, 197, 214
Gallbladder disease, 147-149
Gastrointestinal system (GI):
    age-related changes in, 145-146
    anatomy/physiology of, 141-145, 142
        (figure), 144 (figure)
    colorectal cancer, 149
    constipation, 145, 146-147
    disease-related processes, 146-151
    diverticular disease, 147, 148 (figure)
    gallbladder disease, 147-149
    liver function, 144-145
    obesity, 51, 150-151
    optimal aging and, 152
    periodontal disease, 146
    under-nutrition and, 149-150
Gender, 28
    activities of daily living and, 210, 211
        (figure)
    bone loss and, 106-107
    caregiving and, 299
    health levels and, 29
    heart disease and, 128
    instrumental activities of daily
        living and, 212
    longevity, differences in, 28-29
    mortality rate and, 29-30
    skin cancer and, 102
    social network members and, 286-287
    socioeconomic status and, 40
    stress reactions and, 261-262
Genetic theories of aging. *See* Biological
    processes
Geographic location, 22
    climatic factors in, 22
    independence and, 23
    social support and, 22-23
Gerontology, 3
    cross-sectional studies and, 246

specializations within, 3-4
    weight/mortality debate, 151
Gerotranscendence, 61
Glaucoma, 170
Great Depression, 58-59

Health behavior:
    hostility levels and, 233-234
    See also Health promotion
Health care costs, 19, 216
Health promotion, 217
    community-sponsored programs, 221-222
    environmental competence and, 222-223
    exercise programs, 220-221
    health behavior change models, 217-219
    health screening, 221
    programs for, 219-222
    self-care education, 221
    self-efficacy and, 218, 239-243
    self-regulation model of change, 218-219
    See also Personality processes
Healthy aging. *See* Optimal aging
Hearing, 165-167, 166 (figure)
Heart disease, 41
    coronary heart disease, 128-130, 232-234
    heart failure, 130-131
    hormone replacement therapy
        and, 198
Heart function. *See* Cardiovascular system
Heart rate variability, 235-236, 237, 238
Heat shock proteins (Hsps), 45, 50
Helplessness, 238, 239, 242
High-density lipoproteins (HDLs), 126
HIV/AIDS, 26-27, 205, 278-279
Home health care, 216, 289-290
Honolulu Heart Study, 295
Hormone replacement therapy (HRT), 69
    endocrine functioning and, 197-198
    incontinence and, 157
Hormones. *See* Endocrine system; Nervous
    system
Hospice care, 319-320
Hostility, 232-234
Human immunodeficiency virus (HIV), 205

Hypertension (HT), 34, 125-126, 245
Hypothyroidism, 147

Immune system:
  acquired immunity, 201-203
  age-related changes in, 203-204
  anatomy/physiology of, 198-203
  antibodies in, 203
  autoimmune disorders, 203
  B-cells, 203, 204
  cell-mediated immunity, 201-202
  delayed hypersensitivity reactions, 202-203
  disease-related processes, 205
  exercise and, 206
  HIV/AIDS, 205
  humoral immunity, 203
  innate immunity, 201
  leukemias, 205
  nutritional deficiencies and, 206
  optimal aging and, 205-207
  organs in, 198, 200 (figure)
  stress and, 206-207
  T-cells in, 202-203, 204
  white blood cells, 198, 199 (table)
Incontinence, 156-157
Independent living, 23
Indian Health Service (IHS), 36
Infectious disease, 20
  developing nations and, 26-27
  gastrointestinal infections, 145
  nutrition maintenance and, 161
  pneumonia, 137-138
  respiratory infections, exercise and, 141
  tuberculosis, 139-140
Instrumental activities of daily living (IADLs),
    8, 109, 210-213, 213 (figure), 284
Intergenerational Study, 58-59
Internal organ systems, 120
  cardiovascular system, 120-132
  gastrointestinal system, 141-152
  renal/urinary system, 152-162
  respiratory system, 132-141
International situation, 25, 26 (figure)
  chronic curable illness and, 27-28

demographic transition and, 25-26, 27
    (figure)
  economic resources and, 25-26
  infectious/parasitic diseases and, 26-27
  preventive care and, 28

Kidney function. See Renal/urinary system
Korsakoff's psychosis, 249-250
Kyphosis, 110

Late life, 4-5
Learned helplessness, 239
Leukemias, 205
Life course theory, 58-59
Life expectancy, 6-7, 20, 41-42
  age-specific life expectancy, 20-21, 35-36
  average expectancy, changes in, 21-22
  causes of death, 20
  centenarians, 5, 17, 19, 20-21
  chronic illness and, 21
  compression of morbidity, 21
  educational status and, 40
  ethnicity and, 34-35, 37
  socioeconomic status and, 40-41
  See also Rate of aging
Life Orientation Test (LOT), 243-244
Life span, 6, 21-22, 285
Longevity. See Life expectancy; Rate of aging
Longitudinal Study on Aging, 215
Long-term care, 216
Low-density lipoproteins (LDLs), 126, 234
Lung cancer, 135-136, 140

MacArthur Studies of Midlife, 241
MacArthur Study of Successful Aging, 3
Macular degeneration, 170-171
Magnetic resonance imaging (MRI), 176
Mammography, 34
Marital status, 30
  divorce, 31
  gender imbalance and, 30
  health effects of, 30-31
  mental health and, 32
  widowhood, 31-33

Meals on Wheels program, 150, 224
Medicare/Medicaid, 38, 216
Medications:
    alcohol consumption and, 249
    blood-brain barrier and, 177
    confusional states and, 252
    constipation and, 147
    kidney function and, 161
    ototoxic medication, 165, 167
    potassium homeostasis and, 155
Menopause, 118, 128, 190, 192, 198
Mental health:
    alcohol consumption and, 249-250
    functional health/losses and, 215, 216
    physical health problems and, 251-252
    widowhood and, 32
    See also Personality processes
Mindfulness, 242-243
Morbidity, 7
    compression of morbidity, 21
    functional losses and, 215
    See also Socioeconomic status (SES)
Mortality rate, 7
    anxiety, cardiac death and, 235-236
    body weight and, 151
    depression and, 237
    divorce and, 31
    ethnicity and, 34, 35-37, 36-37 (figures)
    functional losses and, 215-216
    gender and, 29-30
    hip fractures and, 112
    widowhood and, 31-32
    See also Socioeconomic status (SES)
Musculoskeletal system, 104
    age-related changes in, 106-109
    anatomy/physiology of, 104-106
    back pain, 117
    bones, 104-105, 106-108, 107 (figure)
    bursitis/tendonitis, 117
    disease-related processes in, 109-117
    fractures, 110-112, 111 (figure), 113 (figure)
    optimal aging and, 117-119
    osteoarthritis, 114-117, 115 (figure)
    osteoporosis, 109-114

soft tissues in, 105-106, 108-109
Myocardial infarction (MI), 129-130, 237
Myocardial Infarction Onset Study, 233

National Health Interview Survey, 246
National Health and Nutrition Epidemiological
    Survey (NHANES), 151
National Long-Term Care Surveys, 212
National Mortality Followback Survey, 35
Nervous system:
    age-related changes in, 176-178
    Alzheimer's disease, 179-183
    anatomy/physiology of, 171-176
    blood-brain barrier, 177
    brain function, 174-176, 174-175 (figures)
    brain reserve capacity, 178
    cognitive stimulation and, 185
    disease-related processes, 178-184
    localization of function theory, 175-176
    magnetic resonance imaging and, 176-177
    neurotransmitters, 172, 173 (table), 177
    optimal aging and, 184-185
    Parkinson's disease, 183
    pseudodementia/delirium, 184
    stress and, 177
    strokes, 178-179
    tissue plasminogen activator, 179
    See also Endocrine system; Stress
Neurological disorders, 21, 164
Neuronal slowing, 3
Normative Aging Study (NAS), 3, 85, 90-91, 140,
    234, 245, 247
Nursing homes, 23, 239-240, 289-290, 300
Nutrition, 30, 41
    botanicals and, 198
    cardiovascular health and, 131
    diabetes and, 196
    diverticular disease and, 147
    fluid intake, 161
    gastrointestinal health and, 152
    immune system and, 206
    menopause and, 118, 198
    musculoskeletal health and, 117-118
    nervous system health and, 184-185

obesity, 51, 150-151
senior nutrition programs, 150, 224
sensory system health and, 171
under-nutrition, 149-150, 161

Obesity, 51, 150-151
Optimal aging, 2-3, 8, 303
active engagement with life, 307-309
cardiovascular disease and, 131-132
cognitive/physical function and, 307
community involvement, 309
coping strategies, 311
disease avoidance, 305-307
dying process and, 318-321
environmental competence and,
222-223
exercise and, 306-307
functional health and, 216-217
gastrointestinal system and, 152
hormone replacement therapy, 197-198
immune functioning and, 205-207
models of, 303-312
musculoskeletal system and, 117-119
nervous system and, 184-185
nutrition and, 305-306
organizational memberships, 297, 309
osteoarthritis and, 116
renal/urinary system and, 160-162
respiratory system and, 140-141
Rowe/Kahn model of, 304-309
self-development model, 59
sensory system and, 171
skin health, 103-104
SOC (selection/optimization/compensation)
model and, 59
spirituality and, 316-318
Vaillant model of, 309-312
wisdom and, 312-316
Optimism, 243-244
Osteoarthritis, 114, 115 (figure)
disability and, 116
risk factors in, 114, 116
treatment/management of, 116-117
Osteoporosis, 109

fractures and, 110-112, 111 (figure), 113
(figure)
medications for, 113-114
risk factors in, 109

Parasympathetic nervous system (PNS),
256, 257 (figure)
Parkinson's disease, 147, 177, 183
Period effects, 6, 246, 247
Periodontal disease, 146
Peripheral arterial occlusive disease
(PAOD), 127-128
Peripheral nervous system (PNS), 171-172, 177
Peripheral neuropathy, 195
Personality processes, 230-231
anxiety, 234-236
control/self-efficacy, 239-243
emotional stability, 245
hostility, 232-234
optimism, 243-244
physical/mental health problems,
differentiation of, 251-252
psychological protective factors, 239-245
psychological risk factors, 232-239
transactional vs. bidirectional process, 231
type A behavior pattern, 232
type C behavior pattern, 238
Physiological decline. See Biological processes
Pick's disease, 179
Pneumonia, 137-138, 181
Post-traumatic stress disorder (PTSD), 261, 268
Pressure ulcers, 102-103
Preventive care:
developing nations and, 28
See also Health promotion
Preventive Health Care for Older Adults
(PHCA), 221
Prostate gland:
benign prostatic hyperplasia, 157-159, 158
(figure)
prostate cancer, 159-160
Prostatic-specific antigen (PSA)
values, 159
Pseudodementia, 184

Psychological protective factors, 239
    control/self-efficacy, 239-243
    emotional stability, 245
    optimism, 243-244
Psychological risk factors:
    anxiety, 234-236
    depression, 236-238
    hostility, 232-234
Psychomotor performance, 250
Psychosocial risk factors, 63-64, 272-273
Psychosocial theories, 2, 53, 54 (figure)
    classical theories, 54-58
    conscious development, 60-61
    contemporary theories, 58-61
    deviation-amplification theory, 62
    discontinuous development, 56-57
    emotional/cognitive complexity, 60
    gerotranscendence, 61
    goal-oriented models, 59
    interrelationships among, 61-62
    life course theory, 58-59
    ontogenetic models, 54-57
    post-formal operations, 60
    psychosocial risk factors, 63-64
    self-development model, 59
    SOC (selection/optimization/compensation)
        model, 59
    social-breakdown theory, 63
    sociogenic models, 57-58
Psychosomatic illness, 231
Public policy:
    life expectancy and, 22
    preventive care, developing nations and, 28

Quality-of-life, 7, 116, 223
    automobile driving, 169-170
    dying process and, 225-226
    environmental aspects, 223-224
    hearing loss and, 167
    psychological well-being, 224-225
    social well-being, 224

Rate of aging, 4, 5 (figure)
    demographic factors in, 28-41

ethnicity and, 33-37, 33 (figure),
    36-37 (figures)
    gender and, 28-30
    marital status and, 30-33
    socioeconomic status and, 37-41, 39 (figure)
    See also Theories of aging
Regulatory systems:
    endocrine system, 185-198
    immune system, 198-207
    nervous system, 171-185
    sensory system, 163-171
Rehabilitation therapies, 179, 183
Religiosity, 316-318
Renal/urinary system:
    age-related changes in, 154-156
    anatomy/physiology of, 152-154, 153 (figure)
    atherosclerosis and, 154-155
    benign prostatic hyperplasia, 157-159,
        158 (figure)
    bladder function and, 155
    disease-related processes, 156-160
    glomerular filtration rate, 154
    kidney function, 153-154, 160-612
    optimal aging and, 160-162
    prostate cancer, 159-160
    urinary incontinence, 156-157
Research, 3-4, 65-66
    cause/effect research, 72-73
    change, prediction statistics, 86-92
    cohort-sequential designs, 75-76
    cross-lagged panel designs/analyses, 87-89,
        88 (figure)
    cross-sectional vs. longitudinal designs,
        73-74
    cross-sequential designs, 76
    experimental design, 68-69
    ipsative change, 83-86, 85 (figure)
    longitudinal statistics, 77, 78 (table)
    mean-level change, 78-80, 79 (figure)
    meta-analysis, 70-71
    multiple-point longitudinal data, 89-92,
        90-91 (figures)
    quasi-experimental design, 69-71, 73
    relative change, 80-82, 81 (figure)

research designs, 68-73

sequential designs, 75-77, 75 (table)

statistical techniques, 68

statistical terms, 66-68, 67 (table)

structural change, factor analysis, 82-83, 84 (figure)

time-sequential designs, 76-77

two-point designs, 86-87

Respiratory system:

age-related changes, 134-135, 135 (figure)

anatomy/physiology of, 132-134, 133 (figure)

chronic obstructive pulmonary disease, 138-139

disease-related processes, 135-140

forced vital capacity/forced expiratory volume, 134

lung cancer, 135-136

optimal aging and, 140-141

pneumonia, 137-138

tuberculosis and, 139-140

Role strain, 269-270

Rural population, 23

elders as community asset, 24-25

ethnic populations and, 24

farmers, 23-24

retirement relocation and, 24

small community residents, 24

Schedule of Readjustment Rating Scale, 269

Schedule of Recent Events (SRE), 269

Seborrheic keratoses, 101

Self-development model, 59

Self-efficacy, 218, 239-243

Self-rated health, 216-217, 224-225, 240, 244

Self-regulation model of change, 218-219

Senior nutrition programs, 150, 224

Sensory system, 163

age/disease-related changes in, 164-171

hearing, 165-167, 166 (figure)

optimal aging and, 171

smell, 164

taste, 164-165

touch, 164

vision, 167-171, 168 (figure)

Sexual function, 158

Short Portable mental Status Questionnaire, 214

Skeletal kyphosis, 110

Skilled nursing facility (SNF), 289, 293

Skin:

age-related changes in, 99-100, 100 (figure)

anatomy/physiology of, 98

cancer of, 101-102

disease-related processes, 100-103

optimal aging of, 103-104

pressure ulcers, 102-103

seborrheic keratoses, 101

xerosis, 101

Skin cancer, 101-102

Sleep disturbances, 248, 250

Smell, 164

Smoking, 34, 41, 62, 131

Alzheimer's disease and, 183

chronic obstructive pulmonary disease and, 138, 139

lung cancer and, 136

optimal aging and, 140-141

self-efficacy model of change and, 218

SOC (selection/optimization/compensation) model, 59

Social-breakdown theory, 63

Social exchange theory, 292-293

Social integration, 30-31

Social Security, 19, 38

Social support, 234, 276, 283

assessment of, 290-291

caregiving, 298-300

dysfunctional autonomy, 308

formal support, 288-290

functions of, 284

informal-formal blend of care, 290

informal support, 285-287

mortality, social integration and, 295-296

negative effects of, 293-294, 308

network size, changes in, 291-292

network systems in, 284-290

organizational memberships, 297, 309

quasi-formal support, 287-288

reciprocity in, 292-293

recovery from illness and, 296-297
religiosity and, 317
stressful events and, 297
Sociocultural processes, 3
chronic role strain, 269-270
marriage and, 30
rate of aging, culture and, 4, 5 (figure)
Socioeconomic status (SES), 37
control sense, health levels and, 241
gender and, 40
health and, 40-41
life expectancy and, 40-41
poverty rates, 38-40, 39 (figure)
retirement and, 38
Social Security and, 38
Spirituality, 316-318
Spouse caregiving, 298-300
Statistical analysis. *See* Research
Stochastic processes, 47-48
Stress, 254-255
adrenal function and, 258-259,
260 (figure)
age-related changes and, 266-267
aging and, 52-53
allostasis and, 264
biological models of, 52-53
brain function and, 177, 185
cardiovascular health and, 131-132
cardiovascular reactivity to, 233-234, 258
chronic illness and, 262-264
chronic role strain, 269-270
chronic stress, 261-262
daily stressors, 270-271
environmental stress, 267-271
fight-or-flight response, 258, 261-262
immunocompetence and, 206-207
incontinence and, 156-157
individual-contextual transactional stress,
271-273
life events and, 268-269
marriage and, 31
modern theories on, 259-262
optimism and, 244
oxytocin and, 261

physiological state of, 255-267
positive physiological changes
from, 264-266
psychosocial stress, aging and, 272-273
religiosity and, 318
social support and, 297
sympathetic nervous system response to,
255-256, 257 (figure)
traumatic stress, 267-268
triune reactions model, 262, 263 (figure)
voodoo death, 258, 260-261
See also Coping
Strokes, 178-179, 250
Suicide, 236
Sun exposure, 101-102, 104, 170
Sympathetic nervous system (SNS), 256,
257 (figure)
Systems theory model, 44
homeostasis, 51-52
stress, 52-53
wear-and-tear theories, 52

Taste, 164-165
Tendonitis, 117
Theories of aging, 43-45
biological theories, 45-53
chaos theory and, 44-45
deviation amplification model, 44-45
genetic theories, 46-48
molecular/cellular theories, 49-50
systems-level theories, 51-53
systems theory model, 44
See also Rate of aging
Thyroid function, 189-190, 189
(figure), 196-197
Tinnitus, 167
Tissue plasminogen activator (TPA), 179
Total dependency Ratio (TDR), 19-20
Touch, 164
Transactional influences, 3, 271
Transitions Study, 272
Transitory ischemic attacks (TIAs), 178, 179
Traumatic stress, 267-268
Tuberculosis (TB), 139-140

Type A behavior pattern (TABP), 232
Type C behavior pattern, 238

Urinary system. *See* Renal/urinary system

Vascular dementia, 179
Vision, 167-171, 168 (figure)
Voodoo death, 258, 260-261

Wear-and-tear theories, 52
Well-being. *See* Optimal aging; Quality-of-life
Widowhood, 30, 31-33, 40, 236
Wisdom, 8, 312-316, 321

Xerosis, 101

ABOUT THE AUTHORS

Carolyn M. Aldwin (Ph.D.) is Professor of Human and Community Development at the University of California, Davis. She received her doctorate from the University of California, San Francisco, was a postdoctoral fellow in the Program in Social Ecology at the University of California, Irvine, and spent 5 years at the Veterans Administration Normative Aging Study in Boston. She still collaborates with investigators on this study and also directs the Davis Longitudinal Study. She is currently coeditor for *Psychology and Health* and was associate editor for the *Journal of Personality and Social Psychology.* Her research on health and aging has been funded by the National Institute of Aging. She is a fellow of the Gerontological Society of America, as well as a fellow of the American Psychological Association in Divisions 20 (Adult Development and Aging) and 38 (Health Psychology). She enjoys hiking and cycling.

Diane F. Gilmer (Ph.D.) is Lecturer and Postgraduate Researcher in the Department of Human and Community Development at the University of California, Davis. She received a master of science in nursing from the University of Portland, Oregon, and a master of science in education and a doctorate in human development from the University of California, Davis. She is certified as an adult/family nurse practitioner and has worked extensively with the elderly. Currently, she teaches a course on health and aging at the university. She enjoys gardening, walking with her two springer spaniels, and sailing on San Francisco Bay with her husband and adult children.

Michael R. Levenson received his Ph.D. in personality and social psychology from the University of California, Irvine. Dr. Levenson was a postdoctoral fellow at the Alcohol Research Prevention Group and the University of California, Berkeley, and he was Director of Alcohol Studies for the Boston Veterans Administration Normative Aging Study. He has conducted research on personality stability and change in adulthood as well as the relationship of personality to antisocial behavior, stress, health, and alcohol abuse, funded by the National Institute on Alcohol Abuse and Alcoholism. In recent years, he has devoted much of his time to a long-standing interest in higher levels of adult development. He is currently Associate Research Psychologist at the University of California, Davis, where he directs the Wisdom Project. He is an avid cyclist and was once indoor rowing champion for his age group.